SAP PRESS Books: Always on hand

Print or e-book, Kindle or iPad, workplace or airplane: Choose where and how to read your SAP PRESS books! You can now get all our titles as e-books, too:

▸ By download and online access
▸ For all popular devices
▸ And, of course, DRM-free

Convinced? Then go to **www.sap-press.com** and get your e-book today.

IT Service Management in SAP® Solution Manager

 PRESS

SAP PRESS is a joint initiative of SAP and Galileo Press. The know-how offered by SAP specialists combined with the expertise of the Galileo Press publishing house offers the reader expert books in the field. SAP PRESS features first-hand information and expert advice, and provides useful skills for professional decision-making.

SAP PRESS offers a variety of books on technical and business-related topics for the SAP user. For further information, please visit our website: *www.sap-press.com*.

Marc O. Shäfer and Matthias Melich
SAP Solution Manager (3rd Edition)
2011, 403 pp., hardcover
ISBN 978-1-59229-388-9

Tony de Thomasis and Alisdair Templeton
Managing Custom Code in SAP
2013, 351 pp., hardcover
ISBN 978-1-59229-436-7

Frank Föse, Sigrid Hagemann, and Liane Will
SAP NetWeaver AS ABAP System Administration (4th Edition)
2012, 747 pp., hardcover
ISBN 978-1-59229-411-4

Sebastian Schreckenbach
SAP Administration—Practical Guide
2011, 883 pp., hardcover
ISBN 978-1-59229-383-4

Nathan Williams

IT Service Management in
SAP® Solution Manager

Galileo Press

Bonn • Boston

Galileo Press is named after the Italian physicist, mathematician, and philosopher Galileo Galilei (1564—1642). He is known as one of the founders of modern science and an advocate of our contemporary, heliocentric worldview. His words *Eppur si muove* (And yet it moves) have become legendary. The Galileo Press logo depicts Jupiter orbited by the four Galilean moons, which were discovered by Galileo in 1610.

Editor Laura Korslund
Acquisitions Editor Kelly Grace Harris
Copyeditor Julie McNamee
Cover Design Graham Geary
Photo Credit iStockphoto.com/nikitje
Layout Design Vera Brauner
Production Graham Geary
Typesetting SatzPro, Krefeld (Germany)
Printed and bound in the United States of America, on paper from sustainable sources

ISBN 978-1-59229-440-4

© 2013 by Galileo Press Inc., Boston (MA)
1st edition 2013

Library of Congress Cataloging-in-Publication Data
Williams, Nathan, 1982 May 7-
IT service management in SAP solution manager / Nathan Williams. -- 1st edition.
pages cm
ISBN-13: 978-1-59229-440-4
ISBN-10: 1-59229-440-5
1. SAP solution manager. 2. SAP ERP. 3. Management information systems--Computer programs. 4. Business--Data processing--Computer programs. 5. Integrated software. I. Title.
T58.6.W562 2013
658.4'038011--dc23
2012043866

Contents at a Glance

Dear Reader,

It's a bird! It's a plane! It's ... Nathan Williams?!

That's right, dear reader, I just compared the author of this book to a superhero. And superhero he was—in between working more than full time, traveling all over the place, going through at least one go-live, and (I think) playing in a band, Nathan managed to write this lengthy book in record time, which could only be due to superhuman effort and talent. Through it all, he maintained a dry sense of humor that kept the process moving smoothly, and even asked me to nag him about deadlines (trust me, that's *extremely* rare!).

While I could extol Nathan's virtues for a while, I'm sure you want to hear something about this book that you hold in your hands (or are viewing on your screen). Don't be fooled by the serene cover; behind the smoothly sailing ship lies a treasure chest of information that's worthy of the most fearsome IT pirate. Not only will you find all of the information you need to know about what IT Service Management is and does, you'll also find a detailed, step-by-step configuration guide to two essential tools: Application Incident Management and Change Request Management. If you've been searching for a product that gets you through the jargon around SAP Solution Manager and into the meat of what you need to know, then you've come to the right place.

We at SAP PRESS are always eager to hear your opinion. What do you think about *IT Service Management in SAP Solution Manager*? As your comments and suggestions are our most useful tools to help us make our books the best they can be, we encourage you to visit our website at *www.sap-press.com* and share your feedback.

Thank you for purchasing a book from SAP PRESS!

Laura Korslund
Editor, SAP PRESS

Galileo Press
Boston, MA

laura.korslund@galileo-press.com
www.sap-press.com

Contents

PART II: Application Incident Management

6   Integration into Application Lifecycle Management 221

7   Channels for Creating and Resolving Incidents and Problems ... 239

PART III: Change Request Management

13 Additional Features of Change Request Management 615

14 Enabling the Transport Management System for Change Request Management 647

PART IV: Reporting and Analytics

Introduction

The release of SAP Solution Manager 7.1 delivered an improved, sophisticated, and entirely overhauled platform to support customers throughout Application Lifecycle Management (ALM) and beyond—into the operations and optimization of their IT landscapes. Rather than renaming the product to merely keep up with product version standards, the latest release of SAP Solution Manager changes the game in regards to how customers are reacting to, focusing on, and investing in efforts to leverage as much functionality as possible.

With nearly just a year into the general availability of SAP Solution Manager 7.1, the adoption rates of the existing SAP customer base have been overwhelming. SAP's investment in SAP Solution Manager proves that release 7.1 has been a key focus in regards to improvements in technology, openness, and usability. These improvements apply not only to SAP Solution Manager holistically, but also specifically to the new SAP IT Service Management (SAP ITSM) features delivered with release 7.1.

Problems, incidents, service requests, requests for change, and changes to the landscape are all managed from a central platform. The processes across these areas provide automation, efficiency, and flexibility while also ensuring reliance and control from an IT management perspective. Rather than relying on manual processes, third-party tools, or human intervention, SAP Solution Manager provides the tools and control to effectively deliver and manage services related to your IT landscape.

Some key benefits offered with SAP ITSM in SAP Solution Manager 7.1 include an enhanced infrastructure, web UI, and best-in-class messaging capabilities to deliver Application Incident Management (AIM) and Change Request Management (ChaRM) processes that are aligned to ITIL standards. Throughout this book, we will discuss how the following key improvements can be brought to life to enable an SAP ITSM solution for your organization:

► SAP ITSM supports the customer entire solution, beyond just SAP. IT assets such as mobile devices and printers can now be aligned to the processes within

SAP Solution Manager. A single, central platform can be leveraged to manage incidents and changes related to the entire landscape.

▶ The user acceptance rate is astonishing and can be attributed to the increased usability of SAP ITSM features. A flexible, simple, and customizable web UI is available for message processing and dashboard reporting.

▶ Guided procedures, which included automated setup features and integrated documentation, help to deploy the functionality at a more rapid and intuitive manner.

▶ SAP ITSM is not just a capability for the technical teams. Incident Management, Problem Management, Service Request Management, and Change Request Management span the entire IT and business organization.

▶ SAP ITSM is included in enterprise support. As of release 7.1, it's nearly impossible to develop a business case to procure, license, install, and support a third-party SAP ITSM application when SAP Solution Manager offers the same (if not better) capabilities.

Regardless of which application lifecycle phase you may be in or which products comprise your installed base, this book will walk you through the steps of transitioning the benefits of SAP Solution Manager 7.1 into a reality for your organization. This book will help build a strong business case for implementing and/or upgrading to SAP ITSM in SAP Solution Manager.

Who This Book Is For

This book has been developed to reach a wide audience. At a high level, the content within this book is intended for members involved in the delivery of IT services. For implementation projects, this means service strategy teams and stakeholders. For support projects, this typically means members of the Center of Excellence (COE).

The material within this book, depending on the chapter, is relevant to the CIO, IT leadership, service leads, team leads, support staff, and SAP Solution Manager owners and administrators. Certain chapters contain overview material, reporting capabilities, and process descriptions that appeal to managers and executives. On the other hand, a large portion of the book is reserved for how-tos, configuration activities, and lessons learned that will benefit those tasked with leading and implementing SAP Solution Manager.

What This Book Covers

Part I of the book starts with an overview of IT Service Management. We start by describing the processes at a high level to establish a foundational context that supports the overall content of the book. Following, we enter a discussion on the UIs available within the SAP ITSM features in SAP Solution Manager. We discuss the basic setup activities, including post-installation activities and master data setup, in order to prepare you to begin the functional configuration of SAP ITSM processes.

▶ **Chapter 1**

This chapter provides a basic overview of SAP ITSM, ITIL, ALM, and how SAP Solution Manager delivers these functions in an integrated manner from a central platform. Readers who are new to these frameworks and methodologies will be provided with a high-level understanding of the concepts and terminology. The objective of this introduction is to set the foundation for the rest of the material, concepts, and functionalities described within this book.

▶ **Chapter 2**

This chapter introduces you to the new SAP CRM Web Client UI delivered with 7.1 and explain its layout, navigation, and structure. Because Work Centers remain an integral part of SAP Solution Manager, this chapter will also explain the key features, navigation, and the structure of Work Centers.

▶ **Chapter 3**

This chapter provides the post-installation steps that are required before deploying any of the SAP ITSM functionality. SOLMAN_SETUP, as it relates to SAP ITSM functionality and the required prerequisites, is explained in this chapter. This chapter also describes the security authorizations, master data settings, and UI setup required to execute both administration and end-user SAP ITSM functions.

We then begin Part II of the book, Application Incident Management. We provide an overview of Application Incident Management (AIM), discuss the ins and outs of its subprocesses, and describe how it integrates into Application Lifecycle Management (ALM) for SAP. We provide an overview of the features of AIM and then show you how to configure those features.

▶ **Chapter 4**

This chapter provides an overview of AIM, including its goals, infrastructure, changes in the new release, and UI.

▶ **Chapter 5**

This chapter highlights the business partner roles that are delivered in release 7.1 for AIM. Their duties are described in an effort to prepare organizations to begin a role-mapping concept. Additionally, each transaction type's corresponding process flow will be explained in detail.

▶ **Chapter 6**

AIM can be aligned to any or all SAP implementation or operation phases. This chapter identifies when, where, and how AIM can benefit implementation or support teams. Recommendations are given for when and why to adopt AIM processes specific to your organization's requirements.

▶ **Chapter 7**

There are several options for initiating the AIM process (i.e., for an end user to request an incident to be sent to the SAP Solution Manager system). This chapter explains each method available for creating a problem or incident.

▶ **Chapter 8**

This chapter explains the data and functionality contained in the AIM assignment blocks in the SAP CRM Web UI. Many of these functions have been overhauled since release 7.0 with both a different look and feel. This chapter describes each of the functions available for incident/problem creation, processing, and closing. Further, this chapter explains the steps necessary to leverage these functions according to best practices.

▶ **Chapter 9**

This chapter describes some important functionalities within AIM: Time Recording, Service Level Agreements (SLAs), message dispatching, and knowledge articles. These are all important to the process of AIM, and many have new functionality offered in the 7.1 release.

▶ **Chapter 10**

This chapter provides a description, as well as a step-by-step guide, for the configuration settings required to enable AIM. Tips, tricks, and best practices for configuring AIM features will be provided within each subsection.

Part III of the book, Change Request Management, is structured similar to Part II; however, it's tailored to address the ChaRM functionality within SAP Solution Manager. We close the book out by providing an overview of the SAP ITSM reporting and analytics capabilities and lessons learned throughout our prior engagements with SAP Solution Manager.

- **Chapter 11**

  This chapter provides an overview of ChaRM, including its goals, infrastructure, features of the new release, and UI.

- **Chapter 12**

  This chapter highlights the business partner roles that are delivered in release 7.1 for ChaRM. Additionally, each transaction type's corresponding process flow is explained in detail.

- **Chapter 13**

  In addition to the core features of ChaRM, there are several additional features that support change control. This section describes those additional features that support customers who have dual landscapes, non-ABAP systems, and special handling procedures for specific objects.

- **Chapter 14**

  This chapter describes the process and steps to set up Transport Management System (TMS) for a ChaRM environment. Additionally, this chapter describes other basic technical setup activities that aren't covered by the automatic configuration in SOLMAN_SETUP.

- **Chapter 15**

  This chapter provides a description, as well as step-by-step guide, for the configuration settings required to enable ChaRM. Tips, tricks, and best practices for configuring ChaRM features will be provided within each subsection.

- **Chapter 16**

  This chapter describes the maintenance and project administration activities required to begin a ChaRM project. It discusses the projects required to activate ChaRM as well as the steps required to generate a project cycle and a maintenance cycle.

In Part IV, we explain the reporting and analytics capabilities that are provided standard from SAP Solution Manager to support ITSM functions. We'll provide an overview of the capabilities offered to measure ITSM KPIs that support executive leadership roles in the IT organization, down to the support staff. Capabilities that support both AIM and ChaRM will be covered, and we'll also take a look into the SAP NetWeaver BW reporting features delivered with release 7.1.

- **Chapter 17**

  This chapter covers the SAP ITSM reporting and analytics capabilities available within SAP Solution Manager. Interactive reports, powerful search and monitoring capabilities, dashboards, and the SAP Solution Manager plus SAP NetWeaver BW option are discussed.

▶ **Chapter 18**
This chapter describes the main reporting tools available for ChaRM. In addition to reporting on the status of requests for change and change documents, transports objects are collected from the managed systems and presented in SAP Solution Manager as well.

We then provide two supplemental appendices.

▶ **Appendix A**
This appendix provides lessons learned and best practices for implementing AIM and ChaRM for an organization. From strategy and design to go-live and support, this appendix explains how to avoid common pitfalls throughout implementation.

▶ **Appendix B**
In many scenarios, customers will have ChaRM or Service Desk live in a release 7.0 environment. To protect that data, it's recommended that you perform an upgrade to release 7.1. There are several issues to take into consideration when upgrading to release 7.1. This appendix describes what each customer who requires an upgrade will need to know, as well as best practices for making the transition.

All configuration samples and screenshots were prepared using SAP Solution Manager 7.1, Service Pack 07, available at the time of the writing of this book (December 2012).

Part I
Introduction

Part I of this book provides an introduction to the concepts discussed throughout. We'll begin by presenting an overview of IT Service Management, which will provide the foundation for subsequent chapters. We'll discuss frameworks and methodologies respective of the ITSM processes, in addition to how SAP Solution Manager is aligned to drive them from a systematic approach. We waste no time with diving right into the specifics of SAP Solution Manager and how the system supports the delivery of ITSM processes to the organization. An overview of the SAP Solution Manager ITSM user interfaces is provided, along with key activities you'll need to follow to prepare your SAP Solution Manager system to support ITSM functions.

Implementing IT Service Management disciplines is a start, and adopting them brings tangible results. Commitment from leadership, in-house ITIL expertise, attainable goals, and the ability to accept change all must align to your adoption strategy. A vision of how SAP Solution Manager will provide a framework to encompass ITSM should also be established by the leadership functions within the IT organization.

1 An Overview of IT Service Management

The concept of deploying IT Service Management (in this book, often referred to as ITSM) as a discipline within organizations has been around for a while. As a relatively mature philosophy, ITSM has shifted the way an enterprise has traditionally provided support to its customers. Rather than rolling out a technology-based method to contribute to the overall sustainment of the organization, ITSM is a disciplined focus that provides a process-oriented deliverance of services to sustain the end customer.

As an IT organization's installed base broadens across vast user communities and geographies, coupled with business processes that span complex landscapes, the need to provide a better quality of services becomes essential. Obtaining the best-in-class solutions, getting the latest release of products, and exhausting the infrastructure budget increases IT's success margin only so much. The focus on technology alone simply isn't enough, given the aforementioned factors (along with so many more). What makes the IT organization truly valuable in the customer's eyes is the ability to deliver services with a high caliber of quality. In addition, these services must enable and promote the relationship between IT and the business.

At the end of the day, the discipline of IT Service Management doesn't care which product you roll out to your organization. The fundamental principles of ITSM wouldn't necessarily know if you managed problems on Microsoft Excel spreadsheets, logged your incidents in BMC Remedy, or processed requests for change in SAP Solution Manager. As a process-focused discipline, ITSM doesn't care about which tools or technologies enable the management of services; instead, ITSM is concerned with offering the back-office a framework to structure IT service activities, and the related interactions of IT support members with the end user (business or customer).

This chapter will serve as an introduction to IT Service Management and two related and integrated components: IT Infrastructure Library (ITIL) and Application Lifecycle Management (ALM). Although ITSM isn't concerned with tools or technical details of the system, we'll also discuss how Solution Manager plays a part in ITSM. We don't aim to make you experts in these areas. However, understanding these frameworks and methodologies will provide an important foundation to process the rest of the material, concepts, and functionalities within the other chapters.

1.1   Overview of ITIL and IT Service Management

It's difficult to pin-point the exact timeframe in which the term *IT Service Management* came to fruition. Similarly, there isn't necessarily a single owner of the ITSM discipline. One author didn't develop ITSM or coin its methods on his own, no organization developed ITSM from its own leading practices, and certainly no vendor has sold ITSM as its own service.

Although ITSM's origins may be perceived as mildly unclear, the development of its disciplines can be attributed to several factors (including proprietary ones that we won't discuss).

One of the most significant contributing factors of ITSM, and perhaps the most considerable contributing framework, is the Information Technology Infrastructure Library (ITIL). ITIL, simply defined, is the set of practices that supports ITSM. We'll provide an overview of ITIL in Section 1.1.2.

1.1.1   Background

A primary origin of ITSM is based on the need to advance the maturity of traditional IT practices and even farther back to how large-scale mainframe environments were managed. It's obvious that mainframe environments matured decades ago, so it's a safe assumption that the practice of developing traditional IT has matured as well.

Figure 1.1 identifies some practices of traditional IT that were mainly technology driven for managing these mainframe environments. We are not trying to minimalize the importance of technological components and their role in meeting the needs of business users and components. The point is that these components themselves are not the primary focus of ITSM. On the right side of Figure 1.1 are examples of where organizations should aim for, or typically end up, after they have adopted the disciplines within ITSM.

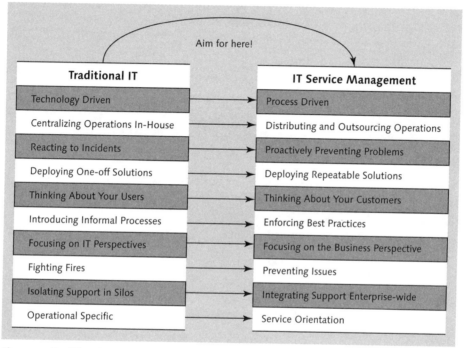

Figure 1.1 Traditional IT Practices Compared to IT Service Management Disciplines

1.1.2 What Is ITIL?

ITIL provides the standard framework and practices necessary to successfully adopt ITSM disciplines. The objective of ITIL is to align ITIL services to meet business requirements.

The framework and practices offered from ITIL are flexible and scalable. ITIL doesn't take notice of one specific IT application or another, nor is ITIL dependent on a specific industry or type of organization. ITIL provides procedures, tasks, and guidelines that can be applied independent of how an organization's IT infrastructure is set up.

Figure 1.2 represents the ITIL framework, also known as the five core publications:

► Service Strategy
► Service Design
► Service Transition
► Service Operation
► Continual Service Improvement

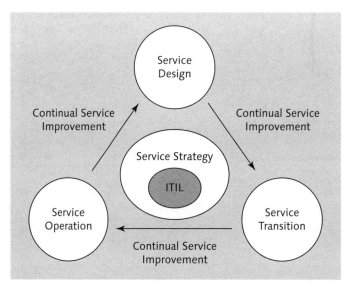

Figure 1.2 ITIL Core Publications

Throughout these 5 core publications, there are 26 overall processes within them. For the purposes of this book, it's important to note that Change Management falls within Service Transition, and that Problem Management, Incident Management, and Service Request Management fall within Service Operation.

1.1.3 IT Service Management Roadmap

So how have organizations evolved from centralized, stand-alone, technology-based practices into distributed, integrated, and process-driven disciplines?

Figure 1.3 provides a high-level roadmap example for organizations to structure an ITSM implementation. This implementation framework consists of five phases and applies to both IT Service Delivery as well as IT Service Support.

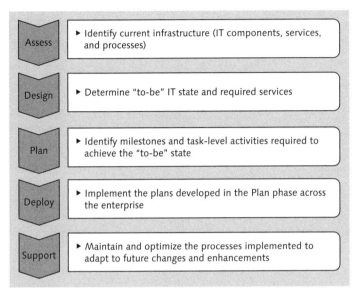

Figure 1.3 ITSM Implementation Framework: Five-Phase Model

1.2 Application Lifecycle Management in SAP

Application Lifecycle Management (ALM) in SAP provides best practices, tools, processes, and services to better manage the delivery of solutions to customers. ALM isn't strictly SAP centric; it provides the components described in the next section to manage both SAP and non-SAP solutions.

Integration is an important factor in the delivery of these best practices, tools, processes, and services throughout the lifecycle of IT applications. SAP Solution Manager is the platform for delivering these components, and it's enabled to deliver them in a manner which serves integration purposes in three key ways:

1. **Tools integration**
   We'll describe more about the tools aspect of ALM in the next section. It's important to note that ALM is scalable in that it supports customers who have third-party tools planned or already deployed to manage various functions.

SAP Solution Manager provides integration capabilities with third-party tools for various activities throughout the application lifecycle. A few examples include the integration to ARIS for process design, the integration to HP Quality Center for testing, and an integration to Remedy for incidents.

A tools analysis and strategy is essential before making the determination to eliminate, integrate, or consolidate tools. Each organization is different in regards to its requirements and enterprise strategy. In many cases, SAP Solution Manager will provide all of the functionality needed to support the implementation of solutions throughout the application lifecycle.

2. **Systems integration**
A fundamental benefit of adopting the capabilities of ALM is integration into systems (both SAP and non-SAP). This is an important part of how SAP Solution Manager delivers the previously mentioned components.

SAP Solution Manager has the ability to technically connect to the managed systems in order to deliver services and provide functionality pertaining to ALM. Incidents created from the managed systems and sent to the IT Service Desk in SAP Solution Manager is just one example.

3. **Process integration**
ALM provides integration across the ITSM processes (this is just one example) to seamlessly transition from Incident Management to Problem Management. Another example is integration between Incident Management and Change Control Management.

ALM delivers all of these best practices, tools, processes, and services across the entire application lifecycle in an integrated manner. From gathering requirements and deploying a project successfully to the optimization of IT solutions, ALM is woven throughout each phase. Rather than focusing on a single phase, it provides a holistic approach to delivering solutions.

The next section will describe the components of ALM, mentioned in the previous list, in greater detail.

1.2.1 Main Components of Application Lifecycle Management

ALM aims to address some of the key challenges faced by IT organizations:

▸ Protecting investments related to IT (technology and process)

▸ Minimizing the impact disruptions have on the business or customer

▶ Promoting innovation

▶ Lowering costs of operation

The components identified in Figure 1.4 are combined, structured, and integrated to address these challenges. The objective is to deliver these components based on a single approach and a central platform—SAP Solution Manager. The goal is to make it easier for IT organizations to receive services offered by SAP.

ALM advances beyond a siloed approach, which focuses only on individual capabilities, toward a more holistic approach for managing the application lifecycle. Rather than improving individual capabilities (e.g., how to create a change request that satisfies our reporting criteria), ALM is focused on improving the end-to-end ITSM processes.

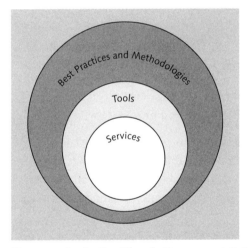

Figure 1.4 Application Lifecycle Management Main Components

We'll discuss the components shown in Figure 1.4 in the following subsections.

Best Practices and Methodologies

Best practices, methodologies, and processes are available within ALM to provide a framework and guidance for delivering IT solutions. These components aim to cover customer requirements for implementing both SAP and non-SAP solutions. Additionally, these frameworks and guidelines span various IT scenarios. For example, ALM's best practices and methodologies can cover implementation activities, operational activities, and upgrade activities.

There are two main examples of these components within ALM:

▸ **SAP standards for solution operations**
These standards enable the various stakeholders (e.g., business process experts and the IT organization) to be prepared to execute the activities required to deploy an SAP solution by describing the different processes of end-to-end solution operations.

▸ **SAP roadmaps**
These provide frameworks to methodically prepare for, implement, and deploy SAP projects. These roadmaps provide a results-driven structure that is recommended and typically required to meet project milestones. Within the SAP roadmaps are templates, accelerators, examples, standards, and best practices to assist with the delivery of tasks throughout each phase.

Tools

Leveraging tools is essential when executing an ALM strategy to manage IT services. Although the focus of this book is SAP Solution Manager as a tool, ALM does not require the sole use of SAP Solution Manager. In fact, it assumes that customers will rely on and integrate multiple SAP and non-SAP tools.

SAP Solution Manager plays the most significant role according to ALM for SAP. SAP Solution Manager provides integration with third-party tools, although it's important to note that SAP Solution Manager is capable of sourcing all ALM capabilities. Although organizations may choose to integrate third-party tools with SAP Solution Manager, it's the anchor for managing IT services and should be considered the system of record and single source of truth for ALM. Finally, SAP Solution Manager is the gateway to SAP Active Global Support (SAP AGS). This integration and collaboration promotes the value between the IT organization and the support engagement with SAP.

Other tools that are capable of providing functions for ALM include the following:

▸ SAP Quality Center by HP (for test management)
▸ SAP Central Process Scheduling by Redwood (for job management)
▸ SAP Productivity Pak by RWD (for e-learning)

Services

Various services are provided exclusively by SAP to help support organizations that adopt and implement ALM. There are three major service offerings available from SAP:

▶ **Expert guided implementation**
This service is performed on the customer's site with the objective of setting up SAP Solution Manager with basic settings. Typically, an expert guided implementation is administered in about five days. Customers are provided with a baseline configuration to help them immediately begin implementing SAP Solution Manager scenarios.

▶ **Consulting services**
Consulting services, provided by SAP, are typically a longer engagement than the setup activities performed by an expert guided implementation. Consulting services (whether delivered by SAP or other firms) focus on deploying an SAP Solution Manager scenario. For example, the consulting services for a ChaRM deployment include the design, configuration, testing, training, and deployment for that specific functionality.

▶ **Training**
Training curriculum programs are developed and lead by SAP in order to provide both SAP partners and customers with educational material on the SAP product suite. Classroom training, virtual training, and certifications are just a few examples of the environments in which SAP training courses are delivered.

1.2.2 ITIL's Six Phases of Application Lifecycle Management

ALM defines the end-to-end process for maintaining the application with six phases, according to ITIL. SAP Solution Manager provides the methodology, tools, and services to support each phase as shown in Figure 1.5. In this chapter, we are describing these phases at a higher level. Although SAP Solution Manager provides tools to enable phases pertaining to implementation and operation, our focus is on those tools specific to ITSM. We'll discuss how the ITSM-related tools align to the six phases of ALM in more detail in Chapter 6.

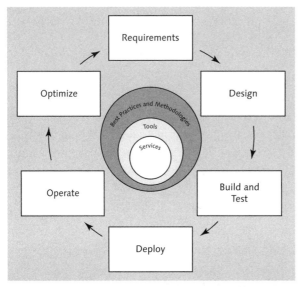

Figure 1.5 Six Phases of Application Lifecycle Management According to ITIL

Brief descriptions of each of the six phases of ALM are provided in the following subsections. We'll discuss these phases, and the tools within SAP Solution Manager that help enable their activities, in more detail in Chapter 6.

Requirements

In the requirements phase, the project team (consulting implementation partner in collaboration with the SAP customer) gathers and documents business requirements. Concepts around SAP standard functionality are introduced in an effort to begin establishing a to-be solution.

Design

In the design phase, the requirements that were gathered in the previous phase are translated into functional design specifications. Design phase activities establish the to-be business processes to be enabled in the holistic IT solution.

Build and Test

During the build and test phase, the functional design specifications are enabled in the system. This is achieved by configuration or custom development within the system. Finally, these settings are tested in the Quality Assurance System (QAS) to be prepared for deployment.

Deploy

During deployment, the tested solution is incorporated into the customer's environment. The solution goes live, and the end users within the business begin using the new system functionality.

Operate

During the operate phase, the services delivered to the SAP customer are monitored to ensure that performance is at the defined Service Level Agreements (SLAs) and key performance indicators (KPIs).

Optimize

During the optimize phase, the outcome of the measured results from the operate phase are reviewed and analyzed. Based on this data, decisions will be made on how to improve the delivery of services. Improvements may come in the form of enhancements to the existing solution or in the introduction of new functionality.

Now that we've discussed ALM, let's move on to consider Incident Management.

1.3   Incident Management

Incidents can be defined as interruptions, which are not planned, to an IT service. Further, a reduction in the quality of service delivered to the business can also be classified as an incident. Restoring normal operations quickly, while minimizing the impact to the business, at a cost-effective manner can be considered the overall objective of Incident Management.

Simply put, an incident is the result of a failure or error within an organization's IT landscape. Incidents can occur in SAP or non-SAP components; however, the process to resolve them—Incident Management—is typically standard regardless of the infrastructure in which the incident occurs.

The concepts and configuration of Incident Management in SAP Solution Manager will be described in detail in subsequent chapters. The purpose of this section is to provide an overview of Incident Management both in general terms (agnostic of a system or framework). We will also discuss Incident Management as it relates to ITIL. Finally, we will align standard Incident Management principles to the functionality and relationship to SAP Solution Manager.

1.3.1 Overview of Incident Management

The process to reach incident resolution must be executed in a formal and phased approach. Because the incident has already occurred and is affecting the business, a predefined process to reach conclusion and restore services must be in place to react to incidents of any type.

Let's examine a simple example of an incident that may occur in an organization's IT landscape. Figure 1.6 represents an example of the lifecycle of an incident. Each step is mapped to an ITIL Incident Management phase, which is explained in the next section.

Incident Management		
Step	Phase	
1. An employee calls the Help Line because his email won't download new messages.	Incident Detection and Recording	Ownership, Monitoring, Tracking, Communication
2. The Help Line agent creates an incident.		
3. The agent classifies the incident.	Classification and Initial Support	
4. The agent checks remotely to see if the employee is connected to the network.		
5. The agent searches for solutions but has no luck finding results.	Investigation and Diagnosis	
6. The agent escalates the issue to the local area network (LAN) team.		
7. A LAN employee receives the incident and checks the email program at the user's workstation.		
8. The LAN employee can fix the issue on-site by adjusting some parameters in the file system.	Resolution and Recovery	
9. The employee is notified that his incident has been completed.	Incident Closure	

Figure 1.6 Example of the Incident Management Process

The following sections describe the ITIL framework regarding Incident Management and how Incident Management is enabled within SAP Solution Manager.

1.3.2 Incident Management According to ITIL

ITIL states that to fully close an incident, there are six main activity areas that must be fulfilled during the lifecycle of an incident. We'll go over each of these areas in the following subsections.

Incident Detection and Recording

Identifying and logging incidents is always the starting point in the phases of Incident Management. Users can manually record an incident from a number of inbound channels (e.g., web portal, direct access to the Incident Management tool, phone call, email). In addition, organizations may set up a workflow that records incidents based on specific triggers (e.g., a threshold is met in business process monitoring that triggers an email notification to a Service Desk).

Classification and Initial Support

After an incident is recorded, it must be classified. Examples of classification values include priority, category, and risk values. Typically, the employee classifying the incident will also play the role of the Level 1 support, or initial support.

Investigation and Diagnosis

If the initial support employee can't quickly and easily resolve the incident on the spot, investigation and diagnosis of the incident will occur. During this phase, the incident is very likely to be escalated to a Level 2 support (e.g., specialized support team) to assist with the diagnosis. The assigned support team may use a number of resources, including their own intellectual resources and knowledge databases, to reach resolution.

Resolution and Recovery

Investigation, diagnosis, and escalation of the incident halts when the incident is resolved. Depending on the resolution details of the incident, it can follow one of these paths:

▶ **Fully closed**
After a period of time passes, and the user who logged the incident is satisfied with the resolution, the incident is completely closed.

▶ **Problem Management**
If the cause of the incident is determined through the Incident Management process but can't be fixed, the Problem Management process will commence.

▶ **Change Management**
If the incident requires a change to the IT landscape, the Change Management process will commence.

Incident Closure

After any one of the aforementioned paths has been completed, the incident is closed. Closed incidents are kept in the system for reference.

Ownership, Monitoring, Tracking, and Communication

Throughout the lifecycle of an incident, these activities occur in an effort to coordinate each step of Incident Management. Each incident must have an owner, be monitored to ensure SLAs are being met, be tracked to ensure the business provided a timely solution, and be communicated to ensure transparency of the incident.

Note

These six areas during the lifecycle of an incident map to the ITIL v3 (2007) subprocess areas for Incident Management. The 2011 version of ITIL decomposes Incident Management into further subprocesses and greater detail. For the purposes of this book, the v3 content is relevant and fully aligns to SAP Solution Manager 7.1.

1.3.3   Incident Management in SAP Solution Manager

As we have described in the beginning of this chapter, ITIL is comprised of a set of processes that supports ITSM. SAP Solution Manager enables ITSM processes and also aligns to the ITIL framework.

SAP Solution Manager provides a user interface, fields, and standard processes to perform the steps throughout Incident Management. Although at times the terminology may be slightly different from the ITIL framework, the meaning and intent of the SAP Solution Manager processes is in alignment. We have described the Incident Management processes within ITIL in the previous section. Figure 1.7 represents the high-level Incident Management process as defined by SAP and as executed from SAP Solution Manager.

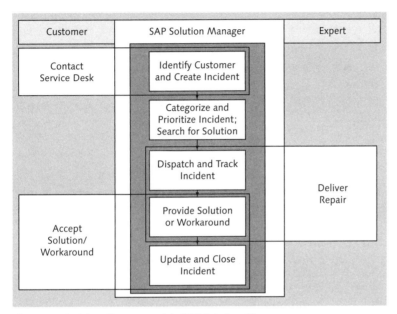

Figure 1.7 Incident Management in SAP Solution Manager

As you can see, the steps and roles shown in Figure 1.7 are closely aligned with the ITIL example shown earlier in Figure 1.6. The delta between these processes is that SAP Solution Manager is included as the central tool to drive the activities within Incident Management.

In addition to providing capabilities to perform Incident Management, SAP Solution Manager provides the ability to integrate into further ALM processes such as Service Request Management and Problem Management as described in the next sections.

1.4   Service Request Management

Service requests are generally defined as a request from a user (e.g. customer, business user, end-user, etc.) to provide new, or a change to existing, IT services. You can think of a service request as a request for change to a service, as opposed to an IT asset as we'll discuss in Section 1.6. The primary objective of Service Request Management is to provide the user with changes to services that are performed in a strict, well-defined, procedural, and controlled manner so that risk is not introduced to degrade business value.

Similar to how we walked through an overview of Incident Management, we will begin by discussing Service Request Management agnostic of any methodologies, frameworks, or systems. We will then highlight the aspects of Service Request Management from an ITIL perspective and conclude the section by discussing how SAP Solution Manager drives Service Request Management activities from the ITSM component.

1.4.1 Overview of Service Request Management

Business users require a clear and well-defined way to create requests that are considered less than major. These minor user requests, resulting in a new or changed service, will fall outside of the immediate responses required from Incident Management or Problem Management. Even though these changes are minor, it's critical to provide a process framework that fulfills these requests so that business requirements can be aligned with the services provided by IT.

Service Request Management handles the fulfillment of requests that are made by the business that require information or a change to service. Some examples include:

▶ New user setup
▶ Password change
▶ Workstation change
▶ New hardware (cell phone, printer, etc.)

1.4.2 Service Request Management According to ITIL

Any solution that involves a formal Service Request Management process should be based on the ITIL best practice framework, similar to the other ITSM processes described within this chapter. In ITIL, Service Request Management is most commonly referred to as *Request Fulfillment*.

According to ITIL, Request Fulfillment is associated with service requests that are considered low cost, low risk, and frequently occurring. As mentioned in our examples in Section 1.4.1, you can probably already identify requests for new users and passwords as classic examples of service requests. In addition to requesting that these services be fulfilled, service requests can also be requests for information. For example, "how do I installed XYZ software?" is a low risk type of question that can be included as part of a service request.

Having a process for fulfilling service requests, separate from Incident and Problem Management, is important. Since these requests for service and information occur frequently from the business and considered low risk, they should not impact the activities involved in processing incidents and problems. While Request Fulfillment is often structured similarly to Incident and Problem Management, Incident and Problem Management should focus on actual incidents that indicate a failure in service, rather than accommodate general questions or requests.

1.4.3   Service Request Management in SAP Solution Manager

Service Request Management has a dedicated transaction type (SMRQ) and workflow within SAP Solution Manager that is aligned to the ITIL best practices framework. In SAP Solution Manager, an end-user (requester) creates a service request document to specify a required service or information. A guided procedure is available for requesters that will walk them through the steps to generate a service request in the SAP Solution Manager system.

The service request is then processed by a message processor. Checklists are used to walk the message processor through the standard, repeatable procedures required in order to fulfill the service request. This checklist is split into one or many tasks, which are assigned to various business partners. Once a particular message process marks a task within the checklist as completed, SAP workflow is triggered, which determines the next message processor. The next message processor is able to view their workflow task within the ITSM Home Page and continue processing the checklist items.

Service Request Management in SAP Solution Manager integrates with the other ITSM processes such as Problem Management and Change Management.

1.5 Problem Management

Problems are generally defined as unknown causes of one or several incidents. Typically, a problem is the result of many incidents that are related in some manner. Problem Management aims to proactively prevent incidents from occurring. A further objective of Problem Management is to minimize the impact of those incidents that can't be prevented.

In this section, we'll discuss Problem Management in a general sense. Similar to how we walked through the overview of Incident Management, we will start with a basic overview describing Problem Management stand alone without the influence of a particular system or framework. We'll then apply the ITIL framework to Problem Management and discuss how industry practices align to the prevention of incidents. Finally, we will align both of these areas to SAP Solution Manager and discuss how Problem Management can be approached systematically.

1.5.1 Overview of Problem Management

If the business users or customers are repeatedly logging incidents that are closely related, you've encountered a problem. As we mentioned, a problem is identified as a condition that is a result of several incidents that exhibit common symptoms. This isn't to say that problems don't arise from a single incident. Problems can be triggered from a single incident or many incidents that are alike.

Unlike incidents, the focus of resolving a problem isn't on how quickly a resolution can be achieved. Because Problem Management is associated with determining and resolving the cause of an incident, the goal is to identify those causes to find a solution so that incidents are not a result of the problem.

Based on what we have described about Incident Management and Problem Management, you might be thinking that resolving incidents is reactive and resolving problems is proactive, but this isn't always the case. While it's very difficult to proactively avoid an incident from occurring, Problem Management can be both reactive and proactive. Deploying Problem Management processes can be proactive in identifying and resolving incidents before they occur. On the other hand, Problem Management can also be reactive in resolving problems in response to incidents.

The bottom line is that Problem Management aims to find and resolve the root cause of problems to prevent future incidents.

Figure 1.8 displays the process flow according to ITIL for Problem Management. We'll provide an overview of each step in the next section.

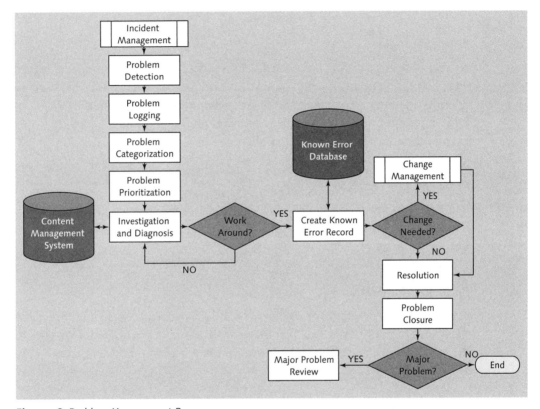

Figure 1.8 Problem Management Process

1.5.2 Problem Management According to ITIL

According to ITIL, there are 11 activities relating to the lifecycle of a problem. We'll provide a brief explanation of each of these activities in the following sub-sections.

Problem Detection

Problems can be detected in many ways. The most common example of problem detection is from one or more incidents logged within a Service Desk tool. Other examples include notifications from outside parties such as vendors or the automated detection of problems from the monitoring infrastructure.

Problem Logging

No matter how a problem is detected, it must be logged in a consistent and logical way. You can think of logging criteria as the minimal yet mandatory fields when entering a problem. For example, every problem should have a short description, long description, date/time logged, priority, and any recovery steps that may have been taken to overcome the problem.

Problem Categorization

Like incidents, problems must be categorized in the same manner. We recommend that problems are categorized with the same metrics and criteria as your incidents are categorized.

Problem Prioritization

Similar to categorization, problems must be prioritized consistently with how incidents are prioritized. Note that these two activities are considered separate in Problem Management, although they essentially occur at the same time by the same resource.

Problem Investigation and Diagnosis

Like the other Problem Management activities, it's especially important to conduct thorough investigation and diagnosis to determine the root cause of the problem. The length of this activity will vary greatly and depend on the impact, urgency, and severity of the problem. Often, a support team member will attempt to recreate the problem. The purpose of recreating the problem is to try to develop a deeper understand of what went wrong and then try different ways to find an efficient resolution to the problem.

Workarounds

Workarounds can be applied to incidents as a temporary fix to the problem. Although a workaround provides a short-term solution to the incident and problem, it's important that the support team continue to conduct investigation and diagnosis to find a permanent resolution. If a workaround is available, the problem record should remain open until a permanent resolution is discovered.

Raising a Known Error Record

If a permanent resolution is the outcome of the support team's investigation and diagnosis, a known error record should be recorded. The purpose of a known error record is to have documentation on-hand that is readily available should similar incidents or problems arise.

Problem Resolution

A resolution should be applied to the problem as soon as it's found. However, in many cases, there are other steps that must occur before a resolution can be applied. Certain organizational activities may require further diligence or activities before a resolution can be applied. Additionally, a resolution may require a change to the IT infrastructure, which, in turn, will prompt the Change Request Management process.

Problem Closure

When the necessary activities and follow-on processes have been completed, the problem can be formally closed. Related incidents that are linked to the problem should be closed as well. Prior to closing these records, a member of the support team (typically the problem manager) should perform a check on these records to ensure that all documentation and details are included.

Major Problem Review

Depending on the organization's priority structure (very high, high, medium, low, etc.), some problems can be considered major. For example, problems classified as very high would be major for an organization. In these cases, a major problem review should be conducted on a periodic basis for all major problems that have been closed. The major problem review is basically a lessons learned activity to identify what was done correctly, areas for improvement, and how to prevent the problem going forward.

Errors Detected in the Development System

New applications (systems or software) are rarely delivered 100% error free. For errors detected during the testing phase, it's important to note and record the details of these errors and how they were resolved before the fix is promoted to production. This can be a formal process or conducted informally by simply classifying the problem as an error detected in the development system.

> **Note**
>
> Similar to Section 1.3.2, the preceding subsections identify the activities within Problem Management according to ITIL v3 (2007).

1.5.3 Problem Management in SAP Solution Manager

SAP Solution Manager aligns to the ITIL framework for Problem Management the same way we previously described the alignment of Incident Management activities. Like Incident Management, SAP Solution Manager provides all of the functionality necessary to execute the process we described in the previous section. Again, some SAP terminology may slightly differ from ITIL; however, the concepts are the same, and SAP Solution Manager is in alignment with the ITIL framework.

Regardless of the IT infrastructure (SAP or non-SAP), SAP Solution Manager can meet almost any organization's requirements for executing Problem Management. In SAP Solution Manager, Problem Management is tightly integrated with the Incident Management process. Further, if a problem requires a change, it's also integrated in the Change Management process in SAP Solution Manager. We'll provide an overview of Change Management in the next section. Both the concepts and the configuration of Problem Management in SAP Solution Manager will be described in detail in subsequent chapters.

Figure 1.9 represents how SAP Solution Manager processes a problem.

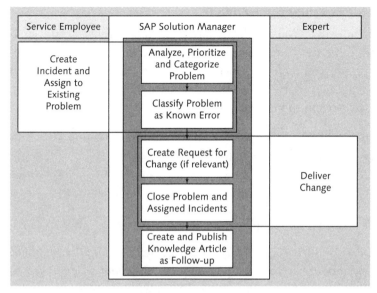

Figure 1.9 Problem Management in SAP Solution Manager

1.6 Change Management

A change is approved by the Change Manager and/or Change Advisory Board. It's implemented, tested, and promoted to a production environment in a controlled way with minimal risk to existing IT infrastructure. As a result, one or more configuration items are updated to provide value to the business by the way of requirements, new enhancements, or maintenance. The objective of managing these changes (i.e., Change Management) is to enable efficient changes with a minimum disruption to the business and IT services.

The overall objective of Change Management is to minimize the impact of any changes that need to occur within the IT environment. Moreover, the objective should be to create zero to minimal incidents as a result of the deployed change.

In this section, we'll provide a general overview of Change Management. Then, we'll discuss Change Management as it relates to the ITIL framework. Finally, we will discuss how SAP Solution Manager provides Change Management capabilities from a systematic approach.

1.6.1   Overview of Change Management

Change Management is an ITSM discipline wherein the objective is to instill standard and efficient procedures to manage changes to an organization's IT environment. The requirements and requests for change can arise based on a number of considerations. The following are just a few examples of why organizations must deploy Change Management to manage changes to their IT environment:

- The user requires additional functionality to execute a business process.
- A break has been introduced that requires a fix.
- External requirements (e.g., legislative) must be met.
- New projects are initiated.
- Service or performance improvements have been made.

Processes that are introduced for Change Management should be standard regardless of the system impacted. Ideally, a single tool should be deployed to manage changes in an effort to prevent redundancy across tracking and reporting changes. While flexibility is important, control is key. Deploying a Change Management solution with these things in mind will help speed the process for managing changes and help minimize the impact of changes to a productive IT environment.

1.6.2   Change Management According to ITIL

In the ITIL framework, Change Management is a part of Service Transition because ITIL considers that a change involves transitioning something that has been developed from Service Design to Service Operations. ITIL assumes that this process will have standard processes and methods so that the new changes are handled efficiently.

The key activities within Change Management according to ITIL include the following:

- Filtering changes
- Managing changes and the change process
- Performing Change Advisory Board (CAB) activities
- Reviewing and closing changes
- Creating reports for management

In the next section, we'll describe how Change Management can be enabled in SAP Solution Manager.

1.7 Integration of ALM and ITSM

So far, we've seen a variety of terms and concepts in this chapter. We've described frameworks, methodologies, and disciplines, as well as provided an overview of the components that make up each of these areas. How do all of these things tie together?

We'll first describe the integration between ALM and ITSM, and then we'll provide a summary in the next section to bring everything together. The important thing to understand—and ultimately what this book is centered around—is that SAP Solution Manager 7.1 enables IT organizations to adopt ALM while providing best-of-breed capabilities to drive ITSM processes.

Figure 1.10 helps visually portray the integration of these areas for past and present software versions of two separate SAP products: SAP Customer Relationship Management (SAP CRM) and SAP Solution Manager.

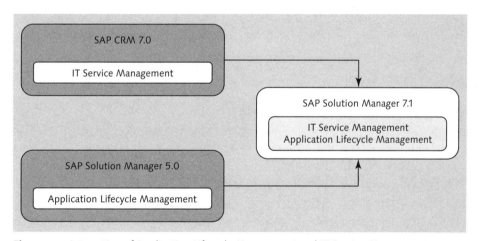

Figure 1.10 Integration of Application Lifecycle Management and IT Service Management

▶ **SAP CRM**

The most current release of the SAP CRM product, 7.0, provides ITSM functionality with best-of-breed messaging capabilities throughout each ITSM process (Incident Management, Change Management, etc.). In other words, SAP CRM does have an IT Service Desk within its infrastructure. SAP CRM also has the Web Client UI, which provides a sleek, flexible, and intuitive way to navigate and administer the functions within that system.

► **SAP Solution Manager**
SAP Solution Manager is delivered with the SAP CRM infrastructure to process transactions related to incidents, change requests, and so on. This is how SAP Solution Manager was able to have a Service Desk and Change Request Management (ChaRM) tool within its own system. A major benefit is that no additional SAP CRM server or SAP CRM license is required to leverage these functions. For organizations that don't have functional SAP CRM in scope, SAP Solution Manager is the tool to process scenarios that require messaging capabilities. The challenge, before the release of SAP Solution Manager 7.1, was that the SAP CRM infrastructure within SAP Solution Manager in prior releases was based on SAP CRM 5.0. Although SAP Solution Manager could facilitate ALM, the messaging capabilities for ITSM were not considered advanced.

Solution Manager 7.1 blends ITSM and ALM together with an upgraded SAP CRM 7.0 infrastructure to drive messaging capabilities. With release 7.1, customers are able to leverage a single platform (SAP Solution Manager) to deploy ALM with best-of-breed functionalities.

1.8   Summary

We've provided many new topics, terms, frameworks, methodologies, and disciplines within this chapter. Recall that the goal isn't to make you experts in ITSM or ITIL, but to describe these concepts at a level so they can be applied when you start to deploy SAP Solution Manager as a tool to drive their respective functions. Remember, you are not just configuring a tool to track and log messages. The objective is to examine the bigger picture and approach your SAP Solution Manager 7.1 implementation with a holistic and integrated approach. Having a basic understanding of the integration between ALM and ITSM, along with how SAP Solution Manager aligns to the ITIL framework, will enable you to offer standardized and integrated approaches for better delivering IT services to your organization.

In the next chapter, we waste no time by getting into some details of ITSM in SAP Solution Manager. We will start our focus on ITSM by identifying and describing some of the key user interfaces that are available when processing ITSM in SAP Solution Manager. Key features, navigation and the architecture of the CRM Web UI and Work Centers for processing messages will be explained.

*As of SAP Solution Manager 7.1, Transactions DSWP and SOLUTION_*
MANAGER are now obsolete. While their activities and functionalities are
available only within the SAP Solution Manager Work Centers, all new
SAP ITSM functions will be available only on the SAP CRM Web user
interface.

2 User Interfaces for SAP ITSM Functions in SAP Solution Manager 7.1

With the 7.1 release of SAP Solution Manager, the mission from SAP was to enhance the product to become more attractive overall. The overhauled interface addresses the challenges related to lacking both functionality and user acceptance.

With 7.1, the SAP CRM Web UI includes best-of-breed messaging capabilities that enable organizations to leverage SAP Solution Manager as a single platform to drive SAP ITSM functions. In addition, the web-based interface (both in the Work Centers and the SAP CRM Web UI) provides SAP customers with a flexible, personal, and intuitive interface that is efficient to use for their day-to-day activities.

This chapter will explain two important concepts concerning how users access the SAP ITSM functions within SAP Solution Manager: the user interfaces known as the SAP CRM Web UI and SAP Solution Manager Work Centers. We'll also discuss the layout, structure, and navigation of the UIs.

2.1 SAP CRM Web User Interface

The SAP CRM Web UI may be considered the most noticeable, practical, and tangible enhancement to the SAP Solution Manager 7.1 product. Enabling your service management users to have access to a SAP CRM-based end-user experience isn't only a big change over the previous interface, but it's also a remarkable way for these users to conduct their daily activities related to SAP ITSM. More savvy SAP users may take a first look and think that they are in fact logged into an SAP CRM 7.0 system.

> **Note**
>
> One of the most significant updates to the SAP Solution Manager infrastructure is an upgraded SAP CRM layer. The prior SAP Solution Manager (version 7.0, Enhancement Package 01) was built on top of an SAP CRM 5.0 layer, whereas release 7.1 has an upgraded SAP CRM 7.0 layer. With this update comes the Web UI recognized in SAP CRM 7.0.

If we take a first glance at viewing a support notification within the Service Desk of SAP Solution Manager 7.0 versus processing an incident in release 7.1, you're able to see the significant difference.

Take notice of the contrast in interface details between Figure 2.1 and Figure 2.2. The interface in Figure 2.2 is web-based and much more professional and advanced. SAP did not take multiple releases or support packages to achieve this delta. This overhaul was delivered in one release, SAP Solution Manager 7.1.

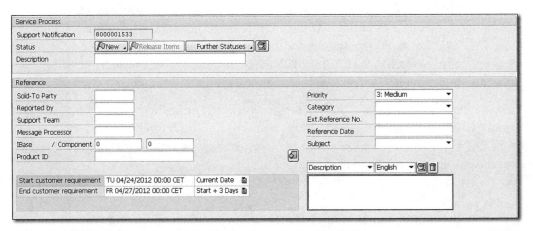

Figure 2.1 Create Support Notification Screen in the SAP GUI

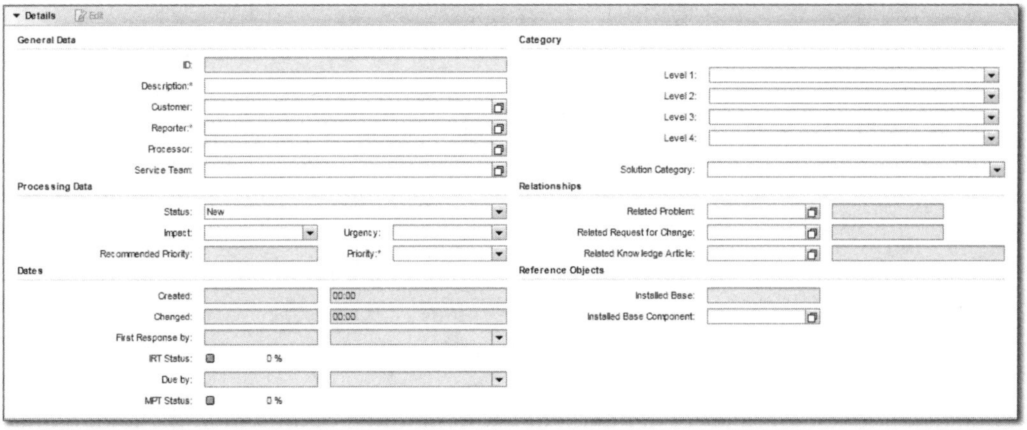

Figure 2.2 Create Incident Screen in the SAP CRM Web UI

2.1.1 Key Features

This section will highlight the key features of the SAP CRM Web UI. We'll discuss the improvements, benefits, and overall value that these features deliver to IT organizations over the standard SAP GUI that we have been familiar with for so long. Together, these features are game-changers in the way SAP Solution Manager is positioned to deliver and manage IT services across your entire organization, down to the business users. The features delivered with the new user interface promote usability, user acceptance, and buy-in from requesters and processors of service tickets.

Completely Web-Based

Customers who have leveraged the Service Desk or Change Request Management (ChaRM) functions of release 7.0 or earlier must note that new transaction types are delivered with release 7.1. If you have adopted 7.0 transaction types and choose to transfer to the 7.1 functionality, you must define a transition strategy to migrate to the new transaction types.

The functionalities these transaction types deliver are only available in the SAP CRM Web UI. All of the functionality that is accessed by the various user groups relating to SAP ITSM functions is now fully web-enabled.

Built on SAP CRM Web UI Framework

As mentioned earlier, one of the other significant enhancements to SAP Solution Manager 7.1 was the infrastructure change from a SAP CRM 5.0 layer to SAP CRM 7.0. With the upgrade of SAP CRM comes all of the benefits of SAP CRM 7.0 messaging capabilities.

We won't list all of the significant features of the SAP CRM 7.0 ITSM capabilities; however, there are two key points to be aware of:

1. The SAP CRM 7.0 environment provides a web-based UI for all messaging-based capabilities. All SAP ITSM functions are created, processed, and managed within a web-based interface.

2. These messaging capabilities are now considered best of breed in SAP Solution Manager, whereas the old SAP CRM 5.0 functionality had difficulty standing up to third-party alternatives for message handling. The SAP CRM 7.0 infrastructure provides SAP customers with messaging capabilities that are Pink Elephant (a globally recognized leader in ITIL and ITSM) certified as well as fully compliant with the ITIL framework.

Web 2.0 Paradigms

Web 2.0 isn't necessarily a new term for those who may be savvy in the web development area. However, Web 2.0 is a new and welcomed concept within SAP Solution Manager.

Web 2.0 creates a rich web experience for users by providing a means for SAP Solution Manager web pages to respond quickly and behave similarly to applications that are a part of your desktop. For example, users can perform functions (such as drag and drop) without requiring the page to reload and deliver new data back to the user. This enables users who are processing transaction types to experience more immediate results when clicking links within the SAP CRM Web UI.

The use of Web 2.0 within SAP Solution Manager's ITSM functions will play an important part in the development of user acceptance for these tools. Prior to release 7.1, activities related to Incident Management and Change Request Management (ChaRM) could be considered anything other than a "rich experience." Web 2.0 will play a significant role in overcoming challenges associated with the adoption of SAP Solution Manager for ITSM functionality.

Business Role Driven

A *business role* can be considered the key to accessing any functions pertaining to SAP ITSM in SAP Solution Manager. Business roles can be customized for the various SAP ITSM components that use the SAP CRM Web UI framework. These business roles are typically copied and assigned to the various user groups that have access to the SAP ITSM components of SAP Solution Manager. For example, you may choose to adapt a business role concept that maps to each user group for your organization.

A developer in the ChaRM scenario may be assigned a comprehensive business role that allows him access to a significant amount of links within the SAP CRM Web UI. A user who can only log problems, on the other hand, may have a much more slimmed down business role with limited access to links.

> **Note**
>
> It's important to note the following concerning business roles:
>
> ▶ Business roles do not take the place of standard security roles in SAP Solution Manager. Standard roles, both individual and composite, are delivered with SAP Solution Manager to control the user group's authorizations. Unlike business roles, the standard security roles control the access to specific authorization objects within SAP Solution Manager.
>
> ▶ You must still define an authorization strategy for end users in your SAP ITSM scenario. Additionally, you must define a business role concept in the SAP Solution Manager system.

Business roles are assigned to the user via a parameter in user maintenance. When users log on to the SAP CRM Web UI, they are able to view the features and functions that are unique to their role. The security roles assigned to the user drive the activities the user can perform in the work center.

We'll discuss more details of the business role concept, including how to customize the standard business roles, in Chapter 3.

Personalized According to User Preference

Most of the functions for SAP ITSM within the SAP CRM Web UI can be personalized according to each user's preference. The functions to uniquely personalize the SAP CRM Web UI are located on the central personalization page.

This page can be started by clicking PERSONALIZE in the header area of the SAP CRM Web UI as shown in Figure 2.3.

Figure 2.3 SAP CRM Web UI Header Area

Note the following differences between SAP CRM objects that can be personalized versus customized:

▶ *Personalizing* the SAP CRM Web UI means to change objects where the results are unique to an individual user's SAP CRM Web UI screens. If an object is personalized by a user, it's local to that user. In other words, it doesn't affect the layout or view of any other user group with access to the same information.

▶ *Customizing* the SAP CRM Web UI means to modify the layout of the screens so that the results are global across all user groups. A customization will impact everyone with access to that information on the screen. Customizing typically requires a transport request as well.

Personalizing the screen layout for SAP ITSM functions is a brand-new power feature in SAP Solution Manager. This feature enables user groups to create views and layouts according to their own preferences, without seeking approval or creating change requests to have a different layout.

Personalizing enables a flexible means to adapt the standard layout of the SAP CRM Web UI according to local requirements. We'll discuss personalizing the SAP CRM Web UI in greater detail in Chapter 3.

Simple Navigation Architecture

The SAP CRM Web UI provides an intuitive way for users to navigate functions associated with their business role. Users who aren't experts in SAP, or users who may be new to SAP, can quickly become familiar with some of the most advanced SAP Solution Manager functions. This feature helps overcome the challenge of mixed user acceptance associated with prior releases of SAP Solution Manager.

As you'll notice in Section 2.1.4, the architecture of the SAP CRM Web UI isn't necessarily complex. The screen is divided into just a few areas, and the buttons aren't scattered all over the screen. Each button has a useful feature and their use is practical.

As with any new application, those familiar with the traditional SAP GUI method of processing SAP ITSM functions will experience a degree of getting used to the new application. However, those users who were accustomed to the SAP GUI should be able to quickly ramp-up to the navigation architecture offered in release 7.1.

Work Center Enabled

Work centers in the SAP CRM Web UI are different from the Work Centers we'll describe in Section 2.2. We aren't purposely trying to confuse you. It just so happens that SAP CRM 7.0 also uses the term *work center* in a different manner than SAP Solution Manager has previously used the term.

> **Note**
>
> To differentiate between the two terms, the lowercased "work center" refers to those in the SAP CRM Web UI, and the uppercased "Work Center" refers to those in Web SAP Solution Manager.

Work centers described within the SAP CRM Web UI are pages that contain a set of shortcuts and provide access to SAP CRM components related to the SAP ITSM scenario. Each SAP ITSM scenario will have its own work center.

Each work center will have many *work center pages*. For example, Incident Management will have its own work center. In fact, every first-level navigation menu item will have its own work center (we'll explain first-level navigation areas in a moment). However, Incident Management will be made up of several work center pages. The Incident Management work center pages will contain links, data, and search areas, as well as reports depending on what activities you're processing within that particular SAP ITSM scenario.

A work center page immediately loads to the work area of the SAP CRM Web UI as soon as the user clicks on an associated link. We'll explain all of these terms in Section 2.1.2.

2.1.2 Navigating the SAP CRM Web UI

In this section, we'll provide an overview of how to navigate to and around the web pages associated with the SAP CRM Web UI. Even if you haven't configured the SAP ITSM processes in SAP Solution Manager, you'll still be able to navigate the layout of the UI to get a sense of how it's organized. There are a couple prerequisites that are required before you're able to navigate to the SAP CRM Web UI. These prerequisites are dependent on one of two scenarios.

Scenario 1: You've Been Assigned the Appropriate Roles to Access the Change Management and/or Incident Management Work Center

Note

Refer to Chapter 3 for details regarding security roles pertinent to SAP ITSM functions, including authorizations required to access SAP CRM UI work centers.

In the case of this scenario, follow these steps:

1. Execute Transaction SOLMAN_WORKCENTER.

2. Choose either the CHANGE MANAGEMENT or INCIDENT MANAGEMENT tab. In Figure 2.4, the CHANGE MANAGEMENT tab is shown.

3. Select the link for IT SERVICE MANAGEMENT in the COMMON TASKS menu area as shown in Figure 2.4.

Figure 2.4 Change Management Work Center

After selecting this link, the SAP SOLUTION MANAGER IT SERVICE MANAGEMENT home screen opens in a new browser window as shown in Figure 2.5.

Figure 2.5 SAP Solution Manager IT Service Management Home Screen in the SAP CRM Web UI

4. Before clicking any of the links on the SAP ITSM home screen, save the initial screen as a favorite or bookmark in your browser. Now you have the ability to access the SAP ITSM platform directly from your browser.

Alternatively, you may still launch out to the SAP CRM Web UI via the Change Management or Incident Management work centers.

Scenario 2: You Aren't Using the Work Centers for SAP ITSM Processing—Instead, You Plan to Launch the SAP CRM Web UI Directly to Execute SAP ITSM Functions

If you haven't been assigned the appropriate roles for the Change Management or Incident Management work centers, or you're simply not using them at all, there is an alternative way to retrieve the URL to access the SAP ITSM home screen. Follow these steps:

1. Log in to the SAP Solution Manager system.

2. In the SAP EASY ACCESS screen, right-click on the FAVORITES folder, and then click ADD OTHER OBJECTS.

3. Select BSP APPLICATION in the subsequent window, and press Enter.

4. When the BSP APPLICATION window appears, enter the values of each field as shown in Figure 2.6. The parameter values for SAP-USER and SAP-PASSWORD must match your SAP Solution Manager logon credentials.

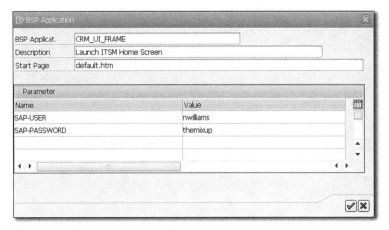

Figure 2.6 BSP Application Details

5. Press ⌶Enter⌷, and the LAUNCH ITSM HOME SCREEN entry will appear in the FAVORITES folder as shown in Figure 2.7.

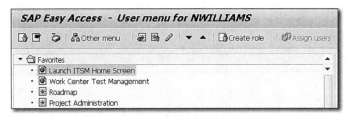

Figure 2.7 SAP GUI Favorites Menu

6. Double-click this entry, and a browser window will open displaying the URL to the SAP ITSM home page (see Figure 2.8). Save this URL as a favorite or bookmark in your browser. Now you have the ability to access the SAP ITSM platform directly from your browser.

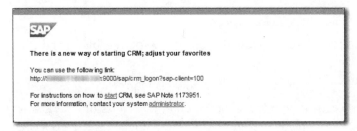

Figure 2.8 SAP CRM Web UI URL Link

> **Note**
>
> You must first activate services defined in the following paths for the SAP ITSM URL to work properly:
>
> ▸ DEFAULT HOST • SAP • BC • BSP • SAP • CRM_UI_START
>
> ▸ DEFAULT HOST • SAP • CRM_LOGON
>
> Services are activated in Transaction SICF for the hierarchy type SERVICE. Simply locate the service, right-click it, and select ACTIVATE SERVICE.

2.1.3 Role-Specific Views

SAP Solution Manager provides two key business roles that deliver views that are specific to both requesters as well as dispatchers (message processors). These two roles are:

▸ SOLMANREQU

▸ SOLMANDSPTCH

> **Note**
>
> These roles are optional for organizations who want to limit the functions and viewable areas within the SAP CRM Web UI for various users. For the majority of the content within our book, we'll present the material based on the business role SOLMANPRO assigned to users.

Figure 2.9 provides a representation of the SOLMANREQU view from the ITSM home page. As you can see, there are options to create incidents as well as service requests, and worklists available right on the home page identifying all of the user's service transactions that they created.

When the user who is assigned the SOLMANREQU business role creates an incident or service request, they're presented with a guided procedure as shown in Figure 2.10.

Each step of the guided procedure is structured to give the end-users (customers, requesters, etc.) a limited amount of fields available to submit the incident. They only are provided and can only see the information that should be submitted by the requester. For example, they are allowed to input the impact and urgency, but not the priority. Additional details, or different details, can be maintained by a support staff member who as the SOLMANDSTCH business role, which we'll explain next.

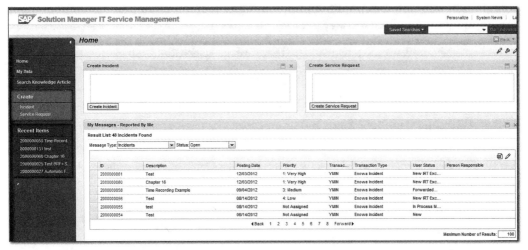

Figure 2.9 SOLMANREQU Home Screen

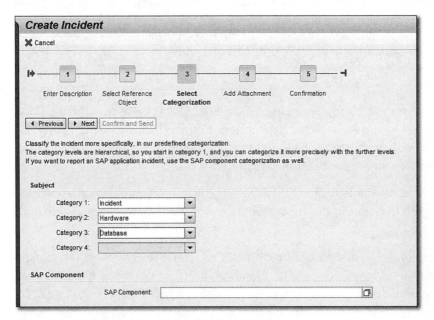

Figure 2.10 Guided Procedure: Create Service Transaction

The example in Figure 2.11 shows an ITSM home screen for a user that has the SOLMANDSPTCH business role assigned to him. As mentioned earlier, these users will typically be the Level 1 or Level 2 message processors in the IT organization. They should have the ability to create service transactions, process them as well as create follow ups, and assign additional information to the documents created by the end user.

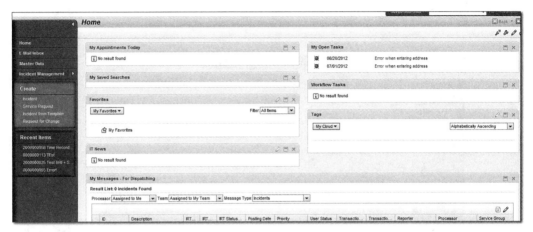

Figure 2.11 ITSM Home Page: SOLMANDSPTCH

Figure 2.12 provides an image of the SOLMANDSPTCH business role with additional processing functions. As you can see, there are additional processing areas available for the message processors when this business role is assigned.

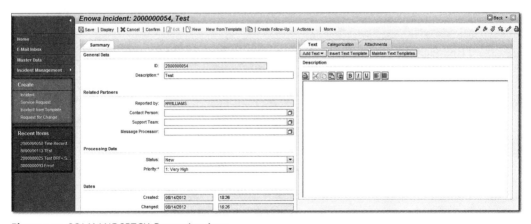

Figure 2.12 SOLMANDSPTCH Processing Area

2.1.4 Architecture

In this section, we'll introduce the main components of the SAP CRM Web UI architecture. There are three key elements to the overall architecture of the SAP CRM Web UI as shown in Figure 2.13:

▶ Header area

▶ Navigation bar

▶ Work area

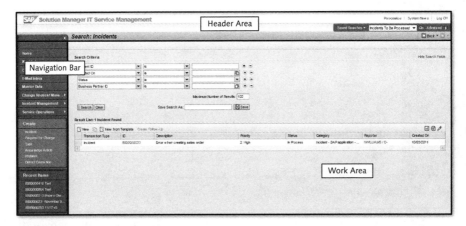

Figure 2.13 SAP CRM Web UI Main Architecture

We'll describe the main components of each of these key elements in the following sections.

Header Area

The header area consists of six subelements as identified in Figure 2.14 and explained here:

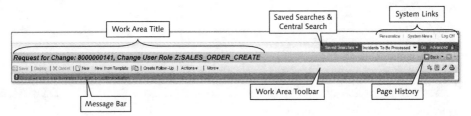

Figure 2.14 SAP CRM Web UI Header Area

▶ **Work area title**

This subelement is dynamic depending on the SAP CRM object or screen that is being viewed. For example, the work area title for an incident would include the incident's number range and corresponding short description.

▶ **System links**

System links, displayed in the upper-right corner of the header area, provide access to SAP CRM Web UI functions that are independent of specific objects or functions. Table 2.1 provides a listing and description of each system link of the SAP CRM Web UI.

System Link	Description
PERSONALIZE	Provides access to the PERSONALIZATION screen
SYSTEM NEWS	Opens a dialog box that displays system news
LOG OFF	Logs the user off the system

Table 2.1 SAP CRM Web UI System Links

▶ **Saved searches and central search**

The saved searches area provides access to a list of predefined search queries. The central search provides access to search queries using a single search field (e.g., search for an incident based on its transaction ID).

▶ **Page history**

Breadcrumbs are visible to the user after selecting the triangle symbol next to the back button on the right side of the screen. A breadcrumb is a SAP CRM term that refers to a recently viewed page. By clicking on a breadcrumb, you're taken to that corresponding page. Figure 2.15 shows the Incident Management work center and home page as two breadcrumbs.

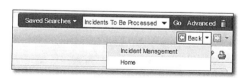

Figure 2.15 History Navigation

▶ **Work area toolbar**

The work area toolbar contains *function buttons* that perform actions related to the entire page displayed in the corresponding work center. For SAP ITSM functions, these function buttons provide access to the following activities as shown in Figure 2.16:

▶ ADD TO FAVORITES

▶ GO TO

▶ PERSONALIZE

▶ PRINT PAGE

Figure 2.16 Function Buttons in the Work Area Toolbar

▶ **Message bar**
The message bar is found directly beneath the work area toolbar as shown in Figure 2.17. However, if no messages are available, this area isn't visible to the user. The message bar will inform the user of errors, warnings, or successful events. The message bar may also appear in other dialog windows such as search windows or tables.

Figure 2.17 Message Bar

Table 2.2 contains a description of each element of the message bar.

Message Bar Element	Description
Message icons	Each message displayed will be marked by an icon. For SAP ITSM functions, the most common message types are marked with the following icons: ▶ Error message (🔲) ▶ Warning message (❗) ▶ Success or general system event message (ⓘ)
Details link	Sometimes, the system will provide additional details about the message. If so, a DETAILS button will appear before the message text providing a link to further documentation about the message.

Table 2.2 SAP CRM Web UI Message Elements

Message Bar Element	Description
Message text	The message text provides a short and simple description of the message.

Table 2.2 SAP CRM Web UI Message Elements (Cont.)

Navigation Bar

The navigation bar consists of four areas:

▶ First-level navigation area

▶ Second-level navigation area

▶ Create area

▶ Recent objects area

The navigation bar can be collapsed or expanded by clicking the inward-facing triangle symbol (◀) near the top-left of the page. Figure 2.18 shows an image of the expanded navigation bar.

Figure 2.18 SAP CRM Web UI Navigation Bar

If you have chosen to collapse the navigation bar, the work area will appear much larger (taking up most of your screen). Furthermore, the only button you'll see from the navigation bar is the button to expand the navigation bar again. Figure 2.19 displays the expanded work area with the navigation bar collapsed. Clicking the outward-facing triangle symbol (▶) will cause the navigation bar to appear again.

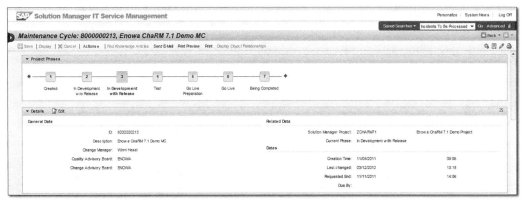

Figure 2.19 Full-Page Work Area View

First-Level Navigation Area

If you take a scenario with a user who has full authorizations for the SAP CRM Web UI profile and a SAP Solution Manager system out-of-the box, the navigation area will have eight entries (as shown earlier in Figure 2.18):

- HOME
- WORKLIST
- CALENDAR
- E-MAIL INBOX
- MASTER DATA
- CHANGE REQUEST MANAGEMENT

- Incident Management
- Service Operations

The navigation area could contain even fewer entries if the SAP CRM Web UI is tailored to meet specific duties for the end user. For example, SAP CRM Web UI authorizations can be adjusted so specific users can see a limited amount of entries within the first-level navigation area. However, the Home entry within first-level navigation is mandatory. Similarly, the navigation area will contain fewer entries if the business roles SOLMANREQU or SOLMANDSPTCH are assigned.

The recommended sequence for first-level navigation entries are as shown in Figure 2.20:

- Home
- Worklist
- Calendar
- E-mail Inbox
- Master Data
- <work centers>

Figure 2.20 SAP CRM Web UI First-Level Navigation Areas

Selecting one of these first-level navigation areas will result in its corresponding work center page to appear in the work area.

Second-Level Navigation Area

Second-level navigation is opened by simply clicking the triangle symbol (▶) near the end of the first-level navigation text. Figure 2.21 displays an example of the Incident Management entry expanded to display its second-level navigation menu.

Figure 2.21 SAP CRM Web UI Second-Level Navigation Areas

Because Incident Management is a work center in the SAP CRM Web UI, the second-level navigation menu will provide the user direct access to links to search pages associated with Incident Management. To close the second-level navigation menu, simply click on the triangle icon again, which will collapse this menu.

Create Area

The CREATE area contains links that will open transaction types in the work area (see Figure 2.22). No content is transferred to the created page unless you have configured the SAP CRM UI to include templates (e.g., incident templates) within the CREATE area. Links within the CREATE area can be personalized depending on the end user's job function. For example, users who just have the ability to log incidents can have their CREATE area personalized to display just the INCIDENT link.

Figure 2.22 SAP CRM Web UI Create Area

Recent Items Area

The RECENT ITEMS area will display the last five objects that the user has accessed by displaying or editing the object (see Figure 2.23). This is helpful in that these objects are kept up to date across sessions. In other words, if the user logs off and then logs on again later, the content of these objects remains available to the user.

Five recent items is the standard. If this isn't sufficient (and, typically, it isn't), the recent objects area can be personalized to include up to 10 of these objects.

Recent items are limited to transaction-level object types. For example, these links provide access to objects such as problems, incidents, and requests for change. You can't access areas such as work centers, search pages, or the home page.

Figure 2.23 SAP CRM Web UI Recent Items

Page Types

The SAP CRM Web UI is made up of numerous elements that allow each user group to display, search for, and maintain various types of data. All of this information is accessible via links and fields within various *page types*. Page types make up the core sections of the SAP CRM Web UI. For the purposes of ITSM in SAP Solution Manager, the page types described in the following subsections will be the main screen areas users will log into to access their information. In this section, we'll introduce the main page types within the SAP CRM Web UI for processing SAP ITSM functions.

Home Page

The user's home page is the first page that should appear when the SAP CRM Web UI is launched from the user's browser (see Figure 2.24). If it doesn't appear, we recommend that you update your URL favorite's link so the home page is accessed right off the bat. The home page is the user's starting point to begin accessing information and processing tasks related to his role in the organization.

The home page should contain only the most important personal information, as well as provide access to the most frequently used tools, specific to the user.

The links to these tools and this information should be determined by the user. Adding this content provides a personalized way to enhance the user's experience within the SAP CRM Web UI. The following links can be added to the user's home page (we'll provide instruction on how to adapt the SAP CRM Web UI to meet your specific requirements in Chapter 3):

- ▶ TODAY'S APPOINTMENTS

- ▶ FAVORITES

- ▶ MY OPEN TASKS

- ▶ WORKFLOW TASKS

- ▶ ALERTS

- ▶ REQUESTS (that belong to the user)

- ▶ WEB LINKS

- ▶ FAVORITE REPORTS

- ▶ SEARCH QUERIES

- ▶ MY SAVED SEARCHES

Links to various tools, information, and reports in the home page can either be *static* or *dynamic*. For example, TODAY'S APPOINTMENTS is an example of dynamic information because it's likely to change on a frequent basis. FAVORITE REPORTS, on the other hand, represents information that can be static. Information that is static isn't likely to change.

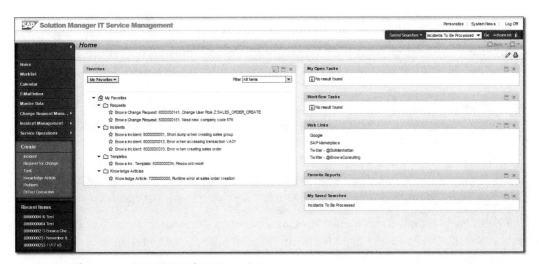

Figure 2.24 SAP CRM Web UI Home Page

Work Center Page

Every first-level navigation entry will link the user to a work center page. The work center page will contain a set of shortcuts and provide the user access to various SAP CRM components associated with the related work center. Figure 2.25

displays the Change Request Management work center with direct access to shortcuts to search and create various components related to ChaRM.

Figure 2.25 SAP CRM Web UI Work Center Page

Search Page

The SEARCH page provides the user with expansive search capabilities for the SAP CRM component in question. Each SEARCH page will offer an area to identify (and personalize) search criteria as well as provide a results list that maps to the specified search criteria.

Figure 2.26 represents a search page for the REQUEST FOR CHANGE component.

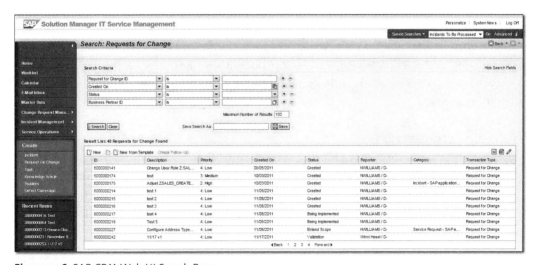

Figure 2.26 SAP CRM Web UI Search Page

Overview Page

The OVERVIEW page is where the lowest level data—transaction data—is viewed and processed. Each SAP CRM component will have an OVERVIEW page that consists of numerous *assignment blocks* depending on which SAP CRM component is being processed (we'll discuss these in the following subsection). Figure 2.27 shows the overview page for a maintenance cycle.

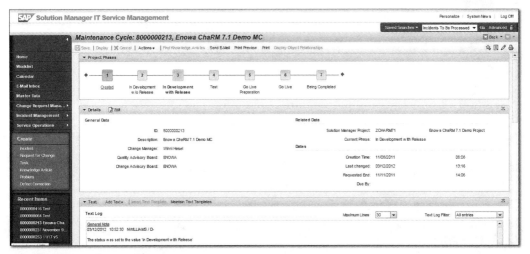

Figure 2.27 SAP CRM Web UI Overview Page

Content Blocks and Assignment Blocks

The *content blocks* and *assignment blocks* screen areas, within the architecture of the SAP CRM Web UI, can be considered the most significant parts of the UI when it comes to organizing and displaying the information within the work center pages.

Content Blocks

The concept of content blocks is very simple: they display different types of information. This can be said about most pieces of SAP architecture, but content blocks are all about displaying information within a work center in an organized and intuitive manner. The information, or links, can come in the form of lists, textual descriptions, or analytical content.

As you can see in Figure 2.28, there are two content blocks within the CHANGE REQUEST MANAGEMENT work center screen. Notice that the links (in this example, they are in the form of a list) are different, but the structure of the content blocks are standardized. This is the case throughout the entire architecture of the SAP CRM Web UI. While the information and links of the content blocks differ within each work center, how a content block is made up remains standard in most ways.

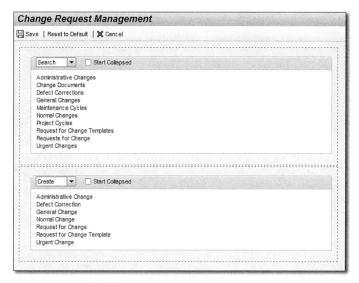

Figure 2.28 Content Blocks

Each content block has the following:

▶ A title that provides a short description of what is available within the content block (e.g., SEARCH or CREATE).

▶ The possibility to have the content block opened or collapsed when the page is loaded. If the START COLLAPSED option is flagged, the content block will appear as a tray when the user opens the work center.

▶ The ability to remove a content block without having to do so in the PERSONAL-IZATION area

▶ A content area that provides the access to lists, textual descriptions, or analytical content.

Assignment Blocks

Assignment blocks are another way to display information. Unlike content blocks, assignment blocks are specific to individual object types. In other words, assignment blocks display and organize information for items such as incidents, requests for change, and change documents.

All objects will have the DETAILS assignment block, as well as numerous other assignment blocks depending on the work center selected. We'll cover assignment blocks in detail later, but Figure 2.29 will give you an idea of what they look like.

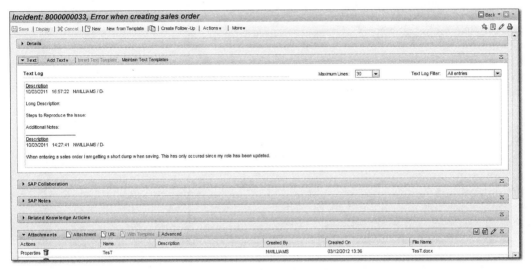

Figure 2.29 Assignment Blocks within an Incident

2.2 Work Centers

For readers who may be newer to the concepts of SAP Solution Manager, it will be helpful to understand what a Work Center is and how it fits in the overall Application Lifecycle Management (ALM) offering within SAP Solution Manager. We've already talked about SAP CRM Web UI work centers, but now it's time to switch gears and understand Work Centers from a fundamental SAP Solution Manager perspective.

> **Note**
>
> Remember, as a way to differentiate in this book, Work Center refers to those in SAP Solution Manager, which is the topic of this section. The lowercased version of the term—work centers—refers to those in the SAP CRM Web UI.

2.2.1   What Is a Work Center in SAP Solution Manager?

An SAP Solution Manager Work Center is a web-based UI—accessible via a single transaction in the SAP Solution Manager system—that provides role-based access to scenarios relevant to individual users. Depending on the user's role, Work Centers provide direct access to the various tools within SAP Solution Manager that execute functions that drive end-to-end solutions operations. In other words, the functionality that can be reached from the Work Centers includes those that span from project implementation all the way to optimization, and all of these functions are integrated among each other.

Organizations that rely heavily on SAP Solution Manager for multiple scenarios find Work Centers to be especially valuable. For example, if SAP Solution Manager is deployed to manage implementation projects, monitor critical business processes, monitor technical operations, used for test management and IT Service Management Work Centers are important. Rather than the end-user having to access and remember several transactions, they can log on to their Work Center (Transaction SOLMAN_WORKCENTER) and have a common view of all of the tasks that relate to their job role.

Work Centers were first introduced in 2008 with SAP Solution Manager 7.0, service pack (SP) 15. They were the first significant improvement to a UI that the market had been exposed to since its initial release. Moreover, Work Centers were the first web-based UI that SAP Solution Manager offered to SAP practitioners. Work Centers provided the market with a sign of hope for Solution Manager: significant improvements and product attention were underway.

2.2.2   Key Features of SAP Solution Manager Work Centers

In this section, we will discuss the key features of SAP Solution Manager Work Centers. Work Centers, while they provide value to organizations that deploy multiple SAP Solution Manager scenarios, are not required for use with the ITSM functions. The Work Centers act as a portal to the ITSM CRM Web UI, which will result in an extra click for those who are not using the Work Centers in the first place. For this purpose, we recommend only using the Work Centers if your user base is used to working with them and rely on them for other SAP Solution Manager scenarios.

Role Based

Typically, the first point that is always established when the topic of Work Centers comes up is that they are *role based*. Role based means that users have direct access to their work based on the authorizations assigned to them in user maintenance. Work Centers have their own unique security roles that are delivered with SAP Solution Manager. In other words, users must be assigned both role-based Work Center roles in addition to the traditional security roles they will require. Just like the traditional security roles assigned in user maintenance, the Work Center roles can be adapted for specific needs of various user groups.

Assigning Work Center roles provides each user view and edit access to various access points within the Work Center home page. Users can be assigned one or many Work Center roles, depending on the needs and requirements of their job duties.

We'll describe the security aspect and identify which roles are relevant for SAP ITSM in Chapter 3.

Intuitive Navigation

Because users are accessing duties specific to their needs and requirements, they're logging onto an interface that only displays information relevant to them. Having a central access point to view only the most pertinent information establishes an environment that is slimmed down and easy to use. The architecture, as described in Section 2.2.4, is very similar to the SAP CRM Web UI. The main screens are divided into three areas for simplicity. Navigation is also intuitive in that the functions are web-based. Additionally, the Work Centers use common structures and content elements that make navigating this environment easy to grasp for end users and administrators alike.

Common Interface

The navigation, buttons, and architecture of the Work Centers are standard, no matter what role your end user plays in SAP ITSM. A common, standardized interface makes things easier when navigating between various Work Centers. Unlike traditional SAP GUI screens or transactions, which vary vastly depending on the associated activities, Work Centers provide a common way to access and process information no matter what job role you may have.

2.2.3 Navigating the Work Centers

From our perspective, there are two key methods to access the Work Centers in SAP Solution Manager, as described in the following subsections.

Access from the SAP GUI

Transaction SOLMAN_WORKCENTER will launch a new SAP screen that almost appears as if it were opening a web browser. What appears like an web browser is in fact a *Web Dynpro for ABAP* application for SAP Solution Manager.

Web Dynpro is the SAP NetWeaver programming model, which is a standard SAP UI technology for developing web-like representations of different applications. In our case, the applications consist of SAP ITSM functions within the SAP Solution Manager environment.

Access from a Web Browser

If you want to display the Work Centers via a URL, as opposed to the Web Dynpro application, you can launch them from a web browser as well by using Transaction SM_WORKCENTER. Executed from the SAP GUI, this transaction will open a web browser that displays all of the work centers the user is assigned to.

2.2.4 Architecture of SAP Solution Manager Work Centers

In this section, we'll provide an introduction to the architecture of the SAP Solution Manager Work Centers. The Work Center architecture is related closely to that of the SAP CRM Web UI architecture. The screen layout is divided into three areas that are navigated almost the same as the SAP CRM Web UI.

Figure 2.30 identifies the three main components of the Work Center architecture. Take note of how similar this architecture is to that of the SAP CRM Web UI. The Work Centers are made up of three main areas, which we'll discuss in the following subsections.

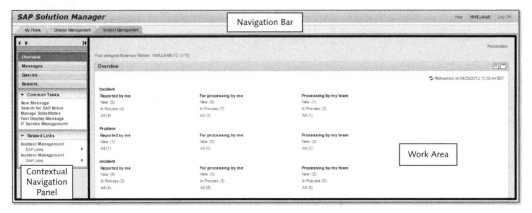

Figure 2.30 Work Center Architecture

Navigation Bar

The navigation bar is how users identify the Work Centers in which they are assigned (see Figure 2.31). (Users will never see the words "Work Center" anywhere on the screen.) The tabs along the navigation bar help users identify which areas they are responsible for.

The Work Center security role that users are assigned will drive which tabs they see and have access to. Each tab contains all of the information and links that users require to perform their job functions. Typically, most information and task execution can be achieved with one click. The Work Centers are designed so that the links provided are the most critical and relevant to accessing the most important activities to the user.

Figure 2.31 Navigation Bar

Contextual Navigation Panel

The contextual navigation panel, located on the left side of the work center, is divided into three areas (see Figure 2.32):

▶ **First-level navigation entries**
  The first-level navigation entries are very similar to the architecture in the SAP

CRM Web UI. These high-level links provide access to the Work Center core components.

▸ **Common tasks**

Common tasks provide direct access to activities that the user typically always accesses according to the specific Work Center. Tasks within this area span the entire Work Center and aren't limited to just one of the first-level navigation areas.

▸ **Related links**

Related links provide access to information and activities that are related to the specific Work Center.

Figure 2.32 Contextual Navigation Panel

Work Area

The work area within each work center contains all of the functions and information required to complete corresponding tasks. Figure 2.33 identifies a work area for processing incidents. In the OVERVIEW area, users are shown all incidents they have reported, those they need to process, and the incidents that belong to their team.

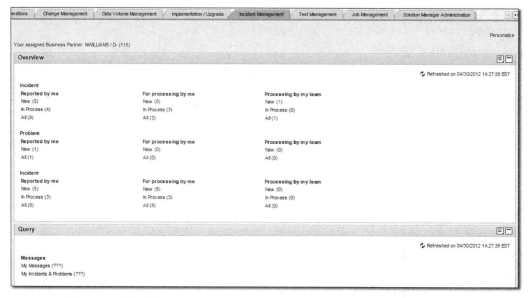

Figure 2.33 Work Area

2.3 Summary

SAP Solution Manager provides web-based user interfaces to support the interaction with activities to support ALM. As you're aware, SAP Solution Manager has evolved from traditional SAP GUI-based screens, to Work Centers, and now to the advanced SAP CRM Web UI to support ITSM functions. The introduction of the SAP CRM Web UI is an instrumental and sophisticated way to illustrate how usability is profoundly enhanced within release 7.1. Its features, ease of use via simple navigation capabilities, and architecture are all designed for a better quality end-user experience. This is especially important when delivering ITSM processes.

In the next chapter, we will begin explaining what you must plan for and execute in order to prepare your SAP Solution Manager system to support ITSM functions. Now that you're aware of the user interfaces to support these functions, we'll begin our discussion on post-installation activities, security, master data setup, and user interface adaption.

Regardless of the size, complexity, or scope of the ITSM functionality you decide to deploy through SAP Solution Manager, there are preparatory activities that must be completed before diving into the functional config- uration. This chapter highlights those activities, and provides use case examples that will help guide you through setting them up.

3 Preparing Your SAP Solution Manager System to Support SAP ITSM Functions

Now that you have a thorough understanding of the integration between Appli- cation Lifecycle Management (ALM) and IT Service Management (ITSM), as well as the supporting frameworks to enable the delivery of IT services, it's time to start standing these processes up in your SAP Solution Manager system. Before we dive into the meat of the SAP ITSM scenarios, we must begin by building a base.

This chapter provides an overview of the prerequisite and basic setup activities that will establish the foundation for subsequent activities related to building out your SAP ITSM strategy in the SAP Solution Manager system. Building this foun- dation consists of the following main areas:

▶ Post-installation and technical setup
▶ Authorization roles and security concept
▶ Master data maintenance
▶ Adapting the SAP CRM Web UI: configuration and personalization

The content described in this chapter spans technical, Basis, security, SAP Solu- tion Manager, and SAP CRM tasks. Although we don't expect you to be an expert in all of these areas, our objective is to provide the information necessary for you to execute and/or lead the completion of tasks related to these areas to prepare your SAP Solution Manager system to receive SAP ITSM.

3.1 Post-Installation and Technical Setup

After the Basis team has finished either upgrading or installing the latest SAP Solution Manager 7.1 system and delivered it as available, you must take the necessary steps to stand up SAP ITSM.

This section provides an overview of the basic configuration steps required prior to configuring the SAP ITSM scenarios in SAP Solution Manager. We'll describe which steps are critical and how to perform them before the SAP ITSM processes can be enabled.

The objective of this section is to provide you with the critical steps required to prepare your SAP Solution Manager system to run SAP ITSM processes. You'll notice a lot of steps and activities that are touch points to other scenarios within SAP Solution Manager. For our purposes, we can ignore those. Additionally, there are cases where the guided procedures include tasks that will be discussed in detail in later chapters.

3.1.1 Overview

Most likely the first transaction you'll execute after the SAP Solution Manager system has been installed is Transaction SOLMAN_SETUP. Transaction SOLMAN_SETUP provides guided procedures to help quickly deploy the basic configuration settings required before incorporating business and IT requirements into the SAP Solution Manager scenarios.

Documentation, accelerators, and direct links to the activities performed within the SAP Solution Manager system are provided within Transaction SOLMAN_SETUP. In many cases, automatic deployment of configuration is available to rapidly apply the configuration. In other cases, which will be noted, you must manually configure the settings. For these cases, documentation is provided along the way with step-by-step instruction.

> **Note**
>
> For guidance on the necessary authorizations to perform the basic configuration, see SAP Note 1560717: ST7.0 and 7.1 SP01 and Higher: Roles for SOLMAN_SETUP.

Figure 3.1 identifies the UI of Transaction SOLMAN_SETUP.

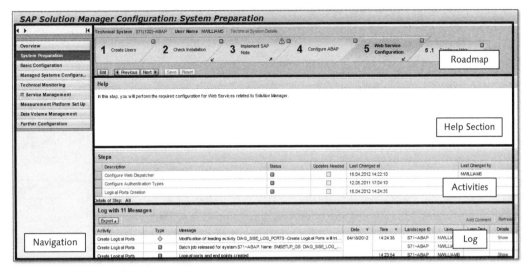

Figure 3.1 SOLMAN_SETUP Architecture

The following components make up the overall architecture of the basic configuration activities:

▶ **Navigation bar**
   Selecting an area within the navigation bar will determine which set of activities get displayed. For the purposes of SAP ITSM and to stick within the scope of activities within this book, we'll focus on the following areas:

   ▶ System Preparation

   ▶ Basic Configuration

   ▶ IT Service Management

   We recommend that the basic configuration activities be completed in their entirety after the SAP Solution Manager system has been installed and/or upgraded. For our purposes, we'll limit the overview and instruction to activities dealing specifically with ITSM.

▶ **Roadmap**
   The roadmap section identifies where you are within the basic configuration steps. Depending on which navigation item you select, the roadmap will update accordingly. At each phase in the roadmap, colored icons will identify the status of each phase (as described in Table 3.1).

Status	Description
▢	Step was performed successfully.
△	Step was performed with warnings (recheck needed).
⚠	Step requires reexecution because of system update.
⊗	Step was performed with errors (recheck and re-execute).

Table 3.1 Transaction SOLMAN_SETUP Status Information Icons

- **Help section**
  Each Transaction SOLMAN_SETUP screen has a HELP section that typically provides background information about the selected activity as well as expected results after the activity has been performed.

- **Activities**
  The ACTIVITIES section provides links to execute both automatic and manual tasks as well as links to the associated documentation. Status information and execution status is recorded to help identify which tasks have been completed successfully.

- **Log**
  The LOG section provides detailed information immediately following the execution of an activity. The log keeps a history of the activity that was performed, by who, when, and the resulting status.

3.1.2 System Preparation

For system preparation, we'll complete the steps described in the following subsections. You'll find a brief overview of each of these steps, as well as instructions on how to configure these basic settings.

Create Users

Creating the SAP Solution Manager users with Transaction SOLMAN_SETUP guided procedures is quick, simple, and automatic. After a few clicks, all of the required system and dialog users, passwords, and their roles are automatically created.

You have the flexibility to perform any of the following maintenance activities, depending on whether the users need to be created or updated. For the following activities, ensure that you're in the SYSTEM PREPARATION • CREATE USERS work area.

▶ CREATE NEW USERS (use one of the following methods)

  ▷ Select the button CREATE ALL USERS.

  ▷ Select each user one by one, and then select the EXECUTE button.

▶ UPDATE AUTHORIZATIONS

  ▷ Select the user that requires the update (Transaction SOLMAN_SETUP will provide status information if this is the case).

  ▷ Select the option to UPDATE AUTHORIZATIONS OF EXISTING USERS in the ACTION field.

  ▷ Click EXECUTE.

▶ UPDATE PASSWORDS

  ▷ Select a system user.

  ▷ Select the option to UPDATE PASSWORD in the ACTION field.

  ▷ Select EXECUTE.

Note

Keep the following in mind when maintaining users and passwords from SAP Solution Manager:

▶ Passwords for dialog users (e.g., SOLMAN_ADMIN) aren't needed and therefore don't require maintenance.

▶ If your system users are controlled via Central User Administration (CUA), they can't be maintained from Transaction SOLMAN_SETUP.

Figure 3.2 identifies the area in Transaction SOLMAN_SETUP for creating users.

Check Installation

In these steps, the SAP Solution Manager automatically performs a series of various checks to validate that those specific parameters, system settings, connections, configurations, and prerequisites are fulfilled prior to configuring the scenarios in SAP Solution Manager.

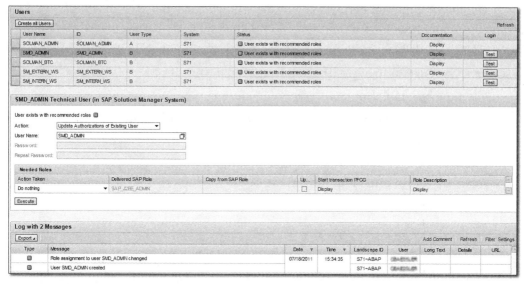

Figure 3.2 Create Users: Transaction SOLMAN_SETUP

To perform these steps, do the following:

1. Ensure you're in the SYSTEM PREPARATION • CHECK INSTALLATION work area of Transaction SOLMAN_SETUP.

2. Select the button EXECUTE ALL.

3. Each activity description below should result in a green status after they have been executed as shown in Figure 3.3. Any errors or warnings will appear in the log in the bottom of the screen. Correct the errors and warnings before proceeding.

Status	Updates Needed	Description
▣	☐	Check TMS Configuration
▣	☐	Check Profile Parameters
▣	☐	Check License Key
▣	☐	Software Prerequisites
▣	☐	Check System Landscape Parameters
▣	☐	Check Service Connection

Figure 3.3 Check Installation Activities Successful

Implement SAP Notes

Implementing the SAP Solution Manager central correction note is absolutely essential before beginning the configuration of SAP ITSM scenarios (or any SAP Solution Manager scenario). The central correction note contains a collection of notes that provides a foundation for configuration as well as fixes to various configurations within SAP Solution Manager. In the guided procedure, you must complete all of the following steps associated with applying the central correction note:

▶ Downloading the note from SAP

▶ Importing the note via Transaction SNOTE

▶ Performing post-processing

Transaction SOLMAN_SETUP provides the central point to launch these activities as well as track the processing status. However, the central correction note is applied via Transaction SNOTE (which you'll notice when you begin to execute these activities).

> **Important!**
>
> Be sure to pay attention, note, and perform all required manual post-processing steps. While Transaction SNOTE will import the majority of the corrections automatically, there will be cases in which manual post-processing is required. Don't overlook or think you can skip these steps. If you don't perform them, you'll encounter issues in the future.

Often, SAP will provide updates (new notes) to the central correction note associated with the support package your SAP Solution Manager system is currently on. There are three different ways to identify the updates:

▶ An information pop-up box appears when you access the SYSTEM PREPARATION activities.

▶ An indicator in the roadmap next to the text IMPLEMENT SAP NOTE warns you that you must reexecute the activity.

▶ The UPDATES NEEDED field is flagged in the steps to implement the note.

Execute these activities by clicking on the relevant links as shown in Figure 3.4. You'll be taken directly to the Transaction SNOTE in the SAP GUI. To complete these activities, adhere to your organization's standard process for implementing SAP Notes.

Figure 3.4 Steps to Implement Central Correction Note

Configure ABAP

This simple, automated configuration performs the following key activities:

▶ Creates SAP Solution Manager as a system in your landscape

▶ Creates the logical systems for SAP Solution Manager

▶ Activates the Service Data Control Center (not relevant for SAP ITSM)

Simply clicking the EXECUTE SELECTED button above the SOLMAN_SETUP activity will achieve these basic configuration settings.

Web Service Configuration

Web Service Configuration, although not directly related to the SAP ITSM functions, should not be skipped because we're configuring all of the SYSTEM PREPARATION tasks within Transaction SOLMAN_SETUP.

These basic configuration settings enable the necessary activation for web services related to SAP Solution Manager; that is, services related to web dispatcher, authentication types, and the creation of logical ports. Because these items are beyond the scope of our book we won't go into depth about the web services.

The web services can be activated by clicking on their respective links and following the related documentation for how to configure them.

Prepare Landscape

The activities within the PREPARE LANDSCAPE section of Transaction SOLMAN_SETUP relate almost exclusively to synching content from the System Landscape Directory (SLD) to the Landscape Management Database (LMDB). The LMDB, which can be considered the "next-wave" System Landscape area (Transaction SMSY), must be populated with the systems SAP ITSM will control.

As of SAP Solution Manager 7.1, certain key activities can't be administered in Transaction SMSY. For example, the creation of Remote Function Call (RFC) connections must be set up in the LMDB. So, to begin configuring the ChaRM scenario within SAP ITSM, your managed systems must be populated within the LMDB.

Administering the SLD and LMDB are technical tasks that the Basis (technical) teams are responsible for. In subsequent chapters, we'll discuss the LMDB further as well as describe how to generate the RFC connections to the managed systems within the LMDB.

In Transaction SOLMAN_SETUP, guided procedures and documentation are available to help you populate the LMDB with your systems via SLD synchronization.

3.1.3 Basic Configuration

In the BASIC CONFIGURATION area of Transaction SOLMAN_SETUP, SAP ITSM is primarily concerned with the tasks within the CONFIGURE AUTOMATICALLY section. Like the other areas of Transaction SOLMAN_SETUP, we recommend that they are all configured as part of post-processing the SAP Solution Manager system. For the purposes of our book, we'll continue to explain the basic configuration steps necessary to begin the configuration of SAP ITSM.

Configure Automatically

Specifically, the following tasks within the CONFIGURE AUTOMATICALLY section are critical for SAP ITSM:

- ACTIVATE PIECE LISTS
- CREATE EXTERNAL ALIASES
- ACTIVATE SERVICES
- PREPARE BUSINESS PARTNER CHANGE
- BUSINESS PARTNER FOR SAP SUPPORT
- GENERATE BUSINESS PARTNER SCREEN

▶ SCHEDULE BACKGROUND JOBS

▶ CONNECTION TO SAP

▶ SCHEDULE STANDARD JOBS

▶ CLEAN-UP PRIORITIES FROM ISSUES SCHEMA

At a minimum, these configuration activities must be completed prior to beginning the configuration of your SAP ITSM scenarios. The documentation within Transaction SOLMAN_SETUP will provide an overview of each of these activities.

To configure them, you can select either the EXECUTE ALL or EXECUTE SELECTED buttons, depending on your configuration approach.

3.1.4   IT Service Management

In this section of the Transaction SOLMAN_SETUP activities, we'll describe the basic configuration specific to SAP ITSM. As previously mentioned, there will be some steps within this section that we'll postpone for now. The postponed steps will be described in more detail in subsequent chapters. We will cover configuration and setup activities, including use case examples, throughout the following chapters:

▶ Chapter 10

▶ Chapter 14

▶ Chapter 15

▶ Chapter 16

Incident and Problem Management

From the main page of SOLMAN_SETUP, select the INCIDENT & PROBLEM MANAGEMENT button shown in Figure 3.5 to begin the guided procedures for the first SAP ITSM scenario.

Figure 3.5 Select Incident Management Guided Procedures

Figure 3.6 shows the Transaction SOLMAN_SETUP areas specific to Incident and Problem Management. The activities shown in the gray boxes are covered in this chapter. When navigating through these areas, you'll see a lot of other tasks that are related to this SAP ITSM scenario. For now, we'll place those activities on hold until we reach a later chapter. For tracking and documentation purposes, you have the option to manually set the execution status for each activity to help you keep track of what still must be performed.

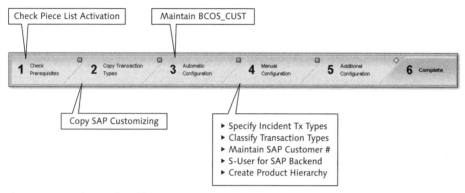

Figure 3.6 Incident and Problem Management Activities

We'll go over the areas shown in the figure in the following subsections.

Check Piece List Activation

This step will run a check to make sure that the piece lists have been activated (we performed the activation in Basic Configuration). After you execute the check, you should receive a log entry as shown in Figure 3.7. If you receive an error or warning, you may have skipped this in Basic Configuration.

Figure 3.7 Piece List Activation Log

Copy Transaction Types

A *transaction type*, also referred to as a document type, defines the attributes and characteristics of a SAP CRM business transaction. Transaction types exist in SAP Solution Manager for any functionality that leverages messaging capabilities. For example, problem messages, incident messages, defect corrections, and requests for change are all transaction types in SAP Solution Manager.

Copying the standard transaction types into a customer namespace ensures that changes (both during implementation and in the future) to Customizing are not overwritten as a result of support packages, upgrades, or related maintenance activities.

SAP Solution Manager 7.1 provides a TRANSACTION TYPE COPY TOOL screen that automatically copies standard transaction types and their associated profiles (e.g., status, partner, action profiles). To use this screen, follow these steps:

1. Launch the TRANSACTION TYPE COPY TOOL screen by selecting the START TRANSACTION button next to the task COPY SAP STANDARD CUSTOMIZING.

2. In the next screen (Figure 3.8), enter the value "SMIN" in the SOURCE TRANSACTION TYPE field, and the value "YMIN" in the TARGET TRANSACTION TYPE field.

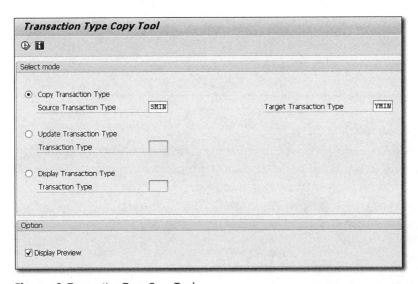

Figure 3.8 Transaction Type Copy Tool

3. On the next page, COPY TRANSACTION TYPE (SMIN → YMIN), select the START COPYING PROCESS button ( ).

4. Confirm all of the prompts to store the Customizing in a transport request.

5. Confirm that your logs contain no errors as shown in Figure 3.9.

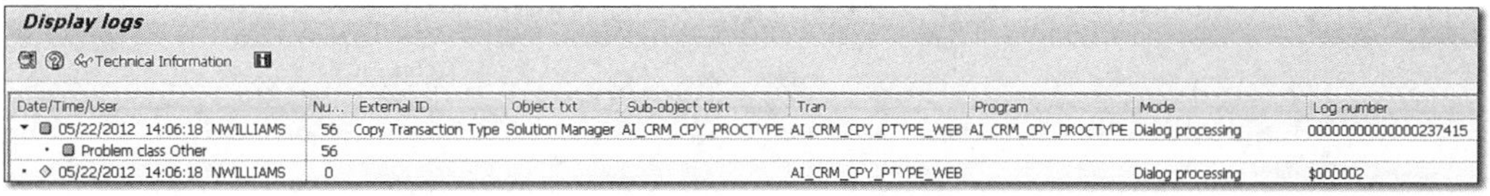

Figure 3.9 Copy Transaction Type Logs

You must repeat this process for each transaction type in scope for your SAP ITSM scenario. Chapter 4 provides an overview of each transaction type relating to SAP ITSM functions.

Maintain BCOS_CUST

In the AUTOMATIC CONFIGURATION section, you execute the automatic activity that populates Table BCOS_CUST with the appropriate entry. For Incident Management, this entry is required when incidents are generated from the HELP • CREATE SUPPORT MESSAGE option.

Specify Transaction Types for Incidents

In the MANUAL CONFIGURATION section, you begin by specifying which transaction type will be triggered when a new incident is created from SAP Solution Manager. Because you have copied the standard SMIN into your customer namespace, you want to call the YMIN incident transaction type.

1. Select the link START TRANSACTION next to the activity SPECIFY TRANSACTION TYPE FOR INCIDENTS.

2. In the SAP GUI screen that appears, maintain your incident transaction type in the PROCESS_TYPE field as shown in Figure 3.10.

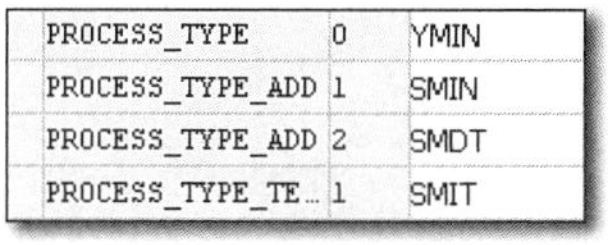

Figure 3.10 Specify Incident Transaction Type

3. Click SAVE.

Classify Transaction Types

In this manual activity, you'll classify the transaction type for Incident Management depending on one of four scenarios:

- Default (normal Incident Management usage)
- Software partner (you get messages from SAP regarding software development)
- Service provider (Incident Management is deployed for several customers)
- SAP Business ByDesign (Incident Management is deployed for SAP Business ByDesign)

Follow these steps:

1. Start the transaction for the activity CLASSIFY TRANSACTION TYPE(S).

2. In the SAP GUI screen that appears, click the NEW ENTRIES button.

3. Enter the details as shown in Figure 3.11, depending on your scenario.

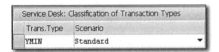

Figure 3.11 Classify Transaction Type for Incident Management

Maintain SAP Customer Number

In this manual configuration activity, you maintain your SAP customer number(s) to use basic SAP Solution Manager functions:

1. Press the START TRANSACTION link to begin the activity MAINTAIN SAP CUSTOMER NUMBER.

2. In the SAP GUI screen that appears, select your customer number from the PROCESSED BY NUMBER field as shown in Figure 3.12.

3. Click EXECUTE.

Figure 3.12 Maintain SAP Customer Number

Maintain S-User for SAP Backend

In this manual configuration activity, you define which SAP Solution Manager users communicate with SAP support when leveraging the backend communication via Incident Management. For these users, their SAP S-user must be maintained in SAP Solution Manager.

Follow these steps:

1. Start the transaction MAINTAIN S-USER FOR SAP BACKEND.

2. Click the NEW ENTRIES button.

3. In the USER column, enter the user ID of the person communicating to SAP.

4. Enter the S-user ID (without the leading zeros) in the CONTACT PERSON column as shown in Figure 3.13.

5. Click SAVE.

Figure 3.13 S-User Assignment

Create Product Hierarchy

In this manual configuration activity, you define a product hierarchy for service in which SAP Solution Manager will assign a subcategory and products. This is a one-time setup activity that is required by SAP Solution Manager. Follow these steps:

1. Start the transaction for CREATE PRODUCT HIERARCHY.

2. In the SAP GUI screen that opens, execute the report.

Change Request Management

To conclude the guided procedures within Transaction SOLMAN_SETUP, you'll perform the basic configuration pertaining to the Change Request Management (ChaRM) scenario of SAP ITSM. As we have previously mentioned with Incident Management, we'll postpone the majority of these tasks for later explanation.

In Transaction SOLMAN_SETUP, select the CHANGE REQUEST MANAGEMENT radio button (Figure 3.14) to display the related tasks.

Figure 3.14 Select Change Request Management Guided Procedures

After selecting this radio button, you'll see activity areas that are similar to those within the Incident and Problem Management guided procedures. The additional activity area is IMPLEMENT SAP NOTE, which is shown in Figure 3.15.

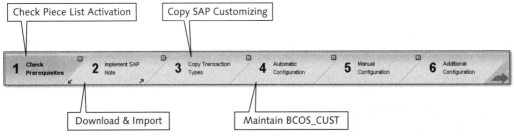

Figure 3.15 Change Request Management Activities

Similar to how we described the Incident and Problem Management activities, we'll walk you through the basic configuration steps that are prerequisites to future content within this book.

Check Piece List Activation

Follow the same instructions as described in the previous section for checking the relative ChaRM piece lists.

Implement SAP Note

Just like the central correction note applied in SYSTEM PREPARATION, SAP Solution Manager delivers a central note for ChaRM activities. The ChaRM central correction note is applied in the same manner. The note is automatically deployed via Transaction SNOTE when launched from Transaction SOLMAN_SETUP.

> **Important!**
>
> Be sure to pay attention, note, and perform all required manual post-processing steps. Although Transaction SNOTE will import the majority of the corrections automatically, there will be cases in which manual post-processing is required. Don't overlook or think you can skip these steps. If you don't perform them, you'll encounter issues in the future.

Copy SAP Customizing

Follow the instructions we provided for this step within the Incident and Problem Management guided procedures for the ChaRM transaction types:

- SMCR (Request for Change)
- SMHF (Urgent Change)
- SMMJ (Normal Change)
- SMTM (Defect Correction)

Maintain BCOS_CUST

In this activity, SAP Solution Manager makes the necessary table updates to Table BCOS_CUST required for ChaRM. You may automatically execute this task, as you previously did for Incident Management. Figure 3.16 shows how Table BCOS_CUST should look after you've completed this step for both scenarios (Incident Management and Change Request Management).

Create Messages: Customizing			
Appl.	+ Dest.	+	+
CHARM	W NONE	CUST620	1.0
CHARM_DEST	W NONE	CUST620	1.0
OSS_MSG	W NONE	CUST620	1.0

Figure 3.16 Table BCOS_CUST (Complete)

Now that we've discussed the preparatory activities that can be completed via SOLMAN_SETUP (or manually from the SAP Solution Manager IMG), we will begin our discussion on authorization roles and security concepts for ITSM.

3.2 Authorization Roles and Security Concept

In this section, we describe which *authorization roles* are required within the SAP ITSM scenarios for technical and end users.

> **Note**
>
> Authorization roles, also referred to commonly as PFCG roles, are used to implement the security concept. With authorization roles, you enable users to perform various activities and restrict users from performing activities outside of their required job duties in the SAP ITSM scenario.

Chapter 5 will discuss details concerning the end user roles within SAP ITSM and their specific job duties according to the process being delivered. The objective of this section is to provide you with role matrices for each SAP ITSM scenario so that you have a basis for assigning these roles to test users.

> **Note**
>
> Details regarding authorization roles in the SAP Solution Manager system can be found within the security guide for SAP Solution Manager 7.1 via the following path to the SAP Service Marketplace: SERVICE.SAP.COM/INSTGUIDES • SAP COMPONENTS • SAP SOLUTION MANAGER • RELEASE 7.1 • SECURITY GUIDE SAP SOLUTION MANAGER 7.1 (beneath OPERATIONS).

3.2.1 Incident Management User Roles

Table 3.2 identifies the authorization roles required to perform Incident Management process activities. Each role involved in Incident Management (e.g., administrator, processor, key user, and display user) will be assigned single roles, based on the matrix in this table. Alternatively, SAP provides *composite roles* that can also be assigned to the users. A composite role consists of several single roles that are related to processing the same set of activities.

Authorization Role	Admin	Pro-cessor	Key User	Display User
SAP_SM_BI_BILO	X	X		X
SAP_BI_E2E	X	X		X
SAP_BW_SPR_REPORTING	X	X		X
SAP_SM_BI_EXTRACTOR	X			X
SAP_SM_BI_ADMIN	X			
SAP_SM_BI_SPR_REPORTING	X			
SAP_SM_BI_DISP		X		X
SAP_SM_CRM_UIU_FRAMEWORK	X	X		X
SAP_SM_CRM_UIU_SOLMANPRO	X	X		X
SAP_SM_CRM_UIU_SOLMANPRO_PROC	X	X		
SAP_SM_CRM_UIU_SOLMANPRO_ADMIN	X			
SAP_SMWORK_BASIC_INCIDENT	X	X	X	X
SAP_SMWORK_INCIDENT_MAN	X	X	X	X
SAP_SUPPDESK_ADMIN	X			
SAP_SUPPDESK_PROCESS		X		
SAP_SUPPDESK_CREATE			X	
SAP_SUPPDESK_DISPLAY				X

Table 3.2 Incident Management Authorization Role Matrix

3.2.2 Change Request Management

Similar to Incident Management, Change Request Management (ChaRM) has roles that must be tied to end users. Table 3.3 identifies the authorization roles and corresponding end-user roles they must be matched to.

▶ A: Administrator
▶ R: Requester
▶ C: Change Manager

- ▶ D: Developer
- ▶ T: Tester
- ▶ I: IT Operator

Authorization Role	A	R	C	D	T	I
SAP_SMWORK_BASIC_CHANGE_MAN	X	X	X	X	X	X
SAP_SMWORK_CHANGE_MAN	X	X	X	X	X	X
SAP_SM_CRM_UIU_FRAMEWORK	X	X	X	X	X	X
SAP_SM_CRM_UIU_SOLMANPRO	X	X	X	X	X	X
SAP_SM_CRM_UIU_SOLMANPRO_CHARM	X	X	X	X	X	X
SAP_SM_CRM_UIU_SOLMANPRO_ADMIN	X					
SAP_CM_SMAN_ADMINISTRATOR	X					
SAP_CPR_PROJECT_ADMINISTRATOR	X					
SAP_CPR_USER	X					
SAP_SOCM_ADMIN	X					
SAP_SOL_PROJ_ADMIN_ALL	X					
SAP_SOLAR01_DIS	X		X			
SAP_SOCM_REQUESTER		X				
SAP_CM_SMAN_CHANGE_MANAGER			X			
SAP_SOCM_CHANGE_MANAGER			X			
SAP_CM_SMAN_DEVELOPER				X		
SAP_SOCM_DEVELOPER				X		
SAP_CM_SMAN_TESTER					X	
SAP_SOCM_TESTER					X	
SAP_CM_SMAN_OPERATOR						X
SAP_SOCM_OPERATOR						X

Table 3.3 Change Request Management Authorization Role Matrix

3.2.3 Security Concept

The standard SAP roles are delivered as templates to support and enable best practices within your IT organization. We recommend that you assign test users—who simulate end users in SAP ITSM—to these roles as a foundation for blueprint and discover. These activities are essential to understanding how the roles and functionalizes within SAP ITSM operate out of the box. After you've gained a level of familiarity with the standards, you can begin to tailor these roles to meet organizational requirements.

> **Important!**
>
> You should never directly modify the standard roles delivered from SAP. Copy authorization roles into a customer namespace beginning with a "Z" or "Y". This will ensure that the roles you tailor specific to your organization's requirements are not affected during an upgrade.

3.3 Master Data Maintenance

Master data in SAP Solution Manager is used the same way in which other SAP products (e.g., SAP ERP) use master data. Like SAP ERP, SAP Solution Manager requires repetitive use of master data to support transaction-based processes and operations.

Common examples of master data in SAP ERP include the customer master, vendor master, pricing data, and bill of materials (BOM). Master data in SAP Solution Manager include the following:

▶ Business partners

▶ Organizational structure

▶ Installed base

▶ Number ranges

This data is intended to be reused over and over throughout the execution of SAP ITSM processes. You'll need test data in your development system to test your configurations. Furthermore, you'll need to establish production master data when it's time to go live with your SAP ITSM processes in SAP Solution Manager. Master data is non-transportable, which means you'll need to establish master data directly within each SAP Solution Manager system you have in your landscape.

We'll go over each of the listed types of master data, as well as how to set them up in the system, in the following sections.

3.3.1 Business Partners

Each member of your IT organization that plays a part in the SAP ITSM processes in SAP Solution Manager will need a business partner ID established for that member's user. First, the system user (with appropriate roles) needs to be set up in Transaction SU01 (User Maintenance). The business partner record is a separate piece that is required for these activities. The business partner ID creates the connection between the system user established in user maintenance and the business partner itself.

There are four key types of business partners that are required to drive Incident Management and ChaRM processes:

- **Sold-to party**
  The *sold-to party*, also known as the *root* of the organizational structure, is the highest level within the organizational structure. The sold-to party is the organization responsible for delivering SAP ITSM. The sold-to party can also be the organization's name itself.

- **Support team**
  A *support team* is an organizational unit that is responsible for processing the incident, problem, or change document.

- **Employee**
  An *employee* is a person responsible for processing the incident, problem, or change document.

- **General (key user)**
  A *general business partner* (or *key user*) is the person who creates the incident, problem, or change document.

Now you're ready to create the employees and key users as business partners in your SAP Solution Manager system. You can create this master data manually or automatically.

Create Users Manually

We'll first walk through the steps to create the business partners manually and then show you how to automatically generate them from SAP Solution Manager. The choice is up to you, and both methods will yield the same results (although the automatic way is much more efficient).

Create a Key User Manually

To use the manual method to create a key user, follow these steps:

1. Execute Transaction BP.

2. On the MAINTAIN BUSINESS PARTNER screen, select BUSINESS PARTNER • CREATE • PERSON. The CREATE PERSON screen will appear.

3. Make sure that the role BUSINESS PARTNER (GEN.) is maintained in the CREATE IN BP ROLE field as shown in Figure 3.17.

Figure 3.17 Create Person Screen

4. On the ADDRESS tab, maintain some data (e.g., FIRST NAME, LAST NAME, CITY, COUNTRY, REGION). The amount of data maintained on the business partner record is up to you. However, we recommend that you maintain the data in our example. This is the data that will appear for your users in SAP ITSM.

5. Select the IDENTIFICATION tab. Enter the following information as shown in Figure 3.18:

   ▶ IDTYPE: "CRM001"

   ▶ DESCRIPTION: "External System Identifier" (this will automatically default)

   ▶ IDENTIFICATION NUMBER: "<System ID> <Installation Number> <Client> <UserID>"

6. Click SAVE.

For the IDENTIFICATION NUMBER entry, you must repeat this string of data for every system and client in which the user is maintained in the managed systems.

Identification Numbers			
External BP number	▓▓ ▓▓ NWILLIAMS	
IDType	Description	Identification Number
CRM001	External System Identifier	▓▓ ▓▓▓▓▓▓▓ 100 NWILLIAMS
CRM001	External System Identifier	▓▓ ▓▓▓▓▓▓▓ 200 NWILLIAMS
CRM001	External System Identifier	▓▓ ▓▓▓▓▓▓▓ 201 NWILLIAMS
CRM001	External System Identifier	▓▓ ▓▓▓▓▓▓▓ 202 NWILLIAMS

Figure 3.18 Maintain System Identification Details

This data will allow the SAP Solution Manager system to determine the business partner by assigning its user ID to the business partner record.

Create an Employee Manually

Now we'll walk through the steps to create an employee (message processor) manually. You don't need to create a separate business partner record if a user is a key user and employee (a common scenario). As shown in Figure 3.19, there is a separate role within the business partner record (EMPLOYEE) that will need to be maintained.

1. In the same screen as you were working in, select the role EMPLOYEE from the CHANGE IN BP ROLE field.

2. Select the IDENTIFICATION tab.

3. Maintain the person's user ID in the USER NAME field.

4. Click SAVE.

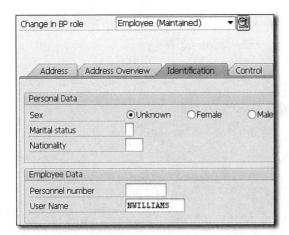

Figure 3.19 Identification Tab, User Master Record

Create Users Automatically

You've probably realized by now that if you have hundreds (or even thousands) of users in your SAP Solution Manager system (and managed systems) who will need business partner records, creating them manually will be a tedious task. To overcome this, SAP Solution Manager provides a way to automatically generate business partners. This method creates the business partner record as both type key user and employee at the time of running the report.

Note

When creating business partners automatically, SAP Solution Manager will read the user master records from the managed systems. A READ RFC destination must have been created (this is a Transaction SOLMAN_SETUP activity) from SAP Solution Manager to the managed systems. Subsequently, a user master record must exist in the managed systems for those business partners to be generated.

To create users automatically, follow these steps:

1. Execute Transaction BP_GEN.

2. In the CREATE BUSINESS PARTNER screen, select the ADD button (as shown in Figure 3.20) to determine all of the systems for which the business partners will be generated.

3. Select the required systems.

4. Press ⌊Enter⌋.

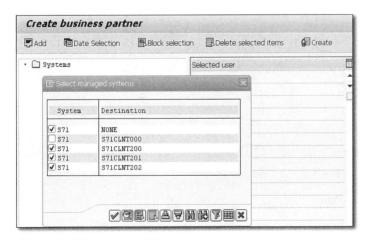

Figure 3.20 Select Managed Systems

5. A folder structure will appear beneath the Systems folder that includes your systems as well as the users in the managed systems that have been read from SAP Solution Manager.

Tips & Tricks

If you don't see your users, you can adjust the dates by selecting the Date Selection button and setting the dates back into the past, as shown in Figure 3.21.

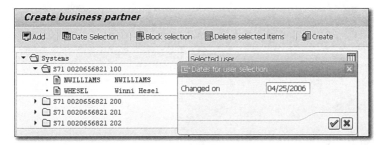

Figure 3.21 Changing Dates for User Selection

6. To create the business partners, simply double click each user on the left side of the screen in the Systems folder structure. Each time you double-click a user, that user will appear in the Selected user table on the right. You have the ability to select multiple users as shown in Figure 3.22.

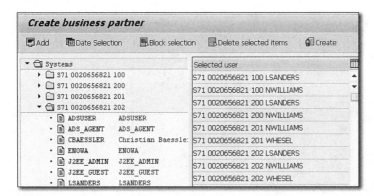

Figure 3.22 Select Users to Be Created as Business Partners

7. When you've selected all of the users to be created, click the Create button.

8. Click YES in the confirmation screen to create the business partners. You'll receive an information message at the bottom of your screen confirming that the business partners have been created.

9. The business partners automatically generated from Transaction BP_GEN can be maintained in Transaction BP. You can search for the business partners by clicking the OPEN button in Transaction BP.

Tips & Tricks

Report AI_SDK_USER_BP_GEN will help the SAP Solution Manager administrator with mass maintenance tasks regarding business partners. With this report you have the ability to do the following:

▶ Compare SAP Solution Manager users with users in the managed systems

▶ List the new users in the managed systems

▶ Automatically create those new users as business partners

▶ Update new users and business partners

3.3.2 Organizational Model

Now that you've created business partners in the form of people (key users and employees), it's time to create business partners in the form of organizational units.

In this section, we'll show you how to build an organizational model in your SAP Solution Manager system that consists of the following components:

▶ Organizational root (also known as the sold-to party)

▶ Organizational objects (support teams and positions)

▶ Assignments of people to the organizational model

The master data element organizational model is an important foundation for driving the processes within SAP ITSM. It controls what is assigned to whom, how support teams will be determined for message processing, and how reports will be driven for analytics.

HR Integration within the Organizational Model

You'll see in the next sections that you'll be creating organizational units in the form of support teams directly within the organizational model. Because the support teams are also business partners, you can create them directly in Transaction BP. Alternatively, you can have the business partner record generated automatically for the organizational objects (support team and people) as you build out the organizational model. This is a key benefit in that it's a way to automatically generate the business partner record for the organizational objects without having to first enter them in Transaction BP.

To enable this functionality, you must first activate HR integration by following these steps:

1. Execute Transaction SM30.

2. In the TABLE/VIEW field, enter the value "T77S0".

3. Click MAINTAIN.

4. Scroll down to find the HRALX/HRAC entry, and enter the value "X" in the VALUE ABBR field as shown in Figure 3.23.

5. Click SAVE.

Figure 3.23 Activating HR Integration

Now, whenever a business partner (person or support team) is created directly within the organizational model, it will automatically generate a business partner record stored in Transaction BP.

Creating the Root for Your Organizational Model

The first step to building the organizational model is to create the root (or sold-to party). Remember, the sold-to party is the overarching entity that "owns" IT. This can be the IT department or the organization itself.

With SAP Solution Manager 7.1, you now have the option to build the organizational model directly within the SAP CRM Web UI. Assuming that you have the correct business role and authorization roles assigned, you can create the organizational model directly within the SAP CRM Web UI by following these steps:

1. Launch the SAP CRM Web UI.

2. Select the SERVICE OPERATIONS work center in the navigation bar as shown in Figure 3.24.

3. Select the ORGANIZATIONAL MODEL link also shown in Figure 3.24.

Figure 3.24 Service Operations Work Center

4. In the SEARCH: ORGANIZATIONAL MODEL screen, select the ROOT ORGANIZATIONAL UNIT button.

5. Make the following selections/entries to the ROOT ORGANIZATIONAL UNIT: NEW screen:

   ▶ DESCRIPTION: Enter name of your sold-to party (e.g., "Enowa Service Management").

   ▶ CODE: Enter short code ID of your sold-to-party (e.g., "ENOWA").

   ▶ FUNCTIONS: Select SERVICE ORGANIZATION.

   ▶ ALLOW ORG UNIT TO BE DETERMINED: Select SERVICE.

   ▶ VALIDITY: Leave all defaulted fields as they are.

6. Click SAVE.

7. An information message will display DATA HAS BEEN SAVED to indicate that your organizational model's root has been created.

8. Select the BACK button to return to the SEARCH: ORGANIZATIONAL MODEL screen. This will be your starting point for the next piece of master data setup.

Create Organizational Objects for Your Organizational Model

Now that a root has been created, it's time to create and assign organizational objects for your organizational model. Organizational objects (positions, support teams, and even users) together with the root comprise the overall organizational model. Together, these components will drive SAP ITSM process activities and functionalities associated with determination as well as reporting and analytics. We'll explain how all of these are orchestrated together in subsequent chapters. Here, we'll walk through the steps of creating and assigning these objects to your organizational model.

1. In the SEARCH: ORGANIZATIONAL MODEL screen, enter the CODE ID of the root you created in the previous steps (e.g., "ENOWA") in the DESCRIPTION field, and click SEARCH.

2. The organizational unit will appear as a result in the table. Select the organizational unit.

3. The details of the organizational unit will appear on the next screen. You'll notice that the example in Figure 3.25 has several support teams already assigned as organizational objects. We'll now create a new organizational object for a security support team.

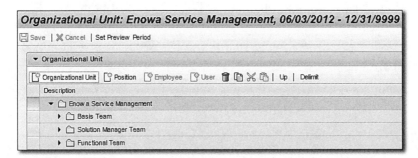

Figure 3.25 Organizational Root and Objects

4. Click the NEW ORGANIZATIONAL UNIT button.

5. Make the following selections/entries in the ORGANIZATIONAL UNIT DETAILS assignment block (leaving the defaulted validity data as is):

   ▸ DESCRIPTION: Enter "Security Team".

   ▸ CODE: Enter "SECURITY".

▶ FUNCTIONS: Select SERVICE TEAM.

▶ ALLOW ORG. UNIT TO BE DETERMINED: Select SERVICE.

6. Click SAVE.

As shown in Figure 3.26, the new organizational object has been created and assigned to the organizational root.

Figure 3.26 New Organizational Object: Security Team

Before you can assign an employee (message processor) to the organizational object, you must first create a position. Follow these steps to do so:

1. Select the NEW POSITION button.

2. Maintain the following information (be sure to accept the default validity data)

▶ DESCRIPTION: "Team Lead"

▶ CODE: "LEAD"

3. Select SERVICE in the FUNCTIONAL ASSIGNMENTS area.

4. Click SAVE.

As you can see in Figure 3.27, the TEAM LEAD position has been created and assigned to the SECURITY TEAM organizational object.

Figure 3.27 Position Assignment to Organizational Object

Now you can assign a message processor to the position by following these steps:

1. Select the ADD EMPLOYEE button.

2. Search for the message processor.

3. Select the user.

4. Click SAVE.

Figure 3.28 shows an organizational model complete with a root, support team, position, and message processor.

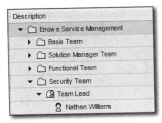

Figure 3.28 Completed Organizational Model

3.3.3 iBase

For all of the processes within SAP ITSM, an installed base (*iBase*) entry in the form of an *iBase component* is required.

The iBase represents all of the systems (SAP and non-SAP) in your landscape. You can consider the iBase as the frontend to the LMDB, which SAP ITSM relies on to classify individual clients within a system.

Because the iBase is determined by the data maintained in the SAP Solution Manager system landscape, it's automatically updated (by performing the activities in the following subsections) whenever a system is added or changed within the system landscape. Non-SAP systems can be manually added to the iBase.

The iBase value itself is classified as "1". Depending on the system ID, installation number, and client of the system's details, a four-digit numerical component is generated to identify the exact client. For example, an iBase component 1234 could identify the unit test client, within the quality assurance system, of SAP ERP. No matter what the iBase component is, the iBase value always remains "1".

Generating the iBase Components

First, let's use an example that the Basis team has added a new system with the system ID S71 to the landscape. This system happens to be an SAP ERP system that will be used in the Incident Management and ChaRM scenarios. You must generate the system and clients as iBase components for it to be used within the SAP ITSM scenarios.

1. Follow the IMG path SAP SOLUTION MANAGER • TECHNICAL SETTINGS • IBASE.

2. Execute the IMG activity CREATE THE COMPONENT SYSTEMS AND ASSIGN AS IBASE COMPONENTS.

3. In the IBASE GENERATION – SAP SYSTEMS (1) screen, select the S71 system as shown in Figure 3.29.

Customer no.	System	Description
☑ ⬛⬛⬛⬛	S71	

Figure 3.29 iBase Generation

4. Click COPY.

A log will appear displaying the results that the iBase components have been generated for the system you selected.

Assign Organizational Root to iBase

For your sold-to party (organizational root that "owns" SAP ITSM) to be linked to the problems, incidents, and ChaRM documents created in SAP Solution Manager, it must be assigned to your iBase components. The sold-to party is determined via the iBase. Follow these steps:

1. Execute Transaction IB52.

2. In the INSTALLED BASE field, enter the value "1" as shown in Figure 3.30.

3. Press [Enter].

4. Highlight the iBase component that is directly involved in your SAP ITSM scenario as shown in Figure 3.31.

Figure 3.30 Change Installed Base: Initial Screen

> **Note**
>
> Production clients are relevant for ChaRM. All clients are relevant for Application Incident Management (AIM). Assign the sold-to party based on this standard.

Figure 3.31 Change Installed Base: Detail Screen

5. Follow the menu path GOTO • PARTNER.

6. In the PARTNER ASSIGNMENT screen, enter the details as shown in Figure 3.32. Search and select for the sold-to party specific to your organization.

Figure 3.32 Partner Assignment Screen

7. Click TRANSFER.

8. Click SAVE.

3.3.4   Number Ranges

Number ranges are used in SAP ITSM processes to numerically classify problems, incidents, and ChaRM documents. After one of these documents is created, SAP Solution Manager will assign a number within the specified range to that document. From each document generated thereafter, the system will assign the next value within that range.

Out of the box, all documents get assigned a number from the same range between 8000000000 and 8999999999. In this section, we'll show you how to set up document-specific number ranges to more easily differentiate between each document type.

> **Note**
>
> Number ranges are master data. The range of numbers will be reused over and over in transactional processing, however, each value within that range will only be assigned once. For this reason, it's highly recommended that after a number range is set up, it isn't maintained going forward. Changing number ranges down the line can have implications such as inconsistent reporting data and inconsistent document sequence, for example.

For this example, we have defined the standards shown in Table 3.4 for how number ranges will be represented in our SAP ITSM processes.

Document	Number Range ID	From Value	To Value
Problem	02	1000000000	1999999999
Incident	03	2000000000	2999999999
Request for Change	04	3000000000	3999999999
Normal Change	05	4000000000	4999999999
Urgent Change	06	5000000000	5999999999
Knowledge Article	07	6000000000	6999999999

Table 3.4 Number Range Values for IT Service Management

Number Range for Problems

First, let's walk through the steps for how to create a number range for problem tickets:

1. Execute Transaction CRMC_NR_RA_PROBLM. The NUMBER RANGE OBJECT FOR CRM SERVICE PROBLEM screen will appear.

2. Click the CHANGE INTERVALS button. The MAINTAIN NUMBER RANGE INTERVALS screen will appear.

3. Select the INSERT INTERVAL button.

4. Maintain the following details based on the data from Table 3.4. Your data should appear as shown in Figure 3.33.

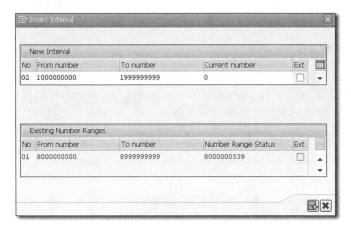

Figure 3.33 Insert Number Range Interval for Problem

5. Click the INSERT button.

6. Click SAVE.

7. Immediately after saving, an information box will remind you that the number ranges are not automatically recorded in a transport. When managing a two- or three-tier SAP Solution Manager landscape, you'll either need to reproduce these steps in the follow-on systems or initiate a transport by selecting INTERVAL • TRANSPORT from the same screen.

8. Click the CONTINUE button to confirm that you're aware of how number ranges must represented in the follow-on system(s).

Number Range for Incidents

Next, you'll create the number range for incidents by following these steps:

1. Execute Transaction CRMC_NR_RA_INCDNT. The Number Range Object for CRM Service Incident screen will appear.

2. Click the Change Intervals button. The Maintain Number Range Intervals screen will appear.

3. Select the Insert Interval button.

4. Maintain the following details based on the data from the Table 3.4. Your data should appear as shown in Figure 3.34.

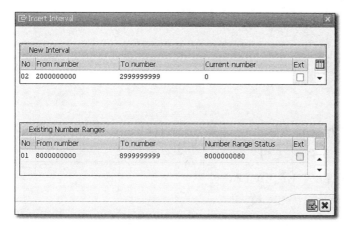

Figure 3.34 Insert Number Range Interval for Incident

5. Click the Insert button.

6. Click Save.

You can also maintain your number range values for service requests within the table displayed in Figure 3.34.

Number Range for ChaRM Documents

Next, you'll create the number ranges for the ChaRM documents (request for change, urgent change, and normal change). All of these number ranges are created within the same transaction by following these steps:

1. Execute Transaction CRMC_NR_RA_SERVICE. The Number Range Object for CRM Service Incident screen will appear.

2. Click the Change Intervals button. The Maintain Number Range Intervals screen will appear.

3. Select the INSERT INTERVAL button.

4. Maintain the details based on the data from Table 3.4, shown previously. Your data should appear as shown in Figure 3.35.

Intervals				
No.	From number	To number	Current number	Ext
01	8000000000	8999999999	8000000539	☐
04	3000000000	3999999999	0	☐
05	4000000000	4999999999	0	☐
06	6000000000	6999999999	0	☐

Figure 3.35 ChaRM Number Range Values

5. Click the INSERT button.

6. Click SAVE.

Number Range for Knowledge Articles

Finally, you'll create the number range for knowledge articles:

1. Execute Transaction CRMC_NR_RA_KA.

2. Select the CHANGE INTERVALS button.

3. Select the INSERT INTERVALS button.

4. Maintain the details shown in Figure 3.36.

Insert Interval					✕
New Interval					
No	From number	To number	Current number	Ext	
01	6000000000	6999999999	0	☐	

Figure 3.36 Insert Knowledge Article Number Range Interval

5. Press SAVE.

Assign Number Range Values to Transaction Types

Now that you've created number ranges for everything in SAP ITSM, you can now assign them to each transaction type (e.g., problem). This will enable the SAP

Solution Manager system to have a link between the number range and transaction type. Follow these steps to assign the number ranges:

1. Follow the IMG path SAP SOLUTION MANAGER • CAPABILITIES (OPTIONAL) • APPLICATION INCIDENT MANAGEMENT (SERVICE DESK) • TRANSACTIONS • DEFINE TRANSACTION TYPES.

2. Select the problem transaction type YMPR, and click the DETAILS button.

3. Choose the appropriate number range value within the INT.NO.RANGE NO field (Figure 3.37), and press ⌷Enter⌷.

Transaction Numbering		
No.Range Object	CRM_PROBLM	CRM Problem
Int.No.Range No	02	
Ext.No.Range No		
☐ Early No. Assgt		

Figure 3.37 Assign Internal Number Range

4. Click SAVE.

5. Repeat these steps to assign the remaining number ranges to the rest of your SAP ITSM transaction types.

Tips & Tricks

The EARLY NO. ASSGT checkbox in the TRANSACTION NUMBERING screen (Figure 3.37) controls when the document will be assigned a value from the number range. If the checkbox isn't checked, the document will only receive a value after it's saved. If it's checked, it will receive an early number assignment which means that a value from the number range will be used even if the document isn't intended to be saved. We recommend that you uncheck this value to preserve numbers and avoid gaps in the transaction numbering.

Figure 3.38 shows the end result for how number ranges are called in SAP Solution Manager. This example is the first incident created within the specified number range.

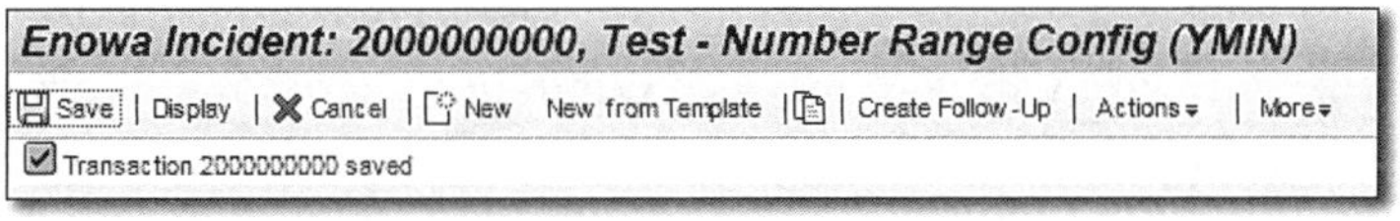

Enowa Incident: 2000000000, Test - Number Range Config (YMIN)

🖫 Save | Display | ✖ Cancel | 🗋 New   New from Template | 🗏 | Create Follow-Up | Actions ▾ | More ▾

☑ Transaction 2000000000 saved

Figure 3.38 YMIN Number Range Example

Number Range for Maintenance

Number ranges are also used for maintenance purposes in ChaRM. For example, different projects and task lists will be assigned number ranges as they are created or generated from SAP Solution Manager. Because the end users never see or encounter these number ranges, it's typically recommended to adhere to the default values provided by SAP. Further, there is rarely a requirement to set up maintenance number ranges that differ from the standard.

To validate or maintain (if required) these number ranges, follow these steps:

1. Execute Transaction SNUM.
2. Specify the object. The options for ChaRM maintenance are as follows:
   - /tmwflow/m: maintenance
   - /tmwflow/d: development
   - /tmwflow/v: variants in task list
3. From here, you can select the DISPLAY or CHANGE buttons depending on whether you want to validate existing values or add new intervals.

3.4 Adapting the SAP CRM Web UI: Configuration and Personalization

The SAP CRM Web UI in SAP Solution Manager provides the flexibility and benefits of having the screens configured and personalized depending on the user group and the specific user. Adapting the SAP CRM Web UI is flexible in that an administrator can control what each role views globally via configuration. Moreover, users can take individual views and personalize them to fit their likes and needs for managing their tasks.

In this section, we'll provide an overview of some basic concepts of adapting the SAP CRM Web UI on these two levels. We'll also provide a few examples on how to both configure and personalize the SAP CRM Web UI based on familiar requirements. The examples we'll share are the most common changes that arise when gathering requirements regarding the view of the SAP CRM Web UI. This section will familiarize you with where to make configurations and how the SAP CRM Web UI can be changed. After you start prototyping different views in your sandbox or development SAP Solution Manager system, you'll find there are countless variations and options for how the SAP CRM Web UI can be adapted to enable your IT organization to manage services.

3.4.1 Business Role SOLMANPRO

A *business role* can be considered similar to an authorization role; however, the business role controls what the user can view in the SAP CRM Web UI. The authorization roles enable or restrict which functions the user can execute in the system. The business role controls what the user views in regards to the navigation bar and logical links in the SAP CRM Web UI. Most importantly, you need to be assigned a business role to access the SAP CRM Web UI.

While you'll always define and maintain multiple authorization roles, an important business role you'll need to copy into your customer namespace is SOLMAN-PRO. With this role, you have the ability to tailor your user's view to structure the navigation bar, work center links, and direct links based on job responsibilities of a specific user group.

> **Note**
>
> SOLMANREQU and SOLMANDSPTCH are also key business roles for ITSM users. Flip back to Chapter 2 to review the UI associated with these two roles.

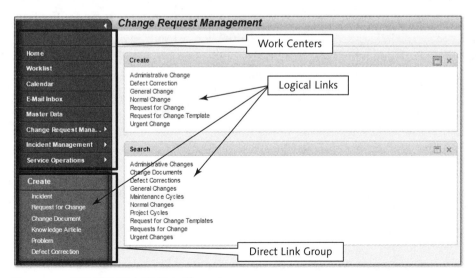

Figure 3.39 SAP CRM Web UI Main Elements

In the next subsections, we'll provide instruction on how to adapt each of these elements of the SAP CRM Web UI. Figure 3.39 provides a reminder of what exactly these elements are. Flip back to Chapter 2 to read more about the features and navigation of the SAP CRM Web UI.

Characteristics

It's important to understand how business roles fit into the big picture of a security concept. The business role SOLMANPRO is assigned to the authorization role SAP_CRM_UIU_SOLMANPRO, so you must first assign each user who is accessing the SAP CRM Web UI this authorization role in Transaction PFCG.

SAP_CRM_UIU_SOLMANPRO contains the business role SOLMANPRO, which allows you access to the SAP CRM Web UI. Adapting the business role occurs in the SAP Solution Manager IMG (which we'll explain in the next sections) and will control which SAP CRM Web UI elements the user groups can view.

Figure 3.40 provides a representation of how these two roles are married together and assigned to the user's master record in Transaction SU01 (User Maintenance). You'll also see that the business role is made up of the following profiles:

▶ NAVIGATION BAR PROFILE
This profile is what we'll focus on the most in the following sections. The Navigation Bar Profile contains the assignment of work centers, work center link groups, direct link groups, and logical links. The Navigation Bar Profile can be specific to a user group. For example, the user group requesters may have a vastly different Navigation Bar Profile than administrators.

▶ LAYOUT PROFILE
The Layout Profile is made up and defines the orientation of the navigation frame. The navigation frame includes the header, footer, work area, and navigation bar. We won't cover this here because we recommend that you stick with the standard.

▶ TECHNICAL PROFILE
The Technical Profile controls the assignment of various technical settings. We'll provide instructions for how to maintain the Technical Profile, but we recommend that every user be assigned the same Technical Profile.

▶ FUNCTION PROFILE

The Function Profile controls the assignment of different functional areas. For example, links that appear in the navigation bar are used with the reporting framework.

▶ ROLE CONFIGURATION KEY

This profile is used to adapt (e.g., add, move, rename fields) various screen elements by using the UI configuration tool.

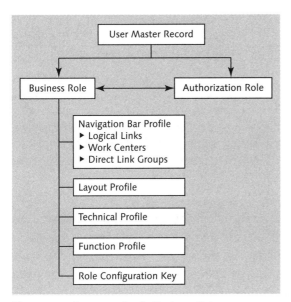

Figure 3.40 Components of a Business Role

3.4.2 Business Role Maintenance

In this section, we'll walk through the prerequisite steps required prior to the activity of adapting the business roles. Before diving into the configuration of the business roles, it's important to follow our security concept and best practices for maintaining roles (for both business and authorization roles). This means copying the following roles into a customer namespace that begins with a "Z" or "Y".

Note

Remember, the roles delivered out of the box are provided as templates only. You'll adapt the roles only in your customer namespace.

To get started, you'll first need to copy the authorization role SAP_SM_CRM_
UIU_SOLMANPRO into a Z or Y role (e.g., ZSAP_SM_CRM_UIU_SOLMANPRO)
and assign it to a user.

Create Requester

You've already copied the authorization role needed to access the SAP CRM Web
UI. Now, we'll walk through how to copy the business role SOLMANPRO to start
adapting the links available in the SAP CRM Web UI. For these examples, we'll
create a business role for a requester (for a request for change document). In
other words, we want to adapt a business role to provide the user group requester
with only the required links.

> **Important!**
>
> The steps within this section are just for the purpose of providing an example on how
> default business roles can be adapted to meet unique requirements. SAP Solution Man-
> ager provides standard business roles out of the box for requesters and dispatchers
> (message processors). Those business roles have been described in Chapter 2.

Figure 3.41 provides the IMG path and activities for configurations related to the
UI framework. Note that they all reside beneath the CUSTOMER RELATIONSHIP MAN-
AGEMENT area in the IMG. The first step is to execute the IMG activity DEFINE BUSI-
NESS ROLE via the path CUSTOMER RELATIONSHIP MANAGEMENT • UI FRAMEWORK •
BUSINESS ROLES • DEFINE BUSINESS ROLE.

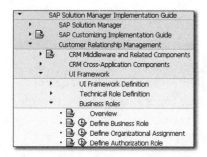

Figure 3.41 IMG Path to UI Framework Customizing

After you select this activity, the CHANGE VIEW "DEFINE BUSINESS ROLES": OVER-
VIEW screen will appear showing the business role SOLMANPRO (see Figure
3.42). Follow these steps:

1. Scroll down to find the business role SOLMANPRO.

2. Select the line for SOLMANPRO.

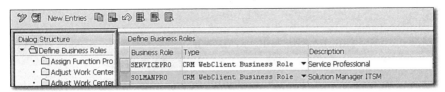

Figure 3.42 Business Role SOLMANPRO Selected

3. Click the COPY AS button (▣).

4. Enter the name for your business role (e.g., "ZREQUESTER"), and then press Enter .

   Now the business role is copied into a new business role based on your naming convention. You'll see the screen as identified in Figure 3.43 with all of the profiles and relative assignments to it.

5. Click SAVE after you reach the screen identified in Figure 3.43.

Business Role	ZREQUESTER
Define Business Roles	
Profile Type	CRM WebClient Business Role
Description	Solution Manager ITSM
Role Config. Key	SOLMANPRO
Nav Bar Profile	SOLMANPRO
Layout Profile	CRM_UIU_MASTER
Technical Profile	DEFAULT_SOLMANPRO
PFCG Role ID	SAP_SM_CRM_UIU_SOLMANPRO
SpecificHelpContext	
☑ SpecHelpFallbck	
Logo Text	Solution Manager IT Service Management

Figure 3.43 Copied Business Role

3.4.3 Adapting the Business Role

Now that you've copied the standard business role into your own ZREQUESTER business role, you're ready to begin adapting the links based on your requirements. First, we'll walk through the steps required to set up the Navigation Bar Profile for the requester.

Navigation Bar Profile

Just like we prepared the business role SOLMANPRO to be adapted by copying it, we'll need to do the same for the profiles within the business role. Follow these steps to copy the Navigation Bar Profile into your customer namespace:

1. Follow the IMG Path CUSTOMER RELATIONSHIP MANAGEMENT • UI FRAMEWORK • TECHNICAL ROLE DEFINITION • DEFINE NAVIGATION BAR PROFILE.

2. Find the Navigation Bar Profile SOLMANPRO, and copy it into a profile called ZREQUESTER. You can do this by highlighting it and clicking the COPY AS button, as described in the steps in Section 3.4.2.

3. Be sure to copy all dependent entries by confirming this in the information box, and then click SAVE.

Now, you can assign the newly created Navigation Bar Profile to your business role by following these steps:

1. Execute the IMG activity DEFINE BUSINESS ROLES.

2. Highlight the ZREQUESTER business role.

3. Click the DETAILS button.

4. Assign the Navigation Bar Profile ZREQUESTER as shown in Figure 3.44.

5. Click SAVE.

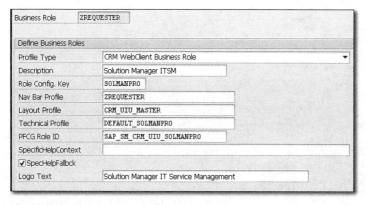

Figure 3.44 Navigation Bar Profile Assignment

Adapting Work Center Visibility

Now that you've copied over the business role and Navigation Bar Profile, it's finally time to start adapting what the requester can see. This is referred to as *visibility*. You'll begin by making a change to the visibility of the requester's work centers with the following steps:

1. Return to the DEFINE NAVIGATION BAR PROFILE IMG activity.

2. Highlight the ZREQUESTER Navigation Bar Profile.

3. Double-click the ADJUST WORK CENTERS folder on the left side of the screen (Figure 3.45).

4. Because the requesters in this example are only accessing the SAP CRM Web UI for creating documents related to SAP ITSM, they need to have a very lean view available for work centers. Make the following work centers in Figure 3.45 inactive by selecting the boxes in the INACTIVE column.

5. Click SAVE.

Dialog Structure	Business Role	ZREQUESTER				
▾ ☐Define Business Roles	Nav Bar Profile	ZREQUESTER				
• ☐Assign Function Profiles						
• ☐Adjust Work Centers	**Adjust Work Centers**					
• ☐Adjust Work Center Group Links						
▾ ☐Adjust Direct Link Groups	WorkCenter	Inactive	Deleted	WC Pos.	WC Pos.	Work Center Title (Nav. Bar)
• ☐Adjust Direct Links	CT-CALENDR	☑	☐	30		Calendar
• ☐Define Keyboard Shortcuts	CT-WORKLST	☑	☐	20		Worklist
• ☐Adjust Central Search Objects	IT-DASH-WC	☑	☐	100		Dashboards and Reports (ITSM)
	IT-SP-HOME	☐	☐	10		Home
	SM-CHANGE	☐	☐	55		Change Request Management
	SM-SRV-MD	☑	☐	40		Master Data
	SM-SUPPORT	☐	☐	65		Incident Management
	SRV-EMAIL	☑	☐	35		E-Mail Inbox
	SRV-OPERAT	☑	☐	90		Service Operations

Figure 3.45 Deactivating Work Centers

Adjusting the Visibility of Direct Links

Now you can adjust the visibility of the direct links for your requesters by following these steps:

1. Execute the IMG activity DEFINE BUSINESS ROLES.

2. Select the ZREQUESTER business role.

3. Double-click the folder ADJUST DIRECT LINK GROUPS on the left. The CHANGE VIEW "ADJUST DIRECT LINK GROUPS": OVERVIEW page will appear as shown in Figure 3.46.

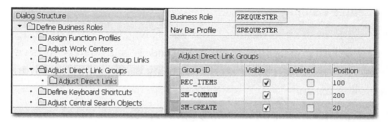

Figure 3.46 SM-CREATE Direct Link Group

4. Scroll down and select the SM-CREATE entry in the GROUP ID field.

5. Double-click the ADJUST DIRECT LINKS subfolder on the left side of the screen.

   Now, you'll see all of the direct links associated with the direct link group SM-CREATE. For the purposes of the requesters in this example, they will only need visibility to create the following document types in SAP Solution Manager:

   ▶ REQUEST FOR CHANGE

   ▶ INCIDENT

   ▶ PROBLEM

   ▶ DEFECT CORRECTION

6. Mark these direct links as visible, as shown in Figure 3.47, and click SAVE.

Adjust Direct Links							
LogLink ID	Visible	Deleted	Position	Position	Icon Name	Icon Name (Role)	Logical Link Title
MD-KNAR-DC	☐	☐	40				Knowledge Article
SLS-APP-DC	☐	☐	10				Appointment
SLS-MAI-CR	☐	☐	30				E-Mail
SLS-TSK-DC	☐	☐	20				Task
SM-CD-DC	☐	☐	7				Change Document
SM-CR-DC	☑	☐	6				Request for Change
SM-IM-DC	☑	☐	5				Incident
SM-PRB-DC	☑	☐	60				Problem
SM-TM-DC	☑	☐	70				Defect Correction
SRV-ORD-DC	☐	☐	100				Service Order
SRV-SCO-DC	☐	☐	80				Service Contract

Figure 3.47 Enabling Visibility to Direct Links

You have successfully adapted the business role and Navigation Bar Profile to slim down the visibility of work centers for a specific user group. Figure 3.48 shows the comparison between the standard work center visibilities with SOLMANPRO versus the adapted ZSOLMANPRO business role.

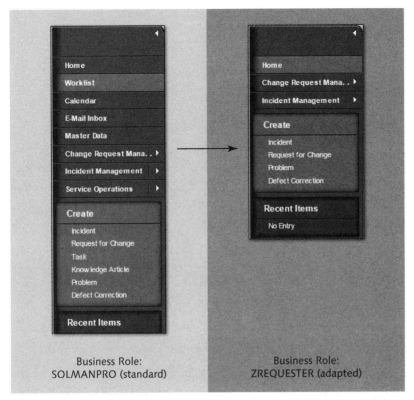

Figure 3.48 Standard Work Center Visibility versus Adapted Work Center Visibility

You can see that for this example, requesters who use SAP Solution Manager for limited use (e.g., just creating IT documents) can be provided with a leaner and more streamlined view for their related work center activities.

Although not required, this method provides a quick way to tailor the view of the SAP CRM Web UI to be more specific and easier to use for various user groups.

Technical Profile

The Technical Profile, as described briefly in Section 3.4.1, controls various settings that relate to the behavior of the Internet browser when the SAP CRM Web UI is accessed. More details can be found in the IMG documentation for the DEFINE TECHNICAL PROFILE IMG activity, but here are a few technical settings this profile controls:

- ▶ Enabling and disabling browser functions such as browser back, frame swapping, and automatic data handling
- ▶ Memory thresholds
- ▶ Time delays
- ▶ System logoff, session end, and timeout specifications
- ▶ Logoff URL

As mentioned before, it's recommended that any changes to the standard Technical Profile should be administered globally. In other words, you should use one Technical Profile for all user groups. It simply doesn't make sense for different user groups to have different technical settings for how their browser behaves when utilizing the SAP CRM Web UI.

Now, we'll walk through the steps of adapting a Technical Profile to deploy some minor technical changes. Just like the business role and its other profiles, we must start by making a copy of the standard Technical Profile, which is DEFAULT_SOLMANPRO, by following these steps:

1. Follow the IMG Path CUSTOMER RELATIONSHIP MANAGEMENT • UI FRAMEWORK • TECHNICAL ROLE DEFINITION • DEFINE TECHNICAL PROFILE.

2. Select the standard Technical Profile DEFAULT_SOLMANPRO, and click the COPY AS button to copy it into your customer namespace (e.g., ZDEFAULT_SOLMANPRO).

3. In our example, we chose to select DISABLE BROWSER BACK SUPPORT as well as update the LOGOFF URL to our own organization's website.

4. Press Enter. You'll then see the results as shown in Figure 3.49.

5. Click SAVE.

You're now able to assign the newly created Technical Profile to your business roles by performing the following steps:

1. Execute IMG Activity DEFINE BUSINESS ROLE.

2. Select the ZREQUESTER business role.

3. Click the DETAILS button.

4. Assign the ZDEFAULT_SOLMANPRO Technical Profile as shown in Figure 3.50.

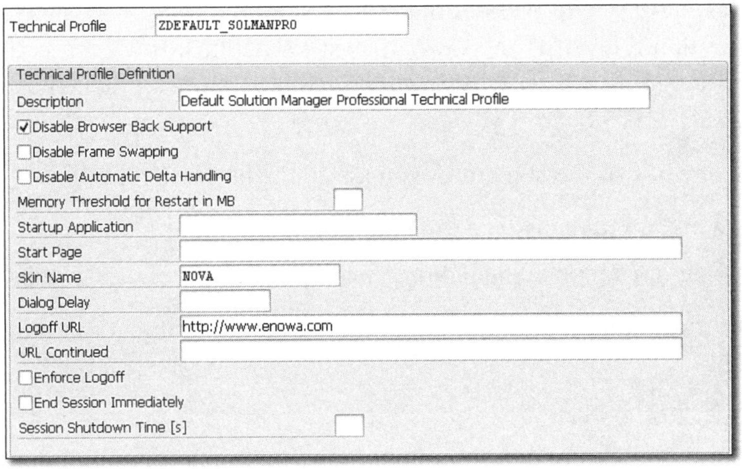

Figure 3.49 Technical Profile Maintenance

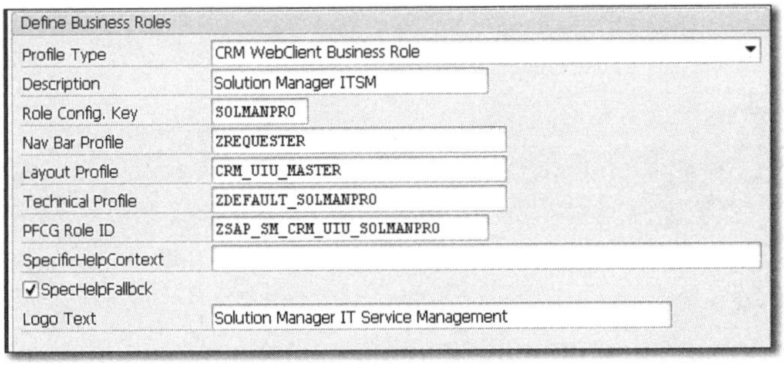

Figure 3.50 Assignment of Technical Profile

> **Important!**
>
> Notice that the PFCG ROLE ID (authorization role), which was copied in the first step, is assigned to the ZREQUESTER business role as well. Ensure that you map your copied authorization role ZSAP_SM_CRM_UIU_SOLMANPRO to the ZREQUESTER business role details as shown in Figure 3.50.

User Assignment

After you've set up business roles for your user groups in the IT organization, including adapting the profiles to satisfy your requirements, you must assign them to your users. Although we have made changes to several profiles, only the business role gets assigned.

Keep in mind that *everyone* who accesses the SAP CRM Web UI *must* be assigned the same authorization role ZSAP_SM_CRM_UIU_SOLMANPRO. However, each user group (or member of the user group) will be assigned its own unique business role (e.g., ZREQUESTER).

You may choose one of two ways in which you assign the business roles:

▸ Assignment via organization (assigned to user groups)

▸ Assignment via authorization (assigned to individual members of user groups)

First, we'll walk through the steps to make the business role assignment based on organizational unit:

1. Launch the SAP CRM Web UI.

2. Select the SERVICE OPERATIONS work center link in the navigation bar.

3. Select the ORGANIZATIONAL MODEL link in the work area as shown in Figure 3.51.

Figure 3.51 Service Operations Logical Links

The SEARCH: ORGANIZATIONAL MODEL screen will appear. By default, the FIND BY field will be populated with ORGANIZATIONAL UNIT.

4. Click the SEARCH button, and the system will retrieve the organizational units created when you first set up this master data.

5. Click the text contained within the first row, which will be the sold-to party. In this example (Figure 3.52), the sold-to party is ENOWA SERVICE MANAGEMENT.

6. Make sure you're in edit mode (select the EDIT button).

7. Select the row that contains the position or organizational unit to which the business role will be assigned as shown in Figure 3.53. For our example, all members of the Basis team will be assigned the business role ZREQUESTER.

Result List: 4 Organizational Units Found

🗋 Root Organizational Unit 🗑 🗋	
Organizational Unit	
Enowa Service Management	
Basis Team	
Solution Manager Team	
Functional Team	

Figure 3.52 Organizational Units

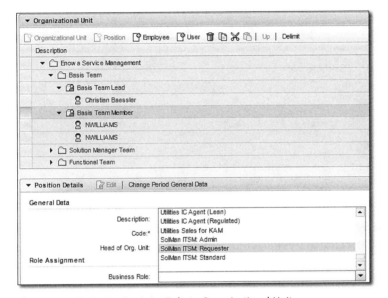

Figure 3.53 Assigning Business Role to Organizational Unit

8. Select the appropriate business role, which is also identified in Figure 3.53.

9. Click SAVE.

Tips & Tricks

The dropdown values for BUSINESS ROLE map to the DESCRIPTION field for your business role (in IMG activity DEFINE BUSINESS ROLE). To identify and assign the appropriate business role in the organizational assignment, you must make the distinction in the DESCRIPTION field in Customizing.

Alternatively, you can also assign business roles based on authorizations. This is done in the user's master record in Transaction SU01 by following these steps:

1. Execute Transaction SU01.

2. Enter the requester's user ID, and click CHANGE.

3. Select the PARAMETERS tab.

4. Enter the "CRM_UI_PROFILE" PARAMETER ID column, and enter "ZRE-QUESTER" in the PARAMETER VALUE column as shown in Figure 3.54.

5. CLICK SAVE.

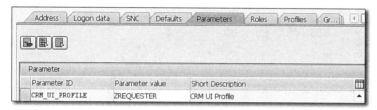

Figure 3.54 Assigning Business Role to Authorization

3.4.4 Personalizing the SAP CRM Web UI Layout

In the previous section, we described how to adapt the views of the SAP CRM Web UI, via configuration, to influence the UI for a specific user group. In our example, we established a business role for requesters. These configuration settings, for SAP Solution Manager, are typically performed by an SAP Solution Manager administrator or consultant responsible for the configuration of SAP Solution Manager. In an actual SAP Solution Manager ITSM implementation, the adaption of business roles expands to include all user groups involved in SAP ITSM.

Personalization, on the other hand, is specific to the end user working within the SAP CRM Web UI environment. Personalization is administered by the end users themselves, without influence or consideration of organizational-specific requirements. Personalization influences the SAP CRM Web UI for the individual user only.

In the following subsections, we'll describe some of the characteristics and features of how end users can use personalization.

Personalization Dialogs

Personalization dialogs are used to adapt the SAP CRM Web UI to user preferences. In other words, after the user accesses an *entry point,* a personalization dialog will launch on the screen to provide the user with several options for personalizing his SAP CRM Web UI.

An entry point can come in one of two forms:

▶ The PERSONALIZE button as indicated by the  icon. This icon can appear within tables, assignment blocks, or within the work center page.

▶ The global application personalization link, PERSONALIZE, as indicated in Figure 3.55.

Figure 3.55 Global Application Personalization Link

Figure 3.56 shows an example of a dialog box for the personalization dialog. This example represents the personalization dialog for a specific table in Incident Management. The user has the option to display specific columns relating to searching for incidents, for example.

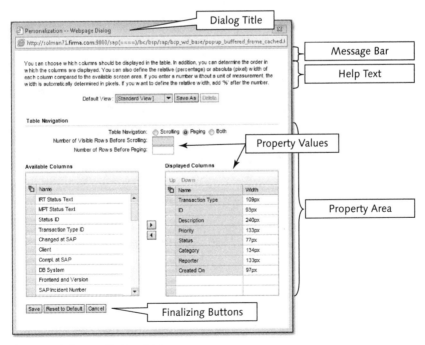

Figure 3.56 Personalization Dialog

Figure 3.57 represents another personalization dialog example. This personalization dialog exists directly within the work center. The PERSONALIZATION button has been executed directly within the work center, and the user is able to personalize the settings and content blocks within a specific work center.

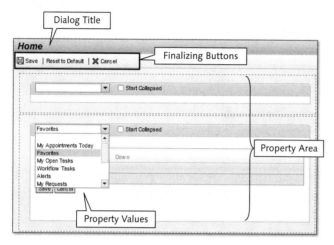

Figure 3.57 Personalization Dialog for Work Center

Drag and Drop

Drag-and-drop functionality enables the user to have fast and direct personalization capabilities without launching a personalization dialog box. Users will be able to utilize the drag-and-drop functionality for the following objects:

▸ **Table columns:** Changing the column width or order.

▸ **Home page and work center page:** Changing the position of the content blocks.

▸ **Overview Page:** Changing the sequence of the assignment blocks.

To use the drag-and-drop capabilities for these personalization objects mentioned, you simply click and hold on the objects and move them to the desired location.

Global Application Personalization

Global application personalization is accessed by clicking the respective link (shown in Figure 3.58). Global application personalization provides multiple capabilities, accessed by the links shown in Figure 3.58, to further personalize the SAP CRM Web UI for the user beyond the details of the SAP ITSM data.

Global application personalization enables the user to personalize their SAP CRM Web UI profile based on several options.

Figure 3.58 Global Application Personalization Screen

3.4.5   Configuring the SAP CRM Web UI Layout

In the last section we discussed the importance of being able to personalize the view of the SAP CRM Web UI layout. Personalizing means that each user can set their own view for what they see in the SAP CRM Web UI. It is unique to each user and not reflected globally once the settings are saved. Configuration, on the other hand, is performed by the SAP Solution Manager administrator. Configuring the SAP CRM Web UI layout prompts a transport request and the objects are transported from SAP Solution Manager development to the follow-on systems. Once the default configuration values are adapted to meet organization requirements (i.e., not a user's specific requirements), they are visible to the end-users of the support organization.

In this section, we'll walk you through the prerequisites you need to be able to adapt the default SAP CRM Web UI layout configurations to meet your own requirements. Some of these requirements may be:

- ▶ Adding fields
- ▶ Hiding fields
- ▶ Changing the field properties (e.g., making a field mandatory)

After we explain the pre-requisites in order to configure the SAP CRM Web UI layout, we will walk you through a configuration example on how to adapt the layout to meet your organization's requirements.

Prerequisites to Perform SAP CRM Web UI Configuration

There are three main pre-requisites in order to configure the SAP CRM Web UI layout:

- ▶ Add configuration mode authorization
- ▶ Enable configuration mode
- ▶ Assign a role configuration key to the user's business role

Add Configuration Mode Authorization

In order to configure the SAP CRM Web UI layout, the configuration mode must be enabled. Before that can be performed the SAP Solution Manager Administrator, or user performing the configuration, must have the appropriate authorization. This user must have the authorization CRMCONFMOD with the ALLOWED=X value maintained in their authorizations. The SAP Solution Manager administrator should communicate this to the security administrator and together they can determine which PFCG authorization role it should belong in.

Enable Configuration Mode

Once the administrator has the CRMCONFMOD object assigned to their authorizations they will be able to enable configuration mode within the SAP CRM WEB UI layout. Configuration mode allows the user to use the configuration tool, which is leveraged to perform configuration on the default settings.

Follow these steps in order to enable configuration mode within the SAP CRM Web UI:

1. Log on to the ITSM Home Page.

2. In the top right corner, select the PERSONALIZE link (Figure 3.59).

Figure 3.59 Select Personalize Link

3. In the SETTINGS area of the PERSONALIZE screen, select the PERSONALIZE SETTINGS button (Figure 3.60).

Figure 3.60 Select Personalize Settings Link

4. Select the option to ENABLE CONFIGURATION MODE (Figure 3.61).

Figure 3.61 Enable Configuration Mode

5. Press SAVE.

You will now notice the CONFIGURATION TOOL buttons ( ) appear in the top right corner of the ITSM Home Page (Figure 3.62).

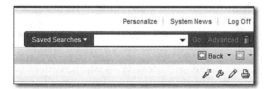

Figure 3.62 Configuration Mode Enabled

Assign Role Configuration Key

Lastly, you will need to assign a role configuration key to the business roles that will need to accept the new configurations. Role configuration keys allow various users to have different configuration views based on their job role.

Follow these steps to navigate to and assign the role configuration key:

1. Follow the IMG path SAP SOLUTION MANAGER IMPLEMENTATION GUIDE • CUSTOMER RELATIONSHIP MANAGEMENT • UI FRAMEWORK • BUSINESS ROLES • DEFINE BUSINESS ROLES.

2. Select the business role that will inherit the new configuration (e.g., SOLMAN-REQU) and press the DETAILS button (Figure 3.63).

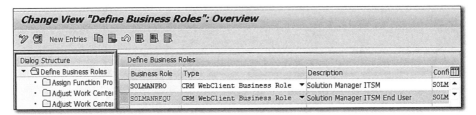

Figure 3.63 View Business Role Details

3. Confirm that a value is maintained in the ROLE CONFIG. KEY field (Figure 3.64).

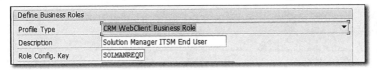

Figure 3.64 Maintain Role Configuration Key

4. Press SAVE

Example: SAP CRM Web UI Configuration

In this example, we will show you how to perform a configuration change to the default SAP CRM Web UI layout values provided by SAP Solution Manager. While there are many options for configuring the SAP CRM Web UI, the objective of this section is to show you how the prerequisite activities and configuration process fit together, as well as point you in the right direction of the configuration tool.

In this example, we will change the TITLE field (Figure 3.65) to read SHORT DESCRIPTION for a requester when he creates an incident.

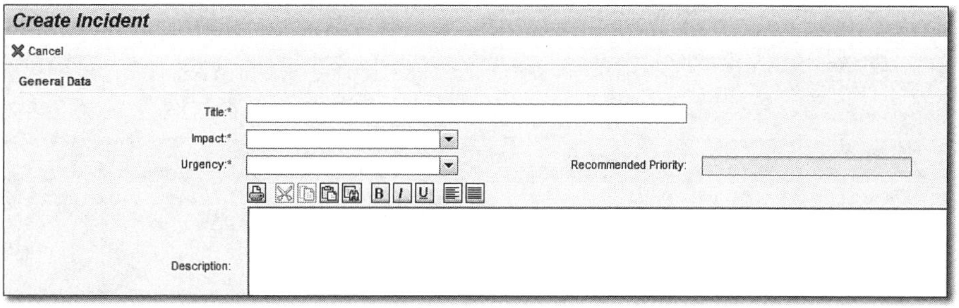

Create Incident

✖ Cancel

General Data

Title:*

Impact:*

Urgency:*   Recommended Priority:

Description:

Figure 3.65 Default SAP CRM Web UI Layout Values

Follow these steps to configure the default values so that the TITLE field has a different name:

1. Select the SHOW CONFIGURABLE AREAS button ( ).

2. Click once in the highlighted area next to the TITLE field (Figure 3.66).

General Data

Title:*

Impact:*

Urgency:*

Figure 3.66 Show Configurable Area

The VIEW CONFIGURATION screen will appear (Figure 3.67). This is where all of the configuration for the selected configurable area is administered.

We will now copy the default configuration. This way, the last view of the SAP CRM Web UI (in this case the default view) is preserved in case we need to revert back to the standard settings.

1. Select the COPY AS button ( ).

2. In the CONFIGURATIONS window (Figure 3.68), you can choose to accept the defaults provided by the system or maintain your own. The ROLE CONFIG. KEY field value will determine which business users will adopt the new SAP CRM Web UI layout configuration settings.

3. Select the TITLE field (it will become highlighted) and click the SHOW FIELD PROPERTIES button (Figure 3.69).

   The field properties for the title field will appear on the right side of the screen.

149

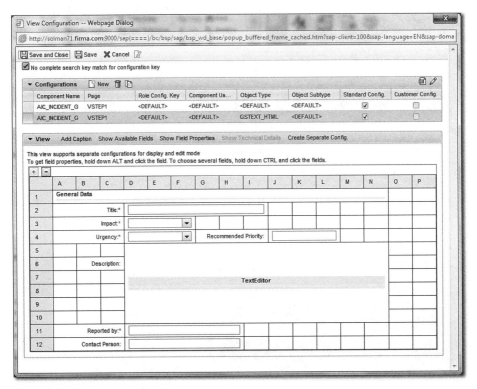

Figure 3.67 View Configuration Screen

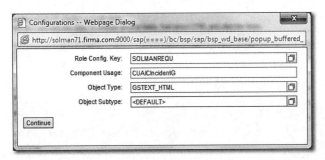

Figure 3.68 Maintain Configurations Settings

4. Change the FIELD LABEL to SHORT DESCRIPTION and select the APPLY button (Figure 3.70).

5. In the CONFIGURATIONS page, select the SAVE AND CLOSE button. You will be prompted to save your changes in a Customizing transport request.

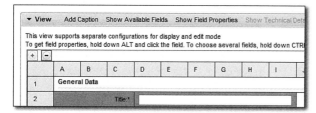

Figure 3.69 Show Title Field Properties

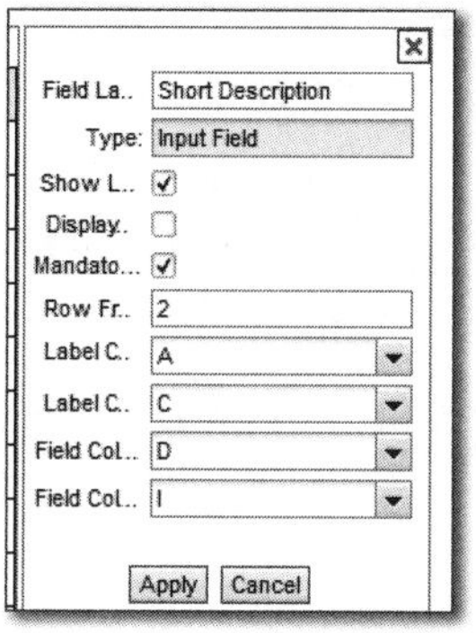

Figure 3.70 Change and Apply New Field Label

6. You will be taken back to the INCIDENT screen. Press the SHOW CONFIGURABLE AREAS button ( ) to exit configuration mode.

As you can see in Figure 3.71, your configuration changes have been applied.

Figure 3.71 Updated Configuration

3.5 Summary

Preparing your SAP Solution Manager system to be configured for SAP ITSM can be a daunting task if you're approaching it for the first time. There are design considerations that involve cross-team collaboration, technical setup activities that require a blend of several skills, and sponsorship activities that must come from the leadership to see the overall strategy through.

While the activities and concepts described in this chapter can be set up rapidly if you have the skills required, we recommend that you put thought into the design and configuration of these basic setup activities.

Transaction SOLMAN_SETUP requires close attention to detail, while the master data maintenance, security concepts, and UI setup require tight collaboration and design. Remember these settings are the foundation and backbone for SAP ITSM. Although these are basic setup configuration tasks, you should treat them as important parts of the process.

In the next chapter we will begin Part II, Application Incident Management. You'll find an overview of Application Incident Management as it relates to the functionality provided in SAP Solution Manager.

Part II
Application Incident Management

You should now have the foundational knowledge required to understand ITSM from a comprehensive view. Part I provided a high-level overview of ITSM from a system-agnostic perspective, with discussions around the methodologies, frameworks, and standard processes relevant to future chapters within this book.

This part of the book will focus specifically on the Application Incident Management scenario within ITSM in SAP Solution Manager. Our main focus will be Problem Management, Incident Management, and Service Request Management, with SAP Solution Manager as the driving platform behind these processes. We'll discuss the end-to-end process flows, how they are integrated throughout the entire ALM scenario, as well as the main features and functionalities. We also provide a comprehensive and detailed chapter dedicated strictly to the functional configuration of Application Incident Management processes.

Application Incident Management, formerly known and also referred to as the Service Desk component of SAP Solution Manager, has evolved considerably over the years. This chapter provides the latest content around the updated service within SAP Solution Manager to process problems, incidents, and service requests throughout your organization.

4 An Overview of Application Incident Management

By now, you should be familiar with the concepts of Incident Management in the sense of overall SAP ITSM. In addition to providing an understanding of these concepts, Chapter 1 explained how the ITIL framework supports the disciplines that have emerged from the Incident Management component of SAP ITSM.

In this chapter, we'll provide an overview of Application Incident Management (AIM) in SAP Solution Manager. First we'll discuss the goals and motivation behind the AIM scenario, as well as provide an explanation of how this scenario is made up in the SAP Solution Manager system. After discussing the architecture and infrastructure, we'll provide an overview of the most significant updates that have been made available to the market with the release of SAP Solution Manager 7.1. Finally, we'll walk through the SAP CRM Web UI components specific to Application Incident Management functionalities.

4.1 Goals and Motivation

In this section, we'll discuss the goals and motivation for releasing a robust SAP ITSM platform, specifically for processing incidents and problems, within SAP Solution Manager. Additionally, the information within this section should provide you, the customer or the administrator, with a goal and motivation to build a business case to adopt AIM.

4.1.1 The Evolution of SAP Service Desk

The central processing and management of tickets related to SAP incidents has been a core function in SAP Solution Manager since its earliest releases. Further, integration into SAP CRM components to deliver functions specific to SAP ITSM are also not new to the SAP Solution Manager platform.

In prior versions of SAP Solution Manager, the Service Desk had all of these components but struggled to match the functionality of third-party incident management tools. Other limitations included poor user acceptance and restrictions to handle SAP applications exclusively.

The tight integration between Application Lifecycle Management (ALM) and SAP ITSM, steered by the ITIL framework and driven by the SAP CRM 7.0 infrastructure, engineers a more robust tool for administering AIM. All of these pieces, layered with an overhauled UI based on the SAP CRM Web Client, deliver an all-new platform within SAP Solution Manager that provides best-of-breed capabilities to deliver AIM.

4.1.2 Application Incident Management in a Nutshell

In this section, we will provide a brief overview of Application Incident Management in SAP Solution Manager. We will highlight the range of capabilities, functionality overview, and motivation from SAP.

Range of Capabilities

AIM provides central message processing capabilities for SAP and non-SAP applications (e.g., non-SAP systems, third-party tools, and network devices). The functionality is flexible in that it can be configured to be a simple repository of messages that have been sent to SAP or a full-blown problem and incident management solution.

Functionality Overview

Using AIM, messages can be created directly within the transaction from which the error was detected in the managed SAP ERP system. SAP Solution Manager automatically captures critical technical details such as the transaction the user is having trouble with, database version, and service pack levels. This information is forwarded to support teams or SAP as an escalation path with workflow and email notifications to streamline resolution. Additionally, external help desks can be connected to your SAP Solution Manager system to support continued use of enterprise tools. AIM includes reporting capabilities to help track key end-user support metrics.

Motivation

Tracking, reporting, and alerting SAP of non-SAP incidents or problems becomes unreliable and inconsistent as tickets are processed across multiple applications (spreadsheets, in-house databases, ticketing tools, etc.). By implementing AIM, you can consolidate support applications, which takes greater advantage of existing SAP license fees and eliminates redundancy across offline or manual tools and processes.

4.1.3 The Goal of Application Incident Management

Implementing business processes across multiple products, the operation of these interconnected processes after they become productive, and optimizing these processes to increase efficiency will require the support of AIM. Like the traditional definition of Incident Management, the goal of AIM within SAP Solution Manager is to restore normal operation of services as quickly as possible without disrupting the business, regardless of the ALM phase.

Throughout each of the phases in ALM, there will be instances when problems and incidents will arise. These problems and incidents must be processed with both SAP ITSM disciplines within a central administration platform.

> **Important!**
>
> SAP Solution Manager 7.1 contains best-of-breed messaging capabilities, ITIL-compliant processes, and an intuitive web UI. The UI is an all-new Service Desk application that aims to meet your requirements for a single platform to perform AIM.

AIM enables all members and customers of the organization to log tickets in SAP Solution Manager when hardware or services aren't functioning as required. Both problems and incidents are handled within this scenario of SAP Solution Manager.

In the next section, we'll provide an overview of the architecture and infrastructure of AIM.

4.2   Architecture and Infrastructure

The architecture and infrastructure of AIM is comprised of all subprocesses that are managed by an organization's IT Service Desk. Additionally, the architecture of AIM includes all external integration points that may be relevant to an IT organization's overall AIM infrastructure. The driving force at the center of all of these integrated components, as shown in Figure 4.1, is the customer.

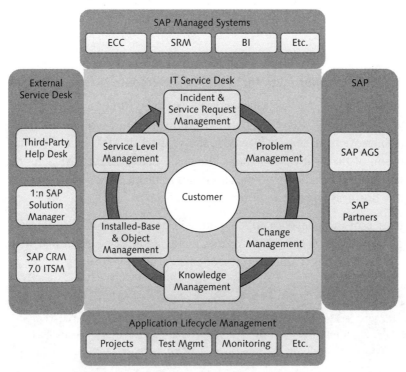

Figure 4.1 Application Incident Management Infrastructure

Remember that in the case of an incident or problem, the goal of AIM is to restore normal service operations with minimal impact to business operations. These components, no matter how few or many an IT organization has, are in place exclusively for the customer or business user. Take away the customer, and there is really no need for an AIM infrastructure to be in place.

Figure 4.2 provides a representation for how the two main AIM processes within SAP Solution Manager feed one another. Because we're heavily concentrated on these two subcomponents of the IT Service Desk in Figure 4.1, it's important to understand how they integrate with one another. Figure 4.2 touches lightly on the process flow and roles involved. We'll explain the process and related roles in detail in Chapter 5.

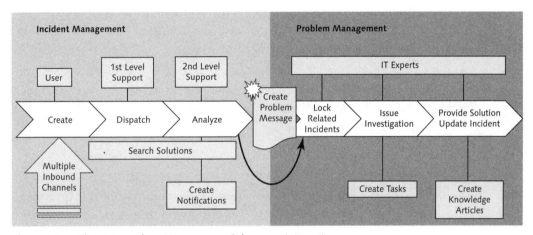

Figure 4.2 Application Incident Management: Subprocess Integration

The following subsections describe the two main components that form the infrastructure of AIM: the IT Service Desk and Operability with Related Components.

4.2.1 IT Service Desk

In general, a *service desk* is a single point of contact to marry the communication methods between users and customers to the personnel within the IT organization. SAP Solution Manager is equipped with the functionality and processes to serve as an organization's IT Service Desk regardless of how the overall service desk is structured.

In the next subsections, we'll quickly go over the different types and components in an IT Service Desk.

IT Service Desk Types

SAP Solution Manager can be enabled to support the following types of service desks:

▶ **Call center**
A *call center* is a central point to receive and process a large volume of tickets via telephone.

▶ **Contact center**
A *contact center* is a central point to receive and process tickets via multiple channels (telephone, fax, email, etc.). Customer interaction by way of delivering solutions directly to the customers is the key differentiator between this type of service desk and a call center.

▶ **Help desk**
A *help desk* is a central point to receive and process tickets closely related to IT assets. Direct communication to the customer or user is typically delivered through a tiered support model.

Components of an SAP IT Service Desk

As shown previously in Figure 4.1, there are five main components (processes) for which an SAP IT Service Desk serves as the central delivery platform. For the purposes of Part II of this book (Application Incident Management) we'll be most concerned with Incident and Service Request Management as well as Problem Management. The other processes will be explained throughout subsequent chapters.

4.2.2 Operability with Related Components

AIM has integration points into four main components. Depending on your IT organization's overall architecture for AIM, any or all of the following components may be integrated into your scenario:

▶ **SAP managed systems**
SAP Solution Manager connects to managed SAP systems that make up your IT organization's installed base. For example, incidents can be raised from any client in any of the systems you choose to connect to the central SAP Solution Manager system.

- **SAP Active Global Support (SAP AGS)**
  SAP Solution Manager connects to SAP AGS to provide service to the customer. For example, incidents that require escalation beyond an IT organization's internal support staff can be forwarded to SAP AGS for resolution.

- **Application Lifecycle Management (ALM)**
  AIM also operates closely with components associated with all phases of ALM. For example, if an alert threshold is exceeded in a business process monitoring scenario, an incident ticket can be automatically generated in the AIM tool.

- **External service desk**
  Other service desks (e.g., third-party or an additional SAP Solution Manager) can be integrated to a central SAP Solution Manager system depending on an IT organization's overall tools architecture. For example, if an organization has BMC Remedy installed for a service desk that handles everything, SAP Solution Manager can be integrated to handle SAP-related messages.

Now that we've covered what AIM means in regards to SAP Solution Manager, we'll describe the key features that are new and enhanced in release 7.1.

4.3 New Features and Enhancements Delivered with SAP Solution Manager 7.1

SAP Solution Manager 7.1 features a major overhaul and update to the majority of the functionality within the system. SAP ITSM accounts for a large portion of the changes and updates. AIM, as part of the overall SAP ITSM scenario, includes many new features and enhancements to the Service Desk features that came with version 7.0.

In this section, we'll cover the key features in AIM that are either new or have been enhanced from the prior versions of SAP Solution Manager. While the objectives of this book aren't to compare prior versions to the current 7.1 release of SAP Solution Manager, it's beneficial to point out the significance of what customers will gain from installing or upgrading their SAP Solution Manager to drive SAP ITSM functions.

First, we'll describe the changes to the transaction types delivered with SAP Solution Manager 7.1. Following an overview of AIM transaction types, we'll guide you through the new and enhanced features available within SAP Solution Manager 7.1 that boost the IT Service Desk functionality.

4.3.1 Release 7.1-Based Transaction Types

A *transaction type*, as briefly defined in Chapter 3, is a SAP CRM component that defines the attributes and characteristics of a business transaction. Transaction types, also called *document types*, exist in SAP Solution Manager for functionalities that leverage messaging capabilities.

Table 4.1 identifies all of the transaction types available to drive the messaging capabilities within ALM. You can see that there is a change in the naming convention of the transaction types from release 7.0 to 7.1. Further, there are many cases in which brand-new transaction types are introduced in release 7.1 (SMIT, SMPR, etc.).

7.0 Based	7.1 Based	Description
SLFN	SMIN	Incident
SISV	SMIS	Incident ISV
SIVA	SMIV	Incident VAR
N/A	SMIT	Incident template
N/A	SMPR	Problem
N/A	SMPT	Problem template
N/A	SMRQ	Service request
N/A	KNAR	Knowledge article

Table 4.1 Application Incident Management Transaction Types

Note

The new 7.1-based transaction types, and their enhanced functionality, are only offered via the SAP CRM Web UI.

Introducing these new transaction types is a significant update included in SAP Solution Manager 7.1. The purpose is to offer better capabilities in regards to messaging from both a user interface (Web UI) and functionality perspective. To achieve this, and adapt to these benefits, customers who have switched to 7.1 must also adopt (or transition) to the new 7.1-based transaction types.

We'll discuss the strategy and best practices for making this transition in Appendix B. In the next section, we'll describe the key new features delivered with SAP Solution Manager 7.1.

4.3.2   New Features in SAP ITSM

With the release of SAP Solution Manager 7.1, the majority of the SAP ITSM functionality is either brand new or has been enhanced. In this section, we'll provide an overview of what we think, based on our experiences deploying IT Service Desk functionality in SAP Solution Manager across multiple customers, are the most significant *new* features included with the 7.1 release.

Text Templates

Text templates are used as a way to rapidly populate information related to the transaction type. Located in the TEXT MANAGEMENT assignment block of AIM, text templates enable you to have an organization-wide standard for how incidents are described.

Rather than counting on the support staff to include all of the long text required for processing a message, text templates can be made available as a standard for inputting text that is critical for message processing.

As shown in Figure 4.3, the support staff has the ability to set the option for USER TEMPLATE or SYSTEM TEMPLATE:

▶ USER TEMPLATE
The *user template* allows the support staff to select from a list of their own user-defined templates.

▶ SYSTEM TEMPLATE
If organization-wide standards are to be used, the user may also select from *system templates*, which are defined at the administrator level.

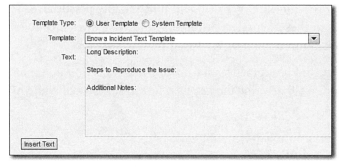

Figure 4.3 Text Template Selection

Incident Templates

Incident templates (transaction type SMIT) offer support teams a quick and efficient way to create incidents that are similar in regards to their characteristics.

Incident templates offer support staff a reusable way to create an incident that they know will be populated with common information. For example, if your IT staff is receiving incidents related to security authorizations, those tickets will typically have the same criteria entered every time (support team, priority, categorization schema, etc.).

This functionality allows your support staff to create these templates ahead of time, so that when the incident is received, they can create the record more rapidly.

As shown in Figure 4.4, incident templates are launched by clicking the NEW FROM TEMPLATE button directly from within the incident. From there, you'll be given the option to search among a database of predefined incident templates.

Figure 4.4 Creating Incidents New from a Template

Follow-Up Documents

Follow-up documents are documents that integrate one ITSM process with another. For example, if you have several incidents that are related, you have a problem. In that scenario, you would create a problem document as a follow-up to the incident. Then, the Problem Management process commences and proceeds within that document. The incident and problem are linked together.

Follow-up documents are available across AIM and ChaRM. They support tight integration and interoperability among other ALM processes. Follow-up documents are a way for your support staff to either continue processing the message, while linking it to the original message, or transition into another ALM process.

For example, if the incident being processed requires a change to a production SAP ERP landscape, a request for change follow-up document can be created to transition to the Change Request Management (ChaRM) process. Similarly, if Problem Management must be initiated, a problem can also be created as a follow-up document.

As shown in Figure 4.5, follow-up documents can be created from within the AIM transaction type. Afterwards, you'll have the option to select which subsequent document type will be initiated.

Figure 4.5 Creating a Follow-Up Document

> **Important!**
>
> This is the new method of generating a request for change document in ChaRM in SAP Solution Manager 7.1.

Solution Categorization

The SOLUTION CATEGORY field in AIM is an additional field delivered with SAP Solution Manager 7.1 to support increased reporting capabilities.

The *solution category*, assigned in the DETAILS assignment block, is used to help document the final resolution criteria of the incident. The values within this drop-down, as shown in Figure 4.6, should be specific to the type of resolution.

As you can see, SAP provides three solution categories out of the box. Keep in mind that these are merely recommendations but can also be considered as a template that can be adapted per your organization's reporting requirements.

Figure 4.6 Solution Category Fields

Recommended Priorities

To more closely align SAP Solution Manager's ITSM functions to ITIL, *recommended priorities* are generated based on a combination of impact and urgency values.

SAP Solution Manager provides an out-of-the box Customizing schema to determine the value generated within the RECOMMENDED PRIORITY field. For example, an IMPACT value of HIGH coupled with an URGENCY of VERY HIGH will result in the RECOMMENDED PRIORITY of HIGH. If your organization's requirements differ from the standard schema, they can be adapted in Customizing.

Recommended priorities, as shown in Figure 4.7, are located in the PROCESSING DATA section within the DETAILS assignment block of the incident. These fields are optional; however, the standard PRIORITY field must be filled out.

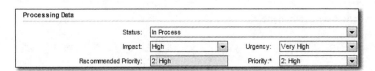

Figure 4.7 Recommended Priorities

Multilevel Categorization

Four levels of category values are available for processing incidents. *Multilevel categorization* allows your organization flexibility and robust capabilities for classifying and reporting on incidents.

As opposed to the SAP Solution Manager 7.0 category options (one field which was global across all transaction types), SAP Solution Manager 7.1 provides a much more adaptable and open mechanism for logging incidents. These values are found in the CATEGORY section of the DETAILS assignment block of the incident.

While you may leverage the multilevel categorization schema that comes standard from SAP (as shown in Figure 4.8), we recommend you spend time collaborating across your IT organization to agree upon and define fields that adapt to your internal reporting criteria.

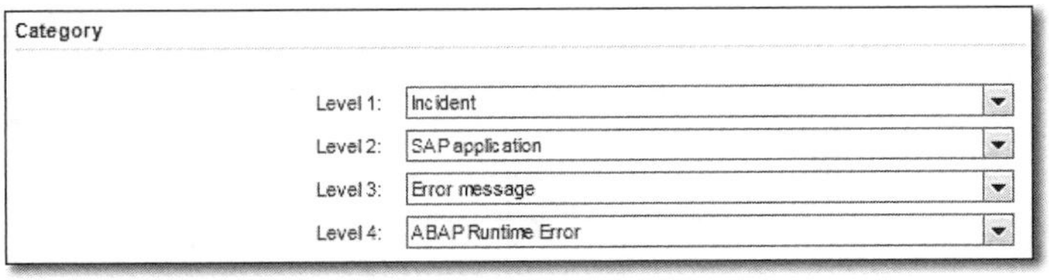

Category	
Level 1:	Incident
Level 2:	SAP application
Level 3:	Error message
Level 4:	ABAP Runtime Error

Figure 4.8 Multilevel Categorization

Observation List

An *observation list* is available to quickly access incidents that are most critical to you, require specific attention, or have the tendency to be accessed more often than others.

There are two options in which incidents can be monitored in an observation list:

▶ **SAP CRM Web UI**
By selecting the ADD TO FAVORITES button (🌟) from within the incident, the incident is then added on the home screen to the FAVORITES folder (Figure 4.9).

▶ **Work centers**
By selecting the ADD TO WATCH LIST button from within the incident, the incident is then added to the MY WATCH LIST section on the OVERVIEW page of the Incident Management work center (see Figure 4.10).

Figure 4.9 SAP CRM Web UI Observation List

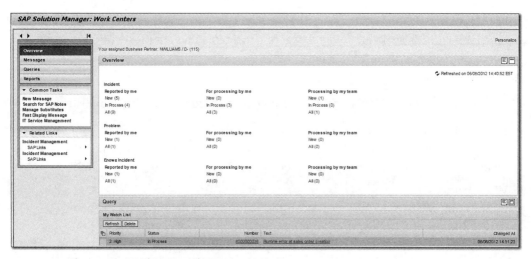

Figure 4.10 Work Center Observation List

Fast Display of Support Messages

This new feature, available in the work center, provides a quick means for users to access an incident based on just the identification number.

By selecting the FAST DISPLAY MESSAGE button in the COMMON TASKS area of the work center (see Figure 4.11), users can go directly to the incident rather than searching for it via the message list. Simply enter the TRANSACTION ID of the incident in the resulting FAST DISPLAY MESSAGE pop-up screen and select OK. You'll be taken directly to that message.

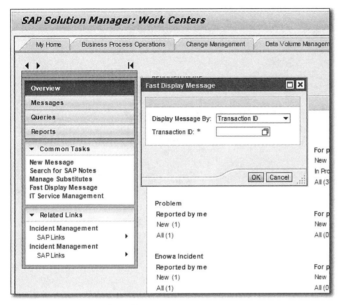

Figure 4.11 Fast Display of Messages

Substitutes for Processing Messages

Substitutes can be configured as a way for people to have a backup if IT support staff members are out of the office. You do this by setting up relationships with the business partners, who are enabled as message processors in your AIM scenario.

After you establish these relationships in Transaction BP, message processors have the ability to manage the substitutes (Figure 4.12) if a scenario requires that their backup provide support for their activities. Here, the SUBSTITUTION screen allows the message processors to maintain which other message processors can substitute them. Also, they can view the message processors that they are designated as substitutes for. Substitutes are managed in the INCIDENT MANAGEMENT work center.

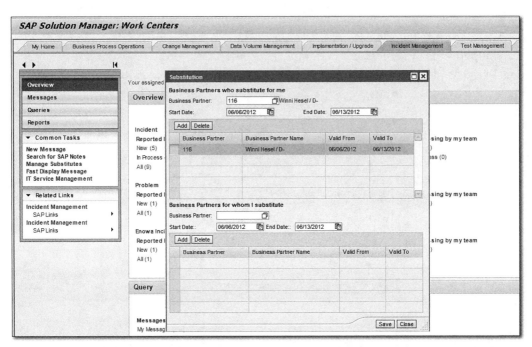

Figure 4.12 Manage Substitutes

Knowledge Articles

Knowledge articles are a new transaction type (KNAR) delivered with SAP Solution Manager 7.1. A knowledge article supports knowledge management in that they provide a way to follow-up on incidents and/or problems by providing documentation relating to the reason or solution.

By building up your Knowledge Management Database (KMDB), knowledge articles are able to promote increased resolution time for future AIM transaction types.

Additionally, knowledge articles can be found automatically when related to specific category values in multilevel categorization. For example, if a specific set of categories has been selected, choosing MORE • FIND KNOWLEDGE ARTICLES in the incident (Figure 4.13) can point the support staff to knowledge articles related to that combination of categories.

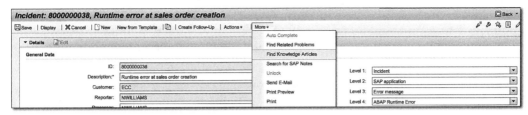

Figure 4.13 Find Knowledge Articles

SAP NetWeaver BW-Based Reporting

With SAP Solution Manager 7.1, reporting based on SAP NetWeaver Business Warehouse (SAP NetWeaver BW) is available to provide analysis of several aspects of AIM (e.g., processing status and historical analysis). Data from the incidents are filtered and refined by means of detailed queries. These queries will respond to analytical requirements by providing data that can be filtered and adjusted.

This analytical capability is based off of web templates on SAP Business Explorer (SAP BEx) web applications. This data is displayed either graphically or in tables. These web templates are called in the SAP NetWeaver BW system in which you apply the queries to the data. Data is pulled from the time of the last extraction.

We'll cover SAP NetWeaver BW-based reporting more extensively in Chapter 17.

Link Support Messages

Incidents can be linked to other incidents or problems with a goal of processing them more efficiently. Also, solutions to future incidents are more easily identified if you have linked related AIM transaction types together.

Within this functionality is the option to lock transactions together. Locking an incident to a problem, for example, will stop the processing of that incident on the individual level. After the corresponding (linked) problem is completed, the incident is closed automatically. This also applies to requests for change that are locked to an incident.

Planning the resolution of a problem and managing the processing of incidents becomes much more efficient when linking these transaction types together.

Figure 4.14 represents how you can link transaction types together. In the RELATED TRANSACTIONS assignment block within the service transaction (incident, problem, etc.), select the INSERT button. You'll have an option to search for the related transaction and link it to the origin. Additionally, these links will be displayed in the RELATIONSHIPS section of the DETAILS assignment block.

Figure 4.14 Linking Transactions

Summary

Although there are many more new features available within AIM in 7.1, those described in this section are the most significant. In the next section, we'll describe functionality that was available in SAP Solution Manager 7.0 but has undergone enhancement to improve the AIM functionalities offered with those features.

4.3.3 Enhanced Features

As with the previous section, our goal is to provide you with a brief overview of the enhanced functionality offered with AIM in release 7.1 of SAP Solution Manager. Many functionalities within this SAP ITSM scenario have been enhanced, but those discussed here are the most significant. Like the new features, we won't describe the configuration aspects just yet. We'll reserve those for later chapters.

Text Management

Text management, administered in the TEXT assignment block within the incident, was a much needed enhancement. As you can see in Figure 4.15, the text area is large and more intuitive than the preceding functionality in prior SAP Solution Manager releases.

The TEXT LOG (where the text is entered and displayed) contains a nice large view for editing and reviewing information. The amount of text visible can be adjusted according to the message processors preference via the MAXIMUM LINES option. The TEXT LOG FILTER allows the user to read specific texts.

Figure 4.15 Text Management

Forward Messages to SAP

If a message requires escalation to SAP, you can send that message to SAP AGS directly from SAP Solution Manager. All communication and details (related to both incident and system), as well as system access, are administered directly from SAP Solution Manager.

With the release of SAP Solution Manager 7.1, problems can now be sent to SAP for additional support. Communication to SAP is maintained in the SAP COLLABORATION assignment block (Figure 4.16).

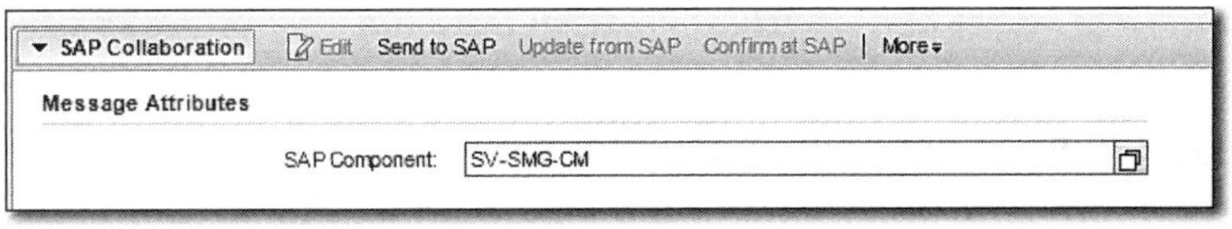

Figure 4.16 SAP Collaboration

Rate Effort of Time Recording Criteria

The reporting criteria have been expanded to enhance time recording. With SAP Solution Manager 7.1, the additional criteria contained in the values for multi-level categorization can be considered in the analytics for time recording.

Last but definitely not least, we can't fail to mention the introduction of the SAP CRM Web UI as considerably the most significant new feature to the SAP Solution Manager platform. Chapter 2 provided a thorough explanation of the key features, architecture, and navigational components of the new SAP CRM Web UI. In the next section, we'll drill down one layer further to provide an overview of how the new SAP CRM Web UI has enhanced the way AIM is executed within SAP Solution Manager.

4.4   SAP CRM Web UI for Creating, Processing, and Tracking

In this section, we'll walk through the areas of the SAP CRM Web UI for creating, processing, and tracking items specific to AIM.

4.4.1   Overview

Chapter 2 provided a thorough explanation of the two key UIs in SAP Solution Manager for administering transaction types, Work Centers, and the SAP CRM Web UI.

There are multiple ways to create incidents and problems beyond the standard SAP Solution Manager interfaces (we'll explain these in Chapter 7). However, you have to decide for which user interface AIM transaction types will be created and processed.

You can choose to create messages in the Incident Management work center or in the SAP CRM Web UI. This choice can be determined based on existing infrastructure or overall preference. Chapter 2 described these choices in detail.

While you have the choice to create in either UI, we recommend that incidents and problems are processed only in the SAP CRM Web UI. This UI is based on the

SAP CRM 7.0 infrastructure and offers a wide range of functionality and personalization to increase the overall AIM processing experience.

4.4.2 Application Incident Management Web UI

In this section, we'll provide a basic overview of what to expect when navigating the AIM portion of the SAP CRM Web UI.

Figure 4.17 displays the INCIDENT MANAGEMENT work center. After the INCIDENT MANAGEMENT work center appears, three work areas (SEARCH, CREATE, and REPORTS) can be accessed specific to the Incident Management transaction types problem and incident.

Additionally, after you select the arrow button ( ) next to the first-level navigation item, the second-level navigation menu opens also (see Figure 4.17). These items give you direct access to key transactions, reports, and templates associated with Incident Management.

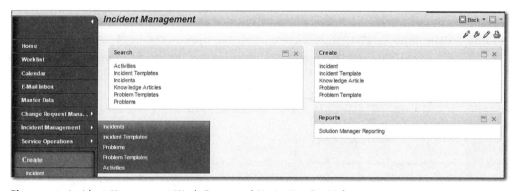

Figure 4.17 Incident Management Work Center and Navigation Bar Links

You can search for problems and incidents by selecting the appropriate search link in the SEARCH work area. The SEARCH: INCIDENTS screen appears as shown in Figure 4.18. From here, search criteria can be entered and saved if necessary to enable a quick search.

Finally, Figure 4.19 shows an example of how an incident or problem may look in your SAP Solution Manager system. The DETAILS assignment block has been expanded to show the key details of the incident. Additional assignment blocks, which are explained in Chapter 8, provide several different types of information relating to the incident that can be used for processing.

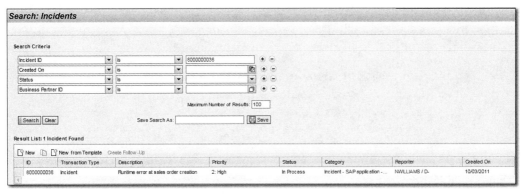

Figure 4.18 Search Screen for Incidents

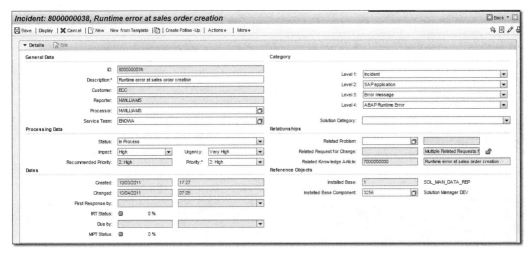

Figure 4.19 An Incident in SAP CRM Web UI

4.5 Summary

As you're now aware, SAP Solution Manager 7.1 delivers Application Incident Management capabilities that have either been completely enhanced or are all new. Whether you're new to managing incidents within SAP Solution Manager or have had experience with the prior Service Desk in SAP Solution Manager, it's easily recognizable that the current release of SAP Solution Manager can be treated as an all-inclusive central platform for handling these activities.

Now that we have provided an overview of what AIM means within SAP Solution Manager, it's important to understand the related subprocesses and user roles. Chapter 5 will provide a detailed explanation of each process within AIM as well as the roles and responsibilities for each user involved throughout the processes.

Several incidents of the same nature create the need for problems to effectively conduct root cause analysis. Integration with the knowledge database, tasks, SAP Support, and Change Management all facilitate the end-to-end lifecycle of an incident and problem.

5 Application Incident Management End-User Roles and Process Flows

You should now have developed a good understanding of the definition, overview, and methodologies associated with Application Incident Management (AIM). In Chapter 1, we introduced the basic concepts of Problem Management, Incident Management, and Service Request Management as related to IT service management (ITSM), ITIL, and Application Lifecycle Management (ALM). In Chapter 1, the material was independent of SAP Solution Manager with the intent of providing a broader history and overview of the concepts. In Chapter 4, we honed in on what AIM means exclusively to SAP Solution Manager.

In this chapter, we'll explain the end-user roles associated with delivering and supporting AIM within SAP Solution Manager. In SAP Solution Manager, AIM consists of Incident Management, Problem Management, and integration points into Knowledge Management (KM). We'll describe the process flows under the AIM umbrella in a step-by-step manner.

Further, we'll describe how Incident Management and Problem Management are executed in an integrated manner within SAP Solution Manager to accomplish end-to-end AIM.

5.1 Roles in Application Incident Management

In this section, we'll describe the roles involved throughout AIM. We'll start by providing an example of what a tiered service organization might look like and then describe how SAP Solution Manager can align to a typical service strategy.

We'll also describe who the players are in the realm of AIM. We'll explain which roles drive the end-to-end process steps in AIM, as well as describe who plays a supporting role in the overall process.

5.1.1 Designing a Tiered Support Structure

Service organizations and service desks are typically designed to have tiers (or levels) in which messages (problems or incidents) follow escalation and analysis/ resolution paths. For example, messages originating from end users are received by a Level 1 service team. If the content within those messages can't be resolved by Level 1 service personnel, the message is forwarded (or escalated) to Level 2. In the case of a service organization that leverages SAP Solution Manager, if the Level 2 service team can't provide resolution, they have the option to forward the message to SAP Active Global Support (SAP AGS), which, in this case, serves as Level 3 support.

Figure 5.1 provides a visual representation of how a tiered support concept would look in conjunction with the use of SAP Solution Manager.

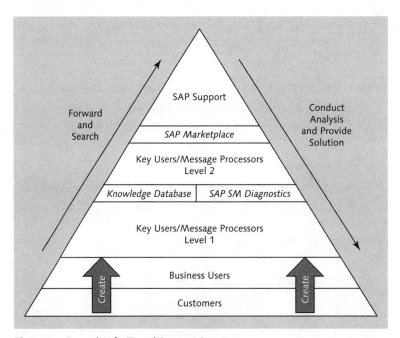

Figure 5.1 Example of a Tiered Support Structure

You can see that there are multiple levels that consist of end-user groups, support levels, and various resources to provide analysis, as well as paths in which messages flow. We'll provide an overview of each of these components that make up the different pieces of our service organization example in the following subsections.

You'll also find an overview of the SAP Solution Manager service organization components as they relate to a tiered support structure, which is driven by SAP Solution Manager to administer AIM. We'll go through a detailed explanation of the end-user roles within these levels in Section 5.1.2.

End Users

As you can identify in the pyramid graphic in Figure 5.1 (or any pyramid diagrams in that sense), the bottom-most layers include the largest population of those involved in the service organization. For the topic at hand, this population includes the end users who create the incidents. We've identified two examples:

▶ **Business users**
These users are also often referred to as "power users" or "super users" in an SAP organization. These users typically have SAP GUI installed on their desktop computers and execute some function of the SAP ERP production process.

▶ **Customers**
Customers can be considered the classic end user. One level below the business users, customers don't see SAP GUI screens. In many cases, customers may not even know what SAP is. They perform their job function on a portal or other interface. Often, they will have the ability to directly create an incident.

Level 1 Support

Level 1 support personnel serve as the initial layer to receive, process, and attempt to resolve messages that are created by the end users. Level 1 support personnel can also be classified as power users or super users.

In many cases, organizations will form Level 1 service teams out of selected business users who have the technical and functional capabilities of processing messages that fall within the scope of Level 1 support.

The main value of Level 1 support is to receive, provide basic processing, and dispatch messages to Level 2. However, Level 1 support may also solve certain types of messages. Examples of Level 1 messages include the following:

► Password resets

► General how-to questions

► Training issues

SAP Solution Manager Resources

Various components of SAP Solution Manager are within reach of the service teams to help with the analysis of incidents and problems. These components are fully integrated within the AIM processes (you'll see the integration when we describe the processes step-by-step in Chapter 7).

Depending on the scope of Level 1 support and the experience the teams have, they may in fact access these resources. More often, as part of message analysis, Level 2 support will tap into these resources more often than the Level 1 support.

There are two main resources within SAP Solution Manager to aid in the analysis and potential resolution of an incident or problem:

► **Knowledge database**
SAP Solution Manager 7.1 offers the capability to manage a repository of knowledge articles. A collection of knowledge articles, linked to incidents and problems with information providing descriptions and solutions, make up the overall knowledge database in SAP Solution Manager. Within the incident or problem, there is a functionality that can automatically determine related knowledge articles based on the four categories within the incident or problem. We'll explain this when we walk through the process in Chapter 9.

► **SAP Solution Manager Diagnostics**
Service teams can also leverage the Diagnostics part of SAP Solution Manager to perform technical root cause analysis on the incident or problem message.

Level 2 Support

Level 2 support will receive messages dispatched from the Level 1 service teams. Resources within Level 2 support typically deal with troubleshooting and analyzing problems that affect multiple users. Additionally, they will process incidents that require a deeper technical understanding to reach a resolution. Throughout the lifecycle of a message, Level 2 support will continue to assist and collaborate with Level 1 support until the problem or incident has been resolved.

Incidents and problems that can be described as non-routine also fall within the responsibility of a Level 2 service team. A few standard examples of messages that are handled exclusively by Level 2 support include the following:

▶ ABAP errors

▶ Performance issues

▶ Downtime/availability issues

▶ Configuration errors

▶ Bug/fix

Level 3 Support

The final level of support in our example is Level 3, SAP AGS. If an error occurs that is an SAP-related bug, the problem or incident can be forwarded directly to SAP AGS for further processing. The act of forwarding, in this case, occurs directly within the message.

All activities associated with processing the message between the service organization and SAP AGS are administered and recorded directly in SAP Solution Manager.

Note
Our example includes two tiers/levels of support within an organization, with Level 3 as an external service team. In many cases, there are up to three or four internal service teams with an additional external service group. The design and organization of a tiered support structure should be developed specific to your organization's requirements and size.

SAP Resources

SAP Solution Manager has direct integration with the SAP Service Marketplace. A search for SAP OSS (Online Service and Support) Notes can be launched directly from the incident or problem. If an SAP OSS Note is found that relates to the message, it can be attached to the incident or problem for further processing and aid in the knowledge management process.

Paths

The arrows within our pyramid diagram in Figure 5.1 represent the different escalation paths associated with a tiered service organization. Messages can be escalated upward throughout the pyramid. Conversely, messages can be passed back downward to facilitate the communication of proposed solutions and the recording of analysis results. The following paths are included in our example of a tiered support structure:

▶ **Create**
According to our example, this path is initiated from the base (end users) and passed to Level 1 support. This isn't to say that Level 1 or Level 2 support members will never create messages. This will definitely be the case. However, from an end-to-end flow, messages that adhere to the support structure start with the end users.

▶ **Forward and search**
Forwarding (dispatching) messages along with searching for solutions to the incident or problem occurs from Level 1 to Level 2 support. These teams will perform these activities as well as tap into the various resources (SAP Solution Manager and SAP) to help facilitate these activities.

▶ **Conduct analysis and provide solution**
The analysis is performed from the very top (Level 3, SAP) all the way to Level 1 support. All service members throughout this pyramid will conduct some sort of analysis, no matter how knowledgeable or technically advanced their skill set is. Even the simplest incidents and problems require an analysis. Furthermore, these members will all play a part in providing a solution back to the end user.

Now that we've described how a three-tiered support structure is designed and administered by SAP Solution Manager, it's time to examine the end-user roles one level deeper. We've described roles in the sense of levels and groups, so now we'll provide an overview of the individual roles that make up these levels of the support organization.

5.1.2 Active Users

In this section, we'll provide an overview of the active users in AIM. Active users execute the end-to-end process steps within Incident Management and Problem

Management directly. In other words, active users have access to SAP Solution Manager and perform tactical functions within AIM.

The following users are considered active users:

▶ Customer

▶ Reporter

▶ Processor

▶ Service team

Figure 5.2 shows a screenshot of an incident. You can identify the active users in the GENERAL DATA area of the DETAILS assignment block of the incident. In the following subsections, we'll provide an overview of each of these active users and the role they play in AIM.

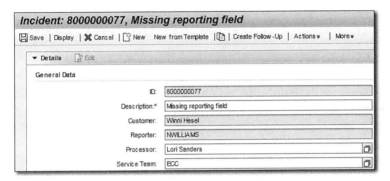

Figure 5.2 Active Users

Customer

The customer is the one that raises the incident or problem. The customer can be an individual, team, or organization.

Reporter

The reporter is the individual that initially records the message. According to our tiered support structure example, reporters mainly consist of end users and business users. This is the case if one of many inbound channels, external to SAP Solution Manager, is used to report the incident. We'll discuss inbound channels in Chapter 7.

If your SAP Solution Manager is utilized as a call center, members of the support team may populate the REPORTER field.

Processor

The PROCESSOR field is populated with the member of the service team who is immediately responsible for handling the message. The PROCESSOR field is typically populated with Level 1 and Level 2 service team members. Others can be IT experts or customer support members that reside within a service team.

The primary responsibility of the processor, as we described in the previous section, is to process the message and forward if necessary to the following service team. Alternatively, if a solution has been potentially found, it's the processor's job to communicate the proposed solution back to the user or original service team.

Service Team

Also referred to as a *service queue* or *customer support team*, the service team consists of multiple processors with the responsibility for processing messages within a similar topic. Additionally, service teams are responsible for processing messages that fall within the scope of their support level.

Service teams can be determined in multiple ways. Most commonly, they are automatically determined based on an SAP component in conjunction with how they are organized in the overall organizational structure. We'll cover how messages are dispatched to service teams in more detail in Chapter 9.

5.1.3   External/Background Roles

In addition to the active users, who play the biggest part in end-to-end AIM, there are also external/background roles that complement Incident Management and Problem Management. Although these roles don't execute functions directly within SAP Solution Manager, they play a supporting role in the overall process. These roles include the following, which we'll describe in the next subsections:

► Sold-to party
► SAP support
► Administrator

Sold-To Party (Owner of System)

The *sold-to party* is the owner of the system. As we described in Chapter 3 (regarding business partners), the sold-to party is typically the organization that owns IT. Often, it's simply the name of the organization.

The purpose of the sold-to party in SAP ITSM is to serve as the root of the overall organizational structure. System assignment is decided upon according to the sold-to party. Furthermore, service teams are aligned to the sold-to party to facilitate reporting, analytics, and dispatching capabilities throughout the SAP ITSM process flows.

SAP Support

SAP Support, as described in the earlier "Level 3 Support" subsection, is SAP Active Global Support (SAP AGS). As stated earlier, if an incident is associated with an error in SAP programming or delivered customization (i.e., the software isn't operating according to standard design), the message can be forwarded directly to SAP AGS from within the message.

The role of SAP Support is to conduct an analysis and facilitate a resolution with the escalating level within the organization's service team. Because there is direct integration between SAP Solution Manager and SAP AGS to perform these activities, SAP Support accesses the managed system landscape via SAP Solution Manager as part of their analysis process.

All activity, communication, and resolution details are stored within the problem or incident.

Administrator

The administrator doesn't have an active role in the end-to-end process for AIM. However, the administrator is responsible for administrative tasks such as the following:

▶ Supporting the design and implementation of the organizational-specific AIM process

▶ Enabling those processes via configuration in the SAP Solution Manager system

▶ Setting up related master data

- Training users
- Providing reports to management
- Implementing fixes or changes to the processes

Now that you have a good understanding of how a service organization is organized using SAP Solution Manager and the end-user roles that play an active support role in AIM, we'll walk through the steps of these processes. First, we'll provide you with a step-by-step overview of the Incident Management process. Following that, we'll describe the steps within Problem Management and how the two processes are tightly integrated.

5.2 Incident Management Process

In this section, we'll provide a description of each step within the Incident Management process as it occurs in SAP Solution Manager. Figure 5.3 provides a high-level representation of the Incident Management process. On the left, you'll notice that inbound channels are inputs to Incident Management. On the right, you'll see that follow-ups provide outputs for administering post-processing tasks to support the closure of incidents and problems, as well as integration into other Application Lifecycle Management (ALM) phases.

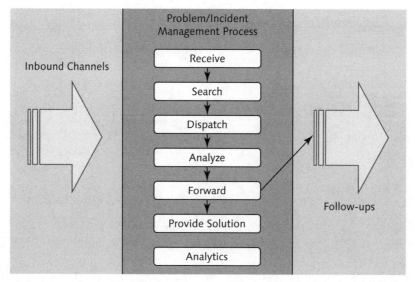

Figure 5.3 High-Level Integrated Problem/Incident Management Process

Throughout Incident Management, several integration points into Problem Management as well as Knowledge Management. We'll discuss both of these processes separately; however, due to the end-to-end design of these processes from SAP, we'll make mention of both processes in each section. The high-level steps within Figure 5.3 apply to both Incident Management and Problem Management. In each respective section, we'll break down this high-level process to point out tasks specific to both Incident Management and Problem Management.

You may or may not choose to incorporate the integration points into other AIM processes. However, to take full advantage of the ITSM capabilities of SAP Solution Manager and implement SAP ITSM/ITIL disciplines within your IT service organization, it's recommended that these processes be leveraged in an integrated matter.

Now, we'll walk through the steps of processing an incident in SAP Solution Manager. First, we'll break down the overall process shown in Figure 5.3 into steps related specifically to Incident Management.

5.2.1   Breaking Down the Process of Incident Management

If your organization is using Problem Management, there's a point in which that process is launched. If your organization is processing incidents only, the Problem Management scenario can be skipped, and the Incident Management process continues until the incident is closed. Figure 5.4 provides a process flow that details steps that occur specifically when processing an incident. We'll use this figure as the basis of our discussion of the process steps.

Like with any standard SAP-delivered element, you should consider these processes to be an ITIL-compliant best practices template for your organization. They provide you with a framework—aligned to standards—that should be adhered to. In many cases, these processes must be altered or expanded to account for organization-specific requirements (e.g., regulatory, audit, or security).

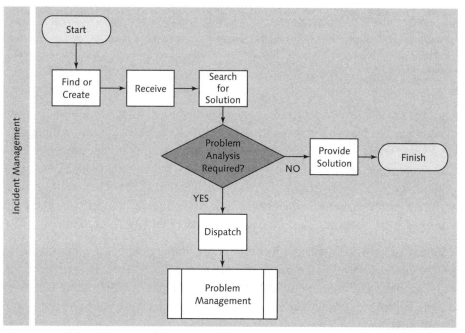

Figure 5.4 Incident Management Process Breakdown

We'll next provide you with a step-by-step description of the template processes delivered with SAP Solution Manager, so you can determine whether the process can be adopted as is or must be adapted to meet your organization's requirements.

5.2.2   Find Incident

The first step in the process is to find the incident (Figure 5.5). Depending on the scenario, this is achieved in one of the following ways:

▶ From a saved search (or the SEARCH: INCIDENTS screen)
▶ From a worklist

The following subsections describe these two methods for finding an incident.

Saved Search

The saved search is a user-defined report. Depending on the user (e.g., IT manager, processor, requester), these searches can be set up accordingly. They don't require Customizing and can be done according to each user's requirements. They aren't global, so every user is able to have many saved searches of their own.

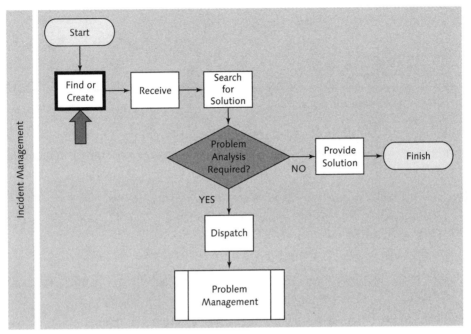

Figure 5.5 Find or Create Process Step: Incident Management

Figure 5.6 provides an example of a HOME screen in the SAP CRM Web UI. You can identify the saved search as a link in the MY SAVED SEARCHES area.

Figure 5.6 My Saved Searches on the Home Screen

Click the link to access the saved search, and the SEARCH: INCIDENTS screen will appear as shown in Figure 5.7. In this screen, you can view information about each incident that falls within the search criteria.

Figure 5.7 Search: Incidents Screen

You can drag and drop the columns to different locations, depending on your preference. When you access the saved search again, the system will remember your preference.

Next, we'll walk through the steps to create a saved search.

Creating a Saved Search

Creating a saved search is simple; just follow these steps:

1. Access the INCIDENT MANAGEMENT work center from the navigation bar in the SAP CRM UI by clicking the link.

2. In the SEARCH area, select the INCIDENTS link as shown in Figure 5.8.

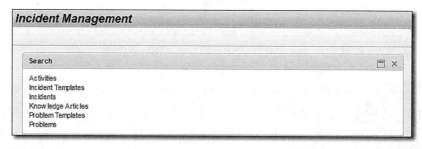

Figure 5.8 Incident Management Work Center Search Options

3. Enter the criteria per your requirements as shown in Figure 5.9.

4. SAP provides four different options for selecting the search criteria. To add more, click the ⊕ button. A new line will appear for entering search criteria.

   The DROP DOWN button (▼) next to each search option will provide several other options you can use to search for the incidents.

Search Criteria

Transaction Type	▼	is	▼	Enow a Incident (Y MIN)	▼	⊕ ⊖
Created On	▼	is on or later than	▼	04/01/2012	🗊	⊕ ⊖
Reported By	▼	is	▼	115	🗗	⊕ ⊖
Business Partner ID	▼	is	▼		🗗	⊕ ⊖

Maximum Number of Results: 100

| Search | Clear | Save Search As: My Q2 2012 Incidents | 🖫 Save |

Figure 5.9 Maintaining Search Criteria

5. Enter the name of your saved search in the SAVE SEARCH AS field.

6. Click SAVE.

7. Access the HOME screen to view your saved search in the MY SAVED SEARCHES work area.

> **Note**
>
> It isn't mandatory that you create a saved search. You can simply search for incidents via the SEARCH: INCIDENTS screen without creating saved searches.

Deleting a Saved Search

When saved search criteria expire, or you no longer have a use for it, you can easily delete the saved search by following these steps:

1. Access the SEARCH: INCIDENTS screen.

2. In the SAVED SEARCHES field in the upper-right corner of the screen, enter your saved search (Figure 5.10).

3. Click the DELETE button (🗑).

Personalize | System News | Log Off

Saved Searches ▼ | My Q2 2012 Incidents ▼ Go Advanced 🗑

🔙 Back ▼ 🔄 ▼

Figure 5.10 Deleting a Saved Search

Worklist

The worklist provides an overview of all business transactions within SAP ITSM. All transaction types (problems, incidents, requests for change, etc.) can be searched for in the worklist.

Like the saved search option, you have the ability to search and filter on multiple criteria to locate the incidents. Further, you have the option to create a saved search based on filtered data within the worklist.

Figure 5.11 shows the WORKLIST screen, which you can access via the WORKLIST link in the navigation bar.

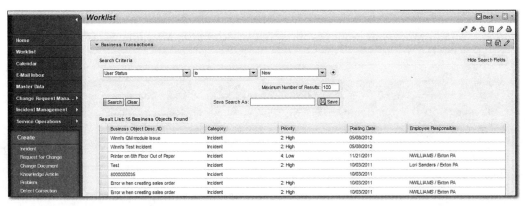

Figure 5.11 ITSM Worklist

5.2.3 Receive Incident

Once found, the incident is then received by the processor (Figure 5.12).

In our example, we'll maintain information within the DETAILS assignment block. Multiple assignment blocks are available for linking other information (SAP Solution Manager project data, documents, URLs, etc.). We'll cover assignment blocks in detail in Chapter 8.

For our example, the processor receives the incident by adding the information, as shown in Figure 5.13, to the incident.

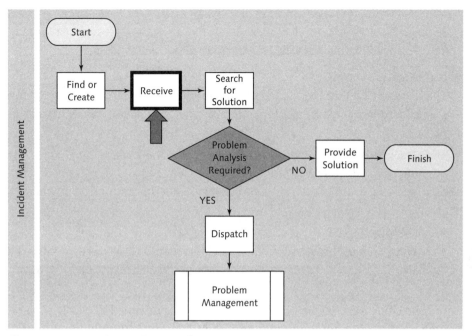

Figure 5.12 Receive Process Step: Incident Management

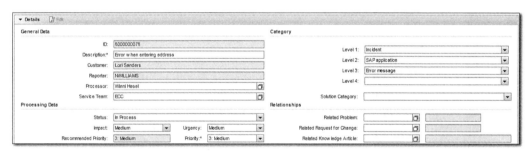

Figure 5.13 Receive Incident: Enter Incident Details

Maintain General Data

The GENERAL DATA area of the DETAILS assignment block (refer to Figure 5.13) includes information such as the identification number of the incident, short description, and the active users (business partners) specifically tied to the incident, as described here.

The following list identifies areas within the GENERAL DATA area of the DETAILS assignment block. Within each of these areas, fields are available for the requester and processor to maintain general information about the incident:

- **Identification number**
  The ID field is determined based on the number range for the incident. After the incident is created from an inbound channel, this value can't be changed.

- **Description**
  The DESCRIPTION field, like the number range value, was created from the inbound channel. However, if the processor identifies an error in the description (spelling, grammar, wrong terminology, etc.), he can update it when he receives the message.

- **Business partners**
  By default, the CUSTOMER and REPORTER fields can't be changed. This setting can be maintained in the partner determination procedure (explained in Chapter 11).

  If dispatching rules (explained in Chapter 9) are maintained, the SERVICE TEAM field will be automatically populated. The PROCESSOR field should be manually entered at this time.

Maintain Processing Data

In the PROCESSING DATA area of the DETAILS assignment block, STATUS, IMPACT, URGENCY, and PRIORITY are maintained by the processor. The entry in the RECOMMENDED PRIORITY field is automatically determined via a combination of the IMPACT and URGENCY field values. Following are the field values:

- **STATUS**
  The STATUS field is updated by the message processor in order to specify the status of the incident (New, In Process, Sent to SAP, etc.).

- **IMPACT**
  The IMPACT level is used to define the effect that the incident will have on the business in regards to how severely service levels will be affected.

- **URGENCY**
  The URGENCY value represents the measure of criticality in which an incident affects business deadlines. The urgency represents the time available to fix the incident before the business is impacted.

▶ PRIORITY

The combination of the IMPACT and URGENCY values should determine the priority of the incident. The priority is then used to identify the required resources and action to take in order to process the incident.

▶ RECOMMENDED PRIORITY

The RECOMMENDED PRIORITY values are determined based on a combination of impact and urgency. The RECOMMENDED PRIORITY values are the same as the standard PRIORITY values. We'll explain how to modify the schema, should your organizational requirements differ from the standard, in Chapter 8.

Maintain Category Values

SAP Solution Manager 7.1 offers four levels of category values (multilevel categorization) to choose for when receiving an incident. The processor will align the scope/content of the incident to the appropriate category values defined by the IT service organization.

Maintain Long Description

After the processor has entered the basic details of the incident in the DETAILS assignment block, the processor should enter descriptive text in the TEXT assignment block (Figure 5.14). Follow these steps:

1. Select the ADD TEXT button.

2. Select the text type from the associated dropdown menu (e.g., DESCRIPTION).

3. Enter some text describing or elaborating upon the incident.

4. Click SAVE.

Figure 5.14 Enter a Description in the Text Assignment Block

To summarize, the process step of receiving an incident consists of maintaining general data specific to the incident that will enable further analysis and dispatching efforts.

The following are the key components of receiving an incident:

▸ Entering incident details such as general data, processing data, and categories

▸ Updating and/or maintaining the long text

5.2.4 Search for Solution

After the processor has performed the activity of receiving the incident, the processor can now begin to search for a solution (Figure 5.15). The search step includes accessing content within the knowledge database and/or leveraging data from SAP Solution Manager Diagnostics.

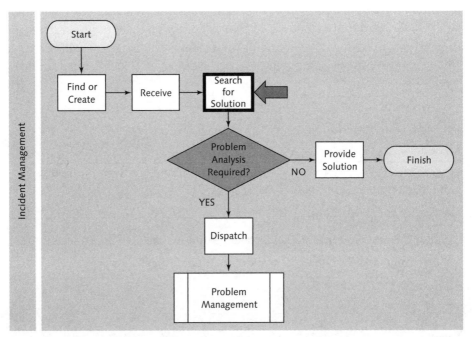

Figure 5.15 Search for Solution Process Step: Incident Management

Because the Diagnostics capabilities are outside the scope of this book, we'll continue along the Incident Management process by searching the database of knowledge articles within SAP Solution Manager.

We'll cover knowledge articles in detail in Chapter 9. The objective of this section is to provide the step-by-step process of Incident Management, which has direct integration into the KM process.

Search for Knowledge Articles

A search for knowledge articles can be conducted directly from the incident by selecting MORE • FIND KNOWLEDGE ARTICLES as shown in Figure 5.16.

Figure 5.16 Search for Related Knowledge Articles

Based on the combination of category values maintained in a multilevel categorization, a matching knowledge article can be found be using this function. Multilevel categorization is maintained not only on the incident but in knowledge articles as well. If a knowledge article contains the same combination of category values in its multilevel categorization schema, SAP Solution Manager will match that knowledge article to the incident.

Therefore, the matching knowledge article will be identified as a relationship on the incident. Figure 5.17 shows the result of SAP Solution Manager finding a related knowledge article.

Relationships

Related Problem:		
Related Request for Change:		
Related Knowledge Article:	7000000010	Errors occur when selecting required in

Figure 5.17 Related Knowledge Articles: Relationships

You can then open the knowledge article via the RELATED KNOWLEDGE ARTICLES assignment block within the incident as shown in Figure 5.18. The processor can access the related knowledge article directly by clicking on the knowledge article's identification number.

Figure 5.18 Related Knowledge Articles: Assignment Block

After clicking on the link to the knowledge article, the knowledge article will open as shown in Figure 5.19.

The processor can filter by text type depending on the purpose for consulting the knowledge article. In the example in Figure 5.19, the processor is reviewing the solution to a knowledge article that relates exactly to the incident.

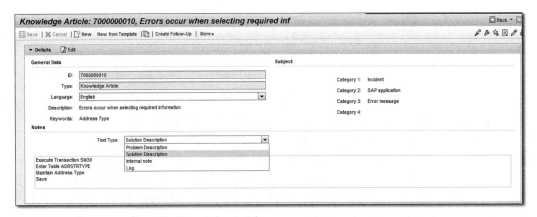

Figure 5.19 Open the Knowledge Article

At this point in the Incident Management process, there can be one of two paths taken depending on whether or not the incident requires further analysis. In other words, this is the point in which Problem Management can be initiated directly from the incident (Figure 5.20).

If the incident requires such analysis, it will be dispatched as described in the Section 5.2.5. However, if the solution discovered in the knowledge article warrants that the processor provide the solution to the requester, the processor may skip the dispatching and proceed directly to the steps in Section 5.2.6 to provide the solution.

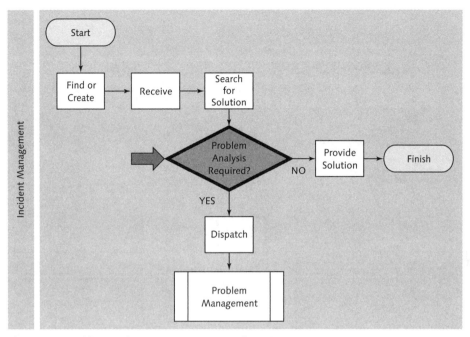

Figure 5.20 Problem Analysis Decision Point: Incident Management

5.2.5   Dispatch Incident

In this section, we'll describe the steps to dispatch the incident to initiate further analysis (refer to DISPATCH in Figure 5.21). As discussed in the following subsections, there are two main activities within the dispatch process step of Incident Management: creating an internal note and creating a follow-up to begin Problem Management.

Create Internal Note

Creating an internal note when dispatching will assist the technician responsible for performing the analysis with background details about the incident. Internal notes are created within the TEXT assignment block. Like all other text types, internal notes provide a way to thoroughly document the communication among processors and between the processors and requesters.

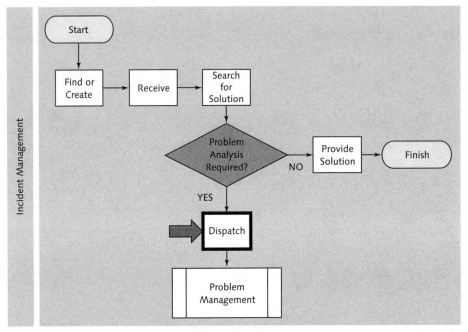

Figure 5.21 Dispatch Process Step: Incident Management

This facilitates a better source of knowledge if similar incidents should arise. Follow these steps:

1. Access the TEXT assignment block within the incident (Figure 5.22).

2. Choose ADD TEXT • INTERNAL NOTE.

Figure 5.22 Enter Internal Note

3. Enter an internal note to describe the background and reason for conducting an analysis.

4. Click SAVE.

Create a Follow-Up Problem Message

After adding an internal note to provide details for your fellow processors, they will need to be notified that an analysis is required. Creating a follow-up problem message will trigger the Problem Management process from within the incident. Follow these steps:

1. In the incident, select the CREATE FOLLOW-UP button as shown in Figure 5.23.

Figure 5.23 Create Follow-Up

In the resulting FOLLOW-UP WEBPAGE DIALOG box, you'll notice a number of different follow-up options that can be selected (Figure 5.24).

2. Select the SMPR PROBLEM entry.

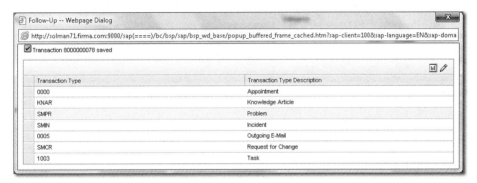

Figure 5.24 Select Problem as the Follow-Up

A new problem message will appear as shown in Figure 5.25. We'll describe the step-by-step details for the Problem Management process in Section 5.3.

Figure 5.25 New Problem

As we mentioned before, if the dispatch step isn't needed (i.e., further analysis via Problem Management isn't required), the process will skip directly to the next step to provide a solution to the requester.

5.2.6   Provide Solution

In this step, the processor takes the necessary steps to provide a solution to the requester (Figure 5.26).

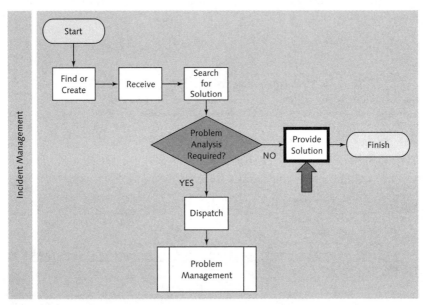

Figure 5.26 Provide Solution Process Step: Incident Management

The proposed solution process step consists of the following key activities, which are discussed in the following subsections:

▸ Notification

▸ Close the incident

Notification

To begin the notification process, the processor selects the PROPOSED SOLUTION value from the STATUS field (Figure 5.27).

Figure 5.27 Select Proposed Solution Status Value

With the following steps, the processor then documents the findings of a proposed solution so that the requester can understand what action to take:

1. Access the TEXT assignment block.

2. Choose ADD TEXT • REPLY (Figure 5.28).

Figure 5.28 Select Reply

3. Enter some text to describe the proposed solution.

4. Click SAVE.

Close Incident

To complete the Incident Management process, the processor closes the incident by selecting the CONFIRMED status value. Confirming (i.e., closing) the incident will lock it from future changes.

Now that we've covered the end-to-end steps specific to the low-level Incident Management process, let's move on to a step-by-step description of Problem Management.

5.3   Problem Management Process

Problem Management can be initiated independently of Incident Management or along with Incident Management. If Problem Management is handled independently of Incident Management, problems are simply created from scratch by reporters who have the appropriate authorization. If Problem Management is handled along with Incident Management, the problem message is created as a follow-up activity as we've described in the previous sections.

As we discussed in Chapter 1, Problem Management is concerned with finding and resolving the root cause of problems in an effort to prevent the occurrence of future incidents. Problem Management performs analyses to determine the cause of the incident(s). If several incidents are related in some way, this is cause to initiate Problem Management.

Problems, in SAP Solution Manager, are classified by transaction type SMPR, while incidents are classified by Transaction SMIN. Each of these transaction types in AIM follow separate workflows and allow the integration of both processes. Further, reporting and analytics can be supported that distinguish the two transaction types from one another.

5.3.1 Breaking Down the Process of Problem Management

Figure 5.29 breaks down the Problem Management process based on the overall AIM process described in Section 5.2.1. Just like the Incident Management process, the Problem Management process has specific steps that are executed in an end-to-end manner. As we mentioned before, Problem Management can be initiated independently of Incident Management. However, we recommend launching Problem Management directly from Incident Management in an effort to provide further analysis.

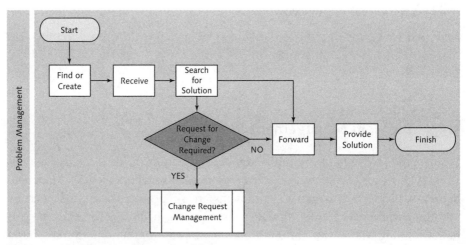

Figure 5.29 Problem Management Breakdown

5.3.2   Find Problem

Just like the commencement of Incident Management, the Problem Management process begins by finding the problem in one of two ways:

▶ From a saved search (or simply the SEARCH: INCIDENTS screen)

▶ From a worklist

The following subsections describe these two methods for finding an incident.

Saved Search or Worklist

Just like finding incidents from the SEARCH: INCIDENTS screen, saved search or worklist problems can be located in the same way. The steps within Section 5.2.3 will help you find problems based on these mechanisms.

From the Incident

Alternatively, problems can be accessed directly from within the incident. In the RELATED TRANSACTIONS assignment block, a link appears to the problem message after it's created as a follow-up. Clicking on the link to the problem message will take you directly to the problem (Figure 5.30).

Figure 5.30 Access Problem Message from the Incident

5.3.3   Receive Problem

In this step of the process (Figure 5.31), the problem is received by the processor. We'll discuss the key activities that occur within the receive process step in the following subsections.

Maintain Problem Details

You'll begin by entering some data in the DETAILS assignment block on the problem message. Because we covered the DETAILS assignment block in detail in Section 5.2.4, we'll touch on these points in broad strokes.

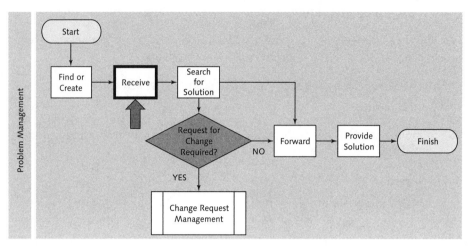

Figure 5.31 Receive Process Step: Problem Management

1. Click the EDIT button (Figure 5.32).

Figure 5.32 Edit Problem Message

2. You'll see a popup screen asking if you want to enter the business partner as the processor. Click YES in the resulting web dialog box (Figure 5.33).

Figure 5.33 Enter Own Business Partner

3. Maintain the fields within the GENERAL DATA section (Figure 5.34).

4. Set the STATUS to IN PROCESS.

5. Click SAVE.

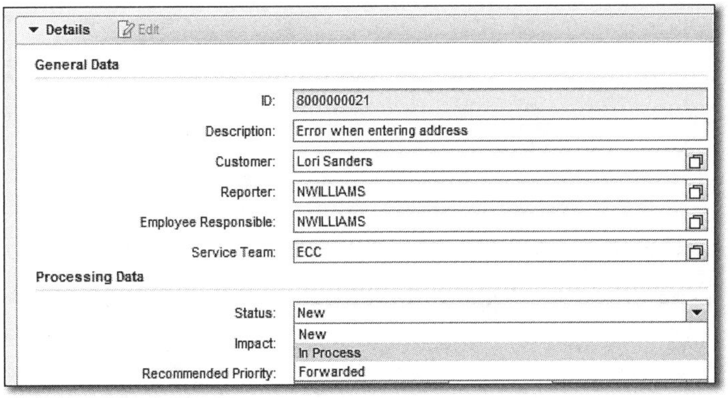

Figure 5.34 Maintain Problem Details

Lock Incident

Locking an incident (or several incidents) to a problem helps support efficient documentation of AIM solutions. There are two main reasons incidents and problems should be linked to one another:

▶ Activities can be more efficiently planned and managed. Locking the messages ensures that messages are handled in a logical sequence or in parallel.

▶ Linking several incidents that relate to a problem aids in faster resolution and more efficient management of multiple messages.

After a problem message is locked to the incident, the incident can't be processed further until some sort of resolution has been reached for the related problem.

If there are several incidents related to a single problem, they shouldn't be closed until the supporting incidents to complete the task have been completed.

To lock an incident to a problem, follow these steps:

1. Access the RELATED INCIDENTS assignment block in the problem.

2. Click the EDIT LIST button.

3. Highlight the incident.

4. Select the LOCK button (Figure 5.35).

At this point in the process, tasks can be created as follow-ups to continue and close out the process. We'll discuss follow-ups in detail in Chapter 7.

Figure 5.35 Lock an Incident

5.3.4 Search for Solution

In this process step, a solution is searched for in one of the following ways:

▶ Object relationships

▶ Root cause analysis tools

These search methods are the same methods we described in Section 5.2.5 for incidents. Access to knowledge articles is available via object relationships (category values) and SAP Solution Manager Diagnostics capabilities provide further technical analysis of root cause.

5.3.5 Forward Problem

In the forward process step for Problem Management, follow-ups are introduced. There are two ways in which problems can be forwarded for further investigation:

▶ Request for change

▶ SAP

We'll describe each of these in Chapter 8, as well as provide step-by-step instructions for how to create the follow-ups.

5.3.6 Provide Solution

The final step in the process (see Figure 5.36) is to provide a solution to the problem. Just like in Incident Management, this occurs within two key activities, notification and closure, which we discuss in the following subsections.

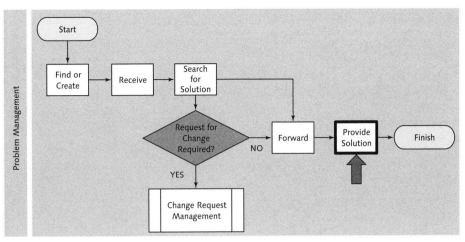

Figure 5.36 Provide Solution Process Step: Problem Management

Notification

During the notification, you provide a solution text to the requester send the requester an email by following these steps:

1. In the TEXT assignment block, select ADD TEXT • SOLUTION (Figure 5.37).

2. Enter some text describing the solution.

3. Click SAVE.

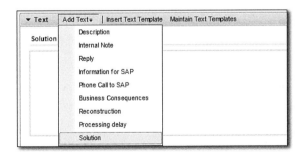

Figure 5.37 Maintain Solution Text

4. Select MORE • SEND E-MAIL (Figure 5.38).

5. In the E-MAIL: NEW screen, enter the details (Figure 5.39).

6. Click SEND.

Figure 5.38 Select Send E-Mail

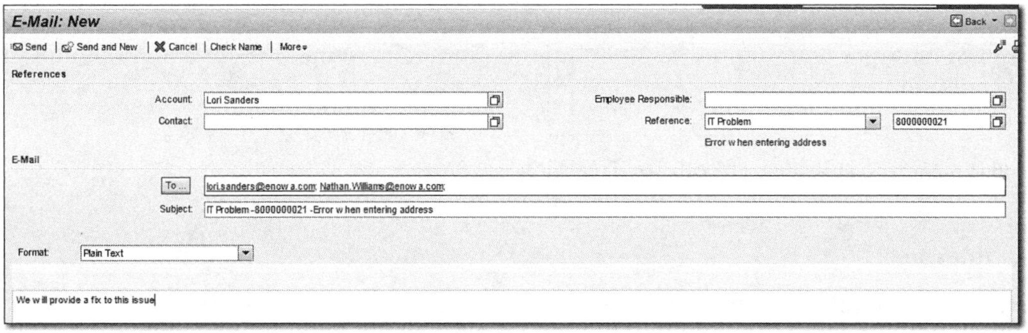

Figure 5.39 Generate Email

Closure

During the final step, the message is closed. This involves maintaining the PROB-LEM CATEGORY field in the SUBJECT area of the problem details. Furthermore, time can be recorded in the TIME RECORDING assignment block. Finally, the processing status is updated to reflect the proposed solution. Follow these steps:

1. In the PROBLEM CATEGORY field, select the appropriate problem category (Figure 5.40). The options shown here are the standard values delivered from SAP. They can be adapted in Customizing per your organization's requirements.

2. Record time spent processing the message in the TIME RECORDING assignment block (Figure 5.41). Time Recording will be covered in detail in Chapter 9.

3. Select the EDIT LIST button.

4. Select the ADD button.

5. Record your time and related information in the appropriate fields (Figure 5.42).

6. Click SAVE.

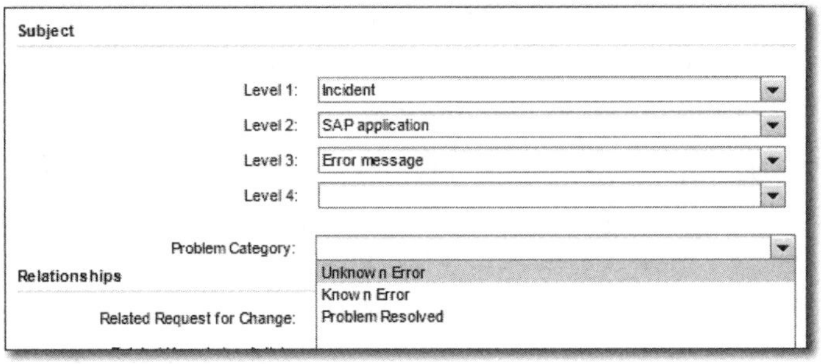

Figure 5.40 Maintain Problem Category

Figure 5.41 Time Recording Assignment Block

Figure 5.42 Maintain Time Recording Information

7. Update the status to PROPOSED SOLUTION in the PROCESSING DATA section of the DETAILS assignment block (Figure 5.43).

8. Click SAVE.

Figure 5.43 Set Status to Proposed Solution

5.4 Service Request Management Process

In this section we will highlight the key steps required in order to fulfill a request (i.e., Service Request Management). The process of fulfilling a service request, as explained in more detail in Chapter 1, is executed for services such as password resets, equipment moves, creation of users, and similar tasks. It's a part of the overall AIM scenario of ITSM in SAP Solution Manager and executed in an end-to-end manner similar to Problem Management and Incident Management.

Similar to the other processes within AIM, the Service Request Management process can integrate into other ITSM processes if needed. For example, problem messages, requests for change, or knowledge articles can be created as follow-ups if there requires further ITSM process integration.

Service requests are represented by their own service transaction, SMRQ. As we have recommend with the other ITSM transaction types, you must copy the standard transaction SMRQ into your own customer namespace (e.g., YMRQ) before beginning any customizing to the workflows or related standard settings. Additionally, the profiles assigned to the transaction type should be copied as well (status profile, action profile, etc.). Remember to use the Transaction Copy tool (described in Chapter 3) to do so.

Now, we will walk you through the main steps in order to fulfill a service request in SAP Solution Manager.

5.4.1 Breaking Down the Process of Service Request Management

Figure 5.44 breaks down the process to fulfill a service request from an SAP Solution Manager standpoint. While this process is high-level, it provides a clear depiction on how requests are fulfilled in an organization. As you can see, there is a clear path from start to finish. Service requests can be opened by an end user (requester, customer, etc.) and closed by a message processor (i.e. technician, dispatcher, support staff, etc.). On the other hand, as we mentioned in the introduction to the section there can be a transition into other processes such as Problem Management or Change Request Management.

The Service Request Management process differs slightly from the overall AIM process we discussed in Section 5.2 and shown in Figure 5.3. Since it is a repeatable and proceduralized process, there is not a need for search, dispatch, or analysis steps as in Problem or Incident Management.

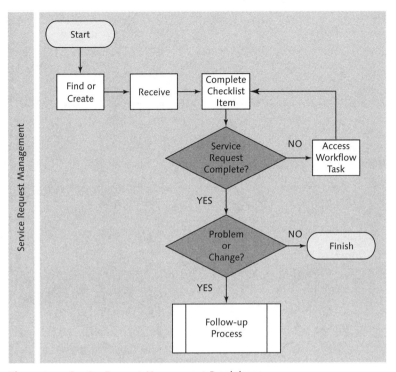

Figure 5.44 Service Request Management Breakdown

5.4.2 Find or Create Service Request

The first step in fulfilling a service request is to either find or create the service transaction. For the purposes of this chapter, which focuses on processing service transactions, we'll assume that the service request has already been created.

Finding the service request can be performed by any of the functions that we have already described in Section 5.2.2 or Section 5.3.2. Message processors can use their worklist or saved searches which they have personalized to find open service requests.

Figure 5.45 provides an image of the worklist from a message processor's home screen. Since they were assigned the SOLMANDSPTCH business role, their open service requests appeared directly on their home screen.

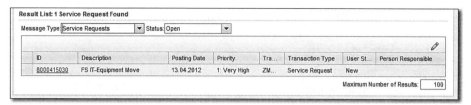

Figure 5.45 Find Service Request from Home Screen

5.4.3 Receive Service Request

In this step of the process, we will briefly highlight the activities performed when a message processor initially receives a service request for processing.

Maintain Service Request Data

Service request data is entered in the DETAILS assignment block (primarily) when a message processor initially receives the service request, similar to receiving an incident or a problem. The message processor will first set the status to In Process and then review the information submitted by the requestor. If the information is accurate and substantial enough for processing, then the message processor can add information relating to processing.

Figure 5.46 shows an image of a service request in processing within the SAP CRM Web UI.

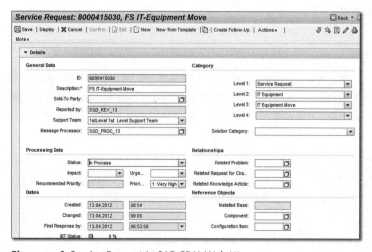

Figure 5.46 Service Request in SAP CRM Web UI

5.4.4 Complete Checklist Item

The next step in the Service Request Management process, as indicated in Figure 5.47, is to complete the first checklist item. Checklists, described in Chapter 8, are used primarily in service requests to support the procedural and standardized process of completing steps in a specific order. Workflow is used in order to identify subsequent steps and processors.

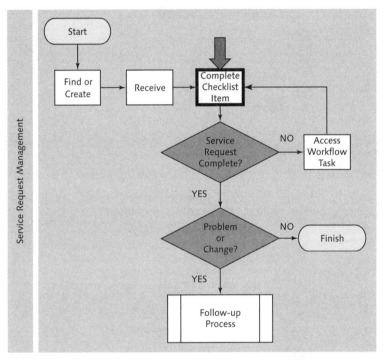

Figure 5.47 Complete Checklist Item Process Step: Service Request Management

Figure 5.48 provides an image of a checklist in SAP Solution Manager. Each step is identified, according with the responsible business partner and status (for example). The workflow we mentioned above is displayed in a graphical process flow format. Once the initial checklist item is completed by the message processor, the workflow triggers the subsequent step.

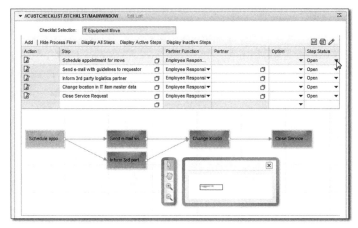

Figure 5.48 Checklist in SAP Solution Manager

5.4.5 Access Workflow Task

Figure 5.49 identifies the final major step in the Service Request Management process breakdown. In this step, the next assigned message processor for the checklist item accesses their workflow task to continue along the process of fulfilling the request.

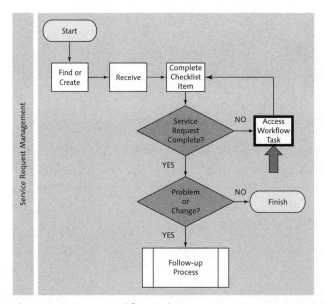

Figure 5.49 Access Workflow Task Process Step: Service Request Management

The next step in the checklist is triggered by the workflow. If another message processor is assigned to that particular checklist step, they will be notified on their ITSM Home Screen within the WORKFLOW TASKS area (Figure 5.50).

Figure 5.50 Find Workflow Tasks

The message process can access the workflow task, which provides all of the details necessary to fulfill the most current open step of the service request (Figure 5.51).

Figure 5.51 Workflow Task

5.5 Summary

SAP Solution Manager supports the entire lifecycle of Incident Management and Problem Management under the umbrella of AIM. While each process can be executed independently of the other, best practices suggest that the two processes should be tied together in an integrated fashion.

As you can see, there are many flavors, variations, and sequences in which AIM can be executed in the SAP Solution Manager system. The information in this chapter provided a solid understanding of how these processes are delivered standard from SAP. Now it's up to your organization to determine how much of your internal processes can be aligned to these standards and what must be adapted to meet enterprise requirements.

Since the release of version 7.1, SAP Solution Manager has increased its ITSM capabilities and architecture to better support all phases of ALM. In the next chapter, we'll discuss how AIM capabilities align and support each phase of ALM.

Incidents will occur well before a service organization has established itself to manage high-volume support desks and call centers. To support these cases, Application Incident Management integrates its processes and capabilities throughout all phases of the application lifecycle.

6   Integration into Application Lifecycle Management

IT services are delivered in all phases of the application lifecycle. While the language and the content in this book are worded toward SAP ITSM for service organizations, it's important to note that SAP ITSM integrates into all phases of Application Lifecycle Management (ALM).

From the design and build phase and all the way to when an application must be deployed and operated, SAP Solution Manager provides the infrastructure and capabilities to manage the delivery of services for the entire organization. Although the customer base may shift as an application progresses through its lifecycle, SAP Solution Manager still provides processes and functionalities that can be adopted at any point.

Although these capabilities aren't mandated and can be selected by the IT organization according to their priorities and existing tools landscape, we recommend leveraging SAP Solution Manager as the central platform and single source of truth for ALM at every phase.

In this chapter, we'll identify how Application Incident Management (AIM) can be integrated throughout ALM beyond purely the optimization of a solution. We'll provide examples of when and how AIM can be adopted throughout the implementation of both SAP and non-SAP applications for the following phases:

▶ Design and build
▶ Test
▶ Deploy
▶ Operate

> **Note**
>
> Note that we have omitted the requirements and optimize phases of ALM from this chapter. Typically, AIM isn't used extensively during the requirements phase. Furthermore, the objective of this chapter is to specifically focus on phases that precede optimization.

6.1 Design and Build Phases

In this section, we'll describe how AIM is integrated into the design and build phases of ALM (see Figure 6.1). In SAP Solution Manager technical terminology, these two phases are referred to as business blueprint and configuration, respectively.

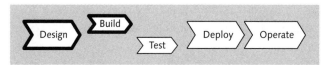

Figure 6.1 Application Incident Management: Design and Build Phases

6.1.1 Design Phase (Business Blueprint)

The *business blueprint* in SAP Solution Manager is most commonly referred to as SOLAR01 (which is the transaction code used to reach the screen to perform blueprint activities).

The business blueprint contains a very important component of the SAP Solution Manager system, the *business process hierarchy* (*BPH*). The BPH is a three-level hierarchal representation of the organization's end-to-end processes as they occur across SAP, non-SAP, and manual steps. The BPH is fundamental to conducting implementation activities in SAP Solution Manager. A few examples are included here:

- ▶ Requirements management
- ▶ Document management
- ▶ Configuration management
- ▶ Development management

- ▶ Test management
- ▶ Issues/AIM
- ▶ End-user training
- ▶ Global rollout functions

As the backbone for subsequent ALM activities, the BPH is intended to bring a business process focus to the implementation and ongoing support for IT applications. By blending organizational-specific terminology with SAP best practices and technical terms, it helps bridge the gap between IT and the business.

Usage

AIM is integrated into the business blueprint transaction of SAP Solution Manager. This integration allows project teams who are using business blueprint functions (requirements gathering, blueprinting, document management, etc.) to create and manage incidents as they may arise during these activities.

In Figure 6.2, the left side of the screen contains the BPH as we have described in the previous subsection. On the right side of the screen are various tabs to align different elements and perform various functions. Selecting a node (e.g., process step) in the BPH on the left and selecting a tab on the right will allow you to maintain information specific to that node.

The tab SERVICE MESSAGES, selected in Figure 6.2, will allow business blueprint users to log incidents that may relate to the particular scenario, process, or process step within the BPH.

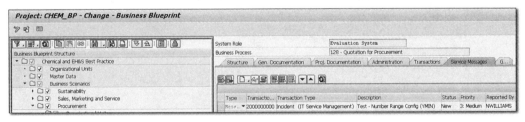

Figure 6.2 Services Messages: SOLAR01 Business Blueprint

Let's go over the two options that you have in the SERVICE MESSAGES tab in the following subsections.

223

Assigning Incidents

Assigning incidents that have already been created is very straightforward. Just follow these steps:

1. Select the value MESSAGE in the TYPE column.

2. Select the dropdown icon (⯆) in the TRANSACTION ID column.

3. Search for the incident.

4. Click SAVE.

5. The incident will appear in the SERVICE MESSAGES tab as shown in Figure 6.3.

Type	Transaction ID		Transaction Type	Description	Status	Priority	
Message ▼	2000000000		▢wa Incident (IT S...	Test - Number Range Config (YMIN)	New	3: Medium	

Figure 6.3 Assigning Incidents in SOLAR01

Creating Incidents

Creating incidents in SOLAR01 is just as straightforward but involves a few more steps, as follows:

1. Select the CREATE button (▢ ⯆).

2. From the dropdown values that appear, select MESSAGE.

3. In the SELECT A TRANSACTION TYPE window (see Figure 6.4), select the appropriate incident transaction type. You can see that the YMIN transaction type we created (see Chapter 3, Section 3.1.4) is available.

Figure 6.4 Select a Transaction Type

The CREATE SUPPORT MESSAGE window appears (Figure 6.5). Users familiar with SAP Solution Manager 7.0 and prior will recognize that this is the same form that is called from Transaction NOTIF_CREATE.

Figure 6.5 Create Support Message

4. Fill out the required fields.

5. Click SAVE. The incident will now be assigned to the associated node on the BPH and be available for processing in the SAP CRM Web UI.

6.1.2 Build Phase (Configuration)

Transaction SOLAR02 accesses the configuration activities in SAP Solution Manager. When accessing the Transaction SOLAR02 screen, you'll notice that the interface is almost identical to the business blueprint screen in Transaction SOLAR01 (Figure 6.6). The key difference is the addition of the CONFIGURATION and DEVELOPMENT tabs to execute and manage activities related to these areas.

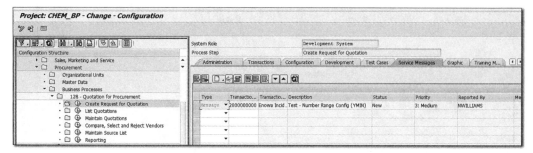

Figure 6.6 Service Messages: SOLAR01 Configuration

The objective for Transaction SOLAR02 is to help project teams document activities related to the configuration and development management. These activities occur during the build phase, which is why they are segregated by means of separate transaction codes in SAP Solution Manager. Activities that are specific to the build phase in SAP Solution Manager include but aren't limited to the following:

▶ Managing configuration documents

▶ Managing functional and technical specification documents (development documents)

▶ Tracking the status of IMG (configuration) objects

▶ Tracking the status of RICEFW (reports, interfaces, conversion, enhancements, forms, and workflow development objects)

Just like in the design/business blueprint phase of an implementation, incidents will arise during the build/configuration phase as well. The option to create or assign incidents to the Service Messages tab is also available in Transaction SOLAR01. The steps to do so are the same as described in Section 6.1.1.

Now that we've described how AIM can be integrated into the design and build phase of ALM, we'll provide an overview of how incidents can be created and managed within the test phase.

6.2 Test Phase

AIM is also tightly integrated within the test phase of ALM. In this section, we'll describe how the AIM functionality within SAP Solution Manager can help support incidents that occur during testing. This section assumes that you have adopted at least some portion of the test management capabilities offered by SAP Solution Manager.

6.2.1 Test Case Errors

A *test case error* is a type of message created when a tester discovers an error in his test case. Identified by transaction type SMDT, test case errors are an all-new transaction type delivered as of release 7.1 of SAP Solution Manager.

The objective of transaction type SMDT is to differentiate between standard incidents (SMIN), defect corrections (SMTM), and test case errors themselves.

> **Note**
>
> Speaking of defect corrections, we'll discuss the specifics about this transaction type (SMTM) in Chapter 13. The defect correction process associated with the SMTM transaction type is specific to defects that are created as a follow-up during the testing phase of the Change Request Management (ChaRM) process.

Creating Test Case Errors

In the following subsections, we'll describe both the prerequisite steps and process in order to create a test case error in SAP Solution Manager.

Prerequisites

To test or leverage the test case error functionality in SAP Solution Manager, there are some general prerequisites that must be satisfied:

▸ A template or implementation project has been defined in Transaction SOLAR01.

▸ Transaction codes and test documents have been uploaded to process steps.

▸ A test plan has been generated with a portion of your BPH hierarchy, with released test documents and transactions.

▸ A test package has been generated based on the scope of the test plan.

▸ A user has been assigned to the test package.

▸ The value for your test customer-defined test case error (e.g., YMDT) must be maintained in Transaction DNO_CUST04 in the PROCESS_TYPE_ADD field.

Additionally, the following services must be activated in Transaction SICF to create test case errors in the Work Center:

▶ SAP • BC • WEBDYNPRO • SAP • AGS_WORK_WITC_CREATE

▶ SAP • BC • WEBDYNPRO • SAP • AGS_WORK_MTC_EXEC

Process Steps for Creating a Test Case Error

You create test case errors in Transaction SOLMAN_WORKCENTER within the Test Management work center. As identified in Figure 6.7, you must be in the TESTER WORKLIST area within the work center. Then, follow these steps:

1. Select a test package in the TEST PACKAGE table.

2. Select a corresponding test case in the ASSIGNED TEST CASES table.

3. Select the RUN button in the same table. The MANUAL TEST CASE screen will appear.

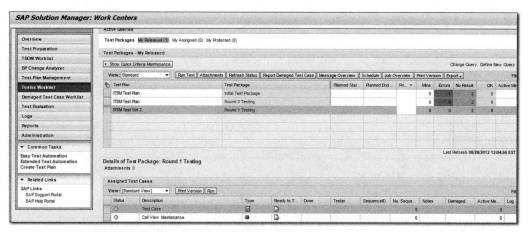

Figure 6.7 Run Test Case

4. Select the MESSAGES tab as shown in Figure 6.8.

5. Select the CREATE button. The CREATE MESSAGE [TEST CASE ERROR] screen will appear as shown in Figure 6.9.

Figure 6.8 Create Message

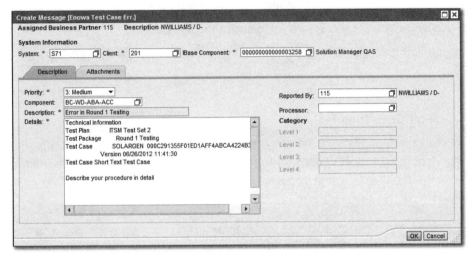

Figure 6.9 Create Test Case Error

6. Enter a value in the SYSTEM field. The values within the CLIENT and IBASE COM-PONENT fields will populate automatically based off of the system information.

7. Enter the other details specific to the error.

8. Click the OK button.

The test case error will now be available within the SAP CRM Web UI for processing. The details and information included when creating the message from the work center will be available when processing the message.

The test case error can be found by searching among the incidents and filtering based on the transaction type SMDT or within your customer namespace. Additionally, it will also be aligned within the test cases of your test package in the work center.

6.2.2 Relating Test Cases to Incidents

You also have the option to create incident transaction types (SMIN) based on test case errors if you would rather stick to one transaction type. If this strategy works better for you, you can still relate the test case to the incident so that there is traceability back to the test case for which the incident occurred. There are two ways in which you can relate test cases to incidents:

▶ Creating incident messages directly from the test case

▶ Assigning previously created incidents to the test case

We'll walk through the steps to accomplish both options in the following sections.

Create Incidents from Test Case

As you can see in Figure 6.10, after running the test case and creating a message (see steps in the "Process Steps for Creating a Test Case Error" section), the CREATE MESSAGE [INCIDENT] screen appears, instead of the CREATE MESSAGE [TEST CASE ERROR].

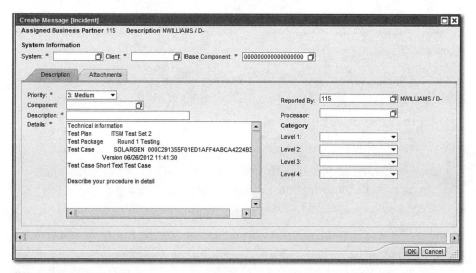

Figure 6.10 Create Incident

To switch from creating transaction type SMDT for test case errors to transaction type SMIN, remove the PROCESS_TYPE_ADD entry for the test case error within the table of Transaction DNO_CUST04.

After clicking OK in the CREATE MESSAGE [INCIDENT] screen, the system sends the incident to be processed further in the SAP CRM Web UI.

In order for the message processor to view the incidents that are associated with a test case, they must update their personalization settings to view the RELATED TEST CASES assignment block. The following steps will illustrate how to update this setting:

1. When processing the incident, select the PERSONALIZE button (✐).

2. In the PERSONALIZATION WEBPAGE DIALOG box that appears, highlight the RELATED TEST CASE entry, and select the MOVE TO RIGHT button (▶) so that it's displayed as an assignment block (Figure 6.11).

3. Click SAVE. (This is a one-time setup activity.)

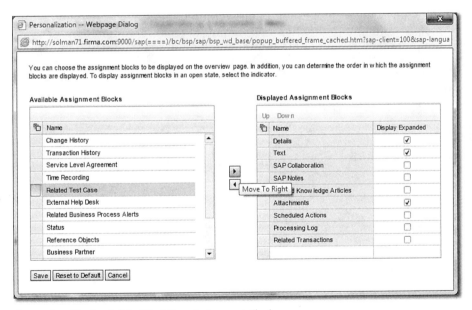

Figure 6.11 Display Related Test Case Assignment Block

The RELATED TEST CASE assignment block is now available when processing incidents. You can see the related incident that has been created from the test case in Figure 6.12.

Figure 6.12 Related Test Case Assigned to Incident

Assign Incidents to Test Case

You can also assign incidents that have previously been created directly to the test case. This situation is helpful if an incident has been created without using the Test Case Error integration functionality. This allows the users to go back, and assign the incidents that relate to the test case.

Follow these steps:

1. In the MESSAGES tab of the MANUAL TEST CASE screen, select the ASSIGN button (Figure 6.13).

Figure 6.13 Assign Message

2. In the ADD MESSAGE window that appears, enter a value in the MESSAGE NUMBER field to which the test case should be assigned.

3. Click OK.

4. Click SAVE in the upper-left corner of the same page (Figure 6.14).

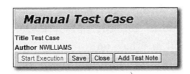

Figure 6.14 Save Message Assignment

As a result, the incident is assigned to the test case, and the test case is mapped to the RELATED TEST CASES assignment block within the incident.

Now that we've described how AIM can be integrated into the test phase of ALM, we'll describe how ALM plays a role in the deploy phase.

6.3   Deploy Phase

Unlike the design, build, test, operate, and optimize phases, the *deploy* phase doesn't have a dedicated scenario in SAP Solution Manager. However, unlike the requirements phase of ALM, components of AIM can still be integrated into the deploy phase.

You still need to manage incidents, problems, and test case errors prior to going live. It's important to have SAP Solution Manager enabled during this phase to serve as a central platform and repository for both incidents and problems related to your IT landscape.

Also during the deploy phase, IT service organizations may start establishing the processes and standing up infrastructure to deliver services during the operate and optimize phase.

Even if you choose to leverage SAP Solution Manager simply as a repository for central SAP OSS Note management, we recommend that you start before go-live with the adoption of AIM. If you've opted not to leverage AIM for the design, build, and testing of your solution, the deploy phase is a perfect time to begin establishing the processes that will sustain the organization and business going forward.

6.4 Operate Phase

AIM is integrated into the *operate* phase (Figure 6.15) of ALM by supporting the monitoring scenarios within SAP Solution Manager. In the operate phase, AIM provides the functionality and workflow to facilitate the resolution of alerts that arise from technical monitoring business process and interface monitoring.

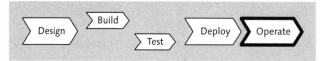

Figure 6.15 Application Incident Management: Operate Phase

In the following sections, we'll describe how incidents can be created manually or generated automatically within both of these monitoring scenarios.

6.4.1 Technical Monitoring Alerts

Because the focal point of this book is SAP ITSM, we won't go too far into detail to describe the monitoring and alerting infrastructure in SAP Solution Manager.

Technical monitoring and alerting helps IT organizations improve the performance and health of systems, no matter how expansively the customer's landscape is set up.

Technical monitoring and alerting falls within the Technical Operations component of SAP Solution Manager. Technical Operations is a work center-based component that provides a rich dashboard to access logs, metrics, graphs, and so on associated with analyzing performance data related to monitoring your entire IT landscape. AIM is integrated into the Technical Operations component of SAP Solution Manager, as incidents can be created based on alerts generated from technical monitoring.

There are two ways in which incidents can be generated, which we'll describe in the next sections.

Create Incidents as Follow-Ups

Incident messages can be created as follow-ups (i.e., manually) directly from the ALERT GROUPS table in the Technical Monitoring work center.

To create an incident as a follow-up to a specific alert, you simply highlight the alert and click the CREATE INCIDENT button. Figure 6.16 in the next subsection shows the screen in which these activities occur.

Create Incidents Automatically

Incidents can be created automatically from alerts by maintaining the incident default settings in Transaction SOLMAN_SETUP (Figure 6.16), and then following these steps:

1. Choose TECHNICAL MONITORING • CONFIGURE INFRASTRUCTURE • DEFAULT SETTINGS.

2. Click the INCIDENT tab.

3. Flag the settings for AUTO-INCIDENTS, and specify the appropriate support component and transaction type for the incident to be created.

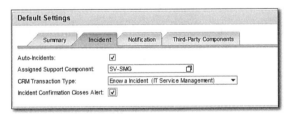

Figure 6.16 Enable Auto-Incidents

In the Technical Monitoring work center, you'll notice that the CREATE INCIDENT button is grayed out (Figure 6.17). When you enable the generation of auto-incidents based on an alert, this feature isn't available.

Rati...	No. ...	Status	Processor	Comments	Incident ID	Incident S...	Start Date Time	End Date Time	Incident...	Notificat...
●	5	Transferred			8000098709	New	23.02.2011 17...	23.02.2011 17...	●	
△	1	Transferred			8000098708	New	23.02.2011 17...	23.02.2011 17...	●	
●	1	Transferred			8000098703	New	23.02.2011 17...	23.02.2011 17...	●	
△	2	Transferred			8000098696	New	23.02.2011 17...	23.02.2011 17...	●	
●	2	Transferred			8000098688	New	23.02.2011 17...	23.02.2011 17...	●	
△	2	Transferred			8000098682	New	23.02.2011 17...	23.02.2011 17...	●	
●	1	Transferred			8000098677	New	23.02.2011 17...	23.02.2011 17...	●	
●	23	Transferred			8000098561	New	23.02.2011 16...	23.02.2011 17...	●	
●	13	Transferred			8000098477	New	23.02.2011 14...	23.02.2011 15...	●	
△	1	Transferred			8000098471	New	23.02.2011 14...	23.02.2011 14...	●	

Figure 6.17 Create Incident Feature Disabled

6.4.2   Business Process Monitoring Alerts

Business process monitoring alerts fall within the SAP Solution Manager business process operations scenario. Like the technical monitoring and alerting infrastructure, business process monitoring alerts support the operate phase of ALM. This is achieved by proactively monitoring an organization's core business processes in an effort to detect problems and resolve them as quickly as possible before they impact the business. Technical and business application-specific functions are monitored on a process-based approach, so that mission-critical business processes can operate smoothly.

If problems identified with business process monitoring can't be resolved, incidents can be sent to AIM for further processing. Information related to the business process and errors (monitoring object, alert details, etc.) are already populated to aid processors in responding to the alert.

Incidents can be created manually or automatically to help support the resolution of a business process monitoring alert, which we'll describe in the following subsections.

Create Incidents as Follow-Ups

Incidents in business process monitoring can be created manually within the Business Process Operations work center. In the BUSINESS CONTEXT section of the screen, on the ALERT tab, you can select one or several alerts to have the incident created for (Figure 6.18).

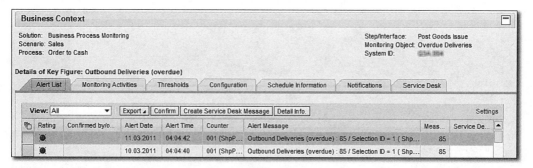

Figure 6.18 Create Incident Manually

236

Clicking the CREATE SERVICE DESK MESSAGE button will produce a dialog box where the incident details can be edited, saved, and sent for processing. The incident ID will be maintained in the SERVICE DESK column as shown in Figure 6.19.

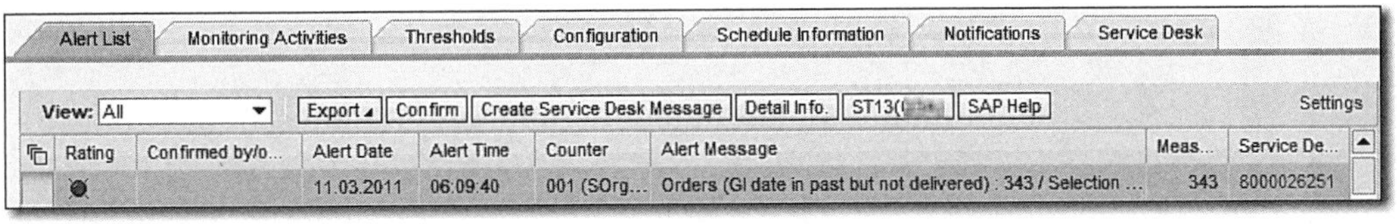

Alert List	Monitoring Activities	Thresholds	Configuration	Schedule Information	Notifications	Service Desk

View: All ▾	Export ▴	Confirm	Create Service Desk Message	Detail Info.	ST13(▪▪▪)	SAP Help				Settings

	Rating	Confirmed by/o…	Alert Date	Alert Time	Counter	Alert Message	Meas…	Service De…	▲
	●		11.03.2011	06:09:40	001 (SOrg…	Orders (GI date in past but not delivered) : 343 / Selection …	343	8000026251	

Figure 6.19 Incident ID

Create Incidents Automatically

Incidents can be created automatically based on business process monitoring alerts. After enabling the configuration (i.e., setting up some parameters for when the incident should be generated), a data collector checks after each run to see if there are any monitoring identifications that require an incident to be created.

After the incident is created, the open alerts will be assigned to the newly created incident. The alert "counter" is reset, and a new incident will be created after the defined thresholds are met again. The incident ID will be populated as it was in Figure 6.19 in the corresponding alert and can be accessed for processing by clicking on the corresponding link.

6.5   Summary

This chapter provided some insight on how AIM integrates into all phases of ALM, beyond purely the optimization of IT applications. The core of this book focuses on SAP ITSM as a whole to efficiently and effective deliver services to the customer in a timely and cost-conscious manner. However, it's important to note that even if you haven't established an IT service organization or if you're purely in implementation mode; AIM within SAP Solution Manager is available leading up to that point.

In the next chapter, we'll continue discussing concepts related to the end-to-end process of AIM and how these processes are administered via SAP Solution Manager. Chapter 5 discussed the process flows for processing incidents and problems after they reach SAP Solution Manager's SAP ITSM platform. Chapter 7 will explain the vehicles for creating these messages, as well as follow-up actions to support post-processing and message closure.

Several inbound channels are available to create and send messages to SAP Solution Manager. This flexibility allows organizations to roll out message creation options depending on their size, complexity, and volume of messages created for Application Incident Management.

7 Channels for Creating and Resolving Incidents and Problems

In Chapter 5, we discussed the steps for processing messages in SAP Solution Manager within the Incident Management and Problem Management processes. The steps, recommendations, and best practices explained for these SAP ITSM processes were specific to how messages were handled after they were received by a service team member. While the SAP CRM Web UI is the central platform for processing messages, organizations have several channels to select from for creating incidents and problems.

In this chapter, we'll describe the various options available to create and send messages to the central SAP Solution Manager system to enable the messages to begin processing. The complexity of the organization, volume of messages being processed, and size of the end-user community with the ability to create messages will play a role in which channel(s) makes most sense for your organization to deploy. Understanding the channels available for creating service transactions will help you determine the strategy for rolling out Application Incident Management to your organization. It will provide you with several options, which can be chosen according to your preference, for initiating the Application Incident Management process.

On the tail end of the process, there are also activities supported by SAP Solution Manager related to the escalation, further processing, and knowledge management to fully confirm the completion of a message. In addition to explaining the methods for creating messages, we'll also describe the follow-up channels that are available to support the post-processing and complete the resolution of a message. These follow-up channels will help you determine the actions that may need to be taken after an incident (for example) is confirmed. For example, integration into the Request for Change process would be required for an incident that requires a change to the SAP application.

7.1   Inbound Channels

In this section, we'll explain the various options organizations may make available to their community of requesters. An inbound channel is a means for how an incident or problem is generated and sent to the SAP Solution Manager system for processing. The *inbound channels* that we'll discuss include the following:

▶ SAP frontend integration

▶ Web self-service: SAP CRM Web UI

▶ Web self-service: work center

▶ Interaction center

▶ Email

Figure 7.1 illustrates the high-level graphical representation of the overall Incident Management and Problem Management processes, which you saw in Chapter 5. Because Incident Management and Problem Management are integrated tightly, the steps in the middle of this graphic summarize what is included in the processing of these related messages.

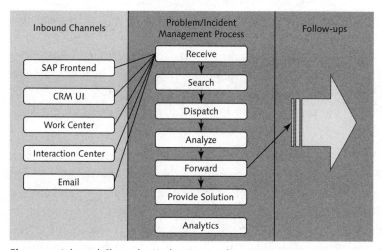

Figure 7.1 Inbound Channels: Application Incident Management

On the left side are the various channels available for creating messages (*inbound channels*). As you can see in Figure 7.1, any of these channels will enable the service team member to receive the message and begin processing.

Organizations may choose to roll out one option or a blend of several inbound channels depending on their environment. First, we'll describe the SAP frontend integration.

7.1.1 SAP Frontend Integration

SAP frontend integration has been an option available to the Service Desk functionality in SAP Solution Manager since its earliest releases. SAP Solution Manager 7.1 has offered the market a best-of-breed processing tool for managing incidents related to both SAP and non-SAP applications. The benefits of AIM in SAP Solution Manager are plenty, especially with the integration of SAP ITSM.

Integration directly into the SAP landscape could not be achieved by another tool. The functionality was impressive, available with minimal customizing, and consistently reliable.

Fast-forward roughly a decade, and this functionality is still available within the most current releases of SAP Solution Manager. Although there are other best-of-breed selling points with SAP ITSM, SAP frontend integration still proves to be one of the most significant benefits of selecting SAP Solution Manager as an organization's single platform for processing messages in AIM.

Overview

SAP frontend integration allows for the creation of messages from any SAP GUI system in the customer landscape. As shown in Figure 7.2, each SAP GUI system has the HELP • CREATE SUPPORT MESSAGE option accessible from the title bar.

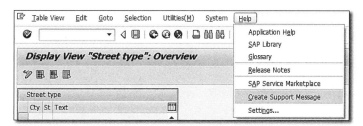

Figure 7.2 Create Support Message Help Option in SAP GUI

SAP frontend integration allows users in any SAP application with the SAP GUI to have a standard channel to create incidents related to the specific screen in which the error occurs. SAP Solution Manager automatically captures system details in the background specific to the time the error was saved and sends those details to the central SAP Solution Manager system.

The message is routed to the appropriate support team based on the SAP component automatically picked up by the system. The system details captured are used to process the message.

In addition to SAP GUI, the following SAP frontends are supported and integrated with AIM in SAP Solution Manager:

▶ SAP NetWeaver Business Client (NWBC)

▶ SAP NetWeaver Portal

▶ SAP CRM Web Client

With the SAP frontend integration option, there are two different kinds of details that are collected at the time the message is created. The functional details include items such as short description and priority. Technical details include information regarding the system at the time the message is created. We'll explain these two areas in the next sections.

Functional Information Captured

First, we will show you how to enter the functional details for the SAP frontend integration.

When selecting the CREATE SUPPORT MESSAGE option, the user is prompted with the CREATE MESSAGE screen as shown in Figure 7.3. In this window, there are four fields to maintain and/or confirm before sending the message to SAP Solution Manager:

▶ COMPONENT
The COMPONENT field is automatically determined based on the SAP application and transaction in which the user encounters the error. The component is used for classifying the incident as well as automatically determining the appropriate support team when it's sent to the SAP Solution Manager system (described in Chapter 9). The component dynamically changes for each screen.

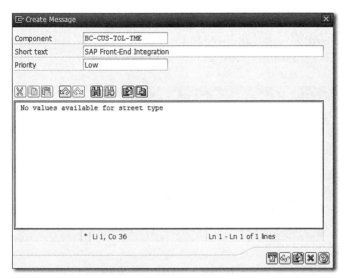

Figure 7.3 Create Message Window

The user may override/change the component prior to sending the message to SAP Solution Manager.

▶ SHORT TEXT
The SHORT TEXT field is maintained by the user and should describe the error at a high level.

▶ PRIORITY
The PRIORITY field defaults to the value LOW. It can be updated by the user. The values and which value is set to default can be changed in Customizing (explained in Chapter 11).

▶ LONG TEXT
The LONG TEXT field should be utilized to thoroughly document and describe the error. You can configure templates to efficiently organize the description. To do this, you must save a text file locally on your computer. The contents of this file will contain the headings, descriptions, etc. that make up the template. You can use the LOAD LOCAL FILE button ( ) to load the text file into the long description area of the message. The contents of the text file can then be further expanded directly within the message.

▶ Additionally, supporting documents can be attached by selecting the ADD FILE button ( ).

Technical Information Captured

Select the DISPLAY ENTIRE MESSAGE button (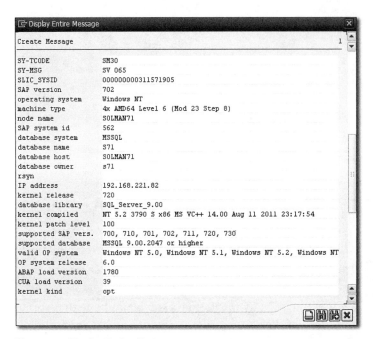) in the CREATE MESSAGE window to produce the DISPLAY ENTIRE MESSAGE screen as shown in Figure 7.4.

Figure 7.4 Display Entire Message

In this window, you can observe all of the technical and system details that are captured at the time the message is created. The figure shows a handful of the many details that are captured by SAP Solution Manager. You can identify by the scroll bar that an immense amount of data related to the SAP application is captured. This information is automatically sent to the SAP Solution Manager system when the user is done filling out the functional details (e.g., SAP component, short text, etc.).

These details can help technical support teams understand the environment at the time the error occurred. Additionally, if the message must be forwarded to SAP Support, these details are also sent.

This is a significant benefit in that SAP Support often won't have to reply (sometimes 24 hours later) with inquiries related to details that have been captured about the system.

Figure 7.5 is the result of the SAP frontend integration. By selecting the SYSTEM DATA button, located in the TEXT assignment block in the incident, you'll produce the technical details that were sent to the SAP Solution Manager system.

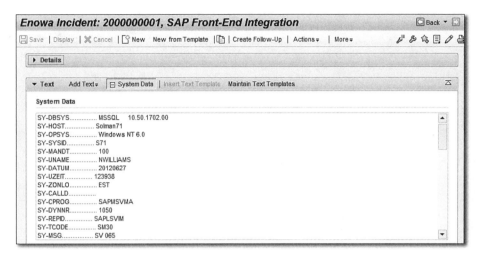

Figure 7.5 System Data in Text Assignment Block

7.1.2 Web Self-Service: SAP CRM Web UI

The SAP CRM Web UI is a universal platform that isn't limited to just message processors and IT professionals seeking out reporting and analytics that are related to SAP ITSM processes. The SAP CRM Web UI can also be enabled to serve as an end-user self-service platform for users who leverage SAP Solution Manager exclusively for creating incidents.

Chapter 2 and Chapter 3 covered the SAP CRM Web UI in detail. Refer to Chapter 2 for details on how to navigate to the SAP CRM Web UI. Refer to Chapter 3 for setup, Customizing, and security specifics. The objective of this section is to identify the SAP CRM Web UI as an inbound channel for creating incidents in SAP Solution Manager.

Business Role for Requester

A standard business role is delivered by SAP Solution Manager specifically for the purpose of an end-user self-service platform. Business role SOLMANREQU provides a slimmed down view of the SAP CRM Web UI, with the objective of providing end users basic and specific tasks related to requesting/creating messages.

Figure 7.6 shows what end users who have been assigned the SOLMANREQU business role will see when they first log on to the ITSM Home Page.

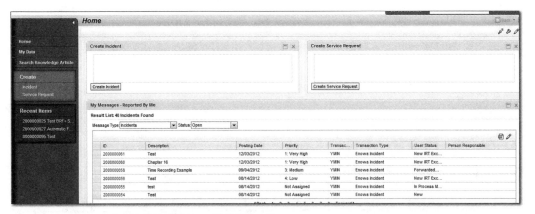

Figure 7.6 SOLMANREQU at ITSM Home Page

This business role can be customized further depending on the IT organization's requirements. Just as we pointed out in Chapter 3, you should create a copy of the standard business role into your own customer namespace (e.g., ZSOLMANREQU). Furthermore, the associated authorization role SAP_CRM_UIU_SRQM_REQUESTER should also be copied into the customer namespace prior to being assigned to the end users.

The SOLMANREQU business role provides a guided procedure that offers a limited number steps and an easy to follow method for creating incidents. Figure 7.7 provides an example of the view which the requesters see when they create an incident with the SOLMANREQU business role assigned to them.

> **Note**
>
> This standard business role creates service requests only. To provide end users with an interface for creating incidents and problems only, follow our configuration example in Chapter 3, Section 3.4.5.

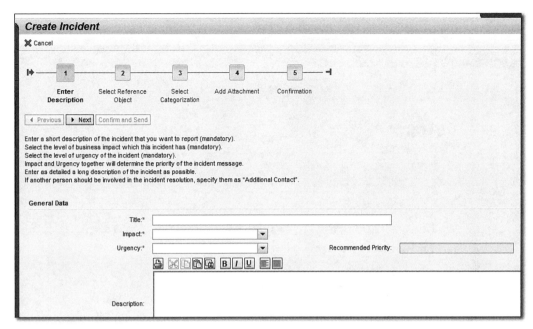

Figure 7.7 Create Incident: SOLMANREQU

7.1.3 Web Self-Service: Work Center

The Work Centers, also described in Chapter 2, are another inbound channel for creating incidents to be received in SAP Solution Manager. This UI, shown in Figure 7.8, provides end users with a role-based platform to perform user-specific activities. Functions within the Work Center are preconfigured to enable the following activities to be performed:

- Search queries definition
- Status reporting
- Watch list monitoring
- Preview incident details

After an incident is selected in the Work Center, the user is taken to the SAP CRM Web UI. Depending on their authorizations as a requestor, they may or may not have the ability to perform subsequent activities in the SAP CRM Web UI.

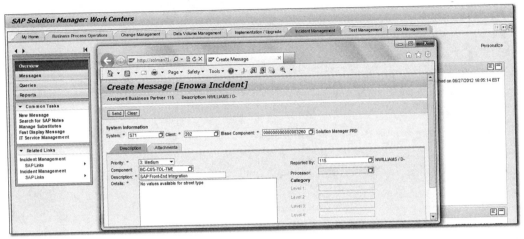

Figure 7.8 Web Self-Service: Work Center

7.1.4 Interaction Center

The *interaction center* is a multifunctional framework offered within SAP ITSM for support team members (specifically referred to as *IT Service Desk agents* in the interaction center) to perform all relevant functions related to a comprehensive and holistic service desk.

The interaction center is accessed by IT Service Desk agents who are assigned the IC_ITSDAGENT business role and corresponding Transaction PFCG role SAP_CRM_UIU_IC_ITSDAGENT in the SAP Solution Manager system.

The INTERACTION CENTER, as shown in Figure 7.9, has a direct integration with SAP Solution Manager's AIM scenario to perform all activities related to processing messages. The interaction center isn't required, but it's available if IT organizations are already using or want to expand on their current SAP ITSM processes.

7.1.5 Email

Within the interaction center, you have the option to generate an incident or problem based on an email. The Email Response Management System (ERMS) in the interaction center allows the automatic creation of incidents and problems based on the details within an email.

Figure 7.9 Interaction Center

As shown in Figure 7.10, you also have the ability to automatically link reply text from the email to the problem in SAP Solution Manager.

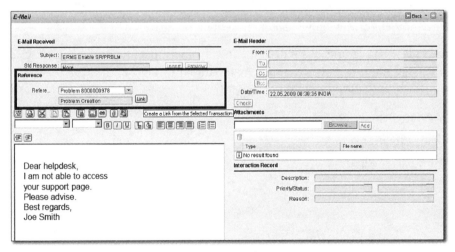

Figure 7.10 Responding to a Problem from the Email Response Management System

7.2   Follow-Ups

In this section, we'll discuss activities and functionalities related to the post-processing of incidents and problems. In disciplines, methodologies, and frameworks such as SAP ITSM and ITIL, processes don't necessarily always have crystal-clear start and end points. Although we often refer to these processes as end to end, and we aim to stand up end-to-end processes for SAP ITSM, the steps at each end aren't always the same for each incident or problem logged.

Depending on the complexity, volume, impact, and outcome of the error, it's rare that incidents and problems are created and completed in a consistent manner on an overall basis. In an SAP ITSM platform such as SAP Solution Manager, which manages SAP and non-SAP incidents and problems, various channels must be available for service organizations to completely process messages to a final resolution.

Referred to as *follow-ups*, these activities are available to service teams to facilitate the following (if required):

▶ Escalation to external support if no resolution can be determined within the IT service organization

▶ Integration into other Application Lifecycle Management (ALM) processes

▶ Development of the knowledge management database

In the following sections, we'll describe the channels that are available to service teams to accomplish these activities. As identified in Figure 7.11, the following channels are available as follow-ups in AIM:

▶ SAP Support

▶ Change request

▶ Third-party help desk

▶ Tasks

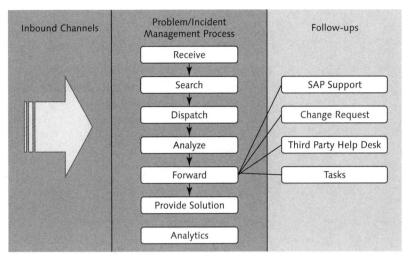

Figure 7.11 Application Incident Management Follow-Ups

7.2.1 SAP Support

In Chapter 5, Section 5.3.5, we introduced you to two options related to the forwarding process step of the Problem Management process (Figure 7.12). If a request for change isn't required, but the problem still can't be resolved at that point, the problem most likely requires further escalation beyond the highest tier within the internal IT service organization.

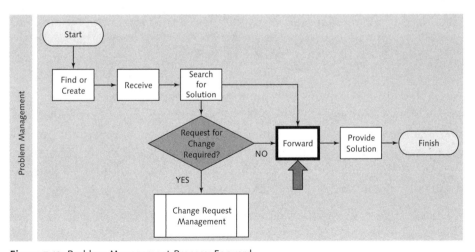

Figure 7.12 Problem Management Process: Forward

Forwarding the problem (or incident) to SAP Support is available directly within the message in SAP Solution Manager. All details that have been entered and automatically captured by SAP are sent to SAP Support for further processing. Dialogue between the processor and SAP Support is communicated within the message as well, providing a fully documented record of communication for future reference.

Communicating with SAP Support is performed in the SAP COLLABORATION assignment block within the incident or problem (see Figure 7.13).

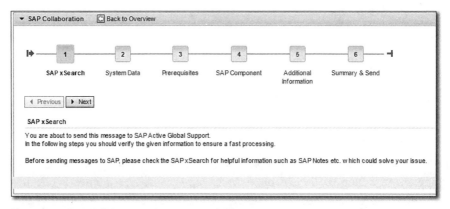

Figure 7.13 SAP Collaboration Assignment Block

> **Note**
>
> In Chapter 8, we'll provide an overview, the prerequisite configuration settings, and step-by-step instructions to enable communication between SAP Solution Manager and SAP Support.

Forwarding the message to SAP Support provides benefits to the IT organization in that services messages can be created directly from the message in SAP Solution Manager. As opposed to reentering all of the details (application related, organization related, error related, etc.) on the SAP Service Marketplace, a processor can use the guided procedure within SAP COLLABORATION to send all of the details already captured quickly to SAP Support.

All details and communications related to the resolution of the error are kept in a single location and available for search and reuse in case similar errors arise in the future.

7.2.2   Request for Change

If an error can only be resolved by making a change to the IT landscape, direct integration into the Change Request Management (ChaRM) process can be initiated by creating a request for change as a follow-up to the problem or incident.

A request for change is associated with changing a component of an IT application. Whether it's SAP related (configuration or development) or non-SAP related (change to an IT asset), SAP Solution Manager's request for change message is provided as a follow-up to incidents and problems.

Example

Let's consider a generic example. Several users are experiencing performance issues (e.g., slow system response). Performance problems across multiple users is a problem in which multiple incidents have already been created in the SAP Solution Manager system. The service team processing the problem has determined that changing parameter XYZ in the production system will increase the response time. To maintain this parameter, they must create a request for change to adjust that setting in the production system.

> **Note**
>
> Part III of our book will explain ChaRM in detail, but here is a sneak preview of how the request for change provides the message processor a way to follow up with an incident or problem in AIM.

1. From the incident or problem, select the CREATE FOLLOW-UP button (Figure 7.14).

Figure 7.14 Create Follow-Up

2. Choose the REQUEST FOR CHANGE transaction type (the standard SMCR transaction type is displayed in Figure 7.15).

3. A new transaction type request for change appears.

4. The requestor fills out the details of the request for change and proceeds according to the ChaRM process described in Part III of this book.

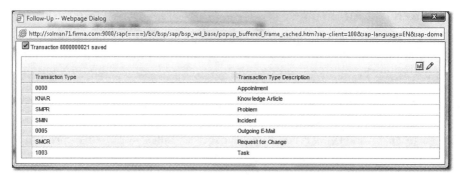

Figure 7.15 Select Request for Change

7.2.3 External Help Desk Integration

SAP Solution Manager provides an open, bidirectional interface that supports the exchange of messages between SAP Solution Manager and the following:

▶ Third-party help desk tools (e.g., HP OpenView, BMC Remedy, IBM Rationale)

▶ In some cases, organizations may have two or more SAP Solution Manager systems that have Application Incident Management enabled. For example, other SAP Solution Manager systems are used within the overall enterprise to process messages related to AIM across geographical areas or business units.

The interface offered by SAP Solution Manager is open (i.e., there is no required or preferred tool by specific companies that must be chosen). Although the interface is open, interface development must occur on the side of the third-party tool.

The interface technology is based on web services, which provide a relatively simple and flexible means for development. Furthermore, it's platform independent, which increases the overall flexibility for developing such an interface.

Common Use Cases

If an organization already has an enterprise-wide help desk in place, SAP Solution Manager is often selected as the central platform for processing second- and third-tier messages related to the IT infrastructure. For organizations that choose to incrementally adopt and deploy SAP Solution Manager functions for AIM, they may begin with leveraging these functionalities strictly for SAP incidents. An even more simplified model for leveraging AIM in SAP Solution Manager is for a repository of messages to be forwarded to SAP Support.

In any of these cases, an enterprise-wide help desk is in place for receiving and routing calls at the first level. For example, medium- to large-sized service organizations typically have a single 1-800 number to collect every call, no matter what the scope is. This central help desk serves as the single source of truth for all messages reported.

This bidirectional interface is provided to support the routing, processing, resolution, and reporting capabilities between SAP Solution Manager and third-party help desks. The objective is to support openness between SAP and non-SAP applications and provide a platform that can seamlessly provide AIM across the entire IT landscape.

Architecture

Because the interface is bidirectional, messages can be forwarded from SAP Solution Manager to a third-party tool, and vice versa. Sending a message to the other system creates a message in the receiving system. Each message has an indicator, so traceability is provided across both systems.

For control purposes, the leading system takes control of the message. When the status changes to CONFIRMED, the related message in the sending system is updated in the same manner. Meanwhile, additional information (such as text types) can be passed between SAP Solution Manager and the third-party help desk.

The following sections identify three common use case examples for leveraging the interface capability for AIM.

SAP as Leading System

In the case that SAP is the leading system, one of the following occurs:

- The message is created directly within SAP Solution Manager via one of the following inbound channels:
  - Web self-service: SAP CRM Web UI
  - Web self-service: work center
  - Interaction center
  - Email

▶ The message is created from a system in the managed SAP ERP landscape:

    ▷ SAP frontend integration

When SAP is the leading system, the use case is as follows (Figure 7.16):

▶ The message is created directly in SAP Solution Manager or received in SAP Solution Manager after it has been generated from SAP frontend integration (❶).

▶ The message is forwarded to the third-party help desk (❷).

▶ A new message isn't automatically created in the third-party help desk.

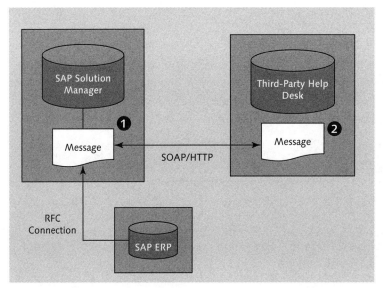

Figure 7.16 SAP as Leading System

Third-Party Help Desk as Leading System

When messages are first created in the third-party help desk (❶), the third-party help desk is the leading system (Figure 7.17). If required, messages are synchronized to the SAP Solution Manager system (❷ for further processing (e.g., the enterprise help desk received an incident that was related to an SAP application). After the message is confirmed in the leading system, it will also be closed in SAP Solution Manager (and vice versa due to the bidirectional interface).

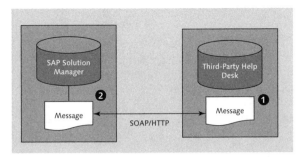

Figure 7.17 Third-Party Help Desk as Leading System

1:n SAP Solution Manager Interface

While the general recommendation is to have a single instance of SAP Solution Manager deployed for the entire enterprise, some organizations have multiple SAP Solution Manager instances. When organizations have several instances of SAP Solution Manager (❶) enabled for AIM (e.g., to support multiple companies, due to mergers or acquisitions, geographical separation, etc.), interfacing can occur between SAP Solution Manager systems (❷).

This concept, referred to as the 1:n SAP Solution Manager interface, can also be used with the integration to third-party help desks as shown in Figure 7.18.

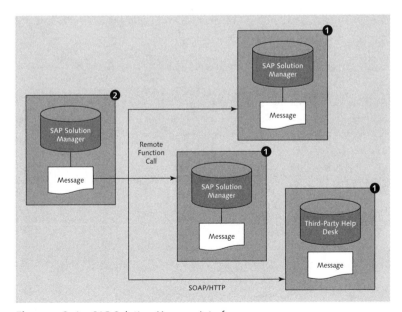

Figure 7.18 1:n SAP Solution Manager Interface

7.2.4 Tasks

As we discussed in Chapter 5, tasks are created as follow-ups during the Problem Management process by the processor after the processor has performed activities related to receiving the problem (e.g., filling out the general problem message details and setting the priority).

Afterwards, the processor can choose to lock incidents to a problem if they are related in order to prioritize activities related to finding a solution and controlling the sequence in how messages are handled.

Tasks are created and assigned to additional processors and contacts in an effort to help manage the activities involved to perform root cause analysis of a problem. They are attached to the problem in the RELATED TRANSACTIONS assignment block where they can be accessed and maintained.

> **Note**
>
> Similar to how incidents and problems are represented by a transaction type (e.g. SMIN and SMPR), a task is also represented by transaction type 1003.

Create a Task

In this section we will describe the steps in order to create a task. The following steps describe the activities of creating a task to help resolve a problem:

1. Select the CREATE FOLLOW-UP button (Figure 7.19).

Problem: 8000000021, Error when entering address

Save | Display | Cancel | New   New from Template | Create Follow-Up | Auto Complete | More

Figure 7.19 Create Follow-Up

2. Select the TASK transaction type in the FOLLOW-UP – WEBPAGE DIALOG window (Figure 7.20).

3. Maintain the details of the task, and click the SAVE AND BACK button (Figure 7.21).

The task is available in the RELATED TRANSACTIONS assignment block of the problem or incident (Figure 7.22).

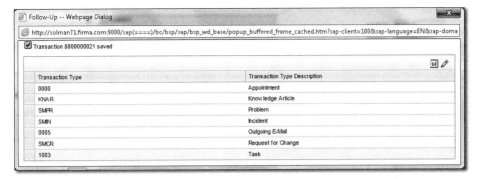

Figure 7.20 Create a Task as a Follow-Up

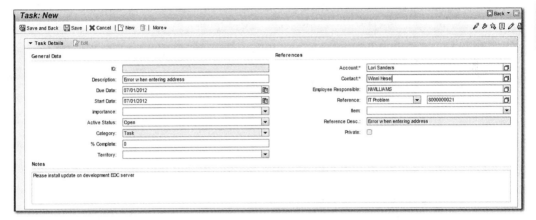

Figure 7.21 Maintain Task Details

Actions	Transaction ID	Transaction	Description	Category	Status	Priority	Transaction Type
	8000000078	8000000078	Error when entering add...	Incident, SAP application...	Proposed Solution	3. Medium	Incident (IT Service Man...
	11		Error when entering add...	Error when entering add...	Open		Task
	12		Error when entering add...	Error when entering add...	Open		Task

Figure 7.22 Tasks as Related Transactions

7.3   Summary

In this chapter, you learned the various options available to initiate Incident Management and Problem Management in SAP Solution Manager. With the release of SAP Solution Manager 7.1, several options are available for end users to create these types of messages to be sent for processing. It's up to the IT organization to determine which inbound channel makes sense to roll out to its user community.

As discussed, it's rare that AIM processes have clear start points and end points across complex messages that are high in volume. For that purpose, follow-ups aid in message resolution and the development of knowledge management within the IT organization. Escalation to SAP Support, integration with other ALM scenarios, and external service desk integration all support the thorough completion and documentation of messages across the AIM lifecycle.

In the next chapter, we'll provide an overview of the core features of AIM. We'll explain the different types of data that can be included in messages as well as discuss the various functionalities available when processing messages. Furthermore, we'll describe the steps necessary to leverage these functions according to best practices.

Application Incident Management in SAP Solution Manager can be adapted to small- and medium-size businesses or scaled to the largest organizations. Business roles provide service team members the appropriate interface for creating and processing service transactions. The SAP CRM 7.0 infrastructure provides robust capabilities to process Application Incident Management for even the most complex environments.

8 Core Features of Application Incident Management

So far, we have discussed what Application Incident Management (AIM) means from an overview perspective. In Chapter 4, we explained why AIM is required to support the efficient delivery of services to the organization. We discussed the architecture and infrastructure, encompassing SAP Solution Manager, which is used to drive the related processes. We identified some of the key new features that were delivered with SAP Solution Manager 7.1, with an emphasis on the SAP CRM Web UI for creating and processing messages. Chapter 5 through Chapter 7 focused strictly on the ins and outs of the processes that make up AIM from an end-to-end perspective. Roles, process flows, touch points into all phases of Application Lifecycle Management (ALM), and inputs/outputs to the process were all described in detail.

Now we'll start to peel back even more layers and get into the meat of AIM. In this chapter, we'll describe the core features within AIM. We'll explain the data and functionality that is contained within screen areas and assignment blocks for incidents, problems, and service requests.

> **Note**
>
> *Assignment blocks* are collapsible and expandable sections of the SAP CRM Web UI screens. Each assignment block effectively organizes data, functionalities, and tasks for each AIM transaction type.

> **Note**
>
> Most assignment blocks are specific to both AIM and Change Request Management (ChaRM). When processing messages related to SAP ITSM, most of the information and functionalities available will be standard across both of these scenarios. We'll cover assignment blocks specific to ChaRM in Part III of this book.

First, we'll describe how and where the data, functionalities, and tasks are segregated via business role assignment. Then, we'll continue to describe the data, functionalities, and tasks available when processing incidents, problems, and service requests in SAP Solution Manager.

8.1 Business Roles and Predefined User Interfaces

In this section, we'll revisit a few basic points on business roles and the aspects of predefined user interfaces (UIs) within the SAP CRM Web UI. Chapter 3 and Chapter 4 covered both of these topics, respectively, in detail. Now, we'll discuss how the business roles and predefined UIs drive the information available to those who use AIM in SAP Solution Manager. Furthermore, we'll discuss the tools and capabilities available within these components to provide a better understanding of the segregation of duties in an IT service organization.

Figure 8.1 provides a graphical representation of the three core business roles available when delivering and processing SAP ITSM scenarios:

▶ SOLMANREQU (SAP ITSM end user)

▶ SOLMANDSPTCH (Level 1 support)

▶ SOLMANPRO (SAP ITSM professional)

For each of these business roles, a predefined UI is provided to those users who are assigned their respective roles.

In the next sections, we'll elaborate further on each of these business roles and provide an understanding of the information and functionalities that are available for each.

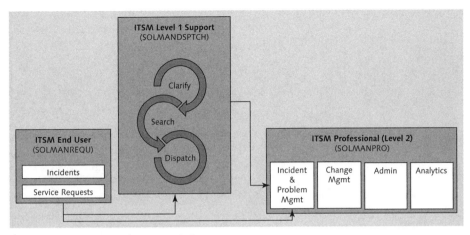

Figure 8.1 SAP ITSM Core Business Roles

8.1.1 SAP ITSM End User

End users in SAP ITSM, also referred to as *requesters*, should be assigned the business role SOLMANREQU.

Note

Remember, business roles are assigned in the PARAMETERS tab of the user's master record (Transaction SU01). The user must have the Transaction PFCG/authorization role SAP_CRM_UIU_SOLMANPRO assigned first. Then, the PARAMETER ID field must be populated with the value CRM_UI_PROFILE. Finally, depending on the user, the PARAMETER VALUE will be entered. In the case of the SAP ITSM end user, the parameter value will be SOLMANREQU.

If you recall from Chapter 3, SOLMANREQU provides SAP ITSM end users with the basic functionalities they need to send an incident or service request to the central SAP Solution Manager system. Because problems should be created as follow-ups to incidents, as part of a root cause analysis process, it's only natural that the SAP ITSM end users are not provided with this ability.

As you can see in Figure 8.2, the business role SOLMANREQU provides a guided procedure that walks the SAP ITSM end user through five basic steps to log the service message:

- ▶ ENTER DESCRIPTION
- ▶ SELECT REFERENCE OBJECT
- ▶ SELECT CATEGORIZATION
- ▶ ADD ATTACHMENT
- ▶ CONFIRMATION

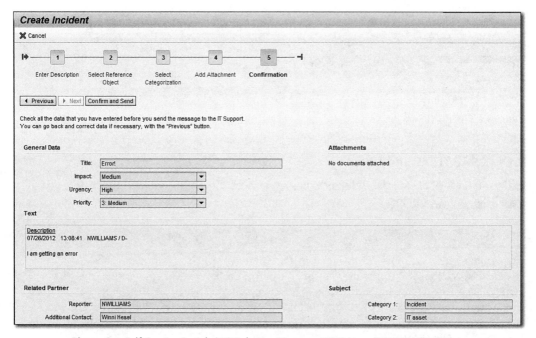

Figure 8.2 Self-Service Portal: SAP Solution Manager ITSM User (SOLMANREQU)

This guided procedure will appear after the SAP ITSM end user clicks on the CRE-ATE INCIDENT or CREATE SERVICE REQUEST in the SAP CRM Web UI (or in the case of the end user, the Self-Service Portal UI).

The guided procedure provides the SAP ITSM end user with a lean, self-service portal for creating incidents and service requests. On the other hand, this guided procedure provides key fields for the Level 1 service team to have a thorough understanding of the nature of the incident or service request.

The following information fields are provided to the SAP ITSM end user when creating a message:

- SHORT DESCRIPTION

- MULTI-LEVEL CATEGORIZATION

- PROCESSING DATA (IMPACT, URGENCY, RECOMMENDED PRIORITY)

- REFERENCE OBJECTS (IBASE COMPONENT, CONFIGURATION ITEM, SOLUTION AND PROJECT DETAILS)

- LONG TEXT

- ATTACHMENTS

- SAP COMPONENT

8.1.2   SAP ITSM Level 1 Support UI

The SOLMANDSPTCH business role should be assigned to Level 1 service team users in an SAP ITSM scenario. This business role provides a predefined UI that gives Level 1 service users the ability to communicate back to the SAP ITSM end users, search for solutions, dispatch, and update the message accordingly.

Figure 8.3 shows the predefined UI delivered with the SOLMANDSPTCH business role.

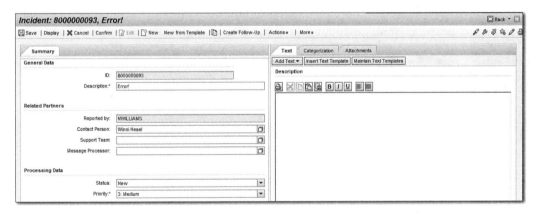

Figure 8.3 SAP ITSM Level 1 Support: Solution Manager SAP ITSM Dispatch (SOLMANDSPTCH)

As you can see from the screenshot, the SOLMANDSPTCH business role is more closely related to a cockpit for adding information and performing activities as opposed to a guided procedure. This predefined UI delivered with this business role allows service users to update the information maintained by the SAP ITSM end user (except the NUMBER RANGE and REPORTED BY fields). In addition, this business role allows for the following added features and functionalities that are specific to the job roles of a service team user:

- Setting the status
- Maintaining the priority
- Determining dates
- Leveraging text templates
- Maintaining related transactions and knowledge articles
- Viewing the change history
- Making time recordings

8.1.3   SAP ITSM Professional UI

The predefined UI delivered with the SAP ITSM professional role (SOLMANPRO) includes a comprehensive suite of information and functionalities that are critical to higher-tiered service users. In other words, the SOLMANPRO business role provides your service teams with everything they need to effectively and thoroughly process SAP ITSM messages.

The SAP ITSM professional UI extends beyond AIM. With this business role and required user authorizations, service team members are able to access information and processing tools related to scenarios beyond AIM:

- ChaRM
- Administration activities
- Reporting and analytics

> **Note**
>
> The SAP ITSM professional UI represents the comprehensive view of information and activities pertaining to AIM as well as ChaRM. For this reason, the remaining sections of this chapter will contain screenshots associated with this particular UI. Keep in mind that while business roles provide role-specific UIs, authorization/Transaction PFCG roles still need to be applied and adapted to use SAP ITSM capabilities.

As shown in Figure 8.4, the SAP ITSM professional UI provides the assignment blocks as described in the beginning of this chapter. The image shows the assignment blocks collapsed, so you can see all of the assignment blocks offered out of the box with the SAP ITSM professional UI.

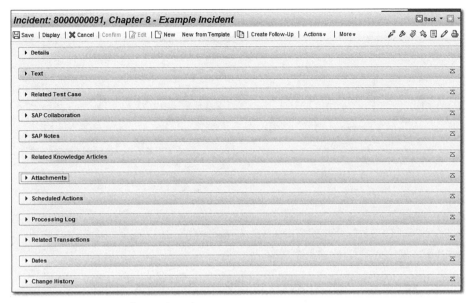

Figure 8.4 SAP ITSM Professional: SOLMANPRO

8.1.4 Hide Unused Assignment Blocks

As you can see already, numerous assignment blocks are available when processing transactions related to SAP ITSM. In fact, the assignment blocks you have available for viewing in your system may be different from our example in Figure 8.4. You can tailor, or slim down, the view of these assignment blocks by clicking the PERSONALIZE button (✎).

When you click this button, the screen in Figure 8.5 will appear.

Depending on your organization's strategy for receiving and processing messages related to SAP ITSM, you have the option of slimming down the view of the assignment blocks that are delivered standard with SAP Solution Manager. The assignment blocks listed in the DISPLAYED ASSIGNMENT BLOCKS table are the currently visible assignment blocks. To move items in and out of this table and the AVAILABLE ASSIGNMENT BLOCKS table, highlight the appropriate row, and click the desired arrow button (⊞).

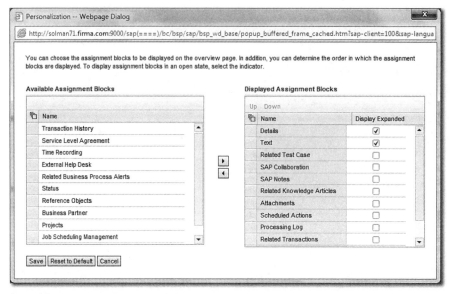

Figure 8.5 Personalize Displayed Assignment Blocks

Now, we'll describe the information and functionalities available within AIM from a UI perspective. Remember, we're saving a select few of the assignment blocks for subsequent chapters.

8.2 Details

The DETAILS assignment block contains the core information about the incident, problem, or service request. In SAP Solution Manager 7.0, the information and functionality within the DETAILS assignment block is similar to that maintained in the FAST ENTRY view of the SAP GUI.

The DETAILS assignment block is segregated by several different screen areas:

▶ GENERAL DATA

▶ CATEGORIZATION

▶ PROCESSING DATA

▶ RELATIONSHIPS

▶ DATE DETERMINATION

▶ REFERENCE OBJECTS

In the following subsections, we'll provide a brief overview of what each of these areas mean in regards to processing a transaction type within AIM. Figure 8.6 identifies how the DETAILS assignment block appears after data is populated within it.

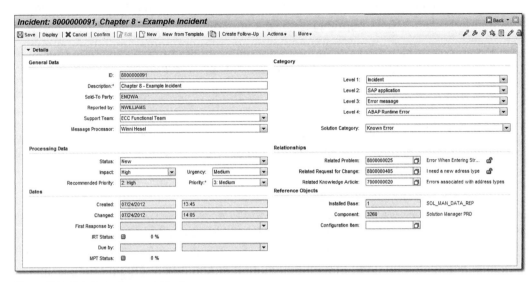

Figure 8.6 Details Assignment Block

> **Note**
>
> This chapter focuses strictly on the description and strategy for information and data maintained in the assignment blocks associated with AIM. We'll cover the configuration approach and steps in Chapter 11. For master data setup (i.e., information maintained within GENERAL DATA), refer back to Chapter 3.

8.2.1 Categorization

Categorization, in SAP ITSM, can be classified in two ways:

▶ Multilevel categorization, which is based on up to four classifications

▶ Solution categorization

We'll discuss these categories in more detail in the following subsections.

Multilevel Categorization

Multilevel categorization enables users, service teams, and IT professionals to report on up to four levels of categories. A categorization schema, configured in the SAP CRM Web UI by the administrator, defines the values within each of these fields/levels.

A standard schema is provided by SAP out of the box. Although these values are a design consideration for the IT organization, the standard example schema is important because it provides the following:

▶ A baseline set of design considerations to start the thought process for how these values can be best used within your organization

▶ A standard configuration example so you have an idea of how these fields are configured

▶ A set of category values that can be activated during the design/build phase of AIM to show the capabilities and flexibility for reporting while demonstrating the overall functionality

Because multilevel categorization is configured via a schema, and not standard table values, each field will depend on the prior field. For example, if a value of INCIDENT is available in LEVEL 1, then the LEVEL 2 values that are selectable will be types of incidents (e.g., SAP application, network, hardware, etc.). LEVEL 3 will also be dependent on LEVEL 2, and so on. Figure 8.7 provides a typical example of an SAP incident based on the standard multilevel categorization schema.

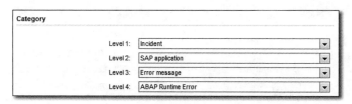

Figure 8.7 Example Categorization Schema: SAP Incident

Multilevel categorization can also be used when you're using SAP Solution Manager to report and manage incidents, problems, and service requests related to non-SAP products. This is often a major question that people have, and it's one of the main areas of focus from SAP regarding release 7.1 of SAP Solution Manager. The answer is yes, SAP Solution Manager does provide the capabilities to manage your entire IT landscape, even beyond SAP.

In Figure 8.8, the four category values maintained provide an example of how an incident related to a printer can be captured.

> **Note**
>
> This is the same multilevel categorization schema that was used in the example in Figure 8.7. This represents the scalability and flexibility that can be provided if the design of these values is well thought out by the organization!

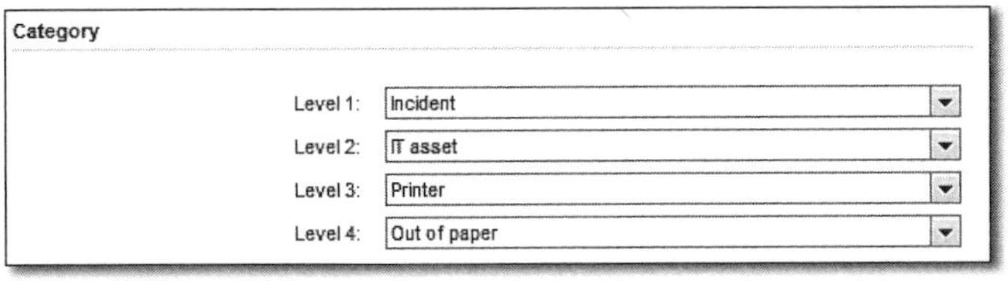

Figure 8.8 Example Categorization Schema: Non-SAP Incident

You also have the option of including a second categorization block within the SAP ITSM professional UI. A second categorization block, as shown in Figure 8.9, is beneficial for organizations that require more precise reporting capabilities across SAP ITSM. The process to add a second categorization block includes additional design discussions as well as UI configuration conducted by the administrator. We'll provide the steps to add a second categorization block in Chapter 11.

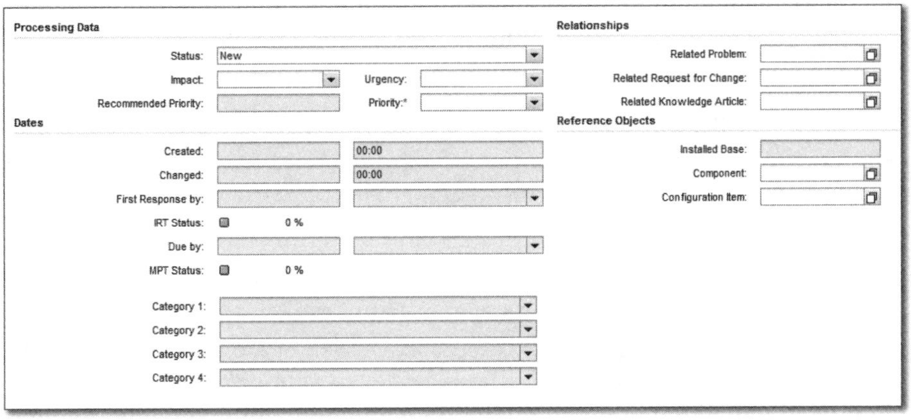

Figure 8.9 Second Categorization Block

Solution Category

SOLUTION CATEGORY is another field that is available when creating and reporting on messages. The solution category is independent of the multilevel categorization fields we described in the prior section. The purpose of this field is to identify the type of solution which was reached when the incident, problem, or service request has been closed.

Figure 8.10 identifies the SOLUTION CATEGORY field within an incident along with its three values that are provided out of the box.

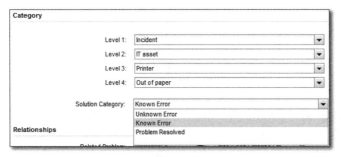

Figure 8.10 Solution Category Field and Values

Design Considerations

Just like any values that must be configured for the fields in AIM, it's important to include the identification and definition of these values within the design/blueprint phase of the overall implementation of these scenarios.

You may have existing tools that are being consolidated, replaced, or integrated with SAP Solution Manager. In this case, most likely you have key field values that are included somewhere in existing tools. It's up to the organization, led by the SAP Solution Manager lead, to determine how existing reporting requirements can be met in SAP Solution Manager. This involves the exercise of mapping these key fields from the legacy systems over to SAP Solution Manager. Multilevel categorization provides the flexibility and scalability to provide key reporting and analytics from SAP Solution Manager.

Alternatively, your organization may be starting out as SAP Solution Manager as the first and only application for AIM. In this case, the design/blueprint sessions will capture which values are necessary for driving reporting and analytics metrics.

8.2.2   Processing Data

The fields available within the PROCESSING DATA screen area classify an incident, problem, or service request based on ITIL standards. In other words, if your organization has adopted or is migrating to ITIL disciplines, SAP Solution Manager supports these standards by providing sufficient fields.

As shown in Figure 8.11, processing data contains information related to the following:

▶ STATUS

▶ IMPACT

▶ URGENCY

▶ PRIORITY

▶ RECOMMENDED PRIORITY

Figure 8.11 Processing Data

We'll provide some information on each of these fields in the following subsections.

Status

The STATUS dropdown contains the following options for processing data:

▶ NEW

▶ IN PROCESS

▶ SENT TO SAP

▶ FORWARDED

▶ CUSTOMER ACTION

▶ PROPOSED SOLUTION

▶ CONFIRMED

▶ WITHDRAWN

Impact

The impact of the message is directly correlated with business criticality. In other words, the IMPACT value is proportional to the number of business users affected by the incident. The standard impact values delivered with SAP Solution Manager are listed here:

▶ DISASTER

▶ HIGH

▶ MEDIUM

▶ LOW

▶ NONE

Because these values can be highly subjective, the recommended practice is to keep an up-to-date configuration management database (CMDB) to determine how many users will be affected by the incident. The CONFIGURATION ITEM field (within the REFERENCE OBJECTS screen area) is intended to capture information that will support a more objective method in selecting an appropriate impact value.

The impact of an incident, problem, or service request is tied closely with how Service Level Agreements (SLAs) are defined, or how they will be affected. This also increases the objectiveness of this value.

Urgency

The URGENCY field is used to identify how quickly the incident should be resolved. Because there is really no way to make a call on urgency completely objective, it's up to the service teams to have the level of knowledge/experience necessary to state the urgency level. Following are the standard URGENCY values delivered with SAP Solution Manager:

▶ EMERGENCY

▶ VERY HIGH

▶ HIGH

▶ MEDIUM

▶ LOW

A common example involves incidents or problems related to the processing of payroll in an HR scenario. If the incident will impact several users having a delay or inaccurate run of payroll, the urgency to complete this incident in a timely matter would be HIGH. Similarly, if an incident indicated that the system could come down unless certain parameters were adjusted, the urgency to adjust the parameters would be high.

Priority

The priority of an incident, problem, or service request is the output of the impact and urgency values. Although there may be other values that can have an influence on the priority (e.g., scope, size, resources required to address, complexity), the main drivers of the priority should be the impact and urgency.

By using these two values, a more objective and accurate priority value is reached. Because the impact and urgency are formulated from more objective sources, service teams can have a more accurate read on which service transactions should be addressed first. Although most users think all of their incidents and problems are very high priority, this usually isn't the case!

The standard PRIORITY values delivered with SAP Solution Manager include the following:

- VERY HIGH
- HIGH
- MEDIUM
- LOW

Entering these values is mandatory in SAP Solution Manager.

> **Important!**
>
> While you have the option to change these values in Customizing, we recommend that you do not change them. These priority values align closely with SAP Active Global Support (SAP AGS) priority values. If you adapt these values and then use the SAP Collaboration functionality, there will be conflicts in how the custom priorities align with standard SAP priorities. Moreover, the PRIORITY field is global across all SAP ITSM transaction types. This means if you change the priority values to be AIM specific, they won't make sense in ChaRM.

Recommended Priority

The service teams often use a simple matrix to set the value of the priority. Because the priority is formed by a combination of impact and urgency, a matrix defines the output (priority) of these two inputs. SAP Solution Manager provides the recommended PRIORITY field as an automated function to suggest the priority based on the impact and urgency values selected. The matrix, in this case, is delivered by SAP Solution Manager. It's preconfigured based on the values identified in Figure 8.12.

		Impact				
		Disaster	High	Medium	Low	None
Urgency	Emergency	Very High	Very High	High	High	Medium
	Very High	Very High	High	Medium	Medium	Low
	High	Very High	High	Medium	Low	Low
	Medium	Very High	High	Medium	Low	Low
	Low	High	Medium	Medium	Low	Low

Figure 8.12 Recommended Priority Determination

The matrix provides priority values based on ITIL standards when combining impacts and urgencies. You should always stick with the standard Customizing. However, if your organization defines priorities slightly differently, the matrix can be updated in Customizing.

8.2.3 Relationships

Relationships to related transaction types (e.g., problems, requests for change, knowledge articles) can be identified in the DETAILS assignment block. These transaction types can be maintained in one of two ways:

▶ Manually by keying in the transaction ID or searching by selection criteria

▶ Automatically if they are created as follow-up transactions

As you can see in Figure 8.13, there is a problem request for change and knowledge article maintained as related transaction types for this particular incident. The LOCK icon (🔒) next to the problem and request for change indicates whether these related transaction types are locked to the incident.

Figure 8.13 Relationships to an Incident

As discussed in Chapter 5, you can lock transactions together. This is valuable when several incidents relate to a single problem; for example, you can lock the incidents to facilitate a more efficient and planned means to reach a resolution. In this particular example, locking several similar incidents at the administrator level supports a controlled way of handling the incidents. If a certain sequence should be followed, whether due to organizational requirements or technical requirements, that can be controlled by locking.

After an incident, problem, or request for change is locked, it can't be edited unless unlocked by the administrator. In the following section, we'll provide additional details about this functionality.

Unlocking

There are two ways a message can be locked or unlocked in SAP Solution Manager. The first, identified in Figure 8.14, is via the MORE button. Simply select MORE, and then choose UNLOCK to enable editing again in the message.

Incident: 8000000091, Chapter 8 - Example Incident	
🖫 Save | Display | ✖ Cancel | Confirm | 🖉 Edit | 🗋 New New from Template |🗋 | Create Follow-Up | Auto Complete | More▾	Find Related Problems
☑ Transaction 8000000032 saved	Find Knowledge Articles
▼ **Details**	Search for SAP Notes
General Data Category	Unlock
ID: 8000000091	Send E-Mail
Description: Chapter 8 - Example Incident	Print Preview
Sold-To Party: ENOWA	Print
Reported by: NWILLIAMS	Display Object Relationships

Figure 8.14 Unlocking an Incident, Option 1

Locks are also displayed in the RELATED INCIDENTS assignment block within the problem message. To lock or unlock an incident and problem, follow these steps:

1. Access the RELATED INCIDENTS assignment block.

2. Select the row with the appropriate incident.

3. Select LOCK or UNLOCK.

The LOCKED column will either be flagged or empty depending on the step you just took, as shown in Figure 8.15.

Figure 8.15 Unlocking an Incident, Option 2

8.2.4 Object Relationships

The OBJECT RELATIONSHIPS section of the DETAILS assignment block is used to reference objects, whether they are SAP or IT assets that relate to the service transaction. SAP reference objects are identified at the client level. For example, an ITSM service transaction can be assigned to client 000 of an SAP ERP system. Non-SAP reference objects can include items such as printers, servers, routers, or others. The non-SAP reference objects can be included with the integration to SAP IT Infrastructure Management, which we'll discuss when we explain the reference to configuration items. Figure 8.16 provides an example of the OBJECT RELATIONSHIPS area referencing an SAP object.

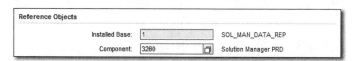

Figure 8.16 SAP Reference Object

If a request for change or other follow-up document is created to integrate into a subsequent ITSM process, these object relationships are automatically copied over. In the Change Request Management scenario, for example, the object relationship can be used to initiate the approval process.

Installed Base

For ITSM functions, an installed base (iBase) must be established in order to represent the system landscape for CRM-based scenarios (e.g. Application Incident Management, Change Request Management, etc.). You can almost think of the iBase as the representation of the system landscape from LMBD, for CRM-specific purposes.

There is typically only a single iBase, in which each system within the SAP landscape is assigned to. In certain situations, separate iBase structures can be assigned, depending on a solution-dependent or solution-independent approach. However, the most common scenario is to use the standard iBase structure which is referred to as SOL_MAN_DATA_REP Installation 1.

Flip back to Chapter 3 for detailed instructions on how to generate the iBase for your CRM-based scenarios. A more technical description of this feature is provided in Chapter 3 as well.

Component

A *component* is a lower level object of the iBase. The component represents products, texts, etc., that can be assigned to the service transaction to pin-point the exact origin or root of where the incident (for example) occurred. A component is represented by a four-character identification number, and represents an SAP system client (e.g., 300) of the respective system.

Depending on how non-SAP products are categorized in SAP Solution Manager, you also have the option of creating products manually as iBase components directly within Transaction IB52. If SAP IT Infrastructure Management is not integrated with your SAP Solution Manager system, this may be a viable option in order to represent your IT assets as reference objects.

Configuration Item

The CONFIGURATION ITEM field can be used specifically to relate IT components within the customer's infrastructure to the incident document in SAP Solution Manager. The intent of this field is to have a link to SAP IT Infrastructure Management so that the Configuration Management Database (CMDB) functionality can be used in conjunction with ITSM.

SAP customers with Enterprise Support can extend ALM seamlessly with SAP IT Infrastructure Management. Extending this functionality allows a link between the incident (for example) and the configuration item that's documented and managed within the CMDB in SAP IT Infrastructure Management.

Now that we've described the features and information recorded in the DETAILS assignment block, we'll continue going down the list of other assignment blocks available in AIM. First, we'll discuss how text is maintained and recorded, as well as how it provides a detailed overview log for all communications throughout the IT organization.

8.3   Text Management

For SAP ITSM functions, there are two main text management sections:

▶ TEXT DESCRIPTION

▶ TEXT LOG

In the next sections, we'll describe what can be included in each of these sections from an information and functionality standpoint.

8.3.1   Text Description

In the TEXT DESCRIPTION section, the text determination procedure is called depending on which transaction type you're maintaining text for. We'll explain the concepts, including step-by-step directions to maintain text determination procedures, in Chapter 11.

There are four different options available in the TEXT DESCRIPTION section, which we'll discuss in the following subsections:

- ADD TEXT
- DISPLAY SYSTEM DATA
- MAINTAIN TEXT TEMPLATES
- INSERT TEXT TEMPLATE

Add Text

Figure 8.17 identifies the standard text types that are available in the incident transaction type. Text types tend to be standard across AIM. However, new text types related to ChaRM are available for that scenario.

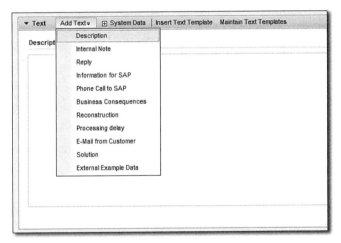

Figure 8.17 Text Types

The objective of segregating text types is to have an organized method to manage the information and dialogue that is exchanged among the requester, service teams, and SAP Support. If managed appropriately, using the text types supports a much more efficient, organized, and understandable audit trail for both the IT organization as well as external auditors (if necessary).

It's important to take note of the following characteristics of two specific text types:

▶ INTERNAL NOTE
Text can be created and classified as internal so that message processors have reference notes to revert back to.

▶ INFORMATION FOR SAP
If an incident or problem must be forwarded to SAP, text must be maintained in the text type INFORMATION FOR SAP.

System Data

Clicking the SYSTEM DATA button will display the technical details that were captured at the time the incident or problem was created, as shown in Figure 8.18. If the message is created from a satellite system, all of the system details from that specific system are collected and sent to the central SAP Solution Manager system.

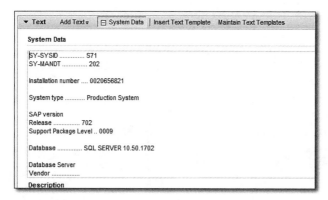

Figure 8.18 System Data

System details, down to the transaction level, are captured if the incident is generated from within the screen the incident or problem occurred. The objective of this is to provide service teams, especially SAP, key system details to speed resolution time. Moreover, responses (which invoke delays) from requesters and internal service teams related to system details aren't needed as much because all of the details are captured in SAP Solution Manager.

Chapter 7, Section 7.1.1, provides additional information about this important feature.

Maintain Text Templates

Text templates are used by requesters and service teams to rapidly insert information about the message that is most important to the IT organization. The information captured in a text template benefits downstream service members as well as the IT organization overall. Using text templates enables standards across how information is captured. Further, they enable completeness and thoroughness in regards to a well-documented trail of information throughout the lifecycle of a message.

There are two different types of text templates that can be enabled in SAP Solution Manager:

▶ User templates

▶ System templates

User Templates

User templates are created and maintained by the individual members involved in the AIM process. They are local, in that they aren't distributed across the entire IT organization.

A common example of a user template, as shown in Figure 8.19, can be an email signature. Because email signatures are specific to each user, it should be created as a user template. The following steps identify how to create a user template:

1. Click the MAINTAIN TEXT TEMPLATES button in the TEXT assignment block.

2. Click the NEW button.

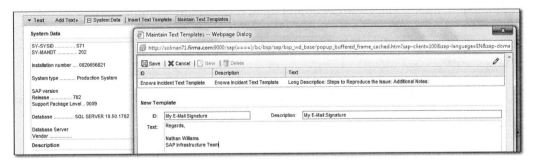

Figure 8.19 Create User Template

3. Enter data in the ID, DESCRIPTION, and TEXT fields.

4. Click SAVE.

System Templates

System templates are created in the SAP Solution Manager IMG by an administrator. Unlike user templates, system templates are global across the transaction type (i.e., incident, problem, or service request). System templates provide standardization across the IT organization in regards to what information is maintained within the message. If all messages are required to have the same information, IT organizations are more likely to have success with well-documented resolutions.

Figure 8.20 provides an example of a basic system template. In this example, requesters and/or service teams are prompted to enter the following information as part of the message text:

▶ LONG DESCRIPTION

▶ BUSINESS IMPACT

▶ STEPS TO REPRODUCE

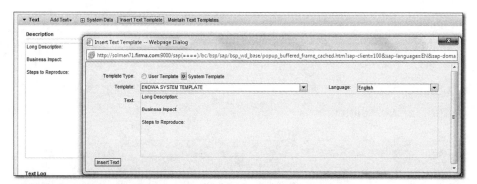

Figure 8.20 Basic System Template

Note

An alternative to the following example is to use existing text types or create custom ones. For your organization, this is a design consideration. You'll want to determine what makes the most sense in regards to your documentation strategy. Keep in mind that text types can be filtered and made mandatory, whereas templates don't provide as much granular flexibility. We'll describe how to control these features when we cover the configuration aspects in Chapter 12.

Insert Text into the Template

Whether you've chosen a user template or system template, when you're ready to insert text into the text template, click the INSERT TEXT TEMPLATE button as shown in Figure 8.21. You'll have the option to either select the user templates that you created locally or select a system template that was configured by the administrator. Follow these steps:

1. Select the radio button for USER TEMPLATE or SYSTEM TEMPLATE.

2. In the TEMPLATE field, select which template will be used.

3. Review the text template in the TEXT field.

4. Click INSERT TEXT.

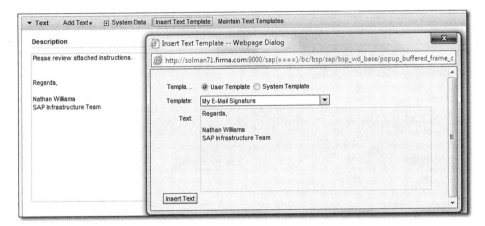

Figure 8.21 Insert Text Template

8.3.2   Text Log

The TEXT LOG within the TEXT assignment block contains the history of all textual dialogue communicated across all roles within AIM (end users, service users, professionals, and SAP support). As soon as text is entered within the text description area, it's captured within the log.

The text log includes the option to filter on text type (e.g., description, reply, internal note, etc.) from the TEXT TYPE field as shown in Figure 8.22. Additionally, you can increase or decrease the size of the text area by adjusting the value within the MAXIMUM LINES field.

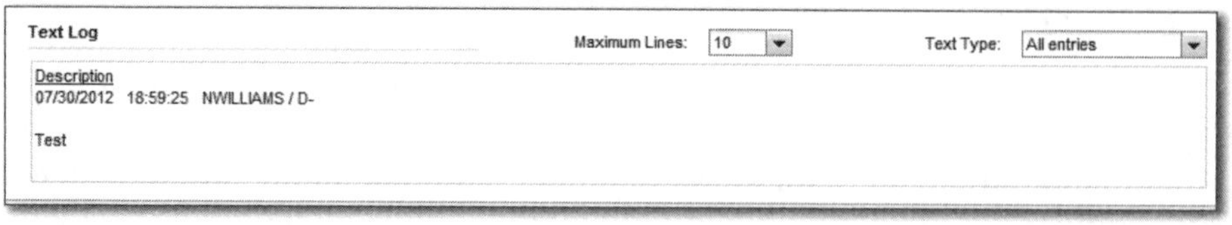

Text Log

Maximum Lines: 10 Text Type: All entries

Description
07/30/2012 18:59:25 NWILLIAMS / D-

Test

Figure 8.22 Text Log

In the next section, we'll describe how specific components of test management can be integrated into the processing of incidents and service requests.

8.4   Related Test Cases

In the RELATED TEST CASE assignment block, you can integrate various components of test management directly within AIM. Because messages associated with test management are yet to be determined as problems and are closely aligned with test defects/errors, this assignment block is only available for the incident transaction type.

> **Note**
>
> For more information on how test management activities can initiate AIM, refer to Chapter 6, where we discussed integration into phases of AIM in detail.

Figure 8.23 shows the result of linking a message associated with a test error or defect directly within the incident in the SAP CRM Web UI. The details of the test management components are recorded (and linked) to the RELATED TEST CASE assignment block.

Actions	Template Type	Template ID	Test Plan	Test Package	Status	Status Text	Test Case Title	Test Object
	Project	CHEM_BP	ITSM Test Set 2	Round 1 Testing	△	Being Processed	Test Case	

Figure 8.23 Related Test Case Assignment Block

As mentioned earlier, several test management components are linked directly within the transaction. Figure 8.23 is an example of how all components can be integrated.

In the next sections, we'll identify how test management components integrate into the incident.

8.4.1 Template ID

Within the TEMPLATE ID field is a link to the SAP Solution Manager project (e.g., CHEM_BP) in which the message was created or assigned. Clicking on the project within this field will open a SAP GUI screen that directs you to the node within the SAP Solution Manager project where the message is recorded. Figure 8.24 is the result of clicking this link. As you can see, a message is maintained on the SER-VICE MESSAGES tab.

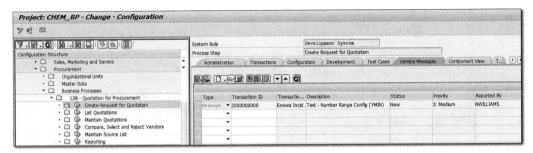

Figure 8.24 Template Project Integration

8.4.2 Test Package

Clicking on the link in the TEST PACKAGE column (e.g., ROUND 1 TESTING) will open the TEST EXECUTION screen. The TEST EXECUTION screen, as shown in Figure 8.25, contains the test package to which the message was assigned (e.g., Transaction STWB_WORK).

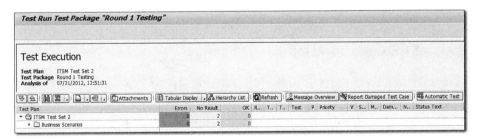

Figure 8.25 Test Package Integration

When you click the MESSAGE OVERVIEW button, the MESSAGE OVERVIEW screen will appear identifying all messages that were associated with this particular test package. In Figure 8.26, three particular errors are associated with this test package.

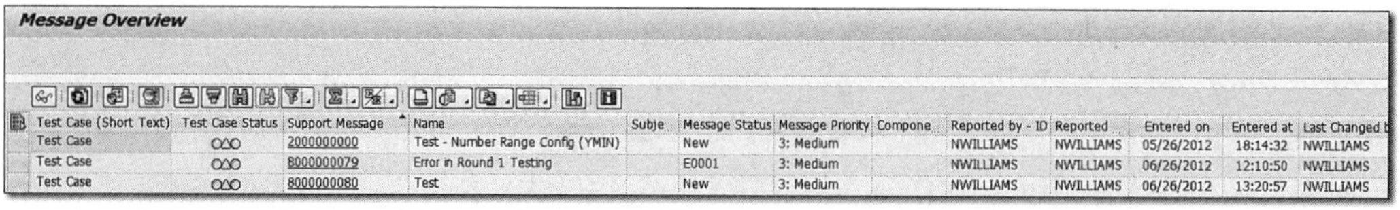

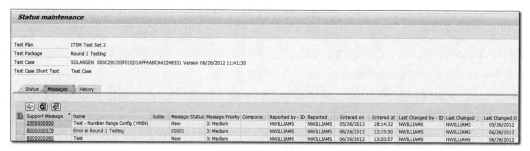

Figure 8.26 Message Overview

8.4.3 Status Text

Clicking on the link within the STATUS TEXT column (e.g., BEING PROCESSED) will launch the STATUS MAINTENANCE screen as shown in Figure 8.27. After selecting the MESSAGES tab, you have another option for viewing all test management messages aligned to the incident.

Figure 8.27 Status Maintenance

In the next section, we'll take a look at how SAP functions and dialogue are documented and administered within SAP Solution Manager.

8.5 SAP Collaboration

In this section, we'll provide an overview of the SAP COLLABORATION assignment block. Further, we'll explain how the capabilities within this assignment block help service teams resolve incidents or problems that must be forwarded to SAP.

> **Note**
>
> SAP Collaboration (within SAP Solution Manager) isn't required, as of Service Pack 05, to receive SAP service. Performing these functions within SAP Solution Manager, as opposed to doing so on the SAP Service Marketplace, is an organizational change management challenge for most technical service team members.

However, we highly recommend migrating toward administering SAP Support directly within SAP Solution Manager. Having the related functions on one platform, integrated into SAP ITSM, is a significant benefit over the prior ways of administering activities related to SAP Support.

8.5.1 Overview

Using SAP Collaboration is a smart, efficient, and valuable way to create and manage SAP Support messages. If your internal service team has discovered a bug associated with standard functionality, an SAP Support message can be created directly within AIM. Additionally, if the highest support tier in your IT service organization is unable to resolve a message, the option to escalate to SAP Support is available.

Problems and/or incidents have the capability to be forwarded to SAP Support as an escalation path. Rather than logging on to the SAP Service Marketplace, service teams can create the SAP Support message directly within SAP Solution Manager. The SAP Support message is linked to the incident or problem, supporting traceability from an end-to-end message resolution perspective.

Moreover, all communication between your internal service team and SAP Support is administered and recorded in the SAP COLLABORATION assignment block. The text dialogue between internal and external service teams furthers the quality, value, and traceability of messages.

Finally, SAP Solution Manager provides a guided procedure and follow-up actions that support all activities associated with communicating with SAP Support. In the following sections, we'll describe the activities in the guided procedure (i.e., the process to send messages and communicate with SAP Support via SAP Solution Manager) as well as the follow-up actions to support a comprehensive tool for administering SAP Support messages.

8.5.2 SAP xSearch

Figure 8.28 shows the guided procedure available within the SAP COLLABORATION assignment block. SAP xSEARCH is the first step to create a message in the SAP Support backbone.

SAP xSearch is an enhanced vehicle for performing a preliminary resource check before actually creating a SAP Support message. The SAP xSEARCH screen will open after you click NEXT.

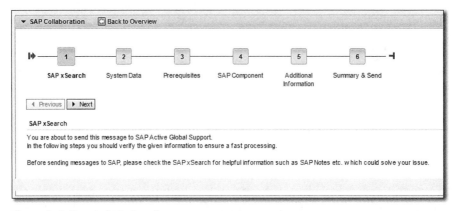

Figure 8.28 Step 1: SAP xSearch

Figure 8.29 shows the initial screen visible to users when the SAP xSearch functionality is launched. Although SAP xSearch isn't mandatory, it's recommended to leverage its search capabilities. After the search criteria are entered, a search is conducted over multiple resources (not just the repository of SAP Notes on the SAP Service Marketplace). In addition to SAP Notes, SAP xSearch uses the SAP Library and SAP Community Network (SCN) as resources.

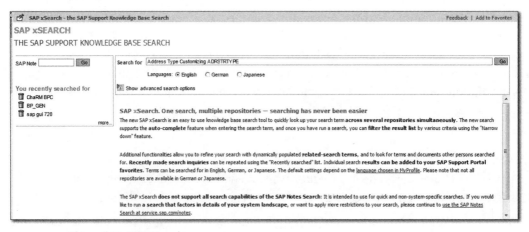

Figure 8.29 SAP xSearch

The objective and benefit of SAP xSearch is to fully exhaust all resources that may help provide a solution before creating a SAP Support message on the SAP Support backbone.

8.5.3 System Data

If no valid results are found from the SAP xSearch, you can continue along the guided procedure by clicking the NEXT button. The next step is to enter the system data as shown in Figure 8.30.

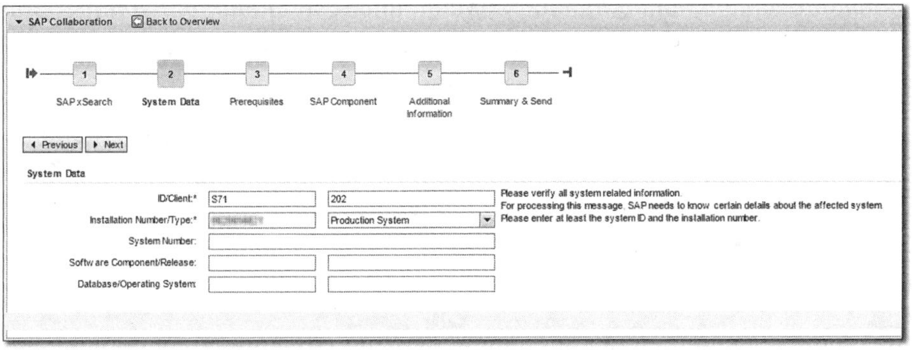

Figure 8.30 Step 2: System Data

In the SYSTEM DATA section, the following information is recorded:

▸ ID/CLIENT (mandatory entry)

▸ INSTALLATION NUMBER/TYPE (mandatory entry)

▸ SYSTEM NUMBER

▸ SOFTWARE COMPONENT/RELEASE

▸ DATABASE/OPERATING SYSTEM

Although the majority of the fields within SYSTEM DATA aren't required, we recommend that they are populated anyway. These values are very simple to find (look within the data of the SYSTEM DETAILS in the TEXT assignment block). More information is always better than less when forwarding support messages to the SAP Support backbone.

Click the NEXT button to advance the guided procedure to step 3, PREREQUISITES.

8.5.4 Prerequisites

The PREREQUISITES step in the guided procedure is offered midway through the process of sending an SAP Support message to the SAP Support backbone. It conducts a prerequisite check, before you get too far in the process, in regards to the following areas:

▶ Information validation

▶ Technical validation

As shown in Figure 8.31, if any information is missing (that is required by the previous step in the guided procedure), you'll be alerted on the leftmost side of the screen. As you can see in the figure, critical details are missing in regards to the installation number and the customer assignment of the installation number.

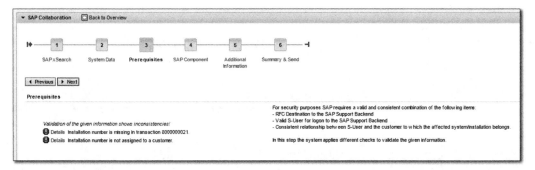

Figure 8.31 Step 3: Prerequisites

Technical details are also validated, as displayed on the rightmost side of the screen in Figure 8.31. There are several prerequisite checks that are performed to ensure that all technical requirements are satisfied. These technical details include the following:

▶ An RFC destination has been generated from the SAP Solution Manager system to the SAP Support backbone.

▶ A valid OSS user ID exists in SAP Solution Manager.

8.5.5 SAP Component

In step 4, you enter the SAP COMPONENT and PRIORITY values that the SAP Support message should be created as.

In SAP ITSM, the SAP Component functionality serves three important functions:

- Determining and dispatching messages to the appropriate support team
- Reporting and analytics (i.e., which SAP application areas are being affected)
- Forwarding SAP Support messages to the SAP Support backbone

SAP COMPONENT is a mandatory field when forwarding a message to SAP. SAP COMPONENT identifies, often down to the screen level, which area of the SAP application is affected.

Let's use a simple example related to SAP Solution Manager to describe the purpose of the SAP Component functionality at a high level. If a message is created with the SAP COMPONENT "SV-SMG-CM", it means an area of ChaRM has been affected.

The first two characters, "SV", identify that an area related to service is affected. The following three characters, "SMG", identify that an SAP Solution Manager component has been affected. Finally, "CM" identifies that ChaRM is affected.

When creating an SAP Support message related to ChaRM, it's always more beneficial to provide a more detailed SAP COMPONENT value. If the lowest level SAP COMPONENT value is provided, the correct service team within SAP Support will be forwarded the message much quicker. If we were to forward the message to SAP Support by simply entering "SV", there would be dialogue required back and forth between SAP and the service team to determine where in the SAP Support backbone the message should be dispatched to. This dialogue can take hours, or days, and can be avoided by entering a unique, detailed SAP COMPONENT value.

An easy way for the end user to provide the SAP COMPONENT value is by accessing the HELP • CREATE SUPPORT MESSAGE option directly within the SAP GUI application and screen in which the error occurred. As shown in Figure 8.32, the SAP COMPONENT value is provided automatically. The user can exit the CREATE MESSAGE window by clicking the CANCEL button ( ).

The SAP COMPONENT value can also be manually selected from a library of components directly within the field.

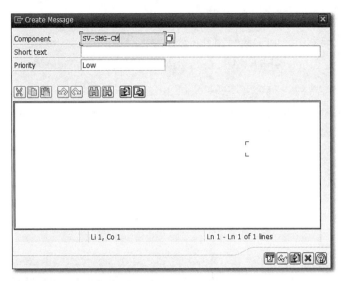

Figure 8.32 Identify the SAP Component

Figure 8.33 shows the step within the guided procedure for maintaining the SAP COMPONENT field. You'll also notice that the PRIORITY field must be maintained as well. Remember that these PRIORITY values are the same as if a message were to be created on the SAP Service Marketplace, so be sure to set them appropriately. If you maintain a value of HIGH or VERY HIGH, you'll also need to maintain the business impact/consequences.

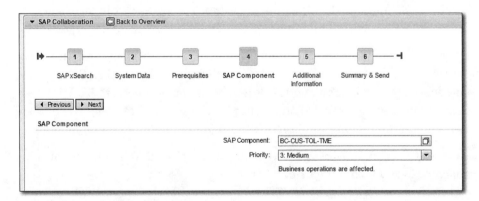

Figure 8.33 Step 4: SAP Component

Click the NEXT button to advance to the subsequent step.

8.5.6 Additional Information

In step 5, ADDITIONAL INFORMATION, you enter text that corresponds with the text type additional information. This information is typically copied from the DESCRIPTION text type by the service user forwarding the message to SAP. Because the description often communicates the description of the incident or problem, this text type is copied. SAP still requires that a unique text type, INFORMATION FOR SAP, be maintained prior to forwarding the message to SAP support.

Figure 8.34 identifies some information for SAP that has been entered as part of this step in the guided procedure.

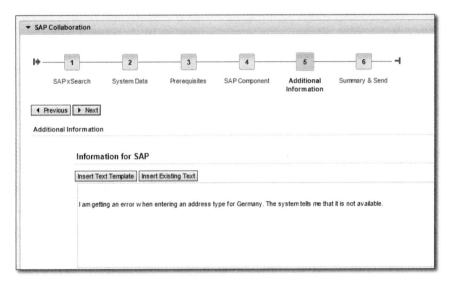

Figure 8.34 Step 5: Additional Information

As shown in Figure 8.35, you have the option for inserting a text template or inserting existing text when maintaining information for SAP.

Figure 8.35 Options to Maintain Information for SAP

Rather than manually copying and pasting the description as your information for SAP, you select it as shown in Figure 8.36. You reach this screen by clicking the INSERT EXISTING TEXT button as shown in Figure 8.35.

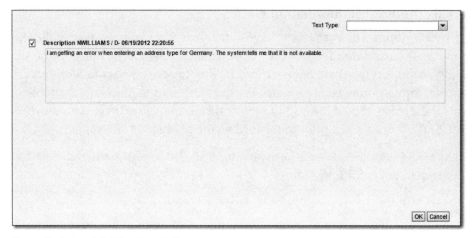

Figure 8.36 Insert Existing Description

Click the OK button to transfer this information.

8.5.7 Summary & Send

In the final step, SUMMARY & SEND, you review the information you've maintained before sending it to SAP. As shown in Figure 8.37, a summary is displayed along with warnings alerting you of what information is missing.

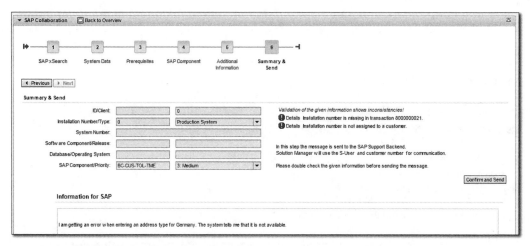

Figure 8.37 Step 6: Summary & Send

When you're satisfied with the information, and all mandatory alerts have been satisfied, clicking the CONFIRM AND SEND button will generate a message in the SAP Support backbone.

8.5.8   Additional Activities

After the message is generated in the SAP Support backbone, follow-up activities and communication with SAP are available. Usually administered in the SAP Service Marketplace, these activities are all integrated and available within the central SAP Solution Manager platform within each service message.

Via the MORE button, as shown in Figure 8.38, service team members have several options integrated within the incident that were once administered on the SAP Service Marketplace:

▶ DISPLAY SAP ACTION LOG

▶ MAINTAIN SAP LOGON DATA

▶ OPEN SYSTEM FOR SAP

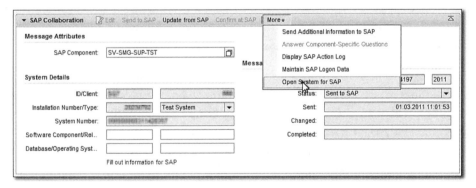

Figure 8.38 Open System for SAP

As shown in Figure 8.39 and Figure 8.40, you have the option to allow system access and open/change connections in the SERVICE CONNECTION OVERVIEW screen.

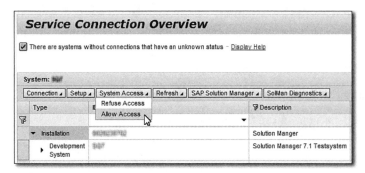

Figure 8.39 Service Connection: Allow Access

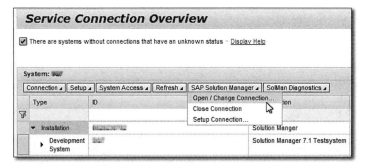

Figure 8.40 Service Connection: Open/Change Connection

SAP message details (e.g., message number, status, time stamps, etc.) are updated by SAP Support within the SAP COLLABORATION assignment block as shown in Figure 8.41. These entries will be automatically updated by SAP as they progress with the analysis, search, and dispatch process on their side. Additionally, SAP will update the text log with their replies. The UPDATE FROM SAP button will refresh the data SAP sends to SAP Solution Manager.

Clicking the CONFIRM AT SAP closes the message on the SAP side. The status in the SAP message details will change to CONFIRMED.

In addition to communicating with the SAP Support backbone, the IT organization can also integrate SAP Solution Manager with SAP Note administration. In the next section, we'll describe how AIM links directly to the SAP Service Marketplace and other components to administer SAP Notes.

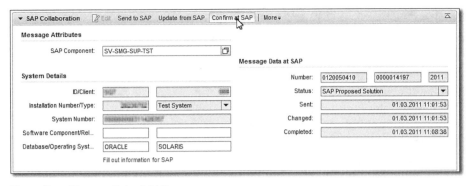

Figure 8.41 Message Data at SAP

8.6 SAP Notes

The SAP Notes assignment block allows both service teams and SAP Support to record and perform activities related to SAP Online Service and Support (OSS) Notes (we just refer to these as SAP Notes throughout the book). With this functionality, there is a direct technical connection to the SAP Service Marketplace to access the SAP Note database. Further, RFC connections enable the integration of SAP Solution Manager to the managed systems for the purposes of the direct application of SAP Notes.

Recording which SAP Notes are applicable to the incident, problem, or service request is beneficial in that it supports a thorough means of documenting how the error was resolved. If a similar incident, problem, or service request arises again, that particular SAP Note can be referenced. If an SAP Note was required to fix a bug, a record is kept directly within the message.

Figure 8.42 shows an SAP Note that has been recorded in this assignment block.

Actions	ID	Description	Details	Status
	1323591	Test plan administration: Test packages and status overview	Details	Status not available

Figure 8.42 Recorded SAP Note

The following sections identify how SAP Notes are logged within the service transaction as well as additional functionalities available for SAP Note administration.

8.6.1   SAP Note Search Options

In addition to supporting the complete documentation of a resolution, the SAP
NOTES assignment block offers added functionalities to support a more seamless
and efficient way of searching for and applying the SAP Notes. You can add SAP
Note numbers manually, or you can leverage the integrated search functions provided by SAP Solution Manager.

In Figure 8.43, the search for SAP Notes can be initiated in three ways, which
we'll discuss in the following subsections.

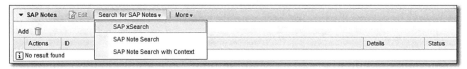

Figure 8.43 Search for SAP Notes Options

SAP xSearch

Launching the SAP xSEARCH browser will perform a search across the SAP Notes
database, SAP Library, and SCN resources. Refer to Section 8.5.2 for more information.

SAP Note Search

Selecting the option for the SAP NOTE SEARCH will open the classic browser on the
SAP Service Marketplace for finding SAP Notes as shown in Figure 8.44.

SAP Note Search with Content

Using the option to search the SAP NOTES WITH CONTENT will prepopulate the SAP
Notes search with content specific to your system. This option's search results are
narrower and more specific to the SAP Notes that are applicable to your system.
Figure 8.45 shows the SYSTEM DATA (although blurred out) area that will have content populated for a more specific SAP Note search.

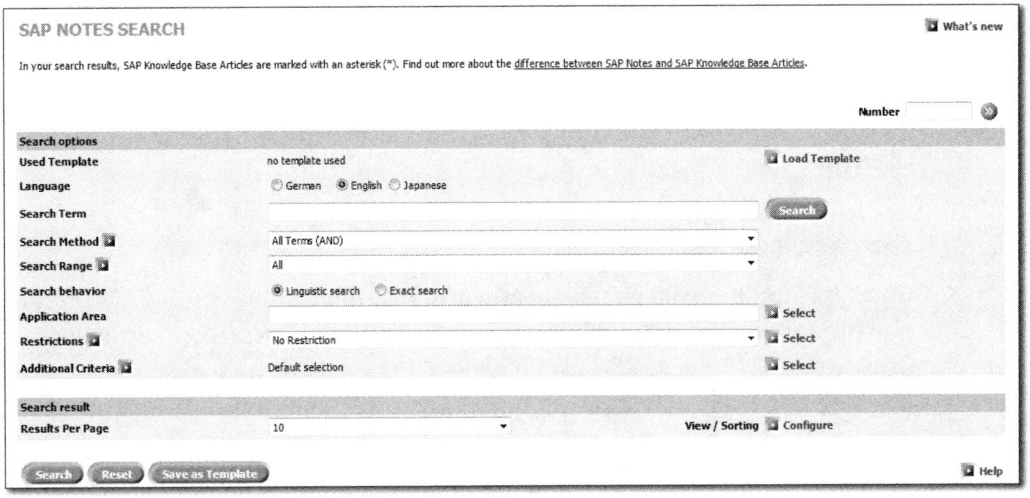

Figure 8.44 SAP Notes Search

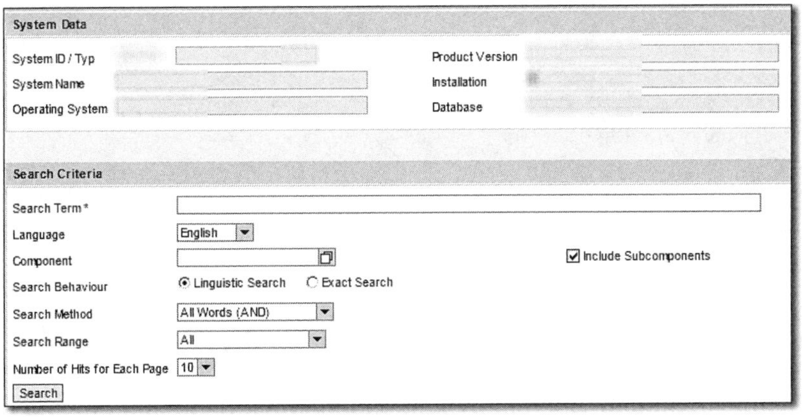

Figure 8.45 SAP Notes Search with Content

8.6.2 Integrated Capabilities

When you click the MORE button in the SAP NOTES assignment block, you're presented with two additional options for processing the SAP Notes. As shown in Figure 8.46, two tools can be called within the assignment block.

Figure 8.46 Integrated Capabilities

SAP Notes Assistant

Depending on the system and client you select, this option will launch Transaction SNOTE to perform SAP Note administration activities. These activities can include the execution or application of the SAP Note in the target system, processing status overview, downloading additional notes, and so on.

When you first select this option, a browser will open as shown in Figure 8.47. The system and client the SAP Note will be applied to in the target system will be entered in these fields.

Figure 8.47 SAP Note Browser Initial Screen

Afterwards, the NOTE ASSISTANT: NOTE BROWSER for that particular system will open as shown in Figure 8.48. The administrator can then proceed with the SAP Note maintenance and administration activities.

Note Assistant: Note Browser		
SAP Note Number		to
Application Component		to
Processing Status		
Implementation Status	Undefined Implement...	
Processors		
Selection		
Software component		
Release		
Sort Order		
⦿ Number		
○ Application Component		

Figure 8.48 SAP Note Browser

System Recommendations

SYSTEM RECOMMENDATIONS is a function of ChaRM that is integrated within AIM. You can perform the system recommendations activity to locate SAP Notes that are valid for a particular technical system. After these SAP Notes are located and identified, they can be downloaded to SAP Solution Manager and recorded within the service transaction. The integration with ChaRM assumes that you first create a request for change to perform the implementation of the SAP Note.

> **Note**
>
> Regarding system recommendations, SAP Notes that are applicable to ABAP can be downloaded and implemented with the SAP Note Assistant. Non-ABAP notes require that Java patches, which can be loaded, are confirmed in the Maintenance Optimizer.

Although the system recommendations functionality is tightly integrated within AIM, selecting the option to perform this activity will launch the user into the CHANGE MANAGEMENT work center as shown in Figure 8.49.

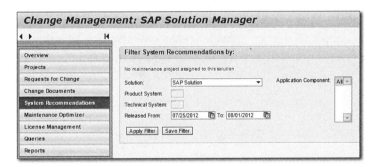

Figure 8.49 System Recommendations

Now that we've described the technical and SAP-related components that can be recorded within a service transaction, we'll discuss how documents and URLs can be recorded as well.

8.7 Attachments

In this section, we'll discuss how attachments, specifically documents and URLs, can be included within the message. Figure 8.50 shows the ATTACHMENTS assignment block without any entries. In this assignment block, you have the option to upload documents locally (i.e., from a hard drive) or link to existing documents that have been uploaded in other scenarios within SAP Solution Manager. Furthermore, URLs can be recorded if documents have been uploaded on a company intranet or Microsoft SharePoint server (for example).

Figure 8.50 Attachments Assignment Block

Adding Attachments and URLs

To add an attachment, click the ADD ATTACHMENT button (Attachment). The ATTACHMENT—WEBPAGE DIALOG screen will appear as shown in Figure 8.51. Within this screen, you have the option to search for a document or upload locally.

If you choose the option to search for a document, the search is conducted over the content server in SAP Solution Manager. In other words, the Knowledge Management Database (KMDB) is scanned to locate documents that fit your search criteria. For example, if you've uploaded a document to a SAP Solution Manager project in Transaction SOLAR01, it can be located and assigned to an incident.

The other option is to simply browse your local hard disk and upload a file.

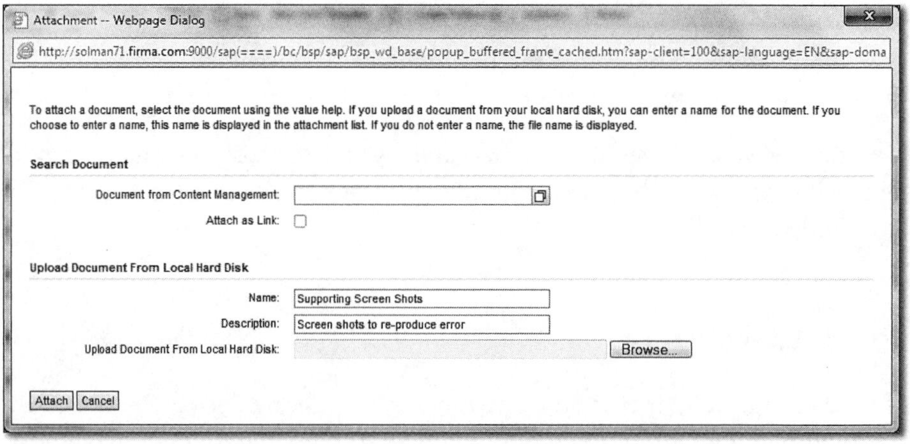

Figure 8.51 Add Attachment

You can also add URLs by selecting the NEW URL button within the assignment block. The NEW URL – WEBPAGE DIALOG screen will appear, as shown in Figure 8.52, where you maintain details about the URL.

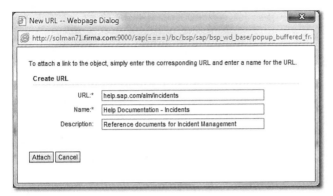

Figure 8.52 Add URL

Figure 8.53 shows an example of how the ATTACHMENTS assignment block will look after an attachment and URL have been uploaded.

Figure 8.53 Populated Attachments

Clicking the ADVANCED button within the assignment block will open a new window as shown in Figure 8.54. Advanced features regarding attachments include the following:

▶ Creating folders to organize the attachments

▶ Check in/checkout functionality

▶ Conducting a where-used list

▶ Viewing the various versions (any changes performed to the attachments are saved in versions)

In the next section, we'll discuss the checklist functionality, which supports the processing and completion of steps needed to fulfill service requests.

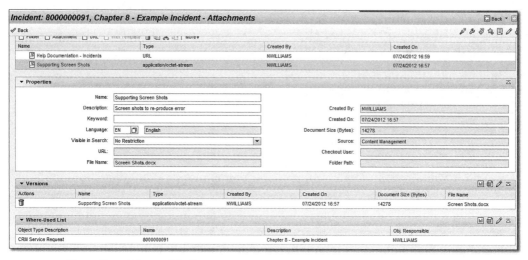

Figure 8.54 Advanced Options

8.8   Checklists

Checklists are used to fulfill all of the steps and activities required to complete a service request. While checklists can be used across ITSM service transactions, the functionality is most commonly deployed for the Service Request transaction type. This is because there are typically defined workflow steps that are assigned to different service request types.

For example, if an end-user requires that a printer be moved to their workstation, it would be classified as an IT Equipment Move. There would be specific steps that the technician (processor) assigned to this particular service request would need to take in order to fulfill that particular service. While a problem and incident requires more of a search, dispatch, and root cause analysis process that is difficult to define concrete steps for, service requests typically fall into specific categories which can be fulfilled by executing standard steps. Some additional examples would include:

▶ Reset password

▶ Report equipment theft

▶ Create user

Checklists can be automatically determined assigned to the service transaction according to rules set up by the SAP Solution Manager administrator. Since each checklist selection type (e.g., reset password, create user) will require different steps, rules can be set up to determine the checklists based on the checklist selection. This, in turn, determines the appropriate process flow and related workflow so that the appropriate message processors are determined.

With checklists, each step is defined for what action must be taken in order to process the service request. As shown in Figure 8.55, the sequential and parallel processing of the checklist activities are represented in graphical format beneath each of the individual checklist activities. Rules and workflow are configured by the SAP Solution Manager Administrator to define how the checklists will be determined as well as how the message processors will be informed that they have a workflow activity assigned to their user. This particular example shows the steps, partner functions, and process flow for an equipment move.

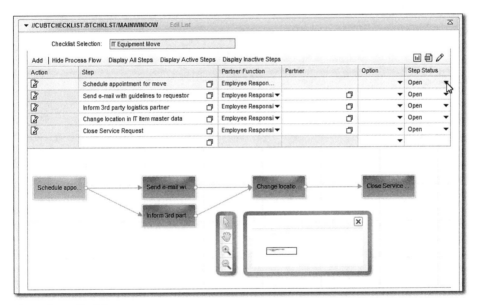

Figure 8.55 Checklist

Once a step is completed by a processor, SAP workflow integration is triggered to determine and inform the subsequent processor. As shown in Figure 8.56, the technician assigned to the next workflow step is informed on their ITSM homepage within the workflow tasks area.

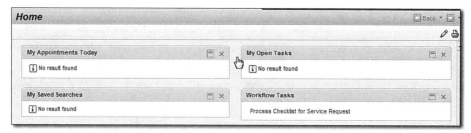

Figure 8.56 Find Workflow Task

Once the technician selects their workflow task, he will be able to view the work instructions in order to process the next step within the checklist. Figure 8.57 provides an example of a workflow task used to support the fulfillment of a service request.

Figure 8.57 Process Workflow Task

In the next section, we'll describe the concept of actions in SAP ITSM. We'll also explain how actions can be triggered, from both a process perspective and manually by IT service team members.

8.9 Scheduled Actions

Actions are preconfigured functions that are triggered to perform various activities in SAP Solution Manager. These actions are built in across each process step in AIM.

Actions are triggered automatically depending on a point in the processor they are executed manually from the ACTIONS button as shown in Figure 8.58. Even the actions triggered from the ACTIONS button are dependent on an exact point in the process because they are driven on which status is current.

Figure 8.58 Actions Button

A few examples of actions include an email being sent, a message being printed, or a status value being updated. There are different action profiles (sets of individual actions) depending on the transaction type. For example, ChaRM will have actions that are different from AIM actions.

In the SCHEDULED ACTIONS assignment block, you can see the processing status of each action that is triggered. Because actions are associated with conditions, they are preconfigured to trigger at various points in time depending on the action. For example, an email condition can state that an email action is only fired when the status is set from NEW to IN PROCESS.

Additionally, you can manually execute these individual actions from this assignment block if they are customized accordingly. All actions are available here, independent of which status is set.

Figure 8.59 shows the SCHEDULED ACTIONS assignment block. You can identify that the SLA ESCALATION action can be, if necessary, manually executed directly from within the assignment block.

Actions	Status	Action Definition	Processing Type	Created By	Status	Created On	Created At	Executable
		E-Mail to Reporter at S...	Mail	NWILLIAMS	Incorrect	07/24/2012	15:58	Done
		Print Message	Print	NWILLIAMS	Incorrect	07/24/2012	15:20	Done
Execute	△	SLA Escalation (MPT)	Mail	NWILLIAMS	Active	07/24/2012	13:42	No
		Start Delta Compilation	Method call	NWILLIAMS	Processed	07/24/2012	13:40	Done
		Start Delta Compilation	Method call	NWILLIAMS	Processed	07/24/2012	13:45	Done

Figure 8.59 Scheduled Actions Assignment Block

In the next section, we'll describe how each component and action with AIM is captured and documented. We'll explain how SAP Solution Manager provides a processing log to capture almost every detail throughout the process.

8.10 Processing Log

The PROCESSING LOG assignment block is the consolidated audit trail for all actions performed in AIM. While the text log provides a consolidated listing of all text types recorded, the processing log is the comprehensive list of everything that is maintained, performed, and recorded while processing the message. The following attributes are recorded as part of the audit capabilities in SAP Solution Manager:

▸ **Executed actions**
Activities triggered by the end user or service team member.

▸ **Attachments**
Documents or URLs that have been uploaded to the message.

▸ **Changed fields**
Fields on the message (e.g., software release, category).

▸ **Linked e-mails**
Email communications linked to the message.

▸ **Notes**
Data maintained within the TEXT assignment block.

▸ **Linked solutions**
Solutions that map to the message.

▸ **Status history**
Status values that have been updated.

▸ **Transaction history**
History of related transaction maintenance.

Figure 8.60 shows the processing log for STATUS HISTORY. The following processing details are recorded within the log:

▸ LOG TYPE
▸ LOG ACTION
▸ NEW VALUE
▸ OLD VALUE
▸ UPDATED BY
▸ UPDATED ON (date)
▸ UPDATED AT (time)

Figure 8.60 Processing Log Assignment Block

Next, we'll describe how a service message integrates with related transactions and how several related transactions can be documented and accessed.

8.11 Related Transactions

In Section 8.2.3 we described how document relationships can be linked within the DETAILS assignment block of the service message. After they are added as a relationship, a link is also established in the RELATED TRANSACTIONS assignment block as shown in Figure 8.61. The RELATED TRANSACTIONS assignment block will also be updated with links to service transaction types if they have been created as a follow-up. For example, if a problem has been created as a follow-up to an incident, it will be recorded as a related transaction.

Actions	Transaction ID	Transaction	Description	Category	Status	Priority	Transaction Type
🗑	8000000025	8000000025	Error When Entering Street Type	Incident, SAP application, Error message	Confirmed		Problem (IT Service Management)
🗑	8000000405	8000000405	I need a new adress type		Implemented	4: Low	Request for Change
🗑	7000000020	7000000020	Errors associated with address types	Incident, SAP application, Error message, ABAP Runtime Error	Draft	4: Low	Knowledge Article

Figure 8.61 Related Transactions Assignment Block

You can directly access the related transactions by clicking on the link within the TRANSACTION ID column. If there is a case in which more transactions are related to the same root case, more transactions can be added in this assignment block. Clicking the EDIT LIST button and the OPEN INPUT HELP button, as shown in Figure 8.62, will allow you to insert multiple related transactions.

If several of the same transaction types are added to a single incident (e.g., two problems are related to a single incident), the relationships will be updated as shown in Figure 8.63.

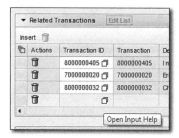

Figure 8.62 Manually Add Several Related Transactions

Figure 8.63 Multiple Related Transactions

8.12 Summary

If you've previously questioned the ability for SAP Solution Manager to serve as your organization's single platform to deliver SAP ITSM processes and disciplines, we hope that you are now starting to be convinced that the capability is at your fingertips. This chapter, while describing core features of AIM, merely scratches the surface of all of the capabilities available when processing incidents, problems, and service requests.

Although we still have more functions to discuss in Chapter 9 and Chapter 10 that are related to AIM, you should have a solid understanding of the value that SAP Solution Manager provides for driving these processes:

▸ Business roles that deliver predefined UIs to enable job-specific functions

▸ Standard functionality, aligned to ITIL standards, which is available out of the box

▸ Availability of components that can be tailored according to your organization's requirements

▸ Integration beyond the SAP managed system, into the SAP Support backbone

▸ Integration into other phases of ALM

- Ability to deliver SAP ITSM functions for non-SAP scenarios
- The ability to have a fully documented resolution processes, with full audit capability

Keep in mind that design considerations are key when rolling a tool out for SAP ITSM. Existing tools, legacy tools, and future scalability must be taken into consideration when designing a central platform for delivering IT services. Be sure to extend these discussions beyond strictly technical teams, as SAP ITSM spans the entire organization.

In the next chapter, we'll discuss more features available within AIM. Chapter 10 will provide an overview of some of the more significant features, which may require more effort in regards to design and configuration.

The scenarios within this chapter will help further your business case to deploy SAP Solution Manager as your single, central platform for Application Incident Management. SAP and ITIL best practices have been aligned to these scenarios to further enable a complete IT Service Management discipline.

9   Additional Features of Application Incident Management

Chapter 8 described the core features that are available when processing service transactions in SAP Solution Manager. Chapter 9 expands upon the capabilities provided to support an organization's Application Incident Management (AIM) scenario. The topics discussed in this chapter are larger scenarios in comparison to the features discussed in the previous chapter. These scenarios will help further your business case to deploy SAP Solution Manager as your single, central platform for AIM. SAP and ITIL best practices have been aligned to these scenarios to further enable a complete SAP IT Service Management (SAP ITSM) discipline.

First we'll discuss the option for message processors to capture the working time spent on incident and problems with the Time Recording feature.

9.1   Time Recording

In this section, we'll discuss the aspects of Time Recording in SAP Solution Manager to capture support efforts for AIM activities.

9.1.1   Overview

Time Recording is an optional function available for organizations who want to track working time per messages directly in SAP Solution Manager as an approach for tracking effort spent processing incidents. Time Recording allows support teams to record the time they spend throughout the lifecycle of messages directly within the transaction. Activities that are related to processing incidents are specifically defined based on your organization's requirements for tracking efforts.

Time Recording can be seamlessly integrated into a Service Desk solution that is already in production. In other words, it can be added at a later time without any impact on current AIM processes. This feature is easily configurable (see Chapter 10 for details), but it will take some design consideration on behalf of the IT organization to determine which metrics and activities should be captured to make best use of the features.

9.1.2 Factors of Time Recording

For the purposes of the Time Recording feature, there are three key factors that must be determined by the IT organization:

- Activity types
- Time recording reminders
- Initial TIME UNIT value

Let's go over each of these factors in the following subsections.

Activity Types

Activity types represent the different points (activities) against which time will be recorded. The SAP Solution Manager system doesn't provide any default activity types. Activity types are strictly a design consideration that must be determined by managers or above within the IT organization.

Activity types should support your current metrics or reporting/analytic strategy for how effort should be captured and calculated for AIM. If there is no current strategy in place to be transferred to the SAP Solution Manager system, the Time Recording feature can be leveraged as a driver to begin these discussions within your organization.

If time is recorded elsewhere (i.e., spreadsheets, third-party tools), a determination should occur for migrating the legacy time-recording processes into SAP Solution Manager. In other words, you must develop and deploy a strategy for how manual (or former) processes will be transitioned into SAP Solution Manager. Furthermore, you must determine how and if time/effort-related data will be migrated to SAP Solution Manager.

Like other configurations to enable AIM, it's recommended that the activity types are determined, agreed upon by all relevant parties, and only updated for critical circumstances. If these activity types are maintained on a regular basis, metrics and reporting/analytics will be uninterrupted.

Figure 9.1 and Figure 9.2 identify two basic examples of how activity types can be defined in SAP Solution Manager. Figure 9.1 is a representation of how activity types can be loosely defined. This particular example may be adopted by organizations that choose to capture and calculate time at a higher level.

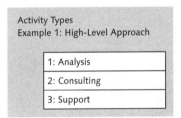

Figure 9.1 High-Level Approach for Activity Type Definition

Figure 9.2, on the other hand, shows how organizations may choose to capture and calculate time at a lower, more granular level of detail. The activity types in this example are based on ITIL activities for AIM.

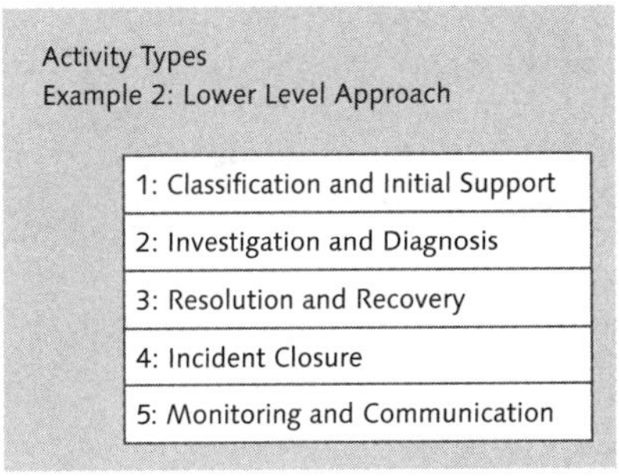

Activity Types
Example 2: Lower Level Approach

1: Classification and Initial Support

2: Investigation and Diagnosis

3: Resolution and Recovery

4: Incident Closure

5: Monitoring and Communication

Figure 9.2 Lower Level Approach for Activity Type Definition

In any event, the activity types you choose to define should be set up to support your requirements to logically record and report on the time spent to measure and support your organization's requirements.

Note
Activity types can be assigned according to business role. For example, the requirements to have Level 1 support team members record their time against different activities than Level 2 support team members can be satisfied by assigning different sets of activity types to different business roles.

Time Recording Reminders

The second factor when determining the strategy for your organization's Time Recording scenario is the time recording reminders. You can enable time recording reminders to remind or prompt message processors to enter their time, depending on how you configure this activity.

Table 9.1 provides a description for each option you have when selecting a time recording reminder.

Option	Time Recording Reminder	Description
1	Inactive	Time recording reminders are not triggered at any point throughout the processing of an incident or problem.
2	Active	Time recording reminders will be triggered every time the SAVE button is clicked within an incident or problem.
3	Active with Status Change	Time recording reminders will be triggered at any point in which the user status is changed within the message. For example, when the status is changed from NEW to IN PROCESS and the message is saved, a reminder will be triggered.

Table 9.1 Options for Time Recording Reminders

Figure 9.3 identifies the reminder in which a support team member will receive in the event that option 2 or option 3 from the preceding table are applicable to your organization's Time Recording strategy.

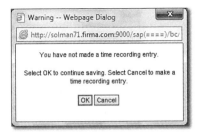

Figure 9.3 Time Recording Reminder

Initial Time Unit Value

Lastly, the initial TIME UNIT value is the final design consideration when establishing a Time Recording approach in SAP Solution Manager. Although this is a minor decision, it's a specification that will need to be accounted for to commence with configuring this scenario.

The initial time unit value is the value (i.e., minutes or hours) that will appear as the default for the message processors when capturing their effort within the incident or problem message. Figure 9.4 provides an example where the TIME UNIT value of MINUTE has been maintained as the initial value.

Figure 9.4 Initial Time Unit Value

9.1.3 Process to Record Time

In this section, we'll walk through the steps to record time for a message. In our example, we'll record working time based on ITIL standards against an incident. Keep in mind that you'll need to follow the configuration activities for time recording as explained in Chapter 10. Follow these steps to record time:

1. Within the incident, navigate to the TIME RECORDING assignment block.

2. Select the EDIT LIST button as shown in Figure 9.5.

   In edit mode, you'll see the ADD button appear as well as a number of different column headings/fields, as shown in Figure 9.6.

Figure 9.5 Select Edit List

Figure 9.6 Select the Add Button

Table 9.2 provides a description of each of the fields provided in the TIME RECORDING assignment block.

Column Name	Description
ACTIONS	Contains a TRASH button after an activity type has been maintained, which the message processor can use to delete the activity type
ACTIVITY TYPE	Specific activity (e.g., analysis, support, etc.) against which time is recorded
DESCRIPTION	Free form text field to provide descriptive text regarding the activity type
TIME SPENT	Free form text field to document the effort, minutes, or hours, spent on an individual activity type
TIME UNIT	Minutes or hours (default based on customized settings)
PROCESSOR	Business partner identification number of the message processor maintaining the activity type
PROCESSOR INFORMATION	General processor information based on data within the processor's business partner record (e.g., name, location, business partner ID)
CHANGED ON	Date in which the activity type was added or maintained (automatically defaults)
STARTED ON	Manual entry to identify when the specific activity type commenced

Table 9.2 Time Recording Standard Field Descriptions

3. Click the ADD button to add an activity type and corresponding details.

Message processors with the "support employee" authorization role have the option to display and update the time for messages that belong to them. However, they don't have this ability for time recording details for messages belonging to other message processors. The "administrator" role contains the authorizations necessary to view and record time regardless of the message processor.

4. Maintain the activity type and related information (e.g., DESCRIPTION, TIME SPENT, TIME UNIT, and STARTED ON date) as shown in Figure 9.7.

Actions	Activity Type	Description	Time Spent	Time Unit	Processor	Processor Information	Changed On	Started on
🗑	01 Classification and Initial Sup ▾	Initial analysis	20	Minute ▾	115	NWILLIAMS / D- (115)	09/04/2012 08:36:13	08/29/2012 00
🗑	02 Investigation and Diagnosis ▾	Reviewed notes and	1	Hour ▾	116	Winni Hesel / D- (116)	09/04/2012 08:36:13	08/29/2012 00
🗑	03 Resolution and Recovery ▾	Provided resolution b	15	Minute ▾	116	Winni Hesel / D- (116)	09/04/2012 08:36:13	08/31/2012 00
🗑	04 Incident Closure ▾	Updated status	5	Minute ▾	116	Winni Hesel / D- (116)	09/04/2012 08:36:13	09/03/2012 00
🗑	05 Monitoring and Communicat ▾	Clarification with use	10	Minute ▾	115	NWILLIAMS / D- (115)	09/04/2012 08:36:13	08/29/2012 00
🗑	05 Monitoring and Communicat ▾	Checked status and	20	Minute ▾	116	Winni Hesel / D- (116)	09/04/2012 08:36:13	08/31/2012 00
🗑	05 Monitoring and Communicat ▾	Notification that issue	5	Minute ▾	116	Winni Hesel / D- (116)	09/04/2012 08:36:13	09/04/2012 00

Figure 9.7 Enter Activity Type and Related Information

5. Click SAVE.

The time captured on the incident or problem message is recorded in Table CRMD_TIMEREP.

In the next section, we'll discuss the concepts of how Service Level Agreement time calculation is performed in SAP Solution Manager.

9.2 Service Level Management

In this section we'll introduce the concept of Service Level Management in SAP Solution Manager. Through this overview, you'll learn how this capability supports AIM, understand important terminology, and gain a basic understanding of the important concepts related to Service Level Management.

It's important to note that Service Level Management is a complex scenario within SAP Solution Manager. An entire book can be dedicated to the ins and outs of Service Level Agreements (SLAs) and all of the various use cases in which SAP Solution Manager supports. The objective of this section is to provide you with the knowledge needed to understand the functionality and make a determination if it should be deployed within your organization.

9.2.1 Overview

Service Level Management provides capabilities to manage and monitor SLAs at the incident message level. After these functions are activated and defined based on your requirements, the system can alert relevant stakeholders (e.g., message processors, managers, support teams, etc.) to inform them of service and response violations. These capabilities help enforce that incidents are handled according to contractually agreed-upon SLAs and that the business is receiving optimal, agreed-upon service from the IT organization.

Service Level Management is available out of the box, mostly preconfigured, from SAP Solution Manager. Given that you've performed the required post-installation steps within SOLMAN_SETUP, Service Level Management contains the bulk of the setup already delivered. Of course, SLAs vary from organization to organization so just like the majority of capabilities in SAP ITSM, you'll need to spend some time gathering or defining SLAs within SAP Solution Manager.

9.2.2 Key Concepts

Now, we'll begin to review some of the key concepts within Service Level Management.

Initial Response Time

The Initial Response Time (IRT) represents the calculated point in time in which the incident is first created (set to status NEW) and the first reaction by the message processor contracted in the SLA. The FIRST RESPONSE BY time stamp will clarify the point in time in which the processor must respond to the incident.

When the message processor begins the processing of the incident (i.e., sets the status to IN PROCESS), the incident is marked by the time stamp FIRST REACTION time stamp, which identifies when the message processor first reacted to the incident.

Figure 9.8 provides a graphical representation of how the IRT, FIRST REACTION time stamp, and status changes relate to one another.

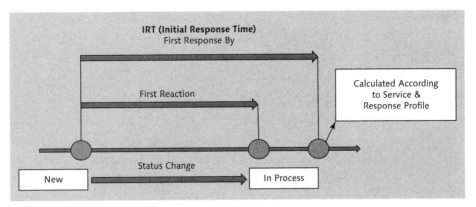

Figure 9.8 Initial Response Time

The IRT will be recalculated if the priority level of the incident is changed. This is based on a defined SLA and determined in Customizing.

Maximum Processing Time

Maximum Processing Time (MPT) refers to the calculated point in between the creation of the incident and the time at which it is closed or confirmed. In other words, the MPT represents the total processing time allowed for an incident based on the contractual details outlined in the customer's SLA.

The time stamp To Do By time stamp represents the MPT. The incident must be processed by this particular time stamp to meet the customer-defined SLA.

When the incident is closed (e.g., withdrawn or confirmed by the reporter), the incident is marked with the time stamp COMPLETED time stamp. This time stamp will identify the actual point in time in which the incident has been completed. Figure 9.9 provides a graphical representation of how the MPT, related time stamps, and status processing all relate to one another.

Similar to IRT, the MPT will be recalculated if the incident priority level changes.

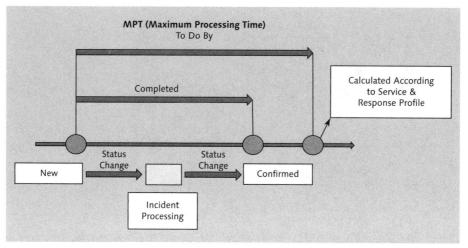

Figure 9.9 Maximum Processing Time

Service and Response Profile

The service profile within Service Level Management specifies the availability times for incident processing. SAP Solution Manager provides for any availability scenario required by an organization for incident processing, such as 5x8 (5 days per week, 8 hours per day) or 7x24 (7 days per week, 24 hours per day) availabilities, among numerous others. You may choose to deploy multiple service profiles for cases in which other purposes must be supported by Service Level Management, for example, single customers, IT items, or multiple service products.

The response profile is where the time allotted between first reaction (IRT) and service end (MPT) is specified. In the response profile, every incident priority is factored in to how this duration is measured. Like service profiles, SAP Solution Manager supports the creation of multiple response profiles. Various response profiles with different priority to duration dependencies offer support for realizing different scenarios.

9.2.3   Assignment Block Details

Details regarding SLA time information for an incident are available in three different areas within the SAP CRM Web UI. These areas are explained in the following subsections.

Details Assignment Block

The first area of the SAP CRM Web UI that displays SLA details is the DETAILS assignment block. IRT, MPT, and status information are displayed within the DATES section as shown in Figure 9.10.

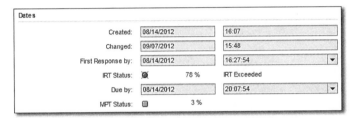

Figure 9.10 SLA Time Information: Details Assignment Block

The IRT and MPT status are displayed in a colored icon (green, yellow, or red), along with a percentage value to identify the status of each duration. This allows the message processor to have a quick, visual representation of the IRT and MPT information when first opening the incident.

The colored icons are defined as followed:

▶ **Green**
Indicates that the defined service time hasn't yet been reached, and agreed-upon SLA times are not affected.

▶ **Yellow**
Indicates a warning that the defined service time is close to reaching the agreed-upon SLA.

▶ **Red**
Indicates a service level violation and that a service time has been exceeded.

The coloring schema for IRT and MPT status can be customized if your organization defines warnings (for example) to occur for a different percentage value than that provided by SAP Solution Manager (see Chapter 10, Section 10.8.6).

Service Level Agreement Assignment Block

The SERVICE LEVEL AGREEMENT assignment block provides more detailed information regarding the SLA time data for an incident. As shown in Figure 9.11, the DATES AND DURATION section of this assignment block displays all SLA date/time information or all of the SLA durations. You're able to switch between these two sets of data by selecting the appropriate dropdown value in the DATE TYPES field.

You can also identify the SERVICE PROFILE and RESPONSE PROFILE, which are used to drive SLA time information for this particular incident, in the SERVICE LEVELS section of the assignment block.

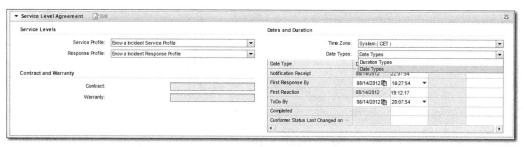

Figure 9.11 SLA Time Information: Service Level Agreement Assignment Block

> **Note**
>
> If the SERVICE LEVEL AGREEMENT assignment block isn't available in your SAP CRM Web UI within the incident, you can add it to the display by clicking the PERSONALIZE button (🖉) at the top-right of your screen and moving the SERVICE LEVEL AGREEMENT entry to the DISPLAYED ASSIGNMENT BLOCKS table.

Dates Assignment Block

Finally, the DATES assignment block is available to provide an even deeper level of detail when viewing SLA time information. The DATES assignment block provides the most comprehensive, detailed view of this data so that message processors or IT managers can analyze SLAs more closely.

As shown in Figure 9.12, this particular assignment block will display all SLA dates, times, and durations for the particular incident. If this assignment block isn't visible for your user, use the PERSONALIZE button to add it to your view. We'll explain more about the concept of dates in the following sections.

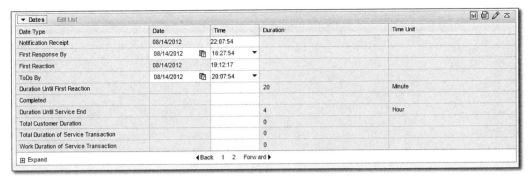

Date Type	Date	Time	Duration	Time Unit
Notification Receipt	08/14/2012	22:07:54		
First Response By	08/14/2012	16:27:54		
First Reaction	08/14/2012	19:12:17		
ToDo By	08/14/2012	20:07:54		
Duration Until First Reaction			20	Minute
Completed				
Duration Until Service End			4	Hour
Total Customer Duration			0	
Total Duration of Service Transaction			0	
Work Duration of Service Transaction			0	

Figure 9.12 SLA Time Information: Dates Assignment Block

9.2.4 Date Types

The date types identified in Figure 9.11 of the previous section are the exact points in time, or time stamps, that are measured when processing an incident. These time stamps and measurements are used to support the overall SLA determination, which rolls up into the summary percentages and statuses within the DETAILS assignment block.

Table 9.3 provides an overview of each of the date types used in SLA time calculation.

Date Type	Description
NOTIFICATION RECEIPT	► Time stamp that identifies when the incident is created by a reporter ► Represents the initialization of the service start ► Basis for all future SLA calculations
FIRST RESPONSE BY	► IRT that represents the calculated point in between the notification receipt and the first time the message processor reacts to it according to SLA contracted information ► Time stamp that clarifies the length of time the processor has, at maximum, to perform an initial reaction
FIRST REACTION	Time at which the message processor initially begins to process the message

Table 9.3 Date Types

Date Type	Description
TO DO BY	▸ MPT represents the calculated point from creation to confirmation according to SLA contracted information ▸ Time stamp that clarifies the length of time the processor has, at maximum, to confirm the message
COMPLETED	When the incident is confirmed or withdrawn by the reporter
CUSTOMER STATUS CHANGED	▸ Time stamp that is set each time the processor changes the status to a status that should not be calculated in the overall SLA calculation ▸ Represents when the incident is handed back to the reporter or third party and outside the message processors hands

Table 9.3 Date Types (Cont.)

9.2.5 Date Durations

In addition to the date type information displayed within the DATES assignment block, time periods identified as *date durations* are also provided. A date duration is a calculation of time specific to the contractual details developed as part of the overall Service Level Management definition. Table 9.4 provides an overview of the date durations used for calculating an SLA in SAP Solution Manager.

Date Duration	Description
DURATION UNTIL FIRST REACTION	▸ Period of time that represents the basis for IRT calculation ▸ Defined within the response profile and based upon incident priority
DURATION UNTIL SERVICE END	▸ Period of time that represents the basis for MPT calculation ▸ Defined within the response profile and based upon incident priority

Table 9.4 Date Durations

Date Duration	Description
TOTAL CUSTOMER DURATION	Period of time when an incident is assigned to the reporter (e.g., customer action, proposed solution, etc.)
TOTAL DURATION OF SERVICE TRANSACTION	Period of time that represents the entire processing of the incident message
WORK DURATION OF SERVICE TRANSACTION	Period of time that represents the entire working duration (i.e., less customer duration) of the incident message

Table 9.4 Date Durations (Cont.)

9.2.6 Calculating IRT and MPT

IRT and MPT are based on organizational (contractual) requirements for SLAs and defined in Customizing for service profiles and response profiles within the SAP Solution Manager IMG. Furthermore, the characteristics of the incident message (e.g., priority values) are defined in Customizing to support SLA time calculation.

Figure 9.13 provides the components that are involved in to calculating IRT and MPT. All of these parameters work together and therefore must be defined for Service Level Management features to work properly in your SAP ITSM scenario.

Incident Message	Service Profile	Response Profile
Notification Receipt ▸ Time stamp of incident creation for initializing the service start ▸ E.g., 2:00 p.m.	**Availability Times** ▸ Office hours of service availability for the incident ▸ E.g., Daily from 8:00 a.m. to 6:00 p.m.	**Duration Until First Reaction** ▸ Defines the duration until first reaction according to incident priority ▸ E.g., Priority 2 = 8 Hours
Priority Level ▸ Incident priority (Very High, High, Medium, Low) and change of incident priority during processing phase (re-calculation of IRT & MRT in case of priority change) ▸ E.g., 2 = High	**Off Time/Exceptions** ▸ Exceptions for service unavailability ▸ E.g., Daily from 6:00 p.m. to 8:00 a.m.	**Duration Until Service End** ▸ Defines the duration until service end according to incident priority ▸ E.g., Priority 2 = 14 Hours
Customer Time Status ▸ Incident status changes that do not affect SLA calculation ▸ E.g., Customer Action, Sent to SAP		

Figure 9.13 Calculating IRT and MPT: Key Parameters

IRT and MPT will be recalculated if one of the following parameters is maintained within the incident message:

▶ PRIORITY LEVEL (will recalculate IRT and MPT)

▶ CUSTOMER TIME STATUS (will recalculate MPT only)

In the next section, we'll cover the details and options related to dispatching messages to the support team along with automatic determination of business partners.

9.3 Dispatching Messages to the Support Team

The dispatching concept allows members of the support organization to access and assign service transactions. This section provides an overview of the functionality, concepts, and options for dispatching so that you can choose the method(s) of dispatching that suit your organization's requirements best.

9.3.1 Overview

Dispatching, in regards to SAP ITSM in SAP Solution Manager, is related to the access and assignment capabilities of service transactions. A synopsis of these two activities are as follows:

▶ **Access of service transactions**
Key master data setup activities (which we'll describe in Section 9.3.2) must be first enabled for message requesters and message processors to have access to the messages that concern them within the worklist. We provided a lot of this detail in Chapter 3, but for the purposes of discussing dispatching specifically, we'll touch on these settings again within this section.

▶ **Assignment of service transactions**
This activity occurs from one message processor to another or one support team to another, and it's based on rules defined by the SAP Solution Manager administrator. These rules, which are flexible and customizable based on your requirements, are provided if a message must be assigned to a different party to speed resolution. For example, if a Level 1 support team member can't resolve a message, the member can dispatch the message to a Level 2 support team member.

Depending on the option your organization adopts for dispatching, the rules will be configured in various manners. We'll describe these options in the following subsections.

9.3.2 Components for Rule Processing

For message dispatching to work properly, the following three core components must be maintained:

▸ Organizational model

▸ Rule definition

▸ Action definition

This section provides an overview of what must be designed and taken into consideration if you determine that message dispatching is a requirement for your SAP ITSM scenario. We'll describe the complete configuration steps and configuration use cases for enabling these components in Chapter 12.

Organizational Model

The SAP CRM organizational model is required to have a root organizational unit, support teams, positions, and business partners (employees) maintained. The organizational model (complete details and setup instructions are explained in Chapter 3) can be either reused from the HR organizational model defined in the SAP ERP system or manually set up specific to your SAP ITSM organization.

The organizational model is required because it maps the positional data and business partner information within the model to a particular user ID within the business partner master record. Together, these items allow the following basic activities to occur:

▸ Key users/requestors (customers) are able to create a service transaction to have it sent to the central SAP Solution Manager system.

▸ These users, in addition to support staff, are able to report/search for messages in the work list based on which team they are working within.

Figure 9.14 provides a graphical representation of how data within the business partner record directly correlates to the business partner details within the SAP CRM organizational mode. In this example, we're showing the support team correlation only. We'll describe how the users play a role in this setup in some of the following sections.

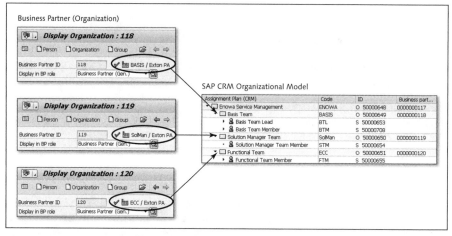

Figure 9.14 Support Team Setup for Message Dispatching

Figure 9.15 provides a closer look at how the SAP CRM organization model data integrates and maps to the data maintained within the business partner record. In the example shown in the figure, a user has been assigned to as BASIS TEAM MEMBER of the support team. For the support team mapping to work, the user's user master ID is maintained in the business partner information as well.

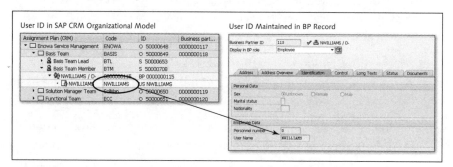

Figure 9.15 User Information in Organizational Model and Business Partner Record

Rule Definition

Next, depending on the options selected for dispatching (described in the next subsection), the rule(s) for message dispatching must be defined. Figure 9.16

provides an example of a completed rule definition. In this example, the organizational model is using the Business Rule Framework plus (which we'll refer to as BRF+) method for automatic dispatching. Specifically, this example represents how BRF+ can be used to automatically determine support teams based on the SAP component entered at the time the message was created. Chapter 10, Section 10.3.5 provides the end-to-end configuration steps to define the rule you see here.

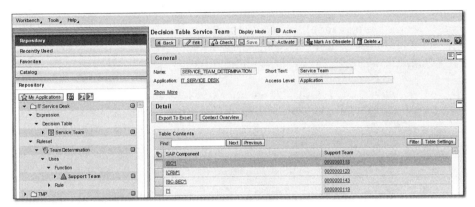

Figure 9.16 Rule Definition with BRF+

At the bottom of Figure 9.16, the table shows that messages will be dispatched based on placeholders in the SAP COMPONENT column as follows:

- [BC*]: Messages for Basis components will be dispatched to support team 118 (Basis Team).

- [CRM*]: Messages for SAP CRM components will be dispatched to support team 120 (Functional Team).

- [BC-SEC*]: Messages for security components will be dispatched to support team 143 (Security Team).

- [*]: All other messages will be dispatched to support team 119 (SAP Solution Manager team).

Action Definition

The last component that must be maintained is an action definition that provides the capability to automatically determine the support team. The actions that are relevant for support team determination within SAP ITSM are as follows (for incident transaction types):

- ▶ SMIN_STD_FIND_PARTNER_FDT

- ▶ SMIN_STD_FIND_TEAM_SEND_EMAIL

This Customizing activity is explained in Chapter 10, Section 10.3.7.

9.3.3 Options for Dispatching

As mentioned previously, several options are available when determining how your organization will adopt and deploy message dispatching. If you are familiar with SAP Solution Manager versions prior to version 7.1, you may already be aware of how dispatching is enabled within the system.

You may also be familiar with Transaction PFAC and the responsibility rules that were enabled to perform automatic dispatching. These methods are still available in the current release of SAP Solution Manager. However, the BRF+ workbench included as of version 7.1 offers a more robust and sophisticated way to control how messages are dispatched.

Table 9.5 provides a brief overview of the dispatching methods available, whether they are automated or manual, and to which release of SAP Solution Manager they are compatible with.

Method	Automatic/Manual	Description	Compatibility
BRF+	Automatic	Message dispatch based on rules defined in BRF+	SAP Solution Manager 7.1
SAP CRM standard dispatch	Manual	Message dispatch based on rule policies defined in the SAP CRM Web UI	SAP Solution Manager 7.1
Dispatch via responsibilities	Automatic	Message dispatch based on the responsibility rule AGS_ICT	SAP Solution Manager 7.0 and 7.1
SAP Solution Manager standard dispatch	Manual	Extended message dispatch based on the responsibility rule AGS_ICT	SAP Solution Manager 7.0 and 7.1

Table 9.5 Options for Message Dispatching

In the following subsections, we'll provide a brief description of the methods available for dispatching.

BRF+

The Business Rule Framework plus (BRF+) is a rule engine that enables users to set up process rules for different scenarios within SAP ITSM. Within AIM, you can deploy the BRF+ functionality to define rules that automatically determine support teams based on criteria such as the following:

▶ SAP component

▶ System identification number

▶ Multilevel categorization

▶ Client

▶ Region/country

For the Change Request Management (ChaRM) scenario, you can create different rules to automatically determine business partners specific to that particular SAP ITSM area. For example, depending on defined criteria, you can automatically enable specific change managers or change advisory boards to be determined within the request for change document.

The BRF+ rules engine became available for use in SAP Solution Manager as of SP01 of release 7.1. As we mentioned, BRF+ offers a more sophisticated, flexible, and robust way to set up the automatic determination of support teams and business partners.

> **Note**
>
> Although other methods of dispatching are available (described next), we recommend that BRF+ is leveraged by your organization when defining and setting up dispatching for your SAP ITSM scenarios. Chapter 12 provides a step-by-step configuration use-case scenario and related configuration steps to realize a BRF+ rules scenario.

SAP CRM Standard Dispatch

Because SAP Solution Manager uses SAP CRM for messaging capabilities, the standard SAP CRM dispatch infrastructure is also available. Rules for dispatching are enabled in the rule modeler. You can access the rule modeler within the SAP CRM Web UI by selecting SERVICE OPERATIONS • RULE POLICIES from the HOME screen.

Similar to the BRF+ dispatching capabilities, the SAP CRM standard dispatch method will determine support teams and business partners for both AIM and ChaRM.

However, unlike BRF+, the SAP CRM standard dispatch functionality isn't automatic. After the Customizing settings (IMG Activity ASSIGN DISPATCHING RULE PROFILE TO TRANSACTION TYPE) are activated, the DISPATCH option will appear within the service transaction type defined in Customizing as shown in Figure 9.17. Clicking this button within the message will trigger the rules defined in the rule modeler and make the appropriate determination.

Figure 9.17 SAP CRM Standard Dispatch

Dispatch via Responsibilities

Dispatching via responsibilities is the only other method, in addition to BRF+, for the automatic determination of support teams and business partners based on rules. With the rule 35000139 (AGS_ICT) in Transaction PFAC, you can define rules and subsequent responsibilities to enable the automatic determination of support teams and business partners.

Dispatch via responsibilities, as mentioned previously, was the method that most organizations leveraged in the previous (pre-7.1) versions of SAP Solution Manager. These responsibilities, while not intuitive to set up, provided a reliable and stable method to satisfy requirements relating to the determination of members in an IT organization.

While we recommend BRF+ as the method to enable dispatching, some organizations may choose to adopt the dispatch via responsibility methods out of familiarity with the setup activities.

SAP Solution Manager Standard Dispatch

The action definition SMIN_STD_MSG_DISPATCH (Automatic Forwarding of Messages) will forward the message to a different support team member based on the same rule as the previously described method. Rule AGS_ICT (35000139) subsequently deletes the current processor of the message and updates the user status defined in the corresponding parameter of the action.

This method for dispatching is manual, in that it must be triggered by a support team member within the action toolbar of the message. Figure 9.18 shows the option that becomes available when this action is activated.

Figure 9.18 SAP Solution Manager Standard Dispatch

Next, we'll provide an overview of the knowledge article functionality to support the overall development of a Knowledge Management Database in SAP Solution Manager.

9.4 Knowledge Articles

In this section, we'll discuss the concepts and related capabilities of knowledge articles as a mechanism to support Knowledge Management within SAP Solution Manager's SAP ITSM processes.

9.4.1 Overview

Knowledge articles are represented by a document/transaction type, KNAR, just the same way as the other messages within SAP ITSM are classified. Knowledge articles are the pieces of information that construct the concept of Knowledge Management within ITIL, as well as SAP Solution Manager.

Essentially, if the same problem occurs repeatedly, its solution should be documented and published to the organization for reference. This is a basic definition of Knowledge Management. Knowledge articles are the means for documenting and publishing solutions within SAP Solution Manager, and they are searchable by various members of the support organization.

Knowledge articles are a cross-function capability, meaning they can be used across SAP ITSM processes. They can be integrated throughout incidents, problems, service requests, and change documents to promote the distribution of knowledge throughout the IT service organization. The objective of this integration as well as distribution of knowledge is to have a single repository of data that represents solutions and follow-ups to related transaction types.

Lifecycle of a Knowledge Article

There are three main phases related to the lifecycle of a knowledge article:

▶ **Creation**
The creation of knowledge articles is the process of documenting solutions to issues that may occur across the IT infrastructure. During this phase, links are established to other message types and objects that are related to the content of the knowledge article. For example, a single knowledge article may be linked to other incidents, reference objects, or even other knowledge articles.

▶ **Classification**
The classification of a knowledge article includes the categorization of the knowledge article. Categorization helps support specific core capabilities of knowledge articles (described a bit later).

▶ **Provision**
The provisioning of knowledge articles involves the publishing of knowledge articles to key groups (e.g., Level 1 support staff, Level 2 support staff, etc.). At the time the knowledge article is provisioned, the user performing these actions will have the opportunity to determine how it will be used (suggested or searched) as well as deliver the solution via email.

Cross-Organizational Benefits

The development of Knowledge Management via knowledge articles aims to benefit all parties involved within the lifecycle of a service message. Message creators (requestors or customers), support staff, and IT Service Desk managers can create and search the database of knowledge articles rather than relying strictly on message processors.

By providing cross-organizational benefits, knowledge articles lessen the dependency and reliance on support staff to discover and provide a solution. While an end-to-end process exists for AIM, knowledge articles provide a means to advance the process more rapidly. For example, a customer who has display access to the knowledge database can search to see if a similar problem has been resolved, rather than generating a new record and having the message processor communicate the existing solution.

Figure 9.19 provides a graphical representation for how knowledge articles can serve various levels within the IT service organization. By supporting the use of knowledge articles, organizational knowledge trickles down to the customer level.

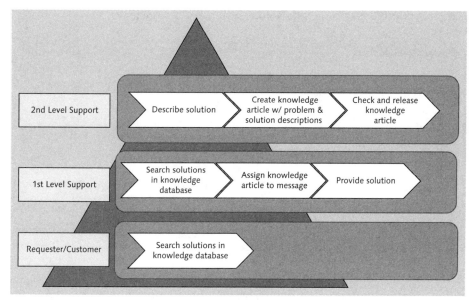

Figure 9.19 Cross-Organizational Knowledge Sharing

Enabling these capabilities throughout the organization will help keep the SAP ITSM organization running at a more efficient rate. For example, resolution time for existing (known) issues is reduced with a thoroughly documented and updated knowledge database. Furthermore, if the IT organization expands its staff, knowledge articles assist in transitioning new message processors into the organization. Training time for new support staff is minimized.

It's important to understand that this concept must be enforced and supported from leadership. Message processors should be trained on the process for creating knowledge articles (explained in the next section) and understand that they are key for enhancing organizational knowledge.

Creating a Knowledge Article

You can create a knowledge article in three key ways, which we'll discuss in the following subsections.

Create Knowledge Article from Scratch

Figure 9.20 displays the INCIDENT MANAGEMENT work center within the SAP CRM Web UI. From this screen, you can select the link for KNOWLEDGE ARTICLE in the CREATE section to create the knowledge article from scratch.

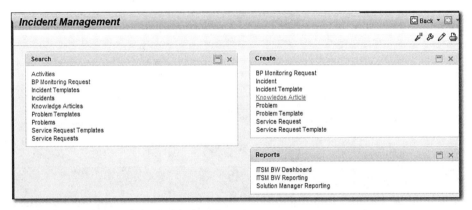

Figure 9.20 Create Knowledge Article from Scratch

After selecting this link, you'll be taken to the knowledge article UI where you can subsequently create, classify, and provision the knowledge article. The UI for the knowledge articles is explained in the next section.

Create Knowledge Article as a Follow-Up

If a service transaction already exists (e.g., a problem message exists for which a solution should be documented), you should create the knowledge article as a follow-up transaction type by following these steps:

1. Within the service transaction, click the CREATE FOLLOW-UP button as shown in Figure 9.21.

2. In the FOLLOW-UP – WEBPAGE DIALOG screen, select the transaction type KNAR with description KNOWLEDGE ARTICLE.

A new knowledge article will then open to which you can create, classify, and provision.

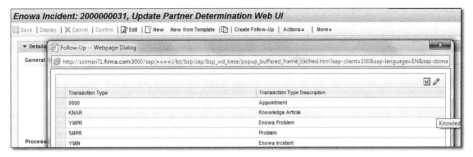

Figure 9.21 Select Knowledge Article as Follow-Up

Create Knowledge Article from a Template

You also have the option of predefining specific details of knowledge articles in the form of knowledge article templates for quicker creation of these documents. Similar to incident or problem templates, knowledge article templates can be leveraged if support staff notices that they are filling out the same details consistently when documenting their solutions.

Knowledge article templates are helpful in that message processors don't have to waste their time with filling out specific information (e.g., language, keywords, status, etc.) that is consistent across knowledge articles. To create a knowledge article based on a template, follow these steps:

1. Select the link from the Incident Management work center to create a knowledge article.

2. In the blank knowledge article that appears, click the NEW FROM TEMPLATE button as shown in Figure 9.22.

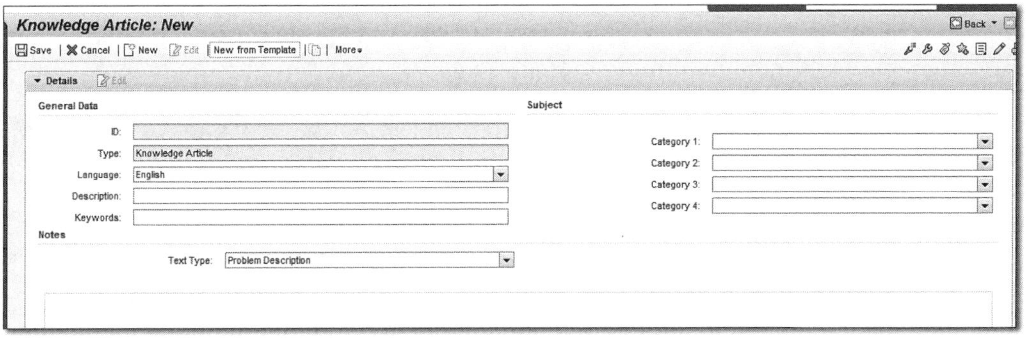

Figure 9.22 Create Knowledge Article from Template

Depending on the templates that you have predefined, you'll be able to select the template that most closely matches your criteria.

9.4.2 User Interface

The UI for knowledge articles is almost exactly the same as the UI for incidents, problems, and service requests. With the exception of fewer assignment blocks and the information captured within the standard assignment blocks, the UI for knowledge articles will look very familiar.

Figure 9.23 provides an image of the DETAILS assignment block within a knowledge article. As you can see, a categorization schema can be assigned to the knowledge article. Assigning categories provides the classification to the knowledge article that drives core capabilities (we'll explain those in the next section).

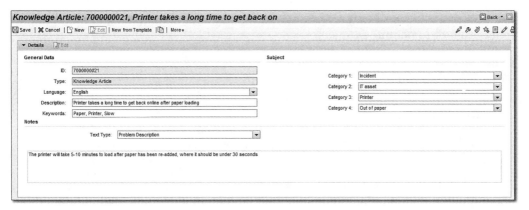

Figure 9.23 Details Assignment Block – Knowledge Article

In addition to a multilevel categorization block, Table 9.6 provides a brief description of the fields within the DETAILS assignment block.

Field	Description
LANGUAGE	To maintain a global SAP ITSM platform, SAP Solution Manager provides the capability to define knowledge articles in an array of languages. Localization is supported with this functionality.
DESCRIPTION	A short description to provide a brief overview of the knowledge article.

Table 9.6 Knowledge Article Details

Field	Description
KEYWORDS	Commonly acknowledged (i.e., obvious) words that relate to the solution within the knowledge article to support streamlined search capabilities.
TEXT TYPE	Classifies the type of knowledge article being created. The following text types are available standard from SAP Solution Manager: ▶ PROBLEM DESCRIPTION ▶ SOLUTION DESCRIPTION ▶ INTERNAL NOTE ▶ LOG
NOTES	Freeform text field to provide additional information, details, and notes in the form of a long description.

Table 9.6 Knowledge Article Details (Cont.)

Figure 9.24 provides an image of the remaining UI of a knowledge article, beyond the DETAILS assignment block.

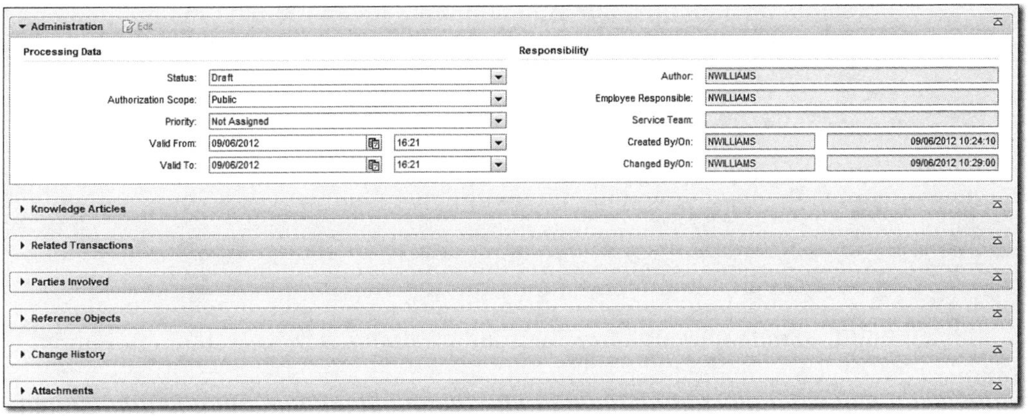

Figure 9.24 Additional Assignment Blocks in a Knowledge Article

Table 9.7 identifies as well as provides a brief overview of the contents of the remaining assignment blocks.

Assignment Block	Description
ADMINISTRATION	Contains processing data that drives the provisioning details of the knowledge article. Additionally, responsibilities are documented (author, owner, service team, and time stamps).
KNOWLEDGE ARTICLES	Enables the integration to other knowledge articles that are similar to the contents of the existing knowledge article.
RELATED TRANSACTIONS	Enables the integration to services messages across various SAP ITSM processes.
PARTIES INVOLVED	Provides the documentation for business partners that may have played a role in the development of the knowledge article.
REFERENCE OBJECTS	Provides a link to the installed base and component that relates to the knowledge article.
CHANGE HISTORY	Provides an audit trail to identify at which changes happened and when.
ATTACHMENTS	Facilities the ability to attach documents or URLs to support the complete documentation of the knowledge article.

Table 9.7 Knowledge Article Additional Assignment Blocks

9.4.3 Core Capabilities

In this section, we'll describe the core capabilities offered when leveraging knowledge articles to build up a KMDB within your IT organization. Specifically, we'll cover the following aspects pertaining to knowledge articles in the following subsections:

▸ Find knowledge article from existing message

▸ Knowledge article integration

▸ Auto-suggest knowledge articles

▸ Authorization scope

Find Knowledge Article from Existing Message

Knowledge articles that have previously been created and classified can be found from existing service transactions. For example, if a message processor (Level 1 or

2) is responding to a message, the processor will have the option to select MORE • FIND KNOWLEDGE ARTICLES from within the message, as shown in Figure 9.25.

If a knowledge article(s) matches certain defined characteristics (defined meaning it has been flagged in Customizing) of the message being processed, it will appear in a popup selection window for the message processor to review. At that point, the message processor can review the related knowledge articles to determine whether the solution helps in the resolution.

Figure 9.25 shows the MORE • FIND KNOWLEDGE ARTICLES option being selected within a service transaction. As you can see, the categorization schema of the incident matches the categorization schema of a previously classified knowledge article. The message processor can now review the contents of the knowledge article to determine if it relates to the incident currently being processed.

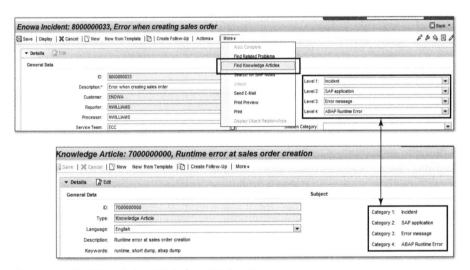

Figure 9.25 Find Knowledge Article from Existing Message

We mentioned that knowledge articles can be found based on various message characteristics. Specifically, if a message matches any one of the follow characteristics within a knowledge article, this capability can be used:

▶ CATEGORY

▶ REFERENCE OBJECT (i.e., IBASE/COMPONENT)

▶ ORG. DATA

▶ SOLD-TO PARTY

Note

To find knowledge articles based on any or all of these characteristics, you must have created an entry in the table within the IMG activity DEFINE SYSTEM PROPOSALS FOR RELATED TRANSACTIONS. A source and target transaction type must be maintained (e.g., source may be your customer incident, and target may be the standard knowledge article). Finally, you can select which of these characteristics will help drive this capability.

Knowledge Article Integration

We made mention of the KNOWLEDGE ARTICLES assignment block in Section 9.4.2. This assignment block allows for other related knowledge articles to be linked to the current knowledge article. As shown in Figure 9.26, you can integrate multiple related knowledge articles to support greater traceability and transparency for the entire KMDB. To do so, simply use the F4 help option within the ID column to pull up a search window to search for additional related knowledge articles.

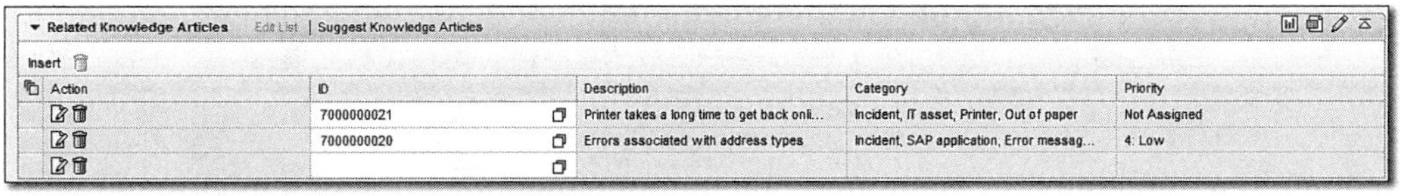

Figure 9.26 Knowledge Article Integration

Additionally, as shown in Figure 9.27, the SUGGEST KNOWLEDGE ARTICLE button is available to help you find related knowledge articles. This feature will propose knowledge articles that are assigned to a category in the categorization schema. The entire schema does not need to be maintained. This feature will suggest knowledge articles for which a single category entry has been defined.

Auto-Suggest Knowledge Articles

In addition to manually finding and suggesting related knowledge articles, you can define specific alerts and rules that will auto-suggest knowledge articles depending on the data entered within the message.

An alert must first be set up to automatically inform the message processor of specific knowledge articles that match the message's categorization specifics. After the alert has been triggered, the message processor will have the ability to review the list of suggested knowledge articles and associated details.

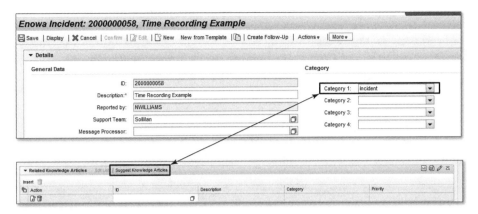

Figure 9.27 Suggest Knowledge Articles

This particular alert is created by executing the CREATE ALERT option within process modeling in the SAP CRM Web UI. Table 9.8 provides the technical details to create this agent.

Name	Description	Language	Navigation Object Type/ Action	Message
AUTOSUGGEST_ KAS	Auto-suggest knowledge articles	EN	Knowledge articles: search	[EVENT$AUTOSUGGEST-KAStart:NumberOfKA] Suggested Knowledge Articles

Table 9.8 Create Alert for Auto-Suggest Articles

A rule policy and set of rules must also be defined to complete this setup. The rule policy and two rules required can be set up in the CREATE RULE POLICY section of the PROCESS MODELING area within the SAP CRM Web UI. Table 9.9 provides the details to set up the rule policy.

Name	Description	Language	Context	Business Roles	IC Events
AUTOKAS	Auto-suggest knowledge articles	EN	Intent driven interaction	Your business role	AutoSuggestKAEnd and AutoSuggest-KAStart

Table 9.9 Create Rule Policy for Auto-Suggest Articles

Finally, two rules must be created. The parameters are defined in Table 9.10.

Name	Rule Definition
Show KA Alert	If Current Event Equals Auto Suggest Knowledge Article Start Then Trigger Alert (Alert Name = AUTO SUGGEST OF KNOWLEDGE ARTICLES; Time Delay (seconds) = "0")
Remove KA Alert	If Current Event Equals Auto Suggest Knowledge Article End Then Terminate Alert (Alert Name = AUTO SUGGEST OF KNOWLEDGE ARTICLES)

Table 9.10 Create Rules for Auto-Suggest Articles

Authorization Scope

This capability acts as an indicator to classify the knowledge articles by the use group/audience in which they are intended. The authorization scope determines which user groups can view the knowledge article. As shown in Figure 9.28, the authorization scope field has three values:

▶ PUBLIC

▶ INTERNAL

▶ CONFIDENTIAL

Figure 9.28 Authorization Scope

Refer to the IMG documentation related to knowledge articles for additional information and Customizing details for the authorization scope settings.

9.5   Summary

In this chapter, you've learned about some of the bigger scenarios that support the AIM processes within SAP Solution Manager. Some of the features described in this chapter are familiar to SAP Solution Manager's earlier versions and some have been made available with the latest support packages within release 7.1.

These scenarios promote SAP ITSM disciplines, enforce ITIL standards, and align with SAP practices. Of course, like any SAP ITSM function or scenario, they must be vetted across your IT organization. Support, enforcement, and decision making must first come from the top. A strategy and roadmap, for any adopted function, must be defined for these functions to fully benefit both the IT organization and the business.

In the next chapter, we'll discuss the functional configuration steps needed for AIM.

In this chapter, you'll learn how to enable both new and essential settings in AIM while understanding the business reasons and expected results.

10 Functional Configuration for Application Incident Management

The activities under the SAP IT Service Management (SAP ITSM) node in the SAP Solution Manager Reference IMG provide a sequential and well-documented roadmap for enabling the process and functional components of Application Incident Management (AIM). SOLMAN_SETUP provides the portal and status tracking capabilities that align with these IMG activities.

In this chapter, we describe, step by step, how to enable the most important and foundational settings for delivering AIM processes in SAP Solution Manager. This chapter will explain the core components necessary to realize the processes for incident, problem, and service request management. The components go beyond the basic requirements to make the vanilla processes work end to end. We'll describe the additional functionalities that enhance AIM and showcase its best-of-breed message abilities.

In addition to explaining the configuration concepts, you'll also find the business reason and expected results for each functionality.

We'll help you understand the two avenues in which configuration can commence:

▶ The guided procedure located in the SAP ITSM section of SOLMAN_SETUP

▶ Directly within the Implementation Guide (IMG) for SAP Solution Manager

While the more progressive and SAP-recommended method of enabling end user settings in AIM is via the guided procedures located within SOLMAN_SETUP, the intent of this chapter is to dive deep into the configuration aspects. For that reason, we'll introduce SOLMAN_SETUP as the portal for initiating configuration. However, when describing the step-by-step instructions to configure these functions, we'll speak from an IMG point of view. The objective of this is to provide you the most detailed, foundational, and comprehensive description of how these particular SAP ITSM processes are realized from SAP Solution Manager.

Whether you opt to leverage the latest functionalities delivered within the guided procedures of SOLMAN_SETUP or go with the traditional configuration methods of following the IMG activities, the content within this chapter is applicable.

10.1 Chapter Overview

We understand that configuration activities are some of the most sought-after pieces of information, especially regarding SAP Solution Manager. It's rare to find a one-stop shop that provides a single source for end-to-end configuration details within such an emerging topic as SAP ITSM. Understanding this point, we've put a great deal of emphasis, detail, and thoroughness on the configuration activities required to enable AIM in SAP Solution Manager. In the following sections, we'll describe a little more about how this chapter is structured, some basic assumptions and prerequisites that you should know about, and some general settings that are important before we get into the meat of functional configuration.

10.1.1 How This Chapter Is Structured

This chapter is intended to be a cut-to-the-chase and show-me-how-it's-done chapter. There are numerous other chapters that go into great detail about methodologies, disciplines, best practices, and informational details. This chapter, on the other hand, will get right into the details of how to enable the functional components within AIM.

While we have tried our best to be short on descriptions, we know it's important to provide structure around what and why you're configuring. For that reason, each configuration activity will include the following subsections, as described next.

Operational Use

The "Operational Use" section for each configuration activity will be more or less in the same context for each configuration. Sometimes, depending on the nature of the configuration, the operational use will vary slightly from activity to activity.

The operational use will briefly describe the function from a straightforward configuration point of view. For example, it may read as the IMG documentation does. Also, the Operational Use section will provide a description of the use case or configuration example we'll use to incorporate sample customer requirements.

The configuration examples, while taken from actual customer scenarios, should be considered as merely examples. You'll need to adapt the concepts and best practices for configuration described in this chapter to the requirements specific to your IT organization.

Configuration Activities

The "Configuration Activities" section of each activity describes, from an end-to-end perspective, how to enable the sample customer requirement/example from the Operational Use section in the SAP Solution Manager system.

Expected Result(s)

The "Expected Result(s)" section will be a quick and pointed reference of what end result should be expected if you have completed the configuration activities successfully. Most often, the expected results will be identified with a screenshot. Sometimes, a short description will provide you with the information needed to validate your configuration settings.

10.1.2 Assumptions

There are a few basic assumptions that we'll cover before you begin configuring AIM. While this chapter is straight to the point in regards to configuration, the previous setup tasks that we've described in other chapters won't be explained here. Furthermore, there are concepts referenced in previous chapters that we'll refer to. Lastly, we'll build upon some of the existing configuration and master data settings previously performed. To that end, it will be helpful to know we aren't exactly starting from scratch with these configuration activities.

The following subsections identify some key assumptions that should be taken into consideration before starting your configuration.

SOLMAN_SETUP

It's important that the guided procedures within SOLMAN_SETUP have been completed prior to the commencement of the functional configuration of the application incident. You must have completed the following sections of SOLMAN_SETUP:

► SYSTEM PREPARATION

► BASIC CONFIGURATION

► MANAGED SYSTEM CONFIGURATION

► IT SERVICE MANAGEMENT (APPLICATION INCIDENT MANAGEMENT)

Important!

The guided procedure for IT Service Management (Application Incident Management) also provides the ability to launch, track, and display documentation associated with the functional configuration areas described in this document. While we encourage you to follow the guided procedure for as many scenarios as possible in SAP Solution Manager, this chapter will explain configuration activities initiated directly from the IMG.

You may cross-reference the configuration activities here with those in SOLMAN_SETUP so you can have a central area to track processing status of each item.

We recommend that you perform any prerequisite checks or automatic configuration available within SOLMAN_SETUP for AIM. Examples include activation of services, background job generation, creation of service product hierarchy, and so on.

Transaction Copy

The Transaction Copy tool is used to automatically copy standard transaction types for AIM (i.e., incidents, problems, and service requests). Additionally, this tool copies all of the profiles associated with the transaction type, applies a customer namespace based on your specifications, and assigns them to the copied transaction type.

We highly recommend that you use the Transaction Copy tool on the AIM transactions prior to performing the configuration activities. The Transaction Copy tool is a step in the guided procedure within SOLMAN_SETUP. Alternatively, you can launch Transaction AI_CRM_CPY_PROCTYPE to reach the Transaction Copy tool.

The following profiles must be copied into a customer namespace (the configuration examples for both transaction and profiles will use the Y* namespace) and assigned to the corresponding transaction type:

▶ Text determination procedure

▶ Partner determination procedure

▶ Status profile

▶ Date profile

▶ Action profile

For purposes of demonstration and example, we'll primarily be using the SMIN incident transaction type for the configuration activities within this section. If you want to introduce these features into another service transaction type (e.g., problem or service request), you must repeat the steps to enable the functionality on the respective transaction type.

Important!

When adapting the standard Customizing, it's important to note that there are two transaction types that are defined as service requests (SRVR and SMRQ). For the purposes of SAP ITSM, the correct transaction type to implement is SMRQ.

Master Data

We highly recommend that you familiarize yourself with these concepts and prepare your SAP Solution Manager system with the master data settings as described in Chapter 3 because they are required for most of the configurations within this chapter.

Security

This chapter assumes that you have the administrator roles in SAP Solution Manager required to perform the various configuration activities described in this chapter. Moreover, it's assumed that the business role assigned to your administrator user allows sufficient authorization to access, maintain, and configure the SAP CRM Web UI screens per the examples within the following sections.

Now, let's get started! First, we'll begin by describing how to configure the functions within the partner determination procedure.

10.2   Partner Determination Procedure

In this section, we'll describe the configuration activities necessary to adapt the partner determination procedure to meet requirements based on sample use-case examples.

As with the other profiles assigned to the AIM transaction types, the partner determination procedure SMIN0001 should have been copied during SOLMAN_ SETUP activities into the customer namespace.

Throughout the following activities, we'll be adapting our customer partner determination procedure YMIN0001 to provide the use-case examples. In this section, we'll describe how to perform the following maintenance activities in regards to partner determination:

▸ Create a new partner function—IT Service Desk Manager.

▸ Assign the new partner function to the partner.

▸ Include the new partner to be in the SAP CRM Web UI.

▸ Specify partner function display in transactions.

▸ Use a standard access sequence to determine the reporter.

For the configuration activities and examples throughout this section, the large majority of the setup is maintained in the IMG within the PARTNER DETERMINATION PROCEDURE area as shown in Figure 10.1.

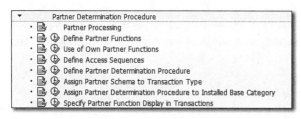

Figure 10.1 Partner Determination Procedure IMG Activities

When we go over adding a new partner function in the SAP CRM Web UI, we'll use the UI Configuration tool directly in the web client.

10.2.1 Create a New Partner Function

Partner functions (e.g., reported by, message processor, support team) are delivered standard with AIM. The partner functions are assigned to a partner determination procedure, which is specific to the SAP ITSM transaction that is being processed. In the case of incidents, problems, and service requests, one partner determination procedure is used (SMIN0001).

Operational Use

Often, organizations will have a requirement to rename a partner function (e.g., from "message processor" to "assigned to") or introduce a new partner function based on how their service organization is established.

In Customizing, both of these capabilities are possible in the DEFINE PARTNER FUNCTIONS IMG activity. In this section, we'll describe how to add a brand-new partner function, IT Service Desk Manager, in SAP Solution Manager to satisfy an organization's requirement to maintain an IT manager directly within the message.

Configuration Activities

Follow these steps to add a new partner function:

1. Execute the IMG activity DEFINE PARTNER FUNCTIONS.

2. Highlight the existing partner function SYSTEM ADMINISTRATOR, and click the COPY AS button (📋) shown in Figure 10.2.

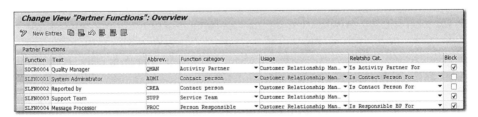

Figure 10.2 Copy Existing Partner Function

3. Maintain the following fields to make the new partner function specific to our example requirement as shown in Figure 10.3:

- ► Function: "YMIN0001"
- ► Text: "IT Service Desk Manager"
- ► Abbrev.: "SDMR"

Figure 10.3 Maintain New Partner Function Details

4. Click Save.

Expected Result(s)

The new partner function IT Service Desk Manager has been created and saved successfully in the Partner Functions table as described in the previous step.

10.2.2 Assign New Partner Function to Partner Determination Procedure

The steps we've just completed created a partner function in the SAP Solution Manager system. This activity defined a function in the overall "bucket" of partner functions across all service processing transaction types.

Operational Use

To make this partner function available for an SAP ITSM process, it must be assigned to the partner determination procedure assigned to the transaction type.

In the next section, we'll assign the new partner function IT Service Desk Manager to the partner determination procedure (YMIN0001). This partner determination procedure was automatically assigned to our incident transaction type (YMIN) when we performed the Transaction Copy tool activities.

Configuration Activities

Follow these steps to assign the new partner function to the partner determination procedure:

1. Execute IMG activity DEFINE PARTNER DETERMINATION PROCEDURE.

2. Highlight the procedure YMIN0001 as shown in Figure 10.4.

3. Double-click the PARTNER FUNCTIONS IN PROCEDURE folder in the dialog structure.

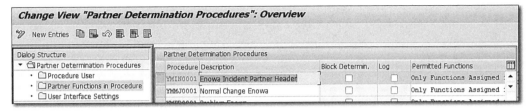

Figure 10.4 Select Partner Determination Procedure

Now, we'll copy an existing partner function from within the partner procedure
and update the details for the IT Service Desk Manager:

1. Highlight the function MESSAGE PROCESSOR as shown in Figure 10.5.

2. Click the COPY AS button.

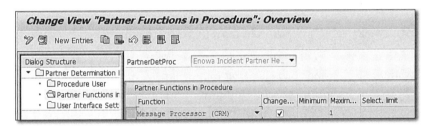

Figure 10.5 Copy Existing Partner Function in Procedure

3. In the CHANGE VIEW "PARTNER FUNCTIONS IN PROCEDURE": DETAILS OF SELECTED
   SET screen, select the new partner function IT SERVICE DESK MANAGER as shown
   in Figure 10.6. You may leave all other details related to the original partner.

Change View "Partner Functions in Procedure": Details of Selected Set

PartnerDetProc	Enowa Incident Partner Header ▼
Partner Function	IT Service Desk Manager (CRM) ▼

Figure 10.6 Update Partner Function

4. Press [Enter].

5. Click Save.

Expected Result(s)

The new partner function should be assigned to the partner determination procedure YMIN0001. To check the expected result, return to the screen to view the Partner Functions in Procedure table. You should now have an entry, along with the standard partners, for the IT Service Desk Manager (CRM) partner function as shown in Figure 10.7.

Partner Functions in Procedure					
Function		Change...	Minimum	Maxim...	Select. limit
Sold-To Party (CRM)	▼	☐		1	
System Administrator (CRM)	▼	☑		1	
Reported by (CRM)	▼	☐	1	1	
Support Team (CRM)	▼	☑		1	
Message Processor (CRM)	▼	☑		1	
IT Service Desk Manager (CRM)	▼	☑		1	

Figure 10.7 View New Partner Function Assigned to Procedure

10.2.3 Specify Partner Function Display in Transactions

Partner functions that have been included as copies from existing partner determinations should be checked to ensure that they will be displayed in the Details assignment block of each transaction. Typically, this is provided out of the box, however, sometimes you may see a partner function in the SAP CRM Web UI appear as a partner number as shown in Figure 10.8.

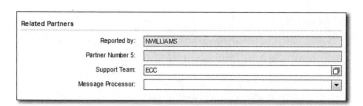

Related Partners	
Reported by:	NWILLIAMS
Partner Number 5:	
Support Team:	ECC
Message Processor:	▼

Figure 10.8 Partner Not Specified to Display in Transactions

Configuration Activities

Follow these steps to configure the partner functions within your Y* partner determination procedure so that they are visible within the Y* service transaction:

1. Execute IMG activity SPECIFY PARTNER FUNCTION DISPLAY IN TRANSACTIONS.

2. Highlight all of the S* entries for an AIM transaction type as shown in Figure 10.9.

> **Note**
>
> In this example, we're selecting all partner functions associated with the standard incident transaction type SMIN. You'll need to repeat this activity for all transaction types.

Change View "Business Partner User Interface Control": Overview

New Entries 🗋 🖫 ⬧ 🗐 🗐 🗐

Business Partner User Interface Control

Trans.Type	Procedure	Order	Function	Role Type	Object Relation Name	F4 Help	
SMHF	SMHF0001	8	▼ SDCD0005	Production Manager	▼ BTPartner_PFT_0005_MAIN	Search: Employee	▼
SMIN	SMIN0001	1	▼ 00000001	Sold-To Party	▼ BTPartner_PFT_0001_MAIN	Search: Sold-To P...	▼
SMIN	SMIN0001	2	▼ SLFN0002	Reported by	▼ BTPartner_PFT_0007_MAIN	Search: Contacts	▼
SMIN	SMIN0001	3	▼ SLFN0003	Support Team	▼ BTPartner_PFT_0016_MAIN	Search: Organizat...	▼
SMIN	SMIN0001	4	▼ SLFN0004	Message Processor	▼ BTPartner_PFT_0008_MAIN	Search: Employee	▼
SMIN	SMIN0001	5	▼ 00000015	Contact Person	▼ BTPartner_PFT_0007_ABBR_CP	Search: Contacts	▼
SMIN	SMIN0001	6	▼ SLFN0001	System Administrator	▼ BTPartner_PFT_0007_MAIN	Search: Employee	▼

Figure 10.9 Select Standard Partner Functions

3. Click the COPY AS button.

4. Replace all of the entries within the TRANS. TYPE and PROCEDURE column with your customer entries (e.g., YMIN and YMIN0001) as shown in Figure 10.10.

Business Partner User Interface Control

Trans.Type	Procedure	Order	Function	Role Type	Object Relation Name	F4 Help	
SMTM	SMTM0001	3	▼ SDCR0002	Change Manager	▼ BTPartner_PFT_0008_ABBR_CHMA	Search: Employee	▼
SMTM	SMTM0001	4	▼ SDCD0004	Current Processor	▼ BTPartner_PFT_0000_ABBR_CPRC	Search: Employee	▼
YMIN	YMIN0001	1	▼ 00000001	Sold-To Party	▼ BTPartner_PFT_0001_MAIN	Search: Sold-To P...	▼
YMIN	YMIN0001	2	▼ SLFN0002	Reported by	▼ BTPartner_PFT_0007_MAIN	Search: Contacts	▼
YMIN	YMIN0001	3	▼ SLFN0003	Support Team	▼ BTPartner_PFT_0016_MAIN	Search: Organizat...	▼
YMIN	YMIN0001	4	▼ SLFN0004	Message Processor	▼ BTPartner_PFT_0008_MAIN	Search: Employee	▼
YMIN	YMIN0001	5	▼ 00000015	Contact Person	▼ BTPartner_PFT_0007_ABBR_CP	Search: Contacts	▼

Figure 10.10 Change Copied Entries to Y* Entries

5. Click SAVE.

6. Create a new entry for your custom partner function (IT Service Desk Manager) as shown in Figure 10.11.

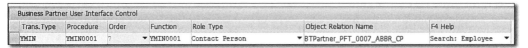

Business Partner User Interface Control						
Trans. Type	Procedure	Order	Function	Role Type	Object Relation Name	F4 Help
YMIN	YMIN0001	7	▼ YMIN0001	Contact Person	▼ BTPartner_PFT_0007_ABBR_CP	Search: Employee ▼

Figure 10.11 Create Interface Control Entry for New Partner Function

7. Click SAVE.

Expected Result(s)

The CONTACT PERSON field will now appear in the SAP CRM Web UI as shown in Figure 10.12, as opposed to PARTNER NUMBER 5.

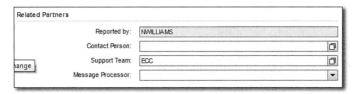

Related Partners

Reported by:	NWILLIAMS
Contact Person:	
Support Team:	ECC
Message Processor:	

hange

Figure 10.12 Partner Functions Displayed in SAP CRM Web UI

10.2.4 Maintain SAP CRM Web UI Settings for Partner Determination

Now that the new partner function is created and assigned to the appropriate partner determination procedure, we'll make settings in the SAP CRM Web UI so it's visible and useable within AIM.

Operational Use

Because the sold-to party partner function is based on our iBase component (Chapter 3), we'll hide this from the standard view and replace it with the new partner function. If you have configured a new partner function, chances are you will want to have this maintainable within the GENERAL DATA area of the incident. Certain partner functions may not be needed and therefore can be replaced by existing partner functions or new ones.

Configuration Activities

In this exercise, we'll walk you through the steps to remove a standard partner function from the GENERAL DATA area of the DETAILS assignment block. We will show you how to add in a new partner function. In this specific example, we'll add the new partner function we created in Section 10.2.1.

1. Access the SAP CRM Web UI with a role that supports UI configuration.
2. Create a new YMIN incident.
3. Click the SHOW CONFIGURABLE AREAS button (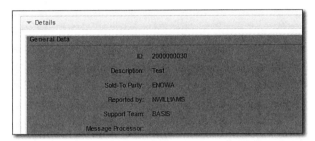).
4. Click somewhere within the DETAILS frame as shown in Figure 10.13.

Figure 10.13 Click Highlighted Area in the Details Frame to Start Configuration

5. Select a partner function (e.g., SOLD-TO PARTY) as shown in Figure 10.14.
6. Select the SHOW AVAILABLE FIELDS button.

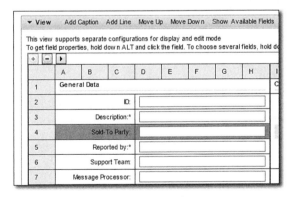

Figure 10.14 Show Available Fields for Partner Functions

7. Maintain any additional partner functions beneath the BTPARTNERSET node in the AVAILABLE FIELDS table as shown in Figure 10.15.

8. Highlight your new partner function, and select the ADD FIELD button.

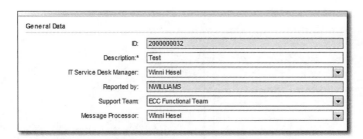

Figure 10.15 Add IT Service Desk Manager Partner Function

9. Use the REMOVE FIELD button to delete the SOLD-TO PARTY from the SAP CRM Web UI view.

10. Click the SAVE AND CLOSE button.

Expected Result(s)

As shown in Figure 10.16, the IT Service Desk Manager partner function will now be available for use in processing. Furthermore, we've removed the SOLD-TO PARTY field because it's automatically determined in the background based on the iBase component.

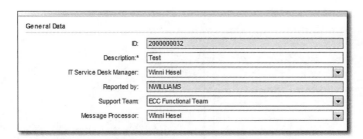

Figure 10.16 New Partner Function in the SAP CRM Web UI

In the next section, we'll discuss how you can enable the Business Rule Framework plus (BRF+) engine to automatically dispatch messages to support teams.

10.3   Support Team Determination

In this section, we'll describe the configuration activities necessary to automatically determine which support team the message should be routed to at the time the requester saves the message. Throughout the following subsections, we'll walk through a use-case scenario for how to use the Business Rule Framework plus (BRF+) rule engine to automatically determine a support team based on the SAP component.

BRF+ is a powerful rule engine that allows users to set up, test, and process rules for various business scenarios to enable determination of objects. The infrastructure of BRF+ includes a vast array of configuration elements such as decision trees, decision tables, value ranges, formulas, and functional cells. The complexity of these computation elements enable organizations to deliver flexible requirements associated with business rules.

Although BRF+ isn't specific to SAP Solution Manager (business rules are commonly required in the managed SAP ERP landscape), the rule engine is included as part of SAP Solution Manager's infrastructure to enable determination rules in SAP ITSM scenarios.

In Incident Management, BRF+ can be enabled (as we'll describe throughout the following sections) to define rules for support team determination. Criteria such as SAP component, system ID, country, and so on can be used to automatically route a message to the support team at message creation. In Change Request Management (ChaRM), BRF+ can enable the automatic determination of business partners. Common requirements in this scenario include the determination of change manager or Change Advisory Board (CAB).

While you still can enable dispatching via Transaction PFAC rules, we recommend using the BRF+ framework as it provides the most robust, flexible, and intuitive method to enable determination of business partners.

10.3.1   Configuration Overview

Configuring the BRF+ rule engine occurs in the SAP CRM Web UI by launching Transaction BRFPLUS from the GUI. Figure 10.17 provides a high-level overview of the configuration process to enable support team determination based on computational elements configured in BRF+.

> **Note**
>
> In this chapter, we'll provide the step-by-step instructions to achieve the configuration steps in boxes ❷ and ❸. A prerequisite to these configurations is to create an organization model with a root, support teams, positions, and assigned business partners. Refer to Chapter 3 for these steps as we're building on the data in that chapter for the BRF+ activities.

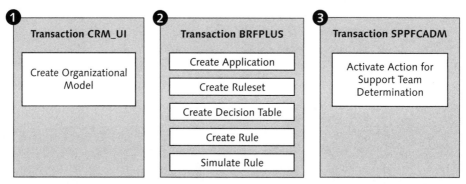

Figure 10.17 Configuration Overview: BRF+

10.3.2 Create Application in the Business Rules Framework

In step one of configuring BRF+, you create an application, which is the highest node (i.e., root) in the structure of BRF+. Throughout the next sections, we'll be creating subnodes that are required to use BRF+ (e.g., expressions, rulesets, etc.).

Configuration Activities

Follow these steps to complete the first step of configuring BRF+:

1. Choose WORKBENCH • CREATE APPLICATION as shown in Figure 10.18.

Figure 10.18 Create Application

2. In the CREATE APPLICATION screen, fill in the following fields in the GENERAL DATA area as shown in Figure 10.19:

- ▶ NAME
- ▶ SHORT TEXT
- ▶ TEXT

The fields in the APPLICATION area should be confirmed as well.

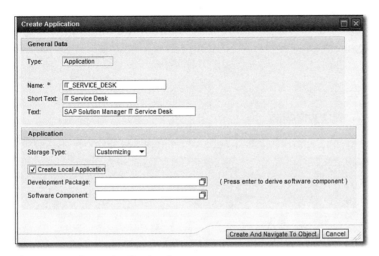

Figure 10.19 Create Application Screen

3. Click the CREATE AND NAVIGATE TO OBJECT button to continue. When you return to the BRF+ main screen, it should appear as shown in Figure 10.20.

4. Click the ACTIVATE button to activate the application.

Figure 10.20 Created Application

Expected Result(s)

Your application, once activated, will be represented with a green ACTIVE icon as shown in Figure 10.21.

Figure 10.21 Activated Application

10.3.3 Create the Ruleset

A ruleset is a container that facilitates the collection of various rules that are required to process an action.

Configuration Activities

To create the ruleset, follow these steps:

1. In the main hierarchy, right-click the root node (e.g., IT SERVICE DESK), as shown in Figure 10.22.

2. Select CREATE • RULESET.

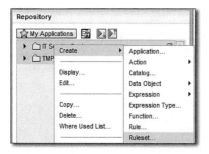

Figure 10.22 Create Ruleset from Root Node

3. In the CREATE RULESET window, maintain the following fields as shown in Figure 10.23:

   ▸ NAME

   ▸ SHORT TEXT

   ▸ TEXT

4. Select the CREATE button. The new ruleset will appear in the hierarchy on the left side of the BRF+ screen as shown in Figure 10.24.

5. Select the ruleset (e.g., TEAM DETERMINATION).

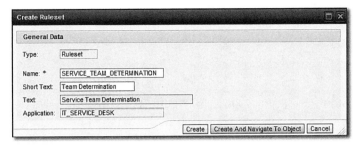

Figure 10.23 Create Ruleset

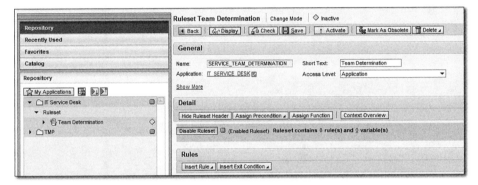

Figure 10.24 BRF+ Screen with Created Ruleset

6. Click the EDIT button so that you're in change mode.

7. Click the ASSIGN FUNCTION button.

8. In the OBJECT QUERY screen, override the contents in the APPLICATION field with the value "SOLMAN" as shown in Figure 10.25.

9. Click the SEARCH button.

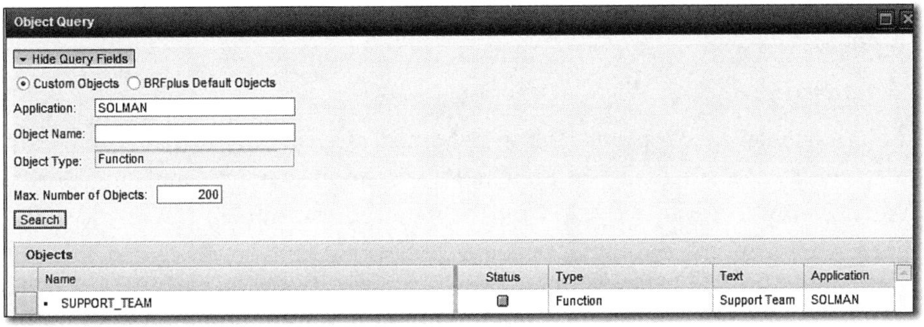

Objects					
Name		Status	Type	Text	Application
• SUPPORT_TEAM			Function	Support Team	SOLMAN

Figure 10.25 Maintain Object Query Details

10. Click the SUPPORT_TEAM entry.

11. Click Save in the main BRF+ screen.

Expected Result(s)

The ruleset will be created and saved as shown in Figure 10.26. Don't activate the ruleset at this point as there are additional configurations required before doing so.

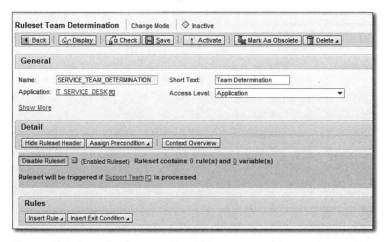

Figure 10.26 Created Ruleset Team Determination

10.3.4 Create the Decision Table

Decision tables are made up of condition and result columns. These two columns are processed sequentially. If all of the conditions are met, the corresponding result values are returned.

Operational Use

In our example, the decision table will be processed in single match mode. In other words, the processing of the columns is stopped immediately at the first matching row. Because a single result is required to return a result, the single match mode works great for support team determination.

Configuration Activities

Follow these steps to create the decision table:

1. Right-click the root of the hierarchy, and select CREATE • EXPRESSION • DECISION TABLE, as shown in Figure 10.27.

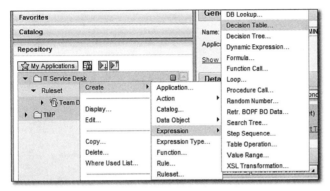

Figure 10.27 Create Decision Table

2. Mark the IS REUSABLE flag, and maintain the following fields in the CREATE DECISION TABLE window as shown in Figure 10.28:

   ▶ NAME

   ▶ SHORT TEXT

   ▶ TEXT

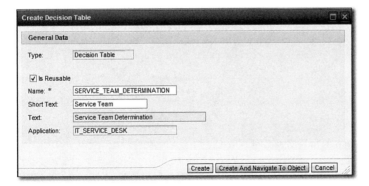

Figure 10.28 Create Decision Table

3. Click the CREATE button.

4. Click SAVE in the main BRF+ screen. The decision table will appear in the structure on the left side of the screen as shown in Figure 10.29.

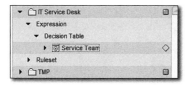

Figure 10.29 Created Decision Table

5. Select the SERVICE TEAM decision table as shown in Figure 10.30.

6. Select the EDIT button so that you're in change mode.

7. Select the TABLE SETTINGS button.

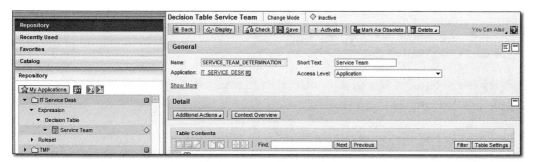

Figure 10.30 Service Team Details

8. In the CONDITION COLUMNS area, right-click on the INSERT COLUMN button, and choose the option FROM CONTEXT DATA OBJECTS as shown in Figure 10.31.

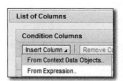

Figure 10.31 Choose Column from Context Data Objects

9. In the resulting CONTEXT QUERY screen, overwrite APPLICATION field contents with the value SOLMAN as shown in Figure 10.32.

10. Click SEARCH.

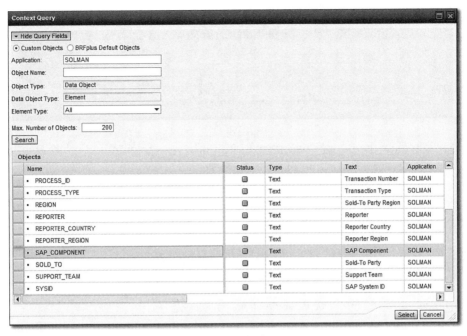

Figure 10.32 Enter value SOLMAN in Application Field

11. Select the SAP_COMPONENT parameter.

12. Click the SELECT button.

> **Note**
>
> Perform these same steps for the RESULT COLUMNS area of the screen. Instead of selecting SAP_COMPONENT, you'll select SUPPORT_TEAM. When you're finished, the results will appear as shown in Figure 10.33.

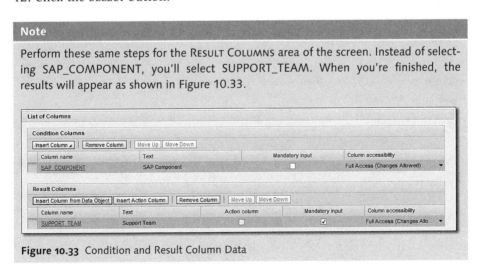

Figure 10.33 Condition and Result Column Data

13. Click OK.

14. In the decision table, select the button INSERT NEW ROW as shown in Figure 10.34.

Figure 10.34 Insert New Row

15. Right-click the button in the SAP COMPONENT column and select DIRECT VALUE INPUT as shown in Figure 10.35.

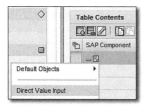

Figure 10.35 Insert Direct Value Input (SAP Component)

16. Select the MATCHES PATTERN option from the drop-down list, and enter the value "BC*" in the field on the right as shown in Figure 10.36.

Figure 10.36 Maintain SAP Component

17. Click OK.

> **Note**
>
> In this example, we're describing how to create a decision table that will enable the determination of the service teams in our organizational model. BC is the highest-level SAP component for Basis, so whenever a message is created from a BC application, the Basis support team will be determined.
>
> The * identifies that this logic will ensure all BC components selected will be routed to the Basis team.

18. In the SUPPORT TEAM column, right-click the ▣ button, and choose the value DIRECT VALUE INPUT as shown in Figure 10.37.

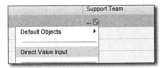

Figure 10.37 Insert Direct Value Input (Support Team)

19. Enter the business partner ID for the service team that should handle all of the BC components as shown in Figure 10.38.

Figure 10.38 Enter Business Partner ID

Tips & Tricks

You'll now need to repeat these steps to set up the decision table for your remaining service teams. Figure 10.39 is an example of a completed decision table with four SAP COMPONENT and SUPPORT TEAM correlations.

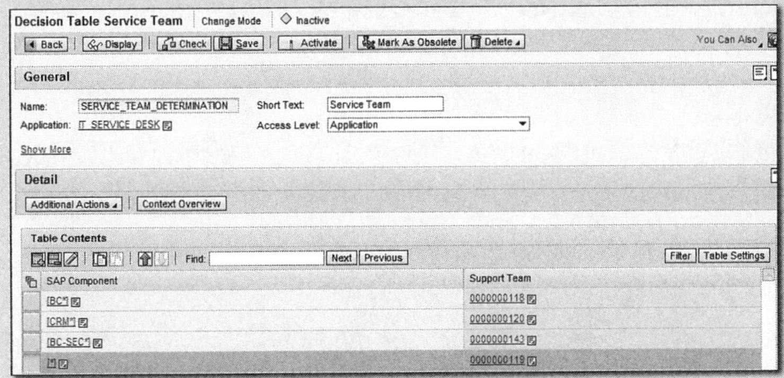

Decision Table Service Team	Change Mode	◇ Inactive

SAP Component	Support Team
[BC*] ▣	0000000118 ▣
[CRM*] ▣	0000000120 ▣
[BC-SEC*] ▣	0000000143 ▣
[*] ▣	0000000119 ▣

Figure 10.39 Completed Decision Table with All Support Teams

The * entry will be assigned to your SAP Solution Manager team as a catch-all rule. In other words, if a message is created outside of these components, the message will still be routed to a service team.

20. Choose the ACTIVATE button.

Expected Result(s)

After you've completed the decision table and activated it, the main BRF+ screen should appear as shown in Figure 10.40. Note the green ACTIVE flag identifying that this step is complete.

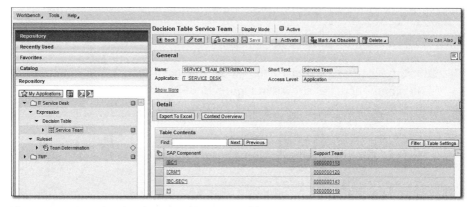

Figure 10.40 Completed and Activated Decision Table

10.3.5 Create the Rule

Now that the ruleset (container and parent node) and the decision table (conditions for how the rule should be triggered) are established, we can create the rule to process the decision table.

Configuration Activities

To create the rule, follow these steps:

1. In the main BRF+ screen, select the TEAM DETERMINATION structure node in the hierarchy as shown in Figure 10.41.

2. Click the EDIT button so that you're in change mode.

3. In the RULES area, select INSERT RULE • CREATE.

4. In the RULE window, enter text in the DESCRIPTION field as shown in the example in Figure 10.42.

5. For the THEN option, select ADD • PROCESS EXPRESSION • SERVICE TEAM as shown in Figure 10.42.

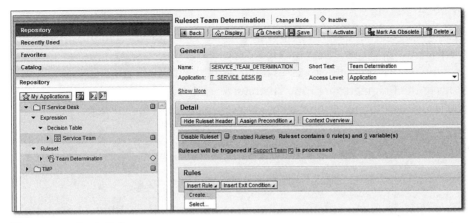

Figure 10.41 Create Rule

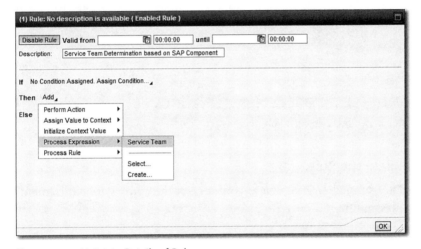

Figure 10.42 Maintain Details of Rule

6. Select the OK button. Now that the rule is created, you can activate the RULESET TEAM DETERMINATION.

7. Select the ACTIVATE button shown in Figure 10.43.

Figure 10.43 Activate Ruleset Team Determination

Expected Result(s)

When you've completed the steps to create the rule and activate the ruleset, your results will appear as shown in Figure 10.44. The RULES section of the screen is identifying that this rule processes the rows of the decision table sequentially and stops at the first matching row. The return value (support team business partner ID) is assigned to the support team partner function of the message.

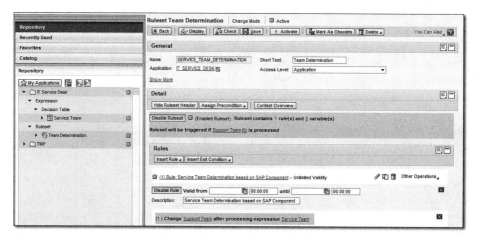

Figure 10.44 Completed and Activated Rule and Ruleset

10.3.6 Simulate the Rule

BRF+ provides a simulation tool where you can test the computational elements within the rules engine.

Operational Use

The simulation tool will run the rule based on criteria that your end users will maintain to determine if the logic has been set up properly.

Activities

Because we're just going to test (simulate) the settings we've maintained for support determination, there are no configuration activities involved. The following activities will simulate the BRF+ components that were enabled in the previous sections.

1. Select TOOLS • SIMULATION in the main BRF+ screen as shown in Figure 10.45.

Figure 10.45 Initiate Simulation

2. In the OBJECT QUERY screen, enter the value "SUPPORT_TEAM" in the OBJECT NAME field as shown in Figure 10.46.

3. Click SEARCH.

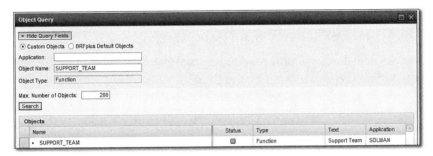

Figure 10.46 Enter Object to be Determined

4. Select the value SUPPORT_TEAM in the OBJECTS table.

5. In the next screen that appears (Figure 10.47), enter a value in the SAP COMPONENT field. In our example, we want to simulate which service team would be determined if this particular SAP component was part of the message details.

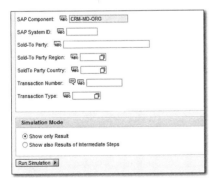

Figure 10.47 Select Run Simulation Button

6. Select the RUN SIMULATION button.

Expected Result(s)

After you've run the simulation for a particular SAP component against the object SUPPORT_TEAM, you'll receive a result as shown in Figure 10.48. If everything was configured properly in BRF+, the service team responsible for the SAP component maintained during the simulation will appear in the results.

Figure 10.48 Support Team Determined in Simulation

10.3.7 Set Actions for Support Team Determination

In this step, we activate the action required to automatically determine the support team based on the logic we defined in BRF+.

Operational Use

This step is required because this action is set to inactive in the standard delivery.

Configuration Activities

To activate the action, follow these steps:

1. Enter Transaction CRMC_ACTION_DEF.
2. Highlight your action profile for incidents (e.g., YMIN_STD), and double-click the ACTION definition node in the structure on the left. The actions relevant to your incident profile will appear as shown in Figure 10.49.

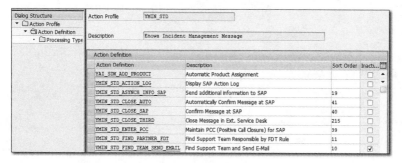

Figure 10.49 Incident Management Action Definitions

3. Ensure that the checkbox in the INACTIVE column isn't marked for the YMIN_ STD_FIND_PARTNER_FDT action definition.

4. Click SAVE.

Expected Result(s)

When a message is created and sent to the central SAP Solution Manager system for processing, the support team will be automatically determined based on the rules configured in BRF+.

This will be the case for any incident that was created with the SAP COMPONENT details maintained. Figure 10.50 shows the end result of an incident in processing wherein the SAP ECC support team has been automatically determined.

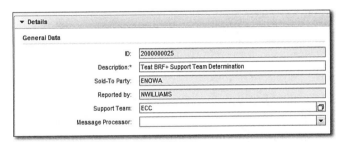

Figure 10.50 SAP ECC Support Team Determined Based on BRF+

10.3.8 Automatic Forwarding of Messages

Independent of BRF+, automatic forwarding of messages provides support team members the ability to rapidly and automatically forward messages based on specific criteria.

Operational Use

As an example, if a message is assigned to the wrong support team (i.e., either the requester entered the wrong information, or the SAP component was intended for a different application area), the message processor can forward the message back to the employee routing the message.

In our example, we'll enable an automatic forwarding action that will be used when a message must be escalated to the next level in the service organization. The message is forwarded so that when a message processor selects the action, the system reacts in the following manner:

▶ Overrides the assigned support team with a Level 2 support team

▶ Deletes the current message processor

▶ Sets the user status to FORWARDED

Configuration Activities

The following steps provide direction on how to configure the incident's action definition settings so that automatic forwarding is enabled:

1. Execute Transaction CRMC_ACTION_DEF.

2. Navigate to the action profile assigned to the transaction type for which you'll enable automatic forwarding (e.g., YMIN_STD).

3. Ensure that you're in change mode by selecting the EDIT button.

4. Ensure that the INACTIVE flag isn't set for the action definition YMIN_STD_MSG_DISPATCH as shown in Figure 10.51.

Figure 10.51 Activate Automatic Forwarding of Messages Action

5. Click SAVE.

6. Double-click the PROCESSING TYPES folder in the dialog structure as shown in Figure 10.52.

Figure 10.52 Access Processing Types

7. In the SETTINGS METHOD CALL area, click the CHANGE button as shown in Figure 10.53.

Figure 10.53 Click Change to Edit Parameters

8. In the CONTAINER EDITOR screen, the system will provide you with the default expressions as a template as shown in Figure 10.54. Enter the values (as we have) in the INITIAL VALUE column based on our examples in Table 10.1.

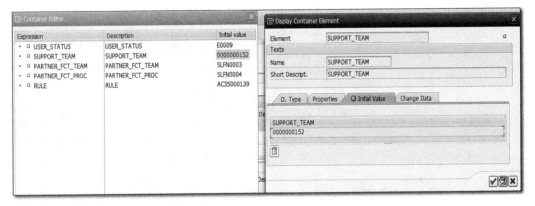

Figure 10.54 Maintain Container Element

Expression	Initial Value	Notes
USER_STATUS	E0009	Status is set when forwarding (i.e., FORWARDED).
SUPPORT_TEAM	0000000152	Support team the message is forwarded to. (You must enter the seven leading zeros.)
PARTNER_FCT_TEAM	SLFN0003	Partner function for the support team assigned to the transaction type.
PARTNER_FCT_PROC	SLFN0004	Partner function for the message processor assigned to the transaction type.
RULE	AC35000139	Rule used for automatic forwarding.

Table 10.1 Parameters for Automatic Forwarding of Messages

9. Double-click on a value within the INITIAL VALUE column to open the DISPLAY CONTAINER ELEMENT screen (Figure 10.54). Within the INITIAL VALUE tab, you can maintain the specific parameter.

10. Click CONTINUE after the parameter has been maintained.

Expected Result(s)

You can test the automatic forwarding functionality directly within AIM for the transaction in which automatic forwarding was activated by selecting ACTIONS • AUTOMATIC FORWARDING OF MESSAGES as shown in Figure 10.55.

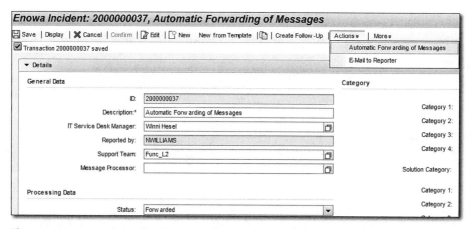

Figure 10.55 Expected Results of Successful Automatic Forwarding of Messages

The following results are to be expected:

▶ The support team is changed to the support team maintained in the parameter (e.g., FUNC_L2).

▶ The status is changed as well per the parameter (e.g., FORWARDED).

▶ The message processor has been deleted.

In the next section, we'll describe the configuration activities necessary to enable the Time Recording functionality to be leveraged in SAP ITSM processes.

10.4 Time Recording

In this section, we'll describe the configuration settings required to enable manual time recording from within a service message. We'll explain how to configure various activities (support, investigation, analysis, recovery, etc.) for your support teams to record their working time against.

The Time Recording functionality is relatively straightforward to configure because it can be achieved with a few simple tasks as identified in Figure 10.56.

Figure 10.56 Time Recording IMG Activities

10.4.1 Define Activity Descriptions and Values

The activity descriptions within configuration activities are general examples based on standard ITIL activities for AIM.

Operational Use

Activity types may vary from organization to organization but generally should be based on standard ITIL processes. Another option is to leverage activities currently used in another tool for recording the time investment spent to process incidents. In any event, the activity descriptions you choose to set up should support your requirements to logically record and report the time spent specific to your support organization's metrics.

Once configured, these activities are available within the TIME RECORDING assignment block when processing messages in the SAP CRM Web UI. Depending on the message processor's activities, they should be assigned to one of the activity descriptions configured by the administrator. The message processor has the option to enter time units in hours or minutes, depending on the task.

Configuration Activities

In the following steps, we'll walk you through the steps in order to configure activity descriptions so that time can be recorded and classified appropriately.

After words we will show you how to set an initial time unit value (i.e. a default value for how time will be recorded in an incident).

Specify Activity Descriptions

1. Execute the IMG activity SPECIFY ACTIVITY DESCRIPTIONS.

2. In the DISPLAY VIEW "IC WEBCLIENT PROFILES": OVERVIEW screen, highlight the business role SOLMANPRO, and double-click the ACTIVITY DESCRIPTION node in the structure on the left as shown in Figure 10.57.

> **Tips & Tricks**
>
> Time recording activity descriptions can be configured based on a specific business role. For example, you can have a set of activities for your Level 1 support teams versus the Level 2 support teams. In our example, we're assigning the activities to the standard SOLMANPRO business role.

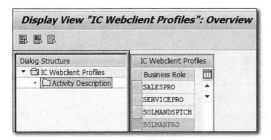

Figure 10.57 Assign Activities to Business Role

3. In the ACTIVITY DESCRIPTION table, maintain the details within the TEXT NO. and TEXT fields as shown in Figure 10.58.

> **Note**
>
> Add sequential numbers (e.g., 01, 02, 03, etc.) in front of each activity description in the TEXT field based on the order you want the activities to appear when recording the support effort. The system won't use the numbers maintained in the TEXT NO. column to sequentially order them in Time Recording, which is why this is necessary.

4. If you have products maintained for your system, add them in the PRODUCT column (however, it isn't required). You'll also notice a FLAG column to the far right. Leave these indicators unmarked.

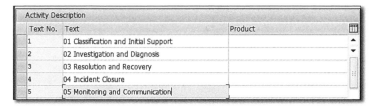

Figure 10.58 Maintain Activity Descriptions

5. Click SAVE.

Specify Initial Time Unit Value

The default time unit value (e.g., minutes or hours) appears at the initial time of recording support efforts. You can record the support effort based on minutes and/or hours; specifying the initial time unit value determines which time unit value is set as default when you initially record your time.

1. Execute the IMG activity SPECIFY INITIAL TIME UNIT VALUE.

2. Choose the NEW ENTRIES button.

3. Assign a TIME UNIT value to the BUSINESS ROLE as shown in Figure 10.59.

4. Click SAVE.

Figure 10.59 Maintain Initial Time Unit Value

Expected Result(s)

The values that you maintained for the activity descriptions will appear in the ACTIVITY TYPE column in the TIME RECORDING assignment block when a user with the relevant business role (e.g., SOLMANPRO) accesses an incident. Further, the TIME UNIT value should be set based on your configurations in the previous step.

Figure 10.60 shows the expected results based on the configuration example in the previous sections.

Figure 10.60 Time Recording in the SAP CRM Web UI

10.4.2 Time Recording Reminders

Time Recording reminders are an optional functionality in AIM.

Operational Use

If these reminders are enabled, support team members will receive a prompt (reminder) to either enter their time immediately or delay the recording for another point in time. These are merely reminders and don't prevent the support team from moving forward in processing the incident if time isn't maintained.

Configuration Activities

In the following steps, we'll show you how to activate Time Recording for your service transaction type.

Activate Time Recording
Follow these steps:

1. Execute Transaction CRMC_ACTION_DEF.

2. Navigate to the action profile used for incidents (in this example, the action profile is YMIN_STD).

3. Confirm that the INACTIVE flag isn't checked for the YMIN_STD_TIME_ REMIND action definition as shown in Figure 10.61.

Figure 10.61 Activate Time Recording

Set Up Reminder
Follow these steps:

1. Select the IMG activity SET TIME RECORDING REMINDER.

2. In the ACTIVITIES window, double-click the option SET UP REMINDER as shown in Figure 10.62.

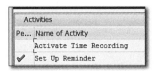

Figure 10.62 Set Up Reminder

3. In the TIME RECORDING REMINDER table, maintain the method for how the processor will be prompted to record their time for each transaction type in AIM as shown in Figure 10.63.

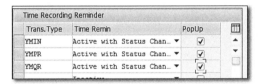

Figure 10.63 Maintain Settings for Time Recording Reminders

4. Mark the box in the POPUP column if the message processors should receive a pop-up notification if they have not entered their time. If this isn't maintained, they will receive a warning message at the top of the screen.

Expected Result(s)

Once activated, Time Recording reminders will appear based on the configuration settings in the previous sections. Figure 10.64 shows the result of activating a Time Recording reminder, upon status change, with a pop-up notification enabled.

Figure 10.64 Pop-Up Time Recording Reminder

In Figure 10.65, you'll see the expected results if pop-ups aren't maintained.

Figure 10.65 Time Recording Reminder without Pop-Ups

In the next section, we'll describe the power behind categorization in SAP Solution Manager.

10.5 Categorization

Configuration activities to enable functionality related to categorization occur both in the IMG and in the SERVICE OPERATIONS section of the SAP CRM Web UI (if you have the SOLMANPRO business role assigned). This area is known as the *category modeler*.

Figure 10.66 and Figure 10.67 provide the IMG activities related to multilevel categorization as well as solution categories. Note that in configuration, they are referred to as PROBLEM CATEGORIES; however, they are displayed as SOLUTION CATEGORIES in the SAP CRM Web UI.

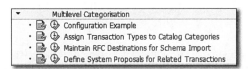

Figure 10.66 Multilevel Categorization IMG Activities

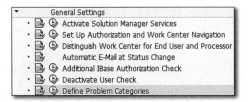

Figure 10.67 Solution (Problem) Categories IMG Activities

Defining category levels, deploying the schema, and performing the updates to follow-on systems occurs directly within the SAP CRM Web UI. From the main ITSM Home Page, follow SERVICE OPERATIONS • CATEGORIZATION SCHEMAS. The CATEGORIZATION SCHEMAS selection will deliver you to the appropriate screen to process these functions.

In this section, we'll describe the configuration steps needed to enable the categorization capabilities in SAP Solution Manager. We'll cover all aspects of how to set up and maintain categorization models and values. The main points covered in this section include the following:

▶ Creating a multilevel categorization schema

▶ Updating and deploying the multilevel categorization schema

▶ Adding levels to an existing schema

▶ Adding a second multilevel categorization block

▶ Importing a categorization schema to a follow-on system

▶ Maintaining solution categories

First, let's go over the prerequisites you'll need to have enabled before you get started.

Prerequisites for SAP CRM Web UI Customization

The UI Configuration tool is used to configure the SAP CRM Web UI screen. The user performing these configurations must have configuration mode enabled. Additionally, the user who is performing these customizations must have the role configuration key assigned to his business role in Customizing.

With the role configuration key parameter, you can create configurations that are dependent on business roles. At runtime, the correct configuration is automatically determined by the business role the user logs in with.

The following steps identify how a user with the appropriate business role assignment can enable configuration mode:

1. Select the PERSONALIZE link in any screen as shown in Figure 10.68.

Figure 10.68 Select Personalize Link

2. In the SETTINGS area of the resulting screen, select the PERSONALIZE SETTINGS link as shown in Figure 10.69.

Figure 10.69 Select Personalize Settings Link

3. Enable configuration mode by marking the appropriate box as shown in Figure 10.70.

Figure 10.70 Enable Configuration Mode

4. Confirm/save the settings.

10.5.1 Baseline Categorization Schema

SAP Solution Manager provides a baseline categorization schema out of the box. This configuration activity is optional. While you'll need to conduct design/blueprint sessions with your IT organization to determine the outcome of your categorization model, it's helpful to have an example schema deployed in your sandbox or development SAP Solution Manager system.

Operational Use

The benefits of leveraging the standard baseline categorizations schema are as follows:

▶ You can see how a multilevel categorization schema is configured.

▶ You can replace the baseline values with your own (i.e., using the baseline schema as a template) so you aren't starting from scratch.

▶ Design/blueprint sessions are facilitated by showing the capabilities of how to classify both SAP and non-SAP service messages.

Configuration Activities

In the following steps, we'll walk you through the steps in order to activate the baseline categorization schema as a configuration example (or template) for your categorization block.

1. Execute the IMG activity CONFIGURATION EXAMPLE.

2. In the ABAP: PROGRAM EXECUTION screen, enter the report "AI_CRM_CREATE_CAT_SCHEMA", and click EXECUTE as shown in Figure 10.71.

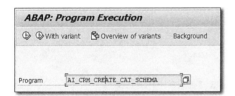

Figure 10.71 Run Configuration Example Report

3. In the following screen (Figure 10.72), select one of these options:

▶ ACTIVATE SCHEMA
SAP Solution Manager activates the schema and assigns it to the default SAP ITSM transaction types (e.g., SMIN, SMPR, SMCR, etc.).

▶ DO NOT ACTIVATE SCHEMA
The system creates the schema, but no transaction types are activated.

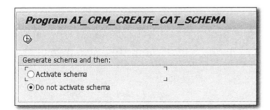

Figure 10.72 Create Schema without Activating Transaction Types

Expected Result(s)

After the program has been executed, you'll see the SAP_SOLUTION_MANAGER_ TEMPLATE available in the search results within the SAP CRM Web UI as shown in Figure 10.73.

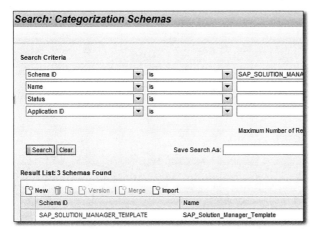

Figure 10.73 Created Baseline Configuration Schema

10.5.2 Assign Transaction Types to Catalog Categories

You must map your customer AIM transaction types (e.g., YMCR) to catalog categories.

Operational Use

This step is required to assign categorization blocks to your transaction type. In addition, the following functionalities for processing messages are enabled within this IMG activity:

▶ FIND RELATED OBJECTS
The system will find, based on the category values maintained, objects that are related to the transaction. For example, problems with the same categorization schema as an incident or request for change will be identified when selecting MORE • FIND RELATED PROBLEMS.

▶ AUTO COMPLETE
This options allows for the transfer of predefined data from a template to a transaction type. For example, you can create a template with predefined text

and business partner information. Then, when an incident is created with the same category values, you select MORE • AUTO COMPLETE, and the system will find a template that has the same categorization.

► ITEM DETERMINATION
This enables the automatic identification of related products for incidents and problems only.

Configuration Activities

In the following configuration activities, we'll provide instructions on how to assign your customer transaction types (e.g. YMIN, YMPR, etc.) to the catalog categories.

1. Execute IMG activity ASSIGN TRANSACTION TYPES TO CATALOG CATEGORIES.

2. Ensure that there are entries available for your customer transaction types, as shown in Figure 10.74. If they're missing, copy them from the standard transaction types.

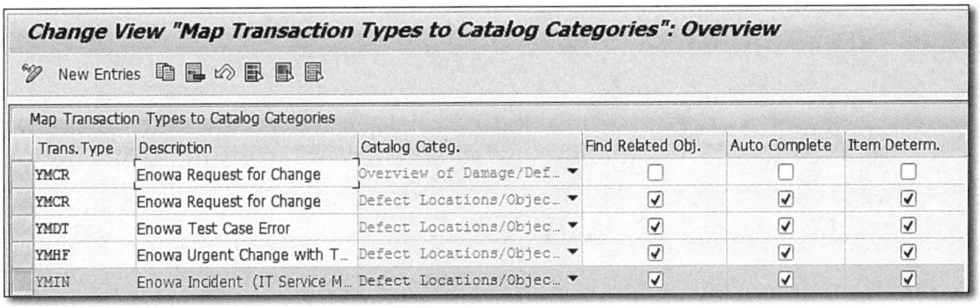

Change View "Map Transaction Types to Catalog Categories": Overview

🖉 New Entries 🗅 🖫 🖾 🖫 🖫 🖫

Map Transaction Types to Catalog Categories					
Trans. Type	Description	Catalog Categ.	Find Related Obj.	Auto Complete	Item Determ.
YMCR	Enowa Request for Change	Overview of Damage/Def... ▼	☐	☐	☐
YMCR	Enowa Request for Change	Defect Locations/Objec... ▼	☑	☑	☑
YMDT	Enowa Test Case Error	Defect Locations/Objec... ▼	☑	☑	☑
YMHF	Enowa Urgent Change with T...	Defect Locations/Objec... ▼	☑	☑	☑
YMIN	Enowa Incident (IT Service M...	Defect Locations/Objec... ▼	☑	☑	☑

Figure 10.74 Map Transaction Types to Catalog Categories

Tips & Tricks

Make sure that your AIM transaction types are assigned to the catalog category DEFECT LOCATIONS/OBJECT PARTS entry.

If you want to enable the FIND RELATED OBJECTS, AUTO COMPLETE, or ITEM DETERMINATION functionalities, mark them in the appropriate fields.

3. Click SAVE.

Expected Result(s)

So far, if you have your customer transaction type assigned to the category catalog, you've achieved the expected results for this configuration activity.

10.5.3 Create/Modify Schema

Creating or modifying the categorization schema occurs when category values have been agreed upon by the IT organization. Similarly, modifying the schema is an activity that occurs when a new category level is required and must be deployed for use.

Operational Use

In the configuration example, we'll leverage the baseline configuration schema created in the previous step to begin tailoring the values. We'll walk through the steps required to add a new level based on the example IT organization's requirements.

Configuration Activities

To add a new level, follow these steps:

1. Navigate to the category modeler by accessing OPERATIONS • CATEGORIZATION SCHEMAS in the SAP CRM Web UI.

2. Select the SAP_SOLUTION_MANAGER_TEMPLATE categorization schema as shown in Figure 10.75 (select the one created from the baseline configuration schema program).

Schema ID	Name	Status	Valid-From Date	Valid-From Time	Valid-To Date	Valid-To Time
SAP_SOLUTION_MANAGER_TEMPLATE	SAP_Solution_Manager_Template	Deployed	07/29/2011	02:17	07/30/2011	14:22
SAP_SOLUTION_MANAGER_TEMPLATE	SAP_Solution_Manager_Template	Deployed	07/30/2011	14:22	08/24/2011	22:05
SAP_SOLUTION_MANAGER_TEMPLATE	SAP_Solution_Manager_Template	Active	08/24/2011	22:05	12/31/9999	23:59
ERMS_DEFAULT_SCHEMA	ERMS Categories	Active	01/23/2004	10:57	12/31/9999	22:59

Figure 10.75 Select Categorization Schema

3. Maintain the following fields in the GENERAL DATA area (refer to the example in Figure 10.76):

▶ SCHEMA ID: Short code of the schema. This is typically created in the customer namespace.

▶ NAME: A short description of the schema.

▶ DESCRIPTION: A description of the schema, if it requires more explanation than the NAME.

▶ LOGICAL STRUCTURE: Select from one of the following

– ATTRIBUTE CATEGORIZATION: Allows for category duplicates to map value combinations.

– HIERARCHICAL CATEGORIZATION: Provides a strict hierarchical arrangement of categories. Each category describes a subject with higher-level categories representing the context of the subject.

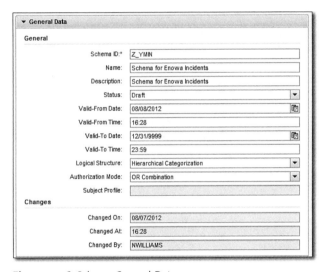

Figure 10.76 Schema General Data

4. Now, we'll expand upon the baseline configuration schema by adding a new ERROR MESSAGE category. Select the line item that contains the ERROR MESSAGE value, and click the NEW button as shown in Figure 10.77.

5. In the GENERAL DATA area (right side of the screen), enter the three values shown in Figure 10.78. For our example, we want to create a category value to represent an error message associated with missing functionality.

6. Click SAVE.

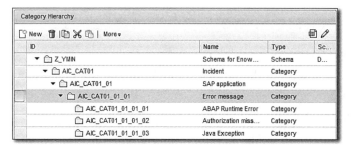

Figure 10.77 Insert New Category

Figure 10.78 New Category Data

Expected Result(s)

You've now added a new category value to the categorization schema. Once saved, your category hierarchy will include the FUNCTIONALITY SPECIFIC value in the appropriate spot as shown in Figure 10.79.

ID	Name	Type	S.
▼ ⌂ Z_YMIN	Schema for Enowa Incidents	Schema	D.
▼ ⌂ AIC_CAT01	Incident	Categ...	
▼ ⌂ AIC_CAT01_01	SAP application	Categ...	
▼ ⌂ AIC_CAT01_01_01	Error message	Categ...	
⌂ AIC_CAT01_01_01_01	ABAP Runtime Error	Categ...	
⌂ AIC_CAT01_01_01_02	Authorization missing	Categ...	
⌂ AIC_CAT01_01_01_03	Java Exception	Categ...	
⌂ AIC_CAT01_01_01_04	Functionality Specific	Categ...	
▶ ⌂ AIC_CAT01_01_02	System message	Categ...	
▶ ⌂ AIC_CAT01_01_03	Masterdata	Categ...	
▶ ⌂ AIC_CAT01_01_04	other	Categ...	
▶ ⌂ AIC_CAT01_02	IT asset	Categ...	
▶ ⌂ AIC_CAT01_03	Hardware	Categ...	
▶ ⌂ AIC_CAT02	Service Request	Categ...	
▶ ⌂ AIC_CAT03	Test Defect	Categ...	
▶ ⌂ AIC_CAT04	Project issue	Categ...	

Figure 10.79 Category Hierarchy with New Value

10.5.4 Assign Application Area

For the multilevel categorization block to be visible for specific transaction types, these transaction types must be assigned to the schema. Don't forget that the prerequisite for this step is to assign your transaction types first to catalog categories in the IMG.

Operational Use

In order for your end-users to be able to display and select the category values intended for your AIM processes, they must be assigned to your customer transaction type.

Configuration Activities

In the following steps we will show you how to assign your customer transaction types to the schema.

1. Enter the category modeler within the SAP CRM Web UI.

2. Access the categorization schema that will be used for your AIM transaction types.

3. Navigate to the APPLICATION AREAS section of the screen as shown in Figure 10.80.

Figure 10.80 Assign Application Areas

Tips & Tricks

In this section, we've deleted all of the standard entries and created entries for our customer transaction types. For incidents and service requests, the application SERVICE REQUEST/INCIDENT should be used. For problems, use the PROBLEM application. Deleting the standard entries isn't required but avoids future warnings of schema overlaps.

---

4. Click SAVE.

Expected Result(s)

Figure 10.80 shows the expected result of assigning application areas to your customer transaction types.

10.5.5 Activate Categorization Schema

Activating the categorization schema essentially means that the schema goes live in your system.

Operational Use

After the schema is activated, users within the SAP ITSM processes will be able to report on and classify service transaction types based on the values configured in the category modeler.

Configuration Activities

In the following steps, we'll show you how to release and activate the categorization schema so it is visible to your SAP ITSM users.

1. Enter the category modeler within the SAP CRM Web UI.

2. Access the categorization schema that will be used for your AIM transaction types.

3. Confirm that the values within the VALID-FROM DATE and VALID-FROM TIME date don't lie in the past.

4. In the GENERAL DATA area, update the STATUS to RELEASED as shown in Figure 10.81.

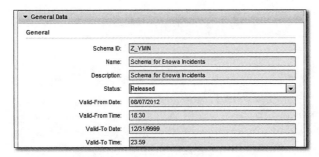

Figure 10.81 Release Categorization Schema

5. Click SAVE.

Expected Result(s)

You can now test the availability and usability of the categorization schema. To do so, simply create a service message based on your customer transaction type within AIM. The values within the levels should not be grayed out anymore. They should have the values defined in the category modeler as shown in Figure 10.82.

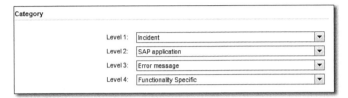

Figure 10.82 Active Categorization Schema

10.5.6 Updating an Active Schema

In this section, we'll show you how to update an active schema, if requirements arise where categories should be added, deleted, or changed.

Operational Use

In certain cases, the IT organization may identify a new requirement regarding how the categorization model should be set up to effectively report on messages. To do so, a new version must be created of the currently active schema.

In the following section, we'll explain the configuration activities necessary to update an already active schema, make a change based on a new version, and deploy those changes back out to the users.

Configuration Activities

Follow these steps to adapt an active schema based on new requirements from the organization.

1. Enter the category modeler within the SAP CRM Web UI.
2. Select the currently active schema, and click the VERSION button as shown in Figure 10.83.
3. Select EDIT to enter change mode.
4. Make a change to the existing schema (e.g., add or remove a level).

Figure 10.83 Create a New Version of the Schema

5. Choose a VALID-FROM DATE and VALID-FROM TIME that is in the near future (e.g., 10 minutes away).

6. Update the status to RELEASED.

7. Click SAVE.

Expected Result(s)

Each schema version represents a combination of its status as well as its validity dates. After you've created a new version and updated its status and validity dates, the new version is in the status of ACTIVE. The previously deployed schema will go into the status of DEPLOYED, as shown in Figure 10.84, and can't be maintained going forward.

After a version has been released and is therefore active, the updated values will be available to the end users in SAP ITSM.

Figure 10.84 Deployed versus Active Schema

10.5.7 Add Additional Category Levels

While four levels of categorization is generous in regards to logging, classifying, and reporting on service transactions, certain organizations may require even more levels of categories. For these scenarios, SAP ITSM provides the ability to incorporate additional category levels into an existing categorization block.

Operational Use

SAP Solution Manager delivers four levels of categories as the standard for classification of service messages based on multilevel categorization. However, if additional category levels are needed, up to 10 can be included within the message.

Configuration Activities

We'll now walk you through the steps of adding an additional category level to an existing categorization block.

1. Select CREATE • INCIDENT, or choose an existing incident.

2. Select the SHOW CONFIGURABLE AREAS button () as shown in Figure 10.85.

Figure 10.85 Show Configurable Areas Button

3. Click the area around the category block as shown in Figure 10.86. Once you click it, it will appear highlighted.

Figure 10.86 Select the Category Block for Configuration

4. Click the SHOW AVAILABLE FIELDS button.

5. Highlight the additional category fields (e.g., CATEGORY 5, CATEGORY 6, etc.) required as shown in Figure 10.87.

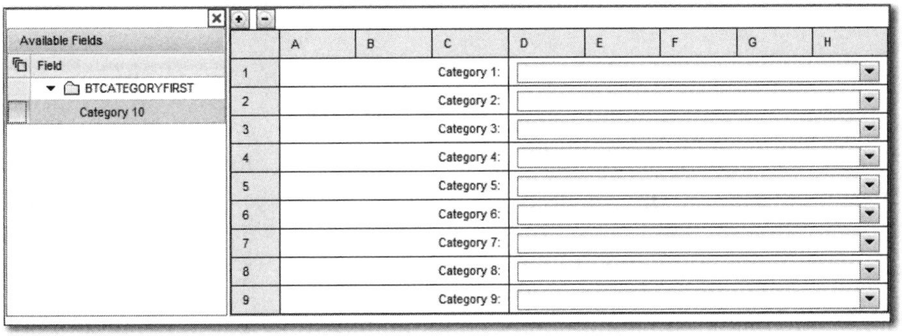

Figure 10.87 Adding Additional Category Fields

6. Click the ADD FIELD button.

7. Save the entries, and close the configuration window.

Expected Result(s)

Based on the additional number of category levels selected, the levels will appear in the CATEGORY block as shown in Figure 10.88. To leverage these fields, a new version of the schema must be created. Furthermore, the extra levels must be defined in the category modeler and released with a new validity date/time so that these changes take effect for the users.

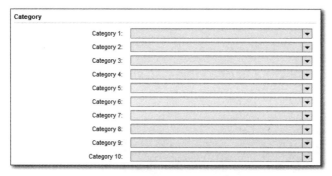

Figure 10.88 Additional Category Levels (Before Activation)

10.5.8 Adding a Second Categorization Block

For service transactions that must be categorized at lower levels (i.e., more precisely), you can add a second categorization block.

Operational Use

This feature is valuable for IT organizations that have more complex reporting/ analytics requirements in which a single category block may not suffice.

In addition to the quantity of category levels achieved, a common example is the way in which category blocks are used within an organization. For example, you can use the first categorization block as a method to describe the subject (i.e., Java exception). You can use a second categorization block to define the reason for this error (i.e., incorrect parameters).

Configuration Activities

In the following sections, we'll describe the configuration activities necessary to add a second categorization assignment block when processing incidents, problems, and service requests. To make these settings, the following configuration activities will be explained:

- ▶ Configuring the SAP CRM Web UI to display an additional categorization block
- ▶ Assigning the transaction types to a second catalog category in the IMG
- ▶ Creating and activating the second schema in the category modeler

Let's get started.

UI Configuration

To configure the UI, follow these steps:

1. Enable the UI Configuration tool by selecting the SHOW CONFIGURABLE AREAS button () as shown in Figure 10.89.

Figure 10.89 Show Configurable Areas button

2. Select the frame within the GENERAL DATA section of the screen as shown in Figure 10.90.

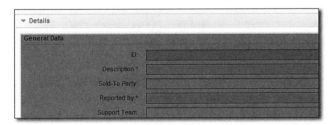

Figure 10.90 Select General Data as the Configurable Area

3. Select the first row within the CONFIGURATIONS table, and click the COPY CONFIGURATION button as shown in Figure 10.91.

Figure 10.91 Copy Configuration

405

4. In the CONFIGURATIONS – WEBPAGE DIALOG screen, enter the role configuration key for the new configuration as shown in Figure 10.92.

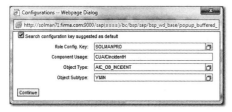

Figure 10.92 Enter the Role Configuration Key

5. Click within the category block, and click the SHOW AVAILABLE FIELDS button as shown in Figure 10.93.

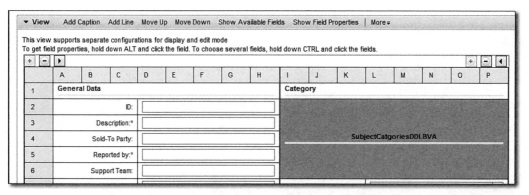

Figure 10.93 Show Available Fields

6. Expand the BLOCKS entry within the AVAILABLE FIELDS, and select the REASON-CATEGORIESDDLBVA entry as shown in Figure 10.94.

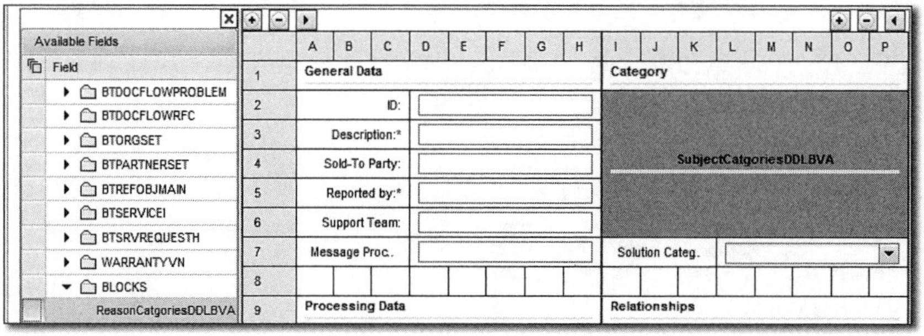

Figure 10.94 Add New Block

7. Click the ADD FIELD button. The new categorization block will now appear in the right side of the UI Configuration tool.

8. Select the new categorization block to drag and drop it so it's placed under the SUBJECTCATEGORIES block as shown in Figure 10.95.

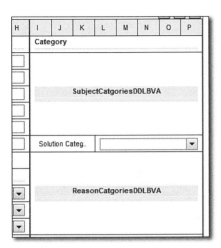

Figure 10.95 Placement of the Second Categorization Block

Assign a Transaction Type to Catalog Category

You need to map the transaction types that will receive the second categorization block to a new catalog category of type C (Overview of Damage/Defects/Reasons). To do this, follow these steps:

1. Execute the IMG activity ASSIGN TRANSACTION TYPES TO CATALOG CATEGORIES.

2. Select an existing transaction type for AIM, and click the COPY AS button as shown in Figure 10.96.

Figure 10.96 Copy Existing Transaction Type to Catalog Category Mapping

3. In the CATALOG CATEGORY column, select the value OVERVIEW OF DAMAGE/ DEFECTS/REASONS as shown in Figure 10.97.

Figure 10.97 Copied Incident with Type C Catalog Category Maintained

4. Uncheck the options to find related objects, auto complete, and item determination because they can't be set for two categorization blocks.

5. Repeat these steps for the transaction types, problems, and service requests to have the second categorization block take affect within these messages types.

6. Click SAVE.

Create and Activate a Second Schema
Now that the transaction types are assigned to the second category catalog, we can create and activate the second schema so that it's visible to the users. Follow these steps:

1. Launch the category modeler in the SAP CRM Web UI.

2. Select the NEW button as shown in Figure 10.98.

Figure 10.98 Create New Schema

3. In the category hierarchy area, build out your requirements for the second categorization schema. (In our example in Figure 10.99, there is only going to be one category level maintained.)

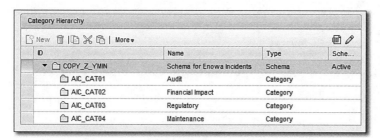

Figure 10.99 Build New Category Hierarchy

4. Assign the appropriate application areas for your AIM transaction types as shown in Figure 10.100. Note that the contents within the VALUE column are the new catalog category values created in the previous step.

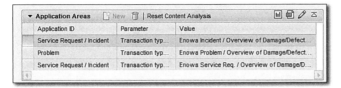

Figure 10.100 Assign Application Areas to New Catalog Category

5. Maintain the validity date and time, and set the status to RELEASED.

6. Click Save.

Expected Result(s)

Based on the steps you just completed, the second categorization block will be available when you create a service message based on your customer transaction types. Figure 10.101 represents the expected result of a completed and activated second categorization block.

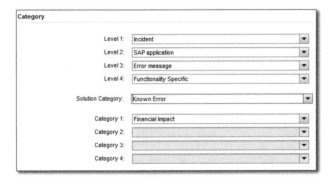

Figure 10.101 Completed and Activated Second Categorization Block

10.5.9 Importing Categorization Schema to Another System

Unlike IMG and SAP CRM Web UI configuration, maintenance associated with building the categorization schema in the category modeler can't be transported to a follow-on quality assurance system (QAS). Objects associated with configuration within the IMG and UI Configuration tool are captured in transport requests and therefore can be transported to other systems. Configuration within the category modeler doesn't generate a transport request and can be considered master data.

Operational Use

To test the schema configuration in the QAS and then promote it to the production system (PRD), SAP Solution Manager provides a way to import the schema based on a remote function call (RFC). This eliminates the need to reenter all of the details associated with the categorization schema and reduces the risk of errors associated with keying in these details manually.

Configuration Activities

> **Important!**
>
> All of the configuration activities associated with the importing of a categorization schema via an RFC connection must be administered in the receiving system.

To import the schema, follow these steps:

1. Execute IMG activity MAINTAIN RFC DESTINATION FOR SCHEMA IMPORT.

2. In the MAINTAIN RFC DESTINATIONS FOR SCHEMA IMPORT TABLE, select the RFC that will be used to import the schema.

3. Provide a description for the RFC DESTINATION. (In the example in Figure 10.102, we have provided the trusted RFC system for the receiving system [i.e., the schema will be imported to client 200 of the S71 system].)

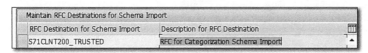

Figure 10.102 Maintain RFC Destination for Schema Import

4. Click SAVE to save the RFC destination table entry.

5. Launch the category modeler (directly in the target/receiving system).

6. Select the IMPORT button as shown in Figure 10.103 (this button will only become available if an entry is made in the RFC table in Customizing).

Figure 10.103 Select the Import Button in the Category Modeler

7. In the SEARCH CRITERIA screen, select the value RFC FOR CATEGORIZATION SCHEMA for the SOURCE field as shown in Figure 10.104.

8. Select the SEARCH button.

9. Highlight the schema that will be imported, and click the IMPORT button.

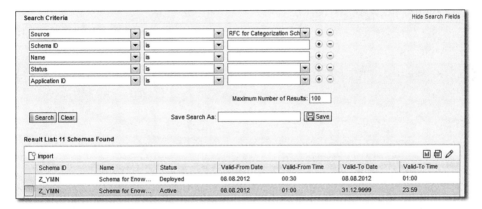

Figure 10.104 Import Schema

10. Assign the schema to the appropriate application area.

11. Set the validity date and time to values in the future.

12. Set the status to RELEASED.

13. Click SAVE.

Expected Result(s)

After you have performed all of the steps in this section, the categorization block should be available and useable in the system in which the schema was imported.

10.5.10 Solution Categorization

Solution categories can be created to classify an incident, problem, or service request's solution. Although they are referred to as *problem categories* in Customizing, they are visible as solution categories across all transaction types in SAP ITSM.

Configuration Activities

In the following steps, we will walk you through the configuration steps to create solution values.

1. Execute IMG activity DEFINE PROBLEM CATEGORIES.

2. In the CHANGE VIEW "PROBLEM CATEGORIES": OVERVIEW screen, select the NEW ENTRIES button.

3. Enter values in the PROBLEM CATEGORY and DESCRIPTION columns as shown in Figure 10.105.

Figure 10.105 Define a New Problem Category

4. Click SAVE.

Expected Result(s)

The new solution category will appear in the list of solution category values in your transaction type. Figure 10.106 shows the example we previously completed.

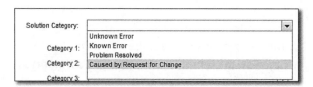

Figure 10.106 New Solution Category in SAP CRM Web UI

In the next section, we'll discuss how text management is administered by way of text determination in SAP Solution Manager.

10.6 Text Management

SAP Solution Manager uses the settings administered in TEXT MANAGEMENT to control which text types are available for specific transaction types for SAP ITSM functions. In addition to text types, TEXT MANAGEMENT drives the behavior of texts as well as how they can be formatted or used in system-wide templates.

As shown in Figure 10.107, the TEXT DETERMINATION PROCEDURE can be configured to enable TEXT MANAGEMENT by a specific group of IMG activities.

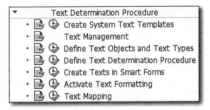

Figure 10.107 Text Management IMG Activities

As you can see in Table 10.2, all transaction types within SAP Solution Manager share the same text determination procedure: SMIN0001. The Transaction Copy tool will have promoted you to copy the standard text determination procedure into your own customer namespace.

413

Transaction Type ID	Transaction Type	Text Determination Procedure
SMIN	Incident	SMIN0001
SMPR	Problem	SMIN0001
SMRQ	Service Request	SMIN0001

Table 10.2 Assignment of Text Determination Procedures to Transaction Types (Standard Assignment)

For the examples within this section, our text determination procedure will be YMIN0001 for all of the transaction types. If needed, you can maintain each text determination procedure differently if you had different requirements (from incident to problem, for example).

10.6.1 Text Determination Procedures

The text determination procedure enables traceability and transparency by supporting the notion of an audit log for various communications and activities throughout SAP ITSM.

Operational Use

The text determination procedure is used by members of the SAP ITSM support teams to record and classify different types of communications that occur throughout the lifecycle of a message. These channels, called text types, can be adapted to meet your organization's requirements for how communication is captured.

Configuration Activities

In the following sections, we'll describe how to add a new text type that should be used by message processors if a message is withdrawn (e.g., Reason for Withdraw). We'll also assign the new text type to the text determination procedure mapped to the transaction type.

Create New Text Type
Follow these steps:

1. Execute the IMG activity DEFINE TEXT OBJECTS AND TEXT TYPES.

2. In the SAPSCRIPT CONTROL TABLES area, mark the radio button for TEXT OBJECTS AND IDS, and click the CHANGE button as shown in Figure 10.108.

Figure 10.108 Change Text Objects and IDs

3. In the CHANGE TEXT OBJECTS screen, double-click on the CRM_ORDERH object as shown in Figure 10.109.

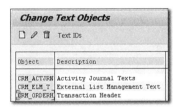

Figure 10.109 Double-Click Text Object CRM_ORDERH

4. Click the CREATE button in the CHANGE TEXT IDS FOR OBJECT CRM_ORDERH screen. Maintain the following fields per the example in Figure 10.110:

 ▹ TEXT ID: The text ID is a four character ID that must start with a Z.

 ▹ DESCRIPTION: The description is what your text type will appear as during message processing.

 ▹ DISPLAY IN TITLE: Select this checkbox to show the ID in the title.

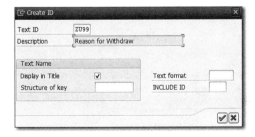

Figure 10.110 Maintain ID Details

5. Press Enter .

The newly created text ID will appear at the bottom of the screen as shown in Figure 10.111.

Figure 10.111 New Text Type

Assign Text Type to Text Determination Procedure

The text type has been created in the bucket of all other text types in SAP Solution Manager. Now, we must assign this text type to be included in the text determination procedure, which is mapped to the transaction types YMIN, YMPR, and YMRQ. Follow these steps:

1. Execute the IMG activity DEFINE TEXT DETERMINATION PROCEDURE.

2. Highlight the object CRM_ORDERH in the TEXT OBJECTS table, and double-click the PROCEDURE node in the dialog structure as shown in Figure 10.112.

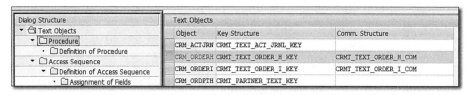

Figure 10.112 Select CRM_ORDERH and Procedure

3. In the next window that appears, highlight the YMIN0001 entry in the PROCEDURE table, and double-click the DEFINITION OF PROCEDURE node in the dialog structure as shown in Figure 10.113.

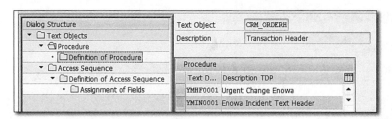

Figure 10.113 Select Customer Defined Procedure and Definition of Procedure

4. In the Change View "Definition of Procedure": Overview screen, select the New Entries button as shown in Figure 10.114.

Change View "Definition of Procedure": Overview
New Entries

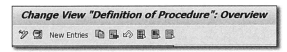

Figure 10.114 Select New Entries

Maintain the definition of the procedure by inserting the details in the following fields per our example in Figure 10.115:

- Text Type
- Sequence (must start with two leading zeros)
- Changes
- Transfer Type

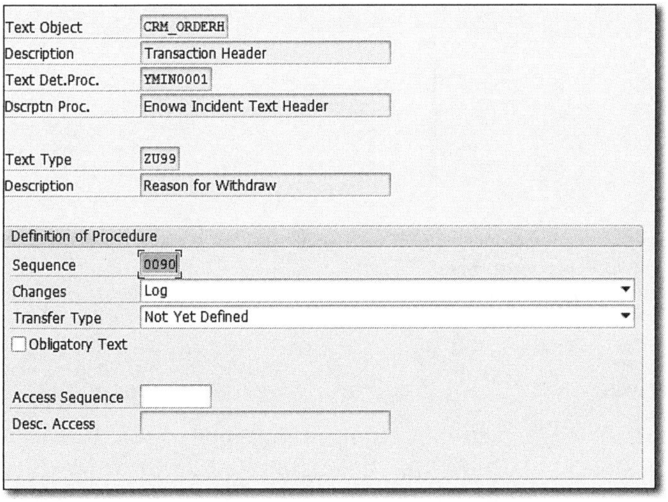

Text Object
CRM_ORDERH
Description
Transaction Header
Text Det.Proc.
YMIN0001
Dscrptn Proc.
Enowa Incident Text Header
Text Type
ZU99
Description
Reason for Withdraw
Definition of Procedure
Sequence
0090
Changes
Log
Transfer Type
Not Yet Defined
Obligatory Text
Access Sequence
Desc. Access

Figure 10.115 Definition of Procedure, Text Type ZU99

5. Click Save.

The newly created text type, ZU99 Reason for Withdraw, has been included in the text determination procedure (see Figure 10.116).

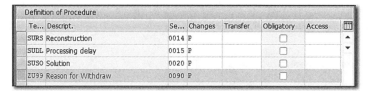

Figure 10.116 New Text Type in Definition of Procedure

Expected Result(s)

As identified in Figure 10.117, the new text type is available within the TEXT assignment block in the transaction. Remember, because all AIM processes share the same text determination procedure, this result is to be expected across all three transaction types.

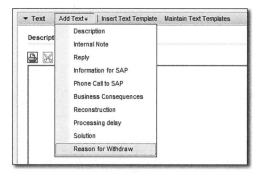

Figure 10.117 Custom Text Type in Message Processing

10.6.2 Text Formatting

Activating text formatting is global across all transaction types in SAP ITSM. In other words, it can't be assigned to a specific transaction type and will be available for AIM as well as ChaRM.

Operational Use

Text formatting can be enabled so that message processors can format text within a message to have bold, italic, or underlined characteristics (for example).

Configuration Activities

We'll walk you through the steps in order to enable the text formatting capability for SAP ITSM.

1. Execute the IMG activity ACTIVATE TEXT FORMATTING.
2. In the CHANGE VIEW "SERVICE DESK CUSTOMIZING": OVERVIEW screen, select the NEW ENTRIES button as shown in Figure 10.118.

Figure 10.118 Select the New Entries Button

Enter values in the following fields based on the example shown in Figure 10.119:

▶ USER NAME: The Solution Manager administrator's user ID
▶ FIELD NAME: "AI_CRM_TEXTEDIT_HTML"
▶ SEQUENCE NUMBER: "15"
▶ DESCRIPTION: "Activate Text Formatting"
▶ FIELD VALUE: "X"

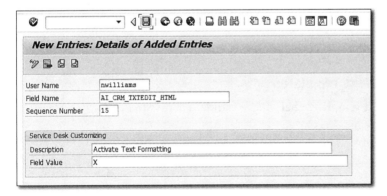

Figure 10.119 Details to Active Text Formatting

Expected Result(s)

The options for text formatting will now appear in the TEXT assignment block for all SAP ITSM transaction types. As you can identify in the icon bar in Figure 10.120, you now have the following options available to format the various text types in your text determination procedure:

► PRINT

► CUT

► COPY

► PASTE

► FIND

► BOLD

► ITALIC

► UNDERLINE

► LEFT ALIGNMENT

► JUSTIFIED

Figure 10.120 Text Formatting Activated

10.6.3 System Text Templates

You can create text templates that can be standard across the IT Service organization.

Operational Use

While the system provides the option for users to create their own user templates, administrators can deploy globally defined and maintained system text templates to support consistency in how messages are documented in SAP ITSM.

Configuration Activities

In this section, we'll describe the configuration activities necessary to create the system text templates as well as activate the templates so they can be leveraged by the end users.

Create Text Templates

To create the templates, follow these steps:

1. Execute the IMG activity CREATE SYSTEM TEXT TEMPLATES.

2. In the CHOOSE ACTIVITY window, double-click the activity CREATE TEXT TEMPLATES as shown in Figure 10.121.

Figure 10.121 Create Text Templates

3. In the DOCUMENT MAINTENANCE: INITIAL SCREEN window, enter a name for the system text template in the NAME field as shown in Figure 10.122.

4. Select the CREATE button. A Microsoft Word template document will open.

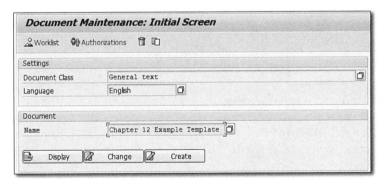

Figure 10.122 Enter the Name of the System Text Template

5. Enter the text that should appear in your system text template. We've included an example in Figure 10.123.

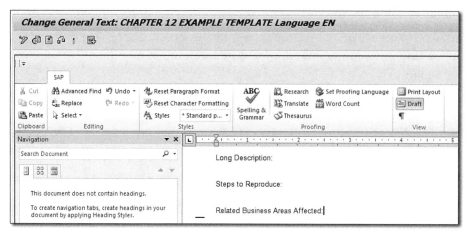

Figure 10.123 Enter Template Criteria

6. Click SAVE.

7. Click the BACK button until you reach the CHOOSE ACTIVITY screen.

Activate Text Templates

To activate the templates, follow these steps:

1. Double-click the activity ACTIVATE TEXT TEMPLATES as shown in Figure 10.124.

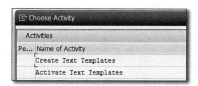

Figure 10.124 Select Activity Activate Text Templates

2. In the CHANGE VIEW "SERVICE DESK CUSTOMIZING": OVERVIEW screen, select the NEW ENTRIES button as shown in Figure 10.125.

Figure 10.125 Create New Entries

3. In the NEW ENTRIES: DETAILS OF ADDED ENTRIES screen, enter values for the following fields per the example in Figure 10.126:

- ▶ FIELD NAME: "SDK_MSG_PROC_AUTO_TEXT"
- ▶ SEQUENCE NUMBER: "99"
- ▶ DESCRIPTION: Description of the system text template
- ▶ FIELD VALUE: The document name you specified in Customizing

New Entries: Details of Added Entries

User Name	
Field Name	SDK_MSG_PROC_AUTO_TEXT
Sequence Number	99

Service Desk Customizing

Description	Chapter 12 Example System Template
Field Value	Chapter 12 Example Template

Figure 10.126 System Text Template Activation Details

4. Click SAVE.

For each system text template you define, you'll need to maintain an entry based on these Customizing steps.

Expected Result(s)

The system text template will now be available after a user in SAP ITSM clicks the INSERT TEXT TEMPLATE button within the TEXT assignment block of any SAP ITSM transaction type.

As shown in Figure 10.127, after the SYSTEM TEMPLATE radio button is selected, the system text templates that have been created and defined are now available in the TEMPLATE dropdown.

After selecting a system text template, clicking the INSERT button will transfer the text values of the template into the text maintenance area in which the SAP ITSM user can fill out the template.

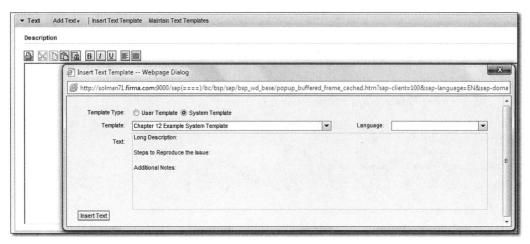

Figure 10.127 System Template in Message Processing

In the next section, we'll provide the step-by-step instructions required to customize the SMIN0001 status profile.

10.7   Status Profile

Status profile settings are enabled in the IMG beneath the STATUS PROFILE main activity group as shown in Figure 10.128.

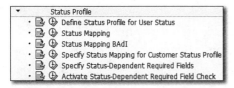

Figure 10.128 Status Profile IMG Activities

As you can see in Table 10.3, each transaction type within AIM is mapped to a single status profile SMIN0001. As part of the Transaction Copy tool activities, you should be working with customer-specific status profiles that have been assigned to your customer-specific transaction type. Throughout the examples in the subsequent sections, we'll be using the status profile YMIN0001 for all maintenance related to status profiles.

Transaction Type ID	Transaction Type	Status Profile
SMIN	Incident	SMIN0001
SMPR	Problem	SMIN0001
SMRQ	Service Request (SAP ITSM)	SMIN0001

Table 10.3 Assignment of Status Profiles to Transaction Types (Standard Assignment)

Status values are made up of a unique ID and a short description. As shown in Table 10.4, the status IDs and short descriptions for status values within the SMIN0001 profile are provided. You can find these values in Table TJ30 in SAP Solution Manager.

User Status ID	Status Value
E0001	NEW
E0002	IN PROCESS
E0003	CUSTOMER ACTION
E0004	SENT TO SAP
E0005	PROPOSED SOLUTION
E0008	CONFIRMED
E0009	FORWARDED
E0010	WITHDRAWN
E0011	IRT EXCEEDED
E0012	IRT WARNING
E0013	MPT EXCEEDED
E0014	MPT WARNING

Table 10.4 Status Profile SMIN0001 (Incident, Problem, and Service Requests)

Note

The last four entries in the table pertain to status values relating to the Service Level Management functionality. These term are discussed in Section 10.8.

In the following sections, we'll describe the configuration aspects specific to status profiles in AIM. We'll provide use cases and configuration examples that will help you understand how you can adapt the configuration and leverage the functionality to meet requirements that are related to reporting based on status. Furthermore, this section will help you develop an understanding of how you can configure status value settings in the SAP Solution Manager system to support authorization concepts and enable controls in your IT service organization.

The following scenarios will be explained with step-by-step configuration instruction:

▶ Creating a new status value
▶ Restricting/enabling specific users to set status values
▶ Mapping user status values to status values in the SAP Support backbone
▶ Setting up mandatory fields based on a status value

Let's get started with the first configuration topic.

10.7.1 Create New Status Value

New status values can be added to your customer status profile in order to accommodate organizational-specific requirements for tracking documents across SAP ITSM. Further, they can be tailored or re-named as well. In this section, we will discuss why status values will be added or changed from the existing status profile as well as walk you through the steps to add a new status value.

Operational Use

In the status profile SMIN0001, SAP Solution Manager provides status values that can scale from small to large IT organizations. The standard status profile rarely needs to be enhanced beyond what is already provided. This is because the status values provided out-of-the box have typically met the requirements of organizations, based on our experience implementing AIM. However, if the standard profile is adapted, usually it's just to rename terminology (i.e., the status value still has the same meaning/reason) or perhaps to add one to two status values to support existing reporting requirements or meet organization-specific metrics.

Furthermore, the status values provided for AIM align closely with ITIL standards for maintaining the processing status for SAP ITSM transactions.

In the following configuration examples, we'll show you how to add a new status value to the status profile.

Configuration Activities

To add a new status value, follow these steps:

1. Execute IMG activity DEFINE STATUS PROFILE FOR USER STATUS.

2. In the CHANGE STATUS PROFILE: OVERVIEW screen, double-click on your customer-specific status profile (e.g., YMIN0001) as shown in Figure 10.129.

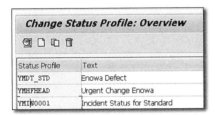

Change Status Profile: Overview

Status Profile	Text
YMDT_STD	Enowa Defect
YMHFHEAD	Urgent Change Enowa
YMIN0001	Incident Status for Standard

Figure 10.129 Select Status Profile

3. In the CHANGE STATUS PROFILE: USER STATUS screen, create a new status value by copying an existing status value and updating the fields. Position your cursor on the status value IN PROCESS, and select the COPY AS button as shown in Figure 10.130.

Change Status Profile: User Status

Object Types

Status Profile	YMIN0001	Incident Status for Standard
Maintenance Language	EN	English

User Status

Stat...	Status	Short Text	Lon...	Init. ...	Lowes...	Highes...	Posi...	Prio...	Auth. code	Tr...
15	WTDR	Withdrawn	☐	☐	15	15	1	1	YMIN_03	FINI
20	PROC	In Process	☐	☐	20	60	1	1	YMIN_04	INPR
21	SAP1	Sent to SAP	☐	☐	20	50	1	1	YMIN_05	INPR
25	DSPT	Forwarded	☐	☐	20	50	1	1	YMIN_06	INPR
30	CACT	Customer Action	☐	☐	20	60	1	1	YMIN_07	INPR
50	SPRV	Proposed Solution	☐	☐	20	60	1	1	YMIN_08	INPR
60	CONF	Confirmed	☐	☐	60	60	1	1	YMIN_09	FINI

Figure 10.130 Copy Existing Status Value

4. In the COPY STATUS window that appears (Figure 10.131), create a status value of ASSIGNED. This is an example of a common requirement that organizations adopt to classify incidents that have been assigned to a message processor but not necessarily have started in process.

5. Maintain details of the status value as shown in Figure 10.131. Table 10.5 provides an overview of the meaning behind these fields.

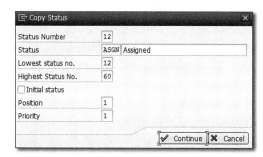

Figure 10.131 Status Value Attributes

Field	Description
STATUS NUMBER	Sequential number that identifies the position of the status value in the message
STATUS	Four-character short code (background use only) and the short description that will appear in the message
LOWEST STATUS NO.	Indicates the lowest status value that can be maintained from this value
HIGHEST STATUS NO.	Indicates the highest status value that can be maintained from this value
INITIAL STATUS	Only mark for status value of NEW
POSITION	Default to 1
PRIORITY	Default to 1

Table 10.5 Status Value Attributes

6. Select the CONTINUE button when you have finished populating the attributes. The newly created status value ASSIGNED will appear in the USER STATUS table as shown in Figure 10.132.

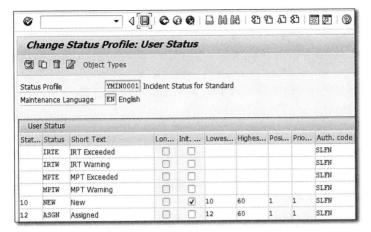

Figure 10.132 New Status Value Created

7. Click SAVE.

Expected Result(s)

In addition to the status value being created in the user status table, it should also be visible in Table TJ30 as shown in Figure 10.133. You'll need to note the status code (e.g., E0015) for future use with authorizations and email notifications.

100	YMIN0001	E0015						12	60	12	01	01	YMIN_02			ASGN	Assigned

Figure 10.133 Table TJ30 Results

Additionally, the status value will be available for selection within the message in the SAP CRM Web UI as shown in Figure 10.134.

Processing Data	
Status:	New
Impact:	New
	Assigned
Recommended Priority:	Withdrawn
	In Process
Dates	Forwarded
	Customer Action
Created:	Proposed Solution

Figure 10.134 Newly Created Status Value

10.7.2 Authorization Keys

Status values should be set according to the SAP ITSM user's job function. Each organization will have different requirements regarding which user can advance or reverse a document to a different status. For example, in some cases the original reporter must be the party that confirms the incident. In other example, only a message processor can advance the status to In Process.

Operational Use

In this section, we'll discuss how authorization keys can be applied to individual status values. Table 10.6 is an example role matrix that identifies which user roles in the IT organization are assigned a specific PFCG role based on standard authorizations for AIM. In the Status Values column, we've provided common examples of which status values can be maintained according to each user.

End User Role	PFCG Role	Status Values
Requester	YSAP_SUPPDESK_CREATE	NEW, CONFIRMED
Message Processor (L1 Support)	YSAP_SUPPDESK_PROCESS_L1	IN PROCESS, CUSTOMER ACTION, PROPOSED SOLUTION, FORWARDED
SAP ITSM Professional (L2 Support)	YSAP_SUPPDESK_PROCESS_L2	IN PROCESS, CUSTOMER ACTION, PROPOSED SOLUTION, FORWARDED, SENT TO SAP
Service Desk Manager (Admin)	YSAP_SUPPDESK_ADMIN	ASSIGNED, WITHDRAWN

Table 10.6 Example Role Matrix with Status Assignment

Configuration Activities

In the following sections, we'll show you how to define authorization keys for each status value in your status profile. Then, we'll show you how to adapt the Message Processor (L1 Support) role so that they can only set the status values identified in the role matrix.

Define Authorization Keys

To define the keys, follow these steps:

1. Execute the IMG activity DEFINE STATUS PROFILE FOR USER STATUS.

2. Access your customer-defined status profile.

3. Select ENVIRONMENT • AUTHORIZATION key as shown in Figure 10.135.

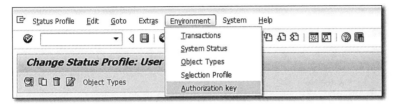

Figure 10.135 Access Status Value Authorization Keys

4. In the CHANGE VIEW "AUTHORIZATION KEY": OVERVIEW screen, ensure that you're in edit mode, and then select the NEW ENTRIES button as shown in Figure 10.136.

Figure 10.136 Select New Entries

5. Enter values within the AUTHKEY and TEXT columns as shown in Figure 10.137.

Tips & Tricks

You'll need to create a unique authorization key, identifiable via transaction type, for each status value that should be controlled by authorizations.

---

6. Click SAVE, and then click the BACK button to return to the YMIN0001 status profile details.

7. In the USER STATUS column, assign the authorization keys you just created to .the corresponding status values in the AUTH. CODE column as shown in Figure 10.138.

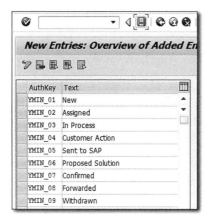

Figure 10.137 Maintain Authorization Code Details

Stat...	Status	Short Text	Lon...	Init. ...	Lowes...	Highes...	Posi...	Prio...	Auth. code	Tr...
	IRTW	IRT Warning	☐	☐					SLFN	
	MPTE	MPT Exceeded	☐	☐					SLFN	
	MPTW	MPT Warning	☐	☐					SLFN	
10	NEW	New	☐	☑	10	60	1	1	YMIN_01	
12	ASGN	Assigned	☐	☐	12	60	1	1	YMIN_02	
15	WTDR	Withdrawn	☐	☐	15	15	1	1	YMIN_03	FINI
20	PROC	In Process	☐	☐	20	60	1	1	YMIN_04	INPR
21	SAP1	Sent to SAP	☐	☐	20	50	1	1	YMIN_05	INPR
25	DSPT	Forwarded	☐	☐	20	50	1	1	YMIN_06	INPR
30	CACT	Customer Action	☐	☐	20	60	1	1	YMIN_07	INPR
50	SPRV	Proposed Solution	☐	☐	20	60	1	1	YMIN_08	INPR
60	CONF	Confirmed	☐	☐	60	60	1	1	YMIN_09	FINI
			☐	☐						

Figure 10.138 Assign Authorization Keys to User Status

Assign Authorization Keys to PFCG Role

Now, we're ready to assign the authorization keys to the authorization (PFCG) role for the Message Processor (L1 Support) personnel.

> **Note**
>
> These tasks are typically performed by a security administrator. We assume that they will be performing these tasks or that you have the required authorizations within your role to maintain roles. Further, we have copied the standard SAP authorization roles to the customer namespace for these configuration examples.

To assign the keys to the role, follow these steps:

1. Execute Transaction PFCG.

2. Enter the role (e.g., "YSAP_SUPPDESK_PROCESS_L1") as shown in Figure 10.139, and select the CHANGE button.

Figure 10.139 Maintain Role

3. In the AUTHORIZATIONS tab, select the CHANGE AUTHORIZATION DATA button.

4. In the CHANGE ROLE: AUTHORIZATIONS screen, select UTILITIES • TECHNICAL NAMES ON.

5. Click the FIND ( ) button.

6. Enter the value "b_userstat" in the AUTHORIZATION object field as shown in Figure 10.140.

7. Click the FIND OBJECT button.

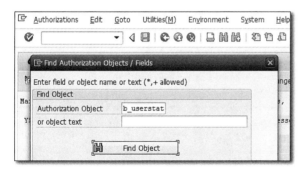

Figure 10.140 Find Object B_USERSTAT

The structure of authorization nodes will expand to identify the authorization objects that match the search for object B_USERSTAT.

8. Maintain the value YMIN0001 in the STATUS PROFILE field, and remove any other status profiles as shown in Figure 10.141.

9. Double-click the contents of the field AUTHORIZATION KEY.

Figure 10.141 Maintain B_USERSTAT

10. In the FIELD VALUES window (Figure 10.142), select only the status values (and corresponding authorization codes) in which the Message Processor (L1 Support) team member should be able to set.

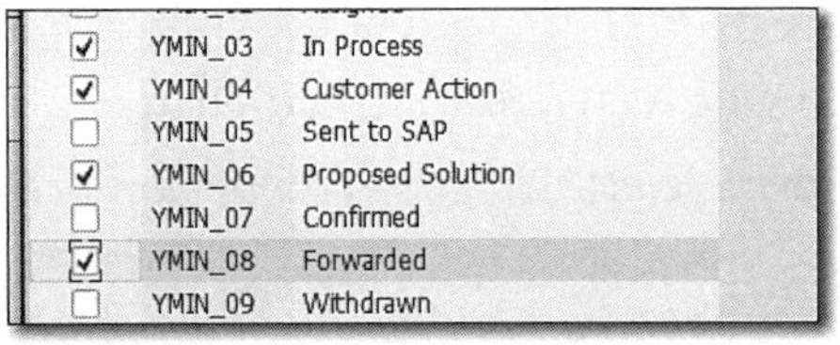

☑	YMIN_03	In Process
☑	YMIN_04	Customer Action
☐	YMIN_05	Sent to SAP
☑	YMIN_06	Proposed Solution
☐	YMIN_07	Confirmed
☑	YMIN_08	Forwarded
☐	YMIN_09	Withdrawn

Figure 10.142 Select Role-Specific Status Values

The values for authorization object B_USERSTAT should now appear as shown in Figure 10.143. For control purposes, we have removed any reference to SMIN* status profiles or authorization keys.

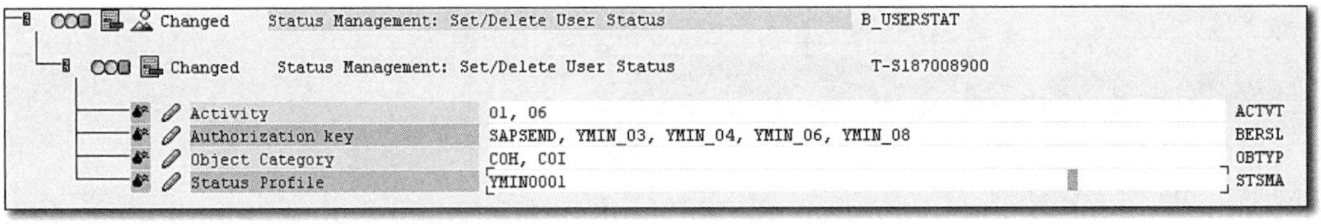

```
┌─ ○○□ 🔲 👤 Changed      Status Management: Set/Delete User Status          B_USERSTAT
 └─□ ○○□ 🔲 Changed      Status Management: Set/Delete User Status          T-S187008900
      ├─ 🔑 ⫽ Activity              01, 06                                              ACTVT
      ├─ 🔑 ⫽ Authorization key     SAPSEND, YMIN_03, YMIN_04, YMIN_06, YMIN_08         BERSL
      ├─ 🔑 ⫽ Object Category       COH, COI                                            OBTYP
      └─ 🔑 ⫽ Status Profile        YMIN0001                                            STSMA
```

Figure 10.143 Customized B_USERSTAT Entry

11. Click the SAVE button.

12. Click the GENERATE button.

Expected Result(s)

The users who are assigned with the YSAP_SUPPDESK_PROCESS_L1 authorization role will only have access to set status values in which they are assigned during processing. If they attempt to set a status value in which they aren't assigned the appropriate authorization key, the system will issue an authorization error in the SAP CRM Web UI.

10.7.3 Status Mapping

Status mapping is delivered standard with SAP Solution Manager to map user status values within AIM status values to SAP if SAP Collaboration is initiated.

Operational Use

For example, status mapping can define that if a message at SAP has the status CUSTOMER ACTION, then the status of the message in SAP Solution Manager will be set to IN PROCESS.

The table identified in Figure 10.144 is informational only. In other words, these customizations are already delivered standard. You may adapt them if you're using different status profiles or if your organization's requirements vary from the standard.

Status Profile	Secondary User Status	Status SAP	Target User Status
YMIN0001		SAP Proposed Solution	E0002
YMIN0001		Customer Action	E0002
YMIN0001		Solution Confirmed	E0002
YMIN0001		In Processing by SAP	E0004
YMIN0001		Confirmed Automatically	E0002
ZMIN0001		SAP Proposed Solution	E0002
ZMIN0001		Customer Action	E0002
ZMIN0001		Solution Confirmed	E0002
ZMIN0001		In Processing by SAP	E0004
ZMIN0001		Confirmed Automatically	E0002

Figure 10.144 Mapping Table for User Status

Configuration Activities

In the following steps, we will show you how to navigate to the standard status mapping configurations provided by SAP:

1. Execute IMG activity STATUS MAPPING.

2. In the CHANGE VIEW "MAPPING TABLE FOR USER STATUS": OVERVIEW screen, as shown in Figure 10.144, you can view or update the standard delivered mapping rules.

Expected Result(s)

If you have adapted the STATUS PROFILE, STATUS SAP, and TARGET USER STATUS values in this table, you'll see the results when SAP updates the status to a message. It's expected that your target user status will reflect the values within this table after the corresponding status at SAP is set.

10.7.4 Status Dependencies

Status dependency is a term used for a function within SAP ITSM where fields are checked during the transition of a status change.

Operational Use

You can identify certain fields in a message that should be flagged to be checked when the status of a transaction is changed. In our configuration example, the requirement is a solution text type that is maintained before the message can be confirmed.

Configuration Activities

In the following steps we will walk you through how to create a status dependency based on a text type.

Check BAdI Activation

First, we need to check that the BAdI `AI_CRM_IM_STATUS_CHECK_CHANGE` has been activated. The UI fields you specify as required will only be checked if this BAdI is activated.

1. Execute the IMG activity ACTIVATE STATUS-DEPENDENT REQUIRED FIELD CHECK.

2. If the BAdI is inactive, make sure you activate it. As shown in Figure 10.145, it has been activated in the system already. Click CANCEL if your system displays the same information box.

Figure 10.145 Active BAdI

Status-Dependent Required Fields

In this section, we'll describe how to enable the solution text type to be required before the status CONFIRMED can be selected.

1. Execute the IMG activity SPECIFY STATUS-DEPENDENT REQUIRED FIELDS.

2. In the CHANGE VIEW "MANDATORY FIELDS FOR STATUS UPDATE": OVERVIEW screen, select the NEW ENTRIES button as shown in Figure 10.146.

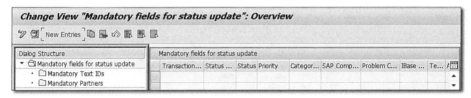

Figure 10.146 Select New Entries

3. In the NEW ENTRIES: DETAILS OF ADDED ENTRIES screen, enter the following values per the example in Figure 10.147:

   ▸ TRANSACTION TYPE: "YMIN"

   ▸ STATUS PROFILE: "YMIN0001"

   ▸ STATUS: "E0008" (confirmed)

   ▸ MANDATORY FIELDS FOR STATUS UPDATE: TEXT TYPE

4. Double-click the MANDATORY TEXT IDs folder in the dialog structure.

5. In the CHANGE VIEW "MANDATORY TEXT IDs": OVERVIEW screen, select the NEW ENTRIES button.

6. Enter the TEXT ID and DESCRIPTION for the text type that is required (i.e., solution) before confirming the message as shown in Figure 10.148.

7. Click SAVE.

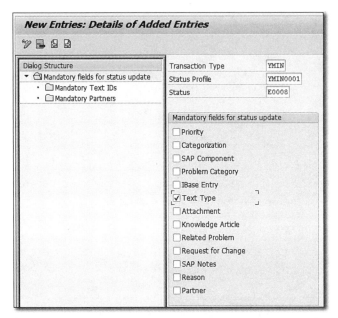

Figure 10.147 Maintain Details for Mandatory Fields for Status Update

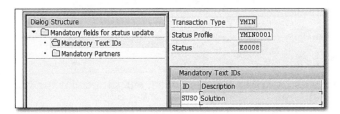

Figure 10.148 Enter Mandatory Text ID

Expected Result(s)

As shown in Figure 10.149, the system will issue a hard stop error if the message processor or requester tries to confirm the message without first entering information within the solution text type.

Figure 10.149 Error is Solution isn't Maintained

In the next section, we'll walk through the steps to enable a simple use case for how Service Level Agreements (SLAs) are determined and escalated in the SAP Solution Manager system.

10.8   SLA Escalation

For the most part, SLA escalation comes preconfigured from SAP Solution Manager to manage SLAs across your SAP ITSM scenarios. There are a few things that must be enabled to the parts working for a particular transaction type; however, for the most part the basic use case is fairly straightforward. On the other hand, depending on an IT organization's requirements for managing SLAs, this functionality can require more effort to design and configure more complex SLAs.

SLA escalation is enabled within the IMG activity group SLA ESCALATION as identified in Figure 10.150. While SLA escalation leverages the configuration items in the DATE PROFILE IMG activity group, we typically don't change these values unless a full-blown SLA escalation strategy with complex organizational requirements is necessary.

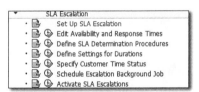

Figure 10.150 IMG Activities for SLA Escalation

In this section, we'll provide an overview of the configuration activities required to get SLA escalation to function for a simple use case. SLA escalation, as mentioned, can be very complex and require a book of its own to describe all of the capabilities and configuration aspects. The objective in this book is to get you in the right area and provide enough basic knowledge so that you're able to expand upon the use case in this section.

10.8.1   Define Service and Response Profiles

Service profiles define the availability times the support team is responsible for processing messages. In other words, you can enable the service profile to map to the holiday/country calendar that your organization follows. SAP Solution Manager provides the flexibility to adapt to most service profiles used by organizations (5x8, 7x24, etc.).

The response profile defines Initial Response Time (IRT), which is the required time duration for the first response to the message, and the Maximum Response Time (MRT), which is the time frame until service end.

Operational Use

In our use-case example, we'll define a service profile in which the support team will be measured based on a Monday through Friday, 9:00 am to 5:00 pm EST schedule (5x8). For our response profile, we'll have the SLA escalation determined based on priority value. Because this is just a configuration example, you'll see that the response times for IRT and MPT are very aggressive.

Configuration Activities

Now, we will walk you through the steps in order to define a service and response profile.

Define Profiles

1. Execute IMG activity EDIT AVAILABILITY AND RESPONSE TIMES.

2. Click the CHANGE button to enter edit mode as shown in Figure 10.151.

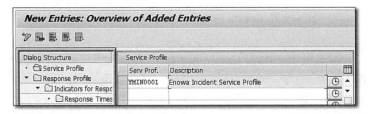

Figure 10.151 Enter Service Profile

3. Click the NEW ENTRIES button.

4. Enter a value within the SERV PROF and DESCRIPTION fields.

5. Click the AVAILABILITY TIME button.

6. Maintain the rule settings per the example in Figure 10.152, or define your own rule settings based on your availability times.

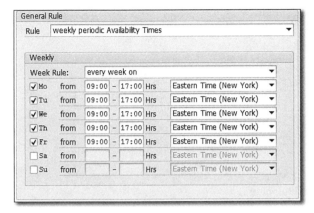

Figure 10.152 Maintain Availability Times

Check the validity date of your factory calendar in Transaction SCAL.

7. Click CONTINUE.

8. Double-click the RESPONSE PROFILE folder in the dialog structure as shown in Figure 10.153.

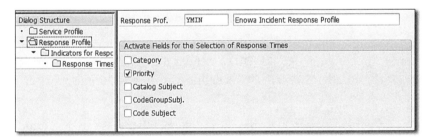

Figure 10.153 Define the Response Profile

9. Define your response profile via your customer transaction type (e.g., YMIN).

10. Mark the PRIORITY box (because our SLA escalation will be determined by the PRIORITY field).

11. Click SAVE.

12. Double-click the INDICATORS FOR RESPONSE TIMES folder in the dialog structure as shown in Figure 10.154.

13. Enter a PRIORITY value (e.g., begin with Very High, which is classified by the numerical value 1).

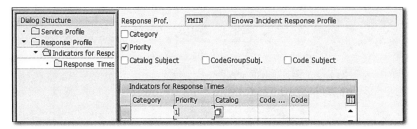

Figure 10.154 Maintain Indicator for Response Times

14. Click SAVE.

15. Highlight the line that contains the priority value, and double-click the RESPONSE TIMES FOLDER in the dialog structure as shown in Figure 10.155.

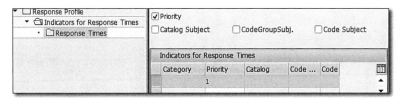

Figure 10.155 Select Response Times

Now we'll create the dependency between the incident's priority values and response times. The duration SRV_RF_DURA defines the duration until first reaction (i.e., IRT). The duration SRV_RR_DURA defines the duration until service end (i.e., MPT).

1. Enter the durations as shown in Figure 10.156. Remember these are just example values and should be adapted according to your organization's requirements.

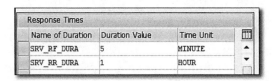

Figure 10.156 Enter Response Times

2. Repeat these steps to maintain dependencies between the remaining priority values and response times.

3. Click Save.

Assign Profiles to Service Product

Because our SLA determination will be based on the service product INVESTIGATION, to cover all scenarios in SAP ITSM, we'll need to assign service and response profiles to this service product.

1. Execute Transaction COMMPR01.

2. Click the Change button to enter edit mode.

3. Select the Service tab as shown in Figure 10.157.

4. Enter your service profiles and response profiles in the respective fields.

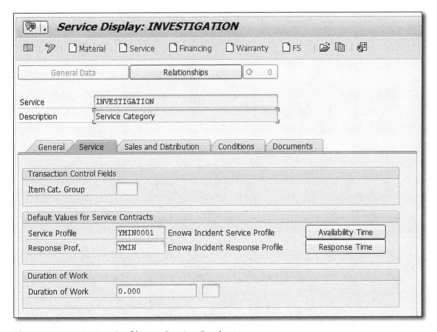

Figure 10.157 Assign Profiles to Service Product

5. Click Save.

Expected Result(s)

You should now have service and response profiles defined with availability times assigned. Furthermore, priority values will have assigned durations. Lastly, your service product must have the service profiles and response profiles that you defined in Customizing.

10.8.2 Define SLA Determination Procedure

As we mentioned in the beginning of this section, SLA escalation and determination is the method in which an organization's service and response times are managed within the system. In the background, this is achieved by the SLA determination procedure and corresponding action profile.

Operational Use

In this section, we'll copy the standard SLA determination procedure into the example customer namespace. Typically, this is all of the Customizing you'll need to do.

Because the SLA determination will be based on the overall service product, it will pick up the service product as part of the access sequence. The other objects in the access sequence will be skipped because we won't configure other objects to be determined by an SLA procedure. As mentioned in Chapter 9, there are multiple other ways (objects) on which to base your SLA determination procedure.

Configuration Activities

In the following steps we will walk you through the configuration required in order to define an SLA determination procedure.

1. Execute the IMG activity DEFINE SLA DETERMINATION PROCEDURE.
2. Select the standard SMIN0001 entry, and copy it into your customer namespace. Figure 10.158 shows the results, displaying the new YMIN0001 value as the copied entry.

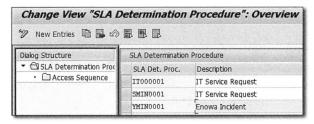

Figure 10.158 Create SLA Determination Procedure

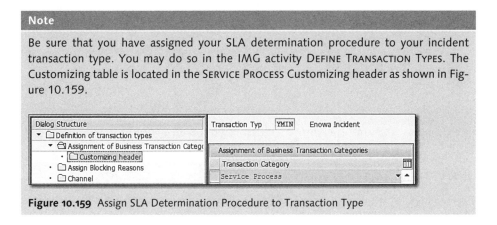

Figure 10.159 Assign SLA Determination Procedure to Transaction Type

3. Double-click the ACCESS SEQUENCE folder in the dialog structure as shown in Figure 10.160.

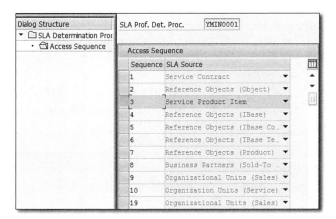

Figure 10.160 Default Access Sequence

The default access sequences were brought over when you copied the standard SLA determination procedure. It's okay to leave this standard Customizing as is. This table will run the following actions, in this sequence, to see if any objects fit these profiles. Because we have only defined our service and response profiles for the service product, the access sequence will determine the SLA determination procedure after it gets to the step highlighted in Figure 10.160.

Expected Result(s)

The expected results for this step are as follows:

▸ A customer-specific SLA determination procedure based on a copy of the SMIN0001 determination procedure.

▸ Default access sequence assigned to your customer SLA determination procedure.

▸ SLA determination procedure assigned to your transaction type.

10.8.3 Define Settings for Durations

The settings for durations define what combination of status profile, status value, and date profile will be used to calculate the durations for the transactions.

Operational Use

When you change the status within a message, SAP Solution Manager will update the date types and durations of the message according to the new status automatically. For example, the system will set the closing date (date type) when you complete a message.

No customization is required because you typically use the standard. However, if you're using a customer-defined status profile, you'll need to copy the values as described in the following configuration activities.

> **Note**
>
> Depending on the support package of your system, please review SAP Note 1675375 and ensure that it's implemented prior to performing the configuration activities.

Configuration Activities

In the following configuration activities, we show you how to define settings for durations.

1. Execute IMG activity DEFINE SETTINGS FOR DURATIONS.

2. Copy the values within the STATUS PROFILE and DATE PROFILE columns into your own customer namespace as shown in Figure 10.161.

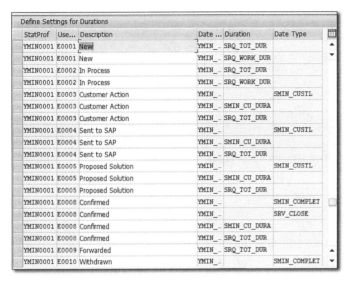

StatProf	Use...	Description	Date ...	Duration	Date Type	
YMIN0001	E0001	New	YMIN _..	SRQ_TOT_DUR		
YMIN0001	E0001	New	YMIN _..	SRQ_WORK_DUR		
YMIN0001	E0002	In Process	YMIN _..	SRQ_TOT_DUR		
YMIN0001	E0002	In Process	YMIN _..	SRQ_WORK_DUR		
YMIN0001	E0003	Customer Action	YMIN _..		SMIN_CUSTL	
YMIN0001	E0003	Customer Action	YMIN _..	SMIN_CU_DURA		
YMIN0001	E0003	Customer Action	YMIN _..	SRQ_TOT_DUR		
YMIN0001	E0004	Sent to SAP	YMIN _..		SMIN_CUSTL	
YMIN0001	E0004	Sent to SAP	YMIN _..	SMIN_CU_DURA		
YMIN0001	E0004	Sent to SAP	YMIN _..	SRQ_TOT_DUR		
YMIN0001	E0005	Proposed Solution	YMIN _..		SMIN_CUSTL	
YMIN0001	E0005	Proposed Solution	YMIN _..	SMIN_CU_DURA		
YMIN0001	E0005	Proposed Solution	YMIN _..	SRQ_TOT_DUR		
YMIN0001	E0008	Confirmed	YMIN _..		SMIN_COMPLET	
YMIN0001	E0008	Confirmed	YMIN _..		SRV_CLOSE	
YMIN0001	E0008	Confirmed	YMIN _..	SMIN_CU_DURA		
YMIN0001	E0008	Confirmed	YMIN _..	SRQ_TOT_DUR		
YMIN0001	E0009	Forwarded	YMIN _..	SRQ_TOT_DUR		
YMIN0001	E0010	Withdrawn	YMIN _..		SMIN_COMPLET	

Figure 10.161 Durations

3. Click SAVE.

Expected Result(s)

The expected results for this configuration activity are as follows:

▶ The standard settings for durations have been copied into your customer namespace.

▶ SAP Note 1675375 has been reviewed and applied if applicable to your system.

10.8.4 Specify Customer Time Status

The status values maintained in this table ensure that SLA calculation isn't affected if the message is set to that status value.

Operational Use

Any status value that is set wherein a message is out of the message processor's hands (i.e., sent to SAP) should not affect SLA calculation. If someone else is holding up the processing of the message, the message processor should not be held accountable based on SLA metrics for the processor's work.

In our example, we'll add the custom status value NOT ASSIGNED (created in Section 10.7.1) to this table.

Configuration Activities

To add the custom status value, follow these steps:

1. Execute the IMG activity SPECIFY CUSTOMER TIME STATUS.

2. Click the NEW ENTRIES button as shown in Figure 10.162.

Figure 10.162 Select New Entries

3. In the STATUS ATTRIBUTES FOR SLA PROCEDURE table, enter the status profile (STATPROF) and user status (USRST) for the ASSIGNED status value as shown in Figure 10.163.

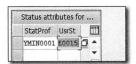

Figure 10.163 Enter Customer Status Assigned

4. Click SAVE.

Expected Result(s)

The status value for which the message processor should not be held accountable in regards to SLA escalation (e.g., ASSIGNED) is added to this table corresponding with your customer status profile.

10.8.5 Adjust Thresholds for IRT and MPT Status

Indicators are delivered with SAP Solution Manager to send warnings and exceeded errors if an IRT or MPT passes a certain threshold. If one of these values passes the 60% threshold, a warning will be issued. If the value exceeds 100%, an exceeded error will be issued.

Operational Use

You can define these thresholds based on your organization's requirements. For this example, we'll stick with the default values because they are sufficient.

Configuration Activities

We will now show you how to navigate to and view the standard IRT and MPT status thresholds.

1. Access Table AIC_CLOCKNAME via Transaction SM30.
2. Review the entries in the CLOCKNAME table in Figure 10.164. Update if necessary.

Clockname	Clockname (Text)	Date Type	Threshold
IRT_ESC	IRT Escalation	SRV_RFIRST	100
IRT_WRN	IRT Warning	SRV_RFIRST	60
MPT_ESC	MPT Escalation	SRV_RREADY	100
MPT_WRN	MPT Warning	SRV_RREADY	60

Figure 10.164 Standard IRT and MRT Threshold Values

3. Click SAVE.

Expected Result(s)

The thresholds for IRT and MPT have been defined in Table AIC_CLOCKNAME.

10.8.6 Schedule Escalation Background Job

An escalation background job is delivered standard with SAP Solution Manager to help facilitate the communication of the results of the SLA determination to the message processors.

Operational Use

If an IRT or MPT threshold is violated, you can enable a standard background job to run that will email the Message Processor (or support team) as a reminder that SLAs are in jeopardy of being met.

Configuration Activities

To enable the background job, follow these steps:

1. Execute IMG activity SCHEDULE ESCALATION BACKGROUND JOB.

2. Select the START CONDITION button as shown in Figure 10.165.

3. Choose the IMMEDIATE button.

4. Mark the flag for PERIODIC JOB.

5. Select the PERIOD VALUES button.

6. Enter a period that the job should run (e.g., every 10 minutes).

7. Click the multiple SAVE buttons until all of the windows close.

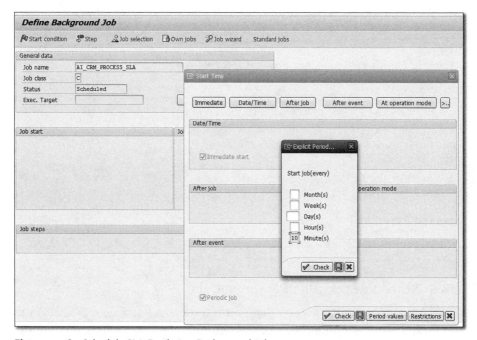

Figure 10.165 Schedule SLA Escalation Background Job

Expected Result(s)

The job should be immediately released. You can check its status in Transaction SM37.

10.8.7 Activate SLA Escalations

The final step to achieve SLA escalation is to activate it based on the steps in the following configuration activities.

Configuration Activities

To activate the escalation, follow these steps:

1. Execute Transaction DNO_CUST04.

2. Make the following entries in the service desk Customizing table as shown in Figure 10.166:

   ▶ FIELD NAME: "SLA_ESCAL_ACTIVE"

   ▶ FIELD VALUE: "X"

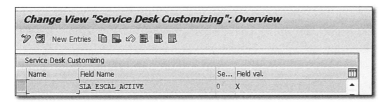

Figure 10.166 Activate SLA Escalations

Expected Result(s)

An entry will be created and saved in Table DNO_CUST04 based on the values just described.

In the next section, we'll describe the concept of actions and conditions as it relates to sending automatic email notifications from the SAP Solution Manager system.

10.9   Actions and Conditions

Actions drive the majority of the components within SAP ITSM. Whether they occur in the background or are executed manually directly from the service message, actions play a big part in how the workflow is enabled throughout these processes. Conditions come into play when you want to schedule and start an action according to specific requirements. We'll discuss the concepts and configuration of actions and conditions throughout subsequent chapters of this book.

For AIM, we'll focus on actions and conditions associated with enabling automatic email notifications from a service message.

10.9.1   Automatic Email Notifications

The E-MAIL TO REPORTER action is available out of the box in the ACTIONS button in the message. This is great for organizations that want to manually trigger emails; however, it's nice to set up automatic emails that are triggered in the background.

Operational Use

In this section, we'll set up an automatic email notification that sends an email to the message processor if the status changes from NEW to IN PROCESS. We'll describe the configuration activities necessary to create this email action, as well as assign the conditions so that it's scheduled and started according to the requirements of the operational use case.

Configuration Activities

The following configuration activities will describe how to adapt the existing standard email action to provide a much more automated and seamless notification method.

Create Action Definition

To create the action definition, follow these steps:

1. Execute Transaction CRMC_ACTION_DEF.

2. Navigate to the action profile assigned to the transaction type from which you'll require an email notification to trigger (e.g., YMIN_STD).

3. Click the CHANGE button to enable edit mode.

> **Tips & Tricks**
>
> In SAP Solution Manager, the action definition and related processing methods for an email notification already exists in the standard action SMIN_STD_MAIL. To send an email based on our requirements, we'll begin by copying this action.

4. Highlight the action definition YMIN_STD_MAIL, and click the COPY AS button shown in Figure 10.167.

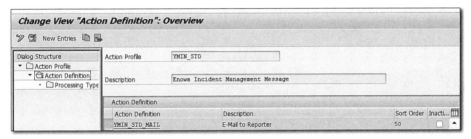

Figure 10.167 Select E-Mail to Reporter Standard Action and Copy

5. In the CHANGE VIEW "ACTION DEFINITION": DETAILS OF SELECTED SET screen, enter a name in the ACTION DEFINITION field and a short description of the action in the DESCRIPTION field as shown in Figure 10.168.

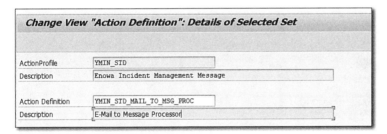

Figure 10.168 Enter Action Definition Name and Description

6. Press [Enter].

7. Click SAVE in the CHANGE VIEW "ACTION DEFINITION": OVERVIEW screen.

8. In the same screen, double-click the action you just copied and saved.

9. In the CHANGE VIEW "ACTION DEFINITION": DETAILS screen, select the flag for the value PARTNER-DEPENDENT as shown in Figure 10.169.

10. Update the values in the action definition based on Figure 10.169.

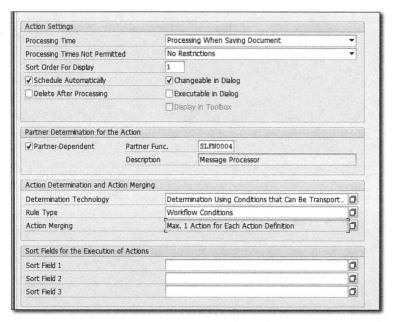

Figure 10.169 Maintain Details of the Action Definition

11. Click on the ACTION DESCRIPTION tab, and provide a description or some notes for the action as shown in Figure 10.170.

Tips & Tricks

If you're enabling your action to fire on a specific status, it may be good to note that in the action description.

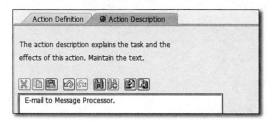

Figure 10.170 Action Description Tab: Add Short Description Here

12. Click SAVE.

13. Double-click the PROCESSING TYPES folder in the dialog structure as shown in Figure 10.171.

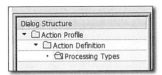

Figure 10.171 Select Processing Types Folder

14. In the CHANGE VIEW "PROCESSING TYPES": OVERVIEW screen, you can view the various processing information associated with the message.

As shown in Figure 10.172, the form AI_CRM_IM_SHORT_TEXT_LINK_FORM is assigned to this email action. This is the Smart Form that will be used as the content when the mail is sent to the message processor. You may copy and modify this particular form, or even create new forms, in Transaction SMARTFORMS. Make sure that you activate the Smart Form and assign it to the action definition for it to be used successfully.

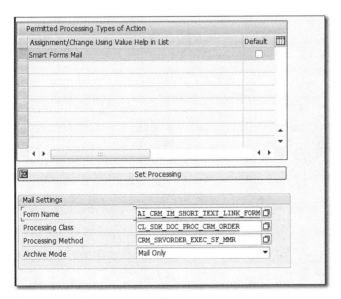

Figure 10.172 View Processing Types

Create Schedule and Start Conditions

Now, we'll create the conditions that will indicate at which point the new action will trigger an email notification to the Message Processor.

1. Execute Transaction CRMC_ACTION_CONF.

2. Click the TECHNICAL NAMES button as shown in Figure 10.173.

3. Scroll to the bottom of the SCHEDULING OF ACTIONS window, and double-click the entry YMIN_STD.

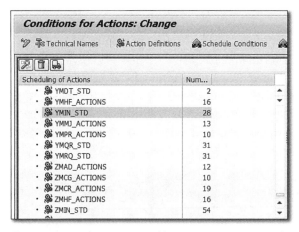

Figure 10.173 Select Action Profile

4. Click the CREATE button (☐ ⬛).

5. From the drop-down list, select the action you created in the previous step— SEND E-MAIL TO MESSAGE PROCESSOR—as shown in Figure 10.174.

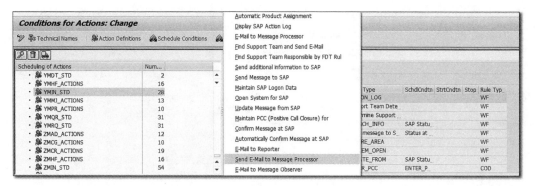

Figure 10.174 Select the Action Send E-Mail to Message Processor

We'll now configure the schedule conditions and start conditions for the email action. The schedule condition identifies when the action should be scheduled. In this example, we want the action to be scheduled when the message is in the status New. The start condition identifies when the action should be triggered. In the example, we want the email notification to be sent to the message processor when the status goes to In Process.

1. Click the Schedule Condition tab as shown in Figure 10.175.

2. Click the Edit Condition button.

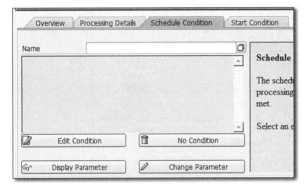

Figure 10.175 Select the Schedule Condition Tab

3. Enter a name for the schedule condition in the Name field as shown in Figure 10.176.

> **Note**
>
> To keep things organized and segregated, we prefer to name the condition based on the name of the action definition as shown in the example. It's important to know that many actions can share the same schedule condition. However, the schedule conditions are linked if you choose to share them among action definitions. In other words, if you make a change to the parameters, that change could affect the processing order of the other actions that share the same condition.

Figure 10.176 Enter the Name of Schedule Condition

4. Click in the CONDITION DEFINITION area to begin the condition configuration.

5. In the CHANGE CONDITION window, create a condition based on the expression, operator, and constant shown in Figure 10.177.

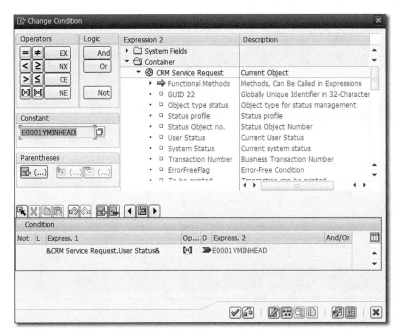

Figure 10.177 Create Schedule Condition

Tips & Tricks

If you want to schedule your action at more than one point (e.g., if it should also be scheduled if the status is in CUSTOMER ACTION, FORWARDED), simply append multiple lines with the same logic separated by an or indicator.

---

6. Press Enter .

7. Confirm that your condition definition appears as shown in Figure 10.178.

Figure 10.178 Completed Schedule Condition

8. Click SAVE.

9. Now, we'll create the start condition. As we already described, the start condition will indicate when the action will trigger. You'll need to create a unique name for your start condition. Perform the same steps you just finished, but make sure you create the start condition within the START CONDITION tab. Your start condition could appear as shown in Figure 10.179. Notice that you'll need to add the error flag line at the end of the start condition.

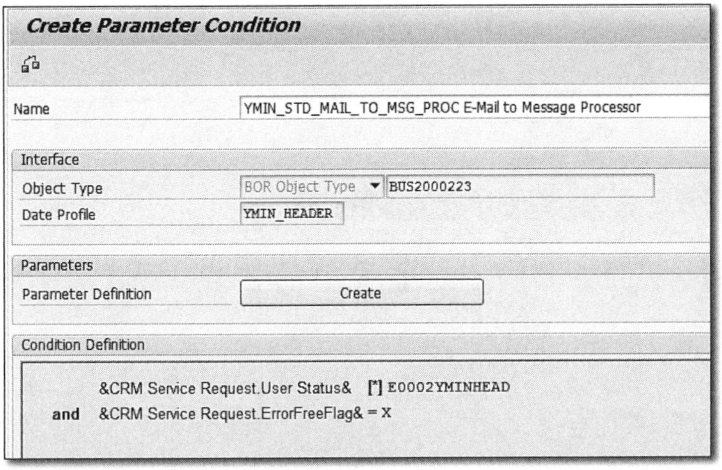

Create Parameter Condition

Name	YMIN_STD_MAIL_TO_MSG_PROC E-Mail to Message Processor

Interface

Object Type	BOR Object Type ▼ BUS2000223
Date Profile	YMIN_HEADER

Parameters

Parameter Definition	Create

Condition Definition

	&CRM Service Request.User Status& [*] E0002YMINHEAD
and	&CRM Service Request.ErrorFreeFlag& = X

Figure 10.179 Start Condition Configuration

10. Be sure to click SAVE. For conditions, it's a good idea to click SAVE multiple times (three times) to be sure every setting is captured.

Maintain SMTP Settings

Now, we'll make the settings necessary for SMTP (simple mail transfer protocol) to deliver the email notification.

1. Execute Transaction SCOT.

2. Double-click the node SMTP as shown in Figure 10.180.

3. In the SAPCONNECT: GENERAL NODE DATA OF NODE SMTP screen, update the settings as shown in Figure 10.181. You'll need to enter the MAIL HOST and MAIL PORT specific to your details.

4. Click the SET button next to the INTERNET flag.

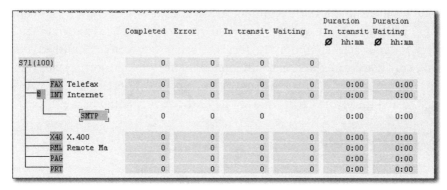

	Completed	Error	In transit	Waiting	Duration In transit ∅ hh:mm	Duration Waiting ∅ hh:mm
S71(100)	0	0	0	0		
FAX Telefax	0	0	0	0	0:00	0:00
INT Internet	0	0	0	0	0:00	0:00
SMTP	0	0	0		0:00	0:00
X40 X.400	0	0	0	0	0:00	0:00
RML Remote Ma	0	0	0	0	0:00	0:00
PAG	0	0	0	0	0:00	0:00
PRT	0	0	0	0	0:00	0:00

Figure 10.180 Select the SMTP Node

Figure 10.181 Click Internet Settings

In the SAPCONNECT: ADDRESS TYPE FOR NODE screen, we've added the details of who can receive emails from SAP Solution Manager. As you can see in Figure 10.182, we've also updated the output of the Smart Forms to send as a .TXT value. This is helpful so the parties receiving the email notification don't have to open a .pdf document.

5. Click CONFIRM, and save your work.

Figure 10.182 Maintain Address Details

Enable SAPconnect

For the emails to send on a periodic basis, you must schedule an SAPconnect job. Follow these steps:

1. In Transaction SCOT, click the SEND JOBS () button as shown in Figure 10.183.

SAPconnect: Administration (system status)

Figure 10.183 Select Send Jobs

2. In the SAPCONNECT: ACTIVE AND SCHEDULED SEND JOBS window, select SCHEDULE JOB • SCHEDULE JOB FOR INT as shown in Figure 10.184.

3. In the SEND JOB: SELECT VARIANT window, define the values in the JOB VALUES section according to your requirements (see Figure 10.185).

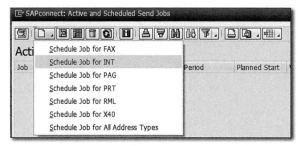

Figure 10.184 Schedule Job for INT

Note

The default values should suffice; however, you should change the BACKGROUND USER setting to a system user.

Figure 10.185 Job Variants

4. Click CONTINUE.

Expected Result(s)

After a message goes from the status of NEW to IN PROCESS, the email will be sent to the queue in Transaction SCOT. After the SAPconnect job has finished, the business partner within the MESSAGE PROCESSOR field will receive the email notification containing the text you have maintained in the Smart Form.

You may use the standard action definition for emails to manually trigger notifications to business partners. Simply copy the existing E-MAIL TO REPORTER action, and update the partner determination details based on your requirements. No maintenance within the conditions is necessary because the action isn't conditional upon a preliminary activity.

In the next section, we'll provide examples and identify the configuration activities necessary to maintain customizations with the priorities in AIM.

10.10   Priorities

Priorities, impact, and urgency configuration activities occur within the two IMG activities identified in Figure 10.186.

Figure 10.186 IMG Activities to Maintain Priorities

In this section, we'll describe the configuration steps required to maintain priority values while processing transactions related to SAP ITSM. In addition to the standard IMG settings, we'll include a configuration example for how to incorporate a new priority value. Further, we'll explain how to default service messages to a particular priority value at message creation. We'll also use Transaction DNO_CUST01 to ensure that the service basis message receives the new priority value.

Furthermore, to set a default priority value, we'll make a Customizing setting in the DEFINE TRANSACTION TYPES IMG activity. We'll also describe how to update the schema for recommended priority values. Urgency, impact, and logic will be covered regarding how priorities are recommended by SAP Solution Manager.

10.10.1   Priority Values

Priority values are global across all SAP ITSM scenarios. In other words, if you make a change to the standard priority values, those changes will appear in incidents, problems, requests for change, and so on. We don't recommend altering the standard priority values for the following reasons:

- They align with ITIL standards for how priority values should be maintained to deliver IT services.
- They align with the SAP Support backbone's priority definition.
- However, you can *add* priority values, which we'll explain in the following subsections.

Operational Use

In the following subsection, we'll describe how to add a priority value of NOT ASSIGNED. This priority value happens to be a common business requirement for IT service organizations to classify service transactions that haven't yet been analyzed and assigned a priority by the support teams. Moreover, ITIL provides a PLANNING priority value in which this NOT ASSIGNED example closely aligns.

Configuration Activities

To add a new priority value, the following activities must be completed:

- Configure priorities of dates
- Configure notification value
- Adjust default values

Now, we'll walk through each of these configuration activities.

Configure Priorities of Dates

To configure priorities of dates, follow these steps:

1. Execute the IMG activity MAINTAIN PRIORITIES OF DATES.

2. In the CHANGE VIEW "PRIORITIES": OVERVIEW screen, select the NEW ENTRIES button as shown in Figure 10.187.

Figure 10.187 Select New Entries Button

3. In the NEW ENTRIES: DETAILS OF ADDED ENTRIES screen, maintain values for the following fields as identified in the example in Figure 10.188:

- ▶ PRIORITY: "*5*"

- ▶ DESCRIPTION: "Not Assigned"

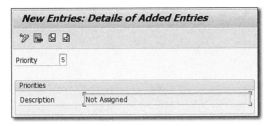

Figure 10.188 Details of Added Priority

4. Click SAVE.

5. Update the PRIORITIES table as shown in Figure 10.189 to include your newly created priority value.

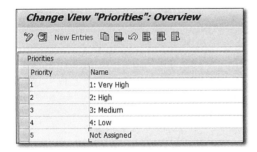

Figure 10.189 Overview of All Priority Values

Configure Notification Value

To configure the notification value, follow these steps:

1. Execute Transaction DNO_CUST01.

2. In the CREATE VIEW "NOTIFICATION TYPE": OVERVIEW screen, highlight the SLF1 entry within the NOTIFICATION TYPE table, and double-click the PRIORITIES folder in the dialog structure as shown in Figure 10.190.

3. In the CHANGE VIEW "PRIORITIES": OVERVIEW screen, select the NEW ENTRIES button as shown in Figure 10.191.

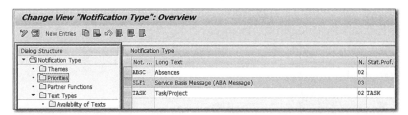

Figure 10.190 Select SLF1 and Priorities

Figure 10.191 Select New Entries

4. In the CHANGE VIEW "PRIORITIES": DETAILS OF SELECTED SET screen, maintain the following fields per the example in Figure 10.192:

▶ NOTIFICAT. TYPE: "SLF1"

▶ PRIORITY: "5"

▶ PRIORITY: "Not Assigned"

▶ PRIORITY: "Priority "Not Assigned""

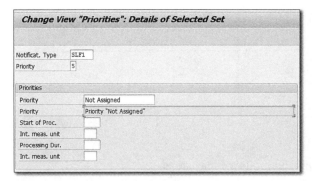

Figure 10.192 Maintain Details of Priorities

5. Click SAVE.

Adjust Default Value

Finally, we'll adjust the default value so that all new messages created will default to the value of NOT ASSIGNED. Note that this particular Customizing can be adapted for a specific transaction type (i.e., it isn't a global Customizing setting).

1. Execute the IMG activity Define Transaction Types.

2. Highlight a transaction type (e.g., YMIN), and double-click the folder Assignment of Business Transactions in the dialog structure as shown in Figure 10.193.

Figure 10.193 Assignment of Business Transactions for YMIN

3. In the next screen, Figure 10.194, highlight the Business Activity value in the Transaction Category table, and double-click the Customizing header folder in the dialog structure.

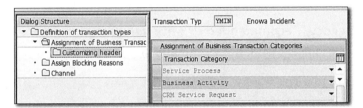

Figure 10.194 Select Customizing Header Business Activity

4. As shown in Figure 10.195, maintain the details within the Default Data for the Priority field (e.g., Not Assigned).

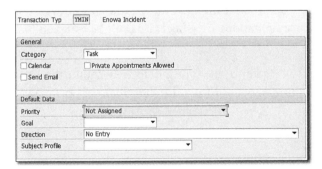

Figure 10.195 Maintain the Default Data for Priority Not Assigned

5. Click Save.

Expected Result(s)

The following are the expected results, based on the three configuration activities we've already described:

▶ All transactions within SAP ITSM will have the newly created priority value of NOT ASSIGNED.

▶ Incidents that have been created will default to the value NOT ASSIGNED as shown in Figure 10.196.

Figure 10.196 New Priority Value Available in Message Processing

10.10.2 Impact, Urgency, Recommended Priority Values

According to ITIL, *priority* should be derived as an output based on both impact and urgency values.

Operational Use

As mentioned in previous chapters, SAP Solution Manager provides a schema delivered standard for recommending priority values based on a combination of impact and urgency. Because the recommended priority logic is aligned with ITIL standards, we recommend that your organization use these values. Moreover, the values (contrary to the IMG documentation) are global and can't be assigned to a particular transaction type.

In this section, we'll help you navigate to the appropriate area within the IMG should your organization's requirements call for a different logic in how priorities are recommended.

Configuration Activities

Define Impact and Urgency Levels

To define the levels, follow these steps:

1. Execute the IMG activity DEFINE IMPACT/URGENCY/RECOMMENDED PRIORITY. As you can see in Figure 10.197, each impact value is given an identification number as well as a description. In this table, you have the option to rename or add impact levels. Again, we recommend that your organization adopt the standards provided by SAP Solution Manager.

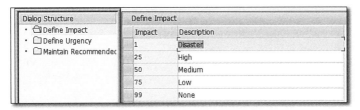

Figure 10.197 Define Impact Values

2. Double-click on the DEFINE URGENCY folder in the dialog structure to navigate to the delivered urgency values as represented in Figure 10.198. Similar to the impact values, the default urgency values are presented in the DEFINE URGENCY table.

Dialog Structure	Define Urgency	
• ☐ Define Impact	Urgency	Description
• ☐ Define Urgency	1	Emergency
• ☐ Maintain Recommended	25	Very High
	50	High
	75	Medium
	99	Low

Figure 10.198 Define Urgency Values

Assign Levels to Priority Value

If you have added a new impact or urgency value, their combinations should be maintained in the MAINTAIN RECOMMENDED PRIORITY table by selecting the corresponding folder in the structure node, as shown in Figure 10.199.

Furthermore, if you disagree with how the system recommends a priority (e.g., you believe that an URGENCY value of EMERGENCY combined with an IMPACT value of HIGH should result in a priority of HIGH as opposed to VERY HIGH), you can adapt the settings here.

Dialog Structure	Maintain Recommended Priority			
• ☐ Define Impact	Urgency	Impact	Prio.	Description
• ☐ Define Urgency	1	1	1	1: Very High
• ☑ Maintain Recommended Priority	1	25	1	1: Very High
	1	50	2	2: High
	1	75	2	2: High

Figure 10.199 Maintain Recommended Priorities

Expected Result(s)

Based on the values in the Customizing tables, you should expect to see your changes take immediate effect within the PROCESSING DATA on the DETAILS assignment block (Figure 10.200) when creating/processing an SAP ITSM transaction.

Additionally, if you have added to or adapted how priorities should be recommended, those changes should be available as well.

Figure 10.200 Processing Data in IT Service Management

In the next section, we'll provide configuration examples and directions on some of the smaller, less complex capabilities in AIM.

10.11   Additional Capabilities

Aside from the main functionalities that are embedded throughout the processing of incidents, problems, and service requests, there are key components that drive value for AIM in SAP Solution Manager. In this section, we'll include a couple of miscellaneous functionalities that lie outside of the core functional configuration that we've described in the previous sections of this chapter.

We'll describe the steps to configure the following:

▶ Setting up customer-specific application components

▶ Enabling the worklist in the SAP CRM Web UI to contain specific transaction types based on business roles

10.11.1 Customer-Specific Application Components

We've previously described the use of SAP components in the realm of forwarding messages to SAP support as well as automatic support team determination based on SAP components.

Customer-specific application components are helpful if you want to have requesters create service messages based on applications that aren't included in the default SAP application components.

Operational Use

In our configuration example, we want to enable the creation of service messages based on the application component Microsoft SharePoint. In other words, if users have an error occur on the SharePoint server, they should be able to identify a specific component for that IT asset. Furthermore, the support team handling non-SAP systems should be determined if this service message is created.

Configuration Activities

The configuration activities for maintaining customer-specific application components can be found in the IMG as shown in Figure 10.201.

Figure 10.201 Customer-Specific Application Components IMG Activities

> **Note**
>
> Before configuring a customer-specific application component, check the default SAP application components to see if the entry is already there. The default components include third-party software (e.g., ARIS), Apple products (e.g., iPad), and so on. The standard application components delivered from SAP will likely meet all of your requirements for creating and processing messages.

Create Application Component

To create an application component, follow these steps:

1. Execute IMG activity MAINTAIN USER APPLICATION COMPONENTS.

2. Maintain the details of the customer-specific application component based on the following values and Figure 10.202:

- ▶ COMPONENT: ID of the component
- ▶ DESCRIPTION: Description of the component
- ▶ COMPONENT LEVEL – Hierarchy level of the component
- ▶ NODE TYPE: "0" for header, and "1" for normal nodes

3. Select the SELECTABLE checkbox.

Figure 10.202 Maintain Details of Component

4. Click SAVE.

Activate BAdI

The BAdI AIC_CUSTOM_COMPONENTS will read the application components that you have maintained in the previous step and add them to the overall list of SAP application components.

1. Execute IMG activity ACTIVATE BADI.

2. Click CONTINUE, as shown in Figure 10.203, to activate the BAdI.

Refresh Component List

Because SAP updates the components on a regular basis, you can refresh them manually with Report DSWP_GET_CSN_COMPONENTS. This report will delete and reintroduce all components (both SAP and non-SAP). The report also allows you to add or maintain your customer-specific application components independently of the SAP application.

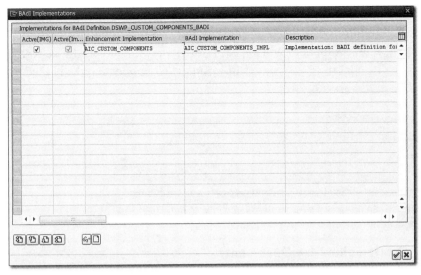

Figure 10.203 Activate the BAdI

1. Execute IMG activity REFRESH COMPONENT LIST.

2. Enter the PROGRAM "DSWP_GET_CSN_COMPONENTS", and click EXECUTE as shown in Figure 10.204.

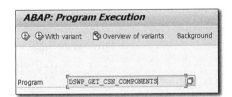

Figure 10.204 Run Refresh Report

3. Select the parameter REFRESH CUSTOMER COMPONENTS as shown in Figure 10.205.

4. Click EXECUTE.

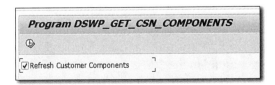

Figure 10.205 Refresh Customer Components

Expected Result(s)

In SAP Collaboration, when maintaining the SAP components, your customer-specific application component will appear in the same structure as the delivered SAP components. Figure 10.206 shows the example component created based on the activities in the previous steps.

Figure 10.206 Customer-Specific Application Components Available

10.11.2 Create Follow-Up Document

Because standard transactions are never really used beyond a proof-of-concept or prototype scenario in which no Customizing is performed, activities need to be performed to link everything together. Also, transaction types can be copied directly in the message in the SAP CRM Web UI. For the system to know which transaction type to be copied to, it needs to be defined in Customizing.

Operational Use

Defining copy control rules (as described in the following subsections) will allow you to control which documents are created as follow-ups to a particular transaction. We need to enable the system so that a customer incident message (YMIN) can trigger a follow-up problem message (YMPR).

Furthermore, we can identify which elements are carried over from one document to another in the mapping rules for copy control. For example, priorities, categories, text, and so on can be brought over (or left behind) to the follow-up document.

Configuration Activities

The configuration activities for setting up how customer transactions and their data flow from one source to the next are found in the FOLLOW-UP DOCUMENT CREATION section of the IMG as shown in Figure 10.207.

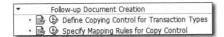

Figure 10.207 Follow-up Document Creation IMG Activities

Define Copying Control for Transaction Types

First, we'll set up how one customer transaction can copy to another customer transaction.

1. Execute the IMG activity DEFINE COPYING CONTROL FOR TRANSACTION TYPES.

2. Select the relevant AIM customer transaction types (source transaction type) that map to a standard transaction type (target transaction type) as shown in Figure 10.208.

3. Select the COPY AS button.

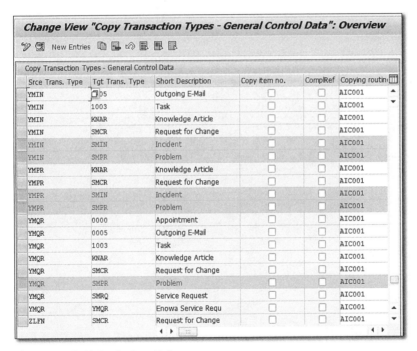

Figure 10.208 Maintain Copy Rules

4. Override the values in the TGT. TRANS. TYPE column with your customer transaction type (e.g., YMPR instead of SMPR) as shown in Figure 10.209.

5. Press Enter .

Copy Transaction Types - General Control Data					
Srce Trans. Type	Tgt Trans. Type	Short Description	Copy item no.	ComplRef	Copying routin
YMIN	YMIN	Enowa Incident	☐	☐	AIC001
YMIN	YMPR	Enowa Problem	☐	☐	AIC001
YMPR	YMIN	Enowa Incident	☐	☐	AIC001
YMPR	YMPR	Enowa Problem	☐	☐	AIC001
YMQR	YMPR	Enowa Problem	☐	☐	AIC001

Figure 10.209 Update Target Transaction Type

6. Click SAVE.

Specify Mapping Rules for Copy Control

Now, we'll set up how one customer transaction can trigger or flow to the follow-up customer transaction. In other words, these steps show you how to not follow-up with a standard SAP transaction type. You can also determine which data flows from one document to the other.

1. Perform the same steps in the IMG activity SPECIFY MAPPING RULES FOR COPY CONTROL as you have for the previous IMG activity. As you can see in Figure 10.210, the table functions in the same manner (e.g., source and target column [SP and TP Type]).

Change View "Copy Control Rules": Overview							
New Entries							
Dialog Structure	**Copy Control Rules**						
▼ 🗀 Copy Control Rules	SP Type	TP Type	Copy Prio.	Copy Cat.	Copy Text	Copy Date	Copy IBase	R
• 🗀 Text ID Mapping	YMIN	SMCR	✓	✓	✓	☐	✓
• 🗀 Dates Mapping	YMIN	SMIN	✓	✓	✓	☐	✓
	YMIN	SMPR	✓	✓	✓	☐	☐
	YMPR	0000	☐	☐	✓	☐	☐
	YMPR	0005	☐	☐	✓	☐	☐
	YMPR	1003	☐	☐	✓	☐	☐
	YMPR	KNAR	✓	☐	✓	☐	☐
	YMPR	SMCR	✓	✓	✓	☐	✓
	YMPR	SMIN	✓	✓	✓	☐	☐
	YMPR	SMPR	✓	✓	✓	☐	✓
	YMQR	0000	☐	☐	✓	☐	☐
	YMQR	0005	☐	☐	✓	☐	☐
	YMQR	1003	☐	☐	✓	☐	☐
	YMQR	KNAR	✓	☐	✓	☐	☐
	YMQR	SMCR	✓	✓	✓	☐	✓
	YMQR	SMPR	✓	✓	✓	☐	☐
	ZLFN	SMCR	☐	☐	☐	☐	☐
	ZMCR	SMAD	✓	✓	✓	✓	✓
	ZMCR	SMAD	✓	✓	✓	✓	✓

Figure 10.210 Select Transaction Types to Define Mapping

2. Override the values in the TP TYPE column with your own customer values as shown in Figure 10.211. At this time, you can determine which data will carry over into the follow-up document.

Figure 10.211 Maintain Target Transaction Type

3. Press Enter.

4. Click SAVE.

Expected Result(s)

When you create a follow-up document based on a customer-defined transaction type, a customer-defined transaction should open rather than an SAP-delivered standard document (Figure 10.212).

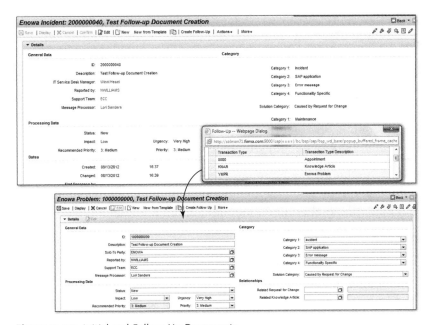

Figure 10.212 Initial and Follow-Up Documents

Also, any data that you marked in the preceding Customizing tables should have carried over from the initial document to the follow-up document.

10.11.3   Processing Log

The processing log, available in the SAP CRM Web UI, is available standard to enable audit/history logs for several characteristics in a message. In Customizing, you can remove specific log types for your transaction, or you can set a default log type to be available when a transaction is accessed.

Operational Use

The Customizing capability is flexible in that you can define change history at the field level as well. In other words, you can define which fields that you want recorded in the processing log.

Configuration Activities

The configuration activities for maintaining settings associated with the processing log can be found in the IMG as shown in Figure 10.213.

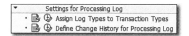

Figure 10.213 Settings for Processing Log IMG Activities

Assign Log Types to Transaction Types

In this configuration activity, we'll set a default log type according to the incident transaction type. If you don't want a default (i.e., you would like all of them to display at run-time), simply don't mark any fields.

1. Execute IMG activity Assign Log Types to Transaction Type.

2. Set the Default flag for the Status Changes entry as shown in Figure 10.214.

Figure 10.214 Set Status Changes Log Type to Default

3. Click Save.

478

Expected Result(s)

When you access an incident (or the transaction type for which you made the processing log settings), you'll see your changes in the PROCESSING LOG assignment block. As you can see in Figure 10.215, the STATUS HISTORY log type is set at default.

Log Type	Log Action	New Value	Old Value	Updated By	Updated On	Updated At
Status History	User Status Changed	Proposed Solution	Customer Action	NWILLIAMS	08/13/2012	07:51
Status History	User Status Changed	Customer Action	In Process	NWILLIAMS	08/13/2012	07:51
Status History	User Status Changed	In Process	Assigned	NWILLIAMS	08/13/2012	07:50
Status History	User Status Changed	Assigned	New	NWILLIAMS	08/13/2012	07:50
Status History	User Status Entered	New		NWILLIAMS	08/13/2012	07:37

Figure 10.215 Status History Log Type as Default in Processing

10.11.4 Worklist

The worklist is a work center within the SAP CRM Web UI used for viewing and accessing various messages related to SAP ITSM. You can customize the worklist to have specific components based on business roles and also to only display transaction types that are specific to your organization.

Operational Use

In this section, we'll provide an example of how to update the worklist configuration settings to include organizational-specific transaction types for AIM. Further, we'll assign these transaction types (and remove the standard SAP transaction types) so that a specific business role can view transactions relative to that role's job function.

Configuration Activities

The configuration activities for settings associated with the worklist can be found in the IMG as identified in Figure 10.216.

Figure 10.216 Worklist IMG Activities

Define Categories

First, we'll define the categories (i.e., transaction types) to be included when viewing messages in the worklist.

1. Execute IMG activity DEFINE CATEGORY GROUPS AND CATEGORIES.

2. Select the SOLMAN-TRANSACTIONS entry within the DEFINE CATEGORY GROUPS table as shown in Figure 10.217.

3. Double-click the DEFINE CATEGORIES FOLDER in the dialog structure.

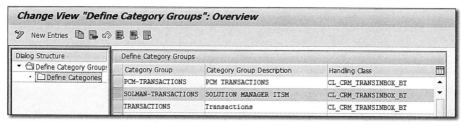

Figure 10.217 Select SOLMAN-TRANSACTIONS

4. In the CHANGE VIEW "DEFINE CATEGORIES": OVERVIEW screen, create new entries based on the values shown in Figure 10.218.

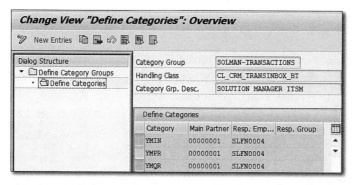

Figure 10.218 Define Customer Categories

5. Click SAVE.

Define Inbox Profile

Now, we'll assign the category values specific to the user's job function by way of business role.

1. Execute IMG activity DEFINE INBOX PROFILES.

2. Highlight the entry SOLMANPRO in the DEFINE INBOX PROFILES table, and double-click the ASSIGN CATEGORIES folder in the dialog structure as shown in Figure 10.219.

> **Note**
>
> In a real-world situation, you would choose to add an entry for a Z business role. We're merely using the standard SOLMANPRO business role as an example.

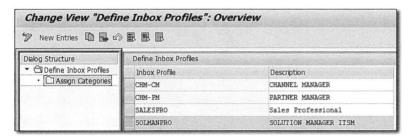

Figure 10.219 Select SOLMANPRO

3. In the ASSIGN CATEGORIES table, we've deleted all values pointing to standard SAP transaction types as shown in Figure 10.220.

> **Note**
>
> This is just an example to show the capabilities and how-to steps for defining an inbox profile. You'll have your own business roles as inbox profiles. Rather than deleting values, you'll simply add your own customer transaction types.

Figure 10.220 Maintain Customer-Specific Transaction Types

Expected Result(s)

When you access the worklist in the SAP CRM Web UI and run a search (without any criteria maintained), the results will yield only the messages based on the transaction types you've previously defined in the inbox profile. Figure 10.221 provides a view of the worklist with the results of customer transaction types.

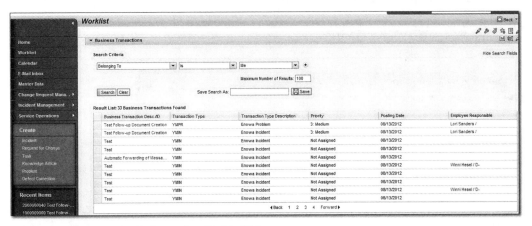

Figure 10.221 Customer-Specific Worklist

10.12 Summary

The objective of this chapter was to quickly ramp you up on the functional components of AIM that showcase the available message capabilities. They are all within SAP Solution Manager; they just need to be adapted and assigned to your customer transaction type.

The basic configuration and system preparation of SOLMAN_SETUP, if completed and enabled, will provide you with a functioning scenario of AIM. Even with customer-defined transaction types and profiles, getting the end-to-end process to work is fairly intuitive with the right master data setup and SOLMAN_SETUP activities completed.

Now that you have the knowledge and direction to configure AIM beyond the standard process, you can really start to identify the power behind the SAP ITSM infrastructure in SAP Solution Manager. Becoming familiar with these configuration activities, adapting the use cases to your own system, and using these use cases as a template to realize your own requirements are the keys to understanding the ins and outs of configuring AIM.

This ends Part II on AIM. In the next chapter, we'll begin the last major section of our book by providing an overview of Change Request Management (ChaRM), followed by an in-depth discussion structured in the same way as the discussion of AIM.

Part III
Change Request Management

The focus of Part III is to dive into the specifics of how ChaRM can control changes and releases that impact your production landscapes. The focus of ChaRM in this book is to provide as much detail as possible concerning how SAP Solution Manager uses existing Transport Management System (TMS) settings to deliver the workflow, approvals, automation, and traceability needed to be your organization's single and only platform for ChaRM.

As you read through Part III, you'll see that we try to structure and organize the content in the same way we did for AIM. Where the majority of the subject matter can map 1:1 from a structuring standpoint, other areas will be explained slightly differently to accommodate ChaRM's unique delivery.

In this chapter, you'll become acquainted with Change Request Management (ChaRM) and find an overview of its goals, infrastructure, features of the new release, and UI.

11   An Overview of Change Request Management

Change Request Management (ChaRM) provides you with the capabilities to manage changes associated with your projects. Project planning, resource management, and software logistics are all covered when you deploy ChaRM for your projects. Whether you are in maintenance or implementation mode, ChaRM provides the end-to-end workflow and functionalities to facilitate the controlled management of changes to both SAP and non-SAP environments.

In this chapter, we'll provide some important introductory details around the Change Request Management (ChaRM) scenario delivered with SAP Solution Manager. Similar to how we introduced Application Incident Management (AIM), we'll explain the goals and motivation of this important component along with how its architecture and infrastructure delivers its processes. We'll jump right in with describing the newest and most important features and enhancements delivered with release 7.1. Finally, we'll revisit the importance of the all-new SAP CRM Web UI, which also extends its benefits and usability into the ChaRM processes.

Whether you're brand new to the ChaRM scenario or you've been exposed to its processes in prior releases of SAP Solution Manager, this chapter is essential to develop the foundational knowledge needed to understand ChaRM in the big picture. You'll find the essential overview needed to understand ChaRM's value holistically while also diving deep into key functionalities.

11.1 Goals and Motivation

We'll start by providing a general overview of ChaRM.

ChaRM is positioned by SAP for customers to deploy a change control tool that is fully integrated into the entire IT landscape as well as various phases across Application Lifecycle Management (ALM). ChaRM is one of the major scenarios within the Change Control Management umbrella within SAP Solution Manager. ChaRM provides the automation, workflows, approvals, and ITIL compliant process flows for implementing changes associated with the IT landscape.

11.1.1 Top Drivers for Change Control

Complex IT landscapes with ever-expanding product bases (both SAP and non-SAP), integrated business processes that span multiple systems, complex requirements from both inside and outside the organization, and the flexibility demanded by the hands-on support teams to keep the business running are just a few of the motivation drivers behind the need for an integrated solution. Of course, we can go on forever about driving factors toward why a tool for managing changes across the landscape is absolutely needed, especially as we start talking about even larger organizations with even more distributed systems and rigorous requirements.

Let's not forget about aligning all of these things to standard SAP IT Service Management (SAP ITSM) disciplines, SAP best practices, and ITIL methodologies. With the requirements and challenges we've already mentioned, these important frameworks must be aligned to your organization's processes for continuous quality and transparency to occur as organizations get larger and systems become more complex.

11.1.2 Addressing the Challenges, Constraints, and Requirements

ChaRM has been available as a change control solution since some of the earliest releases of SAP Solution Manager. Only until recently (SP15 of release 7.0) did it really start gaining attention from the market and implemented instead of even more robust third-party competitors. Regardless of its capabilities in the earlier releases, or how popular it was among the market, it has been a key focus area within SAP for quite some time.

Now, with release 7.1, ChaRM is delivered with a predefined set of workflows and processes that are compliant with ITIL disciplines. We discussed the efforts to stand up SAP ITSM aligned with ITIL disciplines in an organization in Part I. The good news is that they are built in to the standard change processes delivered with ChaRM. If you stick as close to possible to the standards with ChaRM, you're already driving toward an ITIL-compliant solution.

11.1.3 ChaRM in a Nutshell

ChaRM helps coordinate the changes that occur to your IT landscape, SAP, and beyond. It has the capability to manage changes that occur on your SAP systems, non-SAP systems, and various other IT assets. The coordination provided ensures that collisions across changes are identified and potentially avoided so that the business operations aren't interrupted.

The coordination of these changes are all documented (i.e., captured) automatically by the system so that there is full traceability from end to end. You can have an audit log of who approved the change, who handed it off to development, who developed it, who tested it, who approved it for production, and who promoted it to production. All of these details, including dates, times, users, and supporting documentation are housed directly within the change and can be exported at any time depending on your audit needs.

Although we'll focus on ChaRM for maintenance projects specifically (i.e., changes that occur to your production landscape), it also has the ability to control changes across your rollouts, implementations, and upgrades.

Various change types are supported. Whether you're on a defined release schedule or you import transport requests on a one-off basis, ChaRM can support you. Normal changes provide bundling capabilities where changes are collected and moved to production in a single periodic release. Urgent changes are also accommodated in the case of emergencies. Changes can be approved and fast-tracked to production as fast as the users can click through the process. All of these steps support a rapid path to production while still providing the audit capabilities.

ChaRM's workflow and processes use fundamental Transport Management System (TMS) capabilities. Total coverage of change requests and related transport requests are taken into consideration, along with the documentation that ties the functional aspects to the technical drivers.

ChaRM's capabilities enable IT operators (i.e., Basis administrators) to take their hands away from basic TMS activities. Functions such as creating and releasing transport requests and imports to the Quality Assurance System (QAS) all happen behind the scenes. IT operators are involved if there are errors or to perform imports to the production system. These automation capabilities reduce the total workload of IT operators so that they can use their time in other areas.

Taking Advantage of What You Already Own

This point, even though it's just a small section, should actually be dedicated to a single chapter within this book. All of the scenarios we're covering in this book, and all SAP Solution Manager scenarios, are delivered with no additional license fees. ChaRM is a component of SAP Solution Manager, which you're already paying for.

That isn't to say that SAP Solution Manager is free. Education must occur, and internal resources must be used to staff the planning, implementation, and support of ChaRM. Additionally, there may be consultants who are needed to help define the strategy and implement ChaRM if the resources aren't available internally.

However, the considerable cost is absorbed by the license and maintenance fees that you're already paying as part of support. There are no costs associated with procuring, licensing, deploying, or maintaining SAP Solution Manager from a license perspective. The recommendation is to take advantage of what you already own.

SAP Solution Manager 7.1 is here. Whereas prior versions of ChaRM required a close analysis and business case to implement over third-party competitors, version 7.1 provides the robust capabilities needed to deploy SAP Solution Manager's ChaRM component as the single and central platform to administer all changes across your IT landscape.

11.1.4 The Goal of ChaRM

The value and benefits of ChaRM and SAP ITSM as a whole stand on their own legs. Moreover, the benefits of these scenarios speak clearly throughout each chapter. But for the purposes of discussion, there are some key goals from a product standpoint to address the challenges, constraints, and requirements we mentioned in the previous sections.

ChaRM provides full control and transparency over change execution with pre-defined processes, aligned to industry standards, to manage all types of changes across your IT landscape. The goal is for organizations to plan for, implement, deploy, and support a ChaRM solution that is able to offer these capabilities to a full potential. ChaRM helps to realize an IT organization's goals to increase reliability, lower cost of ownership while increasing value, and bridge the gap between IT and the business.

The functionality is there, so the goal is for your organization to uncover the value.

Now that you have a better understanding of ChaRM's potential when it comes to managing changes and releases across production landscapes, we can begin to discuss ChaRM in more detail. In the next section, we'll break down the topic of ChaRM one level deeper by examining the building blocks that enable the goals and motivations to carry forward and drive value for support teams.

11.2 Architecture and Infrastructure

In this section, we'll take a closer look at what ChaRM is made up of from a literal component and methodological point of view. In terms of architecture and infrastructure, we aren't speaking technically (yet). The objective of this section is to take the overview of ChaRM one level deeper before we get into the technical details.

This section will help you understand the pieces of ChaRM and how they are inter-related, dependent, or independent of one another, and how its various layers help support organizations drive change from a holistic and integrated point of view.

11.2.1 Components of Change Request Management

The architecture and infrastructure of ChaRM in SAP Solution Manager is comprised of six main areas as shown in Figure 11.1.

The arrow in Figure 11.1 represents the level to which your organization may choose to adopt ChaRM. For example, Retrofit can be used without leveraging the complete workflow that is available with ChaRM. Depending on your organization, you can choose to adopt ChaRM components at a basic, medium, or full scale.

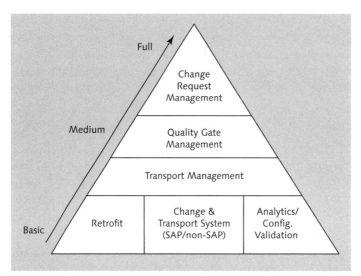

Figure 11.1 Components of Change Request Management

In the following sections, we'll provide a brief overview of each of these areas. Keep in mind that throughout the remainder of the ChaRM chapters, we'll maintain a key focus on the ChaRM component within SAP Solution Manager.

Retrofit

The Retrofit functionality within ChaRM is very important for organizations with dual development systems (one residing with an implementation landscape for project activities and the other residing in a maintenance landscape for production support) that must be kept in sync. This architecture is also referred to as an N, N+1 scenario.

When working in a dual development system scenario, it's important that the implementation team is working in a landscape that is as close to the maintenance production landscape as possible. Because the N+1 landscape will eventually become the "new" N landscape, it's essential to keep the two development systems in sync. The process for keeping these two systems in sync (i.e., applying changes performed in the maintenance landscape to the implementation landscape) is called Retrofit. Rather than manually detecting object conflicts and manually synchronizing between systems, SAP Solution Manager provides the Retrofit feature to automate these activities.

Change and Transport System (CTS)

CTS is a tool that centrally manages changes to Customizing or development objects. Changes are recorded and can be linked together logically or completed independent of one another. In some cases, developers in a single team can use one transport request to group all of their changes together. When the work has been completed, the transport request is released. At this point, changes within the transport request are promoted to other systems (i.e., QAS and PRD). This procedure is automated and known as *transporting*. Transporting allows development in one environment, testing in another, and if the tests are successful, advancement to the production system so the business can accept the changes. Transports are subject to rules controlled by CTS. Transports are logged centrally, and errors are collected to support troubleshooting if imports fail. ChaRM uses CTS throughout the normal, urgent, and defect change processes.

The Enhanced Change and Transport System (CTS+) is the other component, in addition to TMS, that makes up the technical infrastructure of ChaRM. Before CTS+, CTS was the transport capability of SAP NetWeaver AS ABAP. CTS has been enhanced (and identified as enhanced with the + sign) to support non-ABAP objects as well. The goal of CTS+ is to provide all of the transport logistics and monitoring options that are available for the ABAP stack to the Java transports as well.

Analytics/Configuration Validation

Because these functions are independent of our focus on SAP ITSM, we'll briefly discuss this component of Change Control Management.

In short, this component (which has been updated and referenced as a number of terms, so we've consolidated them into the three main ones) is independent of ChaRM. Configuration Validation is used to compare and validate current values of configuration items of a number of systems (compared systems) against a single defined target system (reference system).

The goal is to identify where the inconsistencies lie across systems and have a mechanism to improve the quality of the system landscape wherein the inconsistencies are minimalized or eliminated where it makes sense. End-to-end Change Analysis (Root Cause Analysis) is a prerequisite to enable the functionality and reporting available within this component of SAP Solution Manager.

Transport Management

Native to SAP's process to managing transports within the SAP GUI, the Transport Management System (TMS) is a fundamental component for driving the promotion of transports throughout the landscape for SAP Solution Manager Change Control Management activities. It's one of two components that make up the technical infrastructure of ChaRM.

ChaRM offers workflow, approvals, notifications, auditing, and so on for change and release management activities. However, ChaRM is built on SAP's foundational TMS processes for releasing and importing transport requests from a source system (e.g., development, DEV) to the follow-on target systems (e.g., QAS and PRD).

Rather than executing TMS processes from the SAP GUI, in the managed SAP landscape, ChaRM's infrastructure is woven into the functionality TMS offers. If an SAP landscape is ChaRM enabled, all traditional TMS activities must be executed within the ChaRM environment in SAP Solution Manager.

> **Important!**
>
> TMS doesn't go away with the configuration and activation of ChaRM to manage changes that require transport requests. Although there are different parameters and exceptions (described in Chapter 14) to integrate TMS with ChaRM, ChaRM still depends on TMS for its fundamental intent.

Quality Gate Management

Quality Gate Management (QGM) is a key component within SAP Solution Manager's Change Control Management scenario. QGM enables both implementation and support teams to identify and track changes that occur across the SAP landscape. Reports are available that provide data in respect to all of these changes. Information such as which changes are occurring, which systems, and which owners of the change are outputs of the QGM reports.

The goal of QGM is to maintain control, provide transparency, and meet the quality standards defined by your organization when it comes to promoting changes throughout your landscape.

Milestones, defined by your organization to align to deadlines and specifications, are set in QGM in the form of quality gates (Q-gates). These Q-gates are monitored by either a quality manager or a quality advisory board responsible for advancing changes throughout the landscape. Ultimately, their role is to ensure that the changes that reach production meet the quality standards.

The ChaRM component and QGM component are both standardized change control tools available within SAP Solution Manager. In addition, both of these components have a central transport mechanism and change control system to manage changes across your IT landscape. The differences are as follows:

► QGM focuses on the quality process by means of Q-gates.

► ChaRM provides a process-based workflow for the approval realization of changes.

Change Request Management

Last but certainly not least, ChaRM is a platform within SAP Solution Manager that manages the activities performed throughout the lifecycle of a change. These activities include requesting the change, approving the change, performing the development or configuration of the change, executing the test, and promoting the change to production. In addition to managing these activities, ChaRM provides out-of-the-box processes for handling changes of various scope.

Reporting and analytics are also available to aid various members involved in the Change Management processes to track and have visibility across the various activities. Along similar lines, ChaRM tracks each action along with who performed it and at what point. For example, ChaRM will capture that configuration was tested by Asma on July 20, 2012. These capabilities are beneficial to those organizations seeking better functionality in regards to compliance with auditors.

> **Note**
>
> Using ChaRM to its fullest extent will bring the value of a workflow-enabled change control tool that automates and documents activities within Change Management. However, activating ChaRM for your project will still allow you to adopt basic and medium capabilities. You aren't required to use the workflow.

ChaRM isn't just for managing changes related to SAP. The processes delivered with ChaRM can manage changes across your entire IT landscape. SAP and non-SAP changes, as well as technical and non-technical changes, are supported with the processes delivered with SAP Solution Manager. Further, leveraging these processes delivered with ChaRM align with the Change Management framework defined by ITIL.

11.2.2 The Three Tiers of Change Request Management

Figure 11.2 is a graphical representation of the three tiers of ChaRM. These tiers have been used to describe ChaRM since SAP Solution Manager's earliest releases. The three tiers of ChaRM identify how ChaRM spans beyond the pure technical aspects of moving transports from one system to another.

As you can see, ChaRM provides change administration, project management, and change logistics capabilities. Together, these three tiers enable a comprehensive and end-to-end change control solution that supports all aspects of the support organization.

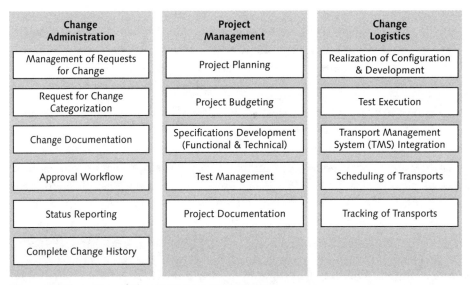

Change Administration	Project Management	Change Logistics
Management of Requests for Change	Project Planning	Realization of Configuration & Development
Request for Change Categorization	Project Budgeting	Test Execution
Change Documentation	Specifications Development (Functional & Technical)	Transport Management System (TMS) Integration
Approval Workflow	Test Management	Scheduling of Transports
Status Reporting	Project Documentation	Tracking of Transports
Complete Change History		

Figure 11.2 Three Tiers of Change Request Management

We'll describe the three tiers of ChaRM in further detail in the following subsections.

Change Administration

Change administration is the messaging capabilities that are offered with ChaRM. The messaging capabilities include everything from the approval to the generation of follow-on documents (transactions) that enable change processes (i.e., normal or urgent).

The change administration tier uses the CRM infrastructure of SAP Solution Manager. In other words, SAP CRM document types are used to drive the workflow settings needed to go from request for change to production import. SAP CRM documents are where you see the business partners involved, the identification number, the description, status values, and basically most everything that we describe in the next section.

ChaRM documents, similar to AIM documents, each have a specific workflow. Consequently, they each have a different action profile and status profile that ultimately drive the traceability by means of an audit trail.

Project Management

Project management, at its highest level, is activating ChaRM for your projects in SAP Solution Manager. For the purposes of our book, we'll focus primarily on the activation of ChaRM for maintenance projects because they are concerned with the production support aspects. However, ChaRM can also be activated for your implementation projects, which means you can bundle transport requests as a group and have them promoted according to the milestones of your implementation project.

Taking it one step further, ChaRM also provides project management capabilities such as serving as an overall document repository. Functional and technical specifications that are specific to the change transaction can be linked to or uploaded directly within the document. Test documentation (instructions and results) can also be uploaded.

The reporting and analytics capabilities within ChaRM help change approvers, Change Advisory Boards (CAB), and release managers better understand the bandwidth across their development teams. This helps from a planning and budgeting perspective. Resources can be assigned and allocated more appropriately based on metrics extracted from ChaRM reports. Further, the assignment of normal changes to a specific release cycle may depend on the availability of the developers within your organization.

Change Logistics

Out of the three tiers, *change logistics* is the technical tier. ChaRM provides the central management of TMS activities across your entire IT landscape. In larger organizations where systems are more complex and span multiple business processes, it's very likely that there will be multiple products and multiple domain controllers. As an IT operator, ChaRM allows you to have central access to all activities associated with the logistics of these components.

Client settings, SCC4 activities, and essentially everything related to TMS is accessible via specific administrator ChaRM screens in SAP Solution Manager. Complete visibility into the transport and change logistics throughout your entire IT landscape is available from SAP Solution Manager.

In the next section, we dive into the key features that are new to release 7.1 of SAP Solution Manager.

11.2.3 An Introduction to Change Transaction Types

Although we have an entire chapter dedicated to describing each change transaction type within ChaRM, we would be missing something if we didn't introduce them as part as the overall composition of this scenario.

We've made mention of change transaction types already, and we'll continue to do so as we begin to describe the new features and enhancements in the next section. Change transactions are the document types, or transaction types, associated with ChaRM. According to standard methodology, ChaRM transaction types are follow-ups to events (incidents, problems, or service requests) that occur during AIM.

Change transaction types define the scope of the work to be done, as well as the workflow (status values, actions, etc.) that is enabled behind the scenes. Each transaction type is different and follows a unique workflow based on its scope. Table 11.1 introduces these transaction types.

> **Note**
>
> Chapter 12 provides a comprehensive overview of these transaction types, including the end-to-end process workflow for each.

Change Type	Highlights
Normal change	▶ Regular maintenance ▶ Related to maintenance cycles ▶ Integrated with TMS
Urgent change	▶ Emergency changes ▶ Ability to fast track to production ▶ Indepedent of maintenance cycles ▶ Integrated with TMS
Administrative change	▶ Administrative activites ▶ Tied to system landscape, not TMS
General change	▶ Changes to IT assets ▶ Not tied to system landscape or TMS
Defect correction	▶ Used during the test phase ▶ Documents test defects and their corrections ▶ Integrated with TMS

Table 11.1 ChaRM Change Transactions

11.3 New Features and Enhancements Delivered with SAP Solution Manager 7.1

For those who are familiar with ChaRM functionality in prior releases, the terminology and benefits will be very familiar in release 7.1. The objective is to display and showcase the powerful functions included in release 7.1 that position SAP Solution Manager to be organization's single platform for processing changes that are required across the IT landscape (even beyond SAP).

For those new to ChaRM, these sections will also be beneficial to you. The terminology may become clearer as we continue through the ChaRM chapters. However, it's important (no matter what level of understanding you may or may not have with ChaRM) to understand the features described in the following sections.

It's impossible to cover everything that is offered from SAP Solution Manager in regards to ChaRM. A multitude of tools, components, and functionalities are both brand new as well as fundamental to ChaRM's core capabilities. The purpose of this section is to provide you with the most significant enhancements and new features delivered with SAP Solution Manager 7.1. Coincidentally enough, they may also be the most powerful yet.

11.3.1 Transaction Types

Similar to AIM, ChaRM processes use transaction types to drive each step and function. By now, you should already be very familiar with what transaction types are as well as their role across SAP ITSM. For the purposes of this section, it's mainly important to understand the deltas between releases 7.0 and 7.1 so you can prepare a strategy to migrate to the new transaction types.

As you can see in Table 11.2, a select few transaction types have no predecessor (i.e., they are brand new). We'll describe their purpose and capabilities as we move through this section of the book.

7.0 Based	7.1 Based	Description
SDCR	SMCR	Request for change
SDMJ	SMMJ	Normal change with TMS
SDHF	SMHF	Urgent change with TMS
SDAD	SMAD	Administrative change without TMS
SDDV	SMDV	For implementation, upgrade, or template projects
SDMM	SMMM	Alternative for task list variant SAP0
SDTM	SMTM	Defect correction
n/a	SMCG	Change of IT assets or legacy systems (general change)
n/a	SMQC	Quality gate Change Management change
n/a	SMCT	Change request template

Table 11.2 Change Request Management Transaction Types

Tips & Tricks

Just as a reminder, the same process and guidelines are applicable for ChaRM transaction types as they were for AIM. It's highly recommended that you copy these over (preferebly with the Transaction Copy tool) into your own customer namespace before adapting them to meet your organizational requirements.

11.3.2 Decoupling and Reassigning Transport Requests

Transport requests contain objects that are attached to change transactions after development or configuration has commenced. There are certain circumstances in which these objects should be decoupled from a change transaction. In other circumstances, they must also be reassigned to another change transaction to satisfy particular requirements.

Use Cases

SAP Solution Manager provides the functionality to decouple and reassign transport requests within normal and urgent change transactions. The following are common use cases that warrant this capability:

▶ A normal change has been created and set to the status of IN DEVELOPMENT. A developer has created a transport request and already assigned development objects to it. The change approver (change manager) has determined that the objects should not go live. The objects must be backed out of the change document.

▶ Functionality contained within the transport request isn't ready to go live with the current maintenance cycle. The objects must be decoupled from the normal change to remove the link to the development objects that shouldn't go live in the current release. If a maintenance cycle must be moved to the go-live phase, and development objects are included within the normal change that aren't ready to go live, they can be decoupled from the normal change using this functionality.

▶ Transport objects that contain emergency fixes within urgent corrections can also be decoupled.

Decoupling a Transport Request

To decouple a request, follow these steps:

1. Highlight the request, and select the option MORE • DECOUPLE TRANSPORT REQUEST from the TRANSPORT MANAGEMENT assignment block (which you can find by scrolling down on the change document) as shown in Figure 11.3.

Figure 11.3 Decouple Transport Request

2. In the DECOUPLE TRANSPORT REQUEST – WEBPAGE DIALOG screen, confirm that the transport request will be decoupled from the change document as shown in Figure 11.4.

Figure 11.4 Confirm Decouple

Important!

After the transport request is decoupled from the change document, it also loses its assignment to a project in the CTS. When there is no CTS project assignment, the transport can be released, in the future, outside of ChaRM. To mitigate this risk, the objects should be assigned to another project as soon as possible, or only specific users should have access to perform this activity.

After the objects have been decoupled from a change document, they should be assigned to another change document immediately to help mitigate the risk just mentioned. This action is performed in the same manner as the objects were decoupled.

3. In a new or different change document, select MORE • ASSIGN TRANSPORT REQUEST from the TRANSPORT MANAGEMENT assignment block as shown in Figure 11.5.

Figure 11.5 Assign Transport Request

The Assign Transport Request – Webpage Dialog screen will appear as shown in Figure 11.6. There are several options for searching for the transport request:

▸ Enter your desired search criteria.

▸ Click the Search button.

▸ Select the appropriate transport request.

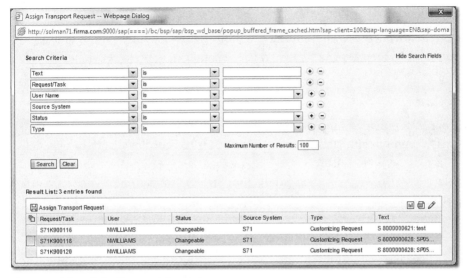

Figure 11.6 Search for Transport Request

The transport request is now assigned to the subsequent change document in the Transport Management assignment block as shown in Figure 11.7.

Figure 11.7 Assigned Transport Request

11.3.3 Change Project Assignment

SAP Solution Manager provides the ability to reassign change documents to different maintenance projects. Often, normal changes that have been assigned to a Release 1 (which goes live on February 15th, for example) requires more time for development and testing. For that reason, the objects associated with that normal change should not go live on the originally intended release date of February 15. Instead, it should be reassigned to Release 2, which goes live on May 15th.

We'll discuss maintenance and project administration in greater detail in Chapter 16. For now, it's important to know that the release date for normal changes depends on the scheduling that occurs within the maintenance cycle. Because maintenance cycles are closely tied to a maintenance project, if a change in release date is required, the project assignment for the normal change must be reassigned.

In the following sections, we'll use a fictional use case to explain our Release 1/2 scenario, and then explain how to switch Maintenance Cycle assignments.

Use Case

Figure 11.8 provides a representation of the use case described previously, which is very common with customers who are trying to coordinate and manage delivery across periodic release cycles. This image is an example of a maintenance cycle/release strategy wherein production imports for normal changes occurred quarterly.

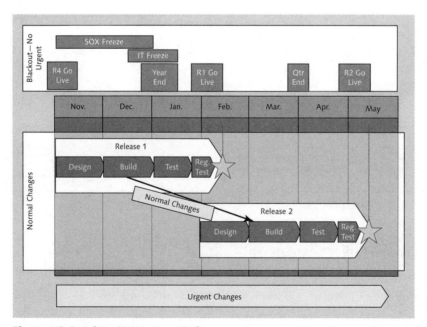

Figure 11.8 Switching Maintenance Cycles

SAP Solution Manager provides the ability for change approvers, depending on the state of the change document, to easily switch between two maintenance cycles.

Table 11.3 provides details about when a normal change can be assigned to another project. After transport objects come into play, they will need to be decoupled (as we described in the previous section) before you can change the project assignment.

After the transport is released, the CHANGE PROJECT ASSIGNMENT option becomes unavailable (as of SP06).

Status	Transport Objects	Change the Project Assignment?	Notes
CREATED	None	Not possible	
IN DEVELOPMENT	None	Yes	For error "Invalid API Call," see SAP Note 1702080
IN DEVELOPMENT	Yes – changeable	Yes	Must decouple objects first
SUCCESSFULLY TESTED	Yes – released	Not possible	

Table 11.3 Criteria for Changing the Project Assignment

Note
For urgent changes, this functionality isn't valid.

Switching between Maintenance Cycles

To switch between maintenance cycles, follow these steps:

1. In the normal change document, select the MORE • CHANGE PROJECT ASSIGNMENT option (Figure 11.9), if your normal change falls within the criteria described in Table 11.3.

2. In the REASSIGN CHANGE TRANSACTION – WEBPAGE DIALOG screen (Figure 11.10), enter your search criteria, or simply click the SEARCH button, to display the list of available maintenance projects.

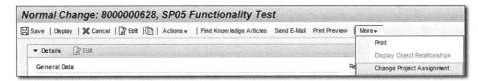

Figure 11.9 Change Project Assignment

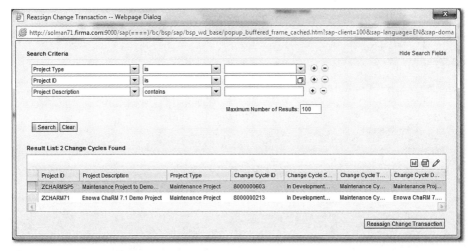

Figure 11.10 Reassign Change Transaction

3. Highlight the appropriate maintenance cycle.

4. Click the REASSIGN CHANGE TRANSACTION button.

As you can see in Figure 11.11, the information details will confirm that your normal change has been reassigned to the new maintenance project. These details are also available within the APPLICATION LOG assignment block.

Figure 11.11 Successful Change of Project Assignment

11.3.4 Status-Dependent Import of Transport Requests

Background jobs that trigger the import of transport requests are mainly concerned with one thing: that the transport request has been released and is awaiting import within the transport buffer. However, certain change document status values are set after the transport request has been released but before it's intended to be imported into production.

In other words, the job(s) that import transport requests into the production system don't care what status the change document is in. As is, the system will import all transport requests that are in the buffer, regardless of document status. This can cause havoc in analytics and reporting in addition to the potential of something breaking in production that was not intended to be promoted at that time. The exception is if you enable the status-dependent import of transport requests functionality in your SAP Solution Manager Customizing.

With this functionality, changes will be imported into the production system based on their status value and not based solely on whether they are in the production buffer. The following are typical examples of where you may find this functionality necessary for your organization:

- Urgent changes imported to production only when their status has reached RELEASED FOR PRODUCTION

- Test messages imported to production only when their status is CONFIRMED

- Normal changes following the preliminary import process (explained in Section 11.3.6) imported to production only when their status is RELEASED FOR IMPORT

11.3.5 Process Improvements

The latest support package releases from SAP Solution Manager 7.1 offer many new functionalities for how changes (SAP, non-SAP, and non-system) can be processed. These functionalities are considered best-of-breed when it comes to creating, processing, and reporting changes. In addition to functions that support organizations in their change and release efforts, process improvements have also been incorporated within release 7.1.

Since the inception of release 7.1 for SAP Solution Manager, there has been a significant overhaul in terms of functions to improve the control of changes in your

IT landscape and to enhance overall user experience. Although there are a vast number of alterations regarding functionality and the UI, the core processes (formally termed normal and urgent corrections) remain the same.

With the exception of a few changes to terminology (e.g., they are now termed *changes* as opposed to *corrections*), there aren't any major changes in how these core processes are executed from a process step perspective.

The exception is the request for change transaction type, which was formally called a change request. The validation feature, as well as the scope extension feature we'll describe next, offers some slight variations (we consider them improvements) to how approvals are reached.

Chapter 12 provides the end-to-end details of these processes, but we'll provide a glimpse of the key improvements offered with 7.1 in the following sections.

Creating Requests for Change

Like AIM, ChaRM has multiple inbound channels. These inbound channels are mechanisms that launch the overall ChaRM process, which starts with initiating a request for change.

It's all about integration with the ALM phases and the other components within SAP Solution Manager that support these phases. The days where requests for change were strictly created from a document type (or form) are over. Now, requests for change are initiated from multiple channels depending on the ALM phase or component the user is working within.

As we mentioned, Chapter 12 will cover the processes with ChaRM extensively, including the inbound channels. For now, it's important to identify these mechanisms as key features that are new in regards to how requests for change are initiated from the end-user ALM community. The inbound channels include the following:

▶ Request for change template

▶ Solution

▶ Implementation or template project

▶ Roadmap

- ▶ Job request

- ▶ AIM

Now we'll discuss the request for change validation feature.

Request for Change Validation

As we mentioned, request for change validation is one change to the former change request process. Validation involves an extra step, which is setting the status to IN VALIDATION via an action as shown in Figure 11.12. The result is that the request for change document status is updated to VALIDATION in which approval can commence.

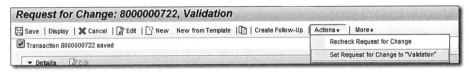

Figure 11.12 Set Request for Change to "Validation"

Validating a change can be considered the first approval layer, prior to the official request for change approval by the CAB. Validation of a request for change, according to SAP, is to be administered by the change approver. The following activities are examples of what the change approver may look for, verify, confirm, and/or update during this step in the request for change process:

- ▶ Appropriate values have been maintained (e.g.,, impact, urgency, priority, category, and business partners).

- ▶ The request is actually a change and not a problem, incident, or training issue.

- ▶ Clarity and completeness of short and long descriptions have been maintained.

- ▶ All required documentation has either been described or uploaded as an attachment.

After the validation step is performed by the change approver, the request for change is released for CAB approval. The request for change is updated to the TO BE APPROVED status, and the workflow continues.

The process diagram in Figure 11.13 provides a snapshot of the request for change process in which the validation and remaining process is identified.

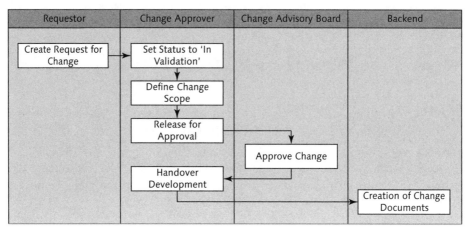

Figure 11.13 Validation Process Steps

Chapter 12 will describe these steps, as well as the initiating steps and user roles, in greater detail.

Scope Extension

Extending the scope of an existing request for change that has already been approved is another process improvement and change to how requests for change are managed in ChaRM. The scope is referred to the type of change document that will be released to the developer after it has been approved by the CAB (e.g., normal, urgent, general change, etc.).

With this functionality, multiple change transaction documents can be tied to the original request for change document. Rather than creating a new request for change document, you have the option to add additional change transactions within the REQUEST FOR CHANGE SCOPE assignment block.

Let's talk about the possible use cases and the steps to extend the scope in the following subsections.

Use Cases

A scenario that is very common, and often unavoidable, is that a request for change requires additional changes after it has reached the testing phase. Several factors may prompt the need for an extension to the original scope:

▶ The developer may determine that what was originally requested in the scope of the change isn't sufficient to meet the business requirements.

▶ Integration effects may require that additional configuration or development is required to complete the change.

▶ Reports may need to be updated.

▶ A break could have been a result of the original request for change.

Extending the Scope

SAP Solution Manager provides functionality to extend the scope of a request for change to accommodate the situations we've described. Follow these steps:

1. As shown in Figure 11.14, you can extend the scope of a request for change by selecting the option EXTEND SCOPE from the ACTIONS button within the request for change document.

Figure 11.14 Extend Scope

After this action is set, the document status is updated to EXTEND SCOPE, and the change approver (or designated support member) can add the additional scope item to the request for change document as shown in Figure 11.15.

Figure 11.15 Add New Scope Item

2. Navigate to the REQUEST FOR CHANGE SCOPE assignment block.

3. Click the INSERT button.

4. Select a value from the CHANGE CATEGORY column.

5. Click SAVE.

Figure 11.16 is a graphical representation of the scope extension process, which is a subprocess (or extension) to the overall request for change process. The process flow shown in Figure 11.16 includes the steps and associated user roles that are used to perform the scope extension according to out-of-the-box SAP standards for ChaRM.

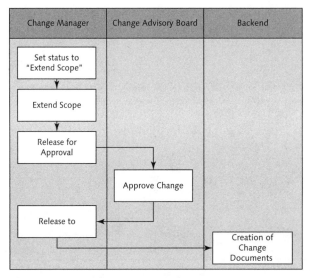

Figure 11.16 Extend Scope Process Flow

As you can see, after the scope is extended, the request for change loops back into the approval procedure. Based on the approval procedure specified for this change request, it will be handed over to development after all of the approval steps have been satisfied by the associated bodies of the CAB or support organization.

11.3.6 Preliminary Import for Normal Changes

Normal changes often become urgent at a moment's notice. At the drop of a hat, the business has made a determination that the once normal change can't wait for the next production release for the change to take effect. It isn't an emergency and must be imported before the maintenance cycle.

SAP Solution Manager 7.1 provides functionality that allows normal changes to follow a preliminary import process, which essentially allows normal changes to operate as an urgent change if the need arises. Furthermore, the documentation and audit traceability for who requested, approved, and imported the preliminary change is captured within the normal change.

Naturally, organizations have felt comfortable with processing urgent changes only. There are controls, intuitive workflow steps, and audit capabilities available to provide enough functionality to operate support organizations with urgent change functionality alone. Moreover, urgent changes provide the flexibility of being able to import a change into the production at any time, and quickly.

Based on our experience, customers would shy away from normal changes because it was extremely difficult to stray away from the one-off process. It was hard to wean off the fact that they didn't have to wait one, two, three, or four weeks for changes to take effect. Moreover, the pain previously associated with backing out normal changes that became urgent gave organizations reasons to stick with urgent changes.

With the latest version of SAP Solution Manager, ChaRM provides a way for organizations to more easily gravitate toward a periodic release cycle because now there is the option to morph a normal change into an urgent change if an emergency arises.

ChaRM provides the controls necessary to ensure that preliminary imports only take effect if the proper channels are followed. Figure 11.17 breaks down the process flow and associated roles available within normal changes should the need for a preliminary import arise.

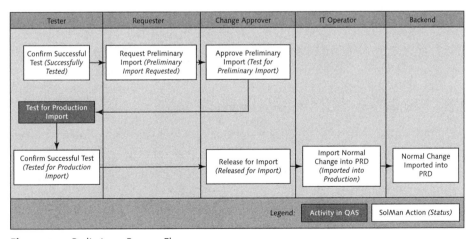

Figure 11.17 Preliminary Process Flow

As you can see from the process diagram, a preliminary import of a normal change into the production system requires its own process, approval, and status values. For this reason, the status schema SMMJHEAD is updated to accommodate this functionality.

Important!

The piece lists must be activated in SOLMAN_SETUP for these changes to take effect. Further, security authorizations must be updated so that your ChaRM users have the appropriate authority to request, approve, test, release, and import the normal change into production prior to its originally intended release date.

11.3.7 Changes Delivered in Assignment Blocks

As the previous sections have identified, there are a lot of new features and enhancements within SAP Solution Manager that vastly changed and improved ChaRM. In this section, we've organized the new features and enhancements that are included as assignment blocks within the SAP CRM Web UI. While the other new features may have been delivered via an action, or were just functionality built into the configuration, the features described in the following sections are called out explicitly in the individual assignment blocks within the request for change or change transaction.

Landscape Accessibility

The LANDSCAPE assignment block, available in the change document, identifies all of the systems that are relevant to the particular change. In other words, it represents the path to production determined by the iBase component specified in the request for change. The iBase component entered is the component identifier for the production client. Once entered, the system knows the related development and test systems based on TMS configuration.

As shown in Figure 11.18, SAP Solution Manager will flag the system that is relevant for logon based on the status of the change document. For example, if the status of the change document is IN DEVELOPMENT, the development system will be flagged as RELEVANT FOR LOGON. At the point of setting the status to IN DEVELOPMENT, the most logical next step is for the developer to start the configuration or development. They can do so immediately by simply scrolling down to this action in the LANDSCAPE assignment block.

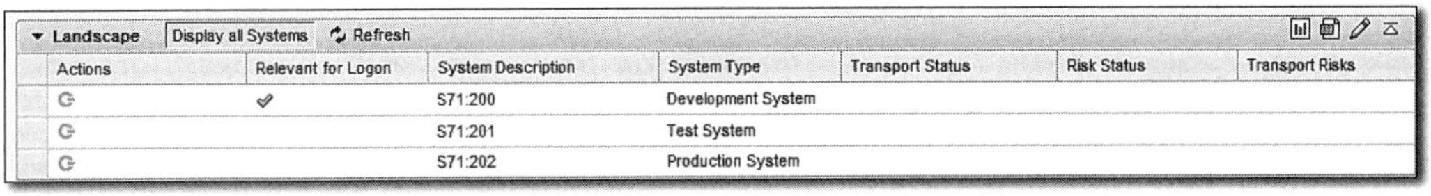

▾ Landscape | Display all Systems | Refresh

Actions	Relevant for Logon	System Description	System Type	Transport Status	Risk Status	Transport Risks
⟳	✓	S71:200	Development System			
⟳		S71:201	Test System			
⟳		S71:202	Production System			

Figure 11.18 Landscape Assignment Block

The DISPLAY ALL SYSTEMS button will expand the data within this assignment block to display all of the systems in which the change will pass through.

The support team member working on the change has the option to access the system directly from the change document by selecting the LOGON TO SYSTEM button located within the ACTIONS column. This allows the developers, testers, IT operators, and so on seamless accessibility to the target system without having to log on from the SAP GUI. Single Sign-On (SSO) is supported so that this logon is truly seamless, as long as trusted RFC connections are established, and your browser settings allow for pop-ups.

Transport Management

Transport requests and their tasks have their own dedicated assignment block, TRANSPORT MANAGEMENT. The following activities and functions related to transport management can be centrally administered directly within the change document:

- Create transport request
- Create a new task
- Create a test transport (for normal changes only)
- Refresh data
- Decouple transport request
- Assign transport request

In addition to the various functions and activities available within this assignment block, you can also view the following key data related to the individual transport requests and related tasks:

- Transport ID
- Request description
- Request type

▶ Owner

▶ Status

▶ Details of critical objects

▶ Details of cross-system object lock (CSOL)

Having this data available within the change document is essential to developers, IT operators, and change managers. It eliminates the need for these parties to log on to the development system and access each individual transport request. In SAP Solution Manager, there is direct traceability and accessibility of TMS data specifically for each change document.

Figure 11.19 shows the Transport Management assignment block populated with two transport requests.

Actions	Transport ID	Request Description	Request Type	Transport of Copies	Tasks	Owner	Status	Critical Objects	CSOL
🔍	S71K900118	S 8000000628: SP05 Functionality Test	Customizin...	0	2	NWILLIAMS	Changeable		
🔍	S71K900125	S 8000000628: SP05 Functionality Test	Customizin...	0	1	NWILLIAMS	Changeable		

Figure 11.19 Transport Management Assignment Block

In the Actions column in Figure 11.20, you can see two icons. The icon that looks like a paper scroll (Show Log icon) directs you to the overview for all of the transport logs associated with the change document's transport. Figure 11.20 shows the results of selecting the Show Log icon.

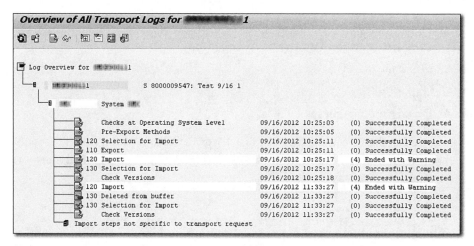

Figure 11.20 Overview of Transport Logs

The second icon, which looks like a magnifying glass, is the SHOW DETAILS icon. Selecting this icon will provide you with an overview of the details of the transport request's task(s). Both icons will launch the user to the associated development system, where the transport request is housed. Figure 11.21 is a result of selecting clicking the SHOW DETAILS icon, or simply selecting the link on the TRANSPORT ID itself.

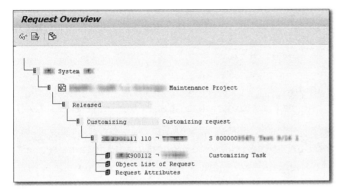

Figure 11.21 Transport Request Overview (Details)

Downgrade Protection

Downgrade protection is an extension (or enhancement) of a fundamental ChaRM component known as cross-system object lock (CSOL). Downgrade protection extends CSOL to provide additional checks to help prevent conflicts of objects in downstream (target) systems.

Downgrade protection provides tracking capability on the objects associated with the change document's transport requests. Conflicts are identified and reported when one of those objects is saved in more than two transport requests that are intended for the same production system.

> **Note**
>
> This functionality is applicable only to ABAP systems in which the CSOL functionality is active on the managed development systems.

In the DOWNGRADE PROTECTION assignment block, you can initiate the downgrade check and review the information related to potential conflicts. Downgrade protection provides these checks for the following change transaction types:

- Maintenance cycles
- Project cycles
- Urgent changes
- Normal changes
- Defect corrections

We mentioned already that the downgrade checks must be initiated. There are three ways in which downgrade checks can be initiated or triggered from the change transactions:

- **Manually**
  Downgrade checks are administered from the DOWNGRADE PROTECTION assignment block by clicking the PERFORM DOWNGRADE CHECK button (Figure 11.22).

- **Automatically**
  Checks can be triggered during the release or import of a transport request. Additionally, they can be triggered automatically if a change document is reassigned to a different maintenance project.

- **From a task list**
  An option is available within the task list to trigger the downgrade check. If a conflict is discovered, a dialog box identifies the conflict to the user and directs the user to the SAP CRM Web UI where the conflict can be further analyzed.

Figure 11.22 Downgrade Protection Assignment Block

Key Features
As we mentioned, there are three options in which downgrade checks can be triggered. If conflicts are reported, SAP Solution Manager will issue a warning type depending on the criticality of the object. The following list identifies the warning types associated with the downgrade checks:

- **Downgrade warning**
  This warning will occur during the export of a transport request and notifies you if identical objects have not yet been imported into the production system.

- **Imminent downgrade**
  This warning will occur during the import of a transport request and notifies

you that identical objects have been released later and already have been imported.

▶ **Overtaker warning**
This warning will occur during the import of a transport request. This warning will notify you of identical objects that have been released earlier but have not been imported yet.

Figure 11.23 provides the results of a downgrade check, the warnings that occurred, and the details of that warning. Based on the results of the check, the status of the conflict is displayed. The status OPEN means that the conflict is waiting to be addressed. If you purposely ignore a conflict, the status is changed to IGNORED.

Details can be displayed for each conflict identified in the DOWNGRADE PROTECTION assignment block. The detail screen (on the right side of Figure 11.23) will provide more information about the conflict. Information regarding the source of the transport and objects involved, for example, will support the developer or IT operator in a better analysis of conflict resolution.

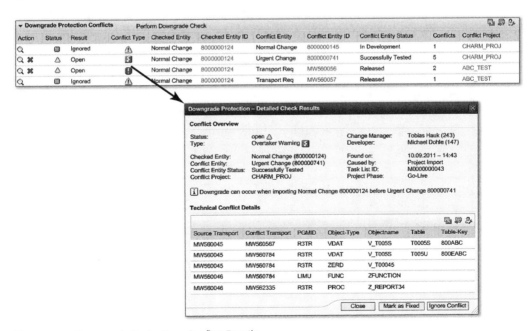

Figure 11.23 Downgrade Protection, Conflict Details

Downgrade checks can be rechecked directly within this assignment block. New conflicts, or unchanged conflicts, will be refreshed, and the developer or IT operator can continue working through each conflict.

Check Types

There are four downgrade check types that are performed by the system during the check:

▶ **Release check**

This check is equivalent to the check provided by CSOL during the saving of objects to the transport requests. If a conflict is detected, the release of the transport is cancelled. The APPLICATION LOG assignment block details are updated as well as the conflict check results within the DOWNGRADE PROTECTION assignment block. If you want to ignore these conflicts, you can check the results on the assignment block, and the release is then triggered again.

▶ **Predecessor check**

Conflicting predecessors (preceding transport requests containing conflicts at the time of importing to the QAS or PRD system) are checked here. Transport requests, as well as transport of copies, are valid during this check. The import will be canceled if the check isn't ignored. Instead of ignoring the conflicts or incurring a canceled import, you may choose to import the predeceding transport request first. Then you may import the follow-on transport request.

▶ **Reassign check**

This check occurs during the reassignment of a change document from one maintenance project to another. Additionally, it's performed during the decouple/reassign transport request activity. Conflicts between the transport requests are reported. You may cancel or continue the activity if conflicts are found. If you choose to continue, the logs will be updated to report that the conflict was ignored.

▶ **Imminent check**

This check identifies impending (imminent) downgrade conflicts when a transport request is imported. This type of conflict is an actual downgrade that would happen if you ignore the conflict.

Important!

It's recommended that you don't ignore imminent downgrade conflicts. Rather, you should restart the import as an alternative. We recommend choosing one of the following options:

▶ Perform a project import of all the transport requests in the correct order, including the newer request and its predecessor (only when the newer request is still included in the project import).

▶ Import by ignoring predecessors via settings appropriate TMS options.

Downgrade Protection Process Flow

The process flow diagram in Figure 11.24 identifies both the user activities and the system actions that are involved during the downgrade checks.

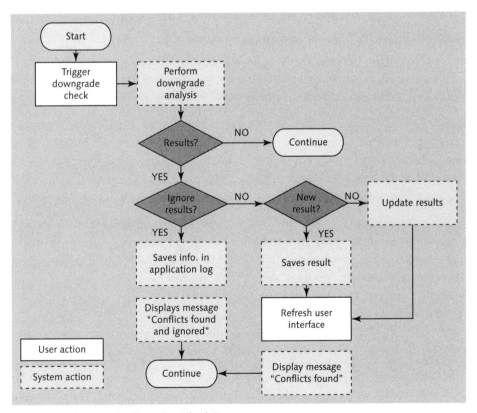

Figure 11.24 Downgrade Protection Check Process

Approval Procedures

When adopting a tool to manage changes to your IT landscape, it's important to have control but also a degree of flexibility. A single approval procedure, as you may have been familiar with in prior releases of SAP Solution Manager, was often too strict. A lack of flexibility limited organizations that required a tool to support multiple approval procedures. SAP Solution Manager 7.1 offers more flexibility in that multiple approvals are supported when processing requests for change. Moreover, they are easily adaptable to meet your requirements for processing requests for change. Standard approval procedure templates are delivered from SAP Solution Manager to give you an idea of how they can be used as well as customized.

Approval procedures are the gateway between the request for change document and the change transaction. They begin after the request for change document has been released for approval and is in the TO BE APPROVED status.

Depending on the organizational requirements for change control, certain approvals may be necessary by certain individuals before a change can be finalized. For example, a change approver and CAB approval are both necessary for requests for change that have a priority value of VERY HIGH.

Approval procedures can involve one or multiple steps. Each of these steps is assigned to a specific business partner function and/or to a specific business partner. When configuring approval procedures, you can define which steps can be executed at the same time. Alternatively, you can also define which steps must depend on another step.

In SAP Solution Manager, approval procedures can be triggered manually by parties within the request for change document, or they can be enabled automatically via rule policies and workflow. We'll explain more about the features of approval procedures in the next section.

Key Features

In the DETAILS assignment block of the request for change, the approval procedure is selected within the CHANGE PLANNING area as shown in Figure 11.25.

The approval procedures are delivered with standard Customizing. They can be adapted to meet your organization's change control requirements for approving requests for change. Depending on the scope of the change, priority, or business area affected, the change can follow the appropriate path to approval.

Change Planning	
Approval Procedure:*	IT Approval Procedure / Change Request Approval Procedure
Project:	
Solution:	

Figure 11.25 Select Approval Procedure

The approvals themselves take place in the APPROVALS assignment block (Figure 11.26). Here, the approval steps and corresponding information (description, partner information, status, time stamps, etc.) can be monitored. Comments, in the form of free text, can be entered as well if a request for change has been rejected (for example). As long as the status of the request for change has not yet been updated to APPROVED, additional information, steps, or approvers can be maintained.

Actions	Step ID	Step Description	Partner Function	Partner ID	Partner Descrip...	Activity	Comments	Entered By	Date	Time
	SMCR000001	Approval Step 1	Change Manager	115	NWILLIAMS	Approved		NWILLIAMS	09/24/2012	17:34

Figure 11.26 Approval Assignment Block

Scope Extension

A scenario that is very common, and often unavoidable, is that a change document requires additional functionality after it has reached testing. The developer may determine that what was originally requested in the scope of the change isn't sufficient to fully execute the implementation.

This is just one example of a case in which the originally requested scope must be extended. Many factors could prompt the need for an extension to the original scope. Alternatively, the change may have integration effects that require additional configuration to accommodate, reports may need to be changed, or a break may have occurred as a result of the change request.

SAP Solution Manager 7.1 provides the ability to extend the scope of a request for change to accommodate those situations in which additional work is needed to complete a change at any point in the process.

As shown in Figure 11.27, you can extend the scope of a change by selecting EXTENDING SCOPE from the ACTIONS button. Subsequently, you can select the scope of the change (e.g., NORMAL or URGENT) from the CHANGE REQUEST SCOPE assignment block. The workflow is then enabled to loop back through your approval procedures and create the follow-on document type.

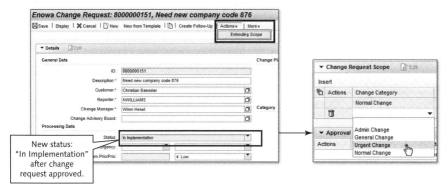

Figure 11.27 Extending Scope

Test Workbench Integration

The test workbench is fully integrated into SAP Solution Manager 7.1 change transaction types. This new feature allows test defects (for example) to link to the associated test plans and test packages directly within the change transaction.

This integration, accessible via the TEST MANAGEMENT assignment block (Figure 11.28), provides direct access to import test information and documentation. You can launch the test package, access the test plan, view the status of the test package, and view the status of each test case within a test package.

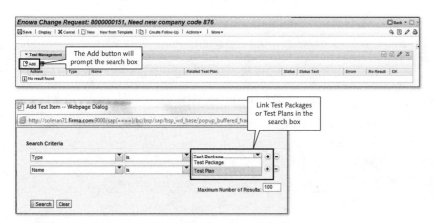

Figure 11.28 Adding Test Workbench Elements to Change Transaction

The new features associated with aligning test management and ChaRM enhance visibility and transparency as well as support the overall integration between ALM and SAP ITSM. Figure 11.29 identifies the various test management details that can be recorded and linked from the test workbench to ChaRM.

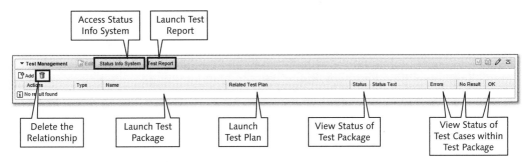

Figure 11.29 Test Management Assignment Block Features

Reference Objects

With SAP supporting more openness when it comes to supporting systems and IT assets outside of the SAP landscape, the need arose for enhancements in the SAP Solution platform to accommodate this strategy. *Reference objects*, in SAP Solution Manager, are products or installations that may require service or change.

Reference objects can include SAP components, non-SAP components, and non-system components. In SAP Solution Manager, several reference objects can be assigned to a single change transaction. Figure 11.30 shows the REFERENCE OBJECTS assignment block included in ChaRM. Reference objects are assigned here for requests for change, and they are assigned in the main processing area in the DETAILS assignment block for change transactions. Even for change documents, they are also represented in the change document's REFERENCE OBJECTS assignment block.

Actions	Installed Base ID	Installed Base Desc.	Component ID	Component Desc.	Object/Product ID	Object/Product Desc.
🗑	1	SOL_MAN_DATA_REP	3254	Solution Manager Controller		
🗑					NORTH AMERICAN PRIN	North American Printer Group
🗑						

Figure 11.30 Reference Objects Assignment Block

Reference objects can also be known for configuration objects or configuration elements. Configuration elements include entities or systems that will eventually require a change and need to be processed through ChaRM. Configuration elements can either reside in the Configuration Management Database (CMDB) or the Landscape Management Database (LMDB). Configuration elements span a broad range of complexity in size. For example, a document can be a configuration element as well as a piece of hardware.

Having the ability to record, maintain, and report on reference objects supports the vision of SAP Solution Manager as a central platform for the delivery of IT services for the entire landscape, even beyond SAP. Functionalities such as these, which are improvements delivered with 7.1, provide IT organizations with the business case for adopting a single tool for SAP ITSM.

In the next section, we'll describe how the power and flexibility of the SAP CRM Web UI for processing messages is extended into the ChaRM processes.

11.4   Web UI for Creating, Processing, and Tracking

In this section, we'll briefly describe how the SAP CRM Web UI capabilities are transferred (or simply made available) to ChaRM's transaction types. As we've described in various chapters associated with AIM, SAP Solution Manager 7.1 delivers SAP ITSM capabilities in a web-based environment, based on the SAP CRM Web UI.

This SAP CRM Web UI is also relevant for all ChaRM transaction types. Figure 11.31 shows the progression from an incident, to a request for change, to a change transaction. While the UI appears the same at an initial glance, the data and fields available for each document are specific to its individual transaction type. This of course goes for the workflow behind the transaction type as well.

Furthermore, the SAP CRM Web UI is enabled for search and monitoring, change documentation, and now managing project phases. Figure 11.32 provides an image of each of these scenarios within the SAP CRM Web UI.

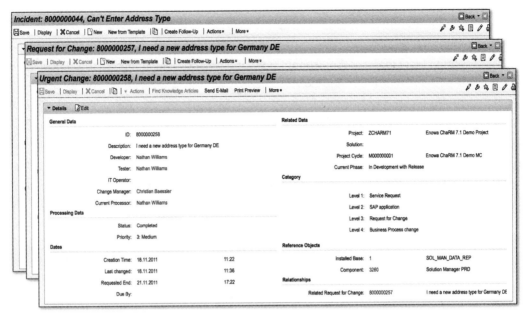

Figure 11.31 Expanding the SAP CRM Web UI Capabilities

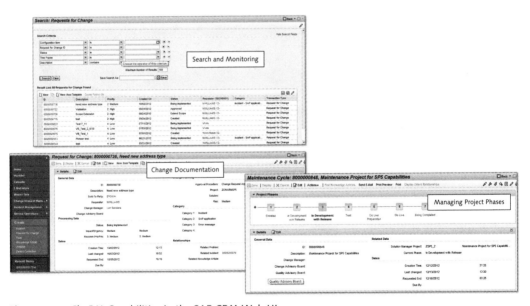

Figure 11.32 ChaRM Capabilities in the SAP CRM Web UI

11.5 Summary

This chapter delivered a lot of information over a wide spectrum of subjects and a high level of detail. You should now understand the big picture of ChaRM as an integral piece of SAP Solution Manager. The motivation behind continual investment, focus, and improvement of this tool hopefully has provided you with an understanding of both the importance and value it brings via its extensive range of capabilities.

Furthermore, you should now have a good understanding of the composition of ChaRM from both a component and process perspective. And finally, we hope that you're excited about the new features and enhancements that are delivered with release 7.1 of SAP Solution Manager. These features alone mark a giant leap forward for how the ChaRM component is now set apart from third-party alternatives. They are proof of the focus and commitment that SAP has invested in providing its customers with a central tool to process changes with full control and transparency.

In the next chapter, we'll provide the details for each individual transaction type in ChaRM. We'll describe the roles throughout the process, as well as explain the end-to-end process for these transaction types.

Integrated with Application Lifecycle Management and Application Incident Management, Change Request Management delivers standard processes to allow for approvals, workflow, control, and traceability across the entire IT landscape (not just SAP).

12 Change Request Management End-User Roles and Process Flows

Chapter 11 provided an overview of SAP Solution Manager's Change Request Management (ChaRM) functionality. We discussed what ChaRM is, and we described the composition of ChaRM and how SAP has been motivated to continually develop and improve its capabilities over the past several years. Chapter 11 also discussed the new features available with release 7.1 in SAP Solution Manager that distinguishes its robust capabilities beyond those of third-party alternatives.

In this chapter, we'll peel back another layer of ChaRM. We'll start by providing an overview of the ChaRM process, from a holistic standpoint. We'll also discuss the players in the ChaRM processes, those who execute each step from requesting a change to promoting the change to production. We'll then explain each change process in detail.

Upon completing this chapter, you'll have a complete understanding of the ChaRM processes from an end-to-end perspective. You'll know who and what is required to deploy a change of any scope into the production system from start to finish.

12.1 ChaRM in the SAP Ecosystem

Before diving in to each individual role and the processes that encompass ChaRM at the singular level, let's take a bird's-eye view of how ChaRM fits not only into SAP IT Service Management (SAP ITSM), but also into the broader SAP ecosystem as well.

In Figure 12.1, we've laid out a very high-level process of the integrated components that serve as inputs, outputs, tools, and techniques to enable end-to-end ChaRM.

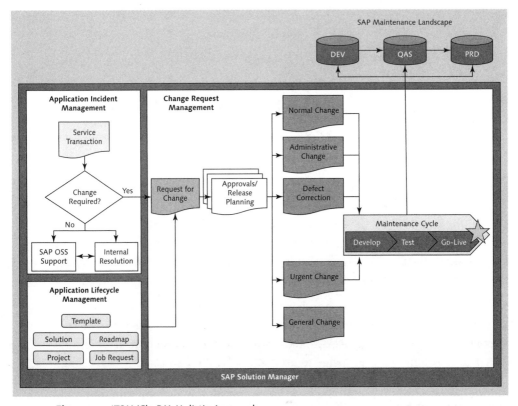

Figure 12.1 ITSM/ChaRM Holistic Approach

If you read this process from left to right, we start by identifying the inputs to ChaRM, or the various options that can trigger a request for change. Starting with Application Incident Management (AIM), if the service transaction type (incident, problem, or service request) doesn't require a change to an SAP component or IT landscape, it follows one path. Either the message can be escalated to the SAP Support backbone for external support, or it's simply resolved within the internal service organization. However, if a change is required, then a request for change document is created based on one of the service transactions we just identified.

If AIM isn't enabled, or the request for change doesn't originate from AIM, ChaRM is connected to various phases across Application Lifecycle Management

(ALM) as well. To that end, the request for change is integrated with the many tools that support ALM. Requests for change can originate from projects, solutions, roadmaps, job requests, and templates.

After the request for change is created, there is a validation and approval procedure that is divided between the change approver and Change Advisory Board (CAB). Depending on the SAP component or IT asset requiring the change, the request for change is approved based on various scope elements. If the change is related to the SAP Transport Management System (TMS) a normal change or an urgent change is required. If the change is related to SAP but not integrated with TMS, an administrative message is appropriate. If the change isn't related to SAP whatsoever, general changes provide the necessary workflow. If errors associated with integration testing occur during the test phase of a release cycle, defect corrections are leveraged.

All of these changes, with the exception of the general change, are linked to the project's maintenance cycle and/or an individual task list. These items control the activities related to the deployment of a change as it's implemented, tested, and ready for go-live. The maintenance cycle uses what has been configured in TMS and is based on your transport track. It's connected to your SAP landscape, which is how SAP Solution Manager controls changes to these systems.

Standard end-user roles and workflows are provided by SAP Solution Manager to perform all activities related to the end-to-end deployment of a change.

This is the comprehensive ChaRM process at a very high level. As we move through this chapter, we'll take each of the process components of ChaRM, including the end-user roles, and describe them piece by piece. We'll kick things off by describing the roles in ChaRM, and then we'll go through each of the ChaRM processes in detail. We'll provide step-by-step instructions along the way, including descriptions of each step and screen captures, to give you a strong understanding of how ChaRM works from a process point of view.

12.2   Roles in Change Request Management

SAP provides a standard workflow for processing requests for change and the follow-on change documents that ultimately deploy the change depending on the scope (i.e., normal, urgent, administrative, etc.). Each step within these processes is aligned to an end-user role, based on SAP best practices and ITIL methodology. Further, SAP provides standard authorization roles that map to each of these end-user roles.

These roles serve as templates and guidelines for your organization when implementing ChaRM to manage changes related to implementation or maintenance projects. Ultimately, the objective and recommendation is for your organization to align your processes and end-user functions to the templates, workflows, and processes provided standard with SAP Solution Manager.

However, due to dynamic differences and various requirements across organizations, sometimes it isn't possible to align strictly to the out-of-the box scenarios provided by SAP Solution Manager. In these cases, your organization will need to map current roles and functions with those in ChaRM and determine how the differences will be bridged.

The end-user roles identified in Table 12.1 are the standard roles that execute the steps necessary for ChaRM processes. We'll explain these further in the remainder of this section.

Role	Description
Requester	Creates the request for change.
Service employee	If the request for change is a result of AIM, the service employee creates the request for change as a follow-up.
Change approver	Categorizes, validates, and monitors requests for change. Approves imports to the production system.
Change Advisory Board (CAB)	Steering committee for the request for change process; approves or rejects requests for change.
Developer	Performs the implementation, documentation, and unit test for changes.
Tester	Tests change and documents results.
IT operator	Supports implementation and maintenance environment. Performs production imports. Handles software logistics.

Table 12.1 ChaRM End-User Roles

12.2.1 Requester

The requester kicks off the entire ChaRM process by creating a request for change. The requester can either create the request for change from scratch, or it can be requested via alternative inbound channels (described in Section 12.3).

Requesters can either be power users of the SAP system, end users (business analyst), or members of the support team (first or second level) who require the authorization to create requests for change based on their job duties. More often than not, requesters will also be developers, testers, and IT operators. On the other hand, some organizations may have only business users as the requesters. It varies across organizations and depends on size, complexity, and organizational structure.

The responsibility of the requester is to provide enough detail about the request for the change approver to thoroughly validate it and position it for approval by the CAB. The requester should fill out, at a minimum, a short description, description of the change, reason for the change, and priority. Depending on the organization and how requesters are trained on ChaRM, they also may provide basic categorization (entering categories, project, risk value, etc.).

12.2.2 Service Employee

Should a service transaction associated with AIM warrant a request for change, it's the responsibility of the service employee (e.g., message processor) assigned to the transaction to create the request for change.

A service transaction can include an incident, problem, or service request. The service employee is a message processor who either serves as Level 1 or Level 2 support for working the service transaction. If the problem, incident, or service requests requires a change to the IT landscape, a request for change document can be created as a follow-up by the service employee.

12.2.3 Change Approver

The change approver is a manager or above level within the IT organization who is responsible for coordinating, managing, and monitoring transport processes. This includes the request for change process, change process, and release management.

In the request for change process, change approvers validate the request for change. They are the first ones to handle the request after it has been created by the requester. Their job is to ensure that it's documented with the required information, follows standard guidelines for Change Management, and contains the required project and scope data so the CAB can evaluate it for approval.

In the change process (i.e., normal or urgent), the change approver role also involves the approval or release of a change to the production system. They facilitate phases within the ChaRM maintenance cycle as well as set the approvals themselves. These actions allow the change approvers to be fully informed and aware of what changes are occurring, or on deck, to the production environment.

12.2.4 Change Advisory Board (CAB)

The CAB in ChaRM approves or rejects requests for change. The CAB representatives should be an equal mix between the business and IT teams so that the decision on what is implemented and promoted to production is unbiased and is made to best serve the holistic organization. Typical CAB members can include, but aren't limited to, the following:

▶ Consultants

▶ Customers

▶ Suppliers

▶ IT staff

▶ Change manager

In ChaRM, the only time the CAB enters the system is during this approval/rejection phase. However, they are the governing body that makes the decisions regarding what should be implemented and when the changes should be released to the production systems. The CAB makes these recommendations based on many factors. Because the CAB is made up of a various mix of representatives across the IT organization, they are able to provide educated and knowledgeable insight on what is approved. They are aware of existing services, costs associated with changes, resource availability/constraints, and other important factors.

12.2.5 Developer

The term *developer* in ChaRM refers to a user who implements changes in the development system. While a developer is often associated with an ABAP programmer who implements workbench requests associated with development, in ChaRM, a developer is someone who is a functional configuration expert.

The role of a developer in a ChaRM maintenance project could be shared across consultants, power users, or Level 1 and Level 2 support members. Their responsibility is to implement changes that are approved as part of the request for change process.

Further, they provide test instructions to the tester as well as document the implementation of the change. They perform the unit tests associated with the change and hand the changes off to the tester when they are finished with their implementation.

12.2.6 Tester

A *tester* in ChaRM is an individual who follows the test instructions provided by the developer and tests the change in the test system. They are responsible for creating the test result, which documents the outcome of the test. If the outcome of the test is successful, they confirm the successful test so it can be approved for production by the change approver. If the test fails, it's the responsibility of the tester to return it back to the developer and update the documentation accordingly.

12.2.7 IT Operator

IT operator is synonymous with the role Basis team member. In ChaRM, the role of the Basis team is more hands off than traditional TMS procedures. A common misconception is that because ChaRM uses the existing TMS infrastructure, then it's a Basis-intensive tool that requires a lot of hands on from the Basis team. In practice, it's the exact opposite.

The workflow (actions and conditions) built into ChaRM's change process triggers the creation and release of transport requests behind the scenes. Further, all imports into the test system are automated. If there are errors associated with the application or transports, they are displayed directly in the change document for the user. Direct access is provided to TMS to view and analyze errors that may occur.

The role of the IT operator is to schedule or trigger the import of normal and urgent changes into production. Per the standard end-to-end processes for change documents, the only time the IT operator logs into ChaRM is to perform this function.

This isn't to minimize the importance that IT operators play in the end-to-end deployment of changes. It's true that if everything is running 100% smoothly, the IT operator's only ChaRM end-user function is to trigger imports into production. However, from a system maintenance perspective, the IT operator plays a major role in ensuring that the system is available and performing in a manner that supports the business. IT operators take care of the software logistics and support the landscape if ChaRM is disrupted in any way.

Now that we've discussed the roles involved, the following section provides an overview of the request for change process in ChaRM.

12.3   Request for Change Process

The objective of this section is to provide you with a thorough understanding of the end-to-end steps involved in the process to create and approve a request for change. We'll provide step-by-step instructions on how to perform this process in SAP Solution Manager, including a mapping of process steps to end-user roles according to SAP best practices.

12.3.1   Process and Tools

A request for change is a document within ChaRM that is used to request a change to a software component or object. It contains its own process steps, business partner responsibilities, and workflow. These process components are independent on the follow-on workflow, should the request for change be approved for implementation. In other words, the request for change applies to the broader IT landscape within an organization. SAP applications, non-SAP applications, and non-system components (i.e., IT assets) are under the umbrella of components that may require a change or enhancement.

The request for change contains details about the request, including items such as description, risk, priority, and so on. Documentation to support the change is uploaded or maintained directly within the request for change, and the scope of the change is also identified (i.e., normal change, urgent change, etc.). The approval procedure is also handled within the request for change. Should the change or enhancement be approved by the change approver and/or CAB, a follow-on document (i.e., the scope maintained) will be generated.

The request for change is classified by transaction type SMCR in the SAP Solution Manager system. As we've advised throughout our book for each transaction type, it's critical to copy the standard transaction type into your customer namespace. The standard Customizing delivered with SMCR should not be adapted to preserve SAP settings. We strongly recommend copying SMCR over to YMCR (or ZMCR).

If you've upgraded from release 7.0 to 7.1 of SAP Solution Manager, transaction type SDCR is still available for processing in the SAP GUI. Transaction type SDCR is the change request document based on the SAP CRM 5.0 infrastructure, which was included in SAP Solution Manager 7.0. Transaction type SMCR is available with SAP Solution Manager 7.1 and can be processed only in the SAP CRM Web UI.

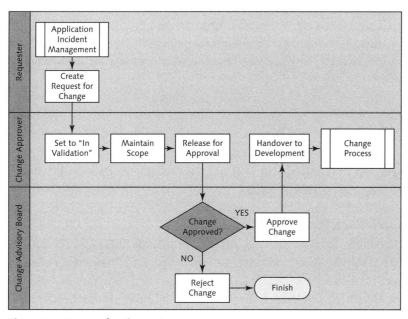

Figure 12.2 Request for Change Process

Figure 12.2 provides the end-to-end process for creating, defining the scope, approving, and handing a request for change off to the developer. Throughout the remainder of this section, we'll provide the step-by-step instructions for how to execute each of these steps in SAP Solution Manager.

Inbound Channels to Trigger Requests for Change

Later in this section, we'll describe the process for creating a request for change. Our examples will demonstrate a requester creating the change from scratch in the SAP CRM Web UI. While this is typically the most common route to create a request for change, it's important to note that ChaRM is integrated with other various tools that support ALM.

Beyond creating a change from scratch, multiple tools are available to generate a request for change depending on the scenario you're working in.

Request for Change Template

Templates can be created by the SAP Solution Manager administrator to quickly and efficiently generate a request for change. Templates eliminate the rekeying of information for changes that occur on a repeatable basis. Changes to security authorizations, for example, typically have details that are shared across related requests for change. The category model, priority, and project could all be pre-populated in a template. Rather than creating a request for change from scratch, the requester can select a template that has all of this information already populated.

Solution

If your organization is using solutions to organize documentation and systems that are in production, you can create a change based on a solution element. Business processes can be checked out and requests for change can be generated based on the business process affected.

Implementation/Template Project

Requests for change can also be created in the Transaction SOLAR01 (Blueprint) or Transaction SOLAR02 (Configuration) within an SAP Solution Manager implementation or template project. If ChaRM is activated for implementation projects, requests for change can be generated from a process in the overall business process hierarchy.

Roadmap

In Transaction RMMAIN, requests for change can also be triggered from an organizational-specific roadmap. The request for change is created on the Service Messages tab and available for processing in the SAP CRM Web UI after it has been created by a requester.

Job Request

If a change to a scheduled job needs to occur, requests for change can be created from the Job Management Work Center. After a job request is selected, the requester has the option to create a request for change. The request for change is now available for processing in the SAP CRM Web UI and contains all of the necessary data about that particular job request.

Application Incident Management

Problems, incidents, and service requests are also triggers for requests for change. This method is also very common with organizations if they are leveraging the full suite of SAP ITSM/ChaRM to manage services within the organization. Depending on the outcome of one of these service transactions, a request for change can be created as a follow-up. It's forever linked to the service transaction.

12.3.2 Starting the Request for Change Process

First, the process begins with a request for change being created. In our scenario, a ChaRM user who has the requester authorizations will create the request for change directly within the SAP CRM Web UI.

Requester: Creates Request for Change

To create the request, the requester follows these steps:

1. Launch the SAP Solution Manager IT Service Management Web UI.

2. Select the link Request for Change in the Create area of the navigation pane as shown in Figure 12.3.

   The SMCR (or ZMCR) document for a request for change appears as shown in Figure 12.4. If you have yet to copy the standard transaction types to a customer namespace, the SMCR standard transaction type will open by default.

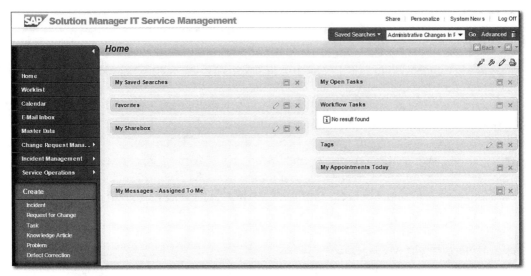

Figure 12.3 Selecting the Request for Change Link

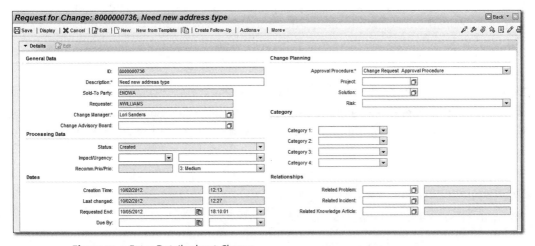

Figure 12.4 Enter Details about Change

3. In the DETAILS assignment block, enter the necessary information about the request for change. Assuming that an end-user type role is creating this, they may only enter basic details (e.g., short description, priority, long description, etc.) about the change.

4. The requester may choose to describe the change in more detail to provide the change approver with enough information to validate and submit the change for approval.

   To do so, ChaRM provides the standard text types DESCRIPTION OF CHANGE and REASON FOR CHANGE so that the change can be described and rationalized thoroughly.

5. In the TEXT assignment block, maintain descriptive text for each of these text types (Figure 12.5).

Figure 12.5 Requester: Enter Descriptive Text

6. When you've finished entering data on the request for change, click SAVE.

The change has been requested. Now the change approver takes over.

Change Approver: Validates Request for Change

After a ChaRM document (request for change or change document) is handed over to another business role, there are two options for the subsequent role to continue the process:

▶ Have each ChaRM user set up saved searches based on when their job role must take action on the ChaRM document.

▶ Set up automatic notifications (email actions) that are triggered at a status change.

These choices are handled on a case-by-case basis and differ across organizations. Some organizations believe that emails can be excessive and that support team members should uphold the periodic activity of monitoring their work queues. On the other hand, some organizations believe that email notifications are a must to maintain tight Service Level Agreements (SLAs).

> **Note**
>
> The examples throughout this chapter walk the users through the steps of accessing messages via saved searches. We created the saved searches, and they should be created at the user level.
>
> Email notifications for ChaRM transactions are enabled the same way as in AIM. The difference is that the actions and conditions are based on SMMJ, SMHF, and so on, rather than SMIN, SMPR, and so on. Refer to Chapter 10 for details on how to configure notifications for SAP ITSM functions.

To validate the request, the change approver follows these steps:

1. Log on to the SAP SOLUTION MANAGER IT SERVICE MANAGEMENT HOME page.

2. Select the NEW REQUESTS FOR CHANGE link in the MY SAVED SEARCHES work area as shown in Figure 12.6.

Figure 12.6 Search for New Change Requests

3. In the SEARCH: REQUESTS FOR CHANGE screen, select the ID link to open a new request for change (Figure 12.7).

Figure 12.7 Select New Request for Change

The request for change document appears.

4. Select the Edit button to begin processing the request.

5. From the Actions menu, select the action Set Request to Change to "Validation" as shown in Figure 12.8.

Figure 12.8 Set Request for Change to "Validation"

6. Click the Save button. The status of the change is now updated from Created to Validation, as shown in Figure 12.9.

7. Fill out the remaining information within the Details assignment block (e.g., impact, urgency, categories, risk, project, approval procedure).

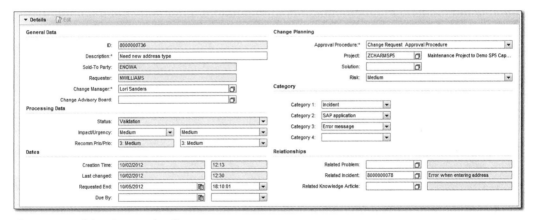

Figure 12.9 Validate Request for Change

8. Click Save.

9. Scroll down to reach the Request for Change Scope assignment block.

10. In the Change Category column, select the scope (i.e., follow-on document) that is appropriate for this change.

Figure 12.10 is an example of a request for change that will be submitted for approval to initiate the normal change process.

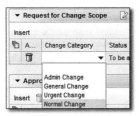

Figure 12.10 Select Request for Change Scope

11. After the scope has been selected, the remaining details are automatically defaulted as shown in Figure 12.11. The system, client, and ccomponent are automatically defaulted based on the project that was assigned in the DETAILS assignment block.

Figure 12.11 Complete Scope

12. Click SAVE.

13. Select the action RELEASE FOR APPROVAL (Figure 12.12).

Figure 12.12 Release for Approval

14. Click SAVE.

The request for change has now been created and, based on the preceding steps, validated by the change approver. The change approver has released the change for approval. As shown in Figure 12.13, the document is now in the status TO BE APPROVED.

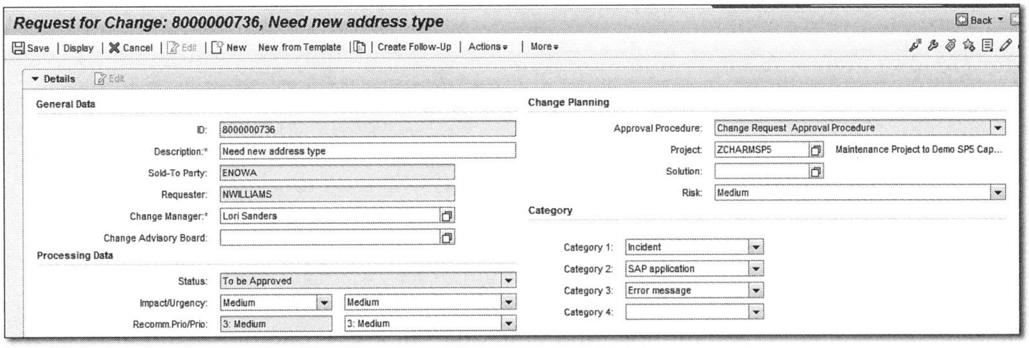

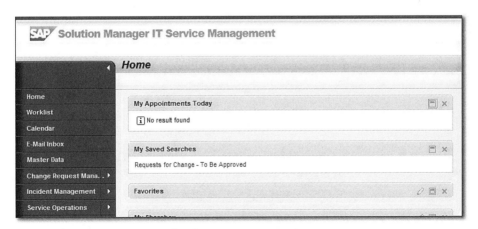

Figure 12.13 Request for Change to Be Approved

Change Advisory Board: Approves Request for Change

Next, the CAB picks up the request to determine if it should be approved, rejected, or passed back to the status VALIDATION for the change approver to maintain further details.

1. As a representative of the CAB, log on to the SAP SOLUTION MANAGER IT SERVICE MANAGEMENT HOME page.

2. Select the link REQUESTS FOR CHANGE – TO BE APPROVED in the MY SAVED SEARCHES work area as shown in Figure 12.14.

Figure 12.14 Search for Requests for Change to Be Approved

3. In the SEARCH: REQUESTS FOR CHANGE screen, select the ID link to open a new request for change (Figure 12.15).

Figure 12.15 Select Request for Change to Be Approved

4. Select the EDIT button to begin processing the change.

5. Scroll down to the APPROVAL assignment block as shown in Figure 12.16.

6. From the ACTIVITY column, select the activity APPROVED.

7. If the message should be sent back to the change approver, select the option to pass it back to VALIDATION status from the ACTIONS menu.

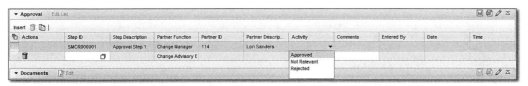

Figure 12.16 Approve Request for Change

8. Click SAVE to trigger the approval and update the status of the document.

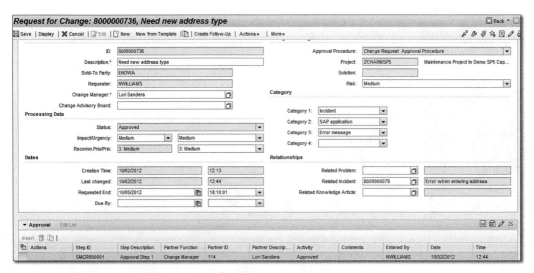

Figure 12.17 Approved Request for Change

As shown in Figure 12.17, the request for change is now in the status APPROVED. Furthermore, you can identify the details of the approval within the APPROVAL assignment block. The business partner, time, and date in regards to the approval are maintained here. Additionally, comments can be entered as free text in the COMMENTS column.

Now that the CAB has approved the change, the final step is handed back to the change approver.

Change Approver: Hands Request for Change over to Development

Now, the change approver will hand this change over to the development team to begin implementation of the change:

1. Log on to the SAP SOLUTION MANAGER IT SERVICE MANAGEMENT HOME page.

2. Select the APPROVED REQUESTS FOR CHANGE link in the MY SAVED SEARCHES work area as shown in Figure 12.18.

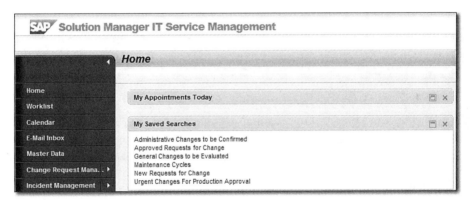

Figure 12.18 Search for Approved Requests for Change

3. In the SEARCH: REQUESTS FOR CHANGE screen, select the ID link to open a new request for change (Figure 12.19).

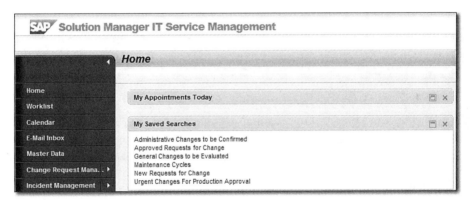

Figure 12.19 Select Approved Request for Change

4. Select the EDIT button.

5. From the ACTIONS menu, select the action RELEASE FOR DEVELOPMENT (Figure 12.20).

Figure 12.20 Select Release for Development

6. Click SAVE.

The request for change's status is now set to BEING IMPLEMENTED. Further, a link to the follow-on normal change is now available in the REQUEST FOR CHANGE SCOPE assignment block as shown in Figure 12.21. After the change approver released the change for development, the normal change (specified scope) was created in the background and linked to this change request.

Figure 12.21 Normal Change Document Created

This concludes the process for creating, validating, and approving a request for change. The immediate next steps are for a developer to begin the implementation of the change, regardless of the scope or software component to be changed.

In the next section, we'll describe the process to extend the scope of a request for change that is already being implemented.

12.3.3 Subprocess: Scope Extension

The scope extension process is a subprocess, or exception process, to the standard request for change process. Extending the scope occurs during the course of the implementation of a change. If additional scope must be added to the original scope to fully meet requirements or avoid breaking existing functionality (for example), the change approver can extend the scope of a request for change for which implementation is already underway.

Extending the scope of an existing request for change allows request for change documents to have multiple change documents (scope items) attached to it. Figure 12.22 identifies the process for extending scope. We'll describe each of these steps in detail in the following sections.

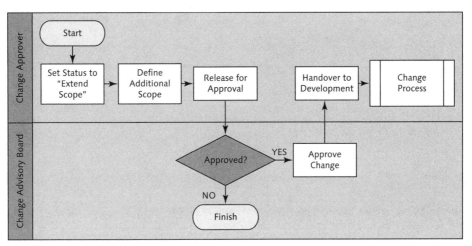

Figure 12.22 Scope Extension Process

Change Approver: Extends Scope

The change approver follows these steps:

1. Select the option EXTEND SCOPE from the ACTIONS button of an existing request for change as shown in Figure 12.23.

Figure 12.23 Extend Scope

2. Click SAVE. The status of the request for change is now updated to EXTEND SCOPE within the DETAILS assignment block.

3. Scroll down to the REQUEST FOR CHANGE SCOPE assignment block. You'll notice, as shown in Figure 12.24, that the original scope item is listed.

4. Click the INSERT button.

5. From the CHANGE CATEGORY column, select the new scope item URGENT CHANGE as shown in Figure 12.24.

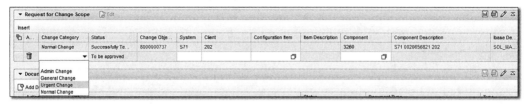

Figure 12.24 Select Extended Scope Item

6. Maintain the system, client, and component information if it doesn't automatically default by the system.

7. From the ACTIONS menu, select the action RELEASE FOR APPROVAL as shown in Figure 12.25.

Figure 12.25 Release for Approval

8. Click SAVE.

The request for change is now updated to the status TO BE APPROVED. Because this is an extension of the scope, it must revisit the CAB approval process.

Change Advisory Board: Approves Scope Extension

If you're a representative of the CAB, you now have the ability to approve, reject, or pass the request for change back to the change approver. Select the option to approve the request for change in the APPROVAL assignment block as shown in Figure 12.26.

The status of the request for change is now updated to APPROVED in the DETAILS assignment block. It's now ready to be handed over to the appropriate developer.

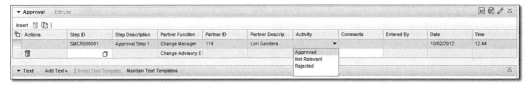

Figure 12.26 Approve Scope Extension

Change Approver: Hands Request for Change over to Development

The change approver hands the request over to development by following these steps:

1. Select RELEASE FOR DEVELOPMENT from the ACTIONS menu as shown in Figure 12.27.

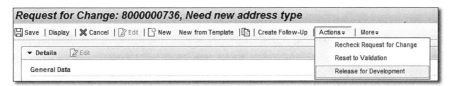

Figure 12.27 Release Extended Scope for Development

2. Click SAVE.

The request for change is now back in the status of BEING IMPLEMENTED. Further, the RELATED TRANSACTIONS assignment block is now updated to include a link to the urgent change document that was created as the extended scope in the background.

Figure 12.28 provides an image of this assignment block within the request for change, which includes the related incident and two change documents that will be implemented to meet the requirements of this change.

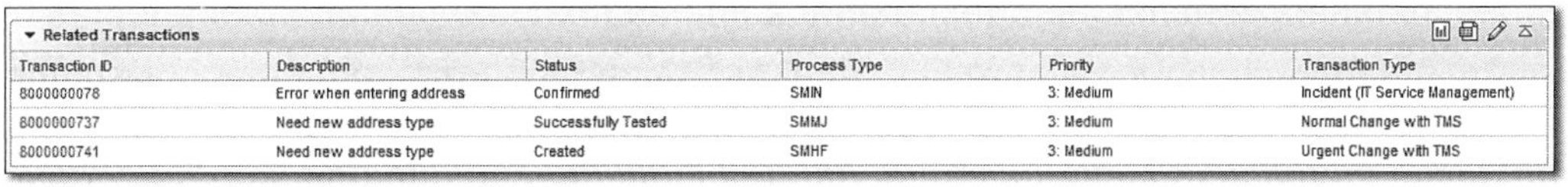

Transaction ID	Description	Status	Process Type	Priority	Transaction Type
8000000078	Error when entering address	Confirmed	SMIN	3: Medium	Incident (IT Service Management)
8000000737	Need new address type	Successfully Tested	SMMJ	3: Medium	Normal Change with TMS
8000000741	Need new address type	Created	SMHF	3: Medium	Urgent Change with TMS

Figure 12.28 Related Transactions Updated

In the next section, we'll explain the differences between normal and urgent changes, before diving into the specifics on how to manage these two different processes.

12.4 Key Differences between Normal and Urgent Changes

There are two different transaction types that support ChaRM for changes specifically tied to TMS in your SAP landscape. In other words, the normal and urgent change transactions are the document types you'll use if you drive a TMS change through the ChaRM process. Basically, if you change an entry in the development SAP ERP system and you're prompted to save your changes to a transport request, this is a change linked to TMS.

In this section, we'll point out the key differences between these two transaction types. In the following two sections, you'll identify some differences between how these two change transactions function in the end-to-end workflow. For example, you'll see some terminology inconsistencies or a few extra steps in the normal change versus the urgent change and vice versa. Here, we'll explain why these two TMS change transaction types must be different in certain aspects to fully support an expansive and holistic ChaRM scenario for your organization.

12.4.1 Transport Request Handling

When processing a normal change, transport requests must be created by selecting the appropriate option within the TRANSPORT MANAGEMENT assignment block. Urgent changes, on the other hand, offer the immediate prompt for transport request creation when the developer sets an urgent change to the status IN DEVELOPMENT.

The Difference

First, transports are created slightly differently in the normal change transaction as opposed to the urgent change transaction. In a normal change, after the document is in the status of IN DEVELOPMENT, the user must scroll down in the SAP CRM Web UI and manually create the transport request in the TRANSPORT MANAGEMENT assignment box via the NEW TRANSPORT REQUEST button.

In the urgent change, after the user sets the status of the document to IN DEVELOPMENT and clicks SAVE, the web dialog box to create a transport request appears automatically. There is no extra step, as there is in the normal change, to manually select a button to create the transport request.

Rationale

The reason that the creation of transport requests is initiated as soon as the document is set IN DEVELOPMENT is to support the notion that this is an urgent change. If this change must be implemented, tested, and promoted to production in an urgent manner, the assumption is that the developer will want the transport request created at the very moment after he sets the status to IN DEVELOPMENT.

A normal change may also be put in the status of IN DEVELOPMENT, however, the actual implementation of the change in the development system might not occur the following moment.

12.4.2 Test Transports

Normal changes use *test transports*, also known as transport of copies, to organize and improve the method in which changes are promoted to the follow-on systems. Urgent changes, based on their inherit urgency, stick with the classic transport request process.

The Difference

Let's take an example scenario to effectively describe the functionality behind test transports in ChaRM.

When a developer adds an object to the transport request, they have two options in a normal change:

▶ Create a test transport manually from the TRANSPORT MANAGEMENT assignment block within the normal change.

▶ Select the PASS NORMAL CHANGE TO TEST action, which creates a test transport in the background.

Both of these options create a test transport based on the objects in the original transport request. The development system then releases the test transport to the

QAS, placing them in the QAS buffer. Typically, an import job to the QAS is scheduled that picks up the released objects in the buffer and imports them into the QAS. Although the test transports have been released, the original transport requests stay in the CHANGEABLE status (i.e., not released).

The test transport is merely a copy of the objects within the original transport request. The two options previously mentioned can depend on the developer's process and preference for testing changes. Some developers may choose to select the first option, which allows them to then log in to the QAS and test the objects themselves. Or, when they select the action PASS NORMAL CHANGE TO TEST, the test transports will be created anyway.

Rationale

Test transports allow the tester to continually pass the change back to the developer if the testing fails. In essence, testers never really know that they are testing test transports. However, it doesn't really matter anyway. The objects are copies of the original objects, stored in a different type of transport request (test transport).

Let's say, for example, the tester and developer exchanges these objects five times. There will be five different transports of copies. When the tester is finally satisfied with the implementation of the required changes, he will select the action CONFIRM SUCCESSFUL TEST. This action consolidates the objects within the latest (i.e., correct) test transport to the original transport request and immediately releases the original transport request. ChaRM does this all automatically in the background via the workflow actions.

The benefit is huge. Even though the objects were changed five times, only one transport request (the original transport request) is queued in the buffer to go to production. Test transports live only until the QAS phase; they never go to production.

The production buffer is protected from being filled up with erroneous transports that will never be imported to the production system. The only transport requests that enter the production buffer are those that are intended on going to the production system.

Because urgent changes must be fast-tracked to the production system, it's assumed that test transports would not be used in this scenario. If an urgent change fails during testing because the transport request was already released, a new transport request must be created, and then the developer can continue with the implementation of the required changes.

> **Note**
>
> Test transports can be used independently of ChaRM. They are simply another transport request type available in the managed SAP ERP system. Using test transports give you the same benefits as we described previously. Some organizations opt to begin using test transports outside of ChaRM, to start operating in a ChaRM-like fashion before adopting the workflow. ChaRM allows for the automated creation, consolidation, and release of both test transports and original transports based on its workflow actions.

12.4.3   Maintenance Cycle

When processing normal changes, the release and import of transport requests are controlled with the various maintenance cycle phases. Transport objects associated with urgent changes can be released and imported independent of maintenance cycle phases. However, objects associated with urgent changes remain in the production buffer until the maintenance cycle goes live.

The Difference

Chapter 16 is dedicated solely to maintenance and project administration in ChaRM; however, it's important to call out key specifics in regards to how normal changes differ from urgent changes in these areas.

The change approver, IT operator, or CAB can control at which point transport requests can be created, released, and imported for ChaRM changes. For normal changes, this is administered via the various phases of the maintenance cycle. For example, one phase allows the development of objects to take place, however, developers are forbidden to release these objects. Another phase only allows for the creation of defect corrections. We'll cover all of these phases in Chapter 16.

For urgent changes, the creation, release, and import of transport requests is controlled at the document level. Each urgent change document has an individual task list (explained in Section 12.6.4); however, these activities are driven from the front-end urgent change document.

While the transports associated with an urgent change can be promoted to the QAS and PRD independent of phase transitions, they will still remain in the production buffer even after they have gone live. Because urgent changes are tied to an individual task list as well as a project (which also means they belong to a maintenance cycle), they will also go live with the overall maintenance cycle. That is to say, they are reimported into the production system after the maintenance cycle goes live. Only at that point are they then taken out of the production buffer.

Rationale

These two methods support the concept that normal changes (i.e., routine, low priority, minor enhancements, etc.) should be bundled and imported to the follow-on systems based on a periodic release cycle. Urgent changes must be supported with a workflow and process that allows the rapid deployment of objects associated with emergencies to production, while still satisfying audit traceability.

The big question is always concerning why urgent changes stick around in the buffer even after they have been approved for production and gone live. Let's take a sample scenario to provide SAP's rationale for designing the ChaRM system to reimport urgent changes into production when its assigned maintenance cycle goes live.

A developer working on a normal change makes a change to Object A and passes it to the QAS via test transports. Object A, which can be considered version 2 of the transport (the original transport being version 1), is awaiting testing.

The same object has broken in production. An urgent change is created that now makes Object A into version 3. Object A, version 3, is now in the PRD. However, Object A, version 2, is still awaiting testing in the QAS.

When the maintenance project (cycle) goes live, there must be a downgrade activity to ensure consistency. If Object A, version 2, is imported into PRD, it would override version 3, which contains the fix to the break the urgent change addressed. For that reason, version 3 is reimported into the production system behind the normal changes that go live with the maintenance cycle.

Even though the urgent changes are independent of the maintenance cycle phases, they are still tied to a maintenance project to ensure overall consistency and proper sequence of transport order. After the maintenance cycle goes live, the urgent changes follow (reimport) and then are cleared from the production buffer.

12.4.4 Task List

Urgent changes use an individual task list that controls the activities related to TMS, which are driven only by the actions executed in the change document. Normal changes don't use individual task lists. Instead, normal changes underneath their maintenance project umbrella share the maintenance cycle activities and functionalities.

Both the individual task list and maintenance cycle represent your transport track for the maintenance or implementation landscape to which ChaRM is activated. The ChaRM infrastructure uses what has been defined in TMS to create the task lists and maintenance cycle. These two elements represent how your TMS has been built.

The Difference

We've discussed some aspects of the maintenance cycle already, and how the urgent and normal changes are both linked to it by an inherent assignment to the maintenance project. We also mentioned that Chapter 16 is reserved for further discussion of maintenance and administrative activities in ChaRM. However, it's important to note that another key difference among these change transactions is the fact that an individual task list is used for urgent changes.

You can think of a task list as a maintenance cycle for urgent changes. The concept to be aware of is that an individual task list gets generated for each urgent change that is created. Another difference is that there is no option to schedule the activities that occur on the individual task list. They must be triggered via the workflow actions in the urgent change document. Finally, administrators and IT operators do not have the ability to manually execute activities within the individual task list. They are locked, forcing ChaRM users to drive urgent changes through QAS and into production via the change document.

Normal changes, on the other hand, are bundled and all assigned to a single maintenance cycle. Some of the activities within the maintenance cycle can be scheduled. Further, they can be manually triggered by the ChaRM users with the appropriate authorizations.

Rationale

The reasoning behind the separation of task lists for urgent changes versus maintenance cycles for normal changes supports both change control as well as end-to-end change deployment and release management. Because normal changes are bundled and implemented, tested, and promoted to production based on a periodic release cycle, there is more flexibility. Certain activities must be activated by the IT operator or change approver outside of the normal change document.

Because there may be a high volume of transport requests and normal change documents for a specific maintenance cycle, there must be flexibility to support some of the chaos that is inherent of supporting a maintenance landscape. Furthermore, scheduling of these tasks is critical and one of the key benefits of using ChaRM for change and release management.

In the urgent change's individual task list, these activities are locked from direct execution at the task list level. As previously mentioned, the creation of transport requests along with their release and import must be triggered based on the workflow actions within the urgent change document. Because SAP Solution Manager provides a rapid path from implementation of changes to production confirmation, it should be assumed that the appropriate users are clicking each button and conforming to the organization's audit and security requirements.

In the next two sections, we'll provide details on both the normal and urgent change processes, respectively.

12.5 Normal Change Process

Now that you understand how requests for change are created, validated, approved, and handed over to development, we'll discuss one of many scenarios regarding how those changes become developed. First, we'll discuss the normal change process. We'll start by explaining what a normal change document is in SAP Solution Manager and provide an overview of the end-to-end process for deploying a normal change into the production system. We'll also provide step-by-step instructions and screenshots on how to administer normal changes from an end-user perspective.

12.5.1 Normal Change Process Overview

Normal changes in ChaRM are relevant whether you're using ChaRM for implementation projects or maintenance projects. For now, we'll stick with the concept of maintenance projects and discuss ChaRM for implementation projects in Chapter 16.

Normal changes support periodic release/cycle management in that they are bundled together in a project and move to production together. To that end, normal changes are assigned to a maintenance project with an agreed upon release date set by the CAB. Phases in the maintenance cycle, also discussed in detail in Chapter 16, control the activities that are allowed throughout the deployment lifecycle of a change. For example, phases can control such things as when transports can be released, when defect corrections can be created, when emergency changes can be created, and so on.

Normal changes are typically used for implementing new features in your managed SAP landscapes. While bug fixes are typically created as urgent changes or defect corrections, normal changes can also be lower priority/risk maintenance activities. Because all changes should not be created as urgent changes, normal changes are important to preserve the stability and continuity of the SAP landscape. Changes are imported as projects, sequenced correctly, and tested rigorously while not compromising the production buffer.

Normal changes are integrated with TMS. Objects associated with the new features or maintenance are assigned to transport requests. Implementation occurs in the development system. When the developer is satisfied with the implementation, he saves those objects to a transport request. A copy of the transport objects (test transport) is imported into the quality assurance system. Once satisfied, the tester consolidates the test transport with the original transport, and the original transport is released. Integration and scenario testing is performed in the quality system and finally transported to production. For a more detailed description of test transports, see Section 12.7.

Figure 12.29 provides the end-to-end process flow for these activities according to ChaRM end-user roles.

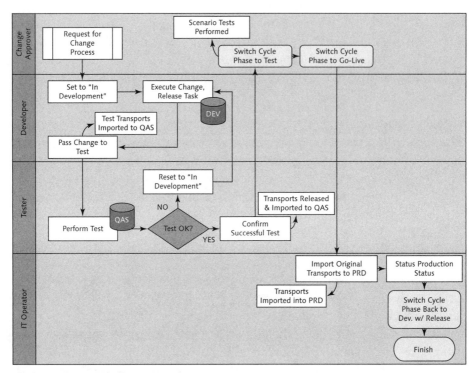

Figure 12.29 Normal Change Process

12.5.2 End-User Roles in the Change Process

When a request for change is approved and handed over to development within the request for change process, the change document is created in the background as described in the previous section. Each change document is delivered with its own unique workflow, status profile, partner profile, action profile, and functionality. In the following sections, we'll walk through the end-to-end process for implementing, testing, and importing normal changes into the production system.

Developer: Implements Change

This step kicks off the normal change process with the actual implementation of the change in the development system. At this point, the phase of the maintenance cycle linked to the normal change must be in the status DEVELOPMENT WITH

RELEASE. The developer will implement the change in the development system, release the task, and create a transport of copies that the developer will test and ultimately pass to the tester for additional verification.

The developer follows these steps:

1. Log on to the SAP Solution Manager IT Service Management Home page.

2. Select the link New Normal Changes in the My Saved Searches work area as shown in Figure 12.30.

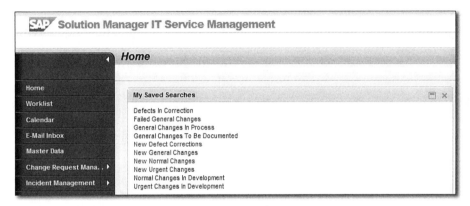

Figure 12.30 Search for New Normal Changes

3. In the Search: Normal Changes screen, select the ID link to open a new normal change (Figure 12.31).

Figure 12.31 Select a New Normal Change

4. Select the Edit button to begin processing the change.

5. From the Actions menu, select the action Set To "In Development" as shown in Figure 12.32.

6. Click Save. The status of the normal change will update from Created to In Development upon saving.

Figure 12.32 Set to "In Development"

At this point, the developer initiates his steps by first reviewing the details and description that was maintained on the request for change document. These details are automatically carried forward into the normal change. Furthermore, the developer can also refer to the DESCRIPTION OF CHANGE and REASON FOR CHANGE, which was added in the TEXT assignment block.

7. Scroll down to the TRANSPORT MANAGEMENT assignment block, and select the NEW TRANSPORT REQUEST button as shown in Figure 12.33.

Figure 12.33 Create New Transport Request

8. In the CREATE TRANSPORT REQUEST – WEBPAGE DIALOG screen that appears, enter information specific to the transport request as shown in Figure 12.34.

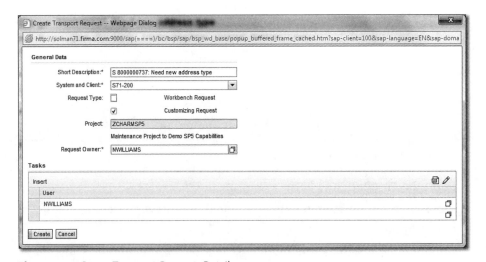

Figure 12.34 Create Transport Request: Details

Note

SAP Solution Manager will automatically default most of the information regarding the transport for you. You can either choose to accept the defaulted information or update it.

9. Deselect the option for WORKBENCH REQUEST because our example involves Customizing only.

10. Click CREATE. The details of the transport request are now updated in the TRANSPORT MANAGEMENT assignment block. As shown in Figure 12.35, no tasks have been created because no development activities have yet occurred. The transport request was created from SAP Solution Manager but resides within the development system.

11. To access the development system, select the LOGON TO SYSTEM button located next to the development system in the LANDSCAPE assignment block (Figure 12.35).

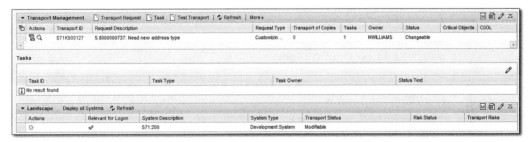

Figure 12.35 Transport Management, Tasks, and Landscape Assignment Blocks

12. The developer is taken to the development system, which is assigned to your maintenance project. Once in the development system, the developer performs the implementation activities required for this specific change. When the developer saves his changes, the PROMPT FOR CUSTOMIZING REQUEST dialog box will open.

13. Select the OWN REQUESTS BUTTON and find the transport request that was created from SAP Solution Manager.

14. Press Enter.

15. The PROMPT FOR CUSTOMIZING REQUEST box will now have the details of the transport request as shown in Figure 12.36.

563

Note

After ChaRM is activated for any development systems, you're restricted from creating or releasing transport requests directly within the managed systems. Creating transport requests and releasing transport requests must occur from ChaRM. This ensures that all changes are based on ChaRM documents and that audit/traceability is preserved.

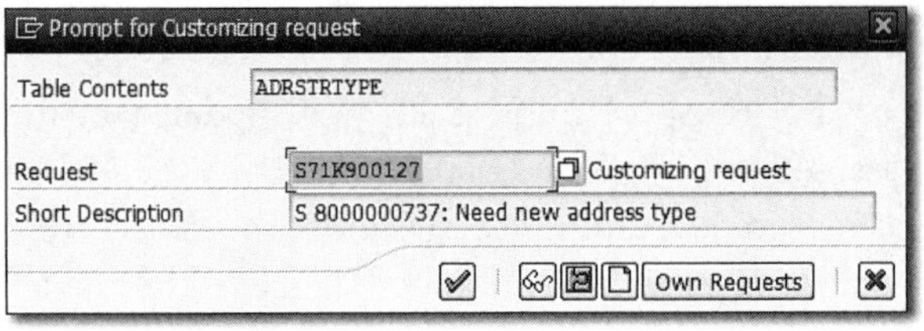

Figure 12.36 Assign Transport Request

As we noted, the developer can't directly release the transport request in the development system. However, the developer must release the task for the normal change process to commence.

16. After assigning the objects to the transport request created from ChaRM, access Transaction SE09 (or Transaction SE10), and release the task(s) associated with this transport request.

17. Return to the normal change document in the SAP CRM Web UI. Before passing the normal change off for testing, the developer may want to enter some instructions for the tester.

18. In the TEXT assignment block, select the ADD TEXT button as shown in Figure 12.37.

19. Select the text type TEST INSTRUCTION.

20. Enter some instructions for the tester.

Figure 12.37 Enter Test Instructions

21. From the ACTIONS menu, select the action PASS NORMAL CHANGE TO TEST as shown in Figure 12.38.

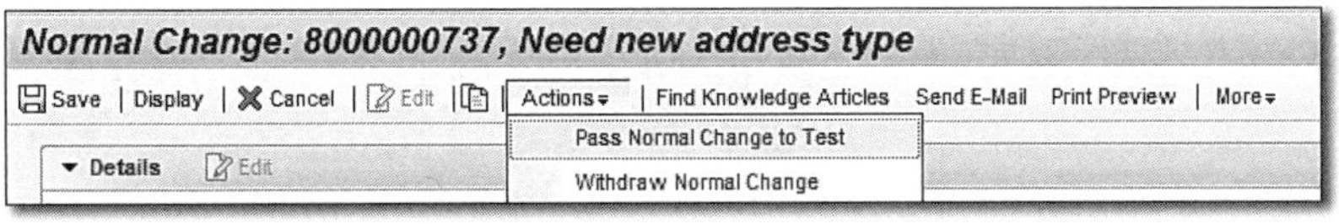

Figure 12.38 Pass Normal Change to Test

22. Click SAVE.

After the developer selects the action to pass the normal change to test and save, the status of the normal change is updated to TO BE TESTED. In the background, a test transport has been created and released to the quality system. In other words, transport objects have been copied to a test transport (transport of copies) and released. We cover test transports in detail in Section 12.7.

The test transport is now ready to be imported into the quality system for testing.

System: Import of Test Transports

Now, the test transports must find their way into the test system. Typically, as part of standard TMS procedures, background jobs are set up that import anything that is in the buffer (i.e., released) to the test system. Whether it be every 5, 15, or 30 minutes, it's very common to have this activity automated. It reduces the effort of the Basis team and also allows the developers/testers to have their objects available in the test system in an automated, timely manner.

On the other hand, you can also provide your ChaRM users permissions to trigger the imports to the test system manually. We recommend that this is granted only for the test system. Production imports should be administered strictly by the IT operators.

Importing transport requests, along with various other TMS activities, is triggered from the task list (within the maintenance cycle). As shown in Figure 12.39, the maintenance cycle is linked to the normal change in the RELATED TRANSACTIONS assignment block.

We'll provide a brief overview of how to trigger these imports manually from within the maintenance cycle, keeping in mind that maintenance and administration activities associated with projects are covered in detail in Chapter 16.

1. Select the link in the TRANSACTION ID column for the maintenance cycle (Figure 12.39).

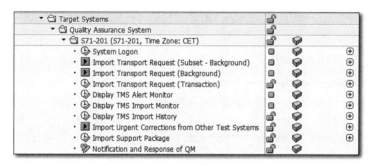

▼ Related Transactions						Ⓜ 🗑 ✎ ☲
Transaction ID	Description	Status	Process Type	Priority	Transaction Type	
8000000603	Maintenance Project to Demo SP5 Capabili	In Development with Release	SMMN	4: Low	Standard,for Task List Variant SAP0	
8000000736	Need new address type	Being Implemented	SMCR	3: Medium	Request for Change	
M000000031	Maintenance Project to Demo SP5 Capabilities				Task List	

Figure 12.39 Access Maintenance Cycle

2. Scroll down to the target systems section of the hierarchy.

3. Right-click the activity IMPORT TRANSPORT REQUEST (BACKGROUND) as shown in Figure 12.40.

Figure 12.40 Import Transport Requests (Background)

From here, you'll see multiple prompts for how to proceed with the import. You can accept the default values or choose to schedule the import. After the import has run, you'll notice a green square if the import was successful.

As a result, the test transports are imported into the quality system. Because we haven't yet released the original transport request, at this point, only the test transports have made their way into the quality system. Remember, the import job will pick up and import all requests that are released, so it makes sense that the original transport requests are left behind for now.

Tester: Tests Change

Now, the tester will test the changes implemented by the developer within the quality system. The tester may not know that he is testing just copies of the original transport requests, but that doesn't matter. Depending on the outcome of the test, the tester can confirm the test to be successful, which consolidates the test transport to the original transport and releases the original transport. Alternatively, he can pass the normal change back to the developer for additional updates. If the normal change is passed back to the developer, an updated test transport will be created and released when the developer passes the normal change back to the tester for a retest.

The tester follows these steps:

1. Log on to the SAP SOLUTION MANGER IT SERVICE MANAGEMENT HOME page.

2. Select the NORMAL CHANGES TO BE TESTED link in the MY SAVED SEARCHES work area as shown in Figure 12.41.

Figure 12.41 Search for Normal Changes to Be Tested

3. In the SEARCH: NORMAL CHANGES screen, select the ID link to open a normal change that is to be tested (Figure 12.42).

Figure 12.42 Select Normal Change to Be Tested

4. Select the EDIT button to begin processing the change.

At this point, the tester reviews the details within the normal change, including the test instructions (Figure 12.43) provided by the developer during implementation. The tester will then test the developer's work.

Figure 12.43 Review Test Instructions

5. In the LANDSCAPE assignment block, select the LOGON TO SYSTEM button for the test system (Figure 12.44).

▼ Landscape	Display all Systems ↻ Refresh						
Actions	Relevant for Logon	System Description		System Type	Transport Status	Risk Status	Transport Risks
⟳	✔	S71:201		Test System			1

Figure 12.44 Log On to Test System

6. The tester will perform the test directly in the test system. When the tester has completed the testing, he will return back to the normal change in SAP Solution Manager.

As shown in Figure 12.45, the tester may want to include some details to the success (or failure) of the test.

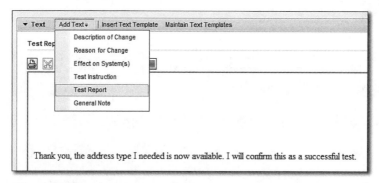

Figure 12.45 Enter Test Report

7. Scroll down to the TEXT assignment block

8. Select the ADD TEXT button.

9. Select the text type Test Report.

10. Enter some details about the test.

11. From the Actions menu, select the action Confirm Successful Test as shown in Figure 12.46.

Figure 12.46 Confirm Successful Test

12. Click Save.

The status of the normal change is now updated to Successfully Tested. As you can see in Figure 12.47, the status of the original transport request has been changed to Released in the Transport Management assignment block. Depending on the number of test transports that were required to fully implement the change properly, the latest objects in the final test transport have been consolidated to the original transport. The original transport is now released to the production buffer, containing only those objects that are intended to go to production.

Figure 12.47 Released Transport Request

Change Approver: Administers Maintenance Cycle

At this point, we'll assume that the background job for importing the transport requests has finished. Alternatively, you may perform the same steps as we just described for importing the requests directly from within the task list.

Now, the original transport requests containing the fully implemented change are imported into the test system. Integration (scenario) testing can now be started.

The change approver will update the phase of the maintenance cycle to the test phase. This will prohibit the creation of new normal changes but also allow for the creation of defects should errors arise from the integration testing.

The change approver follows these steps:

1. Log on to the SAP SOLUTION MANAGER IT SERVICE MANAGEMENT HOME page.

2. Select the link to MAINTENANCE CYCLES in the MY SAVED SEARCHES work area as shown in Figure 12.48.

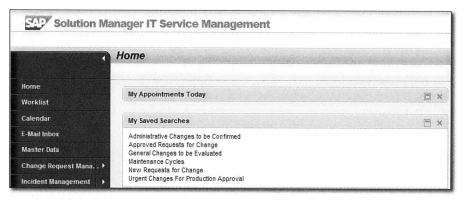

Figure 12.48 Search for Maintenance Cycles

3. In the SEARCH: MAINTENANCE CYCLES screen, select the ID link to open the maintenance cycle (Figure 12.49).

Figure 12.49 Open the Maintenance Cycle

4. Select the EDIT button to begin processing the maintenance cycle.

5. From the ACTIONS menu, select the action SWITCH PHASE TO "TEST" as shown in Figure 12.50.

6. Click SAVE.

The maintenance cycle will be updated to the test phase as shown in Figure 12.51.

At this point, integration testing is performed in the quality system.

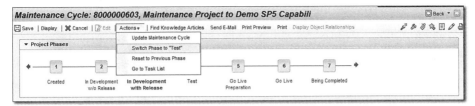

Figure 12.50 Switch Phase to Maintenance Cycle

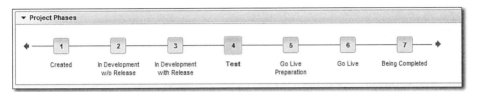

Figure 12.51 Test Phase: Maintenance Cycle

When integration testing is completed, the change approver performs the preceding steps once again in the maintenance cycle to advance the phase to go-live (Figure 12.52). After the maintenance cycle is set to go-live, the import to production can occur.

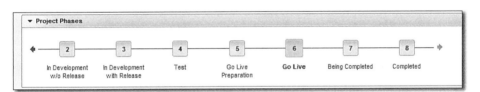

Figure 12.52 Set Phase to Go-Live

IT Operator: Imports Change into Production

Finally, the IT operator schedules (or automatically triggers) the transport requests to the production system. Post-production import, the IT operator will check the transport logs to confirm that no errors were returned. After the IT operator has confirmed that the project's transport requests were imported to production without fail, he will set the PRODUCTION status on the normal change. Finally, the IT operator will reset the phase of the maintenance cycle back to DEVELOPMENT WITH RELEASE where the development phase of the subsequent cycle can commence.

The IT operator follows these steps:

1. Log on to the SAP Solution Manager IT Service Management Home page.

2. Select the link to Maintenance Cycles in the My Saved Searches work area as shown in Figure 12.53.

Figure 12.53 Search for Maintenance Cycles

3. In the Search: Maintenance Cycles screen, select the ID link to open the maintenance cycle (Figure 12.54).

Figure 12.54 Open the Maintenance Cycle

4. In the Related Transactions assignment block, click the link to open the Task List as shown in Figure 12.55.

Figure 12.55 Open the Task List

5. Execute (right-click) the activity Import Transport Requests (Background) as shown in Figure 12.56.

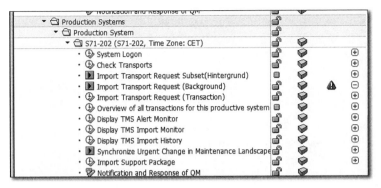

Figure 12.56 Import Transport Requests to Production

Similar to the import to quality, you'll be provided with a series of prompts. You may accept the default values or choose to schedule the import based on your own requirements.

The IT operator follows these steps:

1. Log on to the SAP SOLUTION MANAGER IT SERVICE MANAGEMENT HOME page.

2. Select the link to SUCCESSFULLY TESTED NORMAL CHANGES in the MY SAVED SEARCHES work area as shown in Figure 12.57.

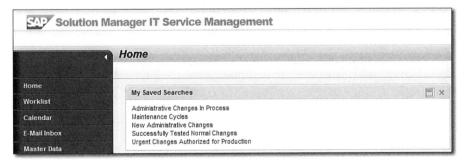

Figure 12.57 Search for Successfully Tested Normal Changes

3. In the SEARCH: NORMAL CHANGES screen, select the ID link to open the successfully tested normal change (Figure 12.58).

4. Select the EDIT button to begin processing the change.

5. From the ACTIONS menu, select the action SET PRODUCTION STATUS as shown in Figure 12.59.

Figure 12.58 Open Successfully Tested Normal Change

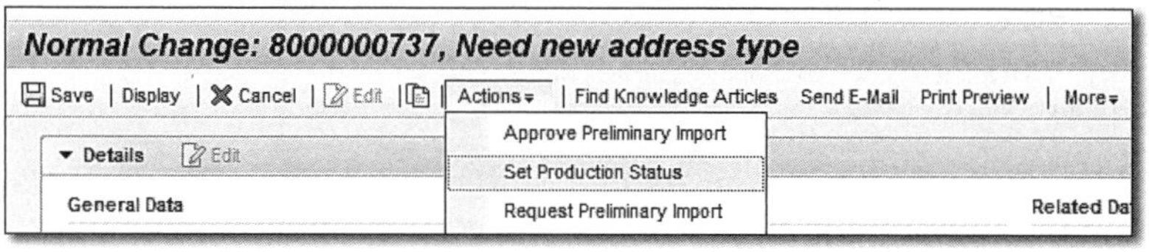

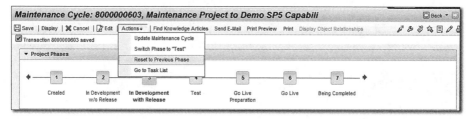

Figure 12.59 Set Production Status

6. Click SAVE. The normal change is now in PRODUCTION status. It's locked from all additional maintenance.

7. Finally, perform a search for maintenance cycles in the SAP CRM Web UI. The maintenance cycle is reverted back to the phase IN DEVELOPMENT WITH RELEASE as shown in Figure 12.60.

Figure 12.60 Reset Phase to Development with Release

The development phase of the next periodic release cycle can now commence. Note that it isn't necessary to completely close out the maintenance cycle with each go-live. Many organizations choose to "recycle" the maintenance cycles after each import into production. Periodically (i.e., bi-annually, annually, etc.), organizations may choose to completely close out the maintenance cycles as part of annual maintenance for ChaRM projects.

Now that you understand how ChaRM can be used to administer changes that are "normal" throughout production maintenance, we'll describe the urgent change process for implementing changes that are emergencies into production.

12.6 Urgent Change Process

Urgent changes in ChaRM are associated with emergencies that must be fast-tracked into the production system. Typically, urgent changes are a break in existing functionality, and fixing the break is a high priority for business continuity to remain uninterrupted.

The workflow behind an urgent change is optimized in that it can be processed through the request for change process, implemented, tested, approved for production, imported into production, and completed in a matter of moments. It really depends on how quickly the support organization can get the documentation, approvals, and implementation of the change completed. In regards to ChaRM, the urgent change will be promoted to production as fast as you can click through the steps in SAP Solution Manager. All of this occurs while using the same tracking and audit capabilities needed to capture who performed each activity, when, and why.

Urgent changes, although assigned to a maintenance project, are independent of the phases within a maintenance cycle. They can be created, imported, and managed regardless of what phase the normal changes are in.

It's up to the CAB to determine and approve what changes constitute the type urgent. Not everything is an urgent change, so it's important to classify and have guidelines for what should be approved as an urgent change. Having too loose of guidelines and approving normal routine maintenance activities as urgent changes creates a risk to your production environment.

Figure 12.61 identifies the end-to-end process for deploying an urgent change into the production system.

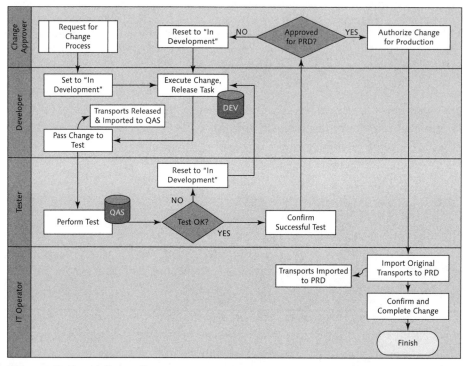

Figure 12.61 Urgent Change Process

Now, we'll walk through each of these steps and explain how urgent changes go from implementation to confirmation.

12.6.1 Developer: Implements Change

To implement the change, the developer follows these steps:

1. Log on to the SAP SOLUTION MANAGER IT SERVICE MANAGEMENT HOME page.

2. Select the NEW URGENT CHANGES link in the MY SAVED SEARCHES work area as shown in Figure 12.62.

3. In the SEARCH: URGENT CHANGES screen, select the ID link to open a new urgent change (Figure 12.63).

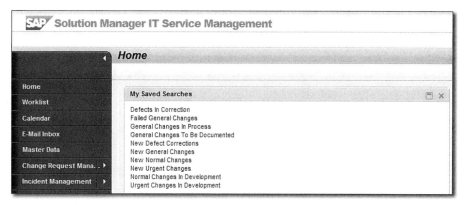

Figure 12.62 Search for New Urgent Changes

Figure 12.63 Open New Urgent Change

4. Select the EDIT button to begin processing the change.

At this point, the developer initiates his steps by first reviewing the details and description that was maintained on the request for change document. These details are automatically carried forward into the urgent change. Furthermore, the developer can also refer to the DESCRIPTION OF CHANGE and REASON FOR CHANGE, which were added in the TEXT assignment block.

5. From the ACTIONS menu, select the action SET TO "IN DEVELOPMENT" as shown in Figure 12.64.

Figure 12.64 Set to "In Development"

6. Click SAVE.

In an urgent change, the CREATE TRANSPORT REQUEST – WEBPAGE DIALOG screen appears immediately after the developer saves the document at this point.

7. In the CREATE TRANSPORT REQUEST – WEBPAGE DIALOG screen that appears, enter information specific to the transport request as shown in Figure 12.65.

   Note that SAP Solution Manager will automatically default most of the information regarding the transport. The developer can either choose to accept the defaulted information or update it.

8. Deselect the option for WORKBENCH REQUEST because this example involves Customizing only.

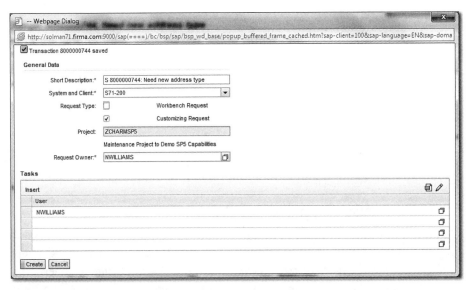

Figure 12.65 Create Transport Request

9. Click CREATE. The status of the urgent change will update from CREATED to IN DEVELOPMENT upon saving.

   The details of the transport request are now updated in the TRANSPORT MANAGEMENT assignment block. No tasks have been created because no development activities have yet occurred. The transport request was created from SAP Solution Manager but resides within the development system.

10. To access the development system, select the LOGON TO SYSTEM button located next to the development system in the LANDSCAPE assignment block (Figure 12.66).

Landscape	Display all Systems ⟳ Refresh						⊍ ⊟ ⌀ ⊼
Actions	Relevant for Logon	System Description	System Type	Transport Status	Risk Status	Transport Risks	
⟲	✓	S71:200	Development System	Modifiable			
⟲		S71:201	Test System				
⟲		S71:202	Production System				

Figure 12.66 Logon to Development System

The developer is taken to the development system that is assigned to the maintenance project. In the development system, the developer performs the implementation activities required for this specific change.

When the developer saves his changes, the PROMPT FOR CUSTOMIZING REQUEST dialog box will open.

11. Select the OWN REQUESTS button, and find the transport request that was created from SAP Solution Manager.

12. Press Enter.

13. The PROMPT FOR CUSTOMIZING REQUEST box will now have the details of the transport request as shown in Figure 12.67.

Figure 12.67 Assign Transport Request to Prompt

14. After assigning the objects to the transport request created from ChaRM, access Transaction SE09 (or Transaction SE10), and release the task(s) associated with this transport request.

15. Return to the urgent change document in the SAP CRM Web UI.

Before passing the urgent change off for testing, the developer may want to enter some instructions for the tester.

16. In the TEXT assignment block, select the ADD TEXT button as shown in Figure 12.68.

17. Select the text type TEST INSTRUCTION.

18. Enter some instructions for the tester.

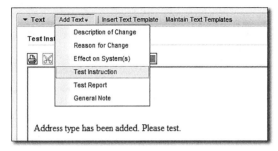

Figure 12.68 Add Test Instruction

19. From the ACTIONS menu, select the action PASS URGENT CHANGE TO TEST as shown in Figure 12.69.

Figure 12.69 Pass Urgent Change to Test

20. Click SAVE.

At this point, the original transport request is released from the development system and imported into the test system. These actions occur behind the scenes as soon as the developer selects the action just mentioned and saves the change document.

Figure 12.70 shows the results within the TRANSPORT MANAGEMENT assignment block. Clicking on the DETAILS button will also refresh the TASKS assignment block and include the details of the transport request's task(s).

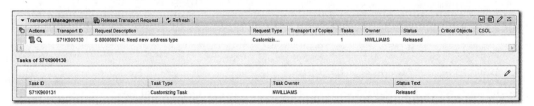

Figure 12.70 Transport Management and Task Details

12.6.2   Tester: Tests Change

Now the tester is ready to begin testing the urgent change within the test system. If the test is successful, the tester will confirm the successful test that the change approver will release for production import. If the test fails, the tester will pass the urgent change back to the developer. Because there are no test transports in the urgent change scenario, the developer will create a new transport request. The developer will implement the fix, release the task(s), and pass the change back to the tester.

The tester will follow these steps:

1. Log on to the SAP Solution Manager IT Service Management Home page.

2. Select the Urgent Changes to Be Tested link in the My Saved Searches work area as shown in Figure 12.71.

Figure 12.71 Search for Urgent Changes to Be Tested

3. In the Search: Urgent Changes screen, select the ID link to open an urgent change that is to be tested (Figure 12.72).

Figure 12.72 Select Urgent Change

4. Select the Edit button to begin processing the change.

At this point, the tester reviews the details within the urgent change, including the test instructions (Figure 12.73) provided by the developer during implementation. The tester will then test the developer's work.

Figure 12.73 Review Test Instructions

5. In the LANDSCAPE assignment block, select the LOGON TO SYSTEM button for the test system (Figure 12.74).

Figure 12.74 Logon to Test System

The tester will perform the test directly in the test system. When the tester has completed the testing, he will return to the urgent change in SAP Solution Manager.

As shown in Figure 12.75, the tester may want to include some details of the success (or failure) of the test.

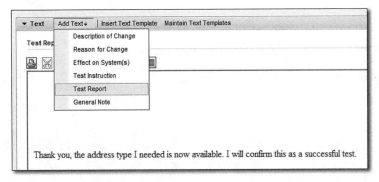

Figure 12.75 Enter Test Report

6. Scroll down to the TEXT assignment block.

7. Click the ADD TEXT button.

8. Select the text type TEST REPORT.

9. Enter some details about the test.

10. From the ACTIONS menu, select the action CONFIRM SUCCESSFUL TEST as shown in Figure 12.76.

Figure 12.76 Confirm Successful Test

11. Click SAVE.

The status of the urgent change is updated to AUTHORIZED FOR PRODUCTION.

12.6.3 Change Approver: Approves Change for Production Import

In this step, the change approver approves the change for production import. The change approver will validate that all of the standardized details about the urgent change have been documented thoroughly to meet requirements for implementation and testing. If something is missing, he has the option to set the urgent change back to IN DEVELOPMENT where it can be updated by the developer and then passed to the tester. If the change approver authorizes the urgent change, it can be imported into production by the IT operator.

The change approver follows these steps:

1. Log on to the SAP SOLUTION MANAGER IT SERVICE MANAGEMENT HOME page.

2. Select the URGENT CHANGES FOR PRODUCTION APPROVAL link in the MY SAVED SEARCHES work area as shown in Figure 12.77.

3. In the SEARCH: URGENT CHANGES screen, select the ID link to open an urgent change that has been successfully tested (Figure 12.78).

4. Select the EDIT button to begin processing the change.

5. From the ACTIONS menu, select the action RELEASE URGENT CHANGE FOR PRODUCTION as shown in Figure 12.79.

6. Click SAVE.

Figure 12.77 Search for Urgent Changes for Production Approval

Figure 12.78 Open Successfully Tested Urgent Change

Figure 12.79 Release Urgent Change for Production

The status of the urgent change document is now updated to AUTHORIZED FOR PRODUCTION.

12.6.4 IT Operator: Imports Change into Production

In this step, the IT operator has the green light from the change approver to import the urgent change into the production system. If the IT operator identifies something wrong, or communication was sent to the IT operator to hold off, the operator also has the option to reset the status of the urgent change back to IN DEVELOPMENT. After the urgent change is imported into production, the IT operator will check the transport logs to confirm that no errors were returned. If everything was successful, the IT operator confirms the change and completes the document.

The IT operator follows these steps:

1. Log on to the SAP Solution Manager IT Service Management Home page.

2. Select the Urgent Changes Authorized for Production link in the My Saved Searches work area as shown in Figure 12.80.

Figure 12.80 Search for Urgent Changes Authorized for Production

3. In the Search: Urgent Changes screen, select the ID link to open the urgent change authorized for production (Figure 12.81).

Figure 12.81 Open Urgent Change Authorized for Production

4. Select the Edit button to begin processing the change.

5. From the Actions menu, select the action Import Urgent Change into Production System as shown in Figure 12.82.

Figure 12.82 Import Urgent Change into Production System

6. Click Save. The status of the urgent change is now updated to Imported into Production.

The IT operator can view the APPLICATION LOG (Figure 12.83) to analyze any errors that may have occurred during the import of the transport requests. Similarly, he will review the transport logs in TMS to ensure that everything went accordingly.

Task Description	Status	Type	Start Date	Start Time	User	Triggered From
Import Transport Request (Online)	▣	Program or transaction	10/03/2012	12:39:21	NWILLIA...	8000000744
Import Transport Request (Online)	▣	Program or transaction	10/03/2012	12:21:44	NWILLIA...	8000000744
Release Transport Request	▣	Job	10/03/2012	12:19:50	NWILLIA...	8000000744
Create Transport Request	▣	Program or transaction	10/03/2012	12:16:53	NWILLIA...	8000000744

Figure 12.83 Review Application Log

7. From the ACTIONS menu, select the action CONFIRM URGENT CHANGE as shown in Figure 12.84.

Figure 12.84 Confirm Urgent Change

8. Click SAVE.

The status of the urgent change is now updated to CONFIRMED.

> **Note**
>
> According to the standard processes from SAP, the IT operator performs the confirmation of the urgent change. Some organizations choose to have the requester or tester confirm that the functionality or fix associated with the urgent change is working properly in the production system. In this case, you'll need to update your authorizations for the appropriate roles to set the status CONFIRMED in an urgent change.

At this point, the urgent change can be completed by the IT operator. Completing the urgent change will perform the necessary checks to complete the individual task list that is associated with the urgent change. After the urgent change is completed, it's locked for future maintenance. Further, all of the activities associated with its task list are also locked. Any new changes related to this urgent change will require a new request for change and urgent change documents.

The IT operator performs these steps:

1. From the ACTIONS menu, select the action COMPLETE URGENT CHANGE as shown in Figure 12.85.

Figure 12.85 Complete Urgent Change

2. Click SAVE.

3. Click the AGREE AND PROCEED button in the COMPLETE TASK LIST screen (Figure 12.86).

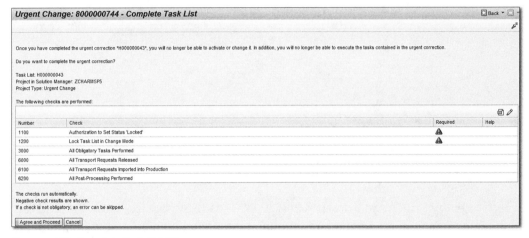

Figure 12.86 Complete Task List (1)

4. After the checks are performed successfully, click the AGREE AND PROCEED button (Figure 12.87).

As shown in Figure 12.88, the urgent change is now completed and locked from further processing.

We'll now describe the administrative change process to handle non-TMS changes.

Figure 12.87 Complete Task List (2)

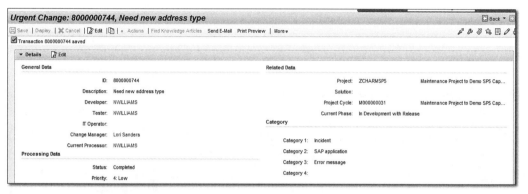

Figure 12.88 Completed Urgent Change

12.7 Administrative Change Process

In this section, we'll describe how ChaRM can help organize, document, and control changes for administrative tasks associated with your SAP landscape. Just as we have done with the normal and urgent changes in ChaRM, we'll then walk through the end-to-end process for implementing, testing, and confirming administrative changes in your SAP landscape.

The administrative change, classified by the standard SAP Solution Manager transaction type SMAD, provides the workflow and documentation needed to process SAP-related changes that aren't directly integrated with TMS. In other words, there are changes that occur in the SAP system that don't require that its changes (objects) are associated with a workbench or a Customizing request. In SAP Solution Manager, these changes are referred to as administrative changes.

The following are just a few typical and common examples of administrative tasks that occur in a SAP landscape:

▶ Updating the patch level of the SAP GUI

▶ Changes to the operating system (OS)

▶ Account number maintenance

▶ Number range maintenance

▶ Browser updates

▶ Service maintenance

▶ Changes to the kernel

Because administrative changes aren't linked to a transport request, they don't follow the standard DEV → QAS → PRD path to production the same way that normal and urgent changes do. Administrative changes can be processed independent of the downstream or upstream systems in either the implementation or maintenance landscape. To that end, they can be created for the non-productive systems (DEV and QAS).

> **Note**
>
> SAP Solution Manager supports the processing of administrative changes for non-productive systems after SP06. If your system is on a support pack preceding SP06, we recommend using the general change (transaction type SMCG) for all SAP non-TMS changes for non-production systems.

While administrative changes are linked to the maintenance project, they can be created independent of the maintenance cycle phases. Furthermore, the option to log on to any system in the project's landscape is available within the administrative change in the SAP CRM Web UI. Similar to normal changes, access to the task list is provided to execute activities related to the process we'll describe in the following sections.

Figure 12.89 provides a graphical representation of the end-to-end process flow for implementing, testing, and confirming an administrative change.

As you can see, the roles are limited between an IT operator (or a developer) and the change approver. Because there is no path to production, there is no need to provide testing and importing. For this reason, the end-to-end process flow for this change document is streamlined. We'll walk through each of these steps in the following sections.

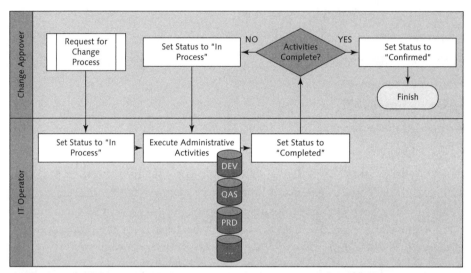

Figure 12.89 Administrative Change Process

12.7.1 IT Operator: Performs Administrative Activities

The first step is for the technician assigned to the administrative change to search for it within his personalized saved searches. In our example, the technician is the IT operator. However, depending on how authorizations are set up in your organization, the developer may in fact be the technician.

The IT operator follows these steps:

1. Log on to the SAP Solution Manager IT Service Management Home page.

2. Select the New Administrative Changes link in the My Saved Searches work area as shown in Figure 12.90.

3. In the Search: Administrative Changes screen, select the ID link to open a new administrative change (Figure 12.91).

Figure 12.90 Search for New Administrative Changes

Figure 12.91 Open New Administrative Change

4. Select the EDIT button to begin processing the request.

5. From the ACTIONS menu, select the action SET TO "IN PROCESS" as shown in Figure 12.92.

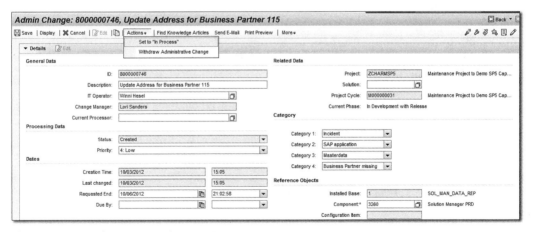

Figure 12.92 Set Administrative Change in Process

6. Click the SAVE button. The status of the administrative change is now updated from CREATED to IN PROCESS.

7. Scroll down to the TEXT assignment block to review the description of change entered by the requester at the time the request for change was created (Figure 12.93).

Figure 12.93 Review Description of Change

8. Scroll down to the LANDSCAPE assignment block. Figure 12.94 identifies the systems relevant to the maintenance project that this administrative change was approved to. Depending on the description and nature of the change, the IT operator will logon to any of these systems to begin the implementation of the change.

9. Select the LOGON TO SYSTEM button for the appropriate system.

Figure 12.94 Logon to System

10. In the target system, perform the required changes and save.

Tips & Tricks

You may enter some additional text (i.e., GENERAL NOTE) in the TEXT assignment block so that the change approver can understand the activities performed during the implementation of the administrative change.

11. When the implementation and documentation is complete, select the action SET TO "COMPLETED" from the ACTIONS menu as shown in Figure 12.95.

The administrative change will now be updated to the status COMPLETED. At this point, the process is handed off to the change approver who will confirm or pass back the administrative change to the IT operator if it requires further implementation.

Figure 12.95 Set Administrative Change to Completed

12.7.2 Change Approver: Confirms Administrative Activities

The change approver will confirm that the changes requested and approved have been implemented according to the requirements by the IT operator. If the implementation isn't correct, the change approver will set the administrative change back to IN PROCESS, to which the IT operator can update the change correctly.

The change approver follows these steps:

1. Logon to the SAP SOLUTION MANAGER IT SERVICE MANAGEMENT HOME page.

2. Select the ADMINISTRATIVE CHANGES TO BE CONFIRMED link in the MY SAVED SEARCHES work area as shown in Figure 12.96.

Figure 12.96 Search for Administrative Changes to Be Confirmed

3. In the SEARCH: ADMINISTRATIVE CHANGES screen, select the ID link to open the completed administrative change (Figure 12.97).

4. Select the EDIT button to begin processing the request.

Figure 12.97 Completed Administrative Change

5. From the Actions menu, select the action Confirm Administrative Change as shown in Figure 12.98.

Figure 12.98 Confirm Administrative Change

6. Click the Save button.

The administrative change is now updated to the status Confirmed as shown in Figure 12.99. No more changes are allowed within this change document because it's locked after the status Confirmed is set.

Figure 12.99 Confirmed Administrative Change

In the next section, we'll provide an overview of the general change process for handling changes that are required outside of the SAP installed base. We'll show you how SAP Solution Manager supports all types of change, even those which occurs on non-SAP systems and non-system IT assets.

12.8   General Change Process

Administrative changes, described in the previous section, have shown us how ChaRM can support changes that don't require transports from source system(s) to target system(s). Now, we'll continue showcasing the broader range of capabilities with ChaRM by explaining the general change transaction type We'll describe what classifies a general change, as well as walk through the end-to-end process for deploying changes across your IT infrastructure.

General changes, introduced in release 7.1 of SAP Solution Manager, are a new change transaction type in the ChaRM scenario. General changes are intended for changes that are not connected to TMS and are not related to the SAP landscape at all.

General changes are used for changes to IT assets such as mobile devices or printers (those being the classic SAP examples for non-SAP IT assets). Of course, general changes aren't limited to these two devices. This change document can manage changes to hardware, non-SAP systems, and legacy systems as well.

Because general changes aren't linked to TMS, it isn't mandatory that they are related to a change project. However, they are still considered a scope item and act as an output change process to the request for change.

Now that ChaRM provides the workflow, documentation, and status values necessary to support changes beyond SAP, we see even more value for selecting SAP Solution Manager over third-party alternatives. General changes support the continual effort to position SAP Solution Manager as the single, central platform to support ALM and SAP ITSM. General changes are one example of how SAP is providing improved flexibility for how IT services are managed and delivered to support business continuity.

Figure 12.100 shows a graphical representation of how to deploy general changes across your IT landscape using SAP Solution Manager's ChaRM scenario. Now, we'll take you through the steps to implement, test, and confirm changes that occur on your IT assets.

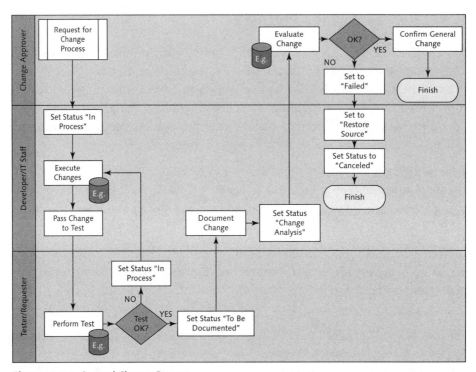

Figure 12.100 General Change Process

12.8.1 Developer: Implements Change

In the first step of the general change process, the developer implements the change that was approved during the request for change process. The developer reviews the details of the request for change as well as the details carried over to the general change document. The implementation occurs on the IT asset identified in the request for change document.

The developer follows these steps:

1. Log on to the SAP SOLUTION MANAGER IT SERVICE MANAGEMENT HOME page.

2. Select the link NEW GENERAL CHANGES in the MY SAVED SEARCHES work area as shown in Figure 12.101.

3. In the SEARCH: GENERAL CHANGES screen, select the ID link to open a new general change (Figure 12.102).

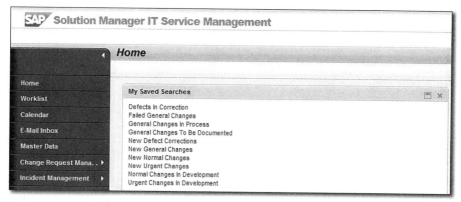

Figure 12.101 Search for New General Changes

Figure 12.102 Open New General Change

4. Select the Edit button to begin processing the change.

5. From the Actions menu, select the action Set To "In Process" as shown in Figure 12.103.

Figure 12.103 Set General Change to In Process

6. Click Save. The general change document's status is updated to In Process upon saving the document.

   Before passing the general change off for testing, the developer may want to enter some instructions for the tester.

7. In the Text assignment block, click the Add Text button as shown in Figure 12.104.

8. Select the text type Test Instruction.

9. Enter some instructions for the tester.

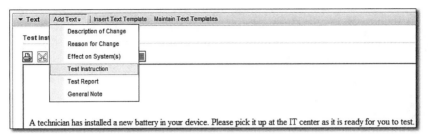

Figure 12.104 Add Text Instruction

Scroll back up and select PASS GENERAL CHANGE TO TEST from the ACTIONS button (Figure 12.105).

Figure 12.105 Pass General Change to Test

10. Click SAVE.

11. The status of the general change is updated to TO BE TESTED. It's now ready for testing.

12.8.2 Tester: Tests Change

In this step, the tester follows test instructions defined by the developer to test the implementation of the required changes to the IT asset. Depending on the outcome of the test, it's passed back to the developer. If it was successful, the developer is required to perform final documentation regarding any additional follow-ups for the general change. If the test fails, the tester puts the general change back to IN PROCESS where the developer can complete the implementation.

The tester follows these steps:

1. Log on to the SAP SOLUTION MANAGER IT SERVICE MANAGEMENT HOME page.

2. Select the GENERAL CHANGES TO BE TESTED link in the MY SAVED SEARCHES work area as shown in Figure 12.106.

Figure 12.106 Search for General Changes to Be Tested

3. In the SEARCH: GENERAL CHANGES screen, select the ID link to open a general change that is to be tested (Figure 12.107).

Figure 12.107 Open General Change to Be Tested

4. Select the EDIT button to begin processing the change.

At this point, the tester reviews the details within the general change, including the test instructions provided by the developer during implementation. The tester will then test the developer's work.

As shown in Figure 12.108, the tester may want to include some details to the success (or failure) of the test.

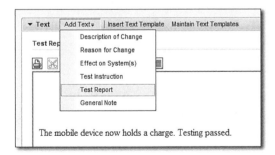

Figure 12.108 Tester Enters Test Report

5. Scroll down to the TEXT assignment block.

6. Click the ADD TEXT button.

7. Select the TEST REPORT text type.

8. Enter some details about the test.

    Now that the change has been tested with successful results, the general change will be passed back to the developer one last time. The purpose is for the developer to update his documentation and record any additional details for the change manager to evaluate and confirm the general change.

9. Scroll back up, and select SET TO "TO BE DOCUMENTED" from the ACTIONS button as shown in Figure 12.109.

Figure 12.109 Select Set to "To Be Documented"

10. Click SAVE.

The status of the general change is now updated to TO BE DOCUMENTED, and the process is handed over to the developer who implemented the change for final documentation.

12.8.3 Developer: Documents Change

In this step, assuming that the test was successful, the developer updates the general change with any follow-ups or information about the change that he implemented. The purpose of this is to provide the change approver with enough detail and information about the general change to be able to analyze and subsequently confirm it.

The developer takes the following steps:

1. Log on to the SAP SOLUTION MANAGER IT SERVICE MANAGEMENT HOME page.

2. Select the GENERAL CHANGES TO BE DOCUMENTED link in the MY SAVED SEARCHES work area as shown in Figure 12.110.

3. In the SEARCH: GENERAL CHANGES screen, select the ID link to open a general change that is to be documented (Figure 12.111).

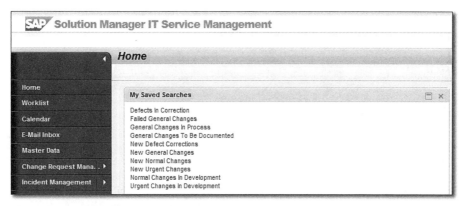

Figure 12.110 Search for General Changes to Be Documented

Figure 12.111 Select General Change to Be Documented

4. Select the EDIT button to begin processing the change.

The developer documents any final details necessary for the change approver to complete his evaluation and ultimately confirm the general change.

5. Scroll down to the TEXT assignment block as shown in Figure 12.112.

6. Click the button ADD TEXT.

7. Select the GENERAL NOTE text type.

8. Update the documentation with any other relevant information and details.

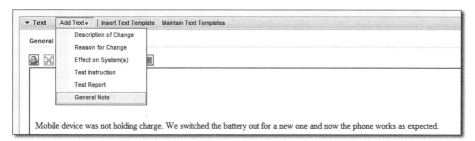

Figure 12.112 Document Change with General Note

601

9. Scroll back up, and select the option to SET TO "CHANGE ANALYSIS" from the ACTIONS button as shown in Figure 12.113.

Figure 12.113 Set to "Change Analysis"

10. Click SAVE.

The status of the general change is updated to CHANGE ANALYSIS. Now the general change is passed to the change approver who does his final analysis and confirms the general change.

12.8.4 Change Approver: Evaluates and Confirms Change

In the final step of the general change process, the change approver reviews the text log that was updated over the course of this process. He analyzes to see that the test was properly documented, the results were documented, and the developer included enough information to satisfy the organization's requirements for implementing a change. If these criteria are met and the change approver is satisfied, he confirms the change, which will close and lock the general change. If not, the change approver has the option of passing back to the developer for further attention.

The change approver follows these steps:

1. Log on to the SAP SOLUTION MANAGER IT SERVICE MANAGEMENT HOME page.

2. Select the GENERAL CHANGES TO BE EVALUATED link in the MY SAVED SEARCHES work area as shown in Figure 12.114.

3. In the SEARCH: GENERAL CHANGES screen, select the ID link to open a general change that is to be analyzed (Figure 12.115).

4. Select the EDIT button to begin processing the change.

5. From the ACTIONS menu, select the action SET TO "CONFIRM GENERAL CHANGE" as shown in Figure 12.116.

6. Click SAVE.

Figure 12.114 Search for General Changes to Be Evaluated

Figure 12.115 Open General Change to Be Analyzed

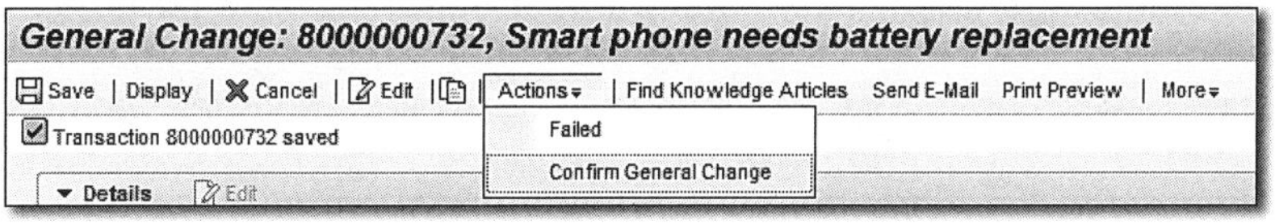

Figure 12.116 Confirm General Change

The general change is now confirmed by the change approver. Subsequently, the status of the general change is updated to CONFIRMED. Further, it's locked from additional processing. This step marks the end of the general change process.

The next section closes out this chapter by jumping back into one final change document linked to TMS. We'll describe how the defect correction ChaRM document can be used to correct test defects found during the integration/scenario testing phase of your release.

12.9   Defect Correction Process

As you're now aware, urgent changes and normal changes are two ChaRM change documents that integrate directly within TMS. You're probably now very familiar with this concept; that is, specific ChaRM documents requiring transport requests and the promotion from development to quality assurance and finally to production.

As we wrap up our chapter on end-user roles and process flows for ChaRM, we'll discuss one final ChaRM document. The defect correction can be added to the short list of change transactions that are linked to TMS. In this section, we'll provide an overview and explanation of the process to deploy a defect correction during the test phase of your release/maintenance cycle.

A defect correction can be thought of as a test error. They are used in conjunction with normal changes and deployed during the test phase of your maintenance project and cycle.

As we've described throughout this chapter, one of the greatest benefits of adopting the normal change process within ChaRM is to gain the advantages associated with the test transport functionality. If you recall from previous sections, test transports allow objects to be passed between development and quality if testing was not successful. This preserved the original transport and protected the production buffer, in that the transport that was released is the transport that is intended on going to production.

With test transports, when the original transport is released, integration (or scenario) testing should yield a high success rate. However, after the import of the original transport request occurs, integration testing begins.

Defect corrections are created if an error occurs during this phase or the test phase of the maintenance cycle. In fact, they can only be created when the change approver (or IT operator) advances the phase of the maintenance cycle to the test phase. These corrections are required in ChaRM because the test phase prohibits new normal changes from being created.

Because the defect correction is used during integration testing, it isn't specific to any single request for change or change transaction. The defect is project specific and affects the overall scope of the maintenance project intended to be deployed into production. For this reason, defect corrections don't require an approval and are created directly by the tester and subsequently implemented by a developer.

Defect corrections allow for the creation and release of transports. The transports associated with a defect correction must be released before the phase of the maintenance cycle is advanced to the next phase.

Figure 12.117 shows a representation of the end-to-end process flow for creating, implementing, and testing a defect correction.

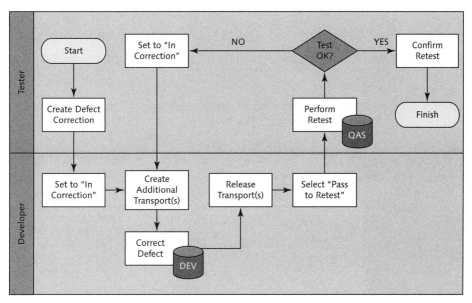

Figure 12.117 Defect Correction Process Flow

As we mentioned, defect corrections are only created in the test phase of the maintenance cycle because that is when integration testing occurs. Figure 12.118 is an image of the maintenance cycle in the SAP CRM Web UI in the test phase. Depending on how your organization administers ChaRM security, this can be set by either the change approver or the IT operator.

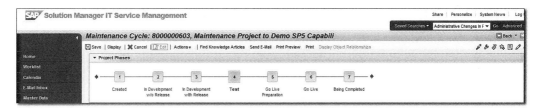

Figure 12.118 Maintenance Cycle in the Test Phase

Now, we'll walk through the steps to create, implement, and test a defect correction in SAP Solution Manager.

12.9.1 Tester: Creates Defect Correction

To initiate the defect correction process, the tester begins by creating a defect correction from scratch in the SAP CRM Web UI by following these steps:

1. Log on to the SAP SOLUTION MANAGER IT SERVICE MANAGEMENT HOME page.

2. Select the CREATE DEFECT CORRECTION link in the CREATE work area as shown in Figure 12.119.

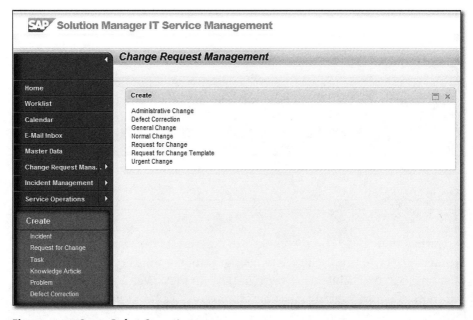

Figure 12.119 Create Defect Correction

The defect correction document appears as a blank template as shown in Figure 12.120.

3. Maintain the header data in the DETAILS assignment block according to your organization's process for creating change documents.

4. Scroll down to the TEXT assignment block.

5. Select the ADD TEXT button as shown in Figure 12.121.

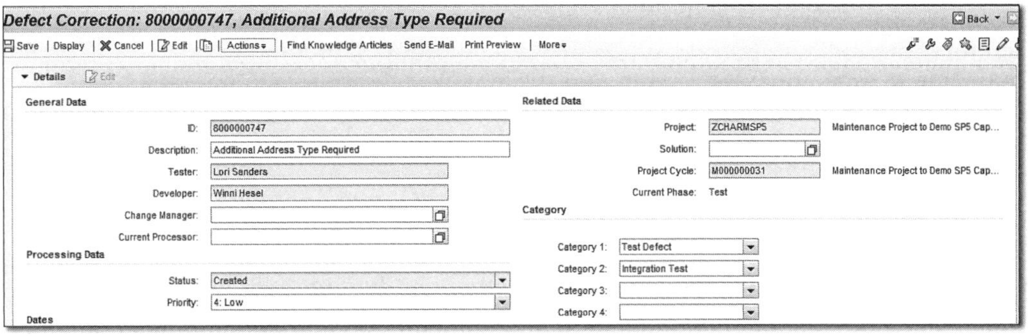

Figure 12.120 Maintain Details of the Defect Correction

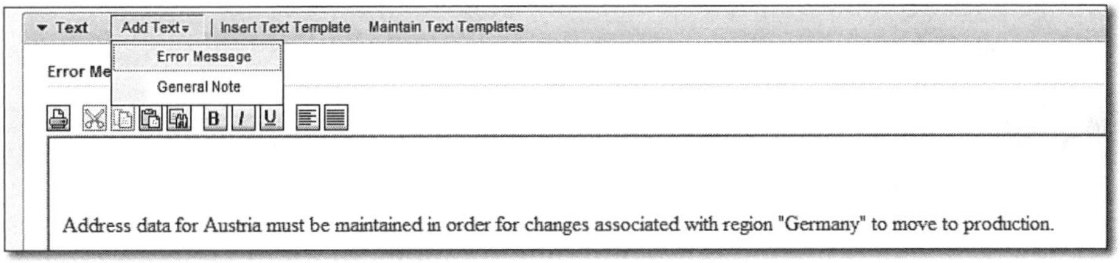

Figure 12.121 Maintain Error Message

6. Select the option ERROR MESSAGE.

7. Provide some descriptive text of the error and why a defect must be created.

8. Click SAVE.

The defect correction is initially saved, and the document status is set to CREATED. Now, the defect correction is passed to the developer to implement the changes required.

12.9.2   Developer: Implements Defect Correction

In this step, the developer takes the defect correction in process to begin implementation. Because the normal changes have been released, and the defect may not be specific to a single normal change, the developer will create new transport request(s) and assign the objects to the request(s). After the developer has completed this work, he will release the transport requests directly in ChaRM and subsequently pass the defect correction back to the tester.

The developer follows these steps:

1. Log on to the SAP SOLUTION MANAGER IT SERVICE MANAGEMENT HOME page.

2. Select the NEW DEFECT CORRECTIONS link in the MY SAVED SEARCHES work area as shown in Figure 12.122.

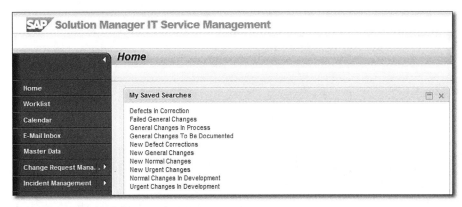

Figure 12.122 Search for New Defect Corrections

3. In the SEARCH: DEFECT CORRECTIONS screen, select the ID link to open a new defect correction (Figure 12.123).

Figure 12.123 Open New Defect Correction

4. Select the EDIT button to begin processing the defect.

5. From the ACTIONS menu, select the action SET TO "IN CORRECTION" as shown in Figure 12.124.

Figure 12.124 Set to "In Correction"

The CREATE TRANSPORT REQUEST – WEBPAGE DIALOG window will appear (Figure 12.125).

6. Enter the details about the transport request. Most of these details will be defaulted for you, but you may choose to update or deselect what is available.

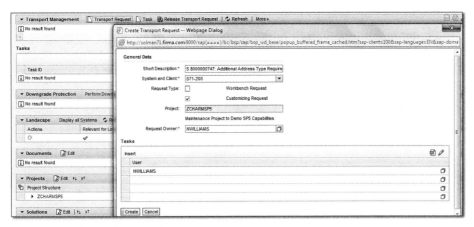

Figure 12.125 Create Transport Request

7. Click CREATE.

8. In the LANDSCAPE assignment block, click the LOGON TO SYSTEM button for the development system as shown in Figure 12.126.

Landscape	Refresh						
Actions	Relevant for Logon	System Description	System Type	Transport Status	Risk Status	Transport Risks	
		S71:200	Development System				
		S71:201	Test System				
		S71:202	Production System				

Figure 12.126 Logon to Development System

The developer is sent to the target development system in the maintenance landscape where he will implement the corrections.

9. When the PROMPT FOR CUSTOMIZING REQUEST window appears, select the OWN REQUESTS button, and search for the transport request that was created in ChaRM.

Once selected, the details of that transport request will become available in that window (Figure 12.127).

10. Press Enter.

609

Figure 12.127 Select Own Request

11. Remaining in the development system, access Transaction SE09 (or Transaction SE10), and release the transport request task associated with the correction. (Remember the transport request itself can't be released directly in the managed system.)

12. Return to the SAP Solution Manager SAP CRM Web UI in defect processing.

13. In the TRANSPORT MANAGEMENT assignment block, click the REFRESH button.

    As shown in Figure 12.128, you'll notice the details and status of the transport request updated to reflect the implemented objects.

Figure 12.128 Transport Management Details Updated

14. Click the button RELEASE TRANSPORT REQUEST.

    The RELEASE TRANSPORT REQUEST – WEBPAGE DIALOG window appears as shown in Figure 12.129.

15. Select the line that contains the transport request to be released.

16. Select the OK button.

Figure 12.129 Release Transport Request

The status of the transport request is now updated to RELEASED in the TRANSPORT MANAGEMENT assignment block (Figure 12.130).

Figure 12.130 Transport Management: Released Transport Request

The transport objects associated with this defect correction are imported into the test system via the standard import jobs that have been set up by the Basis team. Alternatively, this import job can be executed manually from the task list as we've described for the normal changes.

The developer can maintain some descriptive text in the TEXT assignment block if necessary.

17. Scroll back up, and select the option to PASS TO "RETEST" from the ACTIONS button as shown in Figure 12.131.

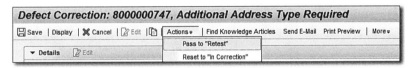

Figure 12.131 Pass to Retest

18. Click SAVE.

The defect correction is now updated to the status TO BE RETESTED. At this point, the process is handed over to the tester who performs the retest.

12.9.3 Tester: Tests Defect Correction

In the final step of the defect correction process, the tester performs a test on the correction(s) implemented by the developer. If the test is successful, the tester will confirm the defect correction, which will close and lock it from additional maintenance. If the test fails, the defect correction is passed back to the developer for additional updates.

The tester follows these steps:

1. Log on to the SAP SOLUTION MANAGER IT SERVICE MANAGEMENT HOME page.

2. Select the DEFECT CORRECTIONS TO BE RETESTED link in the MY SAVED SEARCHES work area as shown in Figure 12.132.

Figure 12.132 Search for Defect Corrections to Be Retested

3. In the SEARCH: DEFECT CORRECTIONS screen, select the ID link to open a defect correction to be retested (Figure 12.133).

Figure 12.133 Select Defect Correction to Be Retested

4. Select the EDIT button to begin processing the defect.

5. In the LANDSCAPE assignment block, click the LOGON TO SYSTEM button for the test system (Figure 12.134).

Figure 12.134 Log On to the Test System

The tester will perform the test directly in the test system. When the tester has completed the testing, he will return to the defect correction in SAP Solution Manager.

6. From the ACTIONS menu, select the action CONFIRM DEFECT CORRECTION as shown in Figure 12.135.

Defect Correction: 8000000747, Additional Address Type Required

Save | Display | ✖ Cancel | 🖉 Edit | 🗐 | Actions ▾ | Find Knowledge Articles Send E-Mail Print Preview | More ▾

Confirm Defect Correction

Reset to "In Correction"

▾ Details   🖉 Edit

Figure 12.135 Confirm Defect Correction

Note

For defect corrections, the TESTER and DEVELOPER fields can't be maintained with the same business partner identification number. For other change documents, this is a "soft" warning that doesn't stop the process. For defect corrections, it's mandatory.

Standard Customizing for the SMTM0001 partner procedure prohibits the changing of business partners. You may want to update these Customizing settings so if these two business partners share the same ID, you can change them.

7. Click SAVE.

The defect correction is now updated to the status CONFIRMED, as shown in Figure 12.136.

Figure 12.136 Confirmed Defect Correction

This marks the end of the defect correction process. All transports associated with this defect are imported into the production system with the remainder of the objects for the project.

12.10   Summary

This chapter illustrates the power, flexibility, and scalability that SAP Solution Manager encompasses in regards to providing an end-to-end change management solution for your entire IT landscape. There literally isn't one scenario that involves changing a component of your IT landscape that isn't supported by SAP Solution Manager. Whether you're a 100% SAP shop, or you're supporting several platforms that include non-SAP assets, ChaRM provides the workflow needed to manage changes from a central platform.

SAP provides the workflow needed to control changes to your software while also allowing the flexibility needed for support team members to perform their jobs. These out-of-the-box processes are ITIL compliant and based on SAP best practices for end-to-end change deployment. While the workflow is there, it's up to your organization to identify what fits, what must be adapted, and what organizational changes must be applied for ChaRM to bring value to your organization. The tools are there, so it's up to your organization to determine when and how these functions will start being rolled out to benefit your teams.

In the next chapter, we'll discuss maintenance activities and project administration. We've touched on the maintenance projects, maintenance cycles, task lists, and ChaRM for implementations in this chapter. Next, we'll discuss these concepts in further detail.

Additional features in Change Request Management provide key function-
alities that proactively detect and centrally handle conflicts that could
cause inconsistencies and risks to your project. We'll discuss four signifi-
cant features that help provide the logistics and coordination needed to
ensure consistency across your SAP projects.

13 Additional Features of Change Request Management

Chapter 11 provided an overview of the major features and functionalities delivered with Change Request Management (ChaRM). Looking all the way back to
Chapter 8 and Chapter 9, many features within Application Incident Management
(AIM) also cross over into the ChaRM scenario. We'll provide a comparison and
explain the cross-over pieces in Chapter 15. In addition to the functional capabilities of ChaRM and the cross-scenario benefits as part of the overall SAP ITSM
framework, you also should have a strong understanding of the end-to-end process flows for each change document available within ChaRM.

In this chapter, we'll describe some of the larger, more robust, and more complex
scenarios that are included with the overall Change Control Management and
ChaRM scenarios within SAP Solution Manager. These additional features of
ChaRM help to organize the coordination, planning, and maintenance efforts
required when there are risks associated with conflicts introduced into projects.

We'll start by providing an overview of the retrofitting capabilities delivered
within the Change Control Management scenario of SAP Solution Manager.

13.1 Retrofit

For the scenario in which the changes applied in the maintenance landscape must
be in sync with the development system, objects are synchronized between the
development system of the implementation landscape and the development system

of the maintenance landscape. The goal is to maintain an up-to-date implementation landscape that contains the latest versions of the objects that have gone live in the maintenance landscape. This needs to happen as quickly, efficiently, and risk-free as possible. This process for synchronizing changes across development systems is called Retrofit.

Because these changes are made across parallel landscapes, they can't all be transported in the traditional manner. Inconsistencies with objects can occur and data can be overwritten if all changes are transported without detecting conflicts or inconsistencies. To avoid the inconsistency of data and loss of required changes, the SAP Solution Manager Retrofit functionality provides automation, control, management, and tracking of changes that must be synchronized in parallel. Rather than transporting objects from the source development system to the target development system, they are repackaged within a transport request on the target system. The objects are merged using various tools depending on the object scenario (we explain these tools in Section 13.1.2).

Within this scenario, SAP Solution Manager provides the functionality to synchronize changes across an N, N+1 scenario (i.e., dual development landscape) using automated tools.

In this chapter, we'll describe the main features of the Retrofit feature, explain how its technical infrastructure drives the process to retrofit objects from a maintenance landscape to an implementation landscape, and go over the steps involved in retrofitting objects.

13.1.1 Overview

Organizations will often require a second development system for larger scale implementation projects while they are supporting a productive maintenance landscape. The main purpose of this is to avoid risks to production associated with implementing large changes within an implementation project as much as possible. Additionally, change management and release management that support the production environment must not interfere with the implementation team's activities.

The classic rationale for this heterogeneous scenario is to provide the flexibility so that developers who work within the maintenance and implementation projects can do so independently. Also, fixes to bugs are commonly preferred to be conducted in a development environment that resembles the productive system as close as possible. Separating these two development scenarios supports the processes of release and change management for the implementation team while simultaneously allowing maintenance to occur following the organization's requirements for support. Most importantly, when the implementation project undergoes cutover into the maintenance landscape, it must not overwrite changes to objects performed as part of normal and urgent production change processes.

Figure 13.1 provides a high-level presentation of a classic N, N+1 scenario in which a three-tier SAP ERP landscape is established to support maintenance of a continuous productive solution. Below that landscape, you'll notice a two-tier implementation landscape to support the implementation of a new solution. Transporting of changes is administered between the target and source systems of the respective landscapes, as they normally would be according to standard transport paths. However, if a change is required to be applied in the parallel development system, the Retrofit tool may be used.

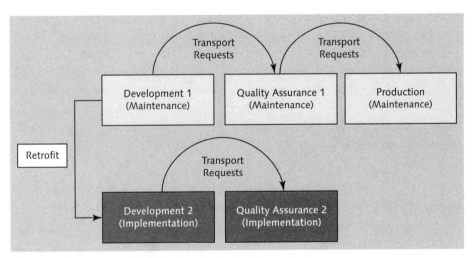

Figure 13.1 Transport and Retrofit Scenario for Parallel Landscapes

The synchronizing of changes to the parallel development system has been a process managed by development teams regardless of the Change Control Management tool in place within the organization. However, this process (without a third-party tool or customer solution) is 100% manual and can be extremely time consuming. Further, errors and inconsistencies are common due to natural human intervention. With SAP Solution Manager, this process can be highly automated by using the Retrofit functionality.

> **Note**
>
> You don't require full ChaRM adoption to use the Retrofit functionality. You can perform retrofitting from the task list, independent of the urgent and normal change documents. In other words, you don't need to adopt the full end-to-end approval and workflows provided with ChaRM. If your scenario includes the workflow, the Retrofit functionality is integrated into the process and can be triggered from the change documents.

13.1.2   Retrofit Process Overview (High-Level)

Figure 13.2 breaks down the process we described in the overview of this section to provide further detail about how the retrofit process works from a technological and scheduling perspective.

We've added a few important details regarding when key retrofit activities occur across the continuous support in a maintenance landscape. For example, the retrofit process initiates after the transport objects are released (❶). After this occurs, the system applies the retrofit data to the implementation landscape (❷) depending on the state of the transport objects. Finally, SAP Solution Manager supports the cutover into the maintenance landscape when the implementation project has gone live (❸). We will discuss the breakdown of this process in detail within the rest of this section.

In the following subsections, we'll describe what happens post-release of transport objects for those that must be synchronized into the parallel development system. We'll discuss the scenarios that you'll come across in regards to how various objects will be handled during the retrofit process. We'll discuss the different tools available to support you in retrofitting, no matter what state the objects are in at the time of retrofit. Finally, we'll discuss how SAP Solution Manager provides the capabilities to support the cutover of changes from the implementation landscape into the maintenance landscape.

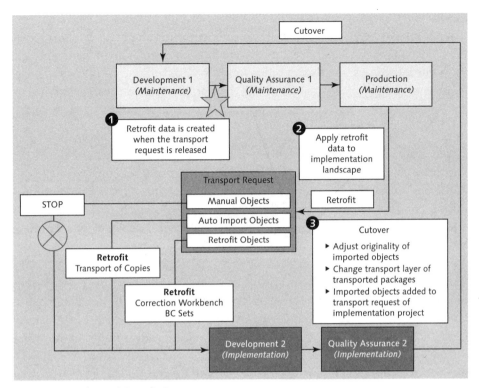

Figure 13.2 High-Level Retrofit Process

Applying Retrofit Data to the Implementation Landscape

After the objects have been released from the development system, they can be retrofitted into the parallel development system of the implementation landscape. If this is being administered from the change document, the RETROFIT option is available according to the status of the document. Urgent changes must be in the status AUTHORIZED FOR PRODUCTION, and normal changes must be in the status TO BE TESTED.

Categories determine how and if the changes originating from the maintenance development system can be systemically synchronized (retrofitted) into the implementation project's development system. There are four categories, which we describe in the following subsections, that cover all scenarios possible within the Retrofit functionality.

Auto Import

If objects have been changed in the maintenance development landscape, yet they have not been changed in the implementation development landscape, the Auto Import scenario is valid. In other words, objects without conflicts in the target system and objects that have not had their original version changed in the target system can be retrofitted using the Auto Import capability.

In this scenario, because the downstream object is original, an automatic import of test transports is released and exported to the development system of the implementation landscape. The test transport (or transport of copies) contains all of the objects required to keep the two parallel landscapes in sync without introducing conflict. All object types are supported (workbench and Customizing) with the Auto Import capability with the exception of SAP NetWeaver Business Warehouse (SAP NetWeaver BW) and Java objects.

SAP Correction Workbench

For repository (workbench) objects that have been changed in the maintenance landscape and should also be reflected in the implementation landscape, the SAP Correction Workbench is used. These include objects with conflicts in the target system as well as objects that have been changed in the target system. You may be familiar with the UI and functionality of the SAP Correction Workbench already because it's the same technology used when applying OSS notes to your SAP systems. Figure 13.3 shows the SAP Correction Workbench in action when used to retrofit changes.

The SAP Correction Workbench, also known as Transaction SCWB, imports workbench objects into the target system if the object does not exist or where it can identify the exact location for the new parts of the object. For these cases, a green traffic light indicates this scenario (Figure 13.4).

> **Note**
>
> The green traffic light does not confirm that 100% of the changes can be copied completely and successfully. If the starting status is different in the maintenance development system and the implementation development system, the green traffic light does not guarantee that copying the changes will result in a program that is syntactically and semantically correct. It's highly recommended that you check the program yourself after the retrofit is complete to ensure that there are no errors.

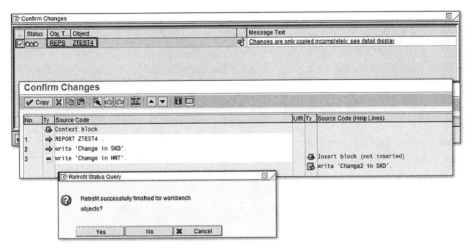

Figure 13.3 SAP Correction Workbench

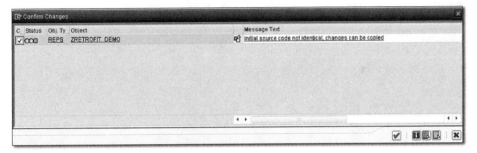

Figure 13.4 Green Traffic Light: Transaction SCWB Import

If this exact location isn't identified by the SAP Correction Workbench, the objects won't be retrofitted, and the user will encounter a warning (yellow traffic light). However, the user can use post-processing tools to perform the retrofit. The yellow warning notifies the user that only part of the changes can be copied using the automated SAP Correction Workbench functionality. For this scenario, a split-screen editor is available to compare and adjust the objects in the source system and the target system. The changes can be adjusted from within the split-screen editor.

Objects that aren't supported by the SAP Correction Workbench will result in a red error. This means that the Retrofit tool can't copy the changes from a systematic, automated perspective.

BC Sets

Similar to how the SAP Correction Workbench is used, the Business Configuration Set (BC Set) tool (Figure 13.5) is used to retrofit Customizing objects from a source development system to a targeted parallel development system. If a Customizing setting was modified in the maintenance and implementation landscape, the Customizing version in the maintenance landscape is recorded in a BC Set. (BC Sets are a collection of customizing settings in which configuration objects are bundled together and loaded into the development system) In the Retrofit tool, it's compared with the object in the implementation landscape and further adjusted.

Figure 13.5 BC Set Tool

Like the SAP Correction Workbench, the BC Set capability will include objects with conflicts in the target system as well as objects that have been changed in the target system. BC Set functionality must be available for the object for the Retrofit tool to synchronize the changes. If the BC Set functionality isn't available (e.g., master data changes), then the retrofit won't occur.

Manual Retrofit

In a world without SAP Solution Manager Retrofit, organizations may have leveraged a third-party Change Control Management tool or an in-house system in order to retrofit transport objects from a maintenance development system to an implementation development system. In the case that no automated tools are available, retrofitting is performed independently of a tool and administered by the developer manually.

Even with the Retrofit tool active when SAP Solution Manager is used, there can be scenarios in which manual retrofitting is required. While the Retrofit tool can automate the majority of changes (i.e., a very high percentage, which differs from organization to organization due to varying object modification), there are cases in which the developers must revert back to their manual process. Manual retrofitting is needed when objects can't be imported automatically and for objects that can't be processed with the post-processing tools. We'll describe why these two scenarios may occur in the following bullet list.

For these cases, the Retrofit tool provides tracking and reporting capabilities so these changes are still traceable in the SAP Solution Manager system.

Some examples of why changes might require manual retrofitting even if SAP Solution Manager is deployed can include the following:

▶ **The object isn't found due to object check.**
Objects are checked before they can be retrofitted into the parallel system. At the time retrofit is performed, the object version in the target system must be identical to the original object version in the source system before the changes are synchronized. This check is to ensure that the change can be copied correctly. If inconsistencies occur in this regard, these objects may not be able to be retrofitted by the tool.

▶ **The objects do not exist.**
If the objects do not exist in the target system, then the Retrofit tool will have nothing to check.

▶ **The objects are locked in a separate request for change.**
If another request for change is controlling the objects that must be retrofitted, they will be locked. In this case, automatic retrofitting cannot occur if transport objects are locked in another document.

▶ **The object to be retrofitted isn't supported for BC Set activation.**
There may be a small percentage (which depends on the scope of your SAP ERP solution) that are not supported by the BC Set activation. In these cases, the automatic retrofitting cannot occur.

▶ **The object to be retrofitted isn't supported in the SAP Correction Workbench.**
There may be a small percentage (which depends on the scope of your SAP ERP solution) that are not supported by the SAP Correction Workbench. In these cases, the automatic retrofitting cannot occur.

Implementation Project Go-Live: Cutover to Maintenance

If a parallel development landscape is used to support a new implementation, the changes completed in the implementation landscape must be transferred to the maintenance landscape. ChaRM provides cutover capabilities to transfer the transport requests from the QAS of the implementation landscape to the development system of the maintenance landscape.

When the changes are introduced into the maintenance landscape, they are packaged together into a small number (one for workbench and one for Customizing) of transport requests. These transport requests are promoted to the QAS of the maintenance landscape where they undergo further testing.

The benefit of this approach is to reduce the number of transport requests associated with an implementation to a smaller number by way of the cutover project. Also, the transport requests containing the changes from the implementation are now sourced from the development system of the maintenance project.

13.1.3 Retrofit in Use

The Retrofit function can be started from the change document (Figure 13.6) or from the task list (Figure 13.7). If the Retrofit function is started from an urgent change, the status of the document must be AUTHORIZED FOR IMPORT. If it's started from the normal change, the status of the document must be CONSOLIDATED. At these two points, the transport requests for the respective change document types have been released. If you choose to retrofit at the change document level, you must take note that the only transport requests that will be retrofitted will be those assigned to that single change document.

Figure 13.6 Start Retrofit from the Change Document

To retrofit transport objects at the project level, you can initiate the process from the task list of the maintenance cycle (see Figure 13.7). In this case, you must perform the activity to release transport requests and select the transport requests that should be retrofitted before starting the process. Right-clicking the START RETROFIT option in the task list and choosing the EXECUTE option will initiate the retrofit process.

Figure 13.7 Start Retrofit from the Task List

After you start the retrofit process, the system will display all of the eligible transport requests for retrofitting (Figure 13.8). These include only those that are released and for which the retrofit has not already finished.

At this point, you'll need to select the option to display the values in the RETROFIT REQUEST column.

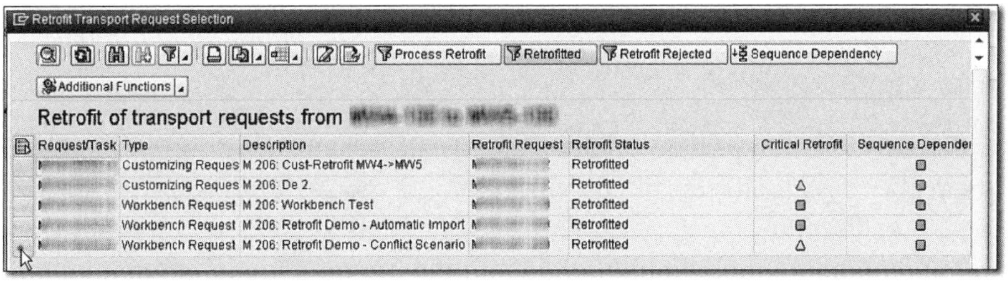

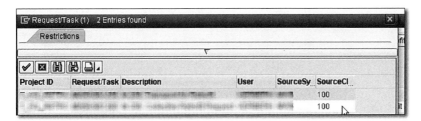

Figure 13.8 Requests Available for Retrofit

After you select this option, you'll be presented with a list of retrofit transport requests (Figure 13.9). These are the transport requests that reside on the retrofit system (i.e., implementation development system) and to which the objects will be synchronized.

Figure 13.9 Select Retrofit Transport Request

At this time, the developer will select the transport request that he created specifically for this retrofit activity.

The developer is now ready to officially retrofit the changes. Prior to retrofitting the change, the developer has the option to perform a consistency check. This feature is located within the ADDITIONAL FEATURES button. The consistency check confirms that a retrofit transport request exists, the sequence dependency checks out okay, and that there are no SAP Note objects within the request that could cause conflicts upon import.

After the consistency check, the developer will select the line item from the table shown in Figure 13.10 and confirm which type of retrofit category will be used (i.e., SCWB, BC SET, etc.).

Figure 13.10 Ready to Retrofit

In this example, the SAP Correction Workbench is being used to retrofit workbench objects. After the retrofit process is started, the SAP Correction Workbench appears and notifies the developer of the object and its associated status (Figure 13.11).

Figure 13.11 Confirm Changes

Confirming again will inform the developer of the inactive objects that will be part of the retrofit process (Figure 13.12).

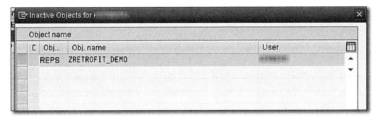

Figure 13.12 Inactive Objects

When the retrofit process has completed, the developer will be given an information screen stating that the request has been retrofitted to the retrofit transport request (Figure 13.13).

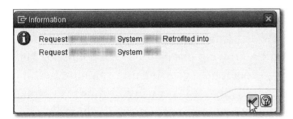

Figure 13.13 Completed Retrofit

In the next section, we'll discuss another feature that is important in ChaRM: cross-system object lock (CSOL).

13.2 Cross-System Object Lock (CSOL)

Cross-system object lock (CSOL) provides the capability to manage conflicts that may occur if there are several projects occurring in which developers are handling the same objects. While CSOL has been a fundamental component of ChaRM, it's resurfacing to be more usable via the DOWNGRADE PROTECTION assignment block.

As described in Chapter 13, SAP Solution Manager 7.1, SP5 enabled CSOL as a key component (and prerequisite) of the Downgrade Protection functionality. CSOL is the "engine" that enables the Downgrade Protection function to track objects stored in transport requests and report conflicts when those objects are saved in more than two transports targeted for the same production system.

Identifying, managing, and avoiding conflict is more efficient and visible to the users with these two components harmonized.

In this section, we'll provide an overview of this feature and discuss the options and scenarios for which this functionality is relevant. Also, we'll show you an example of how to use the features of CSOL in your development environment and manage locks that may occur within the development system's objects in the central SAP Solution Manager system.

13.2.1 Overview

Organizations often have a single implementation landscape or single maintenance landscape that is supported by ChaRM. Due to the nature of large organizations with complex system landscapes, it's not uncommon for several ongoing initiatives to run in parallel. New implementations, upgrades, rollouts, and enhancements will occur to support a growing installed base that must be kept current to support expansion across geographies, growing user communities, and business requirements that demand an updated/fresh installed base. Further, after these implementations enter maintenance or support mode, there are often dual development environments (i.e., N, N+1 scenario) that must be kept in sync.

Based on the common scenarios we've just described, it becomes a question of how you manage changes across these initiatives while avoiding conflicts that occur across development teams.

Prior to ChaRM, developers had the comfort of knowing that their repository (workbench) objects were locked until they were released from the development system. For example, if one developer had modified an ABAP program and collected those objects in a transport request, another developer couldn't maintain that ABAP program until the first developer released the associated transport request. While this remains an important and fundamental piece of the Transport Management System (TMS), it does not apply to Customizing (e.g., table changes) objects.

From a non-systematic approach, this takes an immense amount of collaboration between developers. Especially in the hectic, rapid state in which development occurs, collaboration efforts can be extremely difficult and near impossible. However, it's critical that the same object isn't modified by separate teams when the target production system is shared.

With the CSOL feature, you can identify conflicts between objects in transport requests that have the same production system (or client) as their transport target. SCOL supports both ABAP development objects and Customizing objects. This feature is delivered as part of ChaRM in SAP Solution Manager. For this functionality to work, all transport requests must originate from the change document(s) within the ChaRM or Quality Gate Management (QGM) scenario.

CSOL, when activated, creates locks that are held in the SAP Solution Manager system for any object (workbench and Customizing) that is changed in the managed development system. Depending on the conflict scenario, a developer who needs to make changes to this object in another transport request is prevented from doing so until the lock is released. The lock is released when the transport request is successfully promoted to the production system.

In other words, if John changes an object in the implementation project for HR, Rick can't make a change to that object in the implementation project for FI-CO as long as those two development systems target the same production system. This is just one example of where CSOL prevents conflicts. We'll discuss common use cases of how CSOL manages these conflicts in Section 13.2.2.

Self-Defined Lock Conflict Scenario (Expert Mode)

Lock settings can be set up by the SAP Solution Manager administrator according to the requirements defined by the development leads and change managers (for example). This is determined by the expert mode configuration settings (described in Chapter 15) when setting up CSOL.

Depending on how these locks are set up, they are released according to these requirements. However, the earliest they will be released is after the release of the transport request itself. This enforcement by CSOL ensures that conflicts do not occur at the earlier stages of object development.

You have the choice of labeling conflicts with various message types (e.g., error or warning) depending on your scenario and how much restriction/flexibility should be permitted. Errors restrict the developer from continuing to change the object while warnings can be "skipped." The conflict messages that are displayed to the developers who are attempting to modify objects that are locked contain specific information:

▶ Conflict type (error or warning)

▶ Transport requests affected

▶ Owners of affected transport requests

Categories That Trigger Cross-System Object Lock Errors

We mentioned that there are two message types that label conflicts that are detected by CSOL: errors and warnings. Errors provide a "hard stop" in that if an error is triggered, the developer is prohibited from continuing to change that object type. So what must occur for a lock to deliver an error?

Categories are used by the CSOL functionality to classify how the error conditions are met if a developer attempts to alter an object that has a lock held in the SAP Solution Manager system. If a developer tries to save an object that violates the categories, the error message is triggered, and the developer is prevented from maintaining the object. The following categories classify how the error conditions are met:

▶ **Project relation**
This setting provides the ability to handle objects that have already been saved in a transport request, and will be saved again in another transport request. In regards to the project this object and transport request relate to, there are three different scenarios:

  ▷ **Cross***:* The system ignores the project type that each transport request belongs to.

  ▷ **Specific***:* If the project that the two transports belong to must be the same.

  ▷ **Different***:* If the project that the two transports belong to must be separate.

▶ **Change type relation**
This setting provides the ability to handle objects that have already been saved and must be saved again, taking into consideration the scope of the related change. Here, you must decide whether the objects should be transported as part of routine maintenance (i.e., normal) or imported as an emergency (i.e., urgent). There are three different ways in which change types are classified in this regard:

  ▷ **Urgent only***:* The two transport requests that have the same object belong to two different urgent changes.

- **Partial overlapping**: One of the two transport requests is associated with an urgent change.

- **Overlapping**: The system disregards the change document each transport request belongs to.

- **Object type**
  This setting provides the ability to handle objects that have been saved already and must be saved again that depend on its object type. The object type is whether the object is client-specific or cross-client.

  - **Cross-client**: Only repository objects (ABAP Workbench/development objects) are considered.

  - **Client-specific**: Both repository objects and Customizing objects are considered.

If any three combinations of the characteristics listed under the categories described in the preceding list are met, an error is triggered. Anything else can be considered a warning. Here are a few examples of scenarios that would deliver an error to the developer:

- Cross-Project, Urgent Only, Cross-Client

- Project-Specific, Partial Overlapping, Client-Specific

- Different Project, Overlapping, Cross-Client

Errors versus Warnings

If a hard error should not be an option, a warning message is issued, and the developer uses his discretion to continue with the implementation. Alternatively, the developer may choose to coordinate with the original developer to determine the best time to go forward with the changes.

If a warning is preferred, the SAP Solution Manager administrator will select the WARNING ONLY checkbox when setting up CSOL. This allows the developer to ignore the CSOL settings for how errors are triggered. Instead, only a warning message is displayed, and the developer can proceed to save his work. While the WARNING ONLY feature provides flexibility, you must take caution in knowing that downgrade risks can be associated with not properly coordinating among the other developers. The risk is that new transport requests can take over preceding transport requests sharing the same objects. Therefore, changes intended to be promoted to the target systems will be overridden if proper care isn't taken in this process.

The objective of these categories—and the control of how locks influence the development process—is to maintain consistent and reliable transport objects across your system landscape and throughout parallel projects (whether they be implementation or maintenance).

13.2.2 Common Use Cases

CSOL can be activated as part of your ChaRM solution to support both implementation and maintenance efforts that undergo fast-paced, dispersed, and changing development environments. The goal is to prevent conflicts among transport requests earlier rather than later so that developers can process changes smoothly without interruption or manual intervention to provide coordination activities.

In the following sections, we'll identify the three most common use-case scenarios in which CSOL can detect, avoid, and manage conflicts at an early stage.

Parallel Projects

CSOL provides benefits for customers who are managing multiple (two or more) implementation projects simultaneously, in which all implementation projects share the same system landscape. If a developer in one implementation landscape changes an object that was previously maintained by another developer, the changes made by the first developer are either compromised or lost. If CSOL was activated on the development system of the shared landscape, the developer who accessed the objects secondly would receive an error or warning depending on the category of the lock.

Figure 13.14 provides an example identifying parallel implementation projects for both Finance and Travel Management that share the same logical component (i.e., system landscape). If the objects cross between projects, locks can be maintained in the central SAP Solution Manager system. The logical component of each of these two implementation projects must share the same target production system for the CSOL to work accordingly. The activation of CSOL to support parallel projects is also valid for maintenance projects.

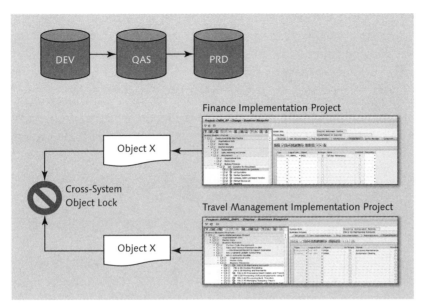

Figure 13.14 Cross-System Object Lock: Parallel Projects

This scenario is also important for organizations that are rolling out a template project to one or many implementation projects in an effort to expand their SAP footprint across geographies or enforce standardization of business processes across the enterprise. In this case, a template project is created in SAP Solution Manager to identify the global processes, documents, attributes, and so on. Subsequently, implementation projects are created for each of the local rollout sites (projects). If the organization is using a common development system for the maintenance of the common scenarios, as well as the local requirements, CSOL fits into the preceding scenario.

Parallel Urgent Changes (Same Project)

The CSOL functionality is also relevant for implementation or maintenance scenarios in which the urgent change document is being used to process emergencies, or frequent one-off transports, into the production system that belong to the same project or maintenance cycle.

Each urgent change document may contain one or more transport requests, which in turn are made of one (or many) objects. If a second developer tries to change objects in an urgent change document that are already maintained in a preceding urgent change document, CSOL will be triggered. The developer making the changes associated with the secondary urgent change document will be notified that he is attempting to change objects that are locked via a preceding urgent change document. These notifications occur, as previously described, in the form of warnings or errors depending on the category of the lock.

Figure 13.15 shows this scenario as it relates to the implementation project activated by ChaRM, the maintenance project, the urgent change documents, and associated system landscape.

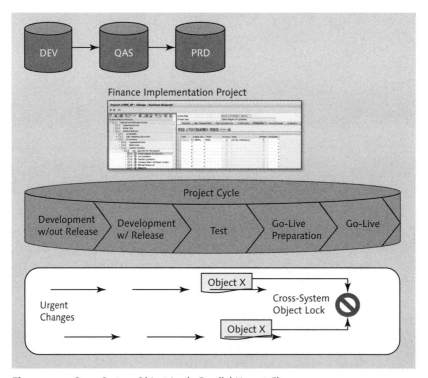

Figure 13.15 Cross-System Object Lock: Parallel Urgent Changes

Different Development Systems

CSOL provides support to manage conflicts when system landscapes require a dual development environment. These scenarios, commonly referred to as N, N+1, support the maintenance of a productive solution while also implementing a new solution that eventually will evolve into the production environment.

Figure 13.16 provides a representation of how this scenario is modeled from a high-level, conceptual standpoint. In this example, the development system from the maintenance landscape and the development system of the implementation landscape must be kept in sync. Avoiding conflicts is critical in this scenario because each development system targets the same production system.

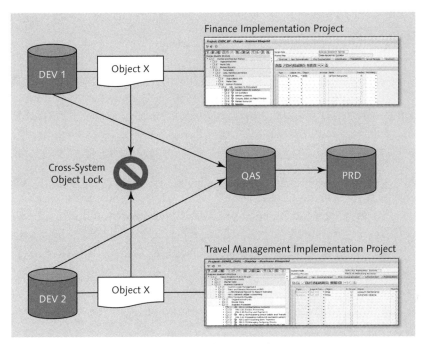

Figure 13.16 Cross-System Object Lock: Different Development Systems

The different development systems scenario would be applicable, for example, when an organization must roll out the standard scenarios to various local implementation sites that have been recently acquired. The acquiring organization already has an SAP maintenance landscape, and the acquired companies run their own SAP landscape. In this case, the organization chooses to keep the development systems isolated in an effort to protect the maintenance landscape. However, because consolidation will occur at some point, these development systems target the same production system. In this case, CSOL will provide support to avoid and manage conflicts should similar objects be maintained across the development systems among the developers.

13.2.3 Cross-System Object Lock in Use

Now, we'll show you what to expect if a developer tries to modify an object that has already been saved by a previous developer with CSOL active. We'll also show you what these locks will look like, and how to access them, as they are created in the central SAP Solution Manager system.

Object Modification

In this example, Developer A has been performing maintenance work on the R3TR program in the SAP ERP development system. He has modified the object TABU as part of a request for change that resulted in an urgent change document during maintenance for SAP ERP production support. As soon as these objects are saved in the transport request of the corresponding urgent change document, a lock entry is created in the central SAP Solution Manager system.

Figure 13.17 shows a table in which testing is conducted for various examples throughout this book. The highlighted entry is the original object maintained by Developer A. A secondary developer (e.g., Developer B) may modify another table entry or create a new table entry, just as long as locks aren't held by associated objects within the SAP Solution Manager system. The point is that CSOL goes to the object level.

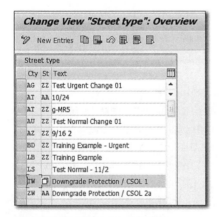

Figure 13.17 Object Level Locking

Shortly afterwards, Developer B accesses the program with the same objects to perform his work as part of a different urgent change. It just so happens that technical specification for that change also calls for TABU modification.

Developer B proceeds with the work, unaware of the fact that Developer A has made changes to the TABU objects that must go to production to ensure business continuity. When Developer B attempts to save his work and collect the same objects in a different transport request, CSOL is put in motion.

As shown in Figure 13.18, Developer B is presented with the CROSS-SYSTEM OBJECT LOCK information box indicating that these objects have been locked by Developer A.

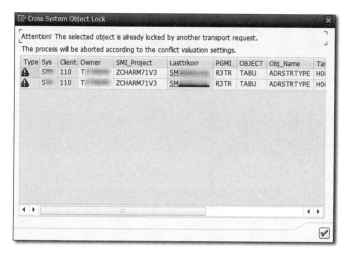

Figure 13.18 Cross-System Object Lock Error/Warning Screen

Developer B must now coordinate with Developer A. First, Developer B would identify who Developer A was based on the OWNER represented in the CROSS-SYS-TEM OBJECT LOCK information screen (Figure 13.18). Developer B would then discuss with Developer A the appropriate course of action, discuss the requirements for changing these objects, and determine how to proceed so that the production system and business community aren't compromised.

If the CROSS-SYSTEM OBJECT LOCK information screen displays only warnings, Developer B can proceed by simply clicking the CONTINUE button at the bottom of the screen. However, if an error is reached, Developer B can't skip past until the lock is removed. We'll explain how to view and release the locks in the following subsection.

Object Lock Monitoring

As described previously, after objects are collected in a transport request, the locks on those objects are held in the SAP Solution Manager system. An SAP Solution Manager administer, or equivalent, can execute Transaction /N/TMWFLOW/LOCKMON to have an overview of all current lock entries held across the development systems in which CSOL is activated.

As shown in Figure 13.19, after this transaction is executed, the OBJECT LOCK MONITOR screen appears. From this screen, you can enter various selection criteria to narrow down the search for the locks held across the development objects. Alternatively, you can leave the search fields blank to view all lock entries.

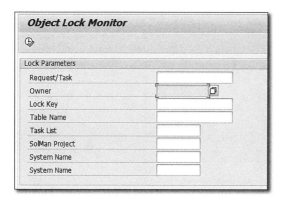

Figure 13.19 Object Lock Monitor: SAP Solution Manager

In the results area, the object locks are divided across two tabs (Figure 13.20): REPOSITORY LOCKS (ABAP development objects) and CUSTOMIZING LOCKS (configuration objects). In this view, the administrator, after being advised by the developers, can select the locks and delete them. After the locks are deleted, follow-on developers are now free to configure objects that would have had hard errors. Conflicts that prompt warnings will also not appear when the respective objects are removed.

In the next section, we'll continue to discuss the benefits that the ChaRM scenario brings to the table by means of object handling and management. Now that you have an understanding of how the CSOL capability provides conflict prevention across development systems that target the same production system, we'll discuss how objects that are critical to the business can be protected from modification attempts by the development team.

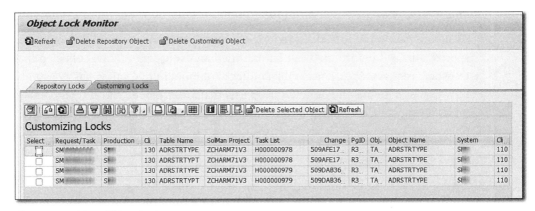

Figure 13.20 View Object Locks

13.3   Critical Object Check

ChaRM, as we've discussed in previous chapters, provides the capability to deliver approval management procedures prior to releasing a change to the developer. The approval management procedure(s) are defined according to the scope of the change as well as according to the change and release management procedures, which provide governance among the support organization. Approval management can be as streamlined and straightforward as the out-of-the-box approval procedure delivered by SAP. On the other hand, approval management can accommodate robust and complex scenarios that often serve the requirements of large organizations.

While the approval management procedures can accommodate nearly any requirements from a Change Advisory Board (CAB) perspective, they are at the process (scope) level only. Often, approval procedures are required at a much lower level. In fact, they are needed at the workbench or Customizing object level. For these detailed requirements, the Critical Object Check functionality is available. In this section, we'll provide an overview of this functionality and how it may relate to your requirements for object level approval. We'll also show, step by step, the expected results that occur when a developer attempts to collect objects in a transport request that are critical to the business and support organization.

13.3.1 Overview

As mentioned in the introduction, critical objects are those objects that require a special approval before they can be modified and subsequently be collected in a transport request. The Critical Object Check component of ChaRM has the ability to collect and define any number of objects that are deemed critical by the enterprise, business unit, IT organization, and so on. If a developer tries to modify an object that is specified as "critical" in the central SAP Solution Manager system, the developer will receive a warning, and a separate approval process must be met before the developer can move forward. The approval must occur before the critical objects can be imported into the target system(s).

Predefined, standard, or delivered critical objects do not exist. Because requirements will vary regarding what is critical from organization to organization, it's up to each customer to identify and define which objects are critical to his business. The process to enter critical objects in the SAP Solution Manager requires effort across the development, change and release management, and project management teams. Together, they must determine which objects should be flagged as critical, and the SAP Solution Manager administrator will maintain them in the SAP Solution Manager system.

The Critical Object Check is valid for Customizing or workbench objects. ChaRM is a prerequisite. If transport requests are created outside of ChaRM (i.e., directly in the development environment), the Critical Object Check isn't valid.

13.3.2 Critical Object Check in Use

In this section, we'll describe a scenario that can be expected if a developer attempts to modify an object that has been flagged as critical in the SAP Solution Manager system.

Developer: Error at Transport Release

At the point in which the developer tries to export the change to the follow-on system, he will receive a warning and an error within the change document as shown in Figure 13.21.

The error will prompt the developer that the transport request contains critical objects and therefore can't be released. In our example, the critical objects are contained within a transport request for an urgent change document. The error provides a hard stop, and the import into the quality assurance system is prevented. The warning notifies the developer that an authorization (approval procedure) must occur before the release can be initiated.

Figure 13.21 Error and Warning at Critical Object Check

If this error is reached, it's up to an approver to process the critical object. The critical object is processed in the TRANSPORT MANAGEMENT assignment block by selecting MORE • PROCESS CRITICAL OBJECT as shown in Figure 13.22.

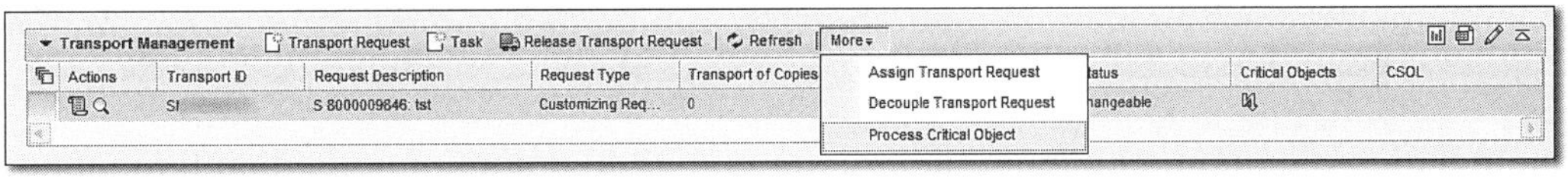

Figure 13.22 Identify Critical Object

As you can see, a flag in the CRITICAL OBJECT column in this particular assignment block identifies a conflict scenario as valid. Per the standard SAP Solution Manager authorization concept, the change approver of the respective request for change document has the authority to process the critical object. We'll highlight both the configuration aspects and authorization details of the Critical Object Check in Chapter 15, when we discuss the functional configuration of ChaRM.

Change Approver: Process Critical Object

Figure 13.22 showed the options available when and if a critical object is identified by ChaRM. It's important to know that only team members who have the appropriate authorizations (change approvers according to standard design) can select the option to process the critical object.

After this option is selected, the PROCESS CRITICAL OBJECTS – WEBPAGE DIALOG screen is displayed (Figure 13.23). Depending on the number of critical objects detected by the transport request at hand, they will be displayed in this window. In our example, one critical object, TABU, has been identified that requires approval.

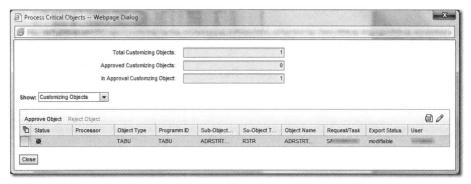

Figure 13.23 View and Process Critical Objects

The critical objects are distinguished by type (i.e., Customizing objects versus workbench objects) in the SHOW field. By default, the workbench objects are displayed at the start. The summary of all critical objects contained in the transport request to be released is contained at the top. Additionally, the object details are collected as well.

To process (approve) the critical objects, follow these steps:

1. Select the critical object(s).

2. Click the APPROVE OBJECT button.

   As a result, the STATUS column will change to a green/successful icon, and the transport requests can now be released.

3. Select the CLOSE button (Figure 13.24) to return to the urgent change document to continue processing the change document.

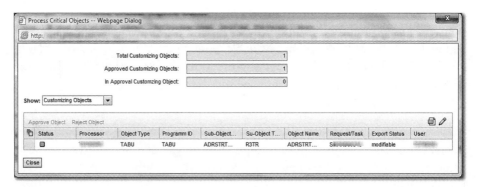

Figure 13.24 Approved Critical Object

In the previous two sections, we discussed how ChaRM provides the ability to centrally manage and control both Customizing and workbench objects. SAP Solution Manager provides object functionality whether coordination of objects must occur for development that eventually reaches the same production system or whether special approval procedures must be in place for critical objects. In the next section, we'll switch gears and highlight the importance of how ChaRM supports the approval, workflow, and ITIL-compliant procedures for objects that extend beyond Customizing and ABAP Workbench-based systems.

13.4　Managing Changes for Non-ABAP Systems

As you're aware by now, Change Control Management in SAP Solution Manager provides organizations with support of changes of any scope and even beyond SAP. With the release of 7.1, SAP is now positioning Change Control Management within SAP Solution Manager as the single source to provide SAP ITSM that scales across any organization.

We've mentioned this vision, and discussed the multitudes of capabilities related to this vision provided by SAP Solution Manager, in every chapter thus far. In fact, we'll continue sharing this message as we move forward into the remaining ChaRM chapters. It's important to know also that Change Control Management provides the ability to manage changes to your non-ABAP systems.

In this section, we'll provide a brief overview of the Enhanced Change and Transport System (CTS+), which can be implemented and integrated into your ChaRM scenario to support your Java-based systems (e.g., SAP Enterprise Portal, SAP NetWeaver Process Integration [SAP NetWeaver PI], SAP Network Development Infrastructure [NWDI], etc.).

13.4.1　Overview

CTS+ has been a fundamental component in SAP systems that has provided the ability for log files associated with Java changes to be attached to transport requests and use the same logistical features used with ABAP transports.

In traditional ABAP TMS, technical objects are attached to transport requests that can then be further modified, exported to a QAS for testing, and then finally promoted to production for use by the business. These technical objects include repository objects, programs, functional objects, user exits, and tables, among many others. Depending on whether they are workbench or Customizing objects, they are placed in their appropriate transport request type. This goes for ABAP-based systems (e.g., SAP ERP, SAP CRM, SAP SRM, etc.)

For non-ABAP systems (i.e., Java systems), there are other technical objects that aren't considered repository objects, like the technical objects in an ABAP system. They include files such as *.epa*, *.doc*, *.jee*, and more. Rather than using transport requests, the Java files are creating archives that are saved to a file which is later deployed to the follow-on system.

With CTS+, you can define these objects to be transported according to the standard SAP ERP transport layer. These archive files are attached to a transport request and use the same logistical capabilities used by the ABAP transport layer. The process to transport and monitor changes, no matter what time, becomes standardized and consistent.

13.4.2 CTS+ Integration into Change Request Management

Implementing CTS+ for your Java systems is an activity conducted by your technical architecture (Basis) teams. It requires skilled expertise in the area of SAP NetWeaver, TMS, and related technical areas. Standing a CTS+ scenario up is a much more complex effort when compared to linking it to ChaRM.

Integrating these two tools will allow non-ABAP systems to use the workflow, approval, and ITIL-aligned process flows delivered with ChaRM. When these two tools are coupled, changes affecting your Java landscape can be processed in the similar end-to-end manner as your ABAP ChaRM transports.

It's important to note that CTS+ isn't a prerequisite to ChaRM. Similarly, ChaRM isn't a prerequisite to leverage the functionality delivered with CTS+. Typically, organizations will implement CTS+ and become familiar with its technology and process prior to integrating it with the ChaRM scenario.

13.5 Summary

In this chapter, you learned about additional features that both complement and enhance the overall ChaRM scenario in SAP Solution Manager. In regards to

Change Control Management, the Retrofit and CTS+ capabilities are available for use without the need to adopt the full end-to-end, ITIL-aligned, process-based workflow that makes up ChaRM. For those organizations that may not be prepared to undergo a shift in process, the Retrofit and CTS+ capabilities may still be used independent of the standard workflows.

Cross-system object lock and the Critical Object Check functionalities will provide the coordination and management efforts needed for organizations that execute implementation projects while simultaneously supporting maintenance efforts. Further, these functionalities support cross-project efforts as well as managing object coordination across urgent changes in the same maintenance project.

In the next chapter, we'll begin with the configuration and setup of ChaRM. Chapter 14 will begin with the fundamental, base configurations by providing an overview of what is needed in regards to setting up TMS and the basic setup of ChaRM.

The Transport Management System is extended so that Change Request Management can control transports and approvals in the managed system landscape. For this to occur, specific settings must be maintained in each domain controller of the system landscape.

14   Enabling the Transport Management System for Change Request Management

In this chapter, we discuss the Transport Management System (TMS) setup activities that must be taken into account when configuring Change Request Management for your managed system landscapes.

The very first steps involve setting up TMS on each domain controller for which transport requests will be controlled by ChaRM.

For the purposes of how our book is structured, we're assuming that the relevant basic configuration, system preparation, and managed system settings within SOLMAN_SETUP have already been completed.

The objective of this chapter is to provide a checklist of TMS activities that are necessary to extend the approval of import of transports so that SAP Solution Manager is the controller. We'll walk through each of these steps and highlight the areas that may be different from setting up TMS independent of ChaRM.

14.1   What You Should Know Before Setting up TMS for ChaRM

In this section, we'll begin by laying out the framework needed to begin setting up TMS for your ChaRM scenario.

14.1.1 Getting Started

It's important to understand who is responsible in configuring TMS settings within your environment. Based on the lessons we've learned and experience working in array of customer environments, we'll provide some lessons learned on where the role of setting up TMS fits in an IT organization. Also, as of the release of SAP Solution Manager 7.1, there are some important strategic changes in the RFC and TMS infrastructure that you should be made aware of. In the following sections, we'll highlight some key "what you need to know" points before getting started with the setup activities.

Who Should Set Up TMS

It's strongly recommended that the activities listed in this chapter are executed by a resource that has a background in SAP Basis and has previously set up TMS in other environments. It's uncommon for a member of the Project Management Office (PMO) or SAP Solution Manager resource without significant Basis knowledge to execute these tasks on his own.

However, the content is relevant for SAP Solution Manager administrators, regardless of their technical background. The activities within this chapter are intended to not only provide the key differences in enabling TMS to support a ChaRM environment, but also to provide those responsible for the ChaRM implementation with a checklist to follow regarding TMS activities. Further, these steps will help those planning for a ChaRM implementation to determine how much effort is required from the Basis team initially.

Navigating TMS Activities from SAP Solution Manager

SAP Solution Manager provides you with the ability to configure TMS directly within the guided procedures found in SOLMAN_SETUP. While the TMS documentation and activities are still available within the SAP Solution Manager IMG, it's recommended that you leverage the capabilities within SOLMAN_SETUP to perform these settings. We recommend that SOLMAN_SETUP is used for the following reasons:

▶ Additional help documentation is provided regarding TMS setup as of release 7.1.

▶ Status tracking is available.

- Updates are flagged when required.
- Task level documentation is provided.
- Log data for the activities is available.

Configuring TMS in SOLMAN_SETUP involves manual activities, which must be performed on the domain controller, client 000, of your managed system landscape (i.e., implementation or maintenance) and not in your SAP Solution Manager system. If there are activities that should be performed in SAP Solution Manager, the standard SAP Solution Manager documentation will state so.

The manual activities for setting up TMS for your ChaRM scenario are found within IT Service Management • Change Request Management • 5 Configure Landscape • 5.1 Configure Transport Management System. Figure 14.1 shows the activities available for setting up TMS for your ABAP systems.

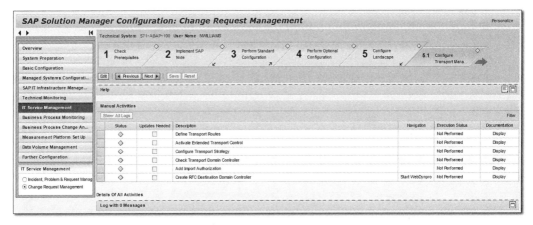

Figure 14.1 SOLMAN_SETUP: TMS Manual Activities

14.1.2 Import Strategy and Changes as of Release 7.1

A new import strategy is available as of release 7.1 of SAP Solution Manager regarding how transports associated with ChaRM projects are imported into target systems. The remote communication has been changed from using a combination of RFC destinations managed in Transaction SMSY and remote infrastructure of TMS to strictly a sole usage of the Transaction SMSY RFC destinations. Changing the remote communication reduces the confusion regarding which infrastructure is used in ChaRM TMS activities.

Sole Usage of RFC Connections for Remote Communication

To transition to using only the Transaction SMSY RFC destination infrastructure, remote enabled APIs must be available in the landscape that ChaRM will control. Applying SAP Note 1384598 — Harmonizing RFC Communication Infrastructure in ChaRM/QGM — will provide the availability of these APIs, and the remote communication going forward will use only the SMSY RFC destinations.

Alternatively, if your SAP_BASIS support package level is equal or greater than the following identified in Table 14.1 on the managed system, the new infrastructure will be in place.

SAP_BASIS Release	SP Level
7.20	SP04
7.11	SP06
7.10	SP11
7.02	SP05
7.01	SP08
7.00	SP23
6.20	SP69
4.6C	SP60

Table 14.1 SAP_BASIS Levels and Releases for Transaction SMSY RFC Destination Infrastructure

If the settings are applicable for your environment, you fall within the scenario described in the SAP Note, Harmonization of RFC Infrastructure.

> **Note**
>
> If SAP Note 1384598 isn't applied in your managed system nor are the SAP_BASIS levels equal or greater to the values in Table 14.1, the legacy remote infrastructure will be used. In this case, there are added TMS activities within the SAP Solution Manager IMG that aren't covered in this chapter. Review the following activities via SAP SOLUTION MANAGER • CAPABILITIES • CHANGE MANAGEMENT • BASIC CONFIGURATION • TRANSPORT MANAGEMENT SYSTEM:
>
> ▶ Activate TMS Trusted Services
> ▶ Activate domain links

Users in Client 000

Another change regarding the SAP Solution Manager 7.1 ChaRM import strategy is that there are no named dialog users needed in client 000. Because the remote communication infrastructure now only uses Transaction SMSY RFC destinations, no dialog users are required in client 000 of the target systems involved with import activities.

These users were typically the IT operators or administrators performing the imports into the follow-on system. Requesting these users to have dialog access into client 000 of the target systems raised concerns, caused confusion, and often violated standard securtity procedures for most organizations. Eliminating the need for dialog users in client 000 of the managed landscape is a major benefit over the prior import strategy and remote communciation infrastructure.

Domain Links

Links from the SAP Solution Manager domain controller to the managed system's domain controller are also *not required* with the latest import strategy in release 7.1. This too is another benefit from the sole usage of Transaction SMSY RFC destinations to enable the harmonization of the ChaRM RFC communication.

Because the remote infrastructure of TMS isn't part of the remote communication, there is no need to create domain links from the SAP Solution Manager system and the managed development system.

Now that you have an understanding of how to access the guided procedures for setting up TMS for your ChaRM solution, as well as the new import strategies of SAP Solution Manager 7.1, we'll begin describing the steps necessary for the actual setup.

14.2 Enabling the Transport Management System for ChaRM

In this section, we'll walk through each of the activities involved with enabling TMS to support a ChaRM implementation or maintenance landscape. Keep in mind that these sections are intended to provide those with less technical knowledge with an overview of these activities. The objective is to provide non-Basis/pure technical resources knowledge around the order and purpose of these steps so that they can be more involved in defining a project plan and guiding a ChaRM implementation.

14.2.1 Define Transport Routes

The first step is for the Basis team to define the transport routes between the development, quality, and production systems. The transport routes are defined within the managed system, as are the remainder of the activities within this section.

For these purposes, we'll assume that knowledge regarding the definition of transport routes is already available within your organization. Therefore, we won't provide a step-by-step description for how to configure TMS. However, if you're new to TMS and want to practice in a sandbox environment (not connected to an implementation or maintenance domain), there are step-by-step guides available on the SAP Help Portal. Lastly, we'll provide examples of transport routes that have been defined within an SAP Solution Manager system and for a managed SAP ERP system.

Key Points to Keep in Mind

When defining the transport routes across your managed systems regarding ChaRM, there are a few key points to acknowledge. You may also refer to these notes in the documentation within the guided procedures of the related task:

▶ Transports are supported in the standard transport layer of each client. When you configure transport routes, note that only consolidation routes that are assigned to the standard transport layer of the relevant exporting client are taken into consideration.

▶ For each exporting client, exactly one target client and one target group are permitted.

▶ We recommend that you assign exactly one development system to a production system and that these two systems are connected by exactly one unique transport track. Development systems and production systems connected by more than one transport track aren't supported by ChaRM.

14.2.2 Activate Extended Transport Control

In this step of the TMS setup process, you activate extended transport control within TMS. Activating extended transport control within the domain controller will allow for the SAP Solution Manager system to take the role as controller.

With the following settings, ChaRM controls the creation and movement of transports throughout the system landscape:

1. Execute Transaction STMS (client 000 in your development system).

2. Select OVERVIEW • SYSTEMS as shown in Figure 14.2.

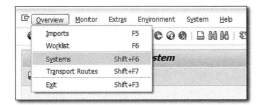

Figure 14.2 Select Overview • Systems

3. In the SYSTEM OVERVIEW screen, double-click a system (Figure 14.3).

Figure 14.3 Select System

4. Make sure you're in change mode.

5. Add the value "1" to the CTC parameter (Figure 14.4).

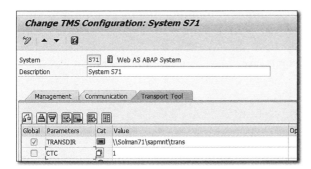

Figure 14.4 Maintain Parameter CTC

6. Click SAVE.

Repeat these steps for each system in the SYSTEM OVERVIEW screen.

14.2.3 Configure Transport Strategy

In this step, we perform two activities that are essential prior to deploying a ChaRM scenario:

▶ Deactivate the quality assurance approval procedure

▶ Activate the single transports strategy

Because ChaRM has its own approval procedure (both in the request for change document and actions required before changes can be promoted to production), the existing quality assurance approval procedure isn't needed in TMS. Also, activating the single transports strategy will ensure that the IMPORT ALL option can't be executed in the Change and Transport System (CTS). Because ChaRM enforces the import of transport requests by project only, that should be the leading strategy for how transports are imported.

Now, we will walk you through the steps in order to deactivate the quality assurance approval procedure and activate the single transport strategy option.

1. Execute Transaction STMS (client 000 in your development system).

2. Choose OVERVIEW • TRANSPORT ROUTES (Figure 14.5).

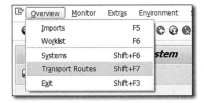

Figure 14.5 Choose Overview • Transport Routes

3. Make sure you're in edit mode.

4. Double-click each system (Figure 14.6).

> **Note**
>
> Figure 14.7 displays a transport route configuration in which three clients within a single SAP Solution Manager system were simulating the role of a development, quality assurance, and production system. In your actual transport route configuration, you'll see multiple systems with respective transport routes.

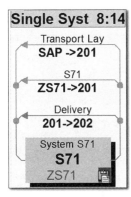

Figure 14.6 Double-Click System (e.g., S71)

5. In the SYSTEM ATTRIBUTES tab, select the option for SINGLE TRANSPORTS (Figure 14.7).

Figure 14.7 Select Single Transports in Transport Strategy

6. In the same tab, de-select the option DELIVERY AFTER CONFIRMATION (Figure 14.8).

Figure 14.8 Deselect Delivery After Confirmation in Quality Assurance

7. Press ⌈Enter⌋.

8. Save and distribute the configuration.

14.2.4 Check Transport Domain Controller

In this step, we'll perform a check on the domain controller to ensure that there are no inconsistencies in the Transaction STMS configuration. In this check, we'll make sure that the transport domain has been configured correctly.

1. Log on on to each of the domain controller's for your ChaRM scenario.

2. Execute Transaction STMS (client 000 in the development system).

The TRANSPORT MANAGEMENT SYSTEM main page should appear with only the information identified in Figure 14.9.

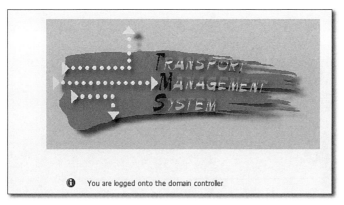

Figure 14.9 Consistent Transport Route Configuration

TMS should not have the errors that are indicated in Figure 14.10. If this is the case, analyze the configuration, and ensure that the setup is consistent.

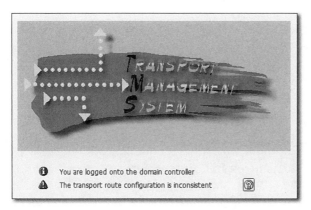

Figure 14.10 Inconsistent Transport Route Configuration

14.2.5   Add Import Authorizations

In this section, we'll add the import authorizations necessary for the users who perform the import of transport requests into the target systems. The manner in which the remote infrastructure is enabled for your domain controller will determine the strategy for how import authorizations are maintained.

Harmonization of RFC Infrastructure Applicable

If you have implemented SAP Note 1384598 in your managed systems, or the SAP_BASIS levels are equal or greater to the values we stated in Section 14.1.2, the RFC infrastructure is harmonized. Therefore, import commands are sent to the logical target client. The operator and administrator users must have the appropriate authorization in all target systems for which imports occur. These users must have the following authorizations in the target clients, respectively (i.e., quality assurance systems and production systems):

▶ SAP_CM_MANAGED_OPERATOR

▶ SAP_CM_MANAGED_ADMIN

Finally, the user IDs within these target systems must match the user IDs within the SAP Solution Manager controller system.

Harmonization of RFC Infrastructure Non-Applicable

If the scenario harmonization of RFC infrastructure isn't applicable regarding your remote infrastructure state, alternative steps must be taken to ensure that the relevant users have the correct authorizations to import transport requests into the target system. In this case, the TMS remote infrastructure is based on RFC connections that are directed solely to client 000 of the target import system. For this reason, the operator and administrator users need to have the import authorizations (listed in the previous section) on client 000 of all target systems.

14.2.6   Create RFC Destination Domain Controller

In this step, you create the READ RFC destination from the SAP Solution Manager system to client 000 of the domain controller (development system). ChaRM must read information, such as transport routes, about the system landscape from each domain controller.

RFC destinations are created and maintained in the system Landscape Management Database (LMDB) in Transaction LMDB.

In the RFC Maintenance area of LMDB, you generate the READ destination to the domain controller as shown in Figure 14.11.

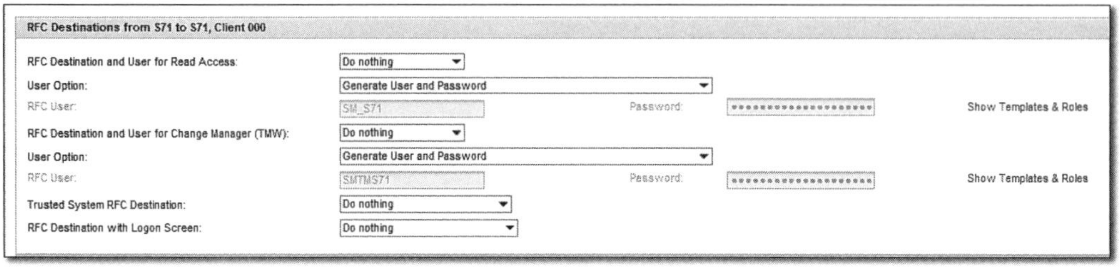

Figure 14.11 Generate READ RFC Destination

14.3 Summary

This chapter provided an overview of the TMS activities that are required within your managed systems domain controller(s) for SAP Solution Manager to control transport approval and import. These steps were the foundational steps (post-SOLMAN_SETUP) to begin configuring ChaRM for your system landscape.

In the next chapter, we'll describe the step-by-step configuration necessary to configure ChaRM.

The standard Change Request Management workflow can be enhanced based on customer-defined transaction types. This chapter builds upon the preparation activities and TMS activities to provide the steps to enable Change Request Management and adapt it for your customer scenario.

15 Functional Configuration for Change Request Management

In this chapter, we describe how to enable the most important and foundational settings for delivering Change Request Management (ChaRM) processes in SAP Solution Manager, step by step. This chapter will explain the core components necessary to realize the processes associated with the request for change and change documents. The components go beyond the basic requirements to make the vanilla processes "work" end to end. We'll describe the additional functionalities that enhance ChaRM and showcase its best-of-breed messaging abilities. Integrating cross-ITSM scenarios, aligning customer namespace entries to standard Change Request Management processes, enhancing the workflow to meet your requirements, and taking advantage of the best-of-breed capabilities based on use case examples from prior engagements are all important take-aways from this chapter.

In addition to explaining the configuration concepts, you'll also find the business reason and expected result(s) for each functionality.

There are two avenues in which configuration can commence:

▶ The guided procedure located in the IT SERVICE MANAGEMENT section of Transaction SOLMAN_SETUP

▶ Directly in the Implementation Guide (IMG) for SAP Solution Manager

While the more progressive, and SAP-recommended method, of enabling end-user settings in ChaRM is via the guided procedures located in Transaction SOLMAN_SETUP, the intent of this chapter is to dive deep into the configuration aspects. For that reason, we'll introduce Transaction SOLMAN_SETUP as the portal for initiating configuration. However, when describing the step-by-step instructions to configure these functions, we'll speak from an IMG point of view. The objective of this is to provide you the most detailed, foundational, and comprehensive description of how these particular SAP IT Service Management (SAP ITSM) processes are realized from SAP Solution Manager.

Whether you opt to leverage the latest functionalities delivered in the guided procedures of Transaction SOLMAN_SETUP or go with the traditional configuration methods of following the IMG activities, the content in this chapter is applicable.

15.1 Chapter Overview

This chapter is intended to be a cut-to-the-chase and show-me-how-it's-done chapter. There are numerous other chapters that go into great detail about methodologies, disciplines, best practices, and informational details. This chapter, on the other hand, will get right into the details of how to enable the functional components in ChaRM.

15.1.1 How This Chapter Is Structured

While we've tried our best to be short on descriptions, we know it's important to provide structure around what and why you're configuring. For that reason, each configuration activity will include the following subsections, as described in the following subsections.

Operational Use

The operational use for each configuration activity will be more or less in the same context for each configuration. Sometimes, depending on the nature of the configuration, the operational use will vary slightly from activity to activity.

The "Operational Use" section will briefly describe what the function is from a straightforward configuration point of view. For example, it may read as the IMG documentation does. Also, this section will provide a description of the use case or configuration example we'll use to incorporate sample customer requirements.

The configuration examples, while taken from actual customer scenarios, should be considered merely examples. You'll need to adapt the concepts and best-practices for configuration described in this chapter to the requirements specific to your IT organization.

Configuration Activities

This section will be light on descriptions and concepts yet heavy on screenshots and configuration steps. The "Configuration Activities" section of each activity describes—from an end-to-end perspective—how to enable the sample customer requirement/example from the "Operational Use" section in the SAP Solution Manager system.

Expected Result(s)

The "Expected Results" section will be a quick and to-the-point reference of what end result should be expected if you've completed the configuration activities successfully. Most often, the expected results will be identified with a screenshot. Sometimes, a short description will provide you with the information needed to validate your configuration settings.

15.1.2 Assumptions

There are a few basic assumptions that we'll cover before you begin configuring ChaRM. While this chapter is straight to the point in regards to configuration, there are other aspects of the book that include setup tasks. Furthermore, there are concepts referenced in previous chapters that we'll refer to. Lastly, we'll build on some of the existing configuration and master data settings previously performed. To that end, it will be helpful to know we aren't exactly starting from scratch with these configuration activities.

The following subsections identify some key assumptions that should be taken into consideration before starting your configuration.

SOLMAN_SETUP

It's important that the guided procedures in SOLMAN_SETUP have been completed prior to the commencement of the functional configuration of ChaRM. You must have completed the following sections of SOLMAN_SETUP:

- ▶ SYSTEM PREPARATION

- ▶ BASIC CONFIGURATION

- ▶ MANAGED SYSTEM CONFIGURATION

- ▶ IT SERVICE MANAGEMENT (CHARM)

  Most of the activities will be described in detail in this chapter, while some of the activities in the ChaRM guided procedure can be automatically enabled from SOLMAN_SETUP.

Important!

The guided procedure for SAP ITSM (ChaRM) also provides the ability to launch, track, and display documentation associated with the functional configuration areas described in this document. While we encourage you to follow the guided procedure for as many scenarios as possible in SAP Solution Manager, this chapter will explain configuration activities initiated directly from the IMG.

You may cross-reference the configuration activities here with those in SOLMAN_SETUP so you can have a central area to track the processing status of each item.

We recommend that you perform any prerequisite checks or automatic configuration available in SOLMAN_SETUP for ChaRM. Examples include implementation of master notes for ChaRM, activation of services, background job generation, and prerequisite checks.

Transaction Copy

The Transaction Copy tool is used to automatically copy standard transaction types for ChaRM (i.e., requests for change, urgent and normal changes, etc.). Additionally, this tool copies all of the profiles associated with the transaction type, applies a customer namespace based on your specifications, and assigns them to the copied transaction type.

We highly recommend that you use the Transaction Copy tool on the ChaRM transactions prior to performing the configuration activities. The Transaction Copy tool is a step in the guided procedure in SOLMAN_SETUP. Alternatively, you can launch Transaction AI_CRM__CPY_PROCTYPE to reach the Transaction Copy tool.

The following profiles must be copied into a customer namespace (the configuration examples for both transaction and profiles will use the Y* namespace) and assigned to the corresponding transaction type:

- Text determination procedure
- Partner determination procedure
- Status profile
- Date profile
- Action profile

For purposes of demonstration and example, we'll primarily be using the SMCR (request for change) and SMHF (urgent change) transaction types for the configuration activities in this section. If you want to introduce these features into another service transaction type (e.g., normal change or general change), you must repeat the steps to enable the functionality on the respective transaction type.

Master Data

We highly recommend that you familiarize yourself with these concepts and prepare your SAP Solution Manager system with the master data settings as described in Chapter 3 because they are required for most of the configurations in this chapter.

Security

This chapter assumes that you have the administrator roles in SAP Solution Manager required to perform the various configuration activities described in this chapter. Moreover, it's assumed that the business role assigned to your administrator user allows sufficient authorization to access, maintain, and configure the SAP CRM Web UI screens per the examples in the following sections.

15.1.3 Cross-ITSM Functionalities

Chapter 10 provided a comprehensive how-to guide explaining how to configure the most important and foundational functionalities to support the processes in Application Incident Management (AIM). While Chapter 10 provided use-case examples that were specific to AIM, the majority of the capabilities highlighted in that chapter span both AIM and ChaRM.

In this chapter, we'll discuss the most critical configuration steps that make up ChaRM exclusively. Because the majority of the functions described in Chapter 10 cross over into ChaRM, it isn't necessary to go over them again. The only difference is that ChaRM transaction types and their associated profiles are used, as opposed to AIM transaction types and profiles.

To that end, you have the ability to leverage the following functions (which we've described in Part II) in the ChaRM scenario. (Keep in mind that you must understand the transaction types and assigned profiles. That is the only difference.)

▶ Partner determination procedure

▶ Support team determination

▶ Time recording

▶ Categorization

▶ Text management

▶ Status profile

▶ SLA escalation

▶ Actions and conditions (note that we'll provide an example specific to ChaRM on how to enhance the workflow using a combination of status values, actions, and conditions later in this chapter)

▶ Priorities

We'll now begin discussing the basic configuration activities and settings for ChaRM.

15.2   Basic Configuration

In this section, we'll explain the configuration activities required to enable the basic configuration settings for ChaRM. Basic configuration settings must be applied in each SAP Solution Manager system in the overall landscape because they aren't transportable. In this section, we'll describe the following activities that make up ChaRM basic configuration:

▶ Activating the integration between the SAP Solution Manager controlling client and ChaRM

▶ Activating the required SAP Solution Manager services to support ChaRM

15.2.1 Overview

The settings we'll describe in this section are maintained in the SAP Solution Manager IMG beneath the BASIC CONFIGURATION node as shown in Figure 15.1.

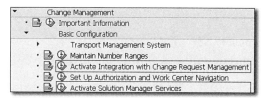

Figure 15.1 Basic Configuration IMG Activities

You'll notice in the IMG activities that we've highlighted the configuration settings we'll discuss later. Refer to Chapter 3 to review the required activities related to number ranges and authorizations.

15.2.2 Integrate Change Request Management with SAP Solution Manager

In order for SAP Solution Manager to have a technical integration with Change Request Management, we must activate the integration between the ChaRM scenario and the SAP Solution Manager client which will control the ChaRM environment.

Operational Use

In this section, we'll activate the integration with ChaRM. This involves three key steps.

First, the SAP Solution Manager controlling client must be activated by ChaRM. The controlling client, also referred to as the ChaRM client after this activation, is the client in which the ChaRM workflow is configured. If you're using three clients as an SAP ERP simulated test-bed, the ChaRM client will be the controller that manages the software logistics across the simulated landscape.

Secondly, we'll specify the RFC destination as part of activating the integration with SAP Solution Manager itself. The RFC destination allows a communication path between the task list and the ChaRM transaction types that are enabled for your scenario.

Finally, we'll maintain table settings to activate the integration with ChaRM.

Configuration Activities

Execute the following configuration activities.

Activate Change Request Management and Set-Up Client

1. Execute the IMG activity ACTIVATE INTEGRATION WITH CHANGE REQUEST MANAGEMENT.

2. In the CHOOSE ACTIVITY window, select the option ACTIVATE CHANGE REQUEST MANAGEMENT AND SET-UP CLIENT (Figure 15.2).

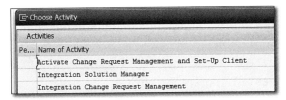

Figure 15.2 Activate Change Request Management and Set-Up Client

3. Specify the client for maintaining ChaRM in the information window that appears (Figure 15.3).

Figure 15.3 Specify Client for Change Request Management

4. Press ⌷Enter⌷.

Activate Integration with SAP Solution Manager

1. Select the INTEGRATION SOLUTION MANAGER option (Figure 15.4).

2. Enter the data in the RFC DESTINATION OF SAP CHANGE MANAGER table as represented in Figure 15.5.

3. Click SAVE.

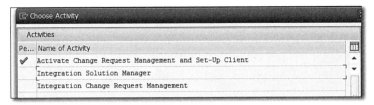

Figure 15.4 Select Integration Solution Manager

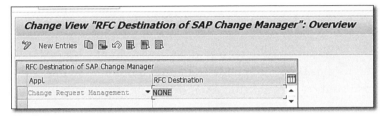

Figure 15.5 Maintain RFC Destination of SAP Change Manager Data

4. Click BACK.

Activate Integration with Change Request Management

Note

You only need to maintain this IMG activity if the Schedule Manager was configured for ChaRM in a client that is different from the request for change.

1. Select the INTEGRATION CHANGE REQUEST MANAGEMENT activity (Figure 15.6).

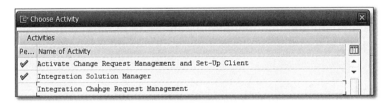

Figure 15.6 Select Integration Change Request Management

2. Update the entry in the CHANGE VIEW "CREATE MESSAGES: CUSTOMIZING": OVERVIEW window according to your requirements (Figure 15.7).

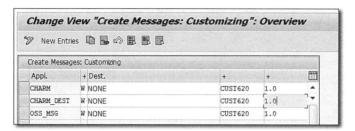

Figure 15.7 Update Table Data

Expected Result(s)

The expected result for this group of configuration activities is a saved configuration with no errors based on the configuration instruction.

15.2.3 Activate SAP Solution Manager Services

Services within the SAP Solution Manager system must be activated in order to use particular web-based applications. SAP Solution Manager provides a report in order to perform these activations automatically.

Operational Use

Activating SAP Solution Manager is critical so that the Web Dynpro applications are enabled in ChaRM. In this configuration activity, we'll execute the SM_CHARM and SM_CRM_UI reports, which activate the required services for Web Dynpro for ChaRM.

Configuration Activities

Follow these steps:

1. Execute the IMG activity ACTIVATE SOLUTION MANAGER SERVICES.
2. Enter the reports "SM_CHARM" and "SM_CRM_UI" in the TECHNICAL NAME fields (Figure 15.8).
3. Click EXECUTE.

Figure 15.8 Execute Reports

Expected Result(s)

The services that fall within the reports executed will display their activation status immediately after the execution. All of the services should show green (successful) as displayed in Figure 15.9.

† Technical Name	Application Component ID	Or	Path
SM_CHARM	SV-SMG	1	/sap/bc/webdynpro/sap/AGS_WORK_CHARM_SCHEDMAN
SM_CHARM	SV-SMG	2	/sap/bc/webdynpro/sap/trp_setup
SM_CRM_UI	SV-SMG	1	/sap/bc/bsp/sap/crm_ui_frame
SM_CRM_UI	SV-SMG	2	/sap/bc/bsp/sap/crm_bsp_frame
SM_CRM_UI	SV-SMG	3	/sap/bc/bsp/sap/gsbirp
SM_CRM_UI	SV-SMG	4	/sap/bc/bsp/sap/thtmlb_scripts
SM_CRM_UI	SV-SMG	5	/sap/bc/bsp/sap/thtmlb_styles
SM_CRM_UI	SV-SMG	6	/sap/bc/bsp/sap/crm_thtmlb_util
SM_CRM_UI	SV-SMG	7	/sap/bc/bsp/sap/bspwd_basics
SM_CRM_UI	SV-SMG	8	/sap/bc/bsp/sap/bsp_wd_base
SM_CRM_UI	SV-SMG	9	/sap/bc/bsp/sap/crmcmp_hdr
SM_CRM_UI	SV-SMG	10	/sap/bc/bsp/sap/crmcmp_hdr_std
SM_CRM_UI	SV-SMG	11	/sap/bc/bsp/sap/uicmp_ltx
SM_CRM_UI	SV-SMG	12	/sap/bc/bsp/sap/bsp_dlc_frcmp
SM_CRM_UI	SV-SMG	13	/sap/bc/bsp/sap/crm_ui_start
SM_CRM_UI	SV-SMG	14	/sap/webcuif/notify
SM_CRM_UI	SV-SMG	15	/sap/webcuif/uif_callback
SM_CRM_UI	SV-SMG	16	/sap/webcuif/uif_export_tab
SM_CRM_UI	SV-SMG	17	/sap/webcuif/uif_feed
SM_CRM_UI	SV-SMG	18	/sap/webcuif/uif_sapgui
SM_CRM_UI	SV-SMG	19	/sap/bc/bsp/sap/ic_base
SM_CRM_UI	SV-SMG	20	/sap/bc/bsp/sap/crm_ui_sysmsg
SM_CRM_UI	SV-SMG	21	/sap/bc/bsp/sap/crm_bsp_fl_help
SM_CRM_UI	SV-SMG	22	/sap/bc/bsp/sap/bsp_crm_btfbse
SM_CRM_UI	SV-SMG	23	/sap/bc/bsp/sap/crm_send_screen
SM_CRM_UI	SV-SMG	24	/sap/crm/crm_send_screen
SM_CRM_UI	SV-SMG	25	/sap/crm/crm_att_provide

Figure 15.9 Activated Services

In the next section, we'll continue with the foundational ChaRM initial configuration activities. The settings in the next section build on the basic configuration activities and are referred to as standard configuration.

15.3 Standard Configuration

In this section, we'll provide step-by-step instructions for how to enable the key standard configuration settings for ChaRM. These standard configuration settings build on the basic configuration settings we discussed in the previous section. While there are many activities under the STANDARD CONFIGURATION area in the IMG, the settings we'll discuss in this section don't relate to adapting the end-to-end ChaRM workflow or any of the core functional capabilities. These settings can be recognized as prerequisite settings before diving into the actual workflow configuration.

15.3.1 Overview

The activities described in this section are performed under the STANDARD CONFIGURATION node in the SAP Solution Manager IMG (Figure 15.10).

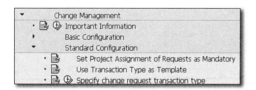

Figure 15.10 Standard Configuration Settings (Prerequisites)

In the following activities, we'll provide step-by-step instructions for these actions:

▸ Set project assignment of requests as mandatory.

▸ Specify change request transaction type.

We won't be discussing the configuration steps related to the IMG activity USE TRANSACTION TYPE AS TEMPLATE. This activity includes documentation covering the process of using standard transaction types as templates, as well as copying their profiles into a customer namespace. We've covered this in the chapter overview.

15.3.2 Set Project Assignment of Requests as Mandatory

Change Request Management provides controlled release over transport requests within your managed system landscape. In order for the technical control to be enabled you must set the project assignment of transport requests as mandatory.

Operational Use

For each managed development system in your ChaRM scenario, you must make the appropriate settings so that transport requests can't be released outside of SAP Solution Manager when ChaRM is activated. You lose transparency, traceability, and control if transports are released in an environment that is supposed to be governed by ChaRM.

For this reason, you configure settings so that project assignment of transport requests is mandatory. This means that the transport request must be assigned to a project for it to be released.

Configuration Activities

Follow these steps:

1. Execute Transaction /TMWFLOW/CMSCONF.

2. In the SYSTEM CHANGE OPTIONS tab of the EXTENDED CONFIGURATION – CHANGE REQUEST MANAGEMENT AND QGM screen, you'll see the managed systems in the SYSTEMS OF PROJECT table (Figure 15.11).

3. For each system controlled by ChaRM, double-click the OPTIONAL text in the PROJECT ASSIGNMENT column.

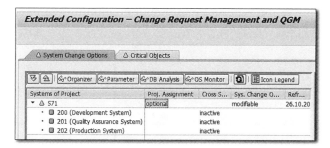

Figure 15.11 Double-Click Optional

4. In the CHANGE ATTRIBUTE DEFINITION window that appears, select the MANDATORY value in the DEFAULT FOR ALL CLIENTS field (Figure 15.12).

> **Note**
>
> You can also enable these settings to be client-specific by specifying the ChaRM-specific clients in the CLIENT-SPECIFIC SETTING area.

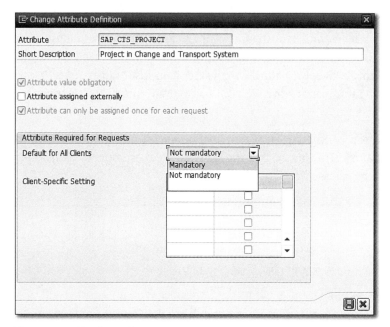

Figure 15.12 Mandatory Project Assignment

5. Click SAVE, and assign your configuration to a workbench request.

The changes that you made for these settings will take effect after you exit and come back into the transaction (see Figure 15.13).

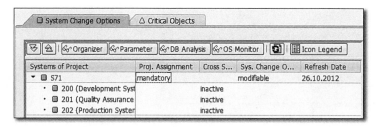

Figure 15.13 Mandatory Project Assignment

Expected Result(s)

If you attempt to release a transport request from the managed development system, and it hasn't been assigned a project (which is done automatically when transport requests are created from ChaRM), you can expect to see the information screen as shown in Figure 15.14. This restricts the user from further releasing the transport request.

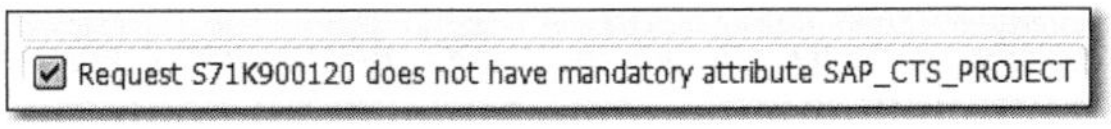

☑ Request S71K900120 does not have mandatory attribute SAP_CTS_PROJECT

Figure 15.14 Project Assignment Mandatory: Information

> **Note**
>
> In the case that ChaRM projects aren't created to enable ChaRM workflow, you may consider creating dummy projects as part of a transition phase activity. This will ensure that development that occurred prior to the activation of ChaRM can still be transported.

15.3.3 Specify Change Request Transaction Type

With new transaction types delivered with release 7.1, you must specify the Change Request Management transaction type that will be used going forward. Specifying the Change Request Management transaction type supports your transition from 7.0 to 7.1. It also informs the system of which transaction type should be the leading transaction type in operation.

Operational Use

In this section, we'll provide the steps necessary to add your new SAP Solution Manager 7.1 request for change transaction type to be included as part of the ChaRM scenario.

Configuration Activities

Follow these steps:

1. Execute the IMG activity SPECIFY CHANGE REQUEST TRANSACTION TYPE.

2. Enter your customer transaction type in the FIELD VAL. column for the parameter CHANGE_REQUEST_NEW. Enter your 7.0-based change request transaction type for the parameter CHANGE_REQUEST. Figure 15.15 provides an example.

3. Click SAVE.

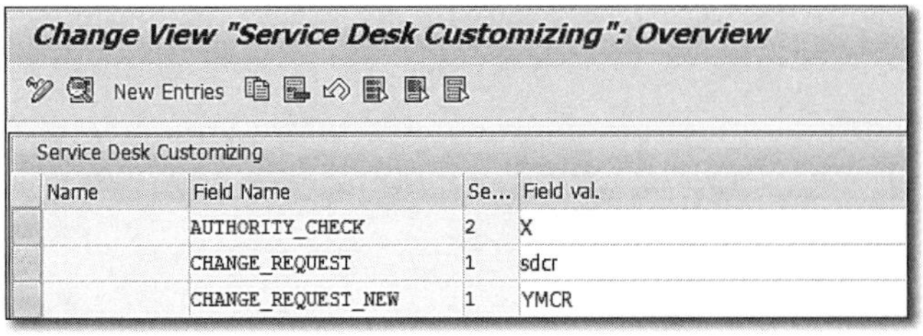

Figure 15.15 Specify Change Request Transaction Type

Expected Result(s)

In direct calls from the SAP CRM_UI, SAP Solution Manager will only use release 7.1-based transaction types (new transaction types).

15.4 Enabling SAP ITSM Process Integration

We've made reference to the fact that SAP Solution Manager provides standard processes to enable AIM and ChaRM for your organization. These processes come preconfigured, in a sense, but they also require configuration to meet organizational requirements for SAP ITSM. While the workflow integrated into the SAP ITSM processes is available out of the box, there is still configuration needed to tie everything together. Specifically, we're talking about technically linking (by configuration) the customer transactions you enabled in AIM (e.g., ZMIN, ZMPR, etc.) to the customer transaction types in ChaRM (e.g., ZMCR).

You've already made the configurations necessary to bring the SAP-delivered transaction types into your own customer namespace. Because the SAP transaction types for AIM and ChaRM are linked from a process perspective out of the box, you'll need to make the appropriate configuration settings to do the same for your customer transaction types.

For example, if you create a follow-on request for change as a result of an incident that requires a change to the IT landscape, you must have the follow-on document created in your own customer transaction type. The ZMIN transaction type must trigger the ZMCR transaction type. The ZMCR transaction type must trigger the Z change documents.

This configuration isn't available out of the box and must be adapted by the customer. In the following sections, we'll perform configuration activities in two areas, both of which are co-located in the SAP Solution Manager IMG:

- **Define copying control for transaction types**
  SAP SOLUTION MANAGER • CAPABILITIES • CHANGE MANAGEMENT • STANDARD CONFIGURATION • TRANSACTION TYPES

- **Define mapping rules for copy control**
  SAP SOLUTION MANAGER • CAPABILITIES • CHANGE MANAGEMENT • STANDARD CONFIGURATION • CHANGE REQUEST MANAGEMENT FRAMEWORK • COPY CONTROL FOR CHANGE REQUEST MANAGEMENT • DEFINE MAPPING RULES FOR COPY CONTROL

15.4.1 Define General Copying Control Rules for Transaction Types

You must link your customer defined transaction types so that the Application Incident Management process and Change Request Management process are integrated. Further, the processes within the Change Request Management must be integrated by defining copying control rules.

Operational Use

In this section, we'll describe how to maintain the general copying control rules for SAP ITSM transaction types. This configuration will provide the framework necessary to specify source and target transaction types when using the SAP ITSM processes in an operational mode.

Table 15.1 identifies a use-case example that includes our customer transaction types as the source and identifies which transaction types they should trigger when the process is handed off between AIM and ChaRM.

Source Transaction Type	As-Is Target Transaction Type	To-Be Target Transaction Type
YMIN: Incident	SMCR: Request for Change	YMCR: Enowa Request for Change
YMCR: Request for Change	SMAD: Admin Change	YMAD: Enowa Admin Change
YMCR: Request for Change	SMCG: General Change	YMCG: Enowa General Change

Table 15.1 Define General Copying Control Rules for ChaRM

Source Transaction Type	As-Is Target Transaction Type	To-Be Target Transaction Type
YMCR: Request for Change	SMCR: Request for Change	YMCR: Enowa Request for Change
YMCR: Request for Change	SMHF: Urgent Change	YMHF: Enowa Urgent Change
YMCR: Request for Change	SMMJ: Normal Change	YMMJ: Enowa Normal Change

Table 15.1 Define General Copying Control Rules for ChaRM (Cont.)

Configuration Activities

Follow these steps:

1. Execute the IMG activity DEFINE COPYING CONTROL FOR TRANSACTION TYPES.

2. Select the SRCE TRANS. TYPE and as-is (existing configuration) TGT TRANS. TYPE (Figure 15.16). Our selections are based on our use-case specifications examples identified in Table 15.1.

3. Click the COPY AS button.

Change View "Copy Transaction Types - General Control Data": Overview

New Entries

Copy Transaction Types - General Control Data

Srce Trans. Type	Tgt Trans. Type	Short Description	Copy item no.	ComplRef	Copying routine
YMCR	SDMJ	Normal Correction	☐	☐	AIC001
YMCR	SMAD	Admin Change	☐	☐	AIC001
YMCR	SMCG	General Change	☐	☐	AIC001
YMCR	SMCR	Request for Change	☐	☐	AIC001
YMCR	SMHF	Urgent Change	☐	☐	AIC001
YMCR	SMMJ	Normal Change	☐	☐	AIC001
YMDT	YMIN	Enowa Incident	☐	☐	AIC001
YMIN	0000	Appointment	☐	☐	AIC001
YMIN	0005	Outgoing E-Mail	☐	☐	AIC001
YMIN	1003	Task	☐	☐	AIC001
YMIN	KNAR	Knowledge Article	☐	☐	AIC001
YMIN	SMCR	Request for Change	☐	☐	AIC001
YMIN	SMIN	Incident	☐	☐	AIC001
YMIN	SMPR	Problem	☐	☐	AIC001
YMIN	YMIN	Enowa Incident	☐	☐	AIC001

Figure 15.16 Select Transaction Types

4. In the CHANGE VIEW "COPY TRANSACTION TYPES – GENERAL CONTROL DATA": DETAILS screen, substitute the value in the TGT. TRANS. TYPE field with your target customer transaction type (Figure 15.17).

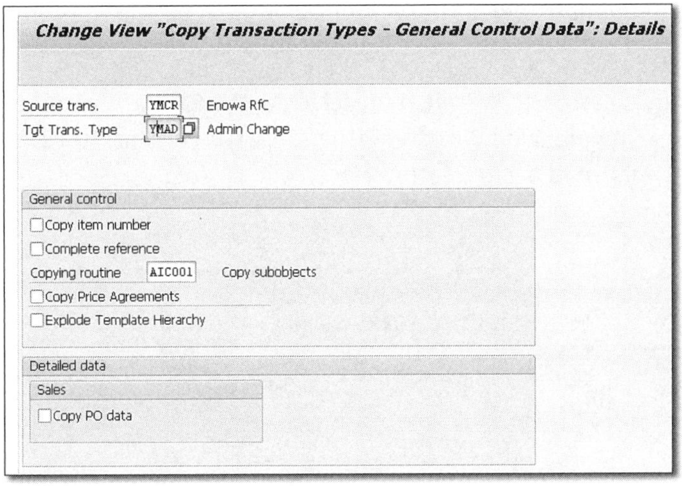

Figure 15.17 Specify Target Transaction Type for Copying Control

5. Press [Enter].

The system will require you to repeat this action until all of the entries you originally selected have been copied into new target transaction types.

When you're finished, your new entries will appear in the Copy Transaction Types – General Control Data table (Figure 15.18).

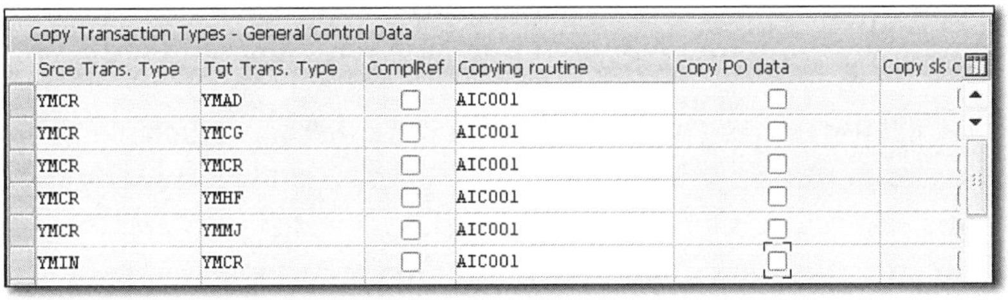

Copy Transaction Types - General Control Data

Srce Trans. Type	Tgt Trans. Type	ComplRef	Copying routine	Copy PO data	Copy sls c
YMCR	YMAD	☐	AIC001	☐	
YMCR	YMCG	☐	AIC001	☐	
YMCR	YMCR	☐	AIC001	☐	
YMCR	YMHF	☐	AIC001	☐	
YMCR	YMMJ	☐	AIC001	☐	
YMIN	YMCR	☐	AIC001	☐	

Figure 15.18 Completed Copying Control Rules

6. Click Save.

Expected Result(s)

Based on the configuration you've made in the previous section, the general copying control rules have been defined that link your customer AIM process with your customer ChaRM process. The tangible result of this configuration will be the ability to create your customer request for change from your customer incident message.

Figure 15.19 represents the expected result(s) for selecting the CREATE FOLLOW-UP button from within a customer incident message. In the FOLLOW-UP WEBPAGE DIA-LOG window that appears, you'll be able to select your customer request for change transaction type.

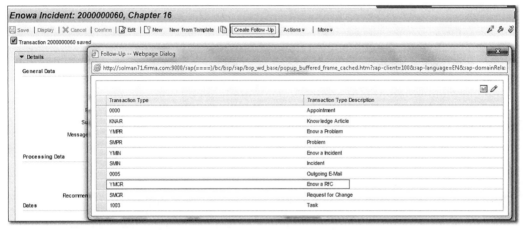

Figure 15.19 Create Customer Request for Change as a Follow-Up

15.4.2 Define Change Request Management Mapping Rules for Copying Control

In this section, we'll use the copying control framework that we completed in the previous section to define mapping rules for our customer ChaRM transaction types. The configuration you saw in Section 15.4.1 achieved the frontend ability to create a follow-on customer request for change from a customer incident.

Operational Use

There are interconnected processes in ChaRM. The request for change document has the validation and approval process that triggers the change process (implementation, testing, and deployment of the change) depending on the scope. In this section, we'll make the configuration settings necessary to tie the interconnecting ChaRM processes together, using your customer-defined transaction types.

Configuration Activities

To successfully define mapping rules, you must have executed the configuration steps described in the "Define General Copying Control Rules for Transaction Types" section.

1. Execute IMG activity DEFINE MAPPING RULES FOR COPY CONTROL.

2. Highlight your customer transaction type for the request for change (e.g., YMCR) in the CREATE PROCEDURE table (Figure 15.20).

3. Double-click the COPY CONTROL RULES folder in the DIALOG STRUCTURE area.

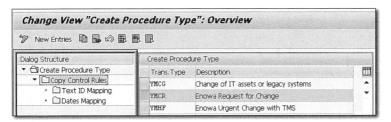

Figure 15.20 Select Customer Request for Change and Copy Control Rules

4. Highlight all of the entries in the COPY CONTROL RULES folder (Figure 15.21).

5. Click the COPY AS button.

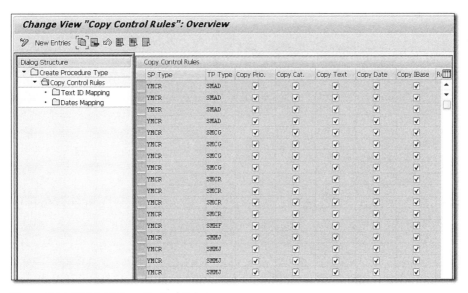

Figure 15.21 Highlight Copy Control Rules

6. Replace all of the entries in the TP TYPE column with your own customer transaction types (e.g., SMAD → YMAD) as shown in Figure 15.22.

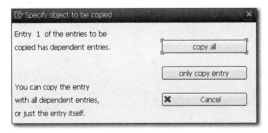

Copy Control Rules							
SP Type	TP Type	Copy Prio.	Copy Cat.	Copy Text	Copy Date	Copy IBase	R
YMCR	YMAD	✓	✓	✓	✓	✓	
YMCR	YMAD	✓	✓	✓	✓	✓	
YMCR	YMAD	✓	✓	✓	✓	✓	
YMCR	YMAD	✓	✓	✓	✓	✓	
YMCR	YMCG	✓	✓	✓	✓	✓	
YMCR	YMCG	✓	✓	✓	✓	✓	
YMCR	YMCG	✓	✓	✓	✓	✓	
YMCR	YMCG	✓	✓	✓	✓	✓	
YMCR	YMCR	✓	✓	✓	✓	✓	
YMCR	YMCR	✓	✓	✓	✓	✓	
YMCR	YMCR	✓	✓	✓	✓	✓	
YMCR	YMCR	✓	✓	✓	✓	✓	
YMCR	YMHF	✓	✓	✓	✓	✓	
YMCR	YMMJ	✓	✓	✓	✓	✓	
YMCR	YMMJ	✓	✓	✓	✓	✓	
YMCR	YMMJ	✓	✓	✓	✓	✓	
YMCR	YMMJ	✓	✓	✓	✓	✓	

Figure 15.22 Replace TP Type Entries with Customer Transaction Types

7. Press Enter .

8. Select the COPY ALL button in the SPECIFY OBJECT TO BE COPIED window (Figure 15.23).

Figure 15.23 Copy All

9. In the INFORMATION window that appears, confirm the copy of the entries by clicking the ENTER button (Figure 15.24).

You'll go through several iterations of selecting the COPY ALL button in the SPEC-IFY OBJECT TO BE COPIED window as well as confirming the entries. Perform this activity until you've finished.

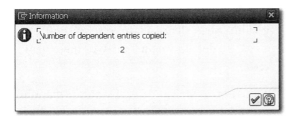

Figure 15.24 Confirm Selection

10. Click SAVE.

11. Click BACK.

12. Highlight all of the entries in the COPY CONTROL RULES table that have your customer transaction types in the SP TYPE column but point to SAP transaction types in the TP TYPE column (Figure 15.25).

13. Click the DELETE button so that the users can't accidentally trigger SAP transaction types from the request for change document.

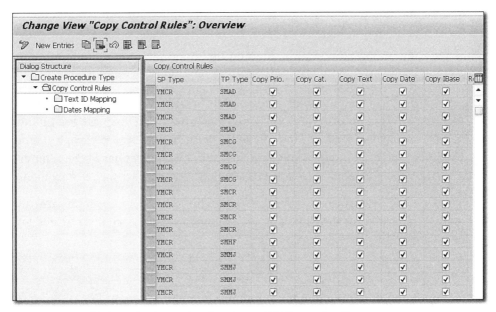

Figure 15.25 Highlight and Delete Values Pointing to SAP Transaction Types

14. Click SAVE.

In the Copy Control Rules table, you also can set the copy rules for details in the document such as priority, category values, text dates, iBase, reference objects, attachments, subject, and context values. By default, the majority of these values are copied over across transaction types.

You can copy the details of text determination as well as dates if separate mapping rules need to be defined for these two variables. The Text ID Mapping and Dates Mapping folders in the Dialog Structure (left side of Figure 15.25) will contain the tables required to enable those specific mapping rules.

Ensure that this activity is also performed so that YMIN is copied over and its target transaction type is YMCR (Figure 15.26).

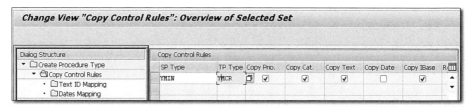

Figure 15.26 Mapping Rules: YMIN Incident

Expected Result(s)

With the result of the preceding configuration, you'll now only have the option to add your customer transactions as change categories in the Request for Change Scope assignment block in your customer-defined request for change (Figure 15.27). All values pointing to standard SAP transaction types have been removed to prevent the accidental selection and creation of a standard change document.

Based on the settings in this section, when the change approver releases the request for change for development, the follow-on change document created will be your customer change document.

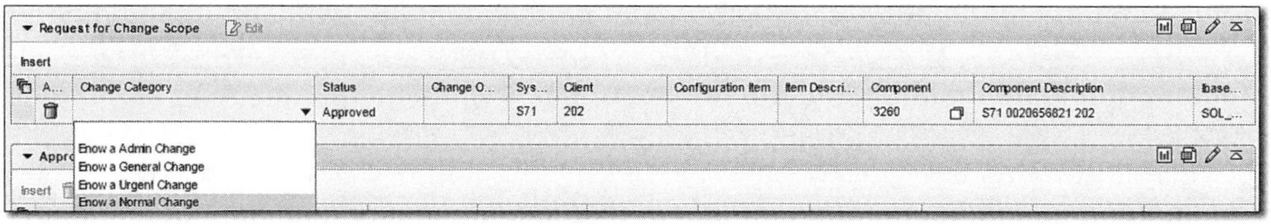

Figure 15.27 Create Customer Change Documents from Request for Change

15.5 Adapting Standard Change Request Management Workflow

In this section, we'll provide end-to-end configuration steps on how to perform a basic enhancement to the standard ChaRM workflow. While SAP Solution Manager includes standard workflows that are preconfigured and ready out of the box, it's often the case that organizations will need to adapt this workflow to meet their own change control requirements.

These requirements can include additional status values, email notifications, approval settings, and field values, for example. In this section, we'll explain the configuration activities involved in adding an additional workflow step into the standard urgent change process. While enhancing the AIM process is as simple as adding a status value, the ChaRM framework relies on action-/status-driven process changes. We'll describe how to enable these settings in the following sections.

15.5.1 Overview

While this example of enhancing the standard workflow for the urgent change process is specific to urgent changes, you can use the concepts and frameworks described to adapt any of the other change documents delivered with ChaRM. We also mentioned that enhancing the standard ChaRM workflow is more complex than simply adding a status value, which is done for AIM. Enhancing the standard workflow for ChaRM is a cross-functional activity. For that reason, we'll cover the following configuration activities that are required to insert an organizational-specific workflow step into the standard processes:

▸ Configuring a new status value and status authorization keys

▸ Updating authorization roles so that the correct user can execute the new workflow step

▸ Creating a new action definition to trigger the new status value

▸ Defining conditions so that the action and status are triggered at the appropriate time

Let's get started with the configuration.

15.5.2 Status Administration

Status administration involves adding, deleting or changing the status values for a particular transaction type. The status values are grouped according to a status profile. Each status value has different attributes that can be adapted to meet your requirements.

Operational Use

In the status profile YMHFHEAD, SAP Solution Manager provides status values that can scale from small to large IT organizations. The standard status profile rarely needs to be enhanced. If it's adapted, usually it's a renaming of terminology (i.e., the status value still has the same meaning/reason) or perhaps one to two status values are added to support existing reporting requirements or meet organization-specific metrics.

Furthermore, the status values provided for ChaRM align closely with ITIL standards for maintaining the processing status for SAP ITSM transactions.

Configuration Activities

In the configuration examples in the following subsections, we'll show you how to add a new status value to the status profile.

Create Status Value

1. Execute IMG activity DEFINE STATUS PROFILE FOR USER STATUS.

2. In the CHANGE STATUS PROFILE: OVERVIEW screen, double-click on your customer-specific status profile (e.g., YMHFHEAD) as shown in Figure 15.28.

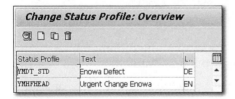

Figure 15.28 Select Status Profile

In the CHANGE STATUS PROFILE: USER STATUS screen, we'll create a new status value by copying an existing status value and updating the fields.

3. Position your cursor on the status value In Development, and click the Copy As button as shown in Figure 15.29.

Change Status Profile: User Status

Object Types

Status Profile	YMHFHEAD	Urgent Change Enowa
Maintenance Language	EN	English

User Status

Stat...	Status	Short Text	Lon...	Init. ...	Lowes...	Highes...	Posi...	Prio...	Auth. code	Tr...	
10	CRTD	Created	☐	☑	10	90	1	1	SMHF_00		
20	PROC	In Development	☐	☐	10	90	1	1	SMHF_01	INPR	
30	TOTE	To Be Tested	☐	☐	20	90	1	1	SMHF_02		
40	Test	Successfully Tested	☐	☐	20	80	1	1	SMHF_03		
50	REL	Authorized for Production	☐	☐	20	80	1	1	SMHF_04		
60	PROD	Imported into Production	☐	☐	20	80	1	1	SMHF_05		
70	Conf	Confirmed	☐	☐	20	80	1	1	SMHF_06		
80	COMP	Completed	☐	☐	80	80	1	1	SMHF_07	FINI	
90	CANC	Withdrawn	☐	☐	90	90	1	1	SMHF_08	FINI	

Figure 15.29 Copy Existing Status Value

4. In the Copy Status window that appears (Figure 15.30), we'll create a status value of Assigned to Developer. This is an example and also a common requirement that organizations adopt to classify change documents that have been assigned to a developer but not necessarily have started the development process.

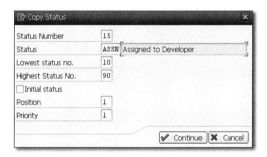

Copy Status		
Status Number	15	
Status	ASSN	Assigned to Developer
Lowest status no.	10	
Highest Status No.	90	
☐ Initial status		
Position	1	
Priority	1	

✔ Continue ✖ Cancel

Figure 15.30 Specify Status Details

5. Maintain details of the status value as we've done in Figure 15.30. Table 15.2 provides an overview of the meaning behind these fields.

Field	Description
STATUS NUMBER	Sequential number that identifies the position of the status value in the message
STATUS	Four-character short code (background use only) and the short description that will appear in the message
LOWEST STATUS NO.	The lowest status value that can be maintained from this value
HIGHEST STATUS NO.	The highest status value that can be maintained from this value
INITIAL STATUS	Only mark for status value of NEW
POSITION	Default to 1
PRIORITY	Default to 1

Table 15.2 Status Value Attributes

6. Click the CONTINUE button when you've finished populating the attributes. The newly created status value ASSIGNED TO DEVELOPER will appear in the USER STATUS table as shown in Figure 15.31.

Stat...	Status	Short Text	Lon...	Init. ...	Lowes...	Highes...	Posi...	Prio...	Auth. code	Tr...
10	CRTD	Created	☐	☑	10	90	1	1	SMHF_00	
15	ASSN	Assigned to Developer	☐	☐	10	90	1	1	SMHF_01	INPR
20	PROC	In Development	☐	☐	10	90	1	1	SMHF_01	INPR
30	TOTE	To Be Tested	☐	☐	20	90	1	1	SMHF_02	
40	Test	Successfully Tested	☐	☐	20	80	1	1	SMHF_03	
50	REL	Authorized for Production	☐	☐	20	80	1	1	SMHF_04	
60	PROD	Imported into Production	☐	☐	20	80	1	1	SMHF_05	
70	Conf	Confirmed	☐	☐	20	80	1	1	SMHF_06	
80	COMP	Completed	☐	☐	80	80	1	1	SMHF_07	FINI
90	CANC	Withdrawn	☐	☐	90	90	1	1	SMHF_08	FINI

Figure 15.31 New Status Value Created

7. Click SAVE.

In addition to the status value being created in the user status table in Table 15.2, it should also be visible in Table TJ30 as shown in Figure 15.32. You'll need to note the status code (e.g., E0011) for future use with authorizations and email notifications.

Data Browser: Table TJ30 Select Entries   10

Table: TJ30
Displayed Fields: 14 of   14   Fixed Columns: ⌐3⌐   List Width 0250

MANDT	STSMA	ESTAT	INIST	STONR	HSONR	NSONR	LINEP	STATP	BERSL	CRM_VRGNG	TXT04	TXT30	LTEXT
100	YMHFHEAD	E0001	X	10	90	10	01	01	SMHF_00		CRTD	Created	
100	YMHFHEAD	E0002		20	90	10	01	01	SMHF_01	INPR	PROC	In Development	
100	YMHFHEAD	E0004		30	90	20	01	01	SMHF_02		TOTE	To Be Tested	
100	YMHFHEAD	E0005		40	80	20	01	01	SMHF_03		Test	Successfully Tested	
100	YMHFHEAD	E0006		60	80	20	01	01	SMHF_05		PROD	Imported into Production	
100	YMHFHEAD	E0007		70	80	20	01	01	SMHF_06		Conf	Confirmed	
100	YMHFHEAD	E0008		80	80	80	01	01	SMHF_07	FINI	COMP	Completed	
100	YMHFHEAD	E0009		50	80	20	01	01	SMHF_04		REL	Authorized for Production	
100	YMHFHEAD	E0010		90	90	90	01	01	SMHF_08	FINI	CANC	Withdrawn	
100	YMHFHEAD	E0011		15	90	10	01	01	SMHF_01	INPR	ASSN	Assigned to Developer	

Figure 15.32 New Status Value in Table TJ30

Create and Assign Status Authorization Key

In the following steps, we'll show you how to define authorization keys for each status value in your status profile. Then, we'll show you how to adapt the change manager role so that it's the only role that can set the new status ASSIGNED TO DEVELOPER.

1. Execute the IMG activity DEFINE STATUS PROFILE FOR USER STATUS.

2. Access your customer-defined status profile.

3. Select ENVIRONMENT • AUTHORIZATION KEY as shown in Figure 15.33.

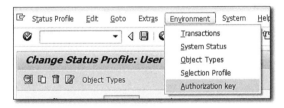

Figure 15.33 Select Environment • Authorization Key

4. In the CHANGE VIEW "AUTHORIZATION KEY": OVERVIEW screen, ensure that you're in edit mode, and then click the NEW ENTRIES button as shown in Figure 15.34.

Figure 15.34 Choose New Entries

5. Enter values in the AUTHKEY and TEXT column as shown in Figure 15.35.

New Entries: Overview of Added Entries

AuthKey	Text
YMHF_00	Created
YMHF_01	Assigned to Developer
YMHF_02	In Development
YMHF_03	To Be Tested
YMHF_04	Successfully Tested
YMHF_05	Authorized for Production
YMHF_06	Imported into Production
YMHF_07	Confirmed
YMHF_08	Completed
YMHF_09	Withdrawn

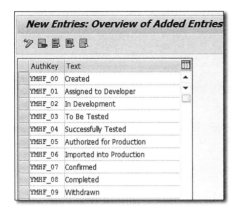

Figure 15.35 Maintain Authorization Key Details

You'll need to create a unique authorization key, identifiable via transaction type, for each status value that should be controlled by authorizations

6. Click Save, and then click the Back button to return to the YMHFHEAD status profile details.
7. In the User Status column, assign the authorization keys you just created to the corresponding status values in the Auth. Code column as shown in Figure 15.36.

User Status

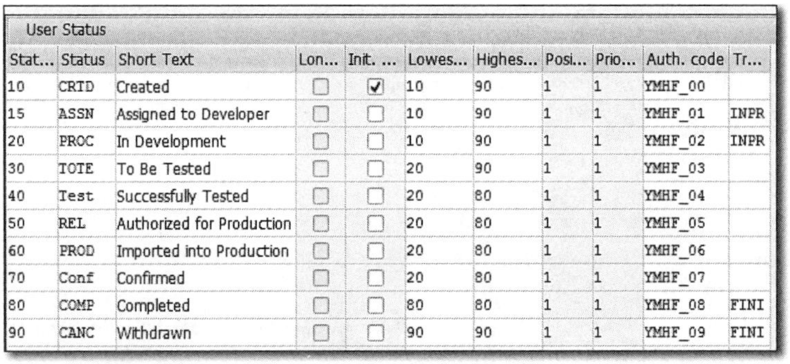

Stat...	Status	Short Text	Lon...	Init. ...	Lowes...	Highes...	Posi...	Prio...	Auth. code	Tr...
10	CRTD	Created	☐	☑	10	90	1	1	YMHF_00	
15	ASSN	Assigned to Developer	☐	☐	10	90	1	1	YMHF_01	INPR
20	PROC	In Development	☐	☐	10	90	1	1	YMHF_02	INPR
30	TOTE	To Be Tested	☐	☐	20	90	1	1	YMHF_03	
40	Test	Successfully Tested	☐	☐	20	80	1	1	YMHF_04	
50	REL	Authorized for Production	☐	☐	20	80	1	1	YMHF_05	
60	PROD	Imported into Production	☐	☐	20	80	1	1	YMHF_06	
70	Conf	Confirmed	☐	☐	20	80	1	1	YMHF_07	
80	COMP	Completed	☐	☐	80	80	1	1	YMHF_08	FINI
90	CANC	Withdrawn	☐	☐	90	90	1	1	YMHF_09	FINI

Figure 15.36 Assign Authorization Keys to User Status

Assign Authorization Keys to the PFCG Role

Now, we're ready to assign the authorization key of the new status value to the authorization (PFCG) role for the change manager.

> **Note**
>
> These tasks are typically performed by a security administrator. We assume that they will be performing these tasks or that you have the required authorizations in your role to maintain roles. Further, we've copied the standard SAP authorization roles to our customer namespace for these configuration examples.

1. Execute Transaction PFCG.

2. Enter the role (e.g., YSAP_SOCM_CHANGE_MANAGER) as shown in Figure 15.37, and select the CHANGE button.

Figure 15.37 Maintain Role

3. In the AUTHORIZATIONS tab, select the CHANGE AUTHORIZATION DATA button as shown in Figure 15.38.

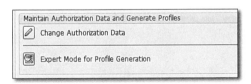

Figure 15.38 Change Authorization Data

4. In the CHANGE ROLE: AUTHORIZATIONS screen, select UTILITIES(M) • TECHNICAL NAMES ON as shown in Figure 15.39.

Figure 15.39 Turn Technical Names On

5. Click the FIND (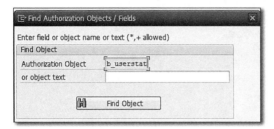) button.

6. Enter the value "b_userstat" in the AUTHORIZATION OBJECT field as shown in Figure 15.40.

Figure 15.40 Find Object B_USERSTAT

7. Click the FIND OBJECT button. The structure of authorization nodes will expand to identify the authorization objects that match the search for object B_USERSTAT.

8. Maintain the value YMHFHEAD in the STATUS PROFILE field, and remove any other status profiles as shown in Figure 15.41.

9. Double-click the contents of the field AUTHORIZATION KEY.

Figure 15.41 Maintain B_USERSTAT

10. In the FIELD VALUES window (Figure 15.42), select the new status values (and corresponding authorization code) that the change manager should now be able to set due to our enhancement to the workflow.

The values for authorization object B_USERSTAT should now appear as shown in Figure 15.43. For control purposes, we've removed any reference to S* status profiles or authorization keys.

11. Click the SAVE button (Figure 15.44).

12. Click the GENERATE button (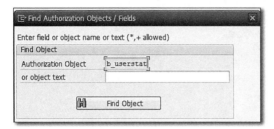).

Figure 15.42 Select Authorization Key

Figure 15.43 Customized B_USERSTAT Activity

Figure 15.44 Save and Generate Authorization Rolex

Expected Result(s)

Now that you've completed the status administration piece of the workflow enhancement process, the following configuration activities are expected to be completed:

- New status value in the appropriate status profile
- Authorization key assigned to the status value
- Relevant authorization roles updated to include permissions to execute the new status value

15.5.3 Maintain Action Profile

The action profile groups action definitions together according to transaction type, similar to the architecture of a status profile. Each action definition has different processing parameters depending on the functionality they provide. For example, some actions trigger email notifications and others trigger the change of a status value within the document.

Operational Use

In ChaRM, status values are only triggered as a result of an action being selected by the user on the change document. Because we've created a brand-new status value, we must now create an action that is dedicated to triggering the status value.

Configuration Activities

Copy Action Definition

1. Execute Transaction CMRC_ACTION_DEF.

2. Click the EDIT button to be in change mode.

3. Highlight the action profile (e.g., YMHF_ACTIONS), and double-click the ACTION DEFINITION folder (Figure 15.45).

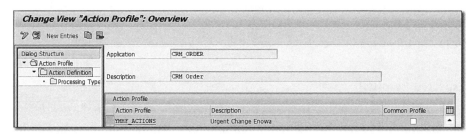

Figure 15.45 Select Action Profile

We'll copy an existing action definition that is related to setting a status in the change document. For this example, we'll copy the existing standard action definition SET TO "IN DEVELOPMENT".

4. Select the action (Figure 15.46).

5. Click the COPY AS button.

6. Enter a value in the ACTION DEFINITION field that conforms to your organization's nomenclature for action definitions (Figure 15.47).

7. Enter a value in the DESCRIPTION field.

8. Press Enter .

Change View "Action Definition": Overview

⟋ ⟋ New Entries ▢ ▢

Dialog Structure		
▾ ▢ Action Profile	Action Profile	YMHF_ACTIONS
▾ ▢ Action Definition		
• ▢ Processing Type	Description	Urgent Change Enowa

Action Definition

Action Definition	Description	Sort Order	Inacti...▦
YMHF_GO_LIVE	Release Urgent Change for Production	40	▢ ▲
YMHF_IN_PROCESS	Set to "In Development"	10	▢ ▾

Figure 15.46 Copy Existing Action

Change View "Action Definition": Details of Selected Set

ActionProfile	YMHF_ACTIONS
Description	Urgent Change Enowa
Action Definition	YMHF_ASSIGNED_TO_DEVELOPER
Description	Set to "Assigned to Developer"

Figure 15.47 Maintain Action Definition ID and Description

9. Select COPY ALL from the window(s) that appear.

10. Confirm the entry in the resulting information box.

11. Click SAVE.

Adapt Action Definition

Now that we've copied an existing action definition into a new name with a new description, we must change a processing parameter in it so the action knows to trigger the new status value.

1. Double-click the newly created action in the ACTION DEFINITION table (Figure 15.48).

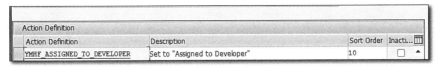

Action Definition

Action Definition	Description	Sort Order	Inacti...▦
YMHF_ASSIGNED_TO_DEVELOPER	Set to "Assigned to Developer"	10	▢ ▲

Figure 15.48 Select New Action

2. Double-click the PROCESSING TYPES folder (Figure 15.49).

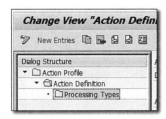

Figure 15.49 Choose Processing Types

3. In the SETTINGS METHOD CALL area of the screen, select the CHANGE option (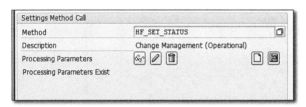)
   next to PROCESSING PARAMETERS (Figure 15.50).

Figure 15.50 Select Change Processing Parameters

4. In the CONTAINER EDITOR window, double-click the existing value in the INITIAL
   VALUE column (Figure 15.51).

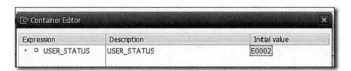

Figure 15.51 Double-Click Initial Value Entry

5. Choose the INITIAL VALUE tab (Figure 15.52).

6. Enter the user status code for the new status value ASSIGNED TO DEVELOPER.
   This will ensure that when the action is selected from the change document,
   the status will be updated accordingly.

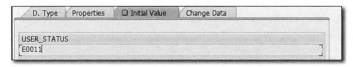

Figure 15.52 Maintain USER_STATUS Parameter

7. Click CONFIRM.

8. Click SAVE.

Expected Result(s)

Based on these configuration activities, you should now have a new action definition in the appropriate action profile for your change transaction type. The unique name of the action, description, and processing parameters should all be updated to reflect the purpose and objectives of the action to enhance the standard workflow.

15.5.4 Maintain Conditions

Conditions are set up for each action definition so that the system knows when to either schedule and/or start the action.

Operational Use

Now that we've created an action definition that will drive our new status value, we must configure conditions that let the SAP CRM infrastructure know where to insert this action. Because there are several steps in each change document, simply creating a status value and an action to determine the status value isn't enough. SAP Solution Manager must know at what point in the workflow the new action and status values will be executed.

In our example, we want to schedule this action to occur when an urgent change is created because that is when a developer is typically assigned in the change process. Further, we'll need to update the conditions of the existing IN DEVELOPMENT status so that it's scheduled at the time our new status value is engaged.

Configuration Activities

Add Action Definition

1. Execute Transaction CRMC_ACTION_CONF.

2. In the CONDITIONS FOR ACTION: CHANGE screen, click the TECHNICAL NAMES button (Figure 15.53).

3. Scroll down and select the appropriate action profile from the SCHEDULING OF ACTIONS column.

4. On the right side of the screen, click the CREATE button, and choose the action you created in the previous section.

Figure 15.53 Select Action Definition

5. Click SAVE.

Define Schedule Condition

1. In the CONDITIONS FOR ACTIONS: CHANGE screen, select the SCHEDULE CONDITIONS tab (Figure 15.54).

2. Click the EDIT CONDITION button.

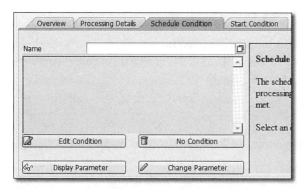

Figure 15.54 Edit Condition

3. Enter a name for the new condition as shown in the example in Figure 15.55.

4. Click in the selection of the screen that reads CLICK HERE TO CREATE A NEW CONDITION.

In the condition editor, you'll need to define a condition based on where the action definition should be scheduled. Because this example (ASSIGNED TO DEVELOPER) should occur when the urgent change is created, we've maintained the schedule conditions as shown in Figure 15.56.

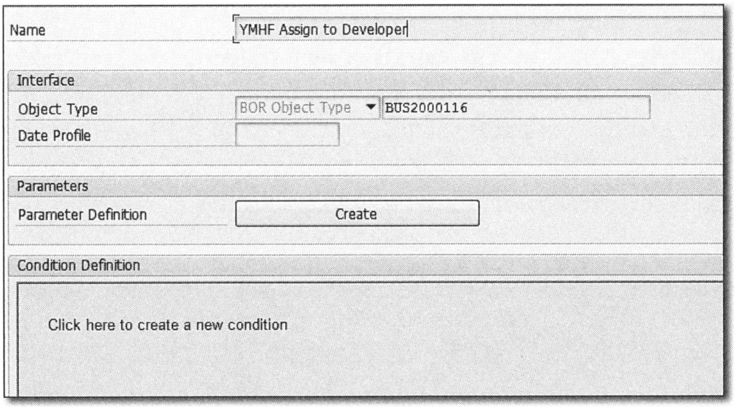

Figure 15.55 Create New Condition

Figure 15.56 Configure Condition Definition

Now, you must also define a condition for when the status is set to ASSIGNED TO DEVELOPER. Because this is a brand-new status with no conditions assigned to it, you must determine what should occur next in the workflow. Logically, it makes the most sense for the document to enter the status IN DEVELOPMENT, after it has been assigned to the developer.

For that reason, we'll create a new condition and assign it to the action definition for the IN DEVELOPMENT status. We've defined the schedule condition so that the IN DEVELOPMENT action will occur at the status ASSIGNED TO DEVELOPER as shown in Figure 15.57.

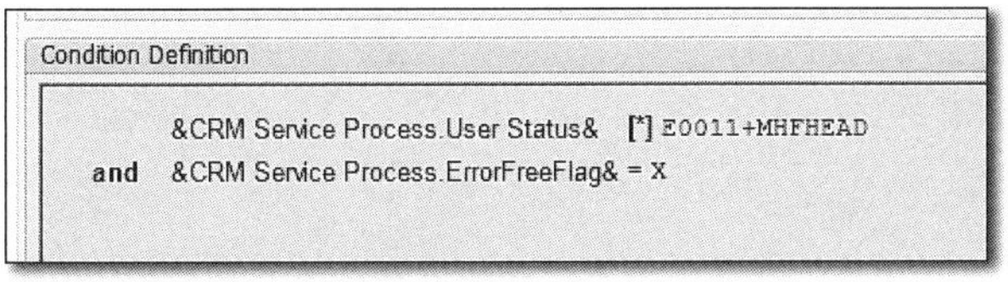

Figure 15.57 Update Conditions at New Status

697

Expected Result(s)

You can check your enhancements to the workflow by testing the new scenario in the workflow. First, you should be able to identify your action definition in the ACTIONS menu at the appropriate status value (according to your schedule conditions). As shown in Figure 15.58, the new action ASSIGNED TO DEVELOPER is available when the urgent change document is in the CREATED status.

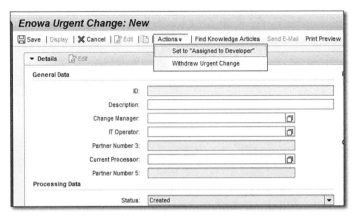

Figure 15.58 New Action Definition Representing Accurate Schedule Conditions

When this action is executed and saved, the new status value will be triggered as shown in Figure 15.59. Based on updating the conditions, the option to SET TO "IN DEVELOPMENT" is available from the ACTIONS menu.

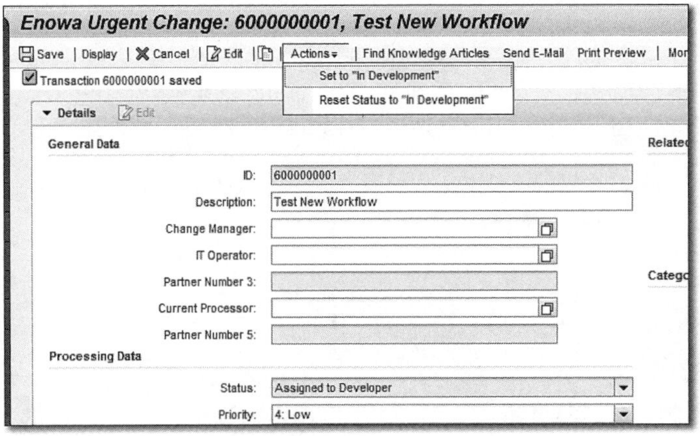

Figure 15.59 New Conditions

This completes the insertion of a new process step to enhance the standard ChaRM workflow.

15.6 Approval Settings

Approval settings, as described in Chapter 12, provide the ability to have a customized procedure in the request for change document to support organizational requirements for approvals. After the request for change is in the status TO BE APPROVED, the approval procedure is engaged, and each approval step is executed, according to the partner function and business partner responsible for the approval.

Multiple approval procedures are supported. For example, requests for change that have a very high risk level may need more approval steps than a request for change with a low risk level. A request for change that requires a workstation change may require less approval than something that affects the SAP ERP production system.

You can enable the configuration so that certain steps must be approved before subsequent steps. For example, you can maintain the configuration so that a change manager must submit his approval before the Change Advisory Board (CAB) can submit its approval. Rule policies can be configured as well in the SAP CRM Web UI to enable automatic determination of the various characteristics of an approval procedure, based on various criteria in the request for change document.

15.6.1 Overview

The configuration activities to enable custom approval settings are found under the APPROVAL SETTINGS node in the SAP Solution Manager IMG (Figure 15.60).

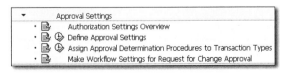

Figure 15.60 Approval Settings Configuration Area

In the following sections, we'll provide step-by-step instructions for how to create your own custom approval procedure and assign it to the YMCR customer request for change transaction type. In this use-case example, we'll configure an approval procedure that has two approval steps. The first is the change manager approval, and the second is the CAB approval. Per our use-case example requirements, the change manager must submit his approval before the CAB can submit its approval.

15.6.2 Define Approval Settings and Assign Procedure to Transaction Type

You can choose to have a default approval procedure which is delivered standard from SAP Solution Manager. If you have a more complex scenario for how requests for changes are approved, you can set up a custom approval procedure with settings specific to your requirements.

Operational Use

In this activity, we'll create a customer approval procedure that will later be assigned to our YMCR request for change transaction type. In this activity, we'll perform the following configuration settings:

▶ Create the approval procedure.

▶ Determine when the approval procedure can be locked from editing.

▶ Define the approval steps.

▶ Assign the approval steps to partner functions.

▶ Specify the order in which the approval steps must be carried out.

▶ Define the determination procedure.

▶ Assign the approval procedure to request for change.

Figure 15.61 represents the main configuration area when defining customer-specific approval procedures. When configuring approval procedures, it's mandatory that each folder in the DIALOG STRUCTURE is completed in the order in which it appears.

We'll go through the each of these folders in order to configure a custom approval procedure based on the requirements defined in our use-case example.

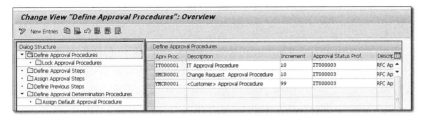

Figure 15.61 Configuration Screen: Define Approval Procedures

Configuration Activities

First, we'll create the approval procedure YMCR0001:

1. Execute the IMG activity DEFINE APPROVAL SETTINGS.

2. In the CHANGE VIEW "DEFINE APPROVAL PROCEDURES": OVERVIEW screen, click the NEW ENTRIES button (Figure 15.62).

Figure 15.62 Click New Entries

3. Fill out the data in the DEFINE APPROVAL PROCEDURES table according to your requirements (APRV PROC. and DESCRIPTION values are just examples) as shown in Figure 15.63.

> **Note**
>
> The standard approval status profile is IT000003. In this status profile, there are three status values specific to approving requests for change: approved, rejected, and not relevant. In our example, we'll leverage the default IT000003 approval status profile. If you require additional status values for a customer approval procedure, you may copy the IT000003 approval status profile in Customizing and adapt it to meet your requirements.

Figure 15.63 Define Approval Procedure

4. Click SAVE.

Next, we'll determine at which point the approval procedure will be locked from editing.

5. In the DEFINE APPROVAL PROCEDURES table, select the approval procedure you just created, and double-click the LOCK APPROVAL PROCEDURES folder in the DIALOG STRUCTURE on the left side of the screen (Figure 15.64).

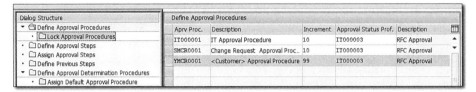

Figure 15.64 Select Lock Approval Procedure

6. Enter new entries based on your requirements and/or the values in Figure 15.65. You can choose whether the approval procedure is locked after the request for change is first saved or after the request for change document is in the status TO BE APPROVED.

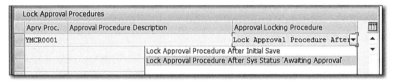

Figure 15.65 Choose Lock Procedure

7. Click SAVE.

Next, we'll define the approval steps in our approval procedure. In our example, there are two approval steps required (one for change manager and another for the CAB).

1. Double-click the DEFINE APPROVAL STEPS folder in the DIALOG STRUCTURE on the left side of the screen (Figure 15.66).

2. Click the NEW ENTRIES button.

3. Enter the approval steps in the DEFINE APPROVAL STEPS table as shown in our example.

4. Click SAVE.

New Entries: Overview of Added Entries

Dialog Structure	Define Approval Steps	
▼ ☐ Define Approval Procedures	Step ID	Step Description
• ☐ Lock Approval Procedures	Y01	Change Manager Approval
• ☐ Define Approval Steps	Y02	Change Advisory Board Approval
• ☐ Assign Approval Steps		
• ☐ Define Previous Steps		
▼ ☐ Define Approval Determination Procedures		
• ☐ Assign Default Approval Procedure		

Figure 15.66 Define Approval Steps

Next, we'll assign the approval steps to the approval procedure, partner functions, sequence, and rule modeler profile.

There are two rule modeler profiles that you can use. Table 15.3 highlights the characteristics of each.

Rule Modeler Profile	Approval Policy	Notes
AI_CM_AP_STEP	AI_CM_CR_RFC_STE	Used to determine which business partner should be entered as the approver automatically for a particular approval step
AI_CM_AP_PRO	AI_CM_CR_RFC_PRO	Used to determine which approval procedure will be used in the request for change

Table 15.3 Rule Modeler Profiles

We're also assigning standard partner functions to our approval procedure. If you choose a partner function, ensure that the partner function is included in the partner determination procedure that is assigned to your request for change transaction type. If not, you may receive errors at processing.

1. Double-click the ASSIGN APPROVAL STEPS folder in the DIALOG STRUCTURE on the left side of the screen (Figure 15.67).

2. Assign your approval steps as shown in our example in the ASSIGN APPROVAL STEPS table.

3. Click SAVE.

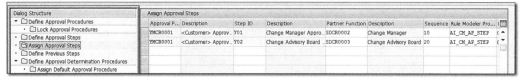

Figure 15.67 Assign Approval Steps

Next, we'll define the steps that must be approved before subsequent steps can be approved. This is called DEFINE PREVIOUS STEPS.

1. Double-click the DEFINE PREVIOUS STEPS folder in the DIALOG STRUCTURE on the left side of the screen (Figure 15.68). For our example, it's required that the change manager approval step (Y01) is performed prior to the CAB approval step (Y02).

2. Enter your requirements in the DEFINE PREVIOUS STEPS table.

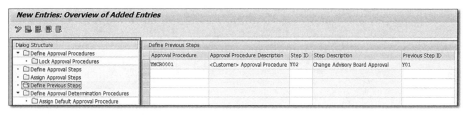

Figure 15.68 Define Previous Steps

3. Click SAVE.

Next, we'll define how our new approval procedure is going to be determined in the request for change document. Approval procedures can either be automatically determined based on criteria defined in rule policies (explained in Section 15.6.3), or the approval procedures can be defaulted according to the request for change transaction type.

1. Double-click the DEFINE APPROVAL DETERMINATION PROCEDURES folder in the DIALOG STRUCTURE on the left side of the screen (Figure 15.69).

2. Click the NEW ENTRIES button.

3. Create a new determination procedure based on data required in Figure 15.69.

4. Click SAVE.

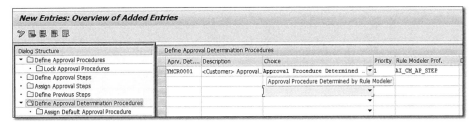

Figure 15.69 Define Approval Determination Procedure

Tips & Tricks

If you selected APPROVAL PROCEDURE DETERMINED BY DEFAULT from the CHOICE column, you can automatically have the approval procedure defaulted into your request for change document at the time it's created. This is known as *standard determination*, and a separate entry in the table must be created as described in the following steps.

5. If you've selected the default CHOICE, highlight the APPROVAL DETERMINATION PROCEDURE you just created in the previous step, and double-click the ASSIGN DEFAULT APPROVAL PROCEDURE folder in the DIALOG STRUCTURE on the left side of the screen (Figure 15.70).

6. Maintain the details in the ASSIGN DEFAULT APPROVAL PROCEDURES table.

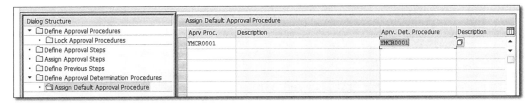

Figure 15.70 Assign Default Approval Procedures

7. Click SAVE.

Finally, we'll need to assign the approval determination procedure to our request for change transaction type:

1. Execute the IMG activity ASSIGN APPROVAL DETERMINATION PROCEDURES TO TRANSACTION TYPES.

2. Select your request for change transaction type, and click the DETAILS button (Figure 15.71).

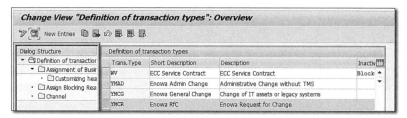

Figure 15.71 View Details of Request for Change

3. In the PROFILES area of the next screen, enter the approval determination procedure you created in the earlier steps in the APRV. DET. PROCEDURE field (Figure 15.72).

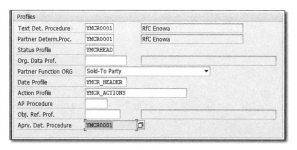

Figure 15.72 Assign Approval Determination Procedure

4. Click SAVE.

Expected Result(s)

You're now able to test your configuration of the new approval procedure in the request for change document. As shown in Figure 15.73, the APPROVAL assignment block shows the two steps in the YMCR0001 approval procedure with the partner functions we defined in Customizing.

You can also see that the CHANGE ADVISORY BOARD approval step is grayed out and not maintainable because the change manager approval is required first.

Figure 15.73 Approval Procedure in Request for Change

As shown in Figure 15.74, after the change manager submits his approval, the CAB is now able to maintain its approval.

Actions	Step ID	Step Description	Partner Function	Partner ID	Partner Descrip...	Activity	Comments	Entered By	Date	Time
	Y01	Change Manag...	Change Manager	116	Winni Hesel	Approved		NWILLIAMS	12/03/2012	22:46
	Y02	Change Adviso...	Change Advisor...	DKOSFELD	Daniel Kosfeld					
			Change Advisory E							

Figure 15.74 Step Two in Approval Procedure Available

15.6.3 Approval Procedures Determined by Rule Modeler

To enable an even more robust approval procedure for your request for change process, you can use the rule modeler in the SAP CRM Web UI to enable automatic determination of approval procedures.

Operational Use

If you've defined an approval determination procedure that will be determined by the rule modeler, you must set up rule policies that determine how the approval procedure and/or characteristics of the request for change document will behave.

Rules are created in the SAP CRM Web UI in the SERVICE OPERATIONS area. Figure 15.75 provides an image of the SERVICE OPERATIONS screen. Click the RULE POLICIES link to access the rule modeler, which is used to configure the rule policies.

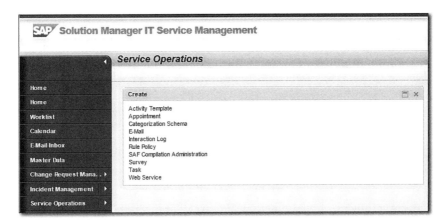

Figure 15.75 Access Rule Policies

Configuration Activities

1. In the SEARCH: RULE POLICIES screen, click the NEW button (Figure 15.76).

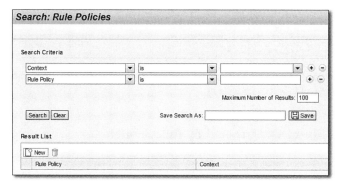

Figure 15.76 Click New

2. In the NEW RULE POLICY – WEBPAGE DIALOG window, enter the CONTEXT "Approval Management", and name the rule policy (Figure 15.77).

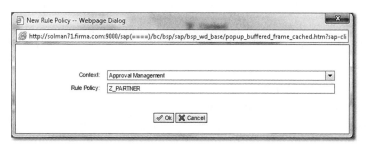

Figure 15.77 Create New Rule Policy

Figure 15.78 provides the standard SAP rule policy as an example. We recommend that you use this rule policy as a template and guide for customizing your own requirements for approval determination based on rules.

Expected Result(s)

The rule policy determination settings enabled in the SAP CRM Web UI should be reflected when you create a request for change document. Alternatively, if you've enabled your approval settings to be dependent on the approval procedure selected, those settings will be updated in the APPROVALS assignment block in the request for change document.

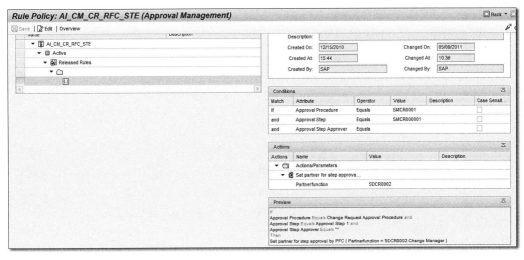

Figure 15.78 Configured Rule Policy

15.7 Extended Configuration

In this section, we'll provide configuration steps for areas that are referred to as extended configuration in the SAP Solution Manager IMG. *Extended configuration* refers to functionalities that support the management, control, and logistics of transport requests and their associated objects (most commonly).

15.7.1 Overview

The extended configuration setup activities are located in its own EXTENDED CONFIGURATION node in the SAP Solution Manager IMG as shown in Figure 15.79.

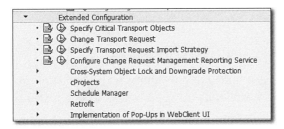

Figure 15.79 Extended Configuration Setup Activities

For the purposes of our discussions regarding ChaRM, we'll provide the configuration setup activities for the following activities:

- Critical transport objects
- Activating cross-system object lock (CSOL) and downgrade protection
- ChaRM reporting service
- Transport request import strategy

15.7.2 Critical Transport Objects

Critical objects require a special approval before they can be modified by a developer. The Critical Object Check tool in ChaRM has the ability to collect and define any number of objects that are deemed critical either by the enterprise, business unit, IT organization, or others.

Operational Use

If a developer tries to modify an object that is specified as "critical" in the central SAP Solution Manager system, a warning is issued, and a separate approval process must be met before the developer can move forward. The approval must occur before the critical objects can be imported into the target system(s).

In this section, we'll show you how to activate/deactivate export checks for critical objects across the managed development systems in your landscape. We'll also show you how to maintain critical object specifications.

> **Note**
>
> Refer to Chapter 13 for a detailed explanation of the Critical Object Check functionality.

Configuration Activities

1. Execute the IMG activity SPECIFY CRITICAL TRANSPORT OBJECTS.
2. Select the CRITICAL OBJECTS tab. Each managed development system connected to the SAP Solution Manager system will be represented in the CRITICAL OBJECTS tab (Figure 15.80).
3. Flag the managed development system(s) that should be activated for the Critical Objects Check functionality in the STATUS column.

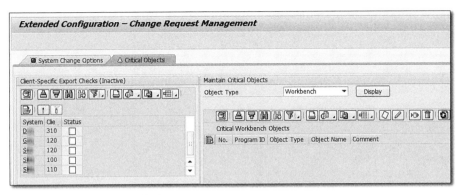

Figure 15.80 Activate Critical Objects

4. In the ACTIVATE A SYSTEM information window, click YES to confirm your selection (Figure 15.81).

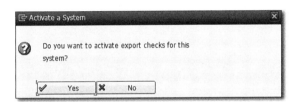

Figure 15.81 Confirm Activation

5. In the right side of the window, click the CREATE button ( ) to maintain critical objects for the activated managed development system (Figure 15.82). You'll notice that in the OBJECT TYPE field, you can toggle between the critical objects maintained for customizing entries as workbench entries.

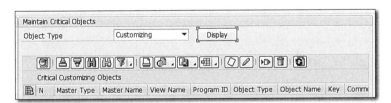

Figure 15.82 Maintain Critical Objects

After clicking the CREATE button, the CRITICAL OBJECTS specifications window will appear as shown in Figure 15.83.

6. Maintain the specifications of the critical objects (Figure 15.83).

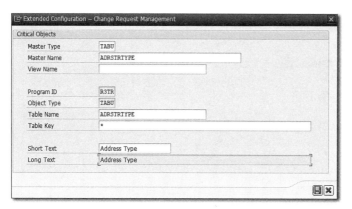

Figure 15.83 Maintain Critical Objects Specifications

> **Note**
>
> For our example, we're maintaining critical objects for Customizing (client-specific objects). For these objects, entries must be maintained in the MASTER TYPE and MASTER NAME fields.
>
> For workbench objects (cross-client objects), the PROGRAM ID, OBJECT TYPE, and TABLE NAME fields are mandatory. Subobjects can be specified by using type LIMU. The export check for modifications can be activated by using the Report /TMWFLOW/CONFIG_ SERVICES.

7. Click SAVE.

You'll be returned to the MAINTAIN CRITICAL OBJECTS screen, where you'll now be able to identify all of the critical objects specified for both Customizing and workbench objects according to each managed system. Figure 15.84 provides an example of critical objects that are currently specified in the SAP Solution Manager system.

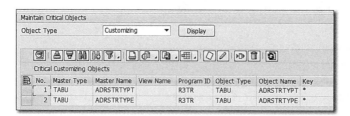

Figure 15.84 Critical Objects Maintained

Expected Result(s)

If a developer tries to export a change to the quality assurance system (e.g., by selecting the ACTION • PASS CHANGE TO TEST), and the object is flagged as critical in the SAP Solution Manager, he will receive the following error and warning messages from in the change document (Figure 15.85).

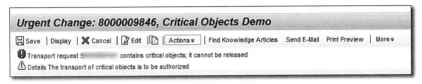

Figure 15.85 Result of Critical Object Check

A change approver, or support staff member with appropriate authorizations, will need to process the critical object. Processing the critical object means that it goes through a separate approval procedure. If approved, the associated transport request can move to the quality assurance system.

> **Note**
>
> Refer to Chapter 14 for additional details on the processing and handling of change documents that contain transport requests with critical objects.

15.7.3 Activate Cross-System Object Lock and Downgrade Protection

Cross-system object lock and Downgrade Protection provide capabilities to proactively identify, monitor, and mitigate collisions that occur among transport request objects.

Operational Use

Cross-system object lock (CSOL) is a tool that provides the ability to identify conflicts between objects in transport requests that have the same production system (or client) as their transport target. When activated, the CSOL creates locks that are held in the SAP Solution Manager system for any object (workbench and Customizing) that is changed in the managed development system. Depending on the conflict scenario, a developer who needs to make changes to this object in another transport request is prevented from doing so until the lock is released.

The lock is released when the transport request is successfully promoted to the production system.

> **Note**
>
> For a detailed overview of the CSOL functionality, refer to Chapter 14.

Configuration Activities

1. Execute the IMG activity Configure and Activate Cross-System Object Lock.

2. Double-click the activity Activate Cross-System Object Lock in Managed Systems (Figure 15.86).

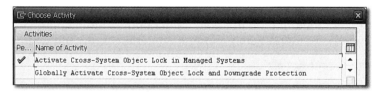

Figure 15.86 Activate Cross-System Object Lock in Managed Systems

3. In the System Change Options tab, expand a development system in the Systems of Project column (Figure 15.87).

4. In the Cross-Sys. Obj. Lock column, double-click the text that reads inactive for each development client that should be controlled by CSOL.

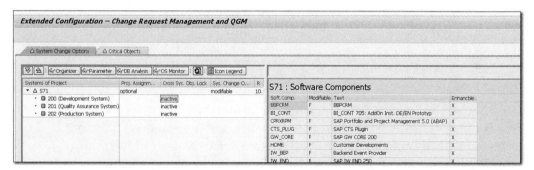

Figure 15.87 Activate Cross-System Object Lock for Development Client

5. In the resulting information box, confirm your selection by clicking Yes (Figure 15.88).

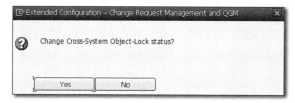

Figure 15.88 Confirm Change of Cros-System Object Lock Status

The text in the Cross Sys. Obj. Lock column will be updated to read ACTIVE, for each development client modified to have this setting (Figure 15.89).

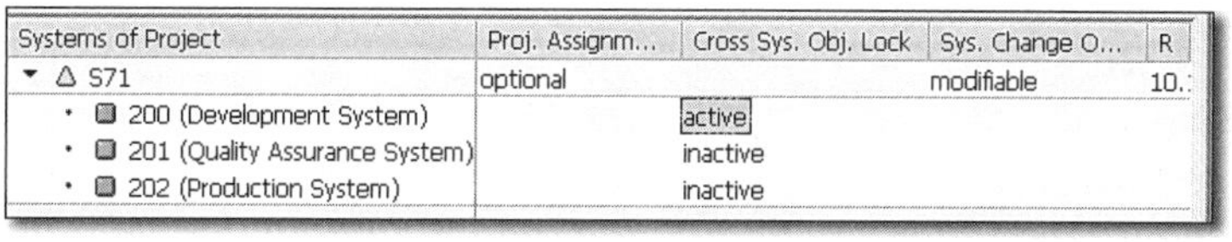

Systems of Project	Proj. Assignm...	Cross Sys. Obj. Lock	Sys. Change O...	R
▼ △ S71	optional		modifiable	10.
• ⬛ 200 (Development System)		active		
• ⬛ 201 (Quality Assurance System)		inactive		
• ⬛ 202 (Production System)		inactive		

Figure 15.89 Active Development Clients (Cross-System Object Lock)

6. Click the BACK button to return to the CHOOSE ACTIVITY screen.

7. Double-click the option GLOBALLY ACTIVATE CROSS-SYSTEM OBJECT LOCK AND DOWNGRADE PROTECTION (Figure 15.90).

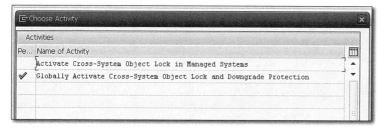

Figure 15.90 Globally Activate Cross-System Object Lock and Downgrade Protection

8. Select the radio button for CROSS-SYSTEM OBJECT LOCK ACTIVE (Figure 15.91).

9. In the CROSS-SYSTEM OBJECT LOCK DETAIL CONFIGURATION area, specify whether the DEFAULT or EXPERT configuration mode should be enabled for the CSOL settings.

Figure 15.91 provides an example of the default value selected.

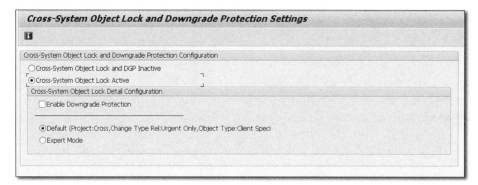

Figure 15.91 Default Configuration Mode

Figure 15.92 provides an example of the EXPERT MODE configuration selected with the various conflict scenarios that can be chosen.

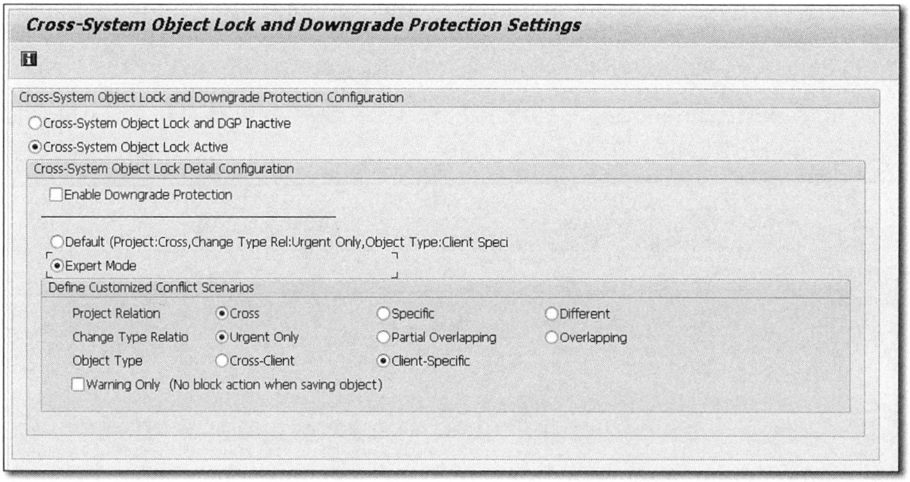

Figure 15.92 Expert Mode

Expected Result(s)

If a developer attempts to modify a transport object in a development client that is activated by CSOL, he will receive errors or warnings depending on how the CSOL was enabled. When the developer attempts to collect and save these objects in a transport request, he will be presented with an error or warning as shown in Figure 15.93.

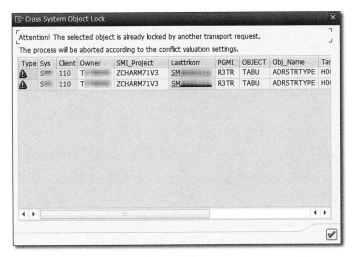

Figure 15.93 Cross-System Object Lock Error Message

15.7.4 Change Request Management Reporting Service

The ChaRM reporting service must be activated if the tracking functionality is used to report on transport objects fetched from the managed development systems.

Operational Use

Reporting data that's related to a project can be automatically fetched by the background job. However, objects that were transported in transport requests can't be reported on unless the object reporting is activated.

In this section, we'll show you the brief activation steps to enable the object reporting for ChaRM tracking. As a reference, the ChaRM tracking report can be accessed via Transaction /TMWFLOW/TRMO. Refer to Chapter 18 for more details about this report.

Configuration Activities

1. Execute IMG activity Configure Change Request Management Reporting Service (or Transaction SE38, alternatively).

2. Enter the Program "/TMWFLOW/CONFIG_SERVICES" as shown in Figure 15.94.

Figure 15.94 Enter Program

3. Click EXECUTE.

4. In the CHANGE MANAGEMENT SERVICES screen, select the radio button next to the OBJECT REPORTING ACTIVE option (Figure 15.95).

Figure 15.95 Activate Object Reporting

5. Click SAVE.

Expected Result(s)

In the ChaRM tracking report, transport objects from the managed systems are fetched successfully when the object reporting is activated. Figure 15.96 provides an example of the results of this report.

Type	Client	Object	Status	Date	CTS Project	Text	Author	SolMan Project	IMG Project	Chg. Proc.	Task List
	200	S71K900026	ES	03/12/2012	S71_P00003	S 8000000231: November 9 ChaRM Webinar - NC	NWILLIAMS	ZCHARM71	ZCHARM71_1	8000000231	M000000001
	200	S71K900028	ES	11/14/2011	S71_P00003	S 8000000222: November 9 ChaRM Webinar - UC	NWILLIAMS	ZCHARM71	ZCHARM71_1	8000000222	H000000002
	200	S71K900031	ES	11/14/2011	S71_P00003	S 8000000237: Test 11/14 v1	NWILLIAMS	ZCHARM71	ZCHARM71_1	8000000237	H000000003
	200	S71K900033	ES	11/14/2011	S71_P00003	S 8000000238: 11/14 NC	NWILLIAMS	ZCHARM71	ZCHARM71_1	8000000238	M000000001
	200	S71K900035	ES	11/14/2011	S71_P00003	S71K900033 : Generated test transport	NWILLIAMS	ZCHARM71	ZCHARM71_1	8000000238	M000000001
	200	S71K900036	ES	11/14/2011	S71_P00003	S71K900033 : Generated test transport	NWILLIAMS	ZCHARM71	ZCHARM71_1	8000000238	M000000001
	200	S71K900038	ES	11/18/2011	S71_P00003	S 8000000256: Demo 11/18 1	NWILLIAMS	ZCHARM71	ZCHARM71_1	8000000256	H000000006
	200	S71K900040	ES	11/18/2011	S71_P00003	S 8000000258: I need a new address type for G	NWILLIAMS	ZCHARM71	ZCHARM71_1	8000000258	H000000007

Figure 15.96 Activated Object Reporting: Fetched Object Data

15.7.5 Transport Request Import Strategy (Status-Dependent Imports)

With the release of SAP Solution Manager 7.1, you can now control the import strategy of the transport requests controlled by Change Request Management based on the status of the change document.

Operational Use

Background jobs that trigger the import of transport requests are concerned only that the transport request has been released and is awaiting import in the transport buffer. However, there are certain change document status values that are set after the transport request has been released but before it's intended to be imported into production. From an operational point of view, the change and release managers don't necessarily want it to go to production just yet. Unfortunately, the status in the change document doesn't prevent this unless you specify the transport request import strategy as we describe here.

With this functionality, changes will be imported into the production system based on their status value and not based solely on whether they are in the production buffer. This can invite risk for urgent change documents, especially because import jobs that run periodically would pick up urgent changes that are in the SUCCESSFULLY TESTED status.

In this use-case example, we'll configure the transport request import strategy so that the transport request in an urgent change can't be promoted to the production system unless the urgent change status reaches the AUTHORIZED FOR IMPORT status.

Configuration Activities

1. Execute the IMG activity SPECIFY TRANSPORT REQUEST IMPORT STRATEGY.

2. Select the NEW ENTRIES button.

3. Maintain the information in the IMPORT STRATEGY table as shown in Figure 15.97.

4. Click SAVE.

5. Highlight the entry you just created in the IMPORT STRATEGY table, and double-click the IMPORT STATUS DEPENDENT folder on the left side of the screen.

Figure 15.97 Maintain New Entries for Import Strategy

6. In the CHANGE VIEW "IMPORT STATUS DEPENDENT": OVERVIEW screen, click the NEW ENTRIES button.

7. In the IMPORT STATUS DEPENDENT table, make the relevant changes so that the appropriate transaction type, status profile, and status are maintained (Figure 15.98).

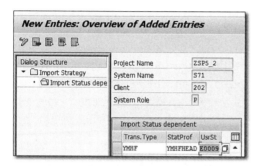

Figure 15.98 Specify Import Status Dependent Data

8. Click SAVE.

Expected Result(s)

When a periodic import job is run that imports released transports into the quality assurance system, transport requests associated with urgent changes can't be picked up by the import job unless the status is set to AUTHORIZED FOR PRODUCTION.

Keep in mind that this example is only to show you the benefit of the functionality and how to enable it for your customer transaction types. Each organization may or may not have a requirement that involves the maintenance of an import strategy that is dependent on status values. If no settings are made in these tables, all released transport requests for change documents will be imported if they are in the buffer when the import job runs, regardless of their document status.

15.8 Additional Features

In this section, we will provide use case examples of additional features within Change Request Management.

15.8.1 View 7.0 Transaction Types in SAP CRM Web UI

For customers that have been using SAP Solution Manager 7.0 Service Desk and ChaRM components, there is an option to have the related transaction types searchable in the SAP CRM Web UI.

Operational Use

While you can have the ability to view 7.0-based transactions in the SAP CRM Web UI, processing must take place in the SAP GUI for 7.0-based transaction types, end users can still have the search and monitoring capabilities in one central location.

In the following configuration activities, we'll provide the steps necessary to view both standard SAP Solution Manager transaction types as well as customer-specific transaction types in the SAP CRM Web UI.

Configuration Activities

View Standard Transaction Types in SAP CRM Web UI

1. Execute the IMG activity DEFINE TRANSACTION TYPES.

2. Select a 7.0-based SAP ITSM transaction type (SD*), and double-click the CHANNEL folder on the left side of the screen (Figure 15.99).

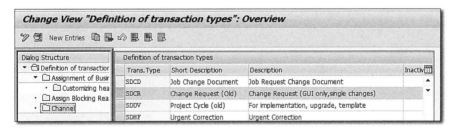

Figure 15.99 Select Channel for 7.0 Transaction Type

By default, the channel table is empty for the 7.0-based transaction types.

3. Click the NEW ENTRIES button (Figure 15.100).

Figure 15.100 Select New Entries

4. Enter the channel "CRM WEBCLIENT UI" (Figure 15.101).

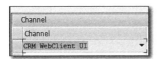

Figure 15.101 Enter Channel

5. Click SAVE.

View Customer Transaction Types in the SAP CRM Web UI

If you've created your own customer transaction types in SAP Solution Manager 7.0, you'll need to connect the Schedule Manager to your 7.0 transaction types using a standard implementation.

1. Execute the IMG activity ASSIGN IMPLEMENTATION TO CHANGE TRANSACTION TYPES.

2. Create your customer transaction types (7.0) in the IMPLEMENTATION OF PROXY INSTANCES table as shown in Figure 15.102. For the appropriate specifications for each transaction type, refer to the standard transaction types and their respective settings.

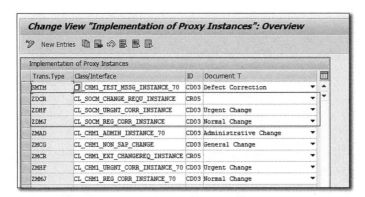

Figure 15.102 Assign Implementation Class to Customer Transaction Types

Expected Result(s)

Based on the configuration activities in this section, you should now be able to view both SD* and ZD* 7.0 SAP ITSM transaction types in the SAP CRM Web UI as shown in Figure 15.103. Release 7.0 transaction types can be searched for, filtered on, and monitored in the SAP CRM Web UI.

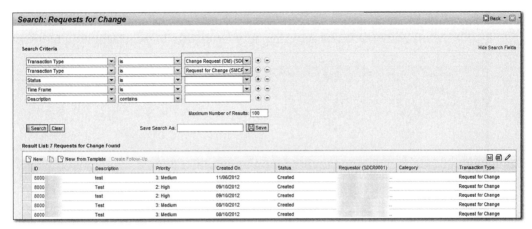

Figure 15.103 7.0 Transaction Types in SAP CRM Web UI

15.8.2 Define Risk Levels

In addition to impact, urgency and priority you also can define different levels of risk which can be assigned to your request for change document.

Operational Use

Risk levels can be configured according to your organization's requirements for tracking and reporting metrics related to the request for change process. SAP Solution Manager doesn't provide standard risk values out of the box because risk criteria typically vary across organizations. In the configuration activities in the next section, we explain how risk levels can be easily configured to support a more thorough reporting service in the request for change process. Further, we provide some examples of risk levels we've seen across various customer use cases.

Risk values aren't assigned to a specific transaction type; they are global settings. Therefore, if you're using more than one request for a change transaction type in the enterprise, you'll need to coordinate with the other departments to agree on a globally accepted standard set of risk values that can be used enterprise-wide.

Configuration Activities

1. Execute the IMG activity DEFINE RISK LEVELS OF REQUEST FOR CHANGE.

2. Click the NEW ENTRIES button (Figure 15.104).

3. Maintain the risk levels according to your Change Management requirements.

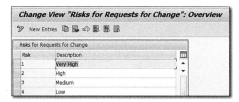

Figure 15.104 Define Risk Levels

4. Click SAVE.

Expected Result(s)

The risk levels will now appear in the RISK field on the request for change document (Figure 15.105).

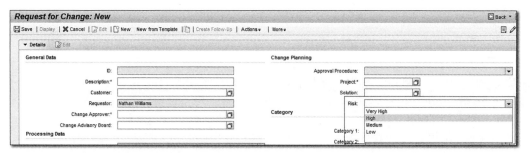

Figure 15.105 Risk Levels in Request for Change

15.8.3 Adjust the Behavior of UI Objects by Status

You have the ability to control, via configuration, the behavior of various object types within the SAP CRM Web UI. Further, these behaviors can be enabled depending on the status of the change document.

Operational Use

Certain SAP CRM Web UI objects in change documents are editable in regards to changeability and visibility. You can choose to deactivate and/or hide certain buttons in specific assignment blocks. Furthermore, you can specify whether fields or pushbuttons can be changed or visible according to document status. If you want certain features available when the status is Create, but you don't want them available when the status is In Development, the Customizing will support that.

Pushbuttons can only be specified as usable. They are either visible and active or visible and inactive depending on the settings. In our example, we'll show you how to hide the Release Transport Request pushbutton from the urgent change document when the urgent change is in the status In Development.

Configuration Activities

1. Execute the IMG activity Adjust UI Objects by User Status.

2. The Customizing process presents two ways to search for the relevant pushbuttons and associated configuration.

3. For our example, select the first option Selection From All Transaction Types (Figure 15.106).

Figure 15.106 Selection from All Transaction Types

4. In the Change View "Transaction Types": Overview screen, highlight the customer transaction type (e.g., YMHF), and double-click the UI Objects folder in the dialog structure (Figure 15.107).

   As shown in Figure 15.108, you must locate the ID of the UI object (this can be cross-referenced in the IMG documentation of this activity).

5. Mark the settings per your requirements. For our scenario, we don't want the field to be editable or visible, so we're setting the value to both fields as False. Further, you can cross-reference the value in the User Status column with the values in Table TJ30 to determine at which point the UI object should reflect your configuration.

Change View "Transaction Types": Overview
New Entries
Dialog Structure
Transaction Types
UI Objects
Transaction Types
Trans.Type
Description
YMCR
Enowa Request for Change
YMHF
Enowa Urgent Change with TMS

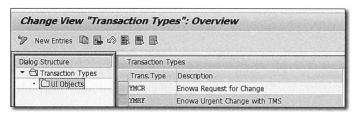

Figure 15.107 Select UI Objects Folder

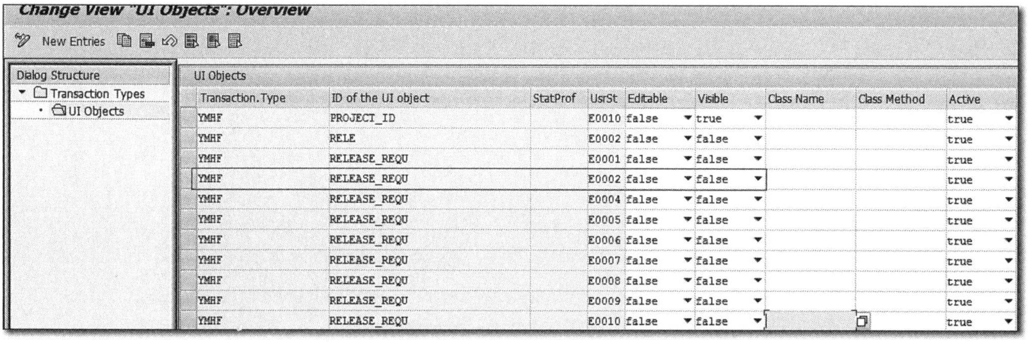

Change View "UI Objects": Overview
New Entries
Dialog Structure
Transaction Types
UI Objects
UI Objects
Transaction.Type | ID of the UI object | StatProf | UsrSt | Editable | Visible | Class Name | Class Method | Active
YMHF | PROJECT_ID | E0010 | false | true | true
YMHF | RELE | E0002 | false | false | true
YMHF | RELEASE_REQU | E0001 | false | false | true
YMHF | RELEASE_REQU | E0002 | false | false | true
YMHF | RELEASE_REQU | E0004 | false | false | true
YMHF | RELEASE_REQU | E0005 | false | false | true
YMHF | RELEASE_REQU | E0006 | false | false | true
YMHF | RELEASE_REQU | E0007 | false | false | true
YMHF | RELEASE_REQU | E0008 | false | false | true
YMHF | RELEASE_REQU | E0009 | false | false | true
YMHF | RELEASE_REQU | E0010 | false | false | true

Figure 15.108 Mark Editable and Visible Fields

6. Click SAVE.

Expected Result(s)

When you execute the associated process from the SAP CRM Web UI, your changes should be reflected per the UI object ID maintained and according to the status for which it was set. As shown in Figure 15.109, the RELEASE TRANSPORT REQUEST button isn't visible in the TRANSPORT REQUEST assignment block during the IN DEVELOPMENT status.

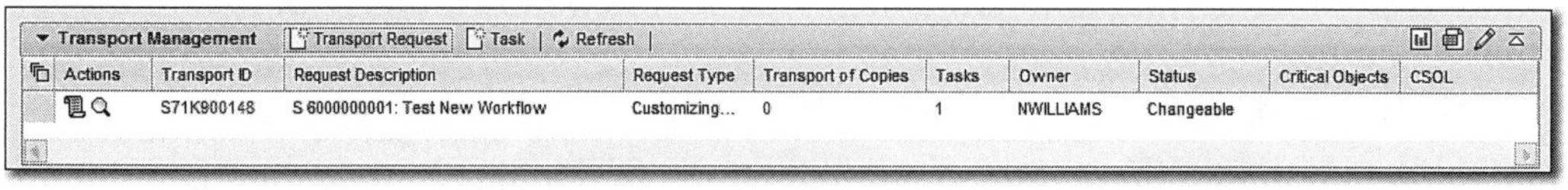

Transport Management
Transport Request
Task
Refresh
Actions | Transport ID | Request Description | Request Type | Transport of Copies | Tasks | Owner | Status | Critical Objects | CSOL
S71K900148 | S 6000000001: Test New Workflow | Customizing... | 0 | 1 | NWILLIAMS | Changeable

Figure 15.109 SAP CRM Web UI Object Modified in the Change Document

15.8.4 Define Which Transaction Types Must Be Completed with a Project Cycle

You can define which change documents must be completely closed before a maintenance cycle or project cycle is completed, whereas default configuration allows open transaction types to be de-coupled from the projects and re-assigned to a subsequent cycle.

Operational Use

When a project cycle or maintenance cycle is completed, change transactions that haven't been completed (e.g., promoted to production or withdrawn from the project) are decoupled from the project. They in turn lose their link to the CTS project as well as the IMG project. These open transaction types therefore can't be completed until a new maintenance cycle or project cycle is reopened from the project. At that point, they are recoupled and can continue with normal processing.

For certain transaction types, this can invoke a risk to software logistics and the integrity of the production system. If the transition between project cycles takes a while, urgent changes that are true emergencies can't be processed.

In this activity, you can identify specific transaction types that must be completed before the project cycle can be closed. In our example, we'll copy the standard urgent change into our customer namespace and flag it as required to be completed for the project cycle to be completed.

Configuration Activities

1. Execute the IMG activity DEFINE TRANSACTION TYPES TO BE COMPLETED WITH A PROJECT CYCLE.
2. Highlight the SMHF transaction type, and click the COPY As button (Figure 15.110).
3. Maintain your customer transaction type in the respective column (Figure 15.111).
4. Place an "X" in the COMPLETION column.
5. Press [Enter].
6. Click SAVE.

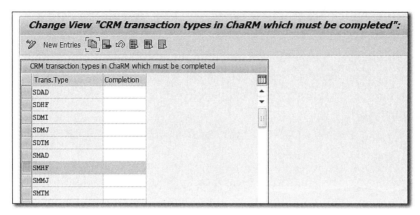

Figure 15.110 Copy Standard Transaction Type

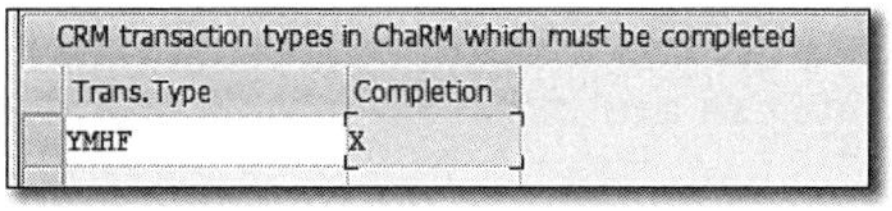

CRM transaction types in ChaRM which must be completed	
Trans. Type	Completion
YMHF	X

Figure 15.111 Specify Completion Flag for Customer Urgent Change

Expected Result(s)

A new value will be entered into the CRM TRANSACTION TYPES IN ChaRM WHICH MUST BE COMPLETED table (Figure 15.112). Further, the SAP Solution Manager system will issue you a hard stop if the IT operator or administrator attempts to advance the project cycle phase to completed, when there are outstanding urgent changes.

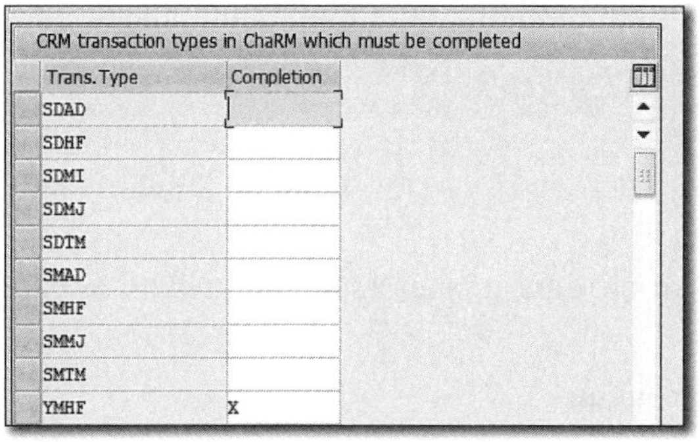

CRM transaction types in ChaRM which must be completed	
Trans. Type	Completion
SDAD	
SDHF	
SDMI	
SDMJ	
SDTM	
SMAD	
SMHF	
SMMJ	
SMTM	
YMHF	X

Figure 15.112 CRM Transaction Types in ChaRM Which Must Be Completed

15.9   Summary

This chapter exposed you to both the foundational and functional configuration steps required to advance your organization's ChaRM scenario to meet specific requirements. You should be familiar with the basic and standard setup activities, which must occur after the prerequisites have been met. You should also have a strong knowledge of how to leverage the use-case examples we've shared to integrate them into your own scenarios.

While ChaRM processes and workflow are configured out of the box, there is still some configuration work to do to get the processes running successfully end to end, in your own customer namespace. From there, explore and practice the functional components that expand the standard workflow into a best-of-breed messaging and change control tool.

In the next chapter, we'll discuss the Maintenance and Project Administration components of Change Request Management. Now that the functional configuration has been completed, it's time to create an SAP Solution Manager project and cycle that is activated by Change Request Management.

Change Request Management deploys maintenance and project adminis-tration functionality to facilitate logistical activities related to transport requests. These functionalities provide the ability to enable a controlled release of transports throughout the implementation and deployment of changes.

16 Maintenance and Project Administration Activities

In Chapter 12 we discussed how ChaRM functions were executed by the ChaRM business partners from an end-user, process-oriented manner. In this chapter, we'll go one level deeper and explain how ChaRM works from a maintenance and administrative perspective. We'll provide information around the abstract layer that is positioned between the process flows executed from the SAP CRM Web UI and the Change and Transport System (CTS) in the managed system.

This layer includes SAP Solution Manager projects and their associated cycles. Within these two components lie other technical areas that support how transport requests are created, implemented, released, and imported throughout the system landscape.

We'll describe all of these components and how they're positioned to support the release of changes to a production system whether you're implementing, upgrading, rolling out, or supporting an SAP solution. In addition to explaining these concepts and features, we'll walk through the steps needed to create an SAP Solution Manager maintenance project and maintenance cycle. First, we'll begin by describing the concepts of implementation and maintenance projects.

16.1 Implementation and Maintenance Projects

We'll begin by discussing the critical aspects of SAP Solution Manager projects and how they are integrated with various architectural components within

ChaRM. We'll provide an overview of how the SAP Solution Manager projects are the basis for providing change control via ChaRM for implementing new solutions as well as maintaining a live solution. We'll then walk through the steps to create a maintenance project in SAP Solution Manager.

16.1.1 Overview and Architecture

SAP Solution Manager projects are used to support the implementation, upgrade, global rollout, and maintenance of SAP solutions. In this chapter, we'll focus on two distinct SAP Solution Manager project types: implementation project and maintenance project.

> **Note**
>
> When we refer to an *implementation project*, we're referring to the implementation of a solution, which can also relate to upgrade or template projects.

Throughout the implementation of new SAP solutions or during the maintenance of an existing solution that has already gone live, changes of various scope will need to be implemented and eventually promoted to production. The variables associated with the scope can include urgency, risk, impact, and criticality directly correlated with reducing downtime in business operations.

SAP Solution Manager projects—activated for ChaRM—provide the functionality to support release approaches for changes that vary in regards to scope. Changes that are deemed urgent have one strategy for release management. This strategy provides a rapid, seamless flow of changes that are imported into the production system as quickly as the actions are selected in the frontend ChaRM application. On the other hand, strict strategies are available for bundling changes in larger, periodic releases to minimalize impact to the production system.

Establishing these projects in the SAP Solution Manager system is a prerequisite before ChaRM can be activated to enable change control. Thus, they are foundational for both production support as well as the implementation of new solutions. These projects can be considered the high-level plan used to balance and manage activities related to planning as well as software logistics, throughout the lifecycle of a change. They provide the basis for the integration of the central repository for all information and activities associated with processing a change.

Processing a change begins with the request for change and continues all the way to bundling changes together for production import.

> **Note**
>
> Project assignment of each transport request is mandatory when your project or maintenance landscape is ChaRM activated. No transport requests can be created or released without being assigned to a project. This results in control over transport requests because they must be created and released via actions driven within the ChaRM component in SAP Solution Manager.

Projects that have been ChaRM activated manage maintenance cycles, described in the next section, which are defined by release management.

Implementation or maintenance projects can be used to distribute changes to one or many SAP landscapes, depending on the strategy of the IT organization and how the Transport Management System (TMS) is set up by the technical infrastructure teams.

Architecture

Figure 16.1 provides a high-level representation of the overall architecture of ChaRM in regards to its foundational project base. An SAP Solution Manager project, depending on the state of the solution, is linked to the cycle. If the solution is being implemented, a project cycle is relevant. If the solution is being maintained in a productive state, a maintenance cycle is relevant.

The cycle is controlled via phases, which we'll discuss in detail in the following section. The activities regarding the implementation and release of changes are controlled and depend on which phase the project or maintenance cycle is in. Similarly, the cycle determines at which point changes can be introduced into the project. As the figure denotes, there are guidelines on when normal changes, defect corrections, and urgent corrections can be introduced according to the phase of the cycle.

Typically, project cycles have a defined start and end period along with defined phase durations. Maintenance cycles, on the other hand, support a continuous process for providing change control to productive solutions. As identified by the dotted arrow, maintenance cycles can continue to run as part of ongoing maintenance to the live solution.

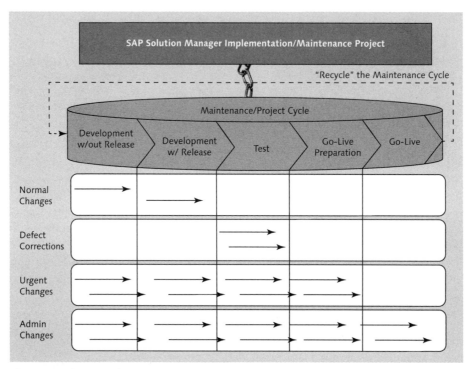

Figure 16.1 ChaRM Architecture

In addition to the maintenance or project cycle (discussed in the next section), there are specific components that comprise the architecture for SAP Solution Manager projects:

▶ **Implementation, template, or upgrade project**
These project types, once activated for ChaRM, support changes that relate to the implementation or upgrade of a solution. The start point, end point, and project phases all have durations defined by project management. Implementation projects have functions to support a project. Template projects have added functions to support a template rollout (global, spin-off, consolidation, merger, etc.). Upgrade projects prepare an organization for accepting new functionality.

▶ **Maintenance project**
A maintenance project supports the ongoing changes that are required to sustain a production system. Like the previously mentioned project types, maintenance projects divide project management and release management activities

into phases. Changes that are emergencies (i.e., urgent changes) can be processed at almost any point in time.

▸ **Logical components**
A logical component contains the systems necessary to provide a production system with changes. A single logical component, for example, would include the system ID and client number (e.g., DSM:100) for each system in the landscape. Multiple logical components could be assigned to a ChaRM project, depending on the scope and strategy of release management. The systems within a logical component are also defined with the appropriate transport routes in TMS.

▸ **IMG project**
The IMG project is created from and identifiable in the SAP Solution Manager system in project administration. However, it's created on and lives within the development system of the assigned logical component. The IMG project groups changes made in the development system into a single project, which is linked to and controlled by the SAP Solution Manager project. If your project has multiple landscapes, an IMG project must be created for each development system of the associated logical components.

▸ **CTS project**
The CTS project is a container in the logical system that bundles transport requests that belong to a single IMG project. A logical system is represented by a system ID: client combination (e.g., DSM:110). A CTS project is created by SAP Solution Manager for each logical system. The CTS project separates itself from the system when the task list is completed and is no longer available after that point.

16.1.2 Implementation, Template, and Upgrade Projects

Implementation, template, and upgrade projects are all project types in SAP Solution Manager. They act as the central repository for business processes (the implementation scope). Additionally, elements such as documentation, transaction, configuration objects, development objects, and end-user training materials are mapped to the business processes. SAP Solution Manager centrally manages and organizes the critical aspects of an implementation, rollout, or upgrade by providing this capability. Further, these projects are integrated into other areas of Application Lifecycle Management (ALM) as well as SAP IT Service Management to support the end-to-end management and deployment of a solution.

Common examples for starting off with any one of these project types include the following:

▶ Implementation project for SAP Funds Management

▶ Upgrade from SAP ECC 4.6 to 6.0

▶ Roll out existing business processes to Italy (for example)

Optionally, these projects can be ChaRM enabled, which means when you activate ChaRM for these project types, all changes associated with the project are controlled and released according to the delivered workflow provided by SAP. The implementation and release activities are divided among various phases of the project cycle. We'll discuss these phases in Section 16.2.4.

Implementation projects are specific to implementing a solution. There is a clear start point for an implementation as well as a defined end point. Moreover, each phase (i.e., development, testing, etc.) has a defined duration according to the overall project plan. SAP Solution Manager provides the workflow, control, and processing functionality to manage and release changes according to each of these phases.

Figure 16.2 is a representation of how implementation projects are structured at a high level. You'll notice that this diagram is very similar to Figure 16.1, with a few differences.

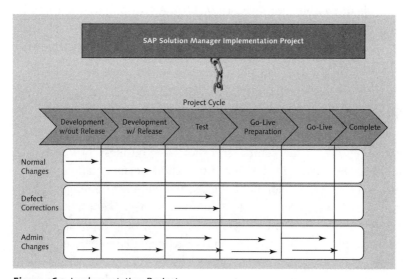

Figure 16.2 Implementation Project

First, you'll notice the absence of urgent changes. Urgent changes aren't permitted in implementation projects because new functionality is not yet in production. Because there is no production system, there are no changes that should be deemed emergencies. Second, you'll notice that the project cycle ends after it's completed (i.e., it's not continuous). Because implementation projects focus on the implementation of a solution, after that solution has gone live, the project is over and therefore can be completed in the SAP Solution Manager system. New implementations should be represented by a new implementation project.

16.1.3 Maintenance Projects

Maintenance projects, another project type in SAP Solution Manager, are used to enable the control of implementation and release activities during production support. After an implementation project goes live, it's recommended that the business processes within that project are migrated to a solution in SAP Solution Manager.

The *solution* is a logical representation of a collection of business functionality deployed in production. It represents all component parts needed to support a business in production. As part of go-live (during cutover or before), it's recommended to migrate the content from your template or implementation projects into the solution. The intent of the solution is to always represent what is in production separately from work in process associated with other projects, standard releases associated with releases, or break fixes (i.e., bug fixes in production or the system not performing as designed).

Like template and implementation projects, the maintenance project has a business process hierarchy (BPH) structure. However, the maintenance project is intended for use in release management for periodic and controlled updates to production. For the most part, these aren't associated with bigger functionality releases or rollouts. You can use the maintenance project for routine maintenance and minor enhancements to the solution that are rolled out per a planned maintenance cycle.

It's recommended to integrate the solution and maintenance project together and use a check-in/check-out functionality should changes arise for a productive business process.

Figure 16.3 provides a representation for how maintenance projects fit in with the overall architecture of ChaRM. In addition to the change transactions supported by implementation projects (i.e., normal, urgent, defect correction, and administrative), maintenance projects also support the handling of urgent changes. Because maintenance projects manage the ongoing changes that occur in a production landscape, the urgent change process is available for emergencies that occur to functionality that is live.

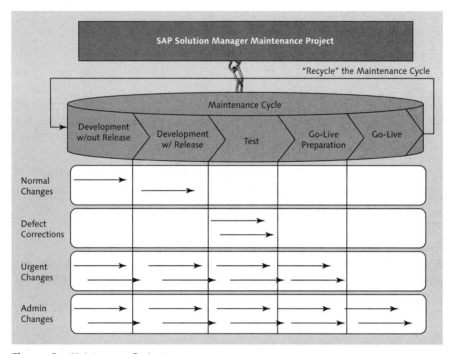

Figure 16.3 Maintenance Project

Like the implementation project, a maintenance project has a defined start. The defined start is at the point in which production support begins or the point in which you activate ChaRM for your maintenance environment. It's recommended that these activities occur immediately following the stability of transport requests post go-live. Typically, this period is 60 days after go-live. Depending on the volume of transports and stability of your maintenance landscape, it's recommended that ChaRM be introduced to your team when transport volume has been reduced and support teams have been accustomed to supporting the live solution.

16.1.4 Creating an SAP Solution Manager Project

Now that you have a basic understanding of the various project types in SAP Solution Manager that can be ChaRM enabled, we'll walk through the steps of creating one of these projects. In the scenario in the following subsections, we'll describe the step-by-step activities required to create a maintenance project in SAP Solution Manager.

Prerequisites

Prior to creating an SAP Solution Manager ChaRM-activated project, there are a few mandatory requirements:

- The managed systems (implementation or maintenance landscape) must be set up to support a ChaRM environment. This means that RFC connections from the SAP Solution Manager system to the managed systems (and back) must be established. Logical components must also be set up in the Landscape Management Database (LMDB). It's recommended that you perform these activities as part of SOLMAN_SETUP. Alternatively, the SAP Solution Manager IMG can point you to the documentation and transactions.

- The basic settings in the SAP Solution Manager IMG must be completed. Cross-reference these settings with those that you've performed in SOLMAN_SETUP; often there are duplicates.

- TMS must be set up for the managed systems according to ChaRM TMS requirements (see Chapter 14). These activities can be found in the CHANGE REQUEST MANAGEMENT section of the IMG.

- Users must be created in the managed systems.

Create Project and Maintain General Details

In this step, we'll walk through the steps to create the "shell" of the SAP Solution Manager project, maintain some general details, and save the project.

1. Execute Transaction SOLAR_PROJECT_ADMIN.

2. In the PROJECT ADMINISTRATION – SAP SOLUTION MANAGER screen, select the CREATE (▯) button as shown in Figure 16.4.

3. In the CREATE PROJECT screen, enter a PROJECT ID and project type (TYP) as shown in Figure 16.5.

Figure 16.4 Project Administration Home Page

> **Note**
>
> The PROJECT ID can be no more than 10 characters. It can't be changed at a later time. It's important to discuss the project ID with members of your team to develop a naming standard that will be consistent when future implementation/maintenance projects are created.

Figure 16.5 Create Project

4. Click the checkmark icon. The project create screen will appear as shown in Figure 16.6. For the purposes of our exercise, we'll walk through the required steps to create the ChaRM project.

5. Enter a name for the project in the TITLE field (the project title can be renamed at any point). Like the project ID, we recommend naming your ChaRM projects in a consistent and standard fashion.

6. Select a language from the PROJECT LANGUAGE field.

7. Click the SAVE button. As soon as you save the project for the first time, you'll see the ENHANCEMENT FOR DOCUMENTS box appear to confirm the knowledge warehouse version (Figure 16.7).

8. Press [Enter] to confirm.

The project is now created with an ID, title, and general data. Remember, these are the bare essentials required to save an implementation or maintenance project. You may explore the other tabs within the project to determine which information and data you'll manage within the project details.

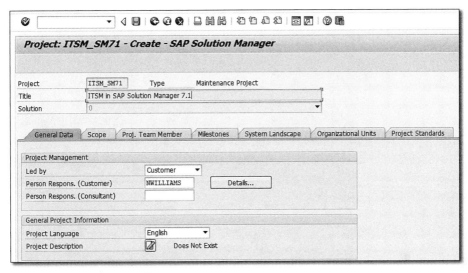

Figure 16.6 Maintain General Project Data

Figure 16.7 Confirm Enhancements for Documents

Add Systems

In this section, we'll add the managed systems that will be controlled by ChaRM. This involves adding the logical component, created as part of the prerequisites, to our newly created project.

1. Assuming you haven't left the project screen, select the SYSTEM LANDSCAPE tab and the SYSTEMS subtab as shown in Figure 16.8.

2. In the LOGICAL COMPONENTS column, select the button to search for available logical components.

3. In the SELECT LOGICAL COMPONENT FOR SYSTEM LANDSCAPE window, select the appropriate logical component (Figure 16.9).

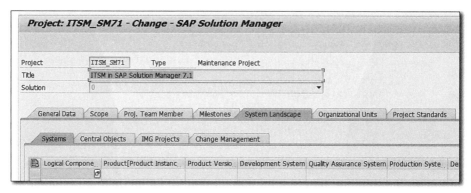

Figure 16.8 Maintain Systems

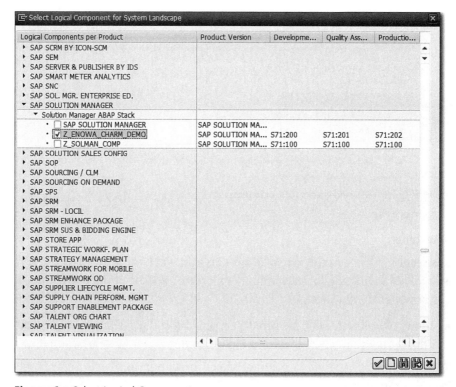

Figure 16.9 Select Logical Component

4. Press ⎡Enter⎤. The logical component entry will now appear in the Systems sub-tab. As shown in Figure 16.10, it will contain the ID of the logical component, the product, version, and system/role assignments.

You may choose to select additional logical components, given the assumption that those system landscapes will be included in the maintenance/project cycle.

Figure 16.10 Logical Component Added to Project

5. Click SAVE.

The logical component is now assigned to your project. The assignment of the logical component enables the project to create the IMG project because a development system has been included in the SYSTEMS tab.

> **Important!**
>
> Any maintenance to the project or maintenance landscape (adding systems, changing systems, deleting systems, etc.) must be scheduled and performed accordingly. Changes to the TMS settings, logical components, system landscape, and so on must be conducted when a maintenance cycle is closed. Inconsistencies and errors may occur if changes of these types occur during the course of a project or maintenance project.

Create IMG Project

In this step, we'll create the IMG project. The IMG project groups changes made in the development system into a single project, which is linked to and controlled by the SAP Solution Manager project.

1. Choose the IMG PROJECTS subtab within the SYSTEMS tab from within your project. You'll see that a logical system is already assigned, which is based on the development system within the logical component.

2. Highlight the logical system as shown in Figure 16.11.

3. Click the CREATE button. (Note there are two CREATE buttons. Select the CREATE button on the far left side.)

4. Select the option NO, LATER when prompted by the system (Figure 16.12). On selecting the NO, LATER option, you'll be immediately logged in to the development system of the logical component you assigned to the project.

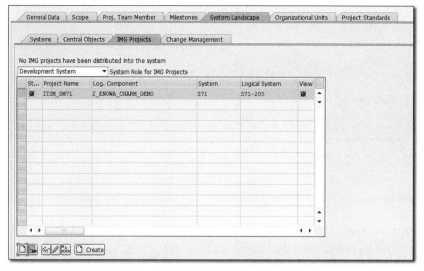

Figure 16.11 Create IMG Project

Figure 16.12 Create Transport Later

Within that system, you'll be within the IMG project (Figure 16.13), otherwise accessible via Transaction SPRO_ADMIN in the development system.

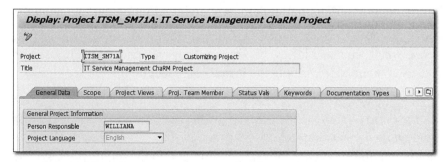

Figure 16.13 Project IMG

There is no action needed in this screen at this time.

5. Select the BACK button within the browser to return to project administration. The IMG project is created via the automatic scheduling of a background job triggered from SAP Solution Manager. When the background job has completed, you'll receive a notification message as represented in Figure 16.14.

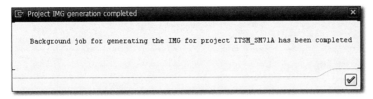

Figure 16.14 Project IMG Generation Completed

6. Press [Enter] to confirm. As shown in Figure 16.15, the IMG project is now identified as complete with the green status. The red status that you see is for the project view. This can be ignored.

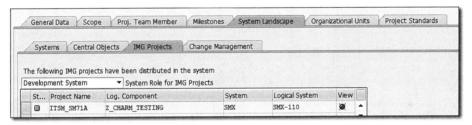

Figure 16.15 Successfully Generated Project IMG

7. Click SAVE.

The IMG project is now successfully generated for the ChaRM project, based on the development system included in the logical component.

Activate Change Request Management

In the final step of creating the ChaRM project, we'll activate the Change Request Management functionality.

1. In the CHANGE MANAGEMENT subtab of the SYSTEM LANDSCAPE tab, select the option to ACTIVATE CHANGE REQUEST MANAGEMENT as shown in Figure 16.16.

2. Confirm your selection in the ACTIVATE CHANGE REQUEST MANAGEMENT window.

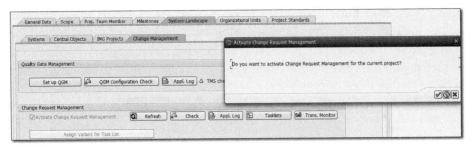

Figure 16.16 Confirm Activation

3. Click SAVE.

Now that we've provided an overview of the projects that can be activated for use by ChaRM, we'll discuss the concept of maintenance and project cycles.

Navigate to Project

After you initially save the SAP Solution Manager project, it can be accessed via the project administration Transaction SOLAR_PROJECT_ADMIN. When this transaction is executed, the PROJECT ADMINISTRATION – SAP SOLUTION MANAGER screen appears as shown in Figure 16.17. To access the project, follow these steps:

1. To navigate to your project, scroll the table entry of all projects in your SAP Solution Manager system to locate it.

2. Double-click the table entry, and you can maintain the settings described in Section 16.1.4.

Figure 16.17 Project Administration Home Page

Now that you understand the concept of SAP Solution Manager projects and how they relate to ChaRM, we'll go over the next piece that's required to use ChaRM to manage changes within your environment: maintenance and project cycles.

16.2   Maintenance and Project Cycles

Maintenance cycles and project cycles are both defined by a SAP CRM document type that controls which software logistic and transport activities can occur throughout the implementation or support of your SAP solution. These cycles are organized according to various phases. Each of these phases control which activities and change documents can be created or executed at any given point during the implementation and release of a change. Further, they group the systems within the logical component assigned to the SAP Solution Manager project. All transport activities and software logistics are based on the logical component(s) assigned to your SAP Solution Manager project.

These phases are delivered standard from SAP Solution Manager and don't require maintenance or configuration from the administrator.

> **Note**
>
> It's highly recommended that the functionalities delivered with the cycle transaction types aren't modified via custom development. The phases provide best practices for Change Control Management and should remain preserved from any changes. For this reason, it's not necessary to copy the standard transaction types for maintenance or project cycles into a Z or Y customer namespace.

In this section, we'll describe the concepts of maintenance and project cycles individually. We'll discuss the components of each of these cycle types, including the activities that can and can't be executed during each of their phases. At the end of the section, we'll walk through the steps to create a maintenance cycle within an SAP Solution Manager maintenance project.

16.2.1   Overview and Architecture

Maintenance cycles and project cycles are created once from within the SAP Solution Manager project. After they have been successfully created, the cycle task list and cycle transaction are also generated in the background as part of the initial generation. Figure 16.18 provides a graphical representation of the overall architecture of these components and how they are interrelated across the landscape.

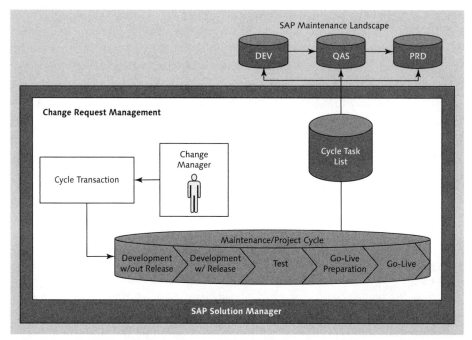

Figure 16.18 Maintenance/Project Cycle Architecture

The following items represent the key components in the preceding overall architecture diagram. We'll discuss these in detail throughout this section:

- **Maintenance/project cycle**
  The layer between the SAP Solution Manager project and the transport track of the managed landscape is structured and organized according to phases that control which activities are performed throughout the implementation and release of transport requests.

- **Cycle transaction**
  This transaction manages the organizational administration of the maintenance or project cycle. The cycle transaction is accessed by the change approver or IT operator to perform phase shifts. Other activities, including monitoring, document management, and reporting, occur within this document.

- **Cycle task list**
  This task list manages the technical administration of the maintenance or project cycle. The cycle task list is based on the systems within the logical component active for the ChaRM project, which is based on TMS configuration.

The time in which your organization enables ChaRM (i.e., implementing a solution or supporting a solution that has gone live) will determine the type of cycle that controls the logistics associated with your SAP landscape. If your organization is in "project" mode and using ChaRM associated with an implementation, template, or upgrade project, then a project cycle controls your project. If your organization is in "support" mode, then a maintenance cycle controls your project.

The maintenance project, according to the scope of the change, is defined by the change approver in the request for change. After the change is approved, and the change document is in the status IN DEVELOPMENT, it's assigned to the cycle specific to the SAP Solution Manager project by the system.

As we've mentioned previously, the type of cycle created depends on the SAP Solution Manager project in which it's created from. Implementation, template, and upgrade projects generate project cycles. Maintenance projects generate maintenance cycles. We'll now take a closer look at each of these cycle types and identify the characteristics of each and how they differ from one another.

Project Cycle

As we've mentioned, project cycles are specific to implementation, template, and upgrade project types.

For these SAP Solution Manager projects, after ChaRM is activated, there is a 1:1 relationship between the project cycle and the project itself. After the changes associated with the project have gone live, the project cycle is completed and therefore closed for that particular implementation. Because implementation projects don't restart, the corresponding cycle should be completed after the changes associated with the implementation have gone live in the production system. Any new implementations will warrant the creation of a new implementation, template, or upgrade project, and therefore a new project cycle will be created.

The project cycle is based on the project landscape. The logical component assigned to your implementation, template, or upgrade project is based on the development, test, and production systems for the solution you're implementing. For the purposes of these project types, the project cycle controls the implementation landscape.

The project cycle is structured according to phases, which are planned by project management. Each project cycle, and the phases that are within it, have a clear start point and end point. The duration is set by project management and enforced when the change manager performs activities according to the project cycle and/or advances its phases. The activities within each of these phases are controlled and therefore support the activities included within each phase of the overall project plan.

We'll describe these activities soon. Figure 16.19 provides an overview of the phases included in a project cycle. You'll also note that this diagram emphasizes that the definite start point and end point to a project cycle.

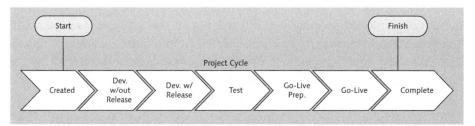

Figure 16.19 Project Cycle Phases

Maintenance Cycle

The maintenance cycle is generated, similar to the project cycle, directly from the SAP Solution Manager maintenance project in the project administration transaction (SOLAR_PROJECT_ADMIN).

The maintenance cycle is a fundamental element for enabling ChaRM for production support. Its start point is the point in which production support for the release period commences. The maintenance cycle's phases and go-live date will be scheduled by the change manager and/or release manager.

Similar to the project cycle, it's the central administrative unit for all transport and software logistics activities. While the project cycle supports the overall project plan, the maintenance cycle supports the organization's maintenance and release strategy. Depending on the maintenance strategy, the maintenance cycle provides the phase control and scheduling capabilities to drive the implementation and deliver the release of these changes into the production system according to defined timelines.

The objective of the maintenance cycle is to centrally manage the distribution of changes to the project systems within the maintenance project to import changes into the production according to a periodic release schedule. It supports routine maintenance with normal changes but also allows for the rapid processing of emergencies with the urgent change functionality.

Urgent changes can be created in all phases of the maintenance cycle. However, they can't be released during the go-live phase of the maintenance cycle. Urgent changes are specific to the maintenance cycle and aren't relevant for the project cycle. Because implementations, upgrades, and rollouts have not yet introduced functionality into a productive environment, there should be no emergencies.

The maintenance cycle can include multiple project tracks within its overall cycle task list (task lists are explained later in this chapter). It can contain one or many SAP ERP tracks, or a blend of products/logical components (i.e., SAP NetWeaver BW, SAP SRM, etc.). While the maintenance cycle can include multiple maintenance landscapes, the relationship between the maintenance cycle and the maintenance project always remains 1:1.

As shown in Figure 16.20, the maintenance cycle shares the same phases that the project cycle uses.

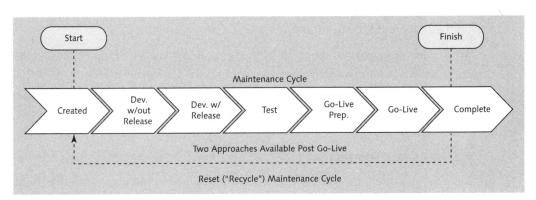

Figure 16.20 Maintenance Cycle Phases

The main differences between the project cycle and the maintenance cycle are as follows:

▶ Maintenance cycles allow for the processing of urgent corrections whereas project cycles don't support urgent changes.

▶ Maintenance cycles can be completed or reset allowing reuse whereas the project cycles must be completed after the import to production occurs.

▶ Maintenance cycles are used for the ongoing support of solutions that have gone live whereas project cycles are used for the implementation, upgrade, or rollout of new solutions within their respective project types.

You'll notice that there is an alternative option after the changes reach the production system. Because maintenance is an ongoing effort, there is an option to reset the phase of the maintenance cycle back to development with release (or development without release) after the changes have gone live. Alternatively, the maintenance cycle can be completed and reopened at go-live. We'll discuss each of these options later in Section 16.3.1.

Similar to the project cycle, the maintenance cycle manages the implementation, release, and import of changes related to a managed system landscape. Software logistics are also maintained. The key difference is that the maintenance cycle manages the production system landscape.

After the maintenance cycle goes live, all of the transport requests within the production buffer (including the urgent changes that have already gone live previously) are imported into the production system. The urgent changes that have previously been imported into the production system are reimported to ensure consistency and synchronization of maintenance changes.

The transport method `IMPORT_PROJECT_ALL` is used to support controlled and consistent transport imports. Transports are imported by project in the order that they are released. This supports consistency and harmonization of transport requests while minimizing risks to the production system.

16.2.2 Cycle Transaction

As we mentioned, the cycle transaction is another component (in addition to the maintenance or project cycle) within the overall architecture. The cycle transaction manages the organizational administration aspects of the project or maintenance cycle. The cycle transaction is represented by a SAP CRM document type. For project cycles, the document is SMDV. For maintenance cycles, the document is SMMN.

As of SAP Solution Manager 7.1, the cycle transaction is processed in the SAP CRM Web UI. You can consider the cycle transaction as the service request for managing the changes that occur to the phases. In addition to changing the phase's documentation, administration, status, and notification occur within the cycle transaction.

Figure 16.21 and Figure 16.22 show a maintenance cycle transaction. As you can see in Figure 16.21, the current project phase is highlighted. The DETAILS assignment block provides organizational information and activity. Business partners, current phase/project, and time stamps are displayed.

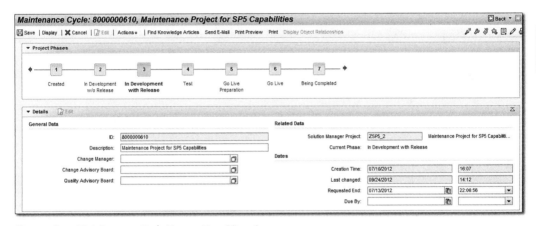

Figure 16.21 Maintenance Cycle Transaction: View 1

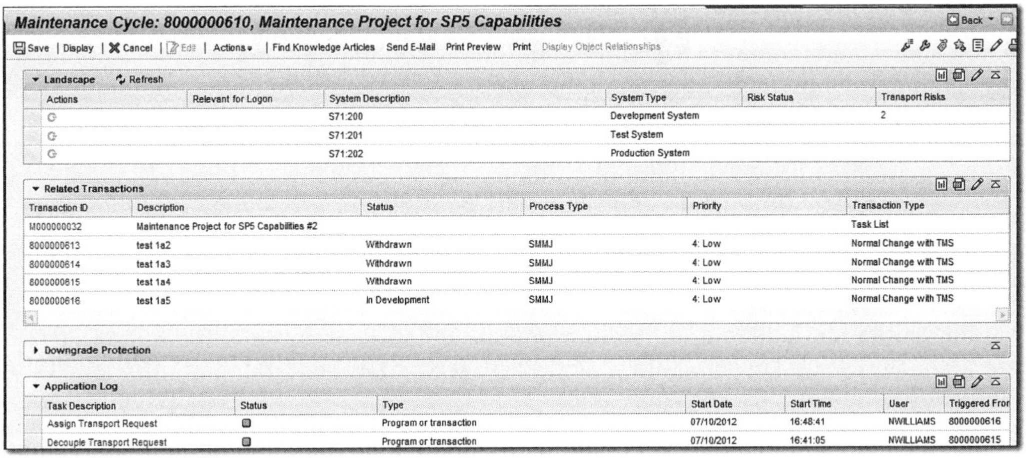

Figure 16.22 Maintenance Cycle Transaction: View 2

In addition to the project phases and details, the landscape data is also included in the cycle transaction. Similar to the change documents, direct logon to the managed landscape is possible within the LANDSCAPE assignment block (Figure 16.22).

In the RELATED TRANSACTIONS assignment block, you're provided with a list of all associated normal changes, urgent changes, administrative changes, and defect corrections that have been assigned to that particular maintenance project. A link is included for direct access to these transactions. The short description, status, priority, transaction type, and process type are just a few characteristics that can be displayed.

Other features, such as the ability to launch downgrade protection and analyze the application log, are also integrated within the SAP CRM Web UI of the cycle transaction.

16.2.3 Cycle Task List

The task list of each project and maintenance cycle manages the technical administration aspects of the respective project. The task list is tightly integrated and based on the configurations maintained in TMS, which are related to the managed system landscape. This means that the task list can control the CTS in the managed system landscape directly from SAP Solution Manager.

The task list provides change and release managers, administrators, and IT operators direct access to activities that need to be performed to meet project planned activities. These activities of course will depend on the authorizations given to these users. These users can see what has been previously scheduled and implemented and when those activities have occurred. The activities are organized by general tasks (tasks that span the entire cycle) and also by system role.

The task list includes a tool referred to as the Schedule Manager to provide an overview of what tasks have been implemented (or attempted to be implemented) and when according to a calendar view. The status is displayed as to whether these tasks have been successfully implemented or failed due to an error (see Figure 16.23).

Double-clicking on these activities will access the application log entry specific to that activity where status analysis can be performed (Figure 16.24).

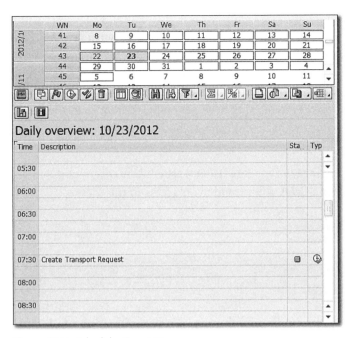

Figure 16.23 Schedule Manager

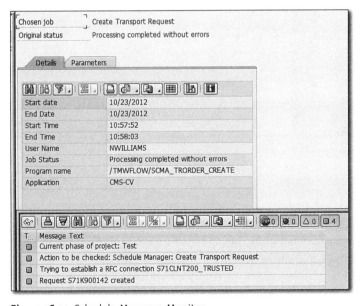

Figure 16.24 Schedule Manager: Monitor

Depending on the role of the user accessing the task list, activities such as creating transports, releasing transports, and importing transports may occur. The automatic logon to the managed systems can occur directly from the task list as well. It's important to note that all of these activities are occurring from the SAP Solution Manager system, which is providing the seamless interface via trusted RFC connections to the managed system. There are general tasks that span the entire landscape, along with activities that are specific to both source systems and target systems.

Figure 16.25 provides an image of the task list and schedule manager of the maintenance cycle. Transaction SCMA will provide you access to this view.

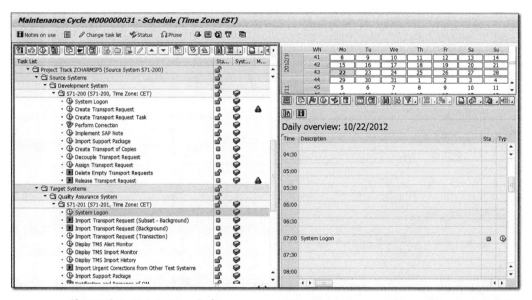

Figure 16.25 Maintenance Cycle

Important!

The cycle task list is a very robust and powerful area in SAP Solution Manager. Most activities involving transport requests can be administered from the cycle task list. It's very important that only administrators, operators, and necessary change managers have authority to access their respective tasks in the cycle task list.

Individual task lists will be generated for urgent changes (i.e., there is a 1:1 relationship for an urgent change and a task list). No manual scheduling or execution of activities can be performed from these task lists because the project track remains locked. The urgent change's task list is closed when the document is set to COMPLETE.

16.2.4 Project and Maintenance Cycle Phases

The activities within the maintenance cycles and project cycles are controlled via their individual phases (i.e., phase control). Phase control is integrated within ChaRM, with each phase being static to the individual project. The objective of phase control is to ensure that transports and software logistics are managed in a controlled manner, according to the project plan and/or maintenance strategy.

Phases control when transport requests can be created, released, or imported, for example. Phases also control which change documents can be created according to the individual phase. For example, defect corrections should only be created when the test phase is set. We'll discuss each of the phases and the activities allowed/not allowed in the upcoming subsections.

The functions within a project may vary slightly depending on the project type. However, each project type shares the same phases. A key example of this concept is that while the phases are the same for an implementation and maintenance project, urgent changes aren't allowed in a project cycle. Project and maintenance cycles are controlled according to the following phases:

- Created
- Development without Release
- Development with Release
- Test
- Go-Live Preparation
- Go-Live
- Being Completed
- Completed

These phases control the activities that can and can't be executed related to the implementation and release of transport requests in to a project. The most important piece of phase control is that only the correct transport activities are permitted according to each phase. This control enables the project, change, and release managers to keep implementation and maintenance activities under control, without introducing conflicts that may prompt negative impacts to the system landscape.

Now, we'll provide a brief overview of each of the phases within a project and maintenance cycle.

Created

When a maintenance or project cycle is first generated from within project administration, it's in the created phase. Because no activities will occur when this status is active, its only purpose is a starting point for either the implementation or maintenance activities. The standard procedure typically involves advancing the phase of the cycle immediately following its creation.

Development without Release

The change manager will set this phase of the cycle at the point in the project in which development can commence. In this phase, transport requests and their tasks can be created but not released. While this provides tight control, it may be too controlled because releasing tasks is part of the standard implementation process for normal changes. In other words, if you're using the normal change type, you won't be able to create test transports or set the action to COMPLETE DEVELOPMENT.

Furthermore, the exports of transport requests aren't permitted. The exception in this case is the export of urgent changes. Normal changes can reach the status IN DEVELOPMENT within this phase, but that's the stopping point.

Based on the restrictions this phase provides in normal changes, it's not uncommon for change managers to skip this phase and advance to the development with release phase.

Development with Release

The most common phase within a maintenance or project cycle is development with release. In this phase, developers are free to create and release transports and their associated tasks. Furthermore, normal changes can be exported to the quality system via the task list or by scheduling the import job in the background.

Because importing transport requests into the quality system is allowed, developers are allowed to perform a unit test both in the development system and the quality system. Because the quality system may contain master data that isn't in the development system, it's beneficial for the developers to test their changes within the quality system before setting the status to Successfully Tested.

As described in Chapter 14, this can be achieved while protecting the production buffer with the test transport functionality. Developers and testers can exchange the change back and forth with the test transport functionality and, when the change is successfully tested, consolidate those changes with the original transport request. Only then is the original transport request, the request intended on reaching production, released from the development system.

Test

Integration, or scenario testing, occurs at the point the change manager switches from the development with release phase to the test phase. At this point, the normal change's transport requests that have been assigned to the maintenance project are released. Any changes that aren't in the status To be Tested can no longer be imported into the quality system. If there are changes that fall into this scenario, the change manager is warned at the time in which the phase is switched within the cycle. This enables a code freeze from the commencement of the test phase.

Normal changes that have unfinished development won't be included in the quality system import or the production import. In the event there are unfinished developments, they can either be tested again, or the normal change can be withdrawn. Alternatively, they can be included in the next import if the cycle is rolled back (reused) to the development with/without release phase or if it's completed.

As we mentioned, testers perform integration testing in the quality system during this phase. Functionality, business relevance, and overall requirements are checked to ensure that the change has been implemented according to the scope within the request for change document.

If errors are found during the test phase, testers can create a defect correction document that allows the developer and tester to work together to introduce a new transport request to correct the error. Because no changes to functionality are relevant, no approvals are necessary for the defect correction. Refer to Chapter 14 for the details of a defect correction document.

New normal changes can be created during the test phase; however, the associated transport requests are prohibited from being exported. Urgent changes are still allowed to be processed as normal, independent of the phases of the maintenance cycle.

The test phase is closed when all of the normal changes and defect corrections have reached the status SUCCESSFULLY TESTED.

Go-Live Preparation

After the normal changes and defect corrections assigned to the maintenance project have been successfully tested, the change manager sets the go-live preparation phase. In the event that additional changes must be introduced within this cycle, transport requests and their tasks can be created, released, and imported during this phase.

These activities aren't performed within requests for change or normal changes and can only be administered from the task list. This means that the facilitation requires special authorizations and will need to be handled by the change approver, IT operator, or administrator.

Urgent changes aren't affected by this phase and can still be processed according to their standard procedures independent of the phase cycle.

Go-Live

The change approver switches the cycle phase to go-live at the point in which the production import will occur. The import involves promoting the entire project buffer into the production system. While we've made several mentions of the release of urgent changes being independent of maintenance or project cycle phases, go-live is the exception. Urgent changes can be created, but they can't be released during this phase. Normal changes and urgent changes are prohibited from being released during the go-live phase of a cycle.

After the entire CTS project buffer is imported into production, no open transports for the project exist, and the transport buffer is clear. Even the urgent changes that were left for reimport after they have been imported are reimported again, and the buffer is reset.

Being Completed

In this phase, the project cycle or maintenance cycle performs additional checks on the change transactions assigned to the SAP Solution Manager project. It will remind you of the change documents that are still in conflicting statuses and therefore will be carried over to the next cycle (Figure 16.26).

Figure 16.26 Warnings and Checks in Maintenance Cycle

Completed

The project or maintenance cycle can be closed when you advance the status to the completed phase. As shown in Figure 16.27, the system will perform a series of checks to remind you of open tasks or activities. You'll then have the option to continue completing the cycle (i.e., ignoring the checks) or addressing them outside of the complete task list wizard.

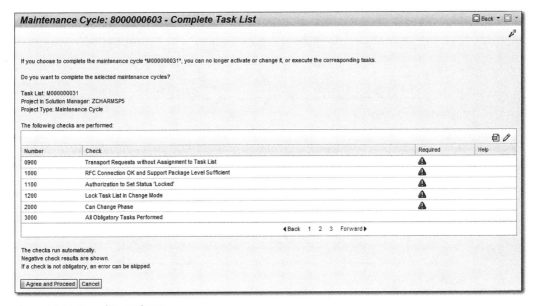

Figure 16.27 Complete Task List

16.2.5 Creating an SAP Solution Manager Maintenance Cycle

In this section, we expand on the previous section that discussed creating an SAP Solution Manager maintenance project. We'll use the example maintenance project from earlier and create a maintenance cycle based on that maintenance project. To create, refresh, and check the status of a maintenance cycle, you'll need to navigate to the SAP Solution Manager project in project administration (Transaction SOLAR_PROJECT_ADMIN).

Create Maintenance Cycle

In the first step, we'll create and name the maintenance cycle. As mentioned before, the name of the maintenance cycle should conform to project nomenclature standards to ensure consistency across projects.

1. In the SYSTEM LANDSCAPE tab and CHANGE REQUEST MANAGEMENT subtab of your project, select the CREATE TASK LIST button (Figure 16.28).

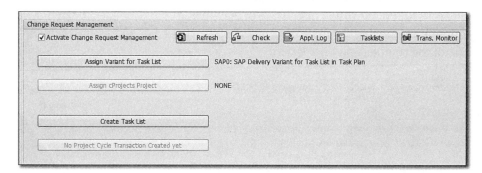

Figure 16.28 Create Task List

2. In the CREATE MAINTENANCE CYCLE screen, enter a name for the maintenance cycle as shown in Figure 16.29.

Figure 16.29 Name Maintenance Cycle

3. Select CONTINUE.

Update Project Phase

In this step, the cycle list and the cycle transaction are generated that build out the overall maintenance cycle. For the developers to begin their work, the change approver must update the maintenance cycle phase status from CREATED to IN DEVELOPMENT WITH RELEASE (or IN DEVELOPMENT WITHOUT RELEASE) in the cycle transaction.

1. After you've confirmed the name of the maintenance cycle, the NEW MAINTENANCE CYCLE screen will appear (Figure 16.30).

2. Select the CHANGE CYCLE button.

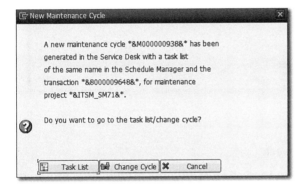

Figure 16.30 New Maintenance Cycle Prompt

> **Note**
>
> As of release 7.1 of SAP Solution Manager, the phases of the maintenance cycle must be set in the cycle transaction. This is performed in the SAP CRM Web UI. After the CYCLE BUTTON is selected, the SAP CRM Web UI is launched taking the change approver to the cycle.

3. Select the EDIT button in the cycle transaction to begin.

4. Advance the phase via the ACTIONS button to the development with release phase (Figure 16.31).

5. Click SAVE.

After saving, the maintenance cycle transaction will be updated to the appropriate phase as shown in Figure 16.32.

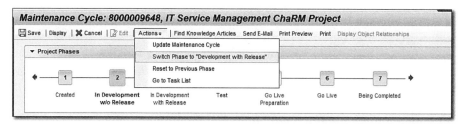

Figure 16.31 Switch Phase to Development with Release

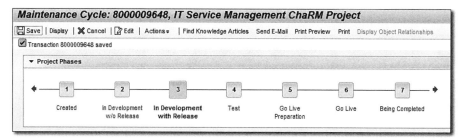

Figure 16.32 Saved Maintenance Cycle

Perform Maintenance Project Check

In this step, we perform a configuration check within the maintenance project to ensure that our configuration is stable with no errors. After we receive all greens within the check, it's safe to begin processing changes through this maintenance project.

In the CHANGE REQUEST MANAGEMENT subtab of our project (Project Administration), select the CHECK button (Figure 16.33).

Figure 16.33 Select Check Button

The system will then perform a series of checks ranging from master data to configuration and even in Transaction STMS. As shown in Figure 16.34, the checks in our project are all successful. BC Sets typically yield yellow warnings. You can review these warnings or ignore them. Typically, warnings will always occur when you deploy BC Sets in the *overwrite all* mode (which is how the system deploys them by default).

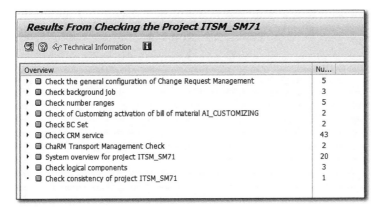

Figure 16.34 Results of Project Check

Unlock Project Track

After cleaning up any red errors associated with the project check, the task list is prepared to support the creation, import, and release associated with development and testing activities.

When a maintenance cycle is first created, the project track of the task list is locked. As a procedural step, the first step after running the project check is to unlock the tasks along the project track. These tasks can be locked at a later point should the associated activities be frozen. Follow these steps:

1. Select the SHOW TASK LIST button (Figure 16.35). Alternatively, the task list can be accessed from Transaction SCMA.

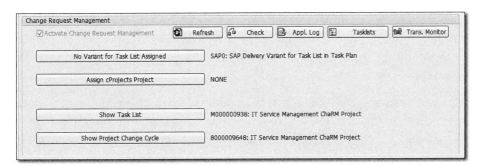

Figure 16.35 Select Show Task List

The task list for the maintenance cycle appears in a new transaction (SCMA).

2. Right-click the lock icon for the top node in the project track.

3. Select the option LOCK/UNLOCK GROUP/SUBSEQUENT GROUPS as shown in Figure 16.36.

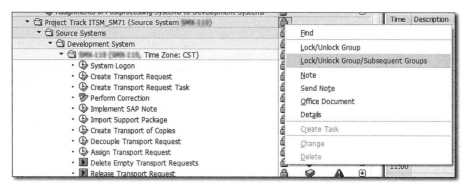

Figure 16.36 Unlock the Project Track

Now the maintenance cycle is ready to begin supporting transport requests and software logistics for your maintenance project.

In the next section, we'll discuss the different options and what to expect when the changes have been imported into the production system.

16.3 Completing the Maintenance or Project Cycle

After the production buffer has been imported into the production system, the maintenance or project cycle can then be closed. For implementation, template, or upgrade projects, completing the project cycle is the next logical step after the transport requests are imported into the production system. Because the implementation of the solution has been completed, the project cycle should be completed too.

For maintenance cycles, there is also the option to complete the maintenance cycle, which ultimately closes it from future activity, similar to the project cycle. The alternative is for the change manager to reset the maintenance cycle phase status back to DEVELOPMENT WITH (or WITHOUT) RELEASE where it can be reused.

16.3.1 Maintenance Cycles: Deciding Whether to Complete or Reuse

Because maintenance projects are intended to support the continual, ongoing maintenance of productive solutions, it makes sense that the phases within the maintenance cycle be continuous and ongoing as well. Resetting the phase status to IN DEVELOPMENT WITH RELEASE after the project has gone live is one option. The second option is to complete it altogether. So which one do you choose?

For simplicity, some organizations choose to keep the current maintenance cycle open by resetting it back to its original development phase. Technically, unlike the project cycle, SAP Solution Manager allows for this to occur. Keep in mind that the task list can't be set back to the status CREATED, and after it's in the status COMPLETED, it can't be changed. Also, prior to completing or resetting the maintenance cycle, each phase of the task list must be run through in order at least one time. Finally, you must finish (not necessarily complete) each task list before beginning a new one.

The second option is to complete the maintenance cycle at the end of the maintenance period. For example, if an organization has a quarterly release strategy, it can choose to complete the maintenance cycle at the end of each quarter. The company will then generate a new maintenance cycle for the original maintenance project at the commencement of the subsequent quarterly release period.

Because SAP Solution Manager provides checks to identify open change transactions and the functionality to automatically have these transactions carried over to the next maintenance cycle, this option is favorable. Most importantly, closing the maintenance cycle after each release supports clearer traceability and more reliable reporting data. If the maintenance cycle is kept open after each production import, it becomes difficult to associate change transactions and transport requests with the maintenance cycle.

Having the open transactions and related transports carry over to the new maintenance cycle is not only technically feasible, it's an option that supports realistic circumstances when supporting changes in periodic release cycles. It's rare that each maintenance cycle will have 100% of the change transactions undergo complete development and therefore will all be imported into production.

16.3.2 Setting the Complete Phase: What to Expect

Technically speaking, when a task list is completed, the CTS project separates itself from the logical system and is no longer available. If you recall from our earlier discussion, the CTS project is the container for the transport requests in each logical system. Closing the task list results in the system saving the open (changeable) transport requests. When you create the new task list, the system automatically copies the transport requests from the previous CTS project to the new CTS project associated with the new task list. The change transactions and associated transport requests are therefore available for processing within the task list of the new maintenance cycle.

Figure 16.37 illustrates what you can expect when completing a maintenance cycle when there are open transactions.

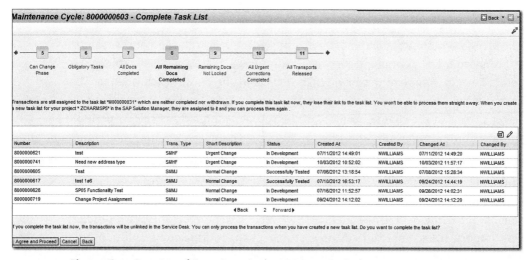

Figure 16.37 Overview of Open Items in the Maintenance Cycle

Maintenance Cycle Checks

Here are a few points to take note of when settings the phase status of the maintenance cycle to COMPLETE:

▶ The system will go through a series of checks that are required before the maintenance cycle can be completed. If the checks are successful, the system will complete the maintenance cycle automatically for you.

▶ For preparation purposes, there is a task in the GENERAL COMPLETION section of the maintenance cycle called CHECK FOR COMPLETION OF MAINTENANCE CYCLE (Figure 16.38). Schedule this job as immediate. When it's completed, double-click it in the Schedule Manager to see the results. Red errors will indicate why you may not be able to complete the maintenance cycle. Yellow warnings can often be skipped.

Figure 16.38 Check for Completion of Maintenance Cycle

▶ When you begin the completion process, the system will initially display all of the checks in an overview dialog box. If the check is marked mandatory, you can't skip it (i.e., you can't complete the maintenance cycle until you address it). You may ignore warnings, however, perform due diligence when doing so.

▶ Objects belonging to the "old" maintenance cycle are automatically decoupled from the maintenance cycle and saved during the completion process. When the new maintenance cycle is created, the system will automatically assign these objects to the new cycle (which you'll generate in Transaction SOLAR_PROJECT_ADMIN) so you can continue to process them. Going forward, these objects must be processed only from the newly created maintenance cycle.

▶ There is a button on the CHANGE REQUESTS tab in project administration called APPL. LOG. You can see the status of the new assignments there (Figure 16.39).

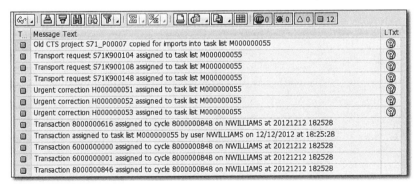

Figure 16.39 Application Log for New CTS Project Assignment

Open Transport Request Handling

Transport requests not released (open/changeable) will lose their link to the initial maintenance cycle. The attribute on the transport SAP_CTS_PROJECT will be deleted because the CTS project will no longer be available in the development system when the maintenance cycle is completed. After you create the new maintenance cycle from the original maintenance project, the transport requests will be automatically assigned to the new maintenance cycle. The transport requests of the new CTS project will have the attribute SAP_CTS_PROJECT, and you can proceed. You can see this behavior also in Figure 16.39 on the first line.

Released Transport Request Handling

Similar to the preceding example, any transport requests that have been released in the initial maintenance cycle can no longer be processed in that maintenance cycle. The good news is, again, after you generate the new maintenance cycle, all handling of those transports going forward will occur there.

> **Note**
>
> It's common to experience an RFC error when completing the maintenance cycle. The cause is that the READ RFC users need to have appropriate authorizations. They will need to have S_TMW_CREATE in all clients.

In the next section, we'll discuss different options and strategies for how to plan for and strategically determine how your release periods will be structured.

16.4 Maintenance Cycle Strategy

As part of every ChaRM implementation, a maintenance cycle strategy must be defined, agreed on, communicated, and strictly adhered to after ChaRM is live for supporting changes to your production environment. A maintenance cycle strategy refers how and when an organization chooses to handle the import of transport requests to the production system. It deals with every aspect of the release.

Some considerations to keep in mind when defining a maintenance cycle strategy include the following:

- ▸ What is the definition of an urgent change for your organization?
- ▸ Is there a distinction between maintenance changes and new enhancements?
- ▸ What is the initial release period (i.e., one day, one week, two weeks, etc.)?
- ▸ What is our target release period (i.e., bi-monthly, quarterly, etc.)?

In the following sections, we'll describe an example of a maintenance cycle strategy.

16.4.1 Example

Let's take the two of the most familiar change transaction types to discuss the idea of a maintenance cycle strategy further.

As you are already aware, normal changes are bundled and move, per a planned release cycle, to the production system together. They are controlled by phases in the maintenance cycle. The phases represent the time that changes are developed, tested, and promoted to production (at a high level). Examples of normal changes may include functionality requests or routine maintenance.

You're also aware that urgent changes are those that are deemed an emergency and must have a fast track to production. They receive their own task list (for workflow purposes) and are independent from the overall maintenance cycle. They remain in the production buffer and are reimported after the maintenance cycle goes live.

For normal changes, the organization must determine the start time as well as the duration of each maintenance cycle phase. Most importantly, the point in which the import to production should occur is also determined.

For example, the development occurs during a two-week window, the testing occurs during a two-week window, and the production import occurs on the last Friday of each quarter. Additionally, the organization must determine exactly what constitutes a normal change and what can be approved as an urgent change. All these strategies, planning efforts, and decisions encompass the maintenance cycle strategy. Figure 16.40 provides a high-level representation of how a maintenance cycle can be defined from a calendar perspective.

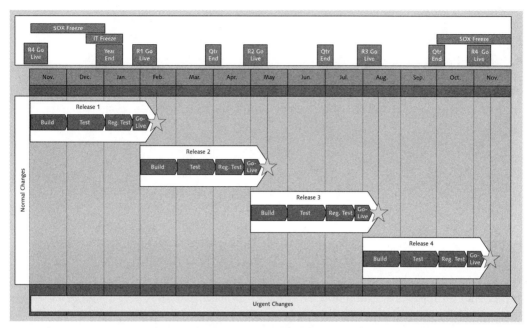

Figure 16.40 Example Quarterly Maintenance Cycle Strategy (Calendar Only)

16.4.2 Common Scenarios

Typically, after an organization activates ChaRM for a maintenance landscape, it starts with a weekly maintenance cycle. In some cases, it's not uncommon for organizations to start off first with only urgent changes. This approach is typically okay (and essential depending on the stability of a newly productive solution) as long as there is a strategy to wean off urgent changes and move into a routine maintenance cycle that eventually processes normal changes.

Going live with ChaRM can be a big organizational change, so sometimes it's necessary to provide more flexibility out of the gate, familiarize the organization with how ChaRM operates in a live environment, stabilize the system, and then gravitate to a more controlled process. The goal should be eventually to get to a bi-weekly maintenance cycle, and then hopefully pushing it to monthly. Of course, this all depends on the stability and size of the landscape. Maintenance cycle strategies across organizations will differ.

Often, organizations get in a rhythm of processing urgent changes and tend to abandon the maintenance cycle strategy after ChaRM is live. Organizations are typically pleased with ChaRM and how it manages production changes. Importantly, auditors are content with the data tracked and managed within ChaRM. Understandably, organizations keep the habit of creating only urgent changes and have a hard time migrating to normal change processes.

To reduce the impact to production operations, you should eventually work toward the normal change process. Having hourly, daily, or one-off imports into production with urgent changes can introduce risk and compromise stability in any production landscape. However, limitations in releases prior to version 7.1 of SAP Solution Manager have kept companies complacent with using only urgent changes.

However with features described in previous chapters (e.g., preliminary import of normal changes, decoupling transport requests, maintenance project reassignment, downgrade protection, etc.), it's much more reasonable to begin processing normal changes and adhere to a periodic maintenance cycle.

In the final section of this chapter, we'll provide an overview of additional project types in the ChaRM scenario: IMG and CTS projects.

16.5 IMG and CTS Projects

Throughout this chapter, we've discussed how cycles, projects, and their related components are integrated to support the implementation and operations of solutions. We started with describing how SAP Solution Manager projects enable these activities and then, throughout the chapter, peeled back layers to determine how ChaRM is maintained and administrated.

Now, we'll describe two final project types. The IMG project and CTS project reside within the managed system landscape. They are technical components that are integrated with the SAP Solution Manager project to support transport management activities. In this section, we'll discuss their purpose and walk through the steps to navigate to them centrally in the SAP Solution Manager system.

16.5.1 Overview and Architecture

We've already discussed and defined the components represented in the diagram shown in Figure 16.41. The objective now is to tie all of these components together and represent them holistically.

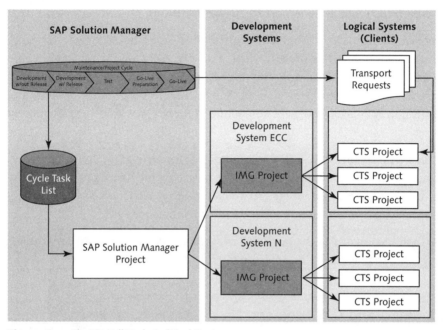

Figure 16.41 ChaRM Full Technical Architecture

As you can see in Figure 16.41, the IMG projects are linked to the SAP Solution Manager project. They reside in the development system and facilitate the coordination of development activities. The changes associated with these development activities are tied to the SAP Solution Manager project, and related activities must be controlled centrally from SAP Solution Manager (ChaRM).

The CTS projects are tied to the IMG project in the logical system and provide a way to group the transport requests for the project.

16.5.2 Navigate IMG Project and CTS Data

The IMG project resides within the development system of the logical component assigned to your ChaRM project. You can access this directly in the development system via Transaction SPRO_ADMIN.

Alternatively, you can access the IMG project directly from project administration (SOLAR_PROJECT_ADMIN) in the SAP Solution Manager system. The CTS project information is also within this area.

Follow these steps to navigate to the IMG project and CTS data:

1. In your SAP Solution Manager project, select the SYSTEMS tab and IMG PROJECTS subtab.

2. Highlight the logical system (see Figure 16.42).

3. Click the DISPLAY button.

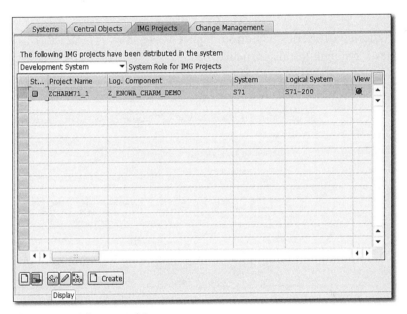

Figure 16.42 Select Logical System

The development system of the logical component will launch, taking you directly to the associated IMG project. The details of the IMG project can be viewed as shown in Figure 16.43.

4. Navigate to the TRANSPORT REQUESTS tab (Figure 16.43).

In this tab, you'll identify key information about the CTS functions. Project data and transport request data (for those assigned to this particular project) are also displayed.

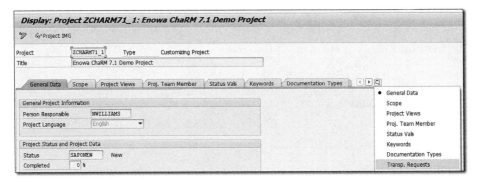

Figure 16.43 Select the Transport Requests Tab

5. Select the ASSIGNED CTS REQUESTS button. Figure 16.44 shows the details of all of the requests assigned to this particular project.

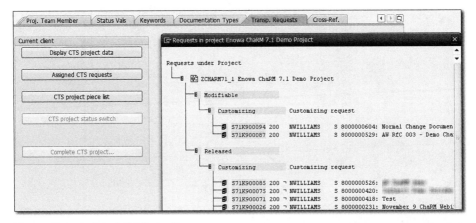

Figure 16.44 Assigned CTS Requests

Selecting the CTS PROJECT STATUS SWITCH button will result in the screen represented by Figure 16.45.

The project status switches of the associated CTS project control specific create, release, and import activities. These activities control the behavior for the transport requests that are assigned to this project. For the items with the red X (all of them), the system is identifying that none of these actions can be performed directly within the logical system. All transport activities must be controlled from SAP Solution Manager.

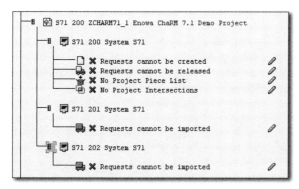

Figure 16.45 CTS Project Status Switch Details

16.6 Summary

SAP Solution Manager's ChaRM functionality is driven not only by the capabilities delivered in the SAP CRM Web UI, but also within the maintenance and project administration activities administered in the SAP GUI. As you've discovered in this chapter, multiple layers make up ChaRM's overall architecture to support change control. In this chapter, you learned about the layer beneath that, which the end user experiences.

Maintenance and project administration in SAP Solution Manager is the backbone for how transport requests and software logistics are handled across the implementation and support of SAP solutions. They provide phase control and best practices for transport management to enable ongoing maintenance and the implementation of new solutions.

We'll now move on to the last part of the book and discuss the reporting and analytics capabilities available in ITSM.

Part IV
Reporting and Analytics

In the last part of the book we'll segue into an important topic: reporting and analytics. Now that you have an understanding of the AIM and ChaRM features and capabilities, as well as the roles and responsibilities in each, it's critical to determine how ITSM KPIs are measured. SAP Solution Manager provides several reporting and analytics capabilities to support all members of the IT organization. From leadership roles such as the CIO and COE lead, to the support staff responsible for creating and processing messages, SAP Solution Manager provides powerful features to report on key metrics within your organization.

In the final two chapters, we'll highlight capabilities that benefit and support all members of the IT organization. These capabilities range from foundational SAP GUI-based reports, to the advanced SAP NetWeaver BW reporting capabilities delivered with release 7.1 of SAP Solution Manager.

Quick, intuitive, and personalized web-enabled search functions provide support staff with a powerful infrastructure to report on and monitor important tickets. Interactive reports, dashboards, and SAP NetWeaver Business Warehouse reporting provide IT leadership with a comprehensive, real-time, graphical way to identify opportunities to improve operational processing.

17 Introduction to SAP IT Service Management Reporting and Analytics: AIM and ChaRM

Release 7.1 of SAP Solution Manager provides significant enhancements in regards to how SAP IT Service Management (SAP ITSM) data and information can be analyzed by stakeholders in the IT organization. As opposed to the traditional SAP GUI-based reporting in prior versions of the system, release 7.1 leans more heavily on the SAP NetWeaver Business Warehouse (SAP NetWeaver BW) content provided as an add-in to the SAP Solution Manager infrastructure. Enhanced search capabilities, based on user-defined personalized criteria, along with interactive monitoring of a user's service transaction types, boost overall usability and acceptance of the tool.

In this chapter, we'll review the options available in the SAP Solution Manager system that provide reporting and analytics capabilities for your SAP ITSM scenario. We'll discuss an overview of the services and then review some examples of SAP NetWeaver BW reporting.

> **Note**
>
> It's important to understand that the functionalities discussed in this chapter can be leveraged across both Application Incident Management (AIM) as well as Change Request Management (ChaRM). Chapter 18 provides content specific to ChaRM reporting in SAP Solution Manager.

17.1   SAP IT Service Management Analytics Overview

This section starts by identifying the key analytics components that enable the SAP ITSM reports from SAP Solution Manager. These components will also be the topics discussed throughout this chapter. We'll make several references to support staff and various stakeholders that have an interest or will want to view SAP ITSM reports in the IT organization. We'll provide an overview of the roles in the IT organization that benefit most from the analytical capabilities provided by SAP Solution Manager, and how they will typically use these reports.

17.1.1   SAP IT Service Management Analytics: Key Components

The key components of SAP ITSM analytics fall across two major areas:

▶ SAP ITSM Analytics on SAP Solution Manager

   ▶ Online transaction reporting (interactive reports)

   ▶ Online monitoring (search and monitor)

▶ SAP ITSM Analytics on SAP Solution Manager with its internal SAP Solution Manager BW system

   ▶ Dashboard reporting

   ▶ SAP NetWeaver BW reporting

If you're counting on just the SAP Solution Manager content for your reporting and analytics, the online transaction processing reporting (interactive reporting) and online monitoring components are available for use. *Interactive reporting* provides wizard-based creation of operational reports based on predefined key performance indicators (KPIs). Interactive reports are created individually from these wizards and then shared across the IT organization. *Online monitoring* refers to the search and monitoring capabilities that provide web-enabled quick searches that can be displayed in a graphical representation and also exported to a spreadsheet for further processing. While interactive reports generally benefit team leads, service leads, and leadership, the online monitoring capabilities are most heavily used by the support staff and team leads.

If you've enabled the SAP NetWeaver BW reporting content in SAP Solution Manager, dashboard reporting and Business Warehouse reporting offer different views that leverage the same data and are based on SAP BusinessObjects Dashboards technology. Predefined dashboard applications are provided standard with SAP Solution Manager and can be tailored/adapted to filter different SAP ITSM processing data depending on your analytics requirements. SAP NetWeaver BW reporting uses historical data that are presented based on predefined web templates. For each of these SAP Solution Manager BW reporting options, you have the ability to report across all service transactions in SAP ITSM. These reports typically benefit IT leadership the most by helping them identify areas of opportunity in regards to SAP ITSM operational processes.

Next, we'll describe some of the roles in the support organization that typically benefit the most from the SAP ITSM analytics capabilities in SAP Solution Manager.

17.1.2 Roles in SAP ITSM Analytics

SAP ITSM reports benefit various members of the IT organization, from the executive level down to the support staff personnel. While each of these roles is concerned with different information, their analyses stem from the same reporting and analytics infrastructure from SAP Solution Manager.

The following roles are those members of the IT organization that will receive the most value from the SAP ITSM reporting and analytics capabilities. These roles are based on IT standards and may be adapted based on the internal roles in your organization.

► **Executive IT leadership**
Executive leadership in the IT organization (e.g., CIO, COE lead, IT Manager, etc.) can leverage the reporting and analytics capabilities offered with SAP ITSM to monitor and identify issues that have occurred, or may occur, in their support environment. Leadership roles in the IT organization are typically concerned with overall trends such as organizational workload analysis, for example. The analytics provided by the SAP ITSM reports service the primary objective of supporting the executive IT leadership in the resolution and preventative measures of issues associated with an IT infrastructure landscape.

► **Service lead**
The service lead (service manager) is responsible for the overall IT service strategy for the support organization. The reporting capabilities in SAP Solution Manager benefit the service lead similar to how they support the leadership. The service lead must analyze the SAP ITSM processes to identify, respond to, and prevent problems/issues across the IT landscape. Further, the service lead

must monitor and track how each service team (e.g., Level 1, Level 2, development teams, configuration teams, etc.) are performing. They service lead tracks this information in an effort to support and maintain Service Level Agreements (SLAs). Further, it's the service lead's responsibility to leverage the data and information extracted from SAP Solution Manager to identify areas of improvement.

▶ **Team lead**
The team lead (or team manager) is responsible for each service team in the IT organization. The team leads analyze the data collected in the SAP Solution Manager to monitor and track the performance of their individual teams. Time spent working on tickets, average workloads assigned to their support staff team members, and overall performance of each team member are all examples of information that team leads extract from the reports offered from SAP Solution Manager.

▶ **Support Staff**
The support staff (i.e., message processors, developers, technicians, etc.) have a personalized view of their own work, based on criteria that works best for them. The support staff can leverage the interactive search and monitoring analytics capabilities to determine their daily tasks and open items. They have the ability to view this information in a highly personalized format with an option to export the data to a spreadsheet or view it in pie or graph formats.

In the next section, we'll begin presenting the reporting capabilities provided by SAP Solution Manager to support SAP ITSM analysis.

17.2 SAP IT Service Management Analytics Capabilities

In this section, we'll discuss the options available for searching, monitoring, and reporting on service transactions across SAP ITSM. These capabilities are typically used by support staff members who must quickly search for and monitor service transactions for which they are responsible. These capabilities are delivered standard (with no setup required) and executable directly from the SAP CRM Web UI.

17.2.1 Search and Monitoring

SAP Solution Manager 7.1 provides powerful search and monitoring capabilities that benefit service leads, team leads, and support staff members who actively view and work on tickets. With the search features, support personnel have quick access to their teams' tickets and their individual tickets. These searches can be saved as a "My Saved Search" for efficient, personalized monitoring.

You can initiate the search from the SAP SOLUTION MANAGER IT SERVICE MANAGEMENT home screen by selecting any of the processes from the navigation pane. Figure 17.1 provides an example of initiating the search for incidents.

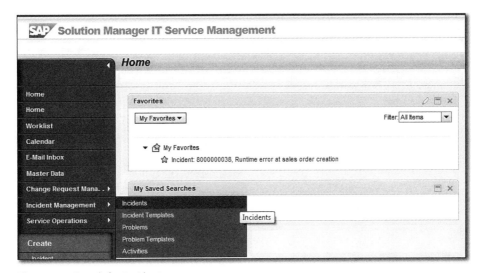

Figure 17.1 Search for Incidents

Depending on which service transaction you're searching on, a resulting search screen will appear. For our example (Figure 17.2), the SEARCH: INCIDENTS screen appears.

From this screen, the user has the following options available for locating various problems, service requests, and incidents.

Search Criteria

Entering the search criteria is the first step to locate incidents. Figure 17.3 provides an image that narrows into the section of the screen where various search categories, operators, and category values are entered to initiate a search.

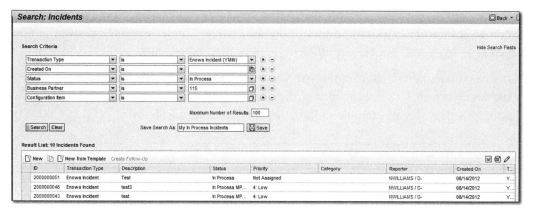

Figure 17.2 Search: Incidents Screen

Figure 17.3 Search Criteria

In the SEARCH CRITERIA area of the SEARCH screen, the user can enter one or many selection criterion to narrow down (or broaden) their search. They can specify the "operator" as well (e.g., IS, IS NOT, IS BETWEEN, IS EARLIER THAN, etc.). Each operator value will depend on the search criteria selected. For example, if CREATED ON is selected as criteria, then the operator values will be IS, IS BETWEEN, IS EARLIER THAN, IS ON OR EARLIER THAN, IS ON OR LATER THAN, and IS LATER THAN. However, if the selection criteria is INCIDENT ID, the operator values will be IS, CONTAINS, or STARTS WITH.

When the user enters the resulting values for the selection criteria, several formats are available depending on the category selected. For example, INCIDENT ID will be a free-form field, STATUS will be a dropdown field, and the CREATED ON category will provide a calendar look-up. Input helps are also used to enable lookups (e.g., for searching for business partners).

The COPY LINE and REMOVE LINE buttons (⊕ ⊖) allow the user to add additional rows or delete them in case of an error when inputting the search criteria.

The Maximum Number of Results can be increased or decreased as well. Further, the Hide Search Fields link can improve the search feature by maximizing space in the screen.

Saved Search

The *saved search* capability allows end users to create personalized, quick-access search queries for various service transactions. For example, developers may want to view change documents that are in the status In Development while testers may want a search query set up to view change documents that are in the status To be Tested. Change approvers would want to see all requests for change that are in status To Be Approved, and IT operators would want to see those that are in status Approved for Production Import. Of course, all of these search capabilities can be tailored down by a number of various search categories and provide these capabilities across all SAP ITSM functions.

The search can be saved by clicking the Save button as shown in Figure 17.4 after entering the search criteria. The saved search is local to each user and defined based on the user's requirements for viewing various information.

Figure 17.4 Create Saved Search

The saved searches appear in the top-right corner of the SAP CRM Web UI. As shown in Figure 17.5, you can quickly access the saved searches by selecting them from a dropdown. The Delete button removes the saved search.

Figure 17.5 Select/Delete Saved Search

A link for the saved searches also appears on the Home screen in the SAP CRM Web UI in the My Saved Searches work center (Figure 17.6).

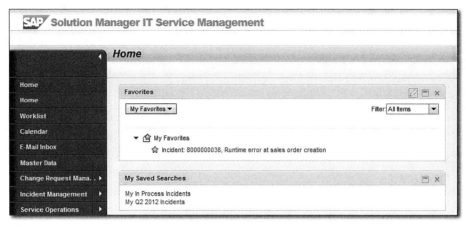

Figure 17.6 My Saved Searches: Home Screen

Personalize Search Criteria View

By selecting the PERSONALIZE button ( ), you can specify the columns you want to view when searching for various service transactions. If there are many search results, this option enables you to determine if the results should be available in a scrolling and/or paging view. The number of visible rows before scrolling and number of rows before paging can also be personalized by the end user. Figure 17.7 provides an image of the PERSONALIZATION web dialog screen, which appears when the user clicks the PERSONALIZE button.

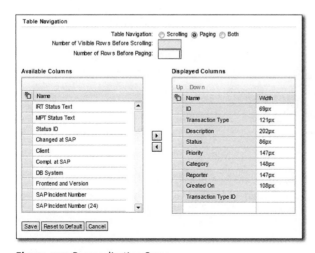

Figure 17.7 Personalization Screen

As shown in Figure 17.8, the user also has the option to drag and drop each of the columns to change the order of how the search criteria is displayed.

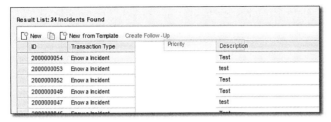

Figure 17.8 Drag-and-Drop Capability

Export Report to Microsoft Excel

The EXPORT TO SPREADSHEET button ( ) allows the user to export the data provided by the search to a Microsoft Excel spreadsheet. This is a basic export that only populates the spreadsheet's cells with the data, without any formatting provided. Exports of the data into spreadsheet format allow for the post-processing of information by the user. For example, follow-ups can be sent to the support staff for incidents that have exceeded the maximum processing time based on SLAs. Figure 17.9 provides an example of a search that was exported to Excel.

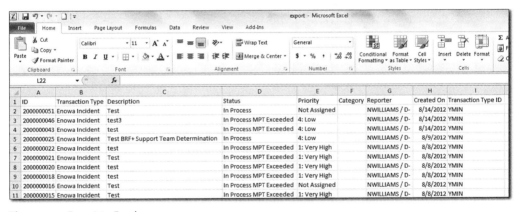

Figure 17.9 Export to Excel

Graphical Representation

Graphical representation of the search results are available in the form of bar charts and pie charts in the SEARCH screen. Selecting the OPEN CHART button ( )

will expand the SEARCH screen to include a chart area toward the bottom of the screen. In this area, you can select the data and the type of chart to be displayed (pie or bar), as well as increase/decrease the size of the chart. Figure 17.10 shows a pie chart that visually displays the priority values of the selected incidents.

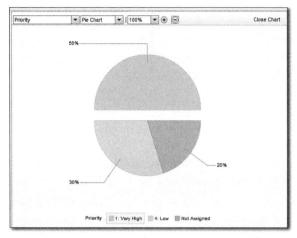

Figure 17.10 Pie Chart

A color-coded legend will display at the bottom of the screen, indicating which sections of the chart are what in regards to the criteria. You can also hover over each section of the chart with your mouse, and the search criteria, number, and percentage will appear.

Figure 17.11 shows the same data, but in a bar chart format.

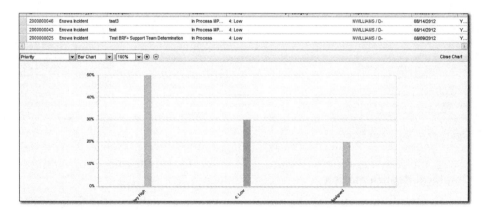

Figure 17.11 Bar Chart

Other Search and Monitoring Features

In addition to the core search and monitoring features just described, there are a few other helpful functionalities in the SAP CRM Web UI that help the support staff quickly search and monitor tickets that they are assigned to, or have an interest in.

▶ **Worklist**

Support staff are typically most concerned with viewing their own tickets. For this reason, SAP Solution Manager provides a worklist in the SAP CRM Web UI.

The user's worklist (Figure 17.12) is a work center that is available from the navigation pane in the SAP ITSM SAP CRM Web UI. The worklist provides a standard search of the transactions belonging to the user. *Belonging* refers to tickets that are both assigned to and opened by a particular user. The search criteria is also provided in the worklist to filter the various results to a more detailed level.

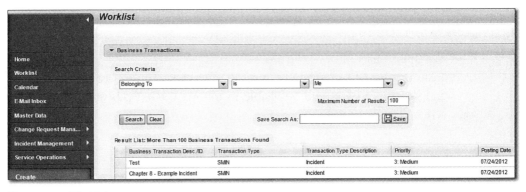

Figure 17.12 Worklist

▶ **Favorites**

Support staff can select the ADD TO FAVORITES button (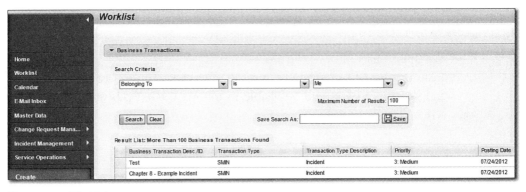) from any service transaction. The incident (for example) now appears in a FAVORITES menu on the home screen (Figure 17.13). This is helpful for support staff members who are working on incidents that are taking a long time to resolve. IT operators also typically flag maintenance cycles as favorites if they need to access the maintenance cycle on a weekly basis for production imports.

Figure 17.13 Favorites

▶ **My Sharebox**
The MY SHAREBOX feature (Figure 17.14) allows support staff to share various items (e.g., favorites, saved searches, or reports) with other support staff members.

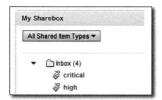

Figure 17.14 My Sharebox

▶ **My Open Tasks**
Tasks that have been opened as a result of changes, service requests, and so on and assigned to you will be visible in the MY OPEN TASKS area of the home screen (Figure 17.15).

Figure 17.15 My Open Tasks

In the next section, we'll cover the other key component in the SAP ITSM analytics area: interactive reporting.

17.2.2 Interactive Reporting

Interactive reporting, also referred to as online transaction processing reporting, refers to reports that are generated and shared based on predefined SAP ITSM KPIs.

Interactive reporting is made up of a class of programs that provides the ability to facilitate and manage transaction-oriented applications. The technical process of facilitating and managing these applications is generally performed for data entry and retrieval transaction processing. With interactive reporting, the report is generated directly from the data of transaction-oriented applications.

An SAP Solution Manager administrator, or someone in charge of analytics in the IT service organization, has the ability to generate interactive reports based on input from the service lead or team leads. The generation of the reports takes place in the SAP CRM Web UI in a guided procedure/wizard. Interactive reports are generated on an individual basis from the wizard and then published (or shared) to the relevant parties from the SAP Solution Manager system.

Figure 17.16 is an example of an interactive report at its initial generation in the wizard in the SAP CRM Web UI of the SAP Solution Manager system. In this wizard, you enter selection criteria in various dropdown selections, tables, fields, and key figures. The data used in the wizard is specific to a single report and represents the information about the service transactions that are being monitored.

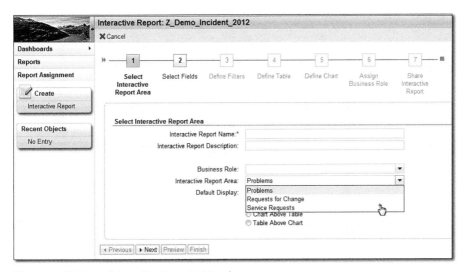

Figure 17.16 Create Interactive Report: Wizard

Interactive reports are presented in real time, allowing members of the support organization to have up-to-date and transparent views of the data across the SAP ITSM processes. These interactive reports are available for monitoring information across problem messages, incidents, requests for change, and other SAP

ITSM areas. The following list identifies a few examples of how interactive monitoring can provide information to be shared across the support personnel:

▶ Number of tickets in process

▶ Number of incidents that have been raised to request for change

▶ Closure rate

▶ Number of service transactions inside or outside the agreed service levels

▶ Average work and total duration

Figure 17.17 provides an example of a published interactive report. In addition to the information and data represented in numbers, percentages can be provided as well.

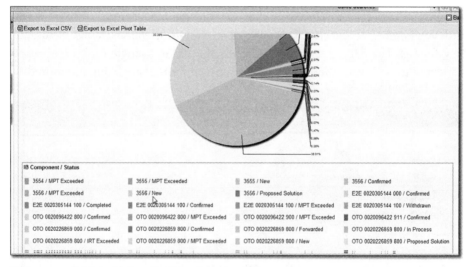

Figure 17.17 Published Interactive Report

In the next section, we'll provide an overview of the SAP Solution Manager plus SAP NetWeaver BW capabilities available to support SAP ITSM analytics.

17.3 SAP Solution Manager with SAP NetWeaver BW

In this section, we'll provide an overview of how the SAP NetWeaver BW reporting infrastructure is used to support reporting and analytics across SAP ITSM functions. Predefined KPIs that are based on BI technology are used to deploy dashboards and various SAP NetWeaver BW reports. While these reports offer different UIs for displaying the information, they leverage the same data.

In the following sections, we'll provide examples of the dashboard reporting and SAP NetWeaver BW reporting capabilities that leverage the SAP NetWeaver BW reporting infrastructure.

17.3.1 SAP NetWeaver BW Integration into SAP ITSM Analytics

SAP Solution Manager 7.1 provides the capability to incorporate the SAP NetWeaver BW reporting infrastructure into SAP ITSM cross-scenario reports. The end-to-end processing of transactions related to AIM and ChaRM can be analyzed based on predefined web templates (which can be extended by the customer). Detailed queries are enabled by the support personnel, and data is extracted and displayed in a graphical format. This real-time, graphical display of SAP ITSM analytics extracted at regular intervals provides IT leadership the opportunity to identify areas for improvement across service delivery.

As mentioned, predefined SAP NetWeaver BW web templates are available based on key analytic criteria. These templates are available per scenario (e.g., Problem Management, Incident Management, etc.). SAP ITSM cross-scenario SAP NetWeaver BW web templates are provided as well to report on the entire SAP ITSM solution. The following are a few examples of the SAP NetWeaver BW web templates that are provided as standard from SAP Solution Manager. We'll also provide visual examples of these web templates a little further in this section.

▶ Average processing time

▶ Workload

▶ Time recording analysis

▶ Total amount

▶ Status iteration analysis

▶ Source analysis

No separate SAP NetWeaver BW system is required to leverage the SAP Solution Manager plus SAP NetWeaver BW reporting capabilities. The SAP NetWeaver stack that comes with the SAP CRM infrastructure provides the ability to execute SAP NetWeaver BW interactive reports from within the same machine. However, you have the option of using a separate client in the SAP Solution Manager system for the SAP NetWeaver BW client. Alternatively, you have the ability to use an existing SAP NetWeaver BW system as well to run the queries and perform data extraction.

Basic setup activities, including system prerequisites, for the SAP NetWeaver BW reporting capabilities are performed with Transaction SOLMAN_SETUP.

Next, we'll describe the SAP ITSM BW dashboards available that provide an application-based view of SAP ITSM information.

17.3.2 SAP ITSM BW Dashboards

SAP ITSM BW dashboards provide IT leadership with an overview of the various SAP ITSM processes based on data intended to help leadership monitor and identify areas of improvement across SAP ITSM scenarios. Standard dashboard applications are delivered that identify the open number of requests for change, the average processing time for a service transaction, and the quality of the overall message processing.

Dashboards are intended to provide access to KPIs in SAP Solution Manager for executive IT leadership (e.g., COE leader, CIO, etc.). The data is presented at a highly aggregated level, facilitating a transparent and open view of the holistic SAP ITSM environment. The objective is to quickly detect areas that are at high risk, causing issues, or requiring overall SAP ITSM process optimization. For example, if there is an average increase of 1,000 urgent changes per month, there is an opportunity for improvement. Having IT leadership identify and eventually remedy this growing number will both improve the stability of the production environment and cut down on the number of hours required to attend to emergencies.

Dashboards are available standard, as previously discussed, but can be tailored to meet the analytics requirements of the IT organization. You have the option to create your own dashboards; however, this involves special SAP BusinessObjects Dashboards (previously Xcelsius) licensing. The delivery of future applications is updated from the management dashboard application store with functional shipments of SAP Solution Manager.

> **Note**
>
> For more information on how to create dashboards with SAP BusinessObjects Dashboards, you can refer to the book *Creating Dashboards with SAP BusinessObjects* by Ray Li and Evan DeLodder (SAP PRESS, 2012).

SAP ITSM BW dashboards are accessible from the SAP CRM Web UI by clicking the ITSM BW DASHBOARD link as shown in Figure 17.18.

Figure 17.18 View ITSM BW Dashboard

In the IT SERVICE MANAGEMENT BW dashboard view, you can see all of the current applications that have already been selected, tailored, and published for the IT leadership (Figure 17.19). As shown in the figure, the dashboards are presented in the form of applications. The WORKLOAD APP and AVERAGE PROCESSING TIME APP are both active.

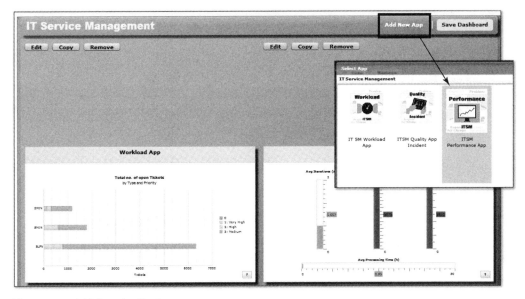

Figure 17.19 Add New Application

New applications can be added via the ADD NEW APP button in the top-right corner of the screen. In this example, the PERFORMANCE APP is being selected.

After the application is added to the IT SERVICE MANAGEMENT BW dashboard view, you must specify the reporting and analysis criteria of the web template. The web templates can be quickly and easily configured by the SAP Solution Manager administrator or staff in charge of reporting and analytics. There are four configuration steps that are administered as part of a guided procedure wizard (Figure 17.20):

▶ Select the application (e.g., workload application, quality application, performance application)

▶ Select priority

▶ Select project

▶ Select transaction type

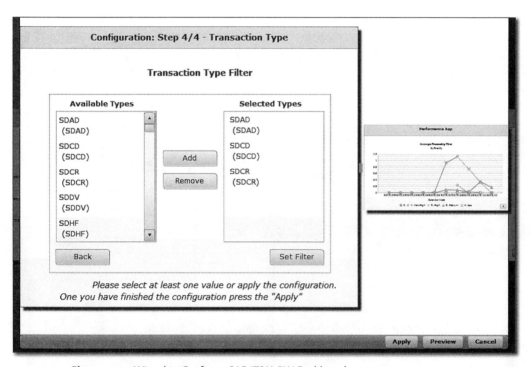

Figure 17.20 Wizard to Configure SAP ITSM BW Dashboard

When you've finished configuring the web templates, the application appears in the IT SERVICE MANAGEMENT BW dashboard as shown in Figure 17.21. You have the ability to select each of these dashboards to view the data in full screen mode.

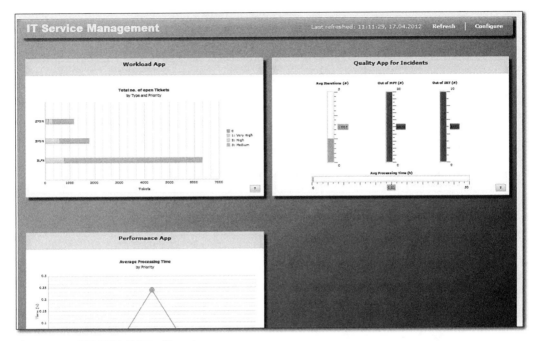

Figure 17.21 SAP ITSM BW Dashboard

Next, we'll provide an overview of the SAP NetWeaver BW reporting capabilities available for SAP ITSM analysis.

17.3.3 SAP NetWeaver BW Reporting

SAP NetWeaver BW reporting provides another view of the data extracted across the SAP ITSM processes. In this section, we'll show you the capabilities available with incorporating the SAP NetWeaver BW reporting infrastructure into the SAP ITSM information for detailed reports. Figure 17.22 shows the SAP NetWeaver BW reports available from SAP Solution Manager in regards to each SAP ITSM process.

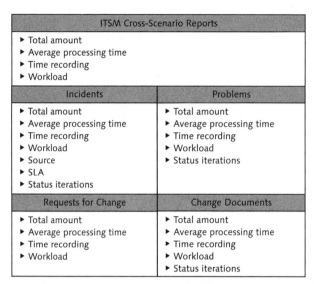

ITSM Cross-Scenario Reports	
▸ Total amount ▸ Average processing time ▸ Time recording ▸ Workload	
Incidents	**Problems**
▸ Total amount ▸ Average processing time ▸ Time recording ▸ Workload ▸ Source ▸ SLA ▸ Status iterations	▸ Total amount ▸ Average processing time ▸ Time recording ▸ Workload ▸ Status iterations
Requests for Change	**Change Documents**
▸ Total amount ▸ Average processing time ▸ Time recording ▸ Workload	▸ Total amount ▸ Average processing time ▸ Time recording ▸ Workload ▸ Status iterations

Figure 17.22 SAP NetWeaver BW Reports Available SAP ITSM

SAP ITSM BW reports are administered by clicking the ITSM BW REPORTING link as shown in Figure 17.23. After the reports have been created, they appear as displayed in the box.

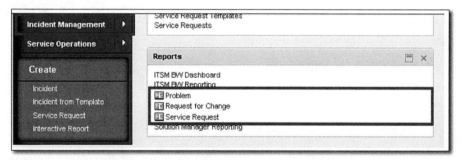

Figure 17.23 SAP ITSM BW Dashboard Administration

The time frame is used to reference the creation of the SAP ITSM tickets. It must be selected for the system to provide the information because it directly affects the basis of the individual analysis of SAP NetWeaver BW reports. Tickets created in the time frame selected will be the only tickets displayed in the SAP NetWeaver BW report after it's published. Figure 17.24 provides the initial screen for specifying the SAP NetWeaver BW report criteria, including the time frame. This screen is known as the ITSM BW Reporting Cockpit.

| Timeframe | This week | ▼ | From | 16.04.2012 | To | 17.04.2012 | CET | Apply Filter |

S▇▇

| **Overview** | Incidents | Problems | Requests for Change | Change Documents |

Total Amount | Average Processing Time | Time Recording | Workload

Click here to load data from Business Warehouse

Figure 17.24 ITSM BW Reporting Cockpit

Conditions are then applied to restrict the data that is applied for the SAP NetWeaver BW report. Standard reports typically provide conditions, but you have the option of determining different analysis conditions depending on the reporting requirements of the organization. After the conditions are saved, you can view the SAP NetWeaver BW report as shown in Figure 17.25. In this example, the total amount of tickets is being reported in regards to priority.

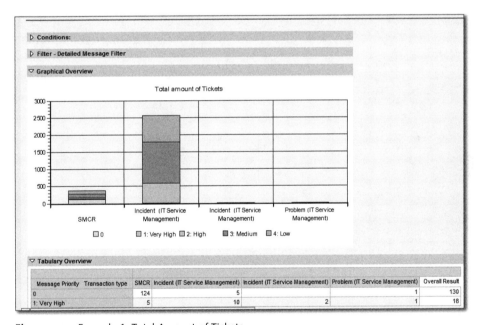

Message Priority	Transaction type	SMCR	Incident (IT Service Management)	Incident (IT Service Management)	Problem (IT Service Management)	Overall Result
0		124	5		1	130
1: Very High		5	10	2	1	18

Figure 17.25 Example 1: Total Amount of Tickets

Graphical and tabular overviews are provided to give you different views of the data.

The FILTER box (Figure 17.26) allows you to define various filter settings and adapt certain characteristics of the SAP NetWeaver BW reports.

Figure 17.26 Filter Box

Figure 17.27 is an example of a SAP NetWeaver BW report that provides an overview of the average processing time of tickets. On the left side of the screen, you have a view of the tickets specified by your selection criteria. Scrolling to the right will present you with a view of the same data, collected against the entire SAP ITSM scenario.

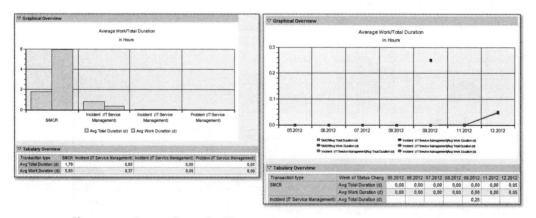

Figure 17.27 Average Processing Time

Time recording is also provided as a standard SAP NetWeaver BW report. Figure 17.28 is an example of how SAP NetWeaver BW reporting can be used to provide analysis for requests for change and incidents in regards to their average working effort.

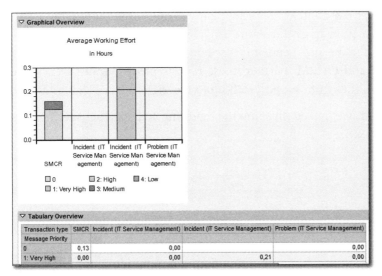

Figure 17.28 Average Working Effort

Total amount is also supported in SAP NetWeaver BW reporting. Figure 17.29 provides an example of a SAP BW report that displays the number of open tickets across SAP ITSM.

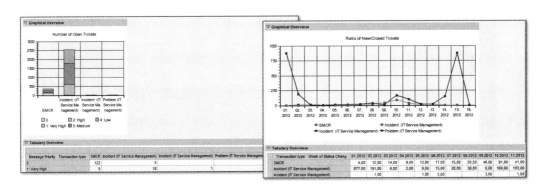

Figure 17.29 Total Amount

17.4 Summary

In this chapter, we've highlighted the key components that are available to support reporting and analytics across SAP ITSM functions. Whether you leverage the content exclusive to SAP ITSM in SAP Solution Manager or choose to enable the SAP NetWeaver BW content, there are plenty of options to thoroughly report on data and information across the entire SAP ITSM solution. Each of the components described can be independently used to analyze data and information across both AIM and ChaRM. Further, these reports provide transparency and monitoring capabilities from support staff up to the CIO.

In the next chapter, we'll deep-dive into the reporting and analytics specifics that are unique to ChaRM.

The Change Request Management reporting service in SAP Solution Manager provides raw data specific to SAP CRM data captured in the central SAP Solution Manager system as well as transport data collected from the managed system landscapes. The data is presented in ALV grids, which provide drill-down ability to convert high-level reporting information into object level details for thorough analysis.

18 Change Request Management Reporting and Analytics

In this chapter, we'll highlight some of the key reporting and analytics capabilities within the Change Request Management (ChaRM) scenario delivered with SAP Solution Manager. These capabilities are delivered across two main areas, which we'll explain and provide examples for in this chapter. The first area is the general ChaRM reporting capabilities that provide the ability to answer typically any question posed by IT leadership. The second area is the transport request tracking capability, which is leveraged by IT managers to identify and manage the logistics in regards to transport requests enabled by your ChaRM scenario.

While you saw a broader base of information in respect to the holistic SAP IT Service Management reporting capabilities in Chapter 17, the objective of this chapter is to find out what questions can be answered and what software logistics can be tracked specifically related to a ChaRM scenario. We'll use a few use-case examples to make our point.

18.1 Introduction to Change Request Management Reporting

In this section, we'll provide an overview of the ChaRM reporting capabilities in SAP Solution Manager. We'll start by discussing the objectives in this particular functionality. Following an overview of the functionality and objectives, we'll discuss the cross-solution reporting capabilities delivered to enable comprehensive ChaRM reporting. We'll also provide some use-case examples in regards to the capabilities offered for reporting and analytics.

Objectives of Reporting in Change Request Management

ChaRM is associated with the end-to-end process for managing changes associated with an IT asset. From the approval of a request for change, the implementation in the development system, the testing cycles in the quality assurance system, and the import to production system, each change is tracked and exported/imported via the functionality in ChaRM. Whether the IT asset effected is related to an SAP component or whether it's an IT asset such as a printer or mobile device, changes are processed in this particular SAP ITSM scenario in SAP Solution Manager.

With the central distribution of changes made to various managed SAP systems and IT assets controlled from SAP Solution Manager, there comes the requirement to collect the related data, summarize it, and make it available for analysis by the organization. This data involves all aspects regarding the events of distributing the change, including logistics, systems, business partners, and status values, among other criteria which we'll describe in Section 18.2 and Section 18.3.

The data collected by SAP Solution Manager from the managed system landscape(s) that are activated by ChaRM support the reporting and analytics requirements from the IT organization. Change and release managers, development and configuration leads, and various other support personnel will have particular interest in this data. The summary of data made available to those parties interested in the results is presented in a series of reports, which you'll see in Section 18.2 and Section 18.3. This data is collected, summarized, and presented with the objective of answering common questions related to ChaRM.

Common questions that are addressed by the change request reporting functionality can include but are not limited to the following:

▶ What is the rejection rate for requests for change?

▶ Which transport objects are associated with a particular change request?

▶ What are all of the change documents associated with my SAP Supplier Relationship Management (SAP SRM) environment?

- How long is it taking for my requests for change to be approved, implemented, and completed?
- How many incidents are resulting in changes to the IT landscape?
- Are the numbers of urgent changes declining as planned?
- How many requests for change are outstanding?

These examples are just a few questions that can be answered by the data collected in the SAP Solution Manager system related to the ChaRM scenario. As you read through this chapter, you'll get a better sense of the expansive and detailed analysis you'll be able to conduct given the reporting and analytic capabilities in ChaRM.

18.2 Components of Change Request Management Reporting

Four main components of the ChaRM reporting service are available in the SAP Solution Manager system. Each of these components plays an important part in how data is collected, available for selection, displayed, and kept up to date.

18.2.1 Data Collection

Data collection refers to the technical process for how information related to the entire ChaRM scenario is gathered and further made presentable to an end user in the form of a report. Data collection includes data that is produced in the central controlling system (SAP Solution Manager) and data that is produced from the managed systems (e.g., the development, quality assurance, and production systems).

The information collected, summarized, and made presentable in relation to the SAP Solution Manager system is kept up to date at all times. This data includes processing information from SAP CRM transactions, business partners, and other ChaRM information that specifically relates to the SAP CRM infrastructure within the SAP Solution Manager environment. An example of SAP Solution Manager transactional data collection is a final report identifying how many normal corrections have been set to the status CONSOLIDATED.

Information from the managed systems, on the other hand, is retrieved via a technical data collector that is scheduled to collect information on a periodic basis. While we refer to the up-to-date collection of data in SAP Solution Manager, there is no technical data collector set up for the SAP CRM transactional information.

The data collector used for the managed systems retrieves reporting specific information from the development, quality assurance, and production systems (for example) involved in your ChaRM scenario. Depending on the reoccurring frequency of the data collector, this information is sent to the central SAP Solution Manager system and stored as persistent data. How frequently you schedule the data collector to run will drive the reporting results sent to the SAP Solution Manager system.

18.2.2 Retrieving the Data

After the data is produced and collected from either the SAP Solution Manager system or the managed system landscape, the results are ready to be accessed. Accessing the data occurs in the SAP Solution Manager and can include the data from the SAP Solution Manager system and/or the managed systems. The results can be analyzed via the standard SAP Solution Manager Report /TMWFLOW/ REP_CHANGE_MANAGER.

You can retrieve the data in this report in three ways. Although there is no one recommended channel for accessing the information, the option you select may be determined by your current or planned strategy for how SAP ITSM scenarios will be accessed. This can also depend on your SAP Solution Manager security authorization procedures (e.g., if you're using Work Centers, etc.). We'll discuss these options in the following subsections.

Option 1: Work Centers

One option is to access the information from the Work Centers. Selecting the REPORTS option on the left-side of the CHANGE MANAGEMENT work center will allow you to select the SOLUTION INDEPENDENT REPORTING option as shown in Figure 18.1. Clicking the REPORT button in the main work area will bring up the data retrieval area.

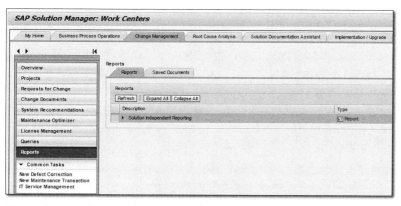

Figure 18.1 Data Retrieval Option 1: Work Centers

Option 2: Transaction SOLAR_EVAL

The second option to retrieve the data produced in the SAP Solution Manager system and collected from the managed systems is via Transaction SOLAR_EVAL. This transaction, known as the analysis transaction, provides a central access point to reports related to multiple scenarios in SAP Solution Manager. You can select the CHANGE REQUEST MANAGEMENT node, as shown in Figure 18.2, to reach the report we mentioned previously.

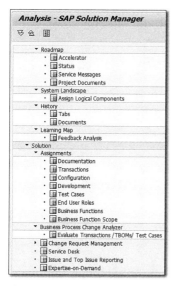

Figure 18.2 Data Retrieval Option 2: SOLAR_EVAL

Option 3: Transaction /TMWFLOW/REPORTINGN

The third option is to assign your users (who should have the authority to view the ChaRM reporting data) access to Transaction /TMWFLOW/REPORTINGN. Executing this transaction from the SAP Solution Manager system will immediately launch the main REPORTING – CHANGE REQUEST MANAGEMENT – SAP SOLUTION MANAGER screen as shown in Figure 18.3. Out of the three options, this option provides the easiest and most direct way to view the reporting information produced and sent to the SAP Solution Manager system.

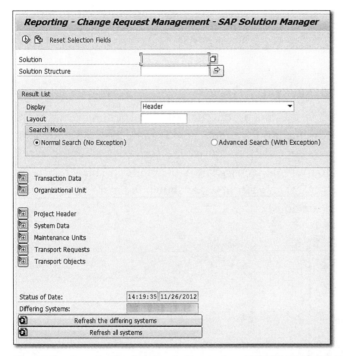

Figure 18.3 Data Retrieval Option 3: Transaction /TMWFLOW/REPORTINGN

From this screen, you have the option to enter criteria specific to the report you want to generate. We'll describe more about the options for reporting in subsequent sections.

18.2.3 Data Display

After the criteria of the report have been filled in (e.g., a release manager who wants to see all requests for change that have been approved this quarter) and the report has been generated, the results are displayed in an ALV grid as shown in Figure 18.4.

Reporting - Change Request Management - SAP Solution Manager

Normal Search: 11 entries found

ID	Transaction Descr.	Trans. Type	Created on	System status	User Status	Chain Link
8000009505	Test	ZMMJ	09/10/2012	Contains Errors In Process	In Development	✖
8000009511	test	ZMMJ	09/10/2012	Contains Errors In Process	In Development	✖
8000009518	Test	ZMMJ	09/11/2012	Contains Errors In Process	In Development	✔

Figure 18.4 Results of Change Request Management Report

From this screen, the results can be filtered or exported to a spreadsheet. You also have the option of removing, adding to, or rearranging the order of columns according to your preference when exporting the data to Microsoft Excel or HTML (for example).

Double-clicking on specific columns will also prompt the system to navigate to details regarding the data in the column. For example, selecting the ID of a transaction type will navigate you to that particular change document, task list, or project in the SAP Solution Manager system.

18.2.4 Status of Data

We mentioned that the data collector must be scheduled for the end users to have information available to them regarding ChaRM activities from the managed system landscape. As a standard setting, the data collector is scheduled to run every hour. The data collector will start running with a subsequent collection process only when the preceding collection process has completed.

As shown in Figure 18.5, the date and time of when the last data collection process is identifiable in the STATUS OF DATA field in the ChaRM report.

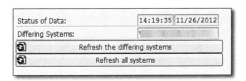

Status of Data:	14:19:35	11/26/2012
Differing Systems:		
	Refresh the differing systems	
	Refresh all systems	

Figure 18.5 Data Collector Information

If the data collector has not executed the collection process in one or more of the managed systems connected to the SAP Solution Manager system, its system identification number is identifiable in the DIFFERING SYSTEMS field. A differing system can be one in which the RFC connections have failed or the system itself is suffering from downtime, for example. You also have the option to update all systems or the differing systems with their respective buttons also shown in this screen.

18.2.5 Change Request Management Reporting: Use-Case Examples

In this section, we'll provide four use-case examples for how the ChaRM service is represented in SAP Solution Manager. For each example, we'll display the selection criteria as well as the delivered results. Keep in mind that these are just basic examples for how the ChaRM report service can be used by IT management. The various combinations in which reports can be created are literally infinite due to the large amount of data reported on in the central SAP Solution Manager system and information collected from the managed systems.

Example 1

Figure 18.6 shows a report in which the change manager wanted to view all open normal change documents that were being processed by developers or configuration architects. As you can see on the left side, the change manager entered the TRANSACTION TYPE "ZMMJ" and the OTHER STATUS "E0002", which is the code for IN DEVELOPMENT for the normal change types.

As you can see, an ALV grid is produced after the report is executed based on the input criteria. All normal change documents based on the selection criteria are displayed. As mentioned before, the change manager has the option to export this data to an Excel spreadsheet (or other file type) or drill down further to view the SAP CRM document.

In the next subsection, we'll show you another common example of how the ChaRM reporting service is used.

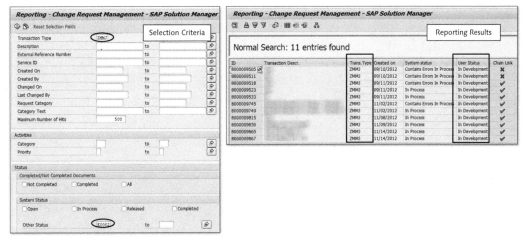

Figure 18.6 Example 1: View Normal Changes In Development

Note

Before continuing it's important that you select the RESET SELECTION FIELDS button (Figure 18.7) before attempting to run a subsequent report.

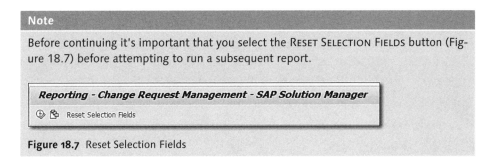

Figure 18.7 Reset Selection Fields

Example 2

In this example, the development lead wants to run a report that provides all of the transport details (i.e., transport request number and objects) associated with a particular change document.

The DISPLAY field in the RESULT LIST section of the selection area can be changed as shown in Figure 18.8. Each of the values determines the layout of the report after it's generated. For basic SAP CRM change document reports, the HEADER entry is appropriate (we used the HEADER entry in Example 1). The HEADER entry provides all of the main details related to the SAP CRM document. The HEADER, PROJECT, TASK LIST, TRANSPORTS, AND OBJECTS value (as shown in Example 2) provides technical details as well as the SAP CRM document information.

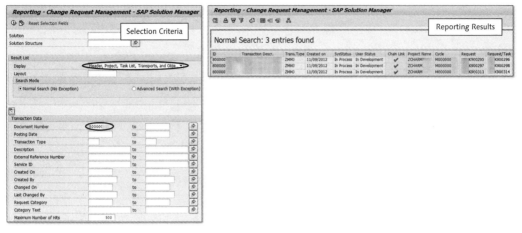

Figure 18.8 Example 2: View Transports and Objects Assigned to a Document

Example 3

Another way the ChaRM reporting service can be used is to determine which change documents are associated with a particular transport request number. As shown in Figure 18.9, the TRANSPORT REQUEST area of the ChaRM report allows you to report on the following details of the transport:

▶ REQUEST/TASK (ID number)

▶ TRANSPORT REQUEST TYPE

▶ REQUEST CATEGORY

▶ REQUEST OWNER

▶ REQUEST TARGET

▶ CHANGED ON

▶ TRANSPORT STATUS

Selection criteria related to transport request information can of course be used in combination with any of the other selection criteria in the ChaRM report.

Example 4

In our final example (again, there are an infinite number of possibilities besides these examples), the release manager wants to view all of the change documents that are associated with a particular production system.

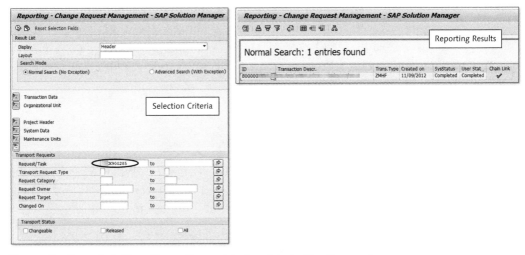

Figure 18.9 Example 3: View Change Documents Associated with a Transport

As shown in Figure 18.10, you have the object of entering selection criteria in the REFERENCE OBJECT area of the report. Specifically, you can enter the exact INSTALLED BASE COMPONENT. This means that in each production landscape ChaRM is activated for, you can narrow down the search for change documents associated to a specific production system. For example, you can report on change documents for just the SAP ERP system or just the SAP NetWeaver BW system.

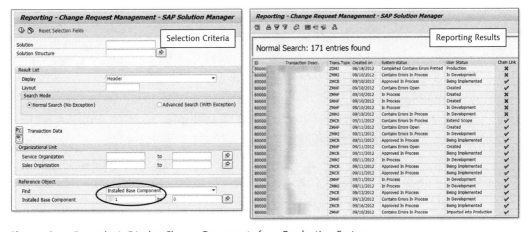

Figure 18.10 Example 4: Display Change Documents for a Production System

In the following section, we'll provide an example of how the transport request tracking report achieves the analysis activities between transport requests in landscapes governed by the ChaRM capability. We'll also identify the key prerequisites for the data from the managed systems to be collected and displayed from the central SAP Solution Manager system.

18.3 Transport Request Tracking

Transport request tracking, accessible via Transaction /TMWFLOW/TRMO in the SAP Solution Manager system, provides data collected from the managed system landscape(s) in regards to transport request information and logistics.

18.3.1 Transport Request Tracking Capabilities

The transport request tracking reports provide the ability to track changes across both SAP Solution Manager and IMG projects. Specifically, these reports support the requirements to have a better understanding of the whereabouts and software logistics of the transport requests in the managed systems. Transport request tracking reporting is divided among three main areas:

1. **System analysis**
   Provides the ability to track transport requests from the exporting system to the importing system. The discrepencies (i.e., in numbers and sequence) are displayed.

2. **Project analysis**
   Transport requests belonging to an SAP Solution Manager maintenance project, implementation project, and so on can be tracked across the logical component(s) that are controlled by ChaRM.

3. **Request analysis**
   Transport request objects, task list, CTS projects, IMG projects, import queues, and transport logs can be viewed centrally from the ChaRM report.

We'll now provide examples of how each of these reports are used to support the tracking of the managed system's transport requests centrally from the ChaRM reporting functionality in SAP Solution Manager.

System Analysis

In Transaction /TMRFLOW/TRMP, support staff involved and concerned with transport request logistics can use its capabilities to analyze transport requests across systems. Missing transport requests are presented in an ALV grid. There is also an option to report on sequence violations that have occurred between the development and quality assurance systems of a managed landscape, for example.

When you execute Transaction /TMWFLOW/TRMO, you're presented with the TRACKING # CHANGE REQUEST MANAGEMENT # SAP SOLUTION MANAGER screen as shown in Figure 18.11.

In the SYSTEM ANALYSIS area, you can enter a source system and comparison system. You also have the option of comparing clients in these systems against each other. Other search criteria such as PROJECT, DATE, and TIME can be selected to narrow the reporting results down to a more granular level.

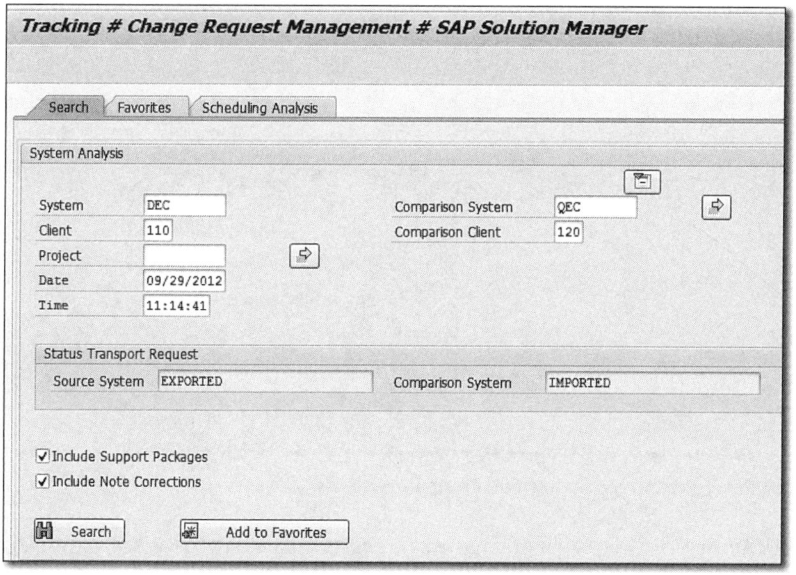

Figure 18.11 Transport Tracking

The status of the transport requests can also be narrowed down according to the following statuses:

▶ EXPORTED

▶ IMPORTED

- ▶ In Import Queue

- ▶ In Import Queue or Imported

- ▶ Open

- ▶ Open or Exported

Finally, you can also include support packages and SAP Note corrections in the results of the transport tracking report. Click the Search button to display the reporting results of your selection criteria.

The results of the tracking report will appear in a split screen view as shown in Figure 18.12. Here, all results are displayed between a development (source) and quality assurance (comparison) system (i.e., Show All Records option). These two tables compare the imported versus exported transport requests between the two systems. Inconsistencies are identifiable via the total number of transports imported or exported, displayed at the top of the table.

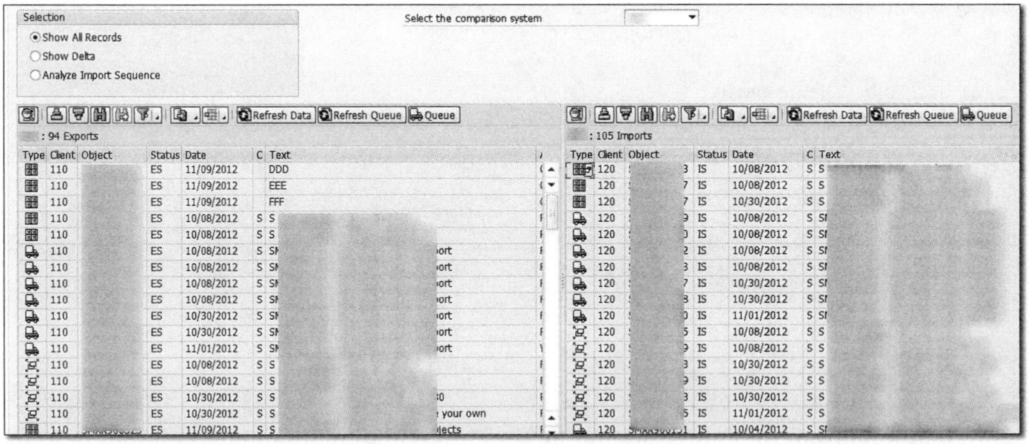

Figure 18.12 All Records between Source and Compare Systems

If you select the option Show Delta, you can see which changes were exported from the source system but not into the comparison system. Alternatively, you can identify which changes were imported into the comparison system but not exported from the source system.

In addition to transport request deltas between source and target systems, import sequence violations are identified by selecting the Analyze Import Sequence option from the Selection area of the results screen (Figure 18.13). Transport requests that violate the import sequence are highlighted in red on the right side of the screen.

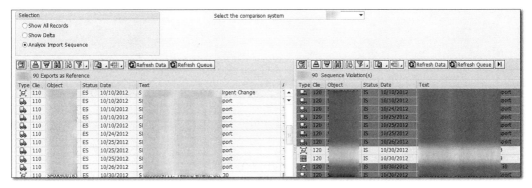

Figure 18.13 Analyze Import Sequence

Import sequence violations are scenarios in which changes were imported into a target system in a different sequence than they were exported from in a source system.

From the two compared ALV grids, the resource analyzing the results has the option to drill further down depending on the data. For example, double-clicking on the IMG project for a particular line item will open Transaction SPRO_ADMIN associated with the particular transport request. The CTS projects, transport request, and task list can also be accessed directly from this report to support further analysis.

Project Analysis

The project analysis report provides a project landscape view specific to the project selected from the hierarchy. This project landscape represents the systems within the logical component(s) assigned to the project. As shown in Figure 18.14, you must enter a PROJECT in the PROJECT ANALYSIS area of the transport request tracking report. You also have the choice of reporting on information based on the SAP Solution Manager project (flagged in Figure 18.14 as shown) or via the IMG project.

After clicking the SEARCH button, the results of the report are generated, and you can double-click a system entry (e.g., production). The tracking results will be updated for that specific system. Figure 18.15 provides an example of transport request tracking data that is updated for the production system.

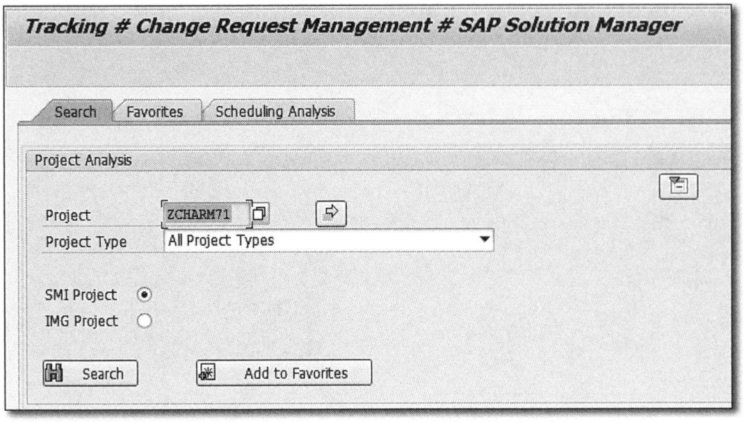

Figure 18.14 Project Analysis Reporting: Selection Criteria

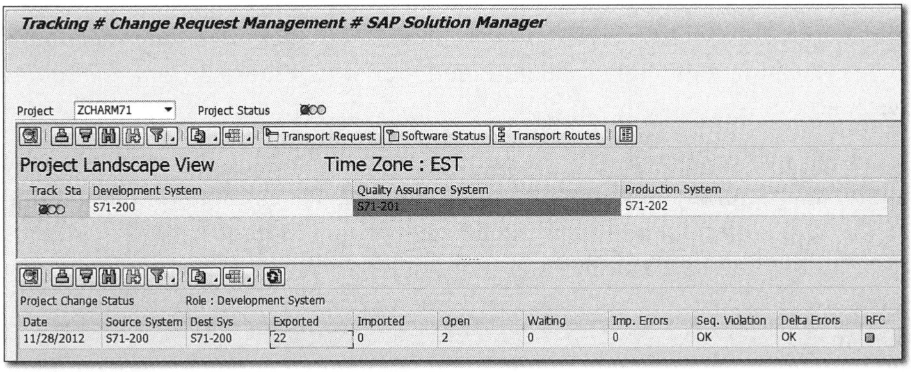

Figure 18.15 Project Analysis

In the results, the source system and destination system are identified. A numerical value represents the number of transports that have been exported, imported, remain open, are waiting, have errors, or include sequence violations/delta errors. The RFC connection is also checked between SAP Solution Manager and the managed system.

You can drill down further; for example, on the number of transport requests imported (Figure 18.16). After the cell is accessed, you'll receive an overview of all objects that have been imported (or exported) into that particular system. You can also drill down further to view the technical details of the transports, CTS projects, and so on.

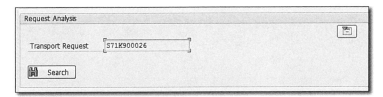

Type	Client	Object	Status	Date	CTS Project	Text	Author	SolMan Project	IMG Project	Chg. Proc.	Task List
	200	S71K900026	ES	03/12/2012	S71_P00003	S 8000000231: November 9 ChaRM Webinar - NC	NWILLIAMS	ZCHARM71	ZCHARM71_1	8000000231	M000000001
	200	S71K900028	ES	11/14/2011	S71_P00003	S 8000000222: November 9 ChaRM Webinar - UC	NWILLIAMS	ZCHARM71	ZCHARM71_1	8000000222	H000000002
	200	S71K900031	ES	11/14/2011	S71_P00003	S 8000000237: Test 11/14 v1	NWILLIAMS	ZCHARM71	ZCHARM71_1	8000000237	H000000003
	200	S71K900033	ES	11/14/2011	S71_P00003	S 8000000238: 11/14 NC	NWILLIAMS	ZCHARM71	ZCHARM71_1	8000000238	M000000001
	200	S71K900035	ES	11/14/2011	S71_P00003	S71K900033 : Generated test transport	NWILLIAMS	ZCHARM71	ZCHARM71_1	8000000238	M000000001
	200	S71K900036	ES	11/14/2011	S71_P00003	S71K900033 : Generated test transport	NWILLIAMS	ZCHARM71	ZCHARM71_1	8000000238	M000000001
	200	S71K900038	ES	11/18/2011	S71_P00003	S 8000000256: Demo 11/18 1	NWILLIAMS	ZCHARM71	ZCHARM71_1	8000000256	H000000006
	200	S71K900040	ES	11/18/2011	S71_P00003	S 8000000258: I need a new address type for G	NWILLIAMS	ZCHARM71	ZCHARM71_1	8000000258	H000000007

Figure 18.16 Project Analysis: Low Level Analysis

Request Analysis

The request analysis feature allows you to view the details of specific transport requests and their assigned data. This data includes type, status, CTS project, IMG project, SAP Solution Manager project, change document, and description.

As shown in Figure 18.17, you can simply enter the transport request ID in the TRANSPORT REQUEST field and click SEARCH.

> **Request Analysis**
>
> Transport Request   [S71K900026]
>
> [⊞] Search

Figure 18.17 Search for Transport Request

The results are shown in Figure 18.18. As you were able to do with the other ChaRM reports, you can further drill down on the various columns in the results to access the SAP CRM document, transport objects, queue, and so on.

Tracking # Change Request Management # SAP Solution Manager

⊗ Configuration ☞ Tracking ☷ Scheduling ⊛ Project Logistics

3 Distribution Event(s) for 1 Requests

Type	Client	Object	Status	Date	CTS Project	Text	Author	SolMan Project	IMG Project	Chg. Proc.	Task Li
	200	S71K900026	ES	03/12/2012	S71_P00003	S 8000000231: November 9 ChaRM Webinar - NC	NWILLIAMS	ZCHARM71	ZCHARM71_1	8000000231	
	201	S71K900026	IE	07/06/2012	S71_P00003	S 8000000231: November 9 ChaRM Webinar - NC	NWILLIAMS	ZCHARM71	ZCHARM71_1	8000000231	
	202							ZCHARM71			

Figure 18.18 Transport Request Analysis Results

18.3.2 Enabling the Change Request Reporting Service

In this section, we'll provide the prerequisite activities required to enable the change request reporting service in your SAP Solution Manager system. In addition to basic Transport Management System (TMS) authorizations, these requirements involve the following key areas, which we'll explain in the following subsections:

▶ Minimum support package levels in the managed systems
▶ Database bandwidth to support data related to transport requests
▶ Object reporting activation

Managed System Landscape Support Package Requirements

To have the transport object data collected and sent to the central SAP Solution Manager system, the managed systems in your landscape must have the required support package levels depending on their release. Table 18.1 provides the requirements for these levels.

Release	Level
4.6C	51
4.6D	42
6.10	45
6.20	56
6.40	15
7.0	06
7.1	06

Table 18.1 Required Levels to Retrieve Data in Managed Systems

Database Storage Space

Transport object information collected from the managed systems is stored directly in the central SAP Solution Manager database. If you're leveraging the reporting services frequently, there is a risk that these tables will fill up quickly unless monitored on a periodic basis by the technical teams. Before activating the object service reporting (explained below), we recommend that you check the following tables to ensure that adequate space is available before using this piece of the ChaRM reporting service:

▶ /TMWFLOW/REP71*

▶ /TMWFLOW/REPE7*

Following activation of the object reporting, we recommend to continue monitoring these tables via standard database monitoring tools to ensure that enough storage space is available to continue producing reports.

Activate Object Reporting

For the change request reporting service to collect information specific to transport objects, you must activate a reporting function from in SAP Solution Manager. To activate the object reporting, follow these steps:

1. Execute Transaction SE38.

2. Enter the PROGRAM "/TMWFLOW/CONFIG_SERVICES" as shown in Figure 18.19.

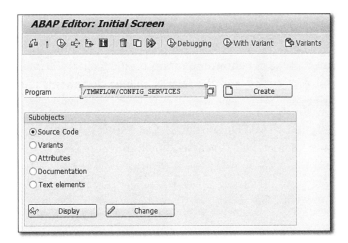

Figure 18.19 Enter Object Activation Report

3. Select the OBJECT REPORTING ACTIVE radio button (Figure 18.20).

4. Click SAVE.

Figure 18.20 Activate Object Reporting

18.4 Other Change Request Management Reports

In this section, we'll identify two other reports that are critical to IT managers, service managers, team managers, and SAP ITSM processors who run various reports in ChaRM. We'll provide a high-level overview of the project logistics report that is used to identify technical and project logistical data across maintenance projects. We'll also discuss the task lists report, which provides a central, consolidated view of all task lists in a ChaRM scenario per project type.

18.4.1 Project Logistics

The project logistics report in SAP Solution Manager, accessible via Transaction /TMWFLOW/PROJ, provides a central platform to report on the technical details of projects, maintenance/project cycles, and the related change documents and associated transport requests.

When you execute Transaction /TMWFLOW/PROJ, the PROJECT LOGISTICS – CHANGE REQUEST MANAGEMENT screen will appear as shown in Figure 18.21.

Figure 18.21 Project Logistics Report

You access data for each project by clicking on an entry in the PROJECTS hierarchy. After clicking on a specific project, data in various tabs will populate that relate to the project. All project types are supported in the project logistics report (i.e., maintenance, implementation, upgrade, etc.). Table 18.2 identifies each tab available per project in the project logistics report and includes a brief description of the information and data captured in each.

Tab	Data/Information Reported (per Project)
SCHEDULING	Displays a daily overview of the maintenance cycle activities and status
TRACKING	Provides project landscape's transport request details (exported, imported, open, waiting, errors, sequence violations)
PLANNING	Displays cProject information if enabled in ChaRM
PROJECT MONITOR	Provides a list of change documents according to pre-defined selection variants
PROJECT STRUCTURE	Identifies maintenance cycle, IMG project, CTS project, and task list identification numbers
CTS STATUS SWITCHES	Displays CTS project status switch information for each system in the project landscape
SYSTEM CHANGE OPTIONS	Provides the ability to enable/disable the cross-system object lock (CSOL) functionality

Table 18.2 Project Logistics Report: Information Displayed

18.4.2 Task Lists

Transaction /TMWFLOW/MAINTINST will provide a consolidated report of all task lists in your ChaRM scenario. As shown in Figure 18.22, the task lists report separates each project type by a different tab. Selecting one of the tabs will display the active task lists for each project type in your ChaRM scenario.

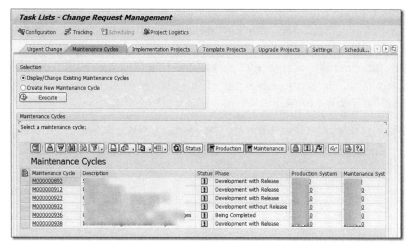

Figure 18.22 Tasks List Report

18.5 Summary

This chapter provided an overview of the ChaRM reporting framework available in the SAP Solution Manager GUI. Whether you're tracking metrics for requests for change or change documents or analyzing the transport objects that are continuously adapted in the managed system landscape, the ChaRM reporting services have a way of centrally presenting you with the results. Having a central platform for tracking data and information exchanged across the ChaRM scenario is critical for IT managers, project managers, and other support staff to monitor metrics and keep productive operations running smoothly. Added value also comes from the simple prerequisites to get the ChaRM reporting services up and running for your system landscape. Finally, a small number of transactions provide the ability to have all information available in single, central, and consolidated reporting areas.

Summarizing the options for Change Request Management reporting and analytics marks an end to our discussion of IT Service Management in SAP Solution Manager. From high-level discussions on methodologies, frameworks, and standards, to detailed configuration steps across Application Incident Management and Change Request Management, you should without a doubt be better equipped to expand upon an existing solution or implement a new ITSM solution within your SAP Solution Manager system.

Appendices

A Lessons Learned When Implementing SAP ITSM Functions

In this appendix, we'll provide some expert advice that we recommend you use when implementing SAP IT Service Management (SAP ITSM) functions for your organization. Because each SAP ITSM implementation is so unique, from the scenarios adopted and the various organizational-specific requirements folded into the standard design, it's nearly impossible to document every single lesson learned and tip within a single book let alone a single chapter.

There are also certain guiding principles that are applicable across the board, regardless of the scope of SAP ITSM functionality delivered and no matter what organization the functions are implemented in. Within this appendix, we'll identify these key guiding principles in the form of lessons learned. These lessons learned can also be considered best practices or expert recommendations.

We've organized these lessons learned across phases of the ASAP Roadmap. We recommend that you execute the implementation activities according to a structured implementation methodology; the ASAP Roadmap is the one we choose when planning for SAP ITSM engagements. Throughout this appendix, we'll provide one to three key lessons learned that relate to each phase of the ASAP Roadmap.

A.1 Organizing an SAP ITSM Implementation

In this section, we'll discuss some key lessons learned that are critical to be aware of before you hit the ground running designing your future-state SAP ITSM solution. Based on our experiences with implementing both Application Incident Management (AIM) and Change Request Management (ChaRM), the topics discussed in this section are absolutely essential before delegating implementation tasks to your team.

We'll discuss how to approach an SAP ITSM implementation using a planned and phased approach, how to develop a SAP Solution Manager landscape that supports testing and prototyping activities, and how to identify team members that will help orchestrate all of these efforts.

A.1.1   Follow Project Methodology

Whether you're implementing an AIM or ChaRM scenario, you must prepare a strategy and plan that takes you from the very initial stages up to the point your SAP ITSM solution is used by your end-user community.

Based on our experiences and lessons learned, we highly recommend that you *develop a project plan for your SAP ITSM project that is based on ASAP Roadmap phases* (at a minimum). At a high level, you can also adapt the various milestones and deliverables that map to the phases of the ASAP Roadmap and scale them down (tailor them) to be specific to SAP ITSM. We'll provide some examples in the following subsections.

The Importance of a Phased Approach

Implementing any facet of the scenarios we just mentioned is an implementation project in and of itself. If you're implementing SAP ITSM in SAP Solution Manager for the first time, or you're replacing or integrating existing enterprise tools to shift toward SAP Solution Manager, you must go through a carefully planned and phased implementation project to be successful.

Following a methodology for implementing your SAP ITSM scenario will help guide you through each phase of the project. This best practice helps to ensure that when the functions are rolled out to your end users, the following key areas are taken into consideration:

▶ Requirements related to the delivery of IT services to the business are covered across the various support and management teams.

▶ Processes, tools, constraints, and restrictions based on existing operations (pre-SAP Solution Manager) have been acknowledged.

▶ Standardization, via best practice workflows delivered from SAP, is enforced across business units, geographies, and vast user communities.

▶ The workflows and requirements have been configured according to best practices and standards within an SAP Solution Manager landscape that is scalable and promotes the ongoing testing and continuous improvement of SAP ITSM functions.

▶ The configuration has been unit tested, integration tested, and user tested by the user community. Defects have been resolved, and the solution is error-free.

▸ Users have been trained according to their role as it relates to SAP ITSM.

▸ The cutover of the SAP ITSM in SAP Solution Manager into a productive state doesn't disrupt current operations.

▸ The productive solution can be supported accordingly.

Choosing a Methodology

In the examples that we've used throughout this book, we've aligned the implementation of SAP ITSM functions closely to the phases tied to Application Lifecycle Management (ALM). We've also based many of our examples and discussions on the ASAP Roadmap, which uses five key phases that serve as the foundation for SAP ERP implementation methodology:

▸ Project Preparation

▸ Business Blueprint

▸ Realization

▸ Final Preparation

▸ Go Live & Support

You don't necessarily have to follow one single methodology to be successful with your SAP ITSM project. For example, we're recommending that you align your SAP ITSM implementation closely to the phases within the ASAP Roadmap. If you want to align your project activities to the phases of ALM or an organizational-specific project methodology, that is perfectly acceptable.

Our recommendation is that you align your SAP ITSM project to some standard software development lifecycle methodology in a fashion that enables success and confirms that all project deliverables and milestones are accounted for. Regardless of a specific methodology, you must set phases (and quality gates) accordingly to facilitate sign off on the preparation, design, build, testing, and final cutover of SAP ITSM functions into a productive state.

Planning: Realization Can't Be the First Phase

A common misconception is that a technical team member can execute the configuration activities related to SAP ITSM, and a productive solution can be up and running for a support organization in no time. Due to the requirements for resources—budget, schedule, and people—along with its impact on current support procedures and cross-team activity, it's important that a plan be developed, and all phases be completed.

First, it's important to note that SAP ITSM configuration isn't typically tasked to a technical (Basis) team member. In other words, it is not strictly Basis that owns all of the ITSM configuration. We'll discuss who typically owns the functional SAP ITSM configuration, and the required skills, when we discuss assembling an implementation team.

Enabling the standard processes from SAP Solution Manager for AIM and ChaRM is perfectly acceptable to do in a silo. This will enable the team member, who may be the owner of SAP ITSM configuration, to get up to speed on both how the workflow operates and the key configuration areas. It will also provide a proof-of-concept or prototype environment that will be beneficial during the Business Blueprint phase. However, at some point, Project Preparation and Business Blueprint phase activities will need to be completed for the stakeholders to provide the buy-in necessary to roll these functions out to end users.

ASAP Roadmap for SAP IT Service Management

As mentioned earlier, the examples and scenarios we've covered in regards to planning an SAP ITSM implementation have been aligned to the phases along the ASAP Roadmap. Figure A.1 aligns some examples of activities that occur throughout an SAP ITSM implementation to the specific ASAP Roadmap phases. Similar to how an SAP ERP implementation is executed, implementing AIM and/or ChaRM requires the same coverage in regards to project methodology. We'll discuss these examples in the following subsections.

Project Preparation

In the Project Preparation phase, there has more than likely been a determination on behalf of the IT leadership to move forward with SAP ITSM. Leadership may not be aware of the detailed capabilities SAP Solution Manager offers, possible gaps between SAP Solution Manager and enterprise requirements, or the fact that SAP Solution Manager provides essentially all of the SAP ITSM functions necessary for large organizations. Furthermore, resources may or may not be identified, scope is yet to be determined, and the schedule/budget might still require approval. However, at a minimum, there has been a decision to prepare for and plan an SAP ITSM initiative leveraging SAP Solution Manager functionality.

The activities within this phase can include, but aren't limited to, those which we've identified in Figure A.1.

Project Preparation	Business Blueprint	Realization	Final Preparation	Go Live & Support
▶ Define Goals & Objectives ▶ Clarify Scope ▶ Define Schedule & Budget ▶ Establish Resources & Assign Responsibilities	▶ Identify Requirements ▶ Conduct Design Workshops ▶ Fit Gap Analysis ▶ Identify Enhancements ▶ Complete Business Design Document ▶ Blueprint Sign-off	▶ Perform Basic Configuration, System Preparation, and Managed System Activities ▶ Configure ITSM Processes ▶ Adapt PFCG Authorization Roles ▶ Test & Correct	▶ User Setup and Role Assignment ▶ End-User Training ▶ Execute Cutover Tasks	▶ Support ▶ Optimization ▶ Next-Wave Planning

Figure A.1 Examples of SAP IT Service Management Activities, Aligned to ASAP

First, *goals* and *objectives* should be defined and documented. SAP Solution Manager may be introduced to reduce complexity and redundancy across existing tools, increase automation, take advantage of existing license/maintenance costs, promote standardization and centralization of SAP ITSM processes, or shift towards an ITIL-based framework for delivering services to the organization. These are just a few examples that can be expanded on in regards to why an organization is undergoing an SAP Solution Manager SAP ITSM implementation.

Second, the *scope* should be identified so that a project plan with appropriate resource allocation can be identified. There are several scope considerations to take into account. Here are just a few examples:

▶ Which AIM processes will be rolled out?

▶ Which ChaRM processes will be rolled out?

▶ Which iBase components will initially be enabled by SAP Solution Manager?

▶ What geographies/user communities will we initially roll SAP ITSM functions out to?

Third, based on the output of the scope decisions, the *schedule* and *budget* must be determined and factored into the project plan for the executing phases. The schedule is typically driven via a target go-live date for the SAP ITSM processes that are being deployed. Go-live dates for SAP ITSM vary from organization to organization and can be based on a number of factors. For example, an upgrade of an SAP ERP system, year-end, or consulting budget may impact or drive the go-live date. After this date is selected, the project plan can be developed accordingly. If outside consulting is required, a budget can be developed based on the resource requirements from blueprint until the go-live date. Further, ample time to support the solution should be taken into consideration as well.

Our final example of Project Preparation activities is in regards to *establishing resources* and *assigning responsibilities*. This includes the internal resources that will play a part in the implementation of SAP ITSM processes. We provide specific examples later in this section. The objective is to identify these team members during the preparatory stages of the implementation and assign responsibilities so there is a clear understanding of who is responsible for what during the remainder of the execution phases. Additionally, outside support by means of system integrators or consulting providers should be determined as well so that on-boarding does not impact the project plan.

Business Blueprint

The Business Blueprint phase of an SAP ITSM implementation is also closely aligned to the outputs and deliverables expected from an SAP ERP implementation. First, *requirements* must be captured from the organization. In the case of SAP ITSM, multiple teams across the business and IT must be involved in the requirements-gathering process. We'll discuss these teams in the next section. Requirements can span audit, security, governance, reporting, and general functionality expected of the tool, among others.

Design workshops are conducted (typically by the SAP Solution Manager architect), to develop future state process flows that leverage SAP Solution Manager to deliver SAP ITSM functionality. Throughout these design workshops, the standard workflows are demonstrated to the core implementation team. Feedback is exchanged to document *future enhancement considerations* or *gaps* that may exist between the original requirements and standard SAP Solution Manager functionality.

Typically, a *business design document* or functional specification is developed throughout the Business Blueprint phase. This deliverable captures the design details necessary to build the solution. Future state process flows are included in this document. Design details can include items such as status values, organizational structure, category values, workflow steps, and approval steps to name just a small sample. This document should give the SAP Solution Manager architect everything he needs to configure the SAP ITSM processes in SAP Solution Manager.

It's recommended that the internal implementation team collectively agree and sign-off on the future state solution prior to the commencement of the Realization phase. A signed off business design document can represent the passing of a quality gate to the Realization phase. This is important because it facilitates participation and requires influence across all SAP ITSM stakeholders. Involving these stakeholders on a Business Blueprint sign-off promotes buy-in of the future state solution and reduces the risk of pushback in later phases. It's highly anticipated that there will be several iterations and versions of the business design document before all parties sign off on it.

Realization

In the Realization phase, the technical and functional configuration of the future state solution commences. This involves the *basic configuration, system preparation,* and *managed systems* configuration areas of SOLMAN_SETUP. Depending on your SAP Solution Manager landscape strategy (explained in Section A.1.2), this must occur in each system (whether the configuration is transported or done within each system individually). Moreover, there are certain automated activation pieces that must be done directly in each system. Typically, as we've mentioned in the earliest chapters on setting up SAP Solution Manager, these activities are done by the Basis team in coordination with the SAP Solution Manager architect.

Following the technical SOLMAN_SETUP activities, the SAP Solution Manager architect responsible for configuration can *configure the SAP ITSM processes*. Depending on their preference/style, they have the option of configuring through

SOLMAN_SETUP (in the SAP ITSM section) or following the activities and documentation directly within the SAP Solution Manager IMG.

Adapting standard PFCG authorization roles is another activity related to the Realization phase. We've recommended that the standard SAP Solution Manager roles are copied into a customer namespace. We've also recommended that the standard transaction types and dependent entries are copied into a customer namespace as well. When this happens, the standard dependent entries within the copied PFCG roles must be adapted to support all of the customer transaction types. Further, system identification numbers are often required in the SAP Solution Manager PFCG authorization roles as well as the roles required on the managed system. To that end, we recommend two to three weeks at a minimum for the adaption, testing, and correction of security roles.

Finally, the workflows you've enabled in SAP Solution Manager and potentially enhanced to meet organizational-specific requirements must be *tested and eventually be defect-free*. We recommend creating test users on your SAP Solution Manager system and prototype clients (explained in Section A.1.2) to simulate a production environment. These test users should have the appropriate authorization roles assigned to them (i.e., roles that will be assigned to "real" end users at go-live). Running through the workflows from end to end and all scenarios in between will serve as an effective way to test the scenario and authorization configurations. The workflow, email notifications, and integration across SAP ITSM scenarios will all be tested in an environment close (if not exactly the same) to production. You may also choose to set up *user acceptance testing* as a way to promote buy-in from the end-user community.

Final Preparation

In the Final Preparation phase of your SAP ITSM implementation, your transports for the workflow configuration and PFCG authorization enablement should be released and imported into your production SAP Solution Manager environment. When this occurs, you can assign the authorization roles to your end users.

End-user training (explained in a Section A.4.1) is conducted in a just-in-time fashion so that end users are trained just a few days before the SAP ITSM functions go live. This ensures that the material and knowledge of the new functions being rolled out are fresh in the users' minds.

Cutover is executed in Final Preparation, which includes tasks related to taking SAP Solution Manager live with SAP ITSM functions. We'll discuss critical cutover considerations and activities in Section A.4.2.

Go Live & Support

Finally, in the Go Live & Support phase, SAP Solution Manager functions are supported if case errors are encountered during productive use by the end users. Typically, the SAP Solution Manager architect, security team member(s), and Basis team member(s) are most involved in the support of SAP ITSM functions after they've gone live. Often, incidents reported by end users are the result of user error and require additional training for the individual user. Other times, security errors or an error missed in testing can require the expertise of SAP Solution Manager support personnel.

The *optimization* of SAP ITSM processes can also occur during the Go Live & Support phase. If there are feedback/requests consistently across end users that are deemed valid by the implementation team, they may choose to have them configured as part of Go Live & Support. For example, an additional email notification may be required so that a quicker response occurs from Level 2 support. In this case, the notification is implemented, and the SAP ITSM solution that has gone live is optimized to further benefit the end user, increase their productivity, and ultimately improve service operations.

Lastly, *next-wave planning* can occur during the Go Live & Support phase. For example, planning initiatives (i.e., budget, schedule, etc.) can be conducted to expand SAP ITSM capabilities beyond the initial scope of the first go-live. Planning efforts can include determining which other systems will be controlled by SAP ITSM (in the case that the initial go-live included a pilot landscape), which other geographies/user communities can be rolled into SAP Solution Manager, which other functions of SAP ITSM can be adopted, when the next SAP Solution Manager support package can be applied, and so on.

A.1.2   Plan a Landscape Strategy

To prepare for Business Blueprint and Realization phase activities of your SAP ITSM implementation, you must discuss how the SAP Solution Manager landscape will be represented. If planned properly, you should be able to establish an environment in the beginning of the project that can support all implementation activities as well as a transition into operations. At a minimum, we recommend establishing a two-tier (development and production) SAP Solution Manager landscape to support an SAP ITSM scenario. Figure A.2 shows how a two-tier SAP Solution Manager landscape would be represented. We'll describe this graphic in the following subsections.

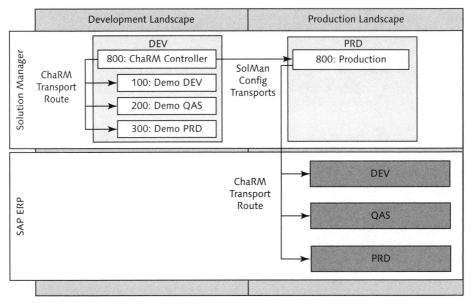

Figure A.2 Example: Two-Tier SAP Solution Manager Landscape Strategy

The Development Environment

Establishing a SAP Solution Manager development system provides a prototype environment for proof of concept (PoC) and testing activities. Furthermore, the development system is where maintenance for the SAP Solution Manager should be applied and tested.

Prototype, Proof of Concept, and Configuration Testing

In our example in Figure A.2, three clients (100, 200, and 300) have been copied from the original Customizing client (800). It's important to inform your Basis team, which typically administers the client copy, that a Customizing copy is acceptable. That way, only a minimum amount of space is used.

Clients 100, 200, and 300 will simulate a DEV → QAS → PRD environment for the ChaRM scenario. You may also choose to have an additional client to simulate a regression testing environment. For this purpose, you must also enable a TMS (TMS) between these clients so that workbench and Customizing transport requests will follow a path that is similar to your SAP ERP maintenance (or implementation) landscape. The objective is that you're able to have a simulated SAP ERP landscape within your SAP Solution Manager development system, which doesn't impact the actual SAP ERP maintenance or implementation landscape.

The original Customizing client (800) represents the SAP Solution Manager controller where all configuration and master data settings are enabled to support the various SAP ITSM workflows. After a transport request, or service transaction, is created based on one of the simulated clients, the controller client drives the process flows to resolution or completion. Security roles, workflow configuration, master data, RFC connections, and various other technical administration activities are performed within clients that will mimic the actual SAP ERP environment. This enables thorough testing and prepares your team for an efficient cutover.

Finally, having an SAP Solution Manager development system dedicated to prototype and proof-of-concept activities facilitates design discussions. Your team is able to view the workflows and various capabilities from an end-to-end perspective. User training and demonstrations are also conducted from within this environment, so that real requests for change and various other service transactions aren't created in the production SAP Solution Manager system.

Maintenance

Just as in an SAP ERP landscape, you would never apply SAP OSS Notes, support packages, enhancement packages, upgrades, and so on directly in the production system. Also, you would never create transport requests to handle bug/fix situations directly in the production system of SAP ERP, for example.

Maintenance to the SAP Solution Manager system is another critical reason why a two-tier SAP Solution Manager landscape is required, at a minimum. There will be SAP Notes, support packages, and the other ideas we mentioned earlier that will need to be applied in a development environment. After they are applied, they will need to be tested. Additional functionality provided with the maintenance fix will be analyzed, and a determination will need to be made whether that functionality will be introduced to the end users.

If your production SAP Solution Manager system is live for SAP ITSM functions, whether AIM or ChaRM, it's essential that normal operations aren't disrupted with maintenance activities. If maintenance compromises current system functionality or if testing requires considerable effort, you must establish a SAP Solution Manager development system to take these considerations into account.

The Production Environment

The workflow configuration, based on the output of your Business Blueprint activities, is performed within the SAP Solution Manager controller client (e.g., 800 from our example). When the configuration is completed, the transport objects should be collected in various workbench and Customizing requests. You have the option of having a single transport request (e.g. SAP ITSM Master Transport Request) for your configuration. After they are released, the transport requests are imported into the second tier of the SAP Solution Manager landscape, that is, the production system.

As displayed previously in Figure A.2, the SAP Solution Manager production system is connected to the SAP ERP implementation and/or maintenance landscape(s). No configuration, testing, or maintenance of any kind is applied directly within the production SAP Solution Manager system with the exception of master data setup and required SOLMAN_SETUP activation. The SAP Solution Manager production system is reserved for use strictly by end users of the SAP ITSM functions in scope for your organization.

The development system and production system should be forever linked by a transport path so that the production and development systems are kept in sync at all times.

Optional: Quality Assurance Environment

A three-tier SAP Solution Manager landscape is an optional approach for those organizations that require a dedicated testing environment. In certain cases (e.g., validated environments) a three-tier SAP Solution Manager landscape is mandatory due to compliance regulations. As mentioned, we recommend a two-tier SAP Solution Manager landscape at a minimum. The ideal scenario would be a three-tier landscape, which allows a true development, quality assurance, and production path strictly for SAP Solution Manager.

In this case, you would need to establish a prototype environment with three client copies and transport routes set up to simulate an SAP ERP landscape similar to what we described in the development system.

Sizing Your SAP Solution Manager Landscape

Depending on the number of end users in your SAP ITSM scenario, you'll need to size your production SAP Solution Manager system appropriately. The usage and volume of service transactions varies from organization to organization, so there isn't a way to make a single recommendation in regards to sizing requirements. For this reason, SAP provides a sizing guide that is available on the SAP Service Marketplace. Organizations can follow this guide to determine the appropriate sizing/hardware specifications needed for their scenario.

It's important to note that the SAP Solution Manage development and/or quality assurance systems don't need to be sized the same way as the production environment. The development and quality assurance system must be able to produce performance results suitable for testing, training, and the ongoing maintenance of SAP ITSM scenarios. The production system, on the other hand, must be able to support multiple users (often thousands) with enough space to handle large volumes of SAP CRM documents without impacting performance.

A.1.3   Identify and Assemble a Team

During the preparatory phase of your SAP ITSM project, it's critical to identify and assemble a team that will support the various phases of the implementation.

It's Not All about Basis

Basis and technical resources play an important role throughout an SAP ITSM implementation. Many of the functions require technical expertise (e.g., RFC connections, LMDB configuration, troubleshooting). Moreover, ChaRM also leverages the TMS, which also requires tight integration and collaboration with the Basis team.

However, it's even more important to note that SAP ITSM in SAP Solution Manager isn't a pure Basis-driven or Basis-focused area. Basis shouldn't be the sole owner or contributor to the SAP ITSM implementation or support activities in regards to ownership.

Implementing SAP ITSM in SAP Solution Manager requires input, collaboration, and contribution across the entire IT service organization. The functions and processes affect the way that Basis supports TMS, how change managers process requests for change, and the way teams configure, develop, and test changes. For this reason, it's important to have cross-team integration when conducting project phase activities.

Identifying a core SAP ITSM implementation team with cross-team representation in the beginning will support success throughout the project and into go-live. Core team members are vital during the design, play-back, and final sign-off of the solution. The roles that are active during the implementation phases eventually evolve into support roles after SAP ITSM in SAP Solution Manager becomes live. Assembling a core team upfront increases buy-in and support from the entire support organization.

Roles in SAP IT Service Management Implementation (Internal)

In this section, we'll identify some of the key roles that may be applicable when planning and assembling a team for your SAP ITSM implementation. Depending on the scope (scenarios, user community, installed base, etc.), these roles may be scaled down or added to. The purpose of this section is to share lessons learned in regards to who is typically involved, from an internal organizational perspective, throughout the implementation phases of SAP ITSM.

Project Sponsor(s)
The project sponsor(s) in the SAP ITSM engagement are typically the key decision makers and influencers in an IT service organization, regardless of the technologies involved. Some examples of activities that they facilitate include, but are not limited to, the following:

► Provides overall project oversight
► Performs oversight and review of deliverables to ensure quality/consistency based on organizational standards
► Gives the final sign-off on the SAP ITSM solution in regards to key phase milestones and deliverables
► Participates in requirements, design, and various other implementation project workshops on a minimal, as-needed basis

Typically, the project sponsor(s) play a minimal role, in regards to total effort, after the project enters the Business Blueprint phase. It's estimated that the project sponsor(s) will be involved roughly 5-10% of the project.

Project Manager

The project manager supports the project sponsor(s) with the activities that we've listed previously. In addition, the project manager is responsible for the following:

▶ Oversight of the schedule and budget to ensure that resources are properly allocated and that the budget isn't compromised

▶ Coordination of approvals by various stakeholders throughout the completion of various phase deliverables

While the project sponsor(s) are responsible from an oversight perspective, the project manager operates at more of a tactical level by coordinating with the rest of the teams It's estimated that the project manager will spend roughly 25% effort throughout the implementation.

Functional Lead

The functional lead plays an important role in the Business Blueprint phase of the SAP ITSM implementation. They are instrumental in that they have detailed knowledge of the existing processes within the organization, or they have the experience that enables them to provide valuable input on the nature of the future state processes. Specifically, the functional lead is responsible for the following key activities:

▶ Support the documentation of current process flows in regards to how incidents and requests for change are handled in the "as-is" environment

▶ Provide input and support the development of the "to-be" state for SAP Solution Manager SAP ITSM functions

▶ Provide input concerning SAP ITSM processes specific to how configuration is managed across functional areas

It's estimated that the functional lead will spend 25% effort throughout the implementation of SAP ITSM functions.

Development Lead

The development lead plays an equally important role as the functional lead, with similar responsibilities. Like the functional lead, they support the documentation and identification of current state processes. They will also support the development of the future-state process flows. However, their focus and effort is in regards to reports, interfaces, conversions, extensions, forms, and workflow (RICEFW) development objects and how those are managed across the ABAP development teams. The input of the development lead during the Business Blueprint phase is just as important as the functional lead and also requires an estimated 25% effort.

Basis Lead

Because an SAP ITSM implementation involves hardware requirements and impacts the TMS, there must be representation from Basis. The Basis lead is responsible for the following key activities throughout an SAP ITSM implementation:

- Supports the documentation of current state process flows in regards to how TMS activities are conducted
- Supports the development of the future-state process flows based on their knowledge of TMS
- Delivers SAP Solution Manager development and production environments to the SAP ITSM implementation team, patched to the latest support package available from SAP

It's estimated that the Basis lead will play a 20% role in regards to total effort of an SAP ITSM implementation.

Security Lead

The security lead is responsible for the following activities and considerations:

- Providing the nomenclature standards for how the SAP Solution Manger PFCG roles will be defined
- Supporting the SAP Solution Manager architect with the definition and maintenance of PFCG authorization roles
- Facilitating end-user setup and role assignment
- Ensuring that standards are enforced when defining security roles

It's estimated that the security lead (or security team member) will require 50% effort during the Realization and Final Preparation phases of the SAP ITSM implementation.

Audit Lead

The audit lead will support the identification of organizational-specific audit-related requirements so they are fully accounted for within the SAP Solution Manager system and SAP ITSM functions in scope. The audit lead will play a part-time role (estimated at 5%) during the implementation. They will provide the requirements during the Business Blueprint phase and also must validate that these requirements have been accounted for during the testing of the final solution.

Service Desk Manager

The Service Desk manager, if represented in your organization, is responsible for the following activities throughout the SAP ITSM implementation:

▸ Supports the documentation of current state process flows in regards to current incident, problem, and service request management

▸ Provides input and supports the development of the future-state AIM processes that will be driven by SAP Solution Manager

▸ Provides input on how the training strategy should be approached when training end users on the AIM functionality in SAP Solution Manager

It's estimated that the Service Desk manager will be used for 20% during the course of the implementation of AIM processes.

Team Member Representatives

Team member representatives from the functional, development, Basis, and security teams should be identified as well to support implementation phase activities. Team member representatives serve as a back-up resource to their respective lead, and also support the SAP Solution Manager architect with their duties to lead design workshops and Realization phase activities.

It's unlikely that the Basis lead would help the SAP Solution Manger architect troubleshoot RFC connection issues. It's also rare that a security lead would help track down specific authorization objects that are required for a role.

For this reason, it's up to the discretion of team leads to appoint team member representatives to assist with the tactical activities that occur throughout the build and test of the SAP ITSM solution. Moreover, team member representatives are those team members who are most familiar with the current state process. They provide value in helping document as-is process flows for SAP ITSM. Finally, team member representatives can be leveraged during user acceptance testing.

It's estimated that team members will be used up to 40% of the time during the implementation of SAP ITSM functions.

Change/Release Manager

The change manager and release manager (sometimes synonymous depending on the organization) will help facilitate the following activities:

▶ Supports the documentation of current state process flows in regards to change and release management efforts

▶ Supports the development of the future-state process flows for ChaRM in SAP Solution Manager

▶ Provides input into the maintenance cycle strategy and other aspects of release management

It's estimated that the change managers and release managers will be leveraged approximately 30% during the course of the ChaRM piece of the implementation.

SAP Solution Manager Owner

The SAP Solution Manager owner is an internal resource that supports the project sponsor and project manager in the delivery of SAP ITSM functions. They may or may not have extensive knowledge and skills in regards to SAP Solution Manager; however, they may evolve into a support resource after the functions are live in the system.

The SAP Solution Manager owner should have a blend of skills across technical, functional, project management, and change/release management. While it's often difficult for organizations to identify an SAP Solution Manager owner, it's better for this resource to have a broad knowledge across multiple work streams/ areas rather than it the responsibility being placed upon a pure Basis, development, or project management resource.

The SAP Solution Manager owner serves as a counterpart with the SAP Solution Manager architect. They support the SAP Solution Manager architect by helping coordinate with internal resources, obtain deliverable sign-off, and manage project issues that require internal knowledge and support to overcome. It's important for these two positions to work closely and collaborate throughout the entire implementation lifecycle. This ensures that after the solution goes live, there is adequate knowledge exchange between the SAP Solution Manager architect and the internal SAP Solution Manager owner.

Roles in SAP ITSM Implementation (External)

Depending on the organization that is approaching an SAP Solution Manager ITSM solution, external help (consulting) may be needed to implement specific functionality. Some organizations are fortunate enough to have internal support that can lead an SAP Solution Manager ITSM. In their case, this position is internal and consulting may not be needed. We'll describe the typical requirements needed for the role required to lead SAP Solution Manager ITSM initiatives.

SAP Solution Manager Architect

A SAP Solution Manager architect is a resource who has extensive knowledge in the area of ALM, ITIL, and SAP ITSM. Moreover, architects have cross-functional and technical skills in SAP Solution Manager as well as security, Basis, project management, and change/release management background. Because SAP ITSM in SAP Solution Manager crosses so many functional, technical, and project management areas, it's helpful to have someone involved in the implementation who has a blend of these skills. Let's also not forget about the SAP CRM 7.0 experience that is required if modifications to the standard SAP workflows are necessary.

That being said, it's important to emphasis again that the responsibility of leading an SAP ITSM engagement should not be placed solely on the Basis team. This isn't recommended or realistic given all of the facets of SAP ITSM.

The SAP Solution Manager architect, in addition to the skills we've just mentioned, first and foremost should be able to develop the project plan and lead the implementation team through the strategy and roadmap for the implementation of SAP ITSM functions. The architect is responsible for executing against the project plan, which involves activities such as the following:

- Providing input and experience related to SAP ITSM to deliverables
- Leading requirements and design workshops
- Facilitating the build of the prototype
- Leading Basis team and coordinating all technical setup of SAP Solution Manager and the managed system landscape
- Performing functional configuration activities for SAP ITSM
- Preparing technical requirements for the Basis team
- Preparing and executing test activities
- Preparing and executing training for end users
- Defining cutover plan and leading cutover activities
- Ensuring a smooth transition to a productive state
- Working to support and optimize the solution after it goes live

The SAP Solution Manager architect is used 100% during the implementation of SAP ITSM activities.

Now that we've discussed some important lessons learned that can be applied during the Project Preparation phase of your SAP ITSM implementation, we'll discuss some key lessons learned that should be considered as you approach the Business Blueprint phase.

A.2   Blueprint and Design Considerations

In this section, we'll provide two key lessons learned that should be taken into consideration in regards to the Business Blueprint phase of your SAP ITSM implementation. The first lesson learned is centered on a two-phase approach for conducting design workshops. The second lesson learned focuses on the importance of adhering to SAP Solution Manager standard workflows and keeping the design efforts minimalistic to ensure a consistent and scalable design.

A.2.1   Business Blueprint Phase: Build and Refine

It's important to structure your SAP ITSM implementation budget to allow for a *proof of concept* and *continuous improvement of design*.

A helpful way to capture requirements for an SAP ITSM solution is to build a proof of concept that supports each function (i.e., AIM, ChaRM) that is going to be implemented. With this proof of concept, you're able to present demos on the functionality. These demos will help foster design discussions as they are refined to represent the future-state solution after each design review. The objective is to keep an up-to-date proof of concept that represents the future-state design as closely as possible. This familiarizes the core implementation team with the functionality as well as supports their buy-in, as they can see their requirements come to fruition at each design review within the SAP Solution Manager system.

To support these efforts, you should divide the SAP ITSM Business Blueprint phase into two parts: build and refine. Figure A.3 provides both a high-level and project plan task level image of how this is conceptually represented. As you're building the prototype and refining based on input from the implementation team, blueprint activities are executed in parallel. This keeps the implementation team engaged, supports the development of a thorough prototype and business design document, and sets the Realization phase up for seamless transition.

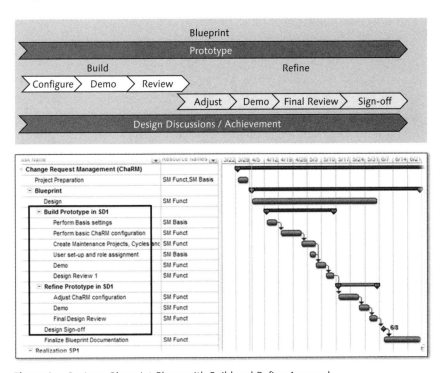

Figure A.3 Business Blueprint Phase with Build and Refine Approach

Build Phase Activities

During the build phase, the SAP Solution Manager architect demonstrates the standard SAP functionality for processing each SAP ITSM scenario in scope. This provides the core implementation team with the appropriate knowledge to understand the capabilities and, in some cases, potential gaps between the organization's requirements and standard delivered functionality.

If enhancements are required to the standard processes to meet requirements, they are documented in the business design document and may be incorporated during the build phase.

Refine Phase Activities

The second phase, refine, occurs after the core implementation team is able to see the future-state solution. The solution is adjusted per any final updates that are based on the team's feedback. Another demo is delivered to confirm expectations, followed by a final review and sign-off of the new change management process.

A.2.2 Workflows: Keep them Standard and Simple

As you're already aware, SAP Solution Manager provides workflows and processes that are readily available to be enabled as standalone items. Whether you're implementing Problem Management, Incident Management, Service Request Management, or any scope of change within ChaRM, there are preconfigured processes available within SAP Solution Manager. We recommend that you adopt the SAP standards and use them as templates, at a minimum, when standing up SAP ITSM within your organization. If you must enhance the workflows, aim to keep them as close to standard as possible and simple in design.

The standards delivered with SAP Solution Manager should be considered SAP best practices and comply with ITIL processes for SAP ITSM. Organizations should strive to execute against these processes, even if it means adapting current processes and procedures.

Adhering to the standards will help drive your organization's IT processes to be more aligned with ITIL-based processes. If additional geographies, user groups, or systems are added to the SAP Solution Manager system, it will be much more of a seamless transition if complex workflows are avoided. Further, SAP will be able to support your SAP ITSM solution in a quicker manner if the standard work-flows are adhered to closely. Finally, upgrades will be less of an effort if the standard workflows are protected.

In certain cases (e.g., an opportunity to decommission a home-grown tool), enhancing the workflow makes sense. In most instances, you can enhance the workflow with Customizing only. Custom development should be avoided as much as possible. Based on our experiences, the majority of customer requirements that were in addition to the features provided by SAP Solution Manager could be met with configuration. We recommend consulting with an experienced SAP Solution Manager architect before attempting custom development. Chances are good that a configurable solution is available.

In the next section, we'll shift to discussing lessons learned as they relate to Realization phase activities for your SAP ITSM implementation.

A.3   System Configuration Approach

The Realization phase of an SAP ITSM engagement transitions the content within the future state business design document (or functional specification document) into system settings within the SAP Solution Manager system. In regards to Realization phase activities, we have two key recommendations based on our lessons learned configuring SAP ITSM functionality.

The first lesson learned is to copy the standard transaction types, and the second is to become very familiar with the SAP Solution Manager security guide.

A.3.1   Copy Standard Transaction Types

We've mentioned this recommendation throughout multiple chapters in this book. However, we find it so important that it should be called out a final time within this appendix. *Copy the standard transaction types* as one of the first configuration steps within the Realization phase.

Copying the standard transaction types into a customer namespace ensures that changes (both during implementation and in the future) to Customizing aren't overwritten as a result of support packages, upgrades, or related maintenance activities.

SAP Solution Manager 7.1 provides a Transaction Copy tool that automatically copies standard transaction types and associated profiles (e.g., status, partner, action profiles). The Transaction Copy tool can be found within the SAP ITSM area of SOLMAN_SETUP and should be used for all transaction copies. Further, this tool enables you to update your customer transaction types with new functionality delivered in applied support packages. If you manually copy the standard transaction types (i.e., from the IMG activities), you won't have the ability to update your customer transaction types. For this reason, we highly recommend that you use the Transaction Copy tool.

As a last and final note, don't use the standard transaction types in your SAP ITSM scenarios. Copy them into a customer namespace and keep the standard transaction types protected and preserved.

A.3.2 Read the SAP Solution Manager Security Guide

As an SAP Solution Manager owner, administrator, or architect, you must *become familiar with the SAP Solution Manager security guide*, specifically those areas within SAP ITSM for which you're enabling in the Realization phase.

There are standard end-user authorizations within the central SAP Solution Manager system, authorizations on the managed systems for these users, as well as authorizations for system-generated users that facilitate TMS activities. The SAP Solution Manager security guide will identify all of the PFCG authorization roles, users, and details you'll need to take into account when building and testing your SAP ITSM scenarios.

Also, we recommend keeping a security matrix updated at all times for the test users and authorizations, with their passwords, for all security-related items in SAP Solution Manager and the managed system landscape. Documenting the setup of security activities thoroughly will save you a lot of time, frustration, and potential defects when you cut over to a productive SAP ITSM solution. This is especially true for ChaRM, where there are multiple users in the background who support the export and import of transport requests.

Most often, errors discovered during testing are a result of RFC connections and/or security authorizations maintained incorrectly. Incorrect, or missing, configuration from either of these two areas may result in the following:

- Transports not released from development or imported into QA

- Login screens appearing where seamless transition should normally occur

- Erroneous errors

- ABAP short dumps

It's important to note that even SAP_ALL and SAP_NEW profiles don't contain specific trusted authorization objects required for testing and using the functionality within SAP ITSM. Reading and understanding the SAP Solution Manager security guide on the SAP marketplace will help you have a better understanding in regards to the specific details on required SAP ITSM authorization objects. You can find the SAP Solution Manager security guide via the following navigation (SAP OSS logon credentials are required): SAP SUPPORT PORTAL • RELEASE & UPGRADE INFO • INSTALLATION & UPGRADE GUIDES • SAP SOLUTION MANAGER • <LATEST RELEASE> • OPERATIONS.

In the next section, we'll discuss some key recommendations and lessons learned associated with turning on your SAP ITSM solution for the end-user community, final preparation, and cutover.

A.4 Positioning Yourself for a Successful Go-Live

In this section, we'll discuss some key recommendations and lessons learned that are associated with turning on the switch for SAP ITSM for your organization. Thorough testing of your requirements and future-state workflows aren't enough to deliver the final solution to your end users. Depending on the SAP ITSM scenario you're deploying, several considerations and factors must be addressed before cutting over into production. This is especially true for going live with a ChaRM solution, as careful precautions must be considered so that current development activities aren't impeded or disrupted in any way.

In this section, we'll highlight some lessons learned in regards to defining a cutover strategy as well as an effective, just-in-time end-user training strategy.

A.4.1 Roll-Out Training, Just-in-Time

As previously mentioned, Basis team members play a vital role in an SAP ITSM implementation; however, the interconnected processes span multiple roles in a support environment. A training strategy must be developed and executed prior to the go-live but not too early on in the implementation. A just-in-time approach to hands-on training will ensure that the end users have the knowledge they'll require when the solution goes live.

To be specific, if SAP ITSM is going live on a Monday, schedule end-user training the week before (preferably later in the week). Delivering training with a just-in-time approach will better ensure that the end users will have the material fresh in their mind.

After the SAP ITSM solution is live within your production environment, make office hours available for one or two weeks. This allows the end users to drop in to receive more focused hands-on help, if needed, and additional training if they remain unfamiliar with the functionality.

Deliver Focused Training Early on to Power Users

We recommend that spot training is given to power users prior to the training of the broader end-user community. Power users, in the case of SAP ITSM, can include those support team members who may have greater influence or demonstrate greater buy-in to the functionality. In the case that SAP Solution Manager is already used, power users can be those users who have become more familiar with the functionality and have demonstrated leadership across the various areas. Delivering spot training to these users ahead of time facilitates good feedback that, when rolled into the functionality, will better the success of training the entire end-user community.

Delivering Effective Training

Training should start with a kick-off meeting. This isn't to be confused with the project kick-off meeting that is held in the project Preparation phase of the implementation. This go-live kick-off meeting should be led by the project sponsor with support from the SAP Solution Manager owner and architect. This meeting will provide a very high-level overview of SAP ITSM in SAP Solution Manager, the vision of how support processes are being streamlined, and expectations for the users (for example).

Following the kick-off meeting, classroom-led training should be conducted for those team members who will be logging into SAP Solution Manager daily to perform SAP ITSM functions. Figure A.4 identifies those roles and examples of various training aspects that should be incorporated into the training material.

Training materials should be developed and kept up to date with potential changes so that end users have a reference point for additional help. The training materials should provide a step-by-step description of each SAP ITSM process in scope. Further, detailed instructions should be described at each step that is specific to the user's job duty.

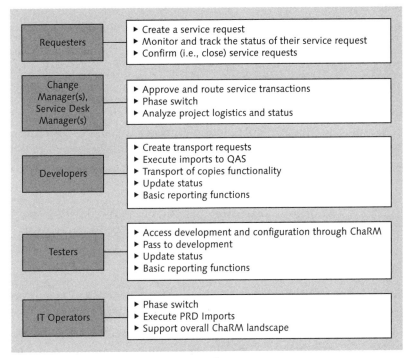

Figure A.4 Sample Training Material Considerations

In addition to published process flows and business process procedures, quick reference guides are also helpful for end users who prefer a "cut to the chase" method of training. Quick reference guides are typically one-page guides, free of screenshots, that include just the specifics needed on how to reach the IT SERVICE MANAGEMENT HOME screen in SAP Solution Manager and process the related service transactions.

A.4.2 Cutover Is Key; Have a Plan

You must have a *well-documented, thoroughly planned,* and *vetted cutover plan* developed weeks prior to the target go-live date. The core implementation team, including the project sponsor and project manager, should be aware of the tasks and assignments within the cutover plan. Owners of action items must be aware of their assigned tasks, the date in which they must be completed, and the risks associated if these activities aren't completed.

Cutover Plan Objectives

A carefully planned and executed cutover may be considered the most important activity in an SAP ITSM implementation. Everything that has been designed, configured, and tested in a development environment will now be controlling processes directly related to your production landscape.

An SAP ITSM cutover plan addresses all open items that must be addressed before transitioning over to a productive SAP Solution Manager. Whether it's a transition from a manual process or from a third-party system, it's important to have a plan that identifies open items as well risks and how they can be mitigated proactively.

The cutover plan can take shape in any form (i.e., Microsoft Word, PowerPoint, Excel, etc.) and can be as simple as a checklist with assigned owners and due dates. If a more elaborate cutover plan is necessary for your organization, it can just be a Word document with a more detailed explanation.

The objective of having a well-documented plan for cutting over to a production is to develop a repository, or bucket list, of everything that must be considered when going live with an SAP ITSM solution. Each one of these items should have an actionable item associated with it, so that risk is mitigated, and issues can be avoided. We'll provide some examples of what is contained in a cutover plan next.

Cutover Activities

The cutover plan will contain several activities that must occur during cutover weekend, assuming that your SAP ITSM solution goes live for your organization on a Monday morning. We'll now provide some examples of some common considerations that are typically taken into account, but you must understand that each organization will have different cutover activities specific to its environment and SAP ITSM solution.

Basis Activities

For the most part, the Basis activities listed here can be completed prior to cutover weekend. However, in our experiences, most organizations determined that the following activities are verified immediately before ChaRM is live:

▶ All TMS activities specific to ChaRM and called out in the SAP Solution Manager IMG have been completed and documented by the Basis team (refer to Chapter 14 for these activities).

▶ The SAP Solution Manager production system is fully connected to/integrated with the managed system landscape. This includes all development, quality, and production systems in scope for the SAP ITSM solution. Trusted connections should be tested and working appropriately.

▶ Transport routes and shipment routes are consistent.

▶ Relative RFC connection and authorizations are tested, and connections are successful.

▶ Import jobs (for quality assurance import) have been scheduled.

Security Activities

In regards to security activities, a checklist should be defined to ensure that related items are acknowledged and accounted for. A few examples of security checklist items include the following:

▶ All final and tested PFCG authorizations defined in the SAP Solution Manager development system have been transported to the SAP Solution Manager production system.

▶ All users within the SAP Solution Manager production system have been generated as business partners.

▶ Email addresses are maintained on both the business partner master record as well as the user master record so that email notifications trigger properly.

▶ All users within the SAP Solution Manager production system have had their appropriate PFCG authorizations roles assigned.

▶ All users within the managed SAP landscape have the PFCG roles related to SAP ITSM activities assigned (compare against the Z* roles in the simulation clients in SAP Solution Manager development).

Transport Requests

For SAP ITSM go-lives that include the ChaRM scenario, your cutover plan should address how open transports will be handled prior to the activation of ChaRM. It's important to note that any transport that is open (i.e., not released) must be merged into a ChaRM transport request after ChaRM goes live. If transports are released before the ChaRM go-live, they are able to follow the normal (i.e., legacy) path to production. In other words, released transport requests don't need to be associated with the ChaRM workflow and can be promoted to production via the manual process.

That being said, we recommend that communication goes out to the development and configuration teams to complete as much of their existing work (tied to transport requests) as possible and release the open transport requests. That way, there will be a smaller volume of transport requests that will undergo the merge process (described in the "Handling Open Transport Requests" section), which is typically preferred by the implementation team.

Depending on the organization, it may choose to "freeze" the creation of new transport requests for the week leading up to the ChaRM go-live. If freezing transport requests isn't an option, significantly reducing the amount may be a more viable way to lower the risk and level of effort associated with merging transport requests during the cutover.

Change Request Management Activation

Another cutover activity that is critical is the activation of ChaRM for the maintenance, implementation, template, or upgrade project that will be controlled with SAP Solution Manager. As covered in Chapter 16, ChaRM activation includes the following activities:

- Create the maintenance or implementation project
- Activate ChaRM
- Generate the maintenance or project cycle

After ChaRM has been activated for a project, a project check analysis is conducted (also discussed in Chapter 16). As part of the cutover schedule, time must be dedicated for troubleshooting and error handling should there be errors associated with potential errors within the project check analysis.

A project check analysis must return positive results with all green lights prior to turning ChaRM over to the support organization. Figure A.5 provides an example of what your results should look like after running the check.

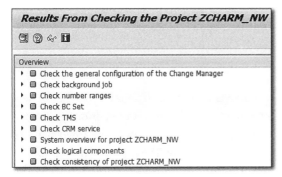

Figure A.5 Successful Project Check Analysis

Mock Run

A "mock run" should be generated as the final cutover activity. A mock run includes creating a request for change within the SAP Solution Manager production system. The follow-on in scope change documents (e.g., urgent change, normal change, etc.) should also be created. The transports associated with these change documents should be promoted to the SAP ERP quality assurance system at a minimum.

For some organizations, "dummy transports" associated with the mock run can be advanced to the SAP ERP production system, just as long as this transport request doesn't impact productive business processes. Typically, a Z table is used to push a workbench request through the mock run, and Z Customizing entries to fill this table are sufficient for a Customizing request.

Test users, or actual ChaRM users with the newly assigned ChaRM roles, should support this effort by using their own SAP IDs. This will provide the final test of security roles, customizing of the solution, TMS, and RFC connections in the actual production SAP Solution Manager system and managed system landscape.

If you're using only the AIM scenario as part of your SAP ITSM go-live, you can simulate each process variant within the SAP Solution Manager production system and managed system landscape as well. Although there won't be any transport requests, you can still create a "mock" incident originating from the managed system(s). Further, you can process this "mock" incident within the central production SAP Solution Manager system and conduct a final test of the various functionalities and process variants.

If each in-scope change document is able to be processed from an end-to-end perspective, and the project check analysis shows all green lights, the SAP ITSM solution is officially ready to be turned over for productive use.

Handling Open Transport Requests

As mentioned previously, transport requests that are in the status of CHANGEABLE prior to the activation of ChaRM must be merged into a ChaRM document at the point ChaRM is activated. This must be considered as part of the cutover plan, so that non-released transport requests are able to follow the controlled path to production. Depending on how the project status switches are enabled within your development environment, open transport requests may or may not be forced to be merged into a ChaRM change document.

For this purpose, the merge functionality is part of basic TMS. As shown in Figure A.6, the contents of transport requests can be merged into a new or open transport request. In the case of ChaRM, the new transport request should be created from a normal or urgent change document so that it can be processed by ChaRM until it reaches the productive SAP ERP system.

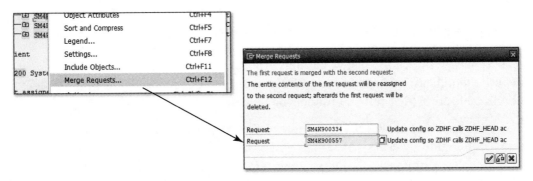

Figure A.6 Merge Requests Functionality

The merge requests functionality is beneficial in that after the objects are merged from the open request to the ChaRM request, the "old" request is deleted, and the locks are removed from the objects. The following points identify the high-level process for using this functionality in relation to ChaRM (available by right-clicking on the original transport request from Transaction SE09 or Transaction SE10):

▶ Create a request for change and the appropriate follow-on correction document (i.e., urgent or normal).

▶ Create the transport request from the change document.

▶ Merge the contents of the "old" pre-ChaRM transport request to the "new" ChaRM transport request.

Now the objects within the open transport request are merged with a ChaRM transport request, and it can follow the standard workflow to the production environment.

A.5 Summary

In this appendix, we've discussed some key guiding principles when planning for an SAP ITSM implementation. The main objective of this appendix was to influence you to use a structured methodology when going about the implementation of SAP ITSM scenarios. Additionally, we hope that you now can take away some key lessons learned in regards to managing each phase of an SAP ITSM implementation.

In Appendix B, we'll discuss some more lessons learned and provide a structured roadmap when upgrading from SAP Solution Manager 7.0 to 7.1. The lessons learned, recommendations, and best practices described within Appendix B are critical for those organizations currently running the Service Desk or ChaRM scenarios within release 7.0 or earlier of SAP Solution Manager.

B   Upgrading to SAP Solution Manager 7.1

In this appendix, we'll help prepare you in your efforts to plan for and upgrade your existing IT Service Management (ITSM) in SAP Solution Manager 7.0 scenarios to the new and improved functionality delivered with release 7.1. While this appendix is geared mostly toward customers who are already operating the Service Desk and Change Request Management (ChaRM) functionalities in an existing SAP Solution Manager 7.0 environment, new customers choosing to perform a fresh installation of 7.1 will benefit from the content as well. This is in regards to determining whether to upgrade to 7.1 or install a new 7.1 environment.

> **Note**
>
> While no automated data or configuration migration is supported, SAP provides multiple options to seamlessly transition to the new and enhanced IT Service Management features delivered in SAP Solution Manager 7.1. No matter your current scenario, you must make a plan to immediately transition to release 7.1 if you haven't done so already.

We'll cover key points you should be aware of when upgrading your SAP Solution Manager landscape to version 7.1. We'll provide insight into the impact on your current SAP ITSM operations and what considerations will be helpful before you request the technical upgrade. We'll explain the primary reasons why upgrading to SAP ITSM in release 7.1 is important and why right now is the appropriate time to make a plan to do so, if you haven't already. Further, we'll discuss the options of upgrading versus performing a fresh installation depending on your existing scenario. If you determine that upgrading is the best option, we'll cover four key transition strategies to seamlessly and efficiently transition to the 7.1-based SAP ITSM functionalities. Finally, we'll provide a configuration roadmap to manually migrate your configuration to the updated release.

First, we'll cover the fundamental basics on what you need to know when approaching a transition to SAP Solution Manager 7.1.

B.1   What You Need to Know to Transition to Release 7.1

In this section, we'll discuss some key points that you must take into consideration prior to upgrading your current SAP Solution Manager landscape to 7.1. The objective of this section is to share what you need to know when transitioning to release 7.1 to significantly minimize (and hopefully reduce) the impact and risk associated with an upgrade to your current SAP ITSM operations. Further, the aspects you'll need to know will also support an upgrade that is planned well and executed efficiently with the goal of leveraging as much functionality delivered with SAP Solution Manager as possible.

We'll first revisit the important aspects of how upgrading your current SAP Solution Manager landscape will impact your current technical infrastructure and operative processes. We'll then provide key information in regards to SAP's maintenance and support strategy, as well as recommend the timing of when you should plan your upgrade to 7.1. Finally, we'll revisit the concept of new transaction types in SAP Solution Manager 7.1 and how you must take this new infrastructure into consideration.

B.1.1   Impact on SAP CRM Messaging Functions

First, let's discuss the impact that release 7.1 will have on your current SAP ITSM processes and functions if you determine to upgrade your current 7.0 SAP Solution Manager landscape. If you're executing processes in a 7.0 environment that are managing incidents, problems, and service requests, you're using the Service Desk functionality. If you're using SAP Solution Manager 7.0 to process change requests and related change documents, ChaRM is still the tool/terminology used.

If you're using these SAP ITSM functions, there are four major areas that you must be aware of that will impact your current environment:

▶ **User interface**
The UI within the SAP Solution Manager 7.1 environment leverages the SAP CRM Web UI. After you upgrade your SAP Solution Manager 7.0 landscape, all new service transactions and their related functionality must be leveraged within the SAP CRM Web UI. Open change transactions can still be processed depending on the SAP ITSM transition strategy chosen by your organization (strategies described in Section B.2).

▶ **Transaction types**

Transaction types that drive the SAP CRM messaging functionalities have been updated in release 7.1 of SAP Solution Manager. Due to the upgraded SAP CRM infrastructure, from release 5.0 to 7.0, the new and enhanced SAP ITSM capabilities are delivered within new transaction types (also referred to as object types and documents).

▶ **Functionalities**

The new functionalities delivered with the updated transaction types are available exclusively within the SAP CRM Web UI for the most part. While processing 7.0-based transaction types may continue depending on the SAP ITSM transition strategy, it's important to note that migration to the updated 7.1-based transaction types is required to leverage the new functionalities.

▶ **Migration restrictions**

There is no automatic data or configuration migration strategy when transitioning to SAP Solution Manager 7.1. While some parts of Customizing and master data may be reused, you must deploy a strategy to migrate to the functionalities and processes delivered with the SAP Solution Manager 7.1 infrastructure.

To help reduce the risk associated with the aforementioned impacts and rapidly take full advantage of the benefits delivered with SAP Solution Manager 7.1, we'll provide our recommendations to plan your transition to release 7.1. Your transition may take form in a technical upgrade from release 7.0 or 7.1 or a new installation of 7.1. We'll describe how to go about planning and transitioning to 7.1 throughout this appendix.

B.1.2 Planning a Transition to Release 7.1

While it's estimated that thousands of SAP customers have either upgraded or installed the latest version of SAP Solution Manager, there are still many customers who may be on the prior release (7.0) of SAP Solution Manager. Among the customers who are currently still running the prior release, each scenario is undoubtedly different. Some may be leveraging Solution Documentation and Solution Implementation only; some may be using Technical Monitoring exclusively, while others are using the Service Desk and ChaRM components for SAP ITSM. Surprisingly, there are also a vast number of customers who are still running early support packages of 7.0 and relying on SAP Solution Manager strictly to download maintenance from the SAP Service Marketplace and to obtain installation keys when installing new SAP products.

Needless to say, there are countless and varying customer scenarios for what functionalities are being leveraged on the prior release of SAP Solution Manager. Our recommendation is to immediately develop a plan to transition to SAP Solution Manager 7.1. This recommendation is regardless of what you're currently running or planning to implement on an existing SAP Solution Manager 7.0 environment. No matter what your current scenario is, if you're still running SAP Solution Manager 7.0, work within your organization and external network to develop a plan to go directly to SAP Solution Manager 7.1.

Four Reasons to Transition Now

Each customer will have a different business case for why the IT organization must invest in the effort to transition its SAP Solution Manager landscape to release 7.1. For example, one customer may define a business case to adopt due to the new SAP ITSM features. The flexibility in ChaRM is required, the user acceptance from the new SAP CRM Web UI will make training easier, and the best-in-class message capabilities will help eliminate redundant tools. On the other hand, another customer leveraging Technical Monitoring may make the business case that the new monitoring and alerting infrastructure will significantly improve the dashboards and support an expanding installed base.

While each business case will be unique and customer-specific, there are key reasons that can be used across the board regardless what the motivation and requirement to advance to SAP Solution Manager 7.1. No matter how your current SAP ITSM scenario is represented in the 7.0 world, these four points should be included to support your business case for launching a 7.1 SAP ITSM transition initiative.

> **Note**
>
> These benefits and reasons are specific to SAP ITSM. Cross-scenario utilization will yield additional benefits.

No New Innovations Deployed on SAP Solution Manager 7.0

If you're using SAP Solution Manager at a very minimal level (i.e., to download maintenance and installation keys, merely to store project documentation, basic technical monitoring, etc.), yet you plan to implement more functionality, you should not do so on release 7.0. There is no point in investing in the planning, implementation, deployment, and support of functionality on a system in which there are no new innovations planned. Regardless of how much you're using, or plan to use, SAP Solution Manager 7.0 functionality, use your next maintenance window to upgrade.

No Upgrade Prerequisites

For customers choosing to upgrade rather than performing a fresh install, your Basis teams can upgrade to SAP Solution Manager 7.1 in one direct shot. Support packages prior to the upgrade aren't needed as part of any prerequisite activities. In fact, it has been consistently reported that the technical upgrade for 7.1 results in downtime similar to a support package upgrade. This means that in most cases, an upgrade to SAP Solution Manager 7.1, with the related post-configuration steps, can occur over a weekend. Of course this does not take into account the handling of complex, existing configuration to the 7.0 workflow, which is the case in some organziations. If 7.0-based SAP ITSM workflow was significantly adapted to meet complex customer requirements, we recommend consulting with an experienced SAP Solution Manager architect to determine the impact and effort required to transition the configuration to 7.1.

Table B.1 identifies the similarities for a typical customer scenario of upgrading to SAP Solution Manager 7.1 compared to a support package implementation.

Initiative	Pre-Processing	Import (Downtime)	Post-Processing (Including Basic Configuration)
Upgrade to SAP Solution Manager 7.1	10 to 20 hours	5 to 10 hours	25 to 30 hours
Install new support package	1 to 2 hours	5 to 8 hours	3 to 4 hours

Table B.1 Upgrade to 7.1 versus Support Package Installation, Common Scenario

SAP Solution Manager 7.1 is Stable and Ready for Use

This book has been printed and includes content at the time Support Package 08 has been delivered for general availability. You can be confident that SAP Solution Manager 7.1, at this support package level, is stable and ready for adoption.

Thousands of customers, as of SP05, have already implemented SAP Solution Manager 7.1 and most have successfully leveraged SAP ITSM in some manner. No matter your priorities or challenges, you have the option of incrementally adopting each piece of SAP Solution Manager to accommodate the requirements within your organization.

SAP Solution Manager 7.1 Functionality Promotes Greater Ease of Use

As compared to prior releases of SAP Solution Manager, upgrading to 7.1 provides project and support teams with greater justification in that the functions are simply easier to use. With simplication, intuitiveness, and ease of use brought to the maket by way of the SAP CRM Web UI, user acceptance rates have been much more positive based on our experiences with upgrading. From an IT managerial standpoint, reporting, metrics, and key performance indicators (KPIs) are traced with greater ease over the prior 7.0 version of SAP Solution Manager.

SAP Solution Manager Maintenance and Support

We've mentioned three key drivers to support a business case for immediately transitioning to SAP Solution Manager 7.1. Another key point to call out specifically relates to SAP's maintenance and support strategy. Mainstream maintenance for SAP Solution Manager is currently planned to cease at the end of 2013, which means customers who are currently operating with SAP Solution Manager 7.0 functionalities can expect no new maintenance or innovations to be delivered within the 7.0 infrastructure. For example, no new functionalities will be introduced regardless of the scenario. Furthermore, after December of 2013, there will be no new SAP OSS Notes created for the 7.0 system. This doesn't mean that support will end for the 7.0 release of SAP Solution Manager. Per enterprise support, or whichever support contract governs the SAP organization, release 7.0 will be supported indefinitely.

Figure B.1 provides a representation of the planned mainstream support schedule for both release 7.0 and 7.1 of SAP Solution Manager. As mentioned, release 7.0's maintenance will end at the close of 2013. Release 7.1, on the other hand, can be expected to be supported (from a maintenance specific perspective) through 2017. This gives SAP Solution Manager customers more than six years to have their investments in 7.1-based scenarios supported with mainstream maintenance.

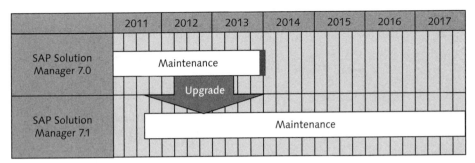

Figure B.1 SAP Solution Manager Mainstream Maintenance Window

Also, as shown in Figure B.1, we recommend that an upgrade (or new installation depending on your scenario) is planned for and executed prior to the end of 2013. This recommendation allows adequate time for customers to begin the planning and upgrade of their 7.0 environment prior to mainstream maintenance ending for 7.0. Due to the availability, stability, and offerings provided by SAP Solution Manager 7.1, we recommend having a plan to transition to 7.1 as soon as possible regardless of your current environment.

Get Experience with Release 7.1 without Impacting Current Activities

We already made a strong recommendation to immediately put in place a plan and strategy to transition your current SAP Solution Manager environment to the latest release. What does that mean in regards to immediate, realistic, and tangible next steps?

You may not have the resources (hardware or personnel) to immediately upgrade or install a 7.1 system. Depending on your organization's schedule, there may be initiatives operating in parallel, unrelated to SAP Solution Manager, that prevent you from immediately putting in place a project plan that gets you up to date with the latest SAP Solution Manager functionality. For these cases, we recommend requesting a sandbox installation of SAP Solution Manager 7.1 from your Basis team to begin gaining some practical experience with release 7.1.

This sandbox or development system doesn't need to be sized according to operating requirements for real-life SAP ITSM. Nor does an installation of this kind require integration into the existing SAP Solution Manager landscape or even the managed SAP ERP landscape. The objective would be for your SAP Solution Manager owner/architect, technical teams, and IT managers to become familiar with release 7.1 before implementing the scenarios for primetime. Practicing with the upgrade or installation, proof-of-concept, and the development of a project plan can all be accomplished with a basic 7.1 environment that doesn't have to connect or impact current operations.

Becoming familiar with the SOLMAN_SETUP activities, SAP ITSM capabilities, and new transaction types will help you get a head start on what it takes to upgrade and/or implement the new features delivered with 7.1. While it may be impossible to transition to 7.1 in the short term, having a 7.1 system in some form to ramp up on knowledge transfer will be a proactive way to kick-start related initiatives. The recommendation is to quickly grasp ahold of the SAP Solution Manager 7.1 capabilities, even if it means the system will be decommissioned at the point you do decide to transition to the latest version.

Upgrade or Install: Which Option Is Right for You?

If you're reading this now, SAP Solution Manager 7.1 has been out for well over a year, stabilizing and continuously being enhanced with innovative functionalities. Most likely your organization's requirements, pain points, and priorities in regards to Application Lifecycle Management (ALM) and SAP ITSM will be addressed by transitioning to SAP Solution Manager 7.1 from release 7.0. If anything, significant value and efficiency brought by the 7.1 functionalities will be the minimum benefits as a result of the transition. The question regarding the transition becomes whether you should upgrade or perform a new installation of release 7.1.

Our recommendation is simple and straightforward. If you have data to protect, we recommending upgrading. If you're using SAP Solution Manager 7.0 for its most basic purposes (e.g., generating installation keys and downloading maintenance components for your managed system, or documentation that can easily be re-uploaded), you should consider a fresh installation.

Upgrading to 7.1, Basic Rationale

In regards to SAP ITSM explicitly, data translates into your SAP CRM 5.0-based incidents, change requests, and other change transactions/documents. Because there is no standard migration path for data and configuration, we highly recommend that you upgrade your SAP Solution Manager landscape so these technical elements are preserved and protected.

When you upgrade to 7.1, your 7.0 transaction types are still available for processing and reference. Further, your 7.0-based configuration (hopefully copied into a Z* customer namespace) is also protected after your system landscape has been upgrade to 7.1. While we don't recommend creating 7.0-based transaction types after your SAP Solution Manager landscape has been upgraded to 7.1, there is still the option of doing so in the SAP GUI (Transaction CMRD_ORDER). We'll provide our recommendations for transitioning from 7.0 transaction types to 7.1 transaction types in Section B.2.

When upgrading, all new and enhanced functionalities are delivered with the new 7.1 transaction types. Furthermore, they are only available within the SAP CRM Web UI. While your 7.0-based transaction types aren't incorporated with these new functionalities, you still have the option to view them in lists/reports in the new SAP CRM Web UI (explained in Chapter 15). While you may not process them in the SAP CRM Web UI, it's an added benefit for support users to have them in a central, searchable location.

Installing a New SAP Solution Manager 7.1, Basic Rationale

As mentioned previously, you should only consider installing a fresh SAP Solution Manager 7.1 system (as opposed to upgrading) if you aren't using SAP Solution Manager 7.0 scenarios to the full capabilities. We've mentioned the example of only using the system for basic monitoring, generating installation keys, or downloading maintenance. Other activities can include basic implementation functionalities that can be easily recreated in a new (7.1) system.

However, if you have multiple projects rich with business process hierarchy (BPH) content (structure, components, documentation, etc.), you should consider an upgrade. Similarly, if you have robust technical monitoring data, you'll want to preserve and protect that infrastructure. SAP ITSM is the same, if not more important, due to its complex workflow and the need to preserve the existing configuration to support a transition phase to 7.1. Moreover, end users and auditors will need to access the data within 7.0 throughout the 7.1 transition period. This transition period can take up to a year, depending on the nature of the organization.

Our lessons learned have proven that for customers already using the 7.0 Service Desk and ChaRM components, upgrading as opposed to newly installing to SAP ITSM in SAP Solution Manager 7.1 is the best option. The end-user acceptance and experience level is much higher when the users don't need to log in to two

SAP Solution Manager systems to both create and process service transactions. While 7.0 transactions can only be searchable in the SAP CRM Web UI, users are automatically brought to the SAP GUI when they attempt to open a 7.0 transaction from the SAP CRM Web UI.

Auditors will also need to log in to two separate SAP Solution Manager systems to perform audit checks related to Application Incident Management (AIM) and ChaRM activities.

On the other hand, a transition to SAP Solution Manager 7.1 can be viewed as a new start to many organizations. Often, for one reason or another, the system has become so messy over the years that organizations may want to shelf it and use it simply as a reference system. Sometimes, starting off with the "fresh clean sheet of paper" is an approach that works for certain organizations. While we're not against this approach, we stick to the notion of upgrading to 7.1 if you're in the position where you must protect existing data and configuration.

Hardware and Sizing Considerations When Upgrading

In Appendix A, we provided some input regarding how the SAP Solution Manager landscape should be designed as well as how to leverage standard tools available from SAP to size each tier (i.e., development, quality assurance, and production) appropriately.

By now, you should be aware that each customer's landscape and sizing specifications will most likely be unique, depending on the scenarios leveraged as well as the volume of end users. While a two-tier SAP Solution Manager landscape may be adequate for most customers, the most preferred and recommended approach is to stand up a three-tier landscape to facilitate the development and regression testing of maintenance and configuration to your SAP ITSM scenario.

If you're upgrading to SAP Solution Manager 7.1, you should be aware of the following considerations and recommendations in regards to hardware and sizing.

Scenario 1: No Hardware Investment Required
If you're currently operating SAP Solution Manager 7.0 and not planning on adding additional scenarios (configuration, data, etc.) or a large number of users, your existing hardware will generally suffice. This consideration is assuming that the performance of your existing SAP Solution Manager 7.0 environment is

acceptable to the current users given the scenarios they are working with on a day-to-day basis.

Also, if you're currently operating SAP Solution Manager 7.0 and have plans to add only a few additional users and perhaps a few additional managed systems post-7.1 upgrade, you'll generally not require investment in additional hardware.

Scenario 2: Hardware Review Is Highly Recommended

On the contrary, if you're planning to change the scope of your SAP Solution Manager environment by adding any of the following, we recommend that you review, reevaluate and take action on your current hardware:

▶ Additional scenarios (e.g., Technical Monitoring, SAP ITSM, Solution Documentation, test management, etc.)

▶ Additional users (e.g., allowing 5,000 end users to log incidents as part of AIM)

▶ Additional managed systems (e.g., adding a large number of additional managed systems to enable an expanded Technical Monitoring, business process monitoring, SAP ITSM, etc. platform)

If you're on an earlier support package of SAP Solution Manager 7.1, we recommend a review and reevaluation of your current hardware specifications. Generally, the guideline for this is support packages that are pre-Enhancement Package 01.

The SAP Solution Manager Sizing Guide, available on the SAP Marketplace, provides the templates and guidelines necessary to administer a sizing exercise. Based on the output of these results, you may consider adding an additional percentage (e.g., 50% or higher) so that a hardware review isn't anticipated in the near-midterm future.

B.2   SAP ITSM Transition Strategy

In this section, we'll discuss three options for transitioning to release 7.1 SAP ITSM transaction types. Your organization's use of SAP ITSM features, the volume of outstanding (open) service transactions, and the ability to organize your support organization to quickly take action on these open transactions will determine the transition strategy that is appropriate for you.

First, we'll discuss the transition strategy we prefer most based on our experiences with customer upgrades. We'll also provide three other viable and recommended options that you should consider when planning your upgrade strategy.

B.2.1 What Is a Release 7.1 Transition Strategy?

When upgrading to SAP Solution Manager 7.1, you must determine a strategy for how to transition from the 7.0-based transaction types to the new and improved 7.1-based transaction types. Because the main purpose of upgrading to SAP Solution Manager 7.1 should be to quickly take advantage of the new SAP ITSM functions, you'll want a plan that allows you to do so quickly while relying less on the old document types. Although your support organization may be very eager to begin creating and processing service transactions based on the 7.1 functionality, you must consider the open 7.0-based transaction types as well. Support teams, IT managers, audit staff, and so on will still need access to these open service transactions to complete business requirements, routine maintenance activities, and various tasks to support the organization from an overall service standpoint.

Figure B.2 provides a representation of how the transition strategy can overlap between your existing SAP Solution Manager 7.0 and future 7.1 environments.

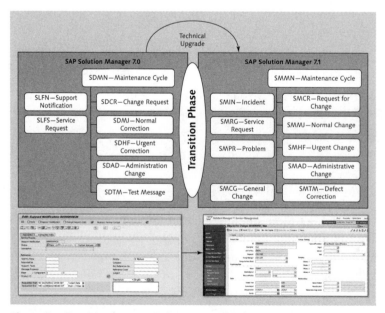

Figure B.2 Transition between Release 7.0 and Release 7.1

A transition strategy defines the approach for eliminating the existence of open 7.0 transaction types so that the functionality delivered in 7.1 can be leveraged across AIM and ChaRM. Depending on your organization, this transition can occur abruptly (i.e., not beginning any 7.1 activity until all 7.0 transactions are closed) or gradually (i.e., parallel processing of 7.0 and 7.1 transaction types). We'll explain how a transition would work relating to both of these examples in the following sections.

To help plan for a smooth transition into using the 7.1-based transaction types for the improved SAP ITSM scenarios, there are four transition strategies available.

B.2.2 Option 1: Parallel Operation of Transaction Types

Based on our customer experiences upgrading SAP Solution Manager landscapes that leverage SAP ITSM scenarios, our preferred transition strategy supports a parallel operation of 7.0 and 7.1 transaction types for an interim period.

As part of this option, after the upgrade to SAP Solution Manager 7.1, the 7.0-based transaction types are still processed and governed by the 7.0 maintenance cycle (e.g., SDMN). However, the requesters' user authorizations are modified so that the creation of 7.0-based service transactions is restricted. New incidents, problems, service requests, and requests for change are created based on the 7.1 transaction types. The new transaction types are therefore governed by the 7.1-based maintenance cycle (e.g., SMMN).

Figure B.3 provides a representation of how parallel operations across 7.0 and 7.1 transactions can be achieved after your SAP Solution Manager landscape has been upgraded. You'll notice that there are four main phases to this transition strategy.

1. **Pre-transition**
   In the pre-transition phase (i.e., before the technical upgrade of 7.1 is performed), SAP ITSM functions are created and processed with the SAP CRM 5.0 transaction types as part of your SAP Solution Manager 7.0 environment.

2. **Beginning of transition**
   The beginning of the transition phase commences after the technical upgrade has been completed and the post-processing/basic configuration is also completed. A maintenance project and maintenance cycle is created (SMMN). At this point, the SAP Solution Manager architect should make the appropriate settings within the system landscape so no new SAP CRM 5.0 service transactions

are created. SAP CRM 7.0 documents should only be created. Processing can continue of the SAP CRM 5.0 documents, thus allowing parallel operation between releases. To facilitate this, the following settings must be made:

- Activity 01 (create) must be removed from authorization object CRM_ORD_PR for all SD* or ZD* messages.
- Activity 01 (create) should be granted for the same authorization object for SM* or ZM* messages.
- Your SM* or ZM* request for change transaction type should be added to the parameter PROCESS_TYPE in Transaction DNO_CUST04.
- The SD* or ZD* change request transaction type should be added to the parameter PROCESS_TYPE_ADD in Transaction DNO_CUST04.

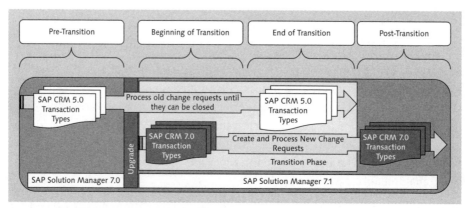

Figure B.3 Transition Strategy: Parallel Operation

Note

Because most authorization objects have been changed due to the new transaction types, we recommend leveraging the PFCG security roles for SAP ITSM in SAP Solution Manager 7.1. After the 7.0-based transaction types have been completed, the corresponding security roles can be decommisioned within the SAP Solution Manager system.

3. **End of transition**

At the end of the transition phase, there are two scenarios that can ocur (your organization will need to determine which scenario is appropriate/realistic):

- End of transition means that all SAP CRM 5.0 transactions have been completed.

- End of transition means that by a specified date, the organization is stating that no further processing can occur on SAP CRM 5.0 transactions. Documents "in flight" can't be processed anymore, and, if needed, they must be recreated in 7.1 format.

Depending on which of these options is selected, the SAP CRM 5.0 documents will be completed by the support teams. If they aren't processed through their appropriate channels, the authorization to change them (authorization object CRM_ORD_PR) should be removed. While the SAP CRM 5.0 documents can no longer be processed, they are still available for viewing. All cycles related to SAP Solution Manager 7.0 (i.e., SDMN) are completed.

4. **Post-transition**
   The post-transition phase commences when all SAP CRM 5.0 documents are restricted from processing. SAP ITSM in SAP Solution Manager 7.1 is fully engaged. The SD* or ZD* transaction types should be deleted from Transaction Type DNO_CUST04 to complete this process.

As you can see, this option allows the flexibility to continue processing 7.0-based transaction types after the technical upgrade of 7.1 is completed and even when leveraging the functionality delivered within the new transaction types. An important benefit is that the legacy transaction types are available for search in the SAP CRM Web UI. The drawback is that the legacy transaction types will open in the SAP GUI, so two UIs will be in use during the transition phase.

Other Transition Strategy Options

While parallel operation of transaction types may be our preferred 7.1 transition strategy, there are other options that may be more preferable depending on your exact scenario, which we briefly discuss in the following sections.

B.2.3 Option 2: Close Everything 7.0 Related Prior to the Upgrade

If you don't want to have 7.0-based transactions supported as part of a parallel transition, option 2 may be preferable to you. In this transition strategy, you need to close all of your open 7.0 transaction types (including the maintenance and project cycles) prior to the technical upgrade to SAP Solution Manager 7.1.

This option may be preferable for those organizations with a limited number of open 7.0 transaction types. Typically, if there are hundreds of open transaction types, this may not be a realistic option. Especially with incidents that require a larger amount of effort or change documents that involve a lot of development effort, it may not be as easy to just close everything.

If you choose to close everything 7.0 related, you must plan the technical upgrade to 7.1 diligently. Because everything will be closed before the upgrade, no access to SAP ITSM capabilities will be available until the 7.1 landscape has been upgraded with post-processing and basic configuration activated and tested.

B.2.4 Option 3: Manual Data Migration

We've previously mentioned that there is neither automated migration path for data, nor for configuration when transitioning to SAP Solution Manager 7.1. There are still customers who want to work with the new transaction types, UI, and related functionality yet still have open 7.0-based transaction types, which require more processing time. They can't simply be closed, and it's not preferred to have parallel processing of 7.0- and 7.1-based transaction types. For this reason, option 3 is available for the manual migration of service transaction data.

In this transition strategy, 7.0-based transaction types that are open at the time of the technical upgrade to 7.1 are manually recreated into 7.1-based transaction types. It would be up to a SAP Solution Manager administrator or a designated support resource to rekey the information contained within the 7.0-based document into the new SAP CRM Web UI.

Depending on the volume of tickets, this may or may not be a realistic option (as was the case for option 2). However, even if there were hundreds of open tickets, this could be a well-received option for an organization that could dedicate two to three resources to rekey data over the course of a cutover weekend. Moreover, the larger the number of open 7.0-based transaction types ironically develops a stronger business case for the manual data migration into 7.1 transactions. The reason is that the larger volume of open tickets reduces the likelihood that they will be fully completed within a reasonable time frame and transition period. More open transaction types increase parallel operation between infrastructures and reduce the likelihood that parallel operation would ever fully come to an end point.

Manual data migration would include the reassignment of attachments, copy and paste of text type descriptions, and assignment of general data, among other manual data entry activities. Further, support personnel who own the tickets may have to advance the status of the document types to accurately reflect the progress of their work and reserve key reporting and metric criteria.

While the upfront effort may be tedious, time consuming, and require the bandwidth of two to three administrators, the return is high. Old tickets are immediately available within the new SAP CRM Web UI. Furthermore, each of these tickets now has the capability of leveraging the SAP ITSM functionality delivered in SAP Solution Manager 7.1.

B.2.5 Option 4: Maintenance Cycle Take Over

Last, but definitely not least, option 4, the maintenance cycle takeover, is also a much preferred transition strategy based on our customer experiences. This option is particularly of interest for those customers leveraging the ChaRM 7.0 functionality.

With this option, the SDMN maintenance cycle is closed immediately following the technical upgrade to SAP Solution Manager 7.1. The activity of completing the SDMN maintenance cycle is part of the post-processing basic configuration process following handover of the upgraded SAP Solution Manager from Basis to the SAP Solution Manager owner/architect.

A new maintenance cycle is generated from the existing maintenance project. Generating a new maintenance cycle from an existing maintenance project is possible after the existing maintenance cycle is advanced to the completed phase. The maintenance cycle that is newly generated is of transaction type SMMN. Unfinished change transactions that were assigned to the previous SDMN maintenance cycle are taken over for further processing by the newly generated SMMN maintenance cycle. Going forward, all new requests for change (and change documents) will be based on the SM* transaction types and therefore controlled by the 7.1-based SMMN maintenance cycle. In conclusion, no new SD* 7.0-based transaction types are created.

Figure B.4 provides a graphical representation of the high-level roadmap for how this functionality plays out for a transitioning ChaRM scenario.

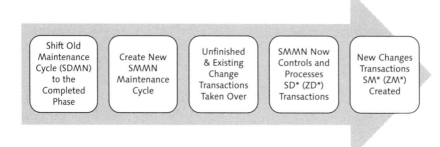

Figure B.4 Maintenance Cycle Takeover

Table B.2 identifies the ChaRM 7.0 transaction types that can be both assigned and processed (i.e., taken over) within the SMMN 7.1 maintenance cycle. Further, this table indicates the prerequisites in regards to which status each transaction type must be advanced to for the takeover functionality to work properly.

Transaction Type	Status
SDMJ (normal correction)	To Be Tested (with open transport requests)
SDHF (urgent correction)	In Development (with open transport requests)
SDAD (administration message)	Confirmed
SDTM (test message)	In Process (with open transport requests)

Table B.2 Status Values Prior to SDMN Completion

The Maintenance Cycle Takeover functionality may be used in conjunction with the option 1 transition strategy, parallel operation of transaction types, in a hybrid approach. With a hybrid approach, the same maintenance project is used and the ChaRM transaction types are processed in parallel until the 7.0-based transaction types are completed.

> **Note**
>
> All maintenance projects created in the SAP Solution Manager 7.0 environment (prior to the technical upgrade to 7.1) will be stored in Table /TMWFLOW/OLDPROJ. After the upgrade to 7.1, you have the ability to enter the newly created project into Table /TMWFLOW/SWITCH. With this entry, 7.0-based transaction types will be created when you generate a task list and cycle transaction from SOLAR_PROJECT_ADMIN.

In the next section, we'll provide a high-level roadmap that includes specific steps that should be taken into account when adapting the 7.1 transaction types to meet your IT organizations requirements.

B.3   Configuration Upgrade Roadmap

We've mentioned that post-processing and basic configuration steps are required after the Basis team has completed their technical upgrade to SAP Solution Manager 7.1. Whether you've previously used the Service Desk or ChaRM components in SAP Solution Manager 7.0, you'll need to determine how existing configuration will be migrated and adapted so that it will be available within the 7.1 environment.

Because the technical upgrade to 7.1 doesn't affect existing 7.0 configuration, your ZD* customer transaction types will be preserved. Due to this protection of previous configuration, the transition strategy options we described earlier are available to help you seamlessly move toward the benefits brought to you by SAP Solution Manager 7.1.

The challenge is that there is no automated migration path for your configuration efforts maintained in the SAP Solution Manager 7.0 environment. While certain settings (some configuration and most master data) can be reused, you'll need to determine a roadmap for how your SAP ITSM requirements will be accommodated within your newly upgraded 7.1 landscape. Figure B.5 provides a high-level roadmap identifying the steps that must be taken after the Basis team has completed the technical upgrade of SAP Solution Manager 7.1.

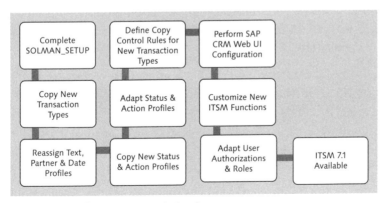

Figure B.5 Configuration Upgrade Roadmap

For some organizations, this can be a chance to revisit their existing SAP ITSM processes. Perhaps in 7.0, the workflow was adapted so far beyond the SAP standards in their SAP Solution Manager landscape that it became unmanageable, convoluted, and inconsistent. On the other hand, the 7.0 workflow may have been missing key audit or governance requirements along with key functionality that would benefit the support organizations.

In these cases, the upgrade to 7.1 can be viewed as a "fresh start" to support organizations. The complex and unmanageable workflow that has been driving existing SAP ITSM processes for years can now be reevaluated and scaled back to support an ITIL-based framework. The improvements and additions to SAP ITSM functionalities delivered with 7.1 can now be rolled into those processes that were previously lacking. Use the configuration upgrade roadmap as a lessons learned and reevaluation tool. While the SAP ITSM functionality in SAP Solution Manager 7.1 provides significant benefits over the prior release, SAP Solution Manager 7.0 has enabled you to learn what works and doesn't work within your support organization. Leverage these lessons learned to your advantage, and take the technical upgrade to release 7.1 as an opportunity to increase the value and return on investment of SAP Solution Manager to your support organization and business community.

B.4 Summary

Transitioning to SAP ITSM in SAP Solution Manager 7.1 is something you should seriously consider, if you haven't already. If you've considered migrating your data and configuration onto the infrastructure provided by SAP Solution Manager 7.1, you should now have the information, options, and roadmaps needed to both plan for and make decisions on how you'll transition to the new and enhanced SAP ITSM functions.

No matter which transition strategy you choose, or whether you decide to upgrade or perform a fresh installation of 7.1, you must at least have a plan to get experience with the processes and functionality delivered with the SAP ITSM platform in SAP Solution Manager 7.1. Starting somewhere is the most important part, even if it's just for your own personal ramp-up knowledge transfer initiative. Chances are, your organization will benefit in the long run.

C   The Author

Nathan Williams is a senior SAP management and technology consultant with a prominent concentration in the area of SAP Application Lifecycle Management and SAP Solution Manager. For nearly seven years, Nathan has supported organizations in their efforts to leverage SAP Solution Manager as an integral component of their SAP Application Lifecycle Management and Run SAP Like a Factory initiatives. Coordinating with IT, business, and program management teams, he has effectively defined strategies and roadmaps to help SAP customers seamlessly transition to SAP Solution Manager processes and capabilities. Nathan is also experienced with all technical configuration aspects of SAP Solution Manager, including security, Basis, and SAP CRM.

Nathan is considered an industry expert and thought leader in regards to SAP Solution Manager. He is a frequent contributor to *SAPexperts* and *SAPinsider*. He is also a regular speaker at SAP TechEd and WIS conferences.

Outside of professional activities, Nathan spends most of his time in New York City where he resides. He is a guitar player in a rock band that plays frequently in New York. Nathan also enjoys running marathons.

Index

Interested in reading more?

Please visit our website for all new
book and e-book releases from SAP PRESS.

www.sap-press.com